Readings in Western Civilization

℧ Vere dignum

University of Chicago Readings in Western Civilization
John W. Boyer and Julius Kirshner, General Editors

University of Chicago
Readings in Western Civilization

John W. Boyer and Julius Kirshner, General Editors

8
Nineteenth-Century Europe:
Liberalism and Its Critics

**Edited by Jan Goldstein
and John W. Boyer**

The University of Chicago Press

Chicago and London

Eric Cochrane, 1928–1985

ἀθάνατος μνήμη
Immortal memory

Jan Goldstein is associate professor of history at the University of Chicago.

John W. Boyer is professor of history at the University of Chicago and editor of the *Journal of Modern History.*

The University of Chicago Press, Chicago 60637
The University of Chicago Press, Ltd., London
© 1988 by The University of Chicago
All rights reserved. Published 1988
Printed in the United States of America
96   5 4 3

Library of Congress Cataloging-in-Publication Data
Main entry under title:

University of Chicago readings in Western civilization.

   Includes bibliographies and indexes.
   Contents: v. 1. The Greek polis / edited by
Arthur W. H. Adkins and Peter White —[etc.]—
v. 5. The Renaissance / edited by Eric Cochrane and
Julius Kirshner —   — v. 8. Nineteenth-century
Europe / edited by Jan Goldstein and John W. Boyer.
   1. Civilization, Occidental—History—Sources.
2. Europe—Civilization—Sources. I. Boyer,
John W. II. Kirshner, Julius.   III. Title: Readings
in Western civilization.
CB245.U64   1986   909'.09821   85-16328
ISBN 0-226-06934-6 (v. 1)
ISBN 0-226-06935-4 (pbk.: v. 1)

ISBN 0-226-06951-6 (v. 8)
ISBN 0-226-06952-4 (pbk.: v. 8)

Contents

Series Editors' Foreword

This series is the result of almost four decades of teaching the History of Western Civilization course at the College of the University of Chicago. The course was founded in its present form in the late 1940s by a group of young historians at Chicago, including William H. McNeill, Christian Mackauer, and Sylvia Thrupp, and has been sustained during the past twenty-five years by the distinguished teaching of Eric Cochrane, Hanna H. Gray, Charles M. Gray, and Karl J. Weintraub. At the time it served as a counterpoint to the antihistorical and positivistic thrust of the general education curriculum in the social sciences in the Hutchins College. Western Civilization has since been incorporated as a year-long course into different parts of the College program, from the first to the last year. It now forms part of the general intercivilizational requirement for sophomores and juniors. It is still taught, as it has been almost constantly since its inception, in discussion groups ranging from twenty to thirty students.

Although both the readings and the instructors of the course have changed over the years, its purpose has remained the same. It seeks not to provide students with morsels of Western culture, nor to nourish their moral and aesthetic sensitivities, and much less to attract recruits for the history profession. Its purpose instead is to raise a whole set of complex conceptual questions regarding the nature of time and change and the intended and unintended consequences of human action and consciousness. Students in this course learn to analyze past events and ideas by rigorously examining a variety of texts. This is in contrast to parallel courses in the social sciences, which teach students to deploy synchronic and quantitative techniques in analyzing society, usually without reference to historical context or process.

Ours is a history course that aims not at imparting relevant facts or exotic ideas but at providing students with the critical tools by which to analyze texts produced in the distant or near past. It also serves a related purpose: to familiarize students with major epochs of that Western historical tradition to which most of them, albeit at times unknowingly, are heirs.

The major curricular vehicle of the course is the *Readings in Western Civilization*, a nine-volume series of primary sources in translation, beginning with Periclean Athens and concluding with Europe in the twentieth century. The series is not meant to be a comprehensive survey of Western history. Rather, in each volume, we provide a large number of documents on specific themes in the belief that depth, not breadth, is the surest antidote to superficiality. The very extensiveness of the documentation in each volume allows for a variety of approaches to the same theme. At the same time the concentrated focus of individual volumes makes it possible for them to serve as source readings in more advanced and specialized courses.

Many people contributed to the publication of these volumes. The enthusiastic collaboration and labors of the members of the Western Civilization staff made it possible for these *Readings* to be published. We thank Barbara Boyer for providing superb editorial direction to the project and Mary Van Steenbergh for her dedication in creating beautifully text-edited manuscripts. Steven Wheatley's advice in procuring funding for this project was invaluable. Members of the University of Chicago Press have given their unstinting support and guidance. We also appreciate the confidence and support accorded by Donald N. Levine, the Dean of the College at the University of Chicago. Above all, we are deeply grateful for the extraordinary dedication, energy, and erudition which our late colleague and former chairperson of the course, Eric Cochrane, contributed to the *Readings in Western Civilization*.

We are grateful to the National Endowment for the Humanities for providing generous funding for the preparation and publication of the volumes.

John Boyer and Julius Kirshner

General Introduction

During the nineteenth century European nations began to work out responses to the long-term agenda set by the French Revolution and the Industrial Revolution: political democratization in the context of sustained economic growth. Because the responses differed markedly among nations, the period invites, indeed almost demands, consideration of several national experiences. This collection of documents therefore divides its attention among Britain, France and Germany, making a short excursion to Italy as well.

Like the other volumes prepared for the Western Civilization course at the University of Chicago, *Nineteenth-Century Europe: Liberalism and Its Critics,* has no pretensions to comprehensive coverage of all the major historical events within its chronological limits. Rather, as its subtitle suggests, it has taken the shifting fortunes of liberalism as its overarching theme. Five separate sections treat aspects of that theme, often putting special emphasis on the nation that best or most richly exemplifies the aspect at hand. The volume thus combines several in-depth case studies with other, carefully selected materials that allow for a comparative, cross-national approach throughout.

Although its beginnings as theory and practice go back to the seventeenth century, *liberalism*—in the "ism" form of the word—first appeared in European languages in the opening decades of the nineteenth century. Like all key words that have been made to bear the weight of historical significance, liberalism has no clear, univocal meaning. It always stands for a doctrine of individual freedom, but the arenas in which this freedom are exercised are various. Liberalism can denote civil liberty, or equality before the law; meritocracy, or the freedom to attain the highest position that one's talents permit; freedom of thought and expression; economic freedom, or the freedom of individuals to pursue their own material interests as they see fit and to meet as competitors in the marketplace; and political freedom, or the liberty to participate, in accordance with a concept of sovereignty of the people, in the processes by which the holders of public authority are determined. This multiplicity of meanings points to some of the internal tensions of liberalism and to some of the problems, foreshadowed during the French Revolution, that it would face again and again during the nineteenth century. Does liberalism logically imply democracy, or can it be stabilized around the other freedoms named above while restricting political freedom? And if it can, should it be? What is the relationship of the doctrine of economic freedom—or, as it was often called in the nineteenth century, the science of political economy—to the ethos of liberalism? That is, if the underlying liberal commitment is to the sanctity of the individual, can liberalism condone a laissez-faire system, which in practice gives some the freedom to get rich and others the freedom to starve? The critics of liberalism referred to in the title of this volume are not only those who, during the course of the nineteenth century, gave other labels to their positions. They are also those who perceived the internal inconsistencies of liberalism and criticized and transformed it from within.

The first section of this volume surveys the varieties of liberalism in its heyday during the first half of the nineteenth century. The case study here is Britain, where the early advance of industrialization presented liberals with both opportunities and problems in abundance. The section opens with Jeremy Bentham's philosophy of utilitarianism, which became the theoretical underpinning of nineteenth-century British political liberalism and distinguished it from its eighteenth-century French counterpart based on natural rights. The popular rhetoric of British liberalism can be heard in journalism on the Crystal Palace and an "industrial biography" by the best-selling author Samuel Smiles; key moments of British liberal practice are represented by a cluster of documents on the suffrage reform of 1832, the anti–Corn Law agitation of the 1840s, and the parliamentary debate of 1846–47 over the Ten Hours Bill regulating factory labor. The view from the other side of the Channel is provided by Victor Cousin, a spokesman for the doctrine of the juste-milieu, the peculiarly cautious and conservative form of liberalism that dominated French politics in the 1830s and 1840s and bore witness to the pall cast over French liberalism by the revolutionary trauma of the previous century. A selection from Hegel illustrates the accentuation of the state that characterized most German political theory, liberal and otherwise, in this period. In addition to furnishing material for a cross-national comparison of liberalisms, section 1 illustrates the range of concerns and projects that engaged the early nineteenth-century liberal imagination: prison reform (Bentham on the Panopticon), the organization of the medical profession, the role and status of women (Thomas Gisborne versus J. S. Mill and Harriet Taylor), Jewish emancipation. That some of these projects were more conducive to restricting than to fostering liberty is a point that bears examination.

In the second section, which focuses on the Revolution of 1848, France is the illustrative case. An important factor leading to the mid-century upheaval was the intellectual ferment in Paris during the preceding two decades, when blueprints for a better society—that is, one that would correct the perceived inadequacies of the liberal order through some principle of association—were put forward with a heady confidence that has been called romantic and utopian. This anti-individualist ferment is represented in the present volume by Charles Fourier's discussion of his model community, the phalanstery; an excerpt from the government's trial of the Saint-Simonians; the socialist feminism of Flora Tristan; and Agricol Perdiguier's autobiographical reminiscence about compagnonnage, the traditional mode of craftsmen's organization which he hoped to refurbish and generalize as an antidote to laissez-faire. The revolutionary events themselves are treated in the trenchant contemporary analyses of Tocqueville and Marx, and two renditions of the passage from democratic republicanism to Caesarism are given—one by Marx and the other by Louis Napoleon himself in his Bordeaux speech announcing the restoration of the empire. In sum, this consideration of France during the tumultuous years 1848–52 shows the emergence of the socialist critique of liberalism as a political force, and also the emergence of the fear of socialism as a counterforce of at least equal strength. The section is rounded out by a document from the Frankfurt Assembly, a key moment of the Revolution of 1848 in Germany, and by two views, by T. B. Macaulay and by Giuseppe Mazzini, of the process of democratization evidently underway.

The third and last case study in this volume is found in section 4, which is wholly devoted to Imperial Germany in the decades immediately after unification. The section explores Bismarck's founding of a national political culture notable for its enmity to the German liberal tradition, thus setting the new Reich on a course significantly different from that of its neighbors to the west. Bismarck's style of leadership and his uncanny ability to manipulate liberal means for authoritarian ends are examined in two of his speeches, one on the creation of the North German Confederation, the other on social insurance and state socialism. Some alternatives to Bismarckian politics are found in short programmatic statements from Bismarck's two principal bourgeois opponents in the 1870s—the National Liberals and the Center party. The section concludes with two selections from prominent academic spokesmen of the 1890s. Whereas Heinrich von Treitschke frankly abandoned his liberal values in the face of mass society, the inaugural address of the young Max Weber offers a tortuous defense of the German liberal tradition by exposing the discrepancy between economic power and social and political prerogatives in late Imperial Germany. In the process it makes a desperate attempt to preserve the connection that older German Liberals postulated between freedom and power and that they found embodied in the ethical culture of the nation. Perceiving from the vantage point of 1895 the inevitability of struggle among national states, the Weber essay also provides a striking contrast to Mazzini's optimistic anticipation of their peaceful cooperation in the 1850s.

The remaining sections in this volume have no single national focus but draw, roughly equally, on material from Britain, France and Germany. Section 3 departs from the usual pattern of the volume in treating a theme that spans the entire century. It takes up one of the great conundrums of nineteenth-century liberalism: the place of religion in the context of "free" thought and "free" politics. Both sides of an impassioned and unending debate, which traced its roots to the eighteenth-century Enlightenment, are presented: those who defended the centrality of religion in official and private capacities (the British Evangelicals, Friedrich Schleiermacher, Leo XIII), and those who sought aggressively to expose the intellectual flaws of traditional religious beliefs and who developed a politics of anticlericalism (Ludwig Feuerbach, Ernest Renan, the leaders of the early Third Republic in France). The two closing documents in the section sound a new, characteristically modern note: existential anxiety, stemming from the conviction that God and religion are no longer credible.

Section 5 treats the rise of mass political movements at the turn of the century, a development produced both by the breakdown of liberal consensus and, ironically, by the very success of the liberal vision. For the mass parties considered here owed their existence to the political democracy that had become the rule in Western Europe by this date, yet they were animated by disdain for the liberal center. The section considers the range of socialist opinion in France (Jean Jaurès) and especially Germany (Engels, Eduard Bernstein, Rosa Luxemburg, Clara Zetkin), emphasizing the issue of socialism's self-definition as a continuator of democratic liberalism or a position radically distinct from it, and touching as well on the division of the nascent feminist movement into bourgeois and socialist wings. The marshaling of anti-Semitism for political purposes by the Right is explored in texts by Maurice Barrès, who espouses it, and Theodor Herzl, who deplores it and proposes Zionism in response to the apparent failure of the liberal policy of Jewish emancipation. Three documents on British imperialism culminate with the populist imperialism set forth by Joseph Chamberlain after he abandoned the Liberal party and its policy of free trade to appeal to the masses as a protectionist and Unionist. Thus the volume ends as the nineteenth century did: with liberalism besieged on all sides and its future uncertain.

A Note on Ancillary Readings

In teaching the nineteenth century as part of the Chicago Western Civilization course, we almost always assign supplementary readings, both to provide necessary chronological background material and to enable more intensive study of particular issues treated in the *Readings*. In the latter category fall Marx and Engels's *The Communist Manifesto,* used either alone or as a prelude to the selection from *The Eighteenth Brumaire* in the *Readings*, and J. S. Mill's *On Liberty* as the classic example of the form British liberalism took in the later nineteenth century.

1
Early Liberal Thought and Practice

1. Jeremy Bentham, *Principles of Legislation*

The work of Jeremy Bentham (1748–1832) left an indelible imprint on nineteenth-century British liberalism. Bentham's intellectual odyssey began when, respecting his father's wish that he become a lawyer, he went to Oxford as a youth to study law. He quickly discovered that he had far more of a penchant to criticize the law than to practice it. What Bentham found so abhorrent about British law, as exemplified in the venerated *Commentaries* of Sir William Blackstone (whose lectures he had attended at Oxford), was its utter reliance upon precedent or, as Bentham sometimes called it, "ancestor-wisdom." His tools for criticism were drawn from his reading of Enlightenment thinkers such as Helvétius, Beccaria and Hartley. From Helvétius in particular he learned the principle of utility—that the source of all human action is the desire to maximize pleasure and minimize pain—and he set about deriving from that principle a new, systematic theory of morality and legislation. The results of this system building were presented in his *Introduction to the Principles of Morals and Legislation* (1789) and in a similar work first published in French in 1802 as *Traités de législation civile et pénale* and retranslated into English in 1864. Our first selection comes from the latter text.

Despite his Enlightenment bent and reformist impulses, Bentham was initially a political conservative. Although momentarily radicalized by the French Revolution, he long trusted in the Tory party to revise the British legal code along the utilitarian lines he had set out, once the compelling reasons for such a revision had been made known. Eventually, however, he despaired of ever winning the Tories over to his viewpoint; by 1808

From Jeremy Bentham, *The Principles of Legislation,* in *The Theory of Legislation,* translated by Richard Hildreth, 8th edition (London: Trubner, 1894), pp. 1–10, 13–15, 27–33, 48, 53–54, 60–79, 81–87.

when he met James Mill (the father of John Stuart Mill), Bentham was ripe for political conversion. Mill senior, leader of the democratically inclined Philosophical Radicals, was persuaded that the cause of that group would be best served by couching its arguments in Benthamite-utilitarian terms; he succeeded in persuading Bentham that, conversely, the tenets of utilitarianism would find their natural expression in a genuinely liberal parliamentary regime with a suffrage base much broader than the one traditional in Britain. The new alliance thus established helped bring about one of the major Liberal victories of the period, the passage of the Great Reform Bill in 1832, the year of Bentham's death.

In addition to legal reform, another of Bentham's pet projects, also justified on utilitarian grounds, was the Panopticon, a peculiar architectural form that could function as a prison, poorhouse, or other public institution. The precise nature of the Panopticon and Bentham's continuing zeal to put his plan into effect is the subject of the second document, an autobiographical reminiscence written by Bentham in 1830–31. Whether the Panopticon embodies a liberal or an antiliberal tendency in Bentham's thought, the project was by no means idiosyncratic to him. Newly designed institutions of incarceration—especially prisons but also insane asylums—were typical Liberal causes throughout Europe during the first half of the nineteenth century.

Chapter 1. The Principle of Utility

THE PUBLIC GOOD ought to be the object of the legislator; GENERAL UTILITY ought to be the foundation of his reasonings. To know the true good of the community is what constitutes the science of legislation; the art consists in finding the means to realize that good.

The principle of *utility,* vaguely announced, is seldom contradicted; it is even looked upon as a sort of common-place in politics and morals. But this almost universal assent is only apparent. The same ideas are not attached to this principle; the same value is not given to it; no uniform and logical manner of reasoning results from it.

To give it all the efficacy which it ought to have, that is, to make it the foundation of a system of reasonings, three conditions are necessary.

First,—to attach clear and precise ideas to the word *utility,* exactly the same with all who employ it.

Second,—To establish the unity and the sovereignty of this principle, by rigorously excluding every other. It is nothing to subscribe to it in general; it must be admitted without any exception.

Third,—To find the processes of a moral arithmetic by which uniform results may be arrived at.

The causes of dissent from the doctrine of utility may all be referred to two false principles, which exercise an influence, sometimes open and sometimes secret, upon the judgments of men. If these can be pointed out and excluded, the true principle will remain in purity and strength.

These three principles are like three roads which often cross each other, but of which only one leads to the wished-for destination. The traveller turns often from one into another, and loses in these wanderings more than half his time and strength. The true route is however the easiest; it has milestones which cannot be shifted, it has inscriptions, in a universal language, which cannot be effaced; while the two false routes have only contradictory directions in enigmatical characters. But without abusing the language of allegory, let us seek to give a clear idea of the true principle, and of its two adversaries.

Nature has placed man under the empire of *pleasure* and of *pain*. We owe to them all our ideas; we refer to them all our judgments, and all the determinations of our life. He who pretends to withdraw himself from this subjection knows not what he says. His only object is to seek pleasure and to shun pain, even at the very instant that he rejects the greatest pleasures or embraces pains the most acute. These eternal and irresistible sentiments ought to be the great study of the moralist and the legislator. The *principle of utility* subjects everything to these two motives.

Utility is an abstract term. It expresses the property or tendency of a thing to prevent some evil or to procure some good. *Evil* is pain, or the cause of pain. *Good* is pleasure, or the cause of pleasure. That which is conformable to the utility, or the interest of an individual, is what tends to augment the total sum of his happiness. That which is conformable to the utility, or the interest of a community, is what tends to augment the total sum of the happiness of the individuals that compose it.

A *principle* is a first idea, which is made the beginning or basis of a system of reasonings. To illustrate it by a sensible image, it is a fixed point to which the first link of a chain is attached. Such a principle must be clearly evident—to illustrate and to explain it must secure its acknowledgment. Such are the axioms of mathematics; they are not proved directly; it is enough to show that they cannot be rejected without falling into absurdity.

The *logic of utility* consists in setting out, in all the operations of the judgment, from the calculation or comparison of pains and pleasures, and in not allowing the interference of any other idea.

I am a partisan of the *principle of utility* when I measure my approbation or disapprobation of a public or private act by its tendency to produce pleasure or pain; when I employ the words *just, unjust, moral, immoral, good, bad,* simply as collective terms including the ideas of certain pains or pleasures; it being always understood that I use the words *pain* and *pleasure* in their ordinary signification, without inventing any arbitrary definition for the sake of excluding certain pleasures or denying the existence of certain pains. In this matter we want no refinement, no metaphysics. It is not necessary to consult Plato, nor Aristotle. *Pain* and *pleasure* are what everybody feels to be such—the peasant and the prince, the unlearned as well as the philosopher.

He who adopts the *principle of utility,* esteems virtue to be a good only on account of the pleasures which result from it; he regards vice as an evil only because of the pains which it produces. Moral good is *good* only by its tendency to produce physical good. Moral evil is *evil* only by its tendency to produce physical evil; but when I say *physical,* I mean the pains and pleasures of the soul as well as the pains and pleasures of sense. I have in view man, such as he is, in his actual constitution.

If the partisan of the *principle of utility* finds in the common list of virtues an action from which there results more pain than pleasure, he does not hesitate to regard that pretended virtue as a vice; he will not suffer himself to be imposed upon by the general error; he will not lightly believe in the policy of employing false virtues to maintain the true.

If he finds in the common list of offences some indifferent action, some innocent pleasure, he will not hesitate to transport this pretended offence into the class of lawful actions; he will pity the pretended criminals, and will reserve his indignation for their persecutors.

Chapter 2. The Ascetic Principle[1]

This principle is exactly the rival, the antagonist of that which we have just been examining. Those who follow it have a horror of pleasures. Everything which gratifies the senses, in their view, is odious and criminal. They found morality upon privations, and virtue upon the renouncement of one's self. In one word, the reverse of the partisans of utility, they approve everything which tends to diminish enjoyment, they blame everything which tends to augment it.

This principle has been more or less followed by two classes of men, who in other respects have scarce any resemblance, and who even affect a

1. Ascetic, by its etymology, signifies *one who exercises.* It was applied to the monks, to indicate their favorite practices of devotion and penitence.

mutual contempt. The one class are philosophers, the other, devotees. The ascetic philosophers, animated by the hope of applause, have flattered themselves with the idea of seeming to rise above humanity, by despising vulgar pleasures. They expect to be paid in reputation and in glory, for all the sacrifices which they seem to make to the severity of their maxims. The ascetic devotees are foolish people, tormented by vain terrors. Man, in their eyes, is but a degenerate being, who ought to punish himself without ceasing for the crime of being born, and never to turn off his thoughts from that gulf of eternal misery which is ready to open beneath his feet. Still, the martyrs to these absurd opinions have, like all others, a fund of hope. Independent of the worldly pleasures attached to the reputation of sanctity, these atrabilious pietists flatter themselves that every instant of voluntary pain here below will procure them an age of happiness in another life. Thus, even the ascetic principle reposes upon some false idea of utility. It acquired its ascendancy only through mistake.[2]

The devotees have carried the ascetic principle much further than the philosophers. The philosophical party has confined itself to censuring pleasures; the religious sects have turned the infliction of pain into a duty. The stoics said that pain was not an evil; the Jansenists maintained that it was actually a good. The philosophical party never reproved pleasures in the mass, but only those which it called gross and sensual, while it exalted the pleasures of sentiment and understanding. It was rather a preference for the one class, than a total exclusion of the other. Always despised, or disparaged under its true name, pleasure was received and applauded when it took the titles of *honour, glory, reputation, decorum,* or *self-esteem.*

Not to be accused of exaggerating the absurdity of the ascetics, I shall mention the least unreasonable origin which can be assigned to their system.

It was early perceived that the attraction of pleasure might seduce into pernicious acts; that is, acts of which the good was not equivalent to the evil. To forbid these pleasures, in consideration of their bad effects, is the object of sound morals and good laws. But the ascetics have made a mistake, for they have attacked pleasure itself; they have condemned it in general; they have made it the object of a universal prohibition, the sign of a reprobate nature; and it is only out of regard for human weakness that they have had the indulgence to grant some particular exemptions.

---

2. This mistake consists in representing the Deity in words, as a being of infinite benevolence, yet ascribing to him prohibitions and threats which are the attributes of an implacable being, who uses his power only to satisfy his malevolence.

We might ask these ascetic theologians what life is good for, if not for the pleasures it procures us?—and what pledge we have for the goodness of God in another life, if he has forbidden the enjoyment of this?

Chapter 3. The Arbitrary Principle; or the Principle of Sympathy and Antipathy

This principle consists in approving or blaming by sentiment, without giving any other reason for the decision except the decision itself. *I love, I hate;* such is the pivot on which this principle turns. An action is judged to be good or bad, not because it is conformable, or on the contrary, to the interest of those whom it affects, but because it pleases or displeases him who judges. He pronounces sovereignly; he admits no appeal; he does not think himself obliged to justify his opinion by any consideration relative to the good of society. "It is my interior persuasion; it is my intimate conviction; I feel it; sentiment consults nobody; the worse for him who does not agree with me—he is not a man, he is a monster in human shape." Such is the despotic tone of these decisions.

But, it may be asked, are there men so unreasonable as to dictate their particular sentiments as laws, and to arrogate to themselves the privilege of infallibility? What you call the *principle of sympathy and antipathy* is not a principle of reasoning; it is rather the negation, the annihilation of all principle. A true anarchy of ideas results from it; since every man having an equal right to give *his* sentiments as a universal rule, there will no longer be any common measure, no ultimate tribunal to which we can appeal.

Without doubt the absurdity of this principle is sufficiently manifest. No man, therefore, is bold enough to say openly, "I wish you to think as I do, without giving me the trouble to reason with you." Every one would revolt against a pretension so absurd. Therefore, recourse is had to diverse inventions of disguise. Despotism is veiled under some ingenious phrase. Of this the greater part of philosophical systems are a proof.

One man tells you that he has in himself something which has been given him to teach what is good and what is evil; and this he calls either his *conscience* or his *moral sense*. Then, working at his ease, he decides such a thing to be good, such another to be bad. Why? Because my moral sense tells me so; because my conscience approves or disapproves it.

Another comes and the phrase changes. It is no longer the moral sense,— it is *common sense* which tells him what is good and what is bad. This common sense is a sense, he says, which belongs to everybody; but then he takes good care in speaking of everybody to make no account of those who do not think as he does.

Another tells you that this moral sense and this common sense are but dreams; that the *understanding* determines what is good and what is bad. His understanding tells him so and so; all good and wise men have just such an understanding as he has. As to those who do not think in the same way, it is a clear proof that their understandings are defective or corrupt.

Another tells you that he has an *eternal and immutable rule of right*, which rule commands this and forbids that; then he retails to you his own particular sentiments, which you are obliged to receive as so many branches of the eternal rule of right.

You hear a multitude of professors, of jurists, of magistrates, of philosophers, who make the *law of nature* echo in your ears. They all dispute, it is true, upon every point of their system; but no matter—each one proceeds with the same confident intrepidity, and utters his opinions as so many chapters of the *law of nature*. The phrase is sometimes modified, and we find in its place, *natural right, natural equity, the rights of man, etc*.

One philosopher undertakes to build a moral system upon what he calls *truth;* according to him, the only evil in the world is lying. If you kill your father, you commit a crime, because it is a particular fashion of saying that he is not your father. Everything which this philosopher does not like, he disapproves under the pretext that it is a sort of falsehood—since it amounts to asserting that we ought to do what ought not to be done. . . .

To sum up;—the *ascetic principle* attacks utility in front. The *principle of sympathy* neither rejects it nor admits it; it pays no attention to it; it floats at hazard between good and evil. The ascetic principle is so unreasonable, that its most senseless followers have never attempted to carry it out. The principle of sympathy and antipathy does not prevent its partisans from having recourse to the principle of utility. This last alone neither asks nor admits any exceptions. *Qui non sub me contra me;* that which is not under me is against me; such is its motto. According to this principle, to legislate is an affair of observation and calculation; according to the ascetics, it is an affair of fanaticism; according to the principle of sympathy and antipathy, it is a matter of humour, of imagination, of taste. The first method is adapted to philosophers; the second to monks; the third is the favourite of wits, of ordinary moralists, of men of the world, of the multitude.

Chapter 4. Operation of These Principles upon Legislation

. . . The principle which has exercised the greatest influence upon governments, is that of sympathy and antipathy. In fact, we must refer to that principle all those specious objects which governments pursue, without having the general good for a single and independent aim; such as good morals, equality, liberty, justice, power, commerce, religion; objects respectable in themselves, and which ought to enter into the views of the legislator; but which too often lead him astray, because he regards them as ends, not as means. He substitutes them for public happiness, instead of making them subordinate to it.

Thus, a government, entirely occupied with wealth and commerce, looks upon society as a workshop, regards men only as productive machines, and cares little how much it torments them, provided it makes them rich. The customs, the exchanges, the stocks, absorb all its thoughts. It looks with indifference upon a multitude of evils which it might easily cure. It wishes only for a great production of the means of enjoyment, while it is constantly putting new obstacles in the way of enjoying.

Other governments esteem power and glory as the sole means of public good. Full of disdain for those states which are able to be happy in a peaceful security, they must have intrigues, negotiations, wars and conquests. They do not consider of what misfortunes this glory is composed, and how many victims these bloody triumphs require. The *éclat* of victory, the acquisition of a province, conceal from them the desolation of their country, and make them mistake the true end of government.

Many persons do not inquire if a state be well administered; if the laws protect property and persons; if the people are happy. What they require, without giving attention to anything else, is political liberty—that is, the most equal distribution which can be imagined of political power. Wherever they do not see the form of government to which they are attached, they see nothing but slaves; and if these pretended slaves are well satisfied with their condition, if they do not desire to change it, they despise and insult them. In their fanaticism they are always ready to stake all the happiness of a nation upon a civil war, for the sake of transporting power into the hands of those whom an invincible ignorance will not permit to use it, except for their own destruction. . . .

Chapter 7. Pains and Pleasures Considered as Sanctions

The will cannot be influenced except by motives; but when we speak of *motives,* we speak of *pleasures* or *pains.* A being whom we could not effect either by painful or pleasurable emotions would be completely independent of us.

The pain or pleasure which is attached to a law form what is called its sanction. The laws of one state are not laws in another because they have no sanction there, no obligatory force.

Pleasures and pains may be distinguished into four classes:

1st. Physical.
2nd. Moral.
3rd. Political.
4th. Religious.

Consequently, when we come to consider pains and pleasures under the character of punishments and rewards, attached to certain rules of conduct, we may distinguish four sanctions.

1st. Those pleasures and pains which may be expected from the ordinary course of nature, acting by itself, without human intervention, compose the *natural or physical sanction.*

2nd. The pleasures or pains which may be expected from the action of our fellow-men, in virtue of their friendship or hatred, of their esteem or their contempt—in one word, of their spontaneous disposition towards us, compose the *moral sanction;* or it may be called the *popular sanction, sanction of public opinion, sanction of honour, sanction of the pains and pleasures of sympathy.*

3rd. The pleasures or pains which may be expected from the action of the magistrate, in virtue of the law, compose the *political sanction;* it may also be called the *legal sanction.*

4th. The pleasures or pains which may be expected in virtue of the threats or promises of religion, compose the *religious sanction.*

A man's house is destroyed by fire. Is it in consequence of his imprudence?—It is a pain of the natural sanction. Is it by the sentence of a judge?—It is a pain of the political sanction. Is it by the malice of his neighbours?—It is a pain of the popular sanction. Is it supposed to be the immediate act of an offended Divinity?—In such a case it would be a pain of the religious sanction, or vulgarly speaking, a judgment of God.

It is evident from this example that the same sort of pains belong to all the sanctions. The only difference is in the circumstances which produce them.

This classification will be very useful in the course of this work. It is an easy and uniform nomenclature, absolutely necessary to distinguish and describe the different kinds of moral powers, those intellectual levers which constitute the machinery of the human heart.

These four sanctions do not act upon all men in the same manner, nor with the same degree of force. They are sometimes rivals, sometimes allies, and sometimes enemies. When they agree, they operate with an irresistible power; when they are in opposition, they mutually enfeeble each other; when they are rivals, they produce uncertainties and contradictions in the conduct of men.

Four bodies of laws may be imagined, corresponding to these four sanctions. The highest point of perfection would be reached if these four codes constituted but one. This perfection, however, is as yet far distant, though it may not be impossible to attain it. But the legislator ought always to recollect that he can operate directly only by means of the political sanction. The three others must necessarily be its rivals or its allies, its antagonists or its ministers. If he neglects them in his calculations, he will be deceived in his results; but if he makes them subservient to his views, he will gain an immense power. There is no chance of uniting them, except under the standard of utility.

The natural sanction is the only one which always acts; the only one which works of itself; the only one which is unchangeable in its principal characteristics. It insensibly draws all the others to it, corrects their deviations, and produces whatever uniformity there is in the sentiments and the judgments of men.

The popular sanction and the religious sanction are more variable, more dependent upon human caprices. Of the two, the popular sanction is more equal, more steady, and more constantly in accordance with the principle of utility. The force of the religious sanction is more unequal, more apt to change with times and individuals, more subject to dangerous deviations. It grows weak by repose, but revives by opposition.

In some respects the political sanction has the advantage of both. It acts upon all men with a more equal force; it is clearer and more precise in its precepts; it is surer and more exemplary in its operations; finally, it is more susceptible of being carried to perfection. Its progress has an immediate influence upon the progress of the other two; but it embraces only actions of a certain kind; it has not a sufficient hold upon the private conduct of individuals; it cannot proceed except upon proofs which it is often impossible to obtain; and secrecy, force, or stratagem are able to escape it. It thus appears, from considering what each of these sanctions can effect, and what they cannot, that neither ought to be rejected, but that all should be employed and directed towards the same end. They are like magnets, of which the virtue is destroyed when they are presented to each other by their contrary poles, while their power is doubled when they are united by the poles which correspond.

It may be observed, in passing, that the systems which have most divided men have been founded upon an exclusive preference given to one or the other of these sanctions. Each has had its partisans, who have wished to exalt it above the others. Each has had its enemies, who have sought to degrade it by showing its weak side, exposing its errors, and developing all the evils which have resulted from it, without making any mention of its good effects. Such is the true theory of all those paradoxes which elevate nature against society, politics against religion, religion against nature and government, and so on.

Each of these sanctions is susceptible of error, that is to say, of some applications contrary to the principle of utility. But by applying the nomenclature above explained, it is easy to indicate by a single word the seat of the evil. Thus, for example, the reproach which after the punishment of a criminal falls upon an innocent family is an error of the popular sanction. The offence of usury, that is, of receiving interest above the legal interest, is an error of the political sanction. Heresy and magic are errors of the religious sanction. Certain sympathies and antipathies are errors of the natural sanction. The first germ of mistake exists in some single sanction, whence it commonly spreads into the others. It is necessary, in all these cases, to discover the origin of the evil before we can select or apply the remedy.

Chapter 8. The Measure of Pleasures and Pains

The sole object of the legislator is to increase pleasures and to prevent pains; and for this purpose he ought to be well acquainted with their respective values. As pleasures and pains are the only instruments which he employs, he ought carefully to study their power.

If we examine the *value* of a pleasure, considered in itself, and in relation to a single individual, we shall find that it depends upon four circumstances,—

1st. *Its intensity.*
2nd. *Its duration.*
3rd. *Its certainty.*
4th. *Its proximity.*

The value of a pain depends upon the same circumstances.

But it is not enough to examine the value of pleasures and pains as if they were isolated and independent. Pains and pleasures may have other pains and pleasures as their consequences. Therefore, if we wish to calculate the *tendency* of an act from which there results an immediate pain or pleasure, we must take two additional circumstances into the account, viz.—

5th. *Its productiveness.*
6th. *Its purity.*

A *productive pleasure* is one which is likely to be followed by other pleasures of the same kind.

A *productive pain* is one which is likely to be followed by other pains of the same kind.

A *pure pleasure* is one which is not likely to produce pains.

A *pure pain* is one which is not likely to produce pleasures.

When the calculation is to be made in relation to a collection of individuals, yet another element is necesssary,—

7th. *Its extent.*

That is, the number of persons who are likely to find themselves affected by this pain or pleasure.

When we wish to value an action, we must follow in detail all the operations above indicated. These are the elements of moral calculation; and legislation thus becomes a matter of arithmetic. The *evil* produced is the outgo, the *good* which results is the income. The rules of this calculation are like those of any other. This is a slow method, but a sure one; while what is called sentiment is a prompt estimate, but apt to be deceptive. It is not necessary to recommence this calculation upon every occasion. When one has become familiar with the process; when he has acquired the justness of estimate which results from it; he can compare the sum of good and of evil with so much promptitude as scarcely to be conscious of the steps of the calculation. It is thus that we perform many arithmetical calculations, almost without knowing it. The analytical method, in all its details, becomes essential, only when some new or complicated matter arises; when it is necessary to clear up some disputed point, or to demonstrate a truth to those who are yet unacquainted with it.

This theory of moral calculation, though never clearly explained, has always been followed in practice; at least, in every case where men have had clear ideas of their interest. What is it, for example, that makes up the value of a landed estate? Is it not the amount of pleasure to be derived from it? and does not this value vary according to the length of time for which the estate is to be enjoyed; according to the nearness or the distance of the moment when the possession is to begin; according to the certainty or uncertainty of its being retained?

Errors, whether in legislation or the moral conduct of men, may be always accounted for by a mistake, a forgetfulness, or a false estimate of some one of these elements, in the calculation of good and evil.

Chapter 9. Circumstances Which Affect Sensibility

All causes of pleasure do not give the same pleasure to all; all causes of pain do not always produce the same pain. It is in this that *difference of sensibility* consists. This difference is in degree, or in kind: in degree, when the impression of a given cause upon many individuals is uniform, but unequal; in kind, when the same cause produces opposite sensations in different individuals.

This difference of sensibility depends upon certain circumstances which influence the physical or moral condition of individuals, and which, being changed, produce a corresponding change in their feelings. This is an experimental fact. Things do not affect us in the same manner in sickness and in health, in plenty and in poverty, in infancy and old age. But a view so general is not sufficient; it is necessary to go deeper into the human heart. Lyonet wrote a quarto volume upon the anatomy of the caterpillar; morals are in need of an investigator as patient and philosophical. I have not courage to imitate Lyonet. I shall think it sufficient if I open a new point of view—if I suggest a surer method to those who wish to pursue this subject.

The foundation of the whole is *temperament,* or the original constitution. By this word I understand that radical and primitive disposition which attends us from our birth, and which depends upon physical organization, and the nature of the soul.

But although this radical constitution is the basis of all the rest, this basis lies so concealed that it is very difficult to get at it, so as to distinguish those varieties of sensibility which it produces from those which belong to other causes.

It is the business of the physiologist to distinguish these temperaments; to follow out their mixtures; and to trace their effects. But these grounds are as yet too little known to justify the moralist or legislator in founding anything upon them. . . .

Chapter 10. Analysis of Political Good and Evil.—How They Are Diffused through Society

It is with government as with medicine; its only business is the choice of evils. Every law is an evil, for every law is an infraction of liberty. Government, I repeat it, has but the choice of evils. In making that choice, what ought to be the object of the legislator? He ought to be certain of two things: 1st, that in every case, the acts which he undertakes to prevent are really evils; and, 2nd, that these evils are greater than those which he employs to prevent them.

He has then two things to note—the evil of the offence, and the evil of the law; the evil of the malady, and the evil of the remedy.

An evil seldom comes alone. A portion of evil can hardly fall upon an individual, without spreading on every side, as from a centre. As it spreads, it takes different forms. We see an evil of one kind coming out of an evil of another kind; we even see evil coming out of good, and good out of evil. . . .

The propagation of good is less rapid and less sensible than that of evil. The seed of good is not so productive in hopes as the seed of evil is fruitful in alarms. But this difference is abundantly made up, for good is a necessary result of natural causes which operate always; while evil is produced only by accident, and at intervals.

Society is so constituted that, in labouring for our particular good, we labour also for the good of the whole. We cannot augment our own means of enjoyment without augmenting also the means of others. Two nations, like two individuals, grow rich by a mutual commerce; and all exchange is founded upon reciprocal advantages.

It is fortunate also that the effects of evil are not always evil. They often assume the contrary quality. Thus, juridical punishments applied to offences, although they produce an evil of the first order, are not generally regarded as evils, because they produce a good of the second order. They produce alarm and danger,—but for whom? Only for a class of evil-doers, who are voluntary sufferers. Let them obey the laws, and they will be exposed neither to danger nor alarm.

We should never be able to subjugate, however imperfectly, the vast empire of evil, had we not learned the method of combating one evil by another. It has been necessary to enlist auxiliaries among pains, to oppose other pains which attack us on every side. So, in the art of curing pains of another sort, poisons well applied have proved to be remedies.

Chapter 12. The Limits Which Separate Morals from Legislation

Morality in general is the art of directing the actions of men in such a way as to produce the greatest possible sum of good.

Legislation ought to have precisely the same object.

But although these two arts, or rather sciences, have the same end they differ greatly in extent. All actions, whether public or private, fall under the jurisdiction of morals. It is a guide which leads the individual, as it were, by the hand through all the details of his life, all his relations with his fellows. Legislation cannot do this; and, if it could, it ought not to exercise a continual interference and dictation over the conduct of men.

Morality commands each individual to do all that is advantageous to the community, his own personal advantages included. But there are many acts useful to the community which legislation ought not to command. There are also many injurious actions which it ought not to forbid, although morality does so. In a word, legislation has the same centre with morals, but it has not the same circumference.

There are two reasons for this difference: 1st. Legislation can have no direct influence upon the conduct of men, except by punishments. Now these punishments are so many evils, which are not justifiable, except so far as there results from them a greater sum of good. But, in many cases in which we might desire to strengthen a moral precept by a punishment, the evil of the punishment would be greater than the evil of the offence. The means necessary to carry the law into execution would be of a nature to spread through society a degree of alarm more injurious than the evil intended to be prevented.

2nd. Legislation is often arrested by the danger of overwhelming the innocent in seeking to punish the guilty. Whence comes this danger? From the difficulty of defining an offence, and giving a clear and precise idea of it. For example, hardheartedness, ingratitude, perfidy, and other vices which the popular sanction punishes, cannot come under the power of the law, unless they are defined as exactly as theft, homicide, or perjury.

But, the better to distinguish the true limits of morals and legislation, it will be well to refer to the common classification of moral duties.

Private morality regulates the actions of men, either in that part of their conduct in which they alone are interested, or in that which may affect the interests of others. The actions which affect a man's individual interest compose a class called, perhaps improperly, *duties to ourselves;* and the quality or disposition manifested in the accomplishment of those duties receives the name of *prudence.* That part of conduct which relates to others composes a class of actions called *duties to others.* Now there are two ways of consulting the happiness of others: the one negative, abstaining from diminishing it; the other positive, labouring to augment it. The first constitutes *probity;* the second is *beneficence.*

Morality upon these three points needs the aid of the law; but not in the same degree, nor in the same manner.

I. The rules of prudence are almost always sufficient of themselves. If a man fails in what regards his particular private interest, it is not his will which is in fault, it is his understanding. If he does wrong, it can only be through mistake. The fear of hurting himself is a motive of repression sufficiently strong; it would be useless to add to it the fear of an artificial pain.

Does any one object, that facts show the contrary? That excesses of play, those of intemperance, the illicit intercourse between the sexes, attended so often by the greatest dangers, are enough to prove that individuals have not always sufficient prudence to abstain from what hurts them?

Confining myself to a general reply, I answer, in the first place, that, in the greater part of these cases, punishment would be so easily eluded, that it would be inefficacious; secondly, that the evil produced by the penal law would be much beyond the evil of the offence.

Suppose, for example, that a legislator should feel himself authorized to undertake the extirpation of drunkenness and fornication by direct laws. He would have to begin by a multitude of regulations. The first inconvenience would therefore be a complexity of laws. The easier it is to conceal these vices, the more necessary it would be to resort to severity of punishment, in order to destroy by the terror of examples the constantly recurring hope of impunity. This excessive rigour of laws forms a second inconvenience not less grave than the first. The difficulty of procuring proofs would be such that it would be necessary to encourage informers, and to entertain an army of spies. This necessity forms a third inconvenience, greater than either of the others. Let us compare the results of good and evil. Offences of this nature, if that name can be properly given to imprudences, produce no alarm; but the pretended remedy would spread a universal terror; innocent or guilty, every one would fear for himself or his connexions; suspicions and accusations would render society dangerous; we should fly from it; we should involve ourselves in mystery and concealment; we should shun all the disclosures of confidence. Instead of suppressing one vice, the laws would produce other vices, new and more dangerous.

It is true that example may render certain excesses contagious; and that an evil which would be almost imperceptible, if it acted only upon a small number of individuals, may become important by its extent. All that the legislator can do in reference to offences of this kind is, to submit them to some slight punishment in cases of scandalous notoriety. This will be sufficient to give them a taint of illegality, which will excite the popular sanction against them.

It is in cases of this kind that legislators have governed too much. Instead of trusting to the prudence of individuals, they have treated them like children, or slaves. They have suffered themselves to be carried away by the same passion which has influenced the founders of religious orders, who, to signalize their authority, and through a littleness of spirit, have held their subjects in the most abject dependence, and have traced for them, day by day, and moment by moment, their occupations, their food, their rising up, their lying down, and all the petty details of their life. There are celebrated codes, in which are found a multitude of clogs of this sort; there are useless restraints upon marriage; punishments decreed against celibacy; sumptuary laws regulating the fashion of dress, the expense of festivals, the furniture of houses, and the ornaments of women; there are numberless details about aliments, permitted or forbidden; about ablutions of such or such a kind; about the purifications which health or cleanliness require; and a thousand similar puerilities, which add, to all the inconveniences of useless restraint, that of besotting the people, by covering these absurdities with a veil of mystery, to disguise their folly.

Yet more unhappy are the States in which it is attempted to maintain by penal laws a uniformity of religious opinions. The choice of their religion ought to be referred entirely to the prudence of individuals. If they are persuaded that their eternal happiness depends upon a certain form of worship or a certain belief, what can a legislator oppose to an interest so great? It is not necessary to insist upon this truth—it is generally acknowledged; but, in tracing the boundaries of legislation, I cannot forget those which it is the most important not to overstep.

As a general rule, the greatest possible latitude should be left to individuals, in all cases in which they can injure none but themselves, for they are the best judges of their own interests. If they deceive themselves, it is to be supposed that the moment they discover their error they will alter their conduct. The power of the law need interfere only to prevent them from injuring each other. It is there that restraint is necessary; it is there that the application of punishments is truly useful, because the rigour exercised upon an individual becomes in such a case the security of all.

II. It is true that there is a natural connection between prudence and probity; for our own interest, well understood, will never leave us without motives to abstain from injuring our fellows. . . .

A man enlightened as to his own interest will not indulge himself in a secret offence through fear of contracting a shameful habit, which sooner or later will betray him; and because the having secrets to conceal from the prying curiosity of mankind leaves in the heart a sediment of disquiet, which corrupts every pleasure. All he can acquire at the expense of security cannot make up for the loss of that; and, if he desires a good reputation, the best guarantee he can have for it is his own esteem.

But, in order that an individual should perceive this connection between the interests of others and his own, he needs an enlightened spirit and a heart free from seductive passions. The greater part of men have neither sufficient light, sufficient strength of mind, nor sufficient moral sensibility to place their honesty above the aid of the laws. The legislator must supply the feebleness of this natural interest by adding to it an artificial interest, more steady and more easily perceived.

More yet. In many cases morality derives its existence from the law; that is, to decide whether the action is morally good or bad, it is necessary to know whether the laws permit or forbid it. It is so of what concerns property. A manner of selling or acquiring, esteemed dishonest in one country, would be irreproachable in another. It is the same with offences against the state. The state exists only by law, and it is impossible to say what conduct in this behalf morality requires of us before knowing what the legislator has decreed. There are countries where it is an offence to enlist into the service of a foreign power, and others in which such a service is lawful and honourable.[3]

III. As to beneficence some distinctions are necessary. The law may be extended to general objects, such as the care of the poor; but, for details, it is necessary to depend upon private morality. Beneficence has its myste-

---

3. Here we touch upon one of the most difficult of questions. If the law is not what it ought to be; if it openly combats the principle of utility; ought we to obey it? Ought we to violate it? Ought we to remain neuter between the law which commands an evil, and morality which forbids it? The solution of this question involves considerations both of prudence and benevolence. We ought to examine if it is more dangerous to violate the law than to obey it; we ought to consider whether the probable evils of obedience are less or greater than the probable evils of disobedience.

ries, and loves best to employ itself upon evils so unforeseen or so secret that the law cannot reach them. Besides, it is to individual free-will that benevolence owes its energy. If the same acts were commanded, they would no longer be benefits, they would lose their attractions and their essence. It is morality and especially religion, which here form the necessary complement to legislation, and the sweetest tie of humanity.

However, instead of having done too much in this respect, legislators have not done enough. They ought to erect into an offence the refusal or the omission of a service to humanity when it would be easy to render it, and when some distinct ill clearly results from the refusal; such, for example, as abandoning a wounded man in a solitary road without seeking any assistance for him; not giving information to a man who is ignorantly meddling with poisons; not reaching out the hand to one who has fallen into a ditch from which he cannot extricate himself; in these, and other similar cases, could any fault be found with a punishment, exposing the delinquent to a certain degree of shame, or subjecting him to a pecuniary responsibility for the evil which he might have prevented? . . .

Chapter 13. False Methods of Reasoning on the Subject of Legislation

It has been the object of this introduction to give a clear idea of the principle of utility, and of the method of reasoning conformable to that principle. There results from it a legislative logic, which can be summed up in a few words. What is it to offer a *good reason* with respect to a law? It is to allege the good or evil which the law tends to produce: so much good, so many arguments in its favour; so much evil, so many arguments against it; remembering all the time that good and evil are nothing else than pleasure and pain.

What is it to offer a *false reason?* It is the alleging for or against a law something else than its good or evil effects.

Nothing can be more simple, yet nothing is more new. It is not the principle of utility which is new; on the contrary, that principle is necessarily as old as the human race. All the truth there is in morality, all the good there is in the laws, emanate from it; but utility has often been followed by instinct, while it has been combatted by argument. If in books of legislation it throws out some sparks here and there, they are quickly extinguished in the surrounding smoke. BECCARIA is the only writer who deserves to be noted as an exception; yet even in his work there is some reasoning drawn from false sources.

It is upwards of two thousand years since Aristotle undertook to form, under the title of *Sophisms,* a complete catalogue of the different kinds of false reasoning. This catalogue, improved by the information which so long an interval might furnish, would here have its place and its use. But such an undertaking would carry me too far. I shall be content with presenting some heads of error on the subject of legislation. By means of such a contrast, the principle of utility will be put into a clearer light.

1. *Antiquity Is Not a Reason.* The antiquity of a law may create a prejudice in its favour; but in itself, it is not a reason. If the law in question has contributed to the public good, the older it is, the easier it will be to enumerate its good effects, and to prove its utility by a direct process.

2. *The Authority of Religion Is Not a Reason.* Of late, this method of reasoning has gone much out of fashion, but till recently its use was very extensive. The work of Algernon Sidney is full of citations from the *Old Testament;* and he finds there the foundation of a system of Democracy, as Bossuet had found the principle of absolute power. Sidney wished to combat the partisans of divine right and passive obedience with their own weapons.

If we suppose that a law emanates from the Deity, we suppose that it emanates from supreme wisdom, and supreme bounty. Such a law, then, can only have for its object the most eminent utility; and this utility, put into a clear light, will always be an ample justification of the law.

3. *Reproach of Innovation Is Not a Reason.* To reject innovation is to reject progress; in what condition should we be, if that principle had been always followed? All which exists had had a beginning; all which is established has been innovation. Those very persons who approve a law to-day because it is ancient, would have opposed it as new when it was first introduced.

4. *An Arbitrary Definition Is Not a Reason.* Nothing is more common, among jurists and political writers, than to base their reasonings, and even to write long works, upon a foundation of purely arbitrary definitions. This artifice consists in taking a word in a particular sense, foreign from its common usage; in employing that word as no one ever employed it before; and in puzzling the reader by an appearance of profoundness and of mystery.

Montesquieu himself has fallen into this fault in the very beginning of his work. Wishing to give a definition of law, he proceeds from metaphor to metaphor; he brings together the most discordant objects—the Divinity, the material world, superior intelligences, beasts and men. We learn, at last, that *laws are relations; and eternal relations.* Thus the definition is more obscure than the thing to be defined. The word *law,* in its proper sense, excites in every mind a tolerably clear idea, the word *relation* excites no idea at all. The word *law,* in its figurative sense, produces nothing but equivocations; and Montesquieu, who ought to have dissipated the darkness has only increased it. . . .

5. *Metaphors Are Not Reasons.* I mean either metaphor properly so

called, or allegory, used at first for illustration or ornament, but afterwards made the basis of an argument.

Blackstone, so great an enemy of reform, that he has gone so far as to find fault with the introduction of the English language into the reports of cases decided by the courts, has neglected no means of inspiring his readers with the same prejudice. He represents the law as a castle, as a fortress, which cannot be altered without being weakened. I allow that he does not advance this metaphor as an argument; but why does he employ it? To gain possession of the imagination; to prejudice his readers against every idea of reform; to excite in them an artificial fear of all innovation in the laws. There remains in the mind a false image, which produces the same effect with false reasoning. He ought to have recollected that this allegory might be employed against himself. When they see the law turned into a castle, is it not natural for ruined suitors to represent it as a castle inhabited by robbers?

A man's house, say the English, is his castle. This poetical expression is certainly no reason; for if a man's house be his castle by night, why not by day? If it is an inviolable asylum for the owner, why is it not so for every person whom he chooses to receive there? The course of justice is sometimes interrupted in England by this puerile notion of liberty. Criminals seem to be looked upon like foxes; they are suffered to have their burrows, in order to increase the sports of the chase.

A church in Catholic countries is the *House of God*. This metaphor has served to establish asylums for criminals. It would be a mark of disrespect for the Divinity to seize by force those who had taken refuge in his house.

The *balance of trade* has produced a multitude of reasonings founded upon metaphor. It has been imagined that in the course of mutual commerce nations rose and sank like the scales of a balance loaded with unequal weights; people have been terribly alarmed at what appeared to them a want of equilibrium; for it has been supposed that what one nation gained the other must lose, as if a weight had been transferred from one scale to the other.

The word *mother-country* has produced a great number of prejudices and false reasonings in all questions concerning colonies and the parent state. Duties have been imposed upon colonies, and they have been accused of offences, founded solely upon the metaphor of their filial dependence.

6. *A Fiction Is Not a Reason*. I understand by fiction an assumed fact notoriously false, upon which one reasons as if it were true. . . .

Blackstone, in the seventh chapter of his first book, in speaking of the royal authority, has given himself up to all the puerility of fiction. The king, he tells us, is everywhere present; he can do no wrong; he is immortal.

These ridiculous paradoxes, the fruits of servility, so far from furnishing just ideas of the prerogatives of royalty, only serve to dazzle, to mislead, and to give to reality itself an air of fable and of prodigy. . . .

But there are fictions more bold and more important, which have played a great part in politics, and which have produced celebrated works: these are *contracts*.

The *Leviathan* of Hobbes, a work now-a-days but little known, and detested through prejudice and at second-hand as a defence of despotism, is an attempt to base all political society upon a pretended contract between the people and the sovereign. The people by this contract have renounced their natural liberty, which produced nothing but evil; and have deposited all power in the hands of the prince. All opposing wills have been united in his, or rather annihilated by it. That which he *wills* is taken to be the will of all his subjects. . . .

Locke, whose name is as dear to the friends of liberty as that of Hobbes is odious, has also fixed the basis of government upon a contract. He agrees that there is a contract between the prince and the people; but according to him the prince takes an engagement to govern according to the laws, and for the public good; while the people, on their side, take an engagement of obedience so long as the prince remains faithful to the conditions in virtue of which he receives the crown.

Rousseau rejects with indignation the idea of this bilateral contract between the prince and the people. He has imagined a *social contract,* by which all are bound to all, and which is the only legitimate basis of government. Society exists only by virtue of this free convention of associates.

These three systems—so directly opposed—agree, however, in beginning the theory of politics with a fiction, for these three contracts are equally fictitious. They exist only in the imagination of their authors. Not only we find no trace of them in history, but everywhere we discover proofs to the contrary. . . .

It is not necessary to make the happiness of the human race dependent on a fiction. It is not necessary to erect the social pyramid upon a foundation of sand, or upon a clay which slips from beneath it. Let us leave such trifling to children; men ought to speak the language of truth and reason.

The true political tie is the immense interest which men have in maintaining a government. Without a government there can be no security, no domestic enjoyments, no property, no industry. It is in this fact that we ought to seek the basis and the reason of all governments, whatever may be their origin and their form; it is by comparing them with their object that we can reason with solidity upon their rights and their obligations, without having recourse to pretended contracts which can only serve to produce interminable disputes.

7. *Fancy Is Not a Reason*. Nothing is more common than to say, *reason decides, eternal reason orders, etc.* But what is this reason? If it is not a distinct view of good or evil, it is mere fancy; it is a despotism, which announces nothing but the interior persuasion of him who speaks. Let us see upon what foundation a distinguished jurist has sought to establish the paternal authority. A man of ordinary good sense would not see much difficulty in that question; but your learned men find a mystery everywhere.

"The right of a father over his children," says Cocceiji, "is founded in reason;—for, 1st, Children are born in a house, of which the father is the master; 2nd, They are born in a family of which he is the chief; 3rd, They are of his seed, and a part of his body." These are the reasons from which he concludes, among other things, that a man of forty ought not to marry without the consent of a father, who in the course of nature must by that time be in his dotage. What there is common to these three reasons is, that none of them has any relation to the interests of the parties. The author consults neither the welfare of father nor that of the children.

The right of a father is an improper phrase. The question is not of an unlimited, nor of an indivisible right. There are many kinds of rights which may be granted or refused to a father, each for particular reasons. . . .

And here we may remark an essential difference between false principles and the true one. The principle of utility, applying itself only to the interests of the parties, bends to circumstances, and accommodates itself to every case. False principles, being founded upon things which have nothing to do with individual interests, would be inflexible if they were consistent. Such is the character of this pretended right founded upon birth. The son naturally belongs to the father, because the matter of which the son is formed once circulated in the father's veins. No matter how unhappy he renders his son;—it is impossible to annihilate his right, because we cannot make his son cease to be his son. The corn of which your body is made formerly grew in my field; how is it that you are not my slave?

8 *Antipathy and Sympathy Are Not Reasons*. Reasoning by antipathy is most common upon subjects connected with penal law; for we have antipathies against actions reputed to be crimes; antipathies against individuals reputed to be criminals; antipathies against the ministers of justice; antipathies against such and such punishments. This false principle has reigned like a tyrant throughout this vast province of law. Beccaria first dared openly to attack it. His arms were of celestial temper; but if he did much towards destroying the usurper, he did very little towards the establishment of a new and more equitable rule.

It is the principle of antipathy which leads us to speak of offences as *deserving* punishment. It is the corresponding principle of sympathy which leads us to speak of certain actions as *meriting* reward. The word *merit* can only lead to passion and to error. It is *effects,* good or bad, which we ought alone to consider. . . .

9. *Begging the Question Is Not a Reason.* The *petitio principii,* or begging the question, is one of the sophisms which is noted by Aristotle; but it is a Proteus which conceals itself artfully, and is reproduced under a thousand forms.

Begging the question, or rather assuming the question, consists in making use of the very proposition in dispute, as though it were already proved.

This false procedure insinuates itself into morals and legislation, under the disguise of *sentimental* or *impassioned* terms; that is, terms which, beside their principal sense, carry with them an accessory idea of praise or blame. *Neuter* terms are those which simply express the thing in question, without any attending presumption of good or evil; without introducing any foreign idea of blame or approbation.

Now it is to be observed that an impassioned term envelops a proposition not expressed, but understood, which always accompanies its employment, though in general unperceived by those who employ it. This concealed proposition implies either blame or praise; but the implication is always vague and undetermined.

Do I desire to connect an idea of utility with a term which commonly conveys an accessory idea of blame? I shall seem to advance a paradox, and to contradict myself. For example, should I say that such a piece of *luxury* is a good thing? The proposition astonishes those who are accustomed to attach to this word *luxury* a sentiment of disapprobation.

How shall I be able to examine this particular point without awakening a dangerous association? I must have recourse to a neuter word; I must say, for example, *such a manner of spending one's revenue* is good. This turn of expression runs counter to no prejudice, and permits an impartial examination of the object in question. When Helvetius advanced the idea that all actions have *interest* for their motive, the public cried out against his doctrine without stopping to understand it. Why? Because the word *interest* has an odious sense; a common acceptation, in which it seems to exclude every motive of pure attachment and of benevolence.

How many reasonings upon political subjects are founded upon nothing but impassioned terms! People suppose they are giving a reason for a law, when they say that it is conformable to the principles of monarchy or of democracy. But that means nothing. If there are persons in whose minds these words are associated with an idea of approbation, there are others who attach contrary ideas to them. Let these two parties begin to quarrel, the dispute will never come to an end, except through the weariness of the combatants. For, before beginning a true examination, we must renounce these impassioned terms, and calculate the effects of the proposed law in good and evil. . . .

If we attempt a theory upon the subject of *national representation,* in following out all that appears to be a natural consequence of that abstract idea, we come at last to the conclusion that *universal suffrage* ought to be established; and to the additional conclusion that the representatives ought to be re-chosen as frequently as possible, in order that the national representation may deserve to be esteemed such.

In deciding these same questions according to the principle of utility, it will not do to reason upon words; we must look only at effects. In the election of a legislative assembly, the right of suffrage should not be allowed except to those who are esteemed by the nation fit to exercise it; for a choice made by men who do not possess the national confidence will weaken the confidence of the nation in the assembly so chosen.

Men who would not be thought fit to be electors, are those who cannot be presumed to possess political integrity, and a sufficient degree of knowledge. Now we cannot presume upon the political integrity of those whom want exposes to the temptation of selling themselves; nor of those who have no fixed abode; nor of those who have been found guilty in the courts of justice of certain offences forbidden by the law. We cannot presume a sufficient degree of knowledge in women, whom their domestic condition withdraws from the conduct of public affairs; in children and adults beneath a certain age; in those who are deprived by their poverty of the first elements of education, etc. etc.

It is according to these principles, and others like them, that we ought to fix the conditions necessary for becoming an elector; and it is in like manner, upon the advantages and disadvantages of frequent elections, without paying any attention to arguments drawn from abstract terms, that we ought to reason in establishing the duration of a legislative assembly. . . .

10. *An Imaginary Law Is Not a Reason. Natural law, natural rights* are two kinds of fictions or metaphors, which play so great a part in books of legislation that they deserve to be examined by themselves.

The primitive sense of the word *law,* and the ordinary meaning of the word, is—the will or command of a legislator. The *law of nature* is a figurative expression, in which nature is represented as a being; and such and such a disposition is attributed to her, which is figuratively called a law. In this sense, all the general inclinations of men, all those which appear to exist independently of human societies, and from which must proceed the establishment of political and civil law, are called *laws of nature.* This is the true sense of the phrase.

But this is not the way in which it is understood. Authors have taken it in a direct sense; as if there had been a real code of natural laws. They appeal to these laws; they cite them, and they oppose them, clause by clause, to the enactments of legislators. They do not see that these natural laws are laws of their own invention; that they are all at odds among themselves as to the contents of this pretended code; that they affirm without proof; that systems are as numerous as authors; and that, in reasoning in this manner, it is necessary to be always beginning anew, because every one can advance what he pleases touching laws which are only imaginary, and so keep on disputing for ever.

What is natural to man is sentiments of pleasure or pain, what are called inclinations. But to call these sentiments and these inclinations *laws,* is to introduce a false and dangerous idea. It is to set language in opposition to itself; for it is necessary to make *laws* precisely for the purpose of restraining these inclinations. Instead of regarding them as laws, they must be submitted to laws. It is against the strongest natural inclinations that it is necessary to have laws the most repressive. If there were a law of nature which directed all men towards their common good, laws would be useless; it would be employing a creeper to uphold an oak; it would be kindling a torch to add light to the sun. . . .

The word *rights,* the same as the word *law,* has two senses; the one a proper sense, the other a metaphorical sense. *Rights,* properly so called, are the creatures of *law* properly so called; real laws give birth to real rights. *Natural rights* are the creatures of natural law; they are a metaphor which derives its origin from another metaphor.

What there is natural in man is means,—faculties. But to call these means, these faculties, *natural rights,* is again to put language in opposition to itself. For *rights* are established to insure the exercise of means and faculties. The right is the *guarantee;* the faculty is the thing guaranteed. How can we understand each other with a language which confounds under the same term things so different? Where would be the nomenclature of the arts, if we gave to the *mechanic* who makes an article the same name as to the article itself?

Real rights are always spoken of in a legal sense; natural rights are often spoken of in a sense that may be called anti-legal. When it is said, for example, that *law cannot avail against natural rights,* the word rights is employed in a sense above the law; for, in this use of it, we acknowledge rights which attack the law; which overturn it, which annul it. In this anti-legal sense, the word *right* is the greatest enemy of reason, and the most terrible destroyer of governments.

There is no reasoning with fanatics, armed with *natural rights,* which each one understands as he pleases, and applies as he sees fit; of which nothing can be yielded, nor retrenched; which are inflexible, at the same time that they are unintelligible; which are consecrated as dogmas, from which it is a crime to vary. Instead of examining laws by their effects, instead of judging them as good or bad, they consider them in relation to these pretended natural rights; that is to say, they substitute for the reasoning of experience the chimeras of their own imaginations. . . .

Is not this arming every fanatic against all governments? In the immense variety of ideas respecting natural and Divine law, cannot some reason be found for resisting all human laws? Is there a single state which can maintain itself a day, if each individual holds himself bound in conscience to resist the laws, whenever they are not conformed to his particular ideas of natural or Divine law? What a cut-throat scene of it we should have between all the interpreters of the code of nature, and all the interpreters of the law of God!

"The pursuit of happiness is a natural right." The pursuit of happiness is certainly a natural inclination; but can it be declared to be a right? That depends on the way in which it is pursued. The assassin pursues his happiness, or what he esteems such, by committing an assassination. Has he a right to do so? If not, why declare that he has? What tendency is there in such a declaration to render men more happy or more wise? . . .

I propose a treaty of conciliation with the partisans of natural rights. If *nature* has made such or such a law, those who cite it with so much confidence, those who have modestly taken upon themselves to be its interpreters, must suppose that nature had some reasons for her law. Would it not be surer, shorter and more persuasive, to give us those reasons directly, instead of urging upon us the will of this unknown legislator, as itself an authority? . . .

All these false methods of reasoning can always be reduced to one or the other of the two false principles. This fundamental distinction is very useful in getting rid of words, and rendering ideas more clear. To refer such or such an argument to one or another of the false principles, is like tying weeds into bundles, to be thrown into the fire.

I conclude with a general observation. The language of error is always obscure and indefinite. An abundance of words serves to cover a paucity and a falsity of ideas. The oftener terms are changed, the easier it is to delude the reader. The language of truth is uniform and simple. The same ideas are always expressed by the same terms. Everything is referred to pleasures or to pains. Every expression is avoided which tends to disguise or intercept the familiar idea, that *from such and such actions result such and such pleasures and pains.* Trust not to me, but to experience, and especially your own. *Of two opposite methods of action, do you desire to know which should have the preference? Calculate their effects in good and evil, and prefer that which promises the greater sum of good.*

2. Jeremy Bentham, *Panopticon Papers*

Outline of the Plan of Construction of a Panopticon Penitentiary House, as Designed by Jeremy Bentham, of Lincoln's Inn, Esq.

Thou art about my path, and about my bed:
and spiest out all my ways
If I say, peradventure the darkness shall cover me,
then shall my night be turned into day.
Even there also shall thy hand lead me; and thy right hand
shall hold me.

                                             Psalm 139

The building *circular*—the cells occupying the circumference—the keepers, etc.—the centre—an *intermediate annular well*, all the way up, crowned by a *sky-light* usually open, answering the purpose of a *ditch* in *fortification*, and of a *chimney* in *ventilation*—the cells, laid *open* to it by an iron *grating*.

The *yards* without, laid out upon the same principle:—as also the *communication* between the building and the yards.

By *blinds* and other contrivances, the keeper concealed from the observation of the prisoners, unless where he thinks fit to show himself: hence, on their part, the sentiment of an invisible omnipresence.—The whole circuit reviewable with little, or, if necessary, without any, change of place.

One station in the inspection part affording the most perfect view of the *two* stories of cells, and a considerable view of another:—the result of a difference of level.

The same cell serving for *all* purposes: *work, sleep, meals, punishment, devotion:* The unexampled airiness of construction conciliating this economy with the most scrupulous regard to health. The minister, with a numerous, but mostly concealed auditory of visitors, in a regular *chapel* in the *centre*, visible to half the cells, which on this occasion may double their complement.

Solitude, or *limited seclusion, ad libitum.*—But, unless for punishment, limited seclusion in assorted companies of two, three, and four, is preferred: an arrangement, upon this plan alone exempt from danger. The degree of *seclusion* fixed upon may be preserved, in all places, and at all time, *inviolate*. Hitherto, where solitude has been aimed at, some of its chief purposes have been frustrated by occasional associations.

From Jeremy Bentham, "Narrative Regarding the Panopticon Penitentiary Project," in *The Works of Jeremy Bentham*, vol. 11, edited by John Bowring (Edinburgh: William Tait, 1843), pp. 96–104.

The *approach, one* only—*gates* opening into a walled *avenue* cut through the area. Hence, no strangers near the building without *leave,* nor without being surveyed from it as they pass, nor without being known to come on *purpose.* The gates, of *open* work, to *expose hostile* mobs: on the other side of the road, a wall with a branch of the road behind, to *shelter peaceable* passengers from the fire of the building. A mode of fortification like this, if practicable in a city, would have saved the *London prisons,* and prevented the unpopular accidents in *St. George's Fields.*

The *surrounding wall,* itself surrounded by an open palisade, which serves as a fence to the grounds on the other side.—Except on the side of the approach, *no public path* by that fence.—A *sentinel's walk* between: on which no one else can set foot, without forcing the fence, and declaring himself a trespasser at least, if not an enemy. To the four walls, four such walks *flanking* and *crossing* each other at the ends. Thus each sentinel has two to check him.

Thus simple are the leading principles.—The application and preservation of them in the detail, required, as may be supposed, some variety of contrivance.

N.B.—The expense of this mode might, it is supposed, be brought *within half* that of the late ingenious Mr. Blackburn's, which was £120 a man.

History of the War between Jeremy Bentham and George the Third, by One of the Belligerents

But for George the Third, all the prisoners in England would, years ago, have been under my management. But for George the Third, all the paupers in the country would, long ago, have been under my management.

The work entitled "Pauper Management," the work to which this brief, and, it is hoped, not altogether uninstructive nor uninteresting history, is designed to serve as an introduction,—would have become law. . . .

No muse shall I invoke: no muse would listen to me. A plain tale is all I have to tell: let others, if any, who may feel disposed and able, stick flowers in it.

Catharine the Second had celebrity, nor that altogether undeserved. In a female body she had a masculine mind. She laid the foundation of a code,—an all-comprehensive code.

My brother, whose loss I had to lament not many years ago,—my only brother, of whose education, he being nine years my junior, the superintendence fell into my hands, when on a traveller's visit to that country, was found possessed of rare talents, was arrested, put into office, and succeeded.

In the year 1786, or 1787, I being on a visit to my brother, of a year and a half, or thereabouts, at Crichoff in White Russia, where he was stationed with a battalion of a thousand men under his command, on an estate then lately purchased by Prince Potemkin, Prime Minister of Russia, under Catharine the Second, the idea presented itself to him of a mode of architecture, to which I gave the name of Panopticon, from the two Greek words,—one of which signified everything, the other a place of sight. A Mr. Pinchbeck, a sort of artist, who enjoyed more or less of the personal favour of George the Third, had either anticipated me, or afterwards followed me, in the employment given to that name.

The purpose to which this rotundo-form was destined to be employed by my brother, was that of a large workshop, in which, with or without the benefit of steam-engine power, occupations capable of being in any degree diversified, might be carried on; partitions in the form and position of radii of the circle being employed in separating from each other such as required to be so separated: in the centre was the apartment, styled, from its destination, the Inspector's Lodge: from thence by turning round his axis, a functionary, standing or sitting on the central point, had it in his power to commence and conclude a survey of the whole establishment in a twinkling of an eye, to use a proverbial phrase. But forasmuch as men had not in these days,—whatsoever may have been the case in the days of Pliny and the traveller Mandeville,—any visual organs seated in the back part of the human frame, it was considered accordingly, that it was material to good order, that the workmen, whose operations were designed to be thus watched, should not be able to know each of them respectively at any time, whether he was or was not at that moment in a state in which the eyes of the inspector were directed to his person in such manner as to take a view of it: accordingly, for the production of this effect, provision was made of an annular screen, pierced in such a manner with slits or holes, that by any person it might be seen whether a person, whom, in this or that other part of the building, he was taking a view of, was knowing whether he was viewed or not.

Taking in hand this idea, I made application of it for the purpose of the case in which the persons subjected to inspection, were placed in that situation, not only for the purpose of being subjected to direction, but also for the purpose of being made to suffer in the way of punishment: in a word, as a place of labour and confinement for convicts.

To the carrying this design into effect, two requisites were necessary:— The first an appropriate form of architecture as above, and an appropriate plan of management, so organized as to draw from that mode of architecture, as far as practicable, all the advantages it was capable of affording. In the course of my reflections on this latter subject, I came to my conclusion, that the customary plan pursued in works instituted by Government, and carried on, on account of Government, was, in an eminent degree, ill adapted to the purpose: though to this general rule, particular exceptions there might be; but to the particular purpose then in hand, they had no application. Accordingly, management by contract, I became convinced, was the only plan that afforded a probability of good success.

In pursuance of the labours of Howard,[1] who died a martyr to benevolence, Sir William Blackstone, the illustrious Commentator on the Law of England,—Sir William Blackstone, in connexion with Mr. Eden, afterwards coroneted by the title of Lord Auckland, devised a plan of architecture and management of a prison for the confinement of convicts, and accordingly drew up for that purpose a Bill which received the official denomination of the *Hard-Labour Bill*. Their plan was in some form or other laid before the public, with such explanations as were thought requisite. The plan of management was—not contract-management, as above, but trust-management: the managing hands, whether one or more, not having any interest in the success: gaining nothing in case of profit, losing nothing in case of loss: in a word, their interest was not to be coincident with their duty. On the contrary, the one was destined to operate in constant opposition to the other: for where a man has nothing to gain by labour, it is his interest to be idle or do anything but labour.

Actuated by these conceptions, I published, anno 1789, a tract, entitled, "View of the Hard-Labour Bill." In this work I took in hand the plan of the two illustrious statesmen, applied to it the above principle, examined it in all its details, and the result was what appeared to me to be a complete demonstration of its inaptitude. Blackstone, notwithstanding the war I had made upon him in my "Fragment on Government,"[2] in answer to the present I made him of a copy of that little work sent me a civil note, acknowledging that he and his cooperator had derived assistance from it: they went to work notwithstanding, and obtained an Act of Parliament, under and by virtue of which they fixed upon a site for the erection. It was a spot of about fourscore acres, in the vicinity of Battersea, and distinguished by the name of Battersea Rise. For ascertaining the sum to be paid for it by Government, a jury, according to custom, was summoned, and assessed the value at a sum between six and seven thousand pounds. On payment of

1. John Howard (1726–90), the celebrated prison reformer, one of Bentham's heroes.—ED.

2. Bentham's first published work (1776), in which he announced the principle of utility in the context of his attack on the mode of legal reasoning in Sir William Blackstone's *Commentaries on the Laws of England*. Given the high esteem in which Blackstone was held, Bentham had prudently published the *Fragment* anonymously, but the secret leaked out.—ED.

that sum it was in the power of Government at any time to take possession of it, and transfer it into any hands at pleasure.

From causes not necessary to bring on this occasion to view, the undertaking lingered, and the verdict of the appraising jury remained without effect. Meantime, my brother remaining still in Russia, I was unable, for want of his assistance, to determine upon the exact form of the edifice, and through want of means, to make a proposal for the performance of the function in question by contract. In the year 1790, the return of my brother to England, furnished me with the requisite architectural skill; and the death of my father, which took place in March 1792, with the addition of assistance from without, supplied the pecuniary means. Accordingly, in March 1792, I sent in to Mr. Pitt, then First Lord of the Treasury; and Mr. Dundas, then Secretary of State, afterwards created Lord Melville, a proposal for the taking charge of convicts to the number of a thousand, according to the above-mentioned plan of construction and management upon the terms therein mentioned. . . .

For giving the requisite powers to the executive authority, an Act of Parliament was necessary. Somehow or other the business lingered: nobody but the King and Prime Minister Pitt knew why. . . . At length came the day, in 1794, on which the act was passed, by which the doing the business by contract was authorized. And the spot at Battersea Rise, which, as above, had been destined to the reception of a penitentiary establishment on the plan of Sir William Blackstone and Mr. Eden, was made to change its destiny, and was transferred to the intended penitentiary to be erected and managed upon my plan. The lingering continued: nobody knew why. Mr. Pitt was shy in speaking of it. After three or four years' interval, the business came upon the carpet in another form. In the year 1797 was instituted the important and influential Finance Committee,—the first by which a report approaching to any such length as that which this Committee gave birth to was produced. . . . Among the members of the committee was Mr., now the Right Honourable Reginald Pole Carew. He had become my friend, and a warm partisan of the Panopticon system, through the medium of my brother, with whom he had become acquainted at Petersburg. The task of making a Report on the Panopticon plan was committed to his hands. The Report he drew up accordingly in favour of the plan was couched in such strong terms, that prudence suggested and produced the suppression of it. It went into other hands,—whose they were I do not at present recollect, if I ever knew—whether those of Mr. Abbot, chairman of the entire committee, or any one else. Of a speech which, on that occasion, Mr. Abbot made in the Committee, the substance was at that time reported to me. Referring to some of the most noted instances of cruelty that history records: "We do not sit here," said he, "to try causes; but the cruelty of the cruelest of those cases was not comparable to that which this man has been suffering." On this occasion the Lords of the Treasury were called upon to say whether or no they were prepared to go on with the plan; and if not, why not?—they answered, in cold terms, in the affirmative.

At this time, however, or before, I was informed that the spot at Battersea Rise, which had formed the basis of the proposal made by me, and acceded to as above, could not be given to me. Two personages [were the parties interested,]—the then Archbishop of York, Dr. Markham, in right of the see, the paramount proprietor; Earl Spencer, as lessee under a long lease from that same see. The Archbishop had been headmaster of Westminster School during the five or six years which I had passed in that seminary: he submitted without reluctance: a civil letter which he wrote to me on that occasion, intimating his consent, is still in my possession. Lord Spencer demurred: he refused to cede the spot to me: but he gave me reason to hope that another part of his estate, called, I believe, Battersea Fields, might be conceded to me. His steward, he said, had informed him that the setting up of an institution of that sort, threatened to be detrimental to other parts of his vast property in that neighbourhood. The spot destined to the institution by Parliament, was an elevated one,—the highest part of it at the same height above the water, by which one boundary of it was bathed,—namely, about ninety-two feet,—as the top of the roof of Westminster Abbey. The spot which I had been led to expect in lieu of it, was also contiguous to the river, but was little, if anything, better than a marsh. By the noble earl I was kept from the cold, in hot water, for about a twelvemonth; at the end of which time I was informed that it never had been his intention that I should have either the one spot or the other: but that should he be compelled to give up part of his estate for the purpose, the choice between the two being at the same time allowed to him, it should be the low, and not the elevated ground.

I was thereupon turned adrift, dislodged from this spot, and sent abroad in quest of another spot: like our first parents, "the world before me,"—but if Providence was my guide, she proved for this time but a blind one. Many were the spots thought of, several visited, and two or three provisionally approved of. . . . At length an opportunity that seemed favourable presented itself; the Earl of Salisbury, of that day, happened to be in want of a sum in ready money,—he had a freehold estate at Millbank,—it had for one of its boundaries a line of about half-a-mile in length, and washed all the way by the Thames.

At length the time was come for putting a final extinguisher upon all hopes. The Millbank estate was now in my possession, all but the one piece of garden-ground, for the buying out of the lease of which £1000 was necessary. The mornings, as usual, were passed in the Treasury Chambers, either in a waiting room,—not unfrequently the board room itself,—or the passages. I had become familiar with three of the chief clerks: one day said one of them to me, "Well, now you will not have long to wait,—the warrant for the £1000 is gone to the king,—his majesty is a man of business,—seldom does a document wait more than twenty-four hours for his signature." The next day came, and the next to that, and so on for three weeks,—a day or two more or less,—all the while the same familiarity and favour in all faces, but the surprise on both parts continually on the increase. On the day that followed, on repairing to the usual haunt, I found everything converted into ice. Upon my putting some question or other, "Mr. Bentham," said the clerk to whom I addressed myself, "you must be sensible that this is a sort of information that is never given, and as seldom asked for." If these were not the very words, this, at any rate, was the very substance. Here ended all hopes of setting up the prison institution. . . .

I come now to another campaign of the war.

In 1797, Pitt the First, [sic] then Prime Minister, brought in his Poor Bill.

Universal was the sensation produced by a measure so important and extensive. It had for its leading idea and groundwork a plan that had been proposed by Mr. Ruggles, a country gentleman of Essex.

I took in hand this bill. I dissected it. I proposed a succedaneum to it: of letters, addressed to Arthur Young, for proposed insertion into the Annals of Agriculture, which had been brought into existence a short time before. They appeared, accordingly, in four successive numbers, in the form of letters, addressed to the editor of these same Annals: the matter of them is that which forms the matter of the body of Pauper Management.

It may be seen to contain a complete system of provision for the helpless and indigent portion of the community of England and Wales included: Local field the same as that of Minister Pitt's above-mentioned Poor Bill. *Mutatis mutandis* plan of architecture the same as that of Panopticon plan—devised for the lodgement, maintenance, and employment of prisoners. Note,—that it was for persons of the unoffending class that this new plan of architecture was originally devised. Principle of universal and constant inspectability the same in both cases: inspectability of the inspectors by the eye of the public opinion tribunal the same in both cases: but actual subjection to inspection in no cases except those in which it was required by the different purposes, or objects in view, of the different, or, in some respects, coincident institutions.

Arthur Young was in a state of rapture: he presented me with 250 copies of those Nos. of his Annals in which the matter was contained. By me they were distributed, at different time, among such persons in whose hands they presented to my conception a promise of being of use . . .

All this while Panopticon for Prison Management remained upon the carpet. One day I received from Mr. Rose an invitation to call upon him— not at his office, but at his house. Days are, on this occasion, of more importance than months, or even years. Notwithstanding the unequivocal and repeated tokens of approbation that had been given to the Panopticon plan by the Planner-General of all the arrangements of the Prime Minister, my intercourse with him had as yet been no otherwise than at arm's length. In demeanour, master and man, *proportions gardées,* were alike cold and haughty: the man was passionate, rough, and coarse. Imagine my astonishment who can, when, after giving me to understand that those on whom the issue depended had read the work [viz., On Pauper Management] and read it with approbation, he concluded with saying, "Come and dine with me here one day the beginning of next week,—Mr. Pitt and Mr. Dundas will meet you,—and we will settle about this plan of yours." The day of the week on which this announcement was made was Friday: I was in the seventh heaven. The Monday passed away—the Tuesday in like manner—the Wednesday eke also. There ended the beginning of the week: on the Thursday I heard, as it were, by accident, by whose mouth I did not long remember, that on the Wednesday, instead of myself, Mr. Ruggles had been the guest: but that the entertainment had closed with mutual dissatisfaction. From the above-mentioned seventh heaven this intelligence cast me down, if not to the bottom of the abyss of despair, at any rate but a little distance from it—a bush of thorns having caught hold of the skirts of my clothing and saved me from absolute destruction.

Before this time I had received intimation from Mr. Rose, that strong as had been the approbation bestowed upon my plan by all those to whose department the business belonged, other persons were there by whom it had been viewed with an eye not altogether favourable: who these persons were was not mentioned, nor any description given of them less mysterious than this. What the power was that thus stood in the way was more than at that time I had any suspicion of. There was an end to my situation of Sub-Regulus of the Poor; but my claim to be Sub-Regulus of the imprisoned part of the population still lingered.

To contract-management was to be substituted trust-management,—in other words, the trustees being constituted authorities, nominees of other superior constituted authorities, management by functionaries in whose instance interest coincided with duty—trustees whose interest was at daggers-drawn with duty.

That everything might be done in due, that is to say, in accustomed form, a committee of Honourable House was duly organized,—number of members, twenty-one, appropriately packed for the purpose. On this occasion what other persons were examined I cannot recollect,—the votes of the time would of course show. I was of course of the number.

This formality being gone through, an act was passed in 1811.

Never does the current of my thoughts alight upon the Panopticon and its fate, but my heart sinks within me: upon the Panopticon in both its branches,—the prisoner branch and the pauper branch: upon what they are now, and what they ought to have been, and would have been, had any other king than this same George the Third been in those days on the throne. According to the calculations which had then been, with close attention, made, the pecuniary value of a child at its birth,—that value which at present is not merely equal 0, but equal to an oppressively large negative quantity, would, under that system of maintenance and education which I had prepared for it, expense of conveyance to the distant site allowed for, have been a positive quantity to no inconsiderable amount.

So much for unoffending indigence. As to the criminally-offending part of the population, no tamer of elephants had a better grounded anticipation of the success of his management than I had of mine, as applied to the offending school of my scholars. Learned and Right Honourable judges I would not then have undertaken,—I would not now undertake to tame: learned gentlemen in full practice I would not have undertaken to tame: noble lords I would not have undertaken to tame: honourable gentlemen I would not have undertaken to tame. As to learned judges under the existing system, I have shown to demonstration, nor has that demonstration ever been contested, nor will it ever be contested, that (not to speak of malevolence and benevolence) the most maleficent of the men whom they consign to the gallows is, in comparison with those by whom this disposition is made of them, not maleficent, but beneficent.

Various were my adventures when, year after year, I was sent or encouraged to go upon a place . . .—a land-hunting—hunting after *terra firma,* which I so oftentimes found slippery as ice,—slipping through my fingers: analogous in some sort was my unhappy chase to that of Fenelon's Telemachus when rambling in quest of his father Ulysses: as often as he thought himself on the point of receiving the paternal embrace, consigned by some delusion or other to final disappointment. But how sadly different the catastrophe,—how opposite in my case to what is called poetical justice!

3. T. B. Macaulay, Speech on Parliamentary Reform (2 March 1831)

Thomas Babington Macaulay (1800–1859) started a promising political career as a member of the Whig party, serving as a member of Parliament from 1830–34 and 1839–47 and as a minister in two Whig cabinets. From 1834 to 1838 he was a member of the Supreme Council of India, where he made major contributions to British colonial rule by helping to formulate a new penal code as well as reforms in the educational system in India. Already in the early 1840s, however, Macaulay was celebrated as the author of the *Lays of Ancient Rome* and *Critical and Historical Essays Contributed to the Edinburgh Review*. When he lost his parliamentary seat in 1847, he turned to the task that had always been closest to his heart since beginning it in 1839: the writing of a history of England from the Revolution of 1688 to the death of George IV, of which four volumes appeared before his death.

Macaulay's *History* celebrates the providential success of the English polity in voluntarily reforming its institutions to avoid the pitfalls of violent revolution. Macaulay believed that the "highest eulogy which can be pronounced on the Revolution of 1688 is this, that it was our last revolution. . . . In all honest and reflecting minds there is a conviction, daily strengthened by experience, that the means of effecting every improvement which the constitution requires may be found within the constitution itself."[1] A work grandly conceived and passionately argued, Macaulay's *History* immediately attained a remarkable popularity (the first two volumes alone sold thirteen thousand copies within four months of publication in November 1848). John Kenyon has aptly characterized the evolution of the Whig ethos that infused Macaulay's writings: "In his early essays Macaulay seemed to be developing into a Whig in what Acton calls the 'Roundhead Tradition,' believing that constitutionalism and democracy had been born in the Civil Wars, betrayed in 1660, and only partially and imperfectly restored by a sordid power transaction in 1688. But from 1832 or thereabouts he turned to the Whiggism of the grandees, of Holland House, Devonshire House, Woburn and Chatsworth, the Whiggism of broad acres and a balanced constitution, to whom 1688, and only 1688, was the Year I of Liberty. This is why, apart perhaps from King William, the heroes of the *History* are moderate, pragmatic con-

From *The Complete Writings of Thomas Babington Macaulay in Ten Volumes*. Vol. 1, *Miscellanies* (Boston, 1901), pp. 1–19.

1. Macaulay, *The History of England*, vol. 2 (London, 1864), p. 242.

stitutionalists like Halifax the Trimmer or the great Lord Chancellor
Somers."[2]

Macaulay was an early supporter of parliamentary reform and on
2 March 1831 delivered an eloquent defense of the bill for electoral
reform sponsored by the Whig cabinet of Earl Grey. This legislation provided for substantial changes in the makeup of the House of Commons—
reducing the number of seats allocated to smaller boroughs and redis-
tributing them in favor of larger boroughs, towns, and the counties. The
franchise was also liberalized in favor of all householders or leaseholders in
the boroughs who inhabited property worth at least ten pounds in annual
rentable value. The bill increased the electorate in the United Kingdom
from under 500,000 to over 800,000. Finally approved by the House of
Lords in June 1832 (in its third version), the bill left Parliament far short
of a truly democratic body, but it did signify the ability of the English
political system in the nineteenth century to adapt to changing social and
political circumstances in an incremental, nonrevolutionary manner.

It is a circumstance, Sir, of happy augury for the motion before the House,
that almost all those who have opposed it have declared themselves hostile
on principle to parliamentary reform. Two Members, I think, have confessed that, though they disapprove of the plan now submitted to us, they
are forced to admit the necessity of a change in the representative system.
Yet even those gentlemen have used, as far as I have observed, no arguments which would not apply as strongly to the most moderate change as to
that which has been proposed by His Majesty's government. I say, Sir, that
I consider this as a circumstance of happy augury. For what I feared was,
not the opposition of those who are averse to all reform, but the disunion
of reformers. I knew that, during three months, every reformer had been
employed in conjecturing what the plan of the government would be. I
knew that every reformer had imagined in his own mind a scheme differ-
ing doubtless in some points from that which my noble friend, the Paymaster of the Forces, has developed. I felt therefore great apprehension that
one person would be dissatisfied with one part of the bill, that another person would be dissatisfied with another part, and that thus our whole
strength would be wasted in internal dissensions. That apprehension is now
at an end. I have seen with delight the perfect concord which prevails
among all who deserve the name of reformers in this House; and I trust that
I may consider it as an omen of the concord which will prevail among reformers throughout the country. I will not, Sir, at present express any opin-

2. John Kenyon, *The History Men: The Historical Profession in England since the Renaissance* (Pittsburgh: University of Pittsburgh Press, 1984), p. 80.

ion as to the details of the bill; but, having during the last twenty-four hours given the most diligent consideration to its general principles, I have no hesitation in pronouncing it a wise, noble, and comprehensive measure, skilfully framed for the healing of great distempers, for the securing at once of the public liberties and of the public repose, and for the reconciling and knitting together of all the orders of the state.

The honorable Baronet who has just sat down,[3] has told us, that the Ministers have attempted to unite two inconsistent principles in one abortive measure. Those were his very words. He thinks, if I understand him rightly, that we ought either to leave the representative system such as it is, or to make it perfectly symmetrical. I think, Sir, that the Ministers would have acted unwisely if they had taken either course. Their principle is plain, rational, and consistent. It is this, to admit the middle class to a large and direct share in the representation, without any violent shock to the institutions of our country. [Hear!] I understand those cheers: but surely the gentlemen who utter them will allow that the change which will be made in our institutions by this bill is far less violent than that which, according to the honorable Baronet, ought to be made if we make any Reform at all. I praise the Ministers for not attempting, at the present time, to make the representation uniform. I praise them for not effacing the old distinction between the towns and the counties, and for not assigning Members to districts, according to the American practice, by the Rule of Three. The government has, in my opinion, done all that was necessary for the removing of a great practical evil, and no more than was necessary.

I consider this, Sir, as a practical question. I rest my opinion on no general theory of government. I distrust all general theories of government. I will not positively say, that there is any form of polity which may not, in some conceivable circumstances, be the best possible. I believe that there are societies in which every man may safely be admitted to vote. [Hear!] Gentlemen may cheer, but such is my opinion. I say, Sir, that there are countries in which the condition of the laboring classes is such that they may safely be entrusted with the right of electing Members of the Legislature. If the laborers of England were in that state in which I, from my soul, wish to see them, if employment were always plentiful, wages always high, food always cheap, if a large family were considered not as an encumbrance but as a blessing, the principal objections to Universal Suffrage would, I think, be removed. Universal Suffrage exists in the United States without producing any very frightful consequences; and I do not believe, that the people of those States, or of any part of the world, are in any good quality naturally superior to our own countrymen. But, unhappily, the laboring classes in

3. Sir John Walsh.

England, and in all old countries, are occasionally in a state of great distress. Some of the causes of this distress are, I fear, beyond the control of the government. We know what effect distress produces, even on people more intelligent than the great body of the laboring classes can possibly be. We know that it makes even wise men irritable, unreasonable, credulous, eager for immediate relief, heedless of remote consequences. There is no quackery in medicine, religion, or politics, which may not impose even on a powerful mind, when that mind has been disordered by pain or fear. It is therefore no reflection on the poorer class of Englishmen, who are not, and who cannot in the nature of things be, highly educated, to say that distress produces on them its natural effects, those effects which it would produce on the Americans, or on any other people, that it blinds their judgment, that it inflames their passions, that it makes them prone to believe those who flatter them, and to distrust those who would serve them. For the sake, therefore, of the whole society, for the sake of the laboring classes themselves, I hold it to be clearly expedient that, in a country like this, the right of suffrage should depend on a pecuniary qualification.

But, Sir, every argument which would induce me to oppose Universal Suffrage, induces me to support the plan which is now before us. I am opposed to Universal Suffrage, because I think that it would produce a destructive revolution. I support this plan, because I am sure that it is our best security against a revolution. The noble Paymaster of the Forces hinted, delicately indeed and remotely, at this subject. He spoke of the danger of disappointing the expectations of the nation; and for this he was charged with threatening the House. Sir, in the year 1817, the late Lord Londonderry proposed a suspension of the Habeas Corpus Act. On that occasion he told the House that, unless the measures which he recommended were adopted, the public peace could not be preserved. Was he accused of threatening the House? Again, in the year 1819, he proposed the laws known by the name of the Six Acts. He then told the House that, unless the executive power were reinforced, all the institutions of the country would be overturned by popular violence. Was he then accused of threatening the House? Will any gentleman say that it is parliamentary and decorous to urge the danger arising from popular discontent as an argument for severity; but that it is unparliamentary and indecorous to urge that same danger as an argument for conciliation? I, Sir, do entertain great apprehension for the fate of my country. I do in my conscience believe that, unless the plan proposed, or some similar plan, be speedily adopted, great and terrible calamities will befall us. Entertaining this opinion, I think myself bound to state it, not as a threat, but as a reason. I support this bill because it will improve our institutions; but I support it also because it tends to preserve them. That we may exclude those whom it is necessary to exclude, we must admit those whom it may be safe to admit. At present we oppose the schemes of revolutionists with only one half, with only one quarter of our proper force. We say, and we say justly, that it is not by mere numbers, but by property and intelligence, that the nation ought to be governed. Yet, saying this, we exclude from all share in the government great masses of property and intelligence, great numbers of those who are most interested in preserving tranquillity, and who know best how to preserve it. We do more. We drive over to the side of revolution those whom we shut out from power. Is this a time when the cause of law and order can spare one of its natural allies?

My noble friend, the Paymaster of the Forces, happily described the effect which some parts of our representative system would produce on the mind of a foreigner, who had heard much of our freedom and greatness. If, Sir, I wished to make such a foreigner clearly understand what I consider as the great defects of our system, I would conduct him through that immense city which lies to the north of Great Russell Street and Oxford Street, a city superior in size and in population to the capitals of many mighty kingdoms; and probably superior in opulence, intelligence, and general respectability, to any city in the world. I would conduct him through that interminable succession of streets and squares, all consisting of well built and well furnished houses. I would make him observe the brilliancy of the shops, and the crowd of well appointed equipages. I would show him that magnificent circle of palaces which surrounds the Regent's Park. I would tell him, that the rental of this district was far greater than that of the whole kingdom of Scotland, at the time of the Union. And then I would tell him, that this was an unrepresented district. It is needless to give any more instances. It is needless to speak of Manchester, Birmingham, Leeds, Sheffield, with no representation, or of Edinburgh and Glasgow with a mock representation. If a property tax were now imposed on the principle that no person who had less than a hundred fifty pounds a year should contribute, I should not be surprised to find that one half in number and value of the contributors had no votes at all; and it would, beyond all doubt, be found that one fiftieth part in number and value of the contributors had a larger share of the representation than the other forty-nine fiftieths. This is not government by property. It is government by certain detached portions and fragments of property, selected from the rest, and preferred to the rest, on no rational principle whatever.

To say that such a system is ancient is no defence. My honorable friend, the Member for the University of Oxford,[4] challenges us to show, that the Constitution was ever better than it is. Sir, we are legislators, not anti-

4. Sir Robert Harry Inglis.

quaries. The question for us is, not whether the Constitution was better formerly, but whether we can make it better now. In fact, however, the system was not in ancient times by any means so absurd as it is in our age. One noble Lord[5] has to-night told us that the town of Aldborough, which he represents, was not larger in the time of Edward the First than it is at present. The line of its walls, he assures us, may still be traced. It is now built up to that line. He argues, therefore, that as the founders of our representative institutions gave Members to Aldborough when it was as small as it now is, those who would disfranchise it on account of its smallness have no right to say that they are recurring to the original principle of our representative institutions. But does the noble Lord remember the change which has taken place in the country during the last five centuries? Does he remember how much England has grown in population, while Aldborough has been standing still? Does he consider, that in the time of Edward the First the kingdom did not contain two millions of inhabitants? It now contains nearly fourteen millions. A hamlet of the present day would have been a town of some importance in the time of our early Parliaments. Aldborough may be absolutely as considerable a place as ever. But compared with the kingdom, it is much less considerable, by the noble Lord's own showing, than when it first elected burgesses. My honorable friend, the Member for the University of Oxford, has collected numerous instances of the tyranny which the kings and nobles anciently exercised, both over this House and over the electors. It is not strange that, in times when nothing was held sacred, the rights of the people, and of the representatives of the people, should not have been held sacred. The proceedings which my honorable friend has mentioned, no more prove that, by the ancient constitution of the realm, this House ought to be a tool of the king and of the aristocracy, than the Benevolences and the Ship-money prove their own legality, or than those unjustifiable arrests, which took place long after the ratification of the great Charter, and even after the Petition of Right, prove that the subject was not anciently entitled to his personal liberty. We talk of the wisdom of our ancestors: and in one respect at least they were wiser than we. They legislated for their own times. They looked at the England which was before them. They did not think it necessary to give twice as many Members to York as they gave to London, because York had been the capital of Britain in the time of Constantius Chlorus; and they would have been amazed indeed if they had foreseen, that a city of more than a hundred thousand inhabitants would be left without representatives in the nineteenth century, merely because it stood on ground which, in the thirteenth century, had been occupied by a few huts. They framed a representative

5. Lord Stormont.

system, which, though not without defects and irregularities, was well adapted to the state of England in their time. But a great revolution took place. The character of the old corporations changed. New forms of property came into existence. New portions of society rose into importance. There were in our rural districts rich cultivators, who were not freeholders. There were in our capital rich traders, who were not liverymen. Towns shrank into villages. Villages swelled into cities larger than the London of the Plantagenets. Unhappily, while the natural growth of society went on, the artificial polity continued unchanged. The ancient form of the representation remained; and precisely because the form remained, the spirit departed. Then came that pressure almost to bursting, the new wine in the old bottles, the new society under the old institutions. It is now time for us to pay a decent, a rational, a manly reverence to our ancestors, not by superstitiously adhering to what they, in other circumstances, did, but by doing what they, in our circumstances, would have done. All history is full of revolutions, produced by causes similar to those which are now operating in England. A portion of the community which had been of no account expands and becomes strong. It demands a place in the system, suited, not to its former weakness, but to its present power. If this is granted, all is well. If this is refused, then comes the struggle between the young energy of one class and the ancient privileges of another. Such was the struggle between the Plebeians and the Patricians of Rome. Such was the struggle of the Italian allies for admission to the full rights of Roman citizens. Such was the struggle of our North American colonies against the mother country. Such was the struggle which the Third Estate of France maintained against the aristocracy of birth. Such was the struggle which the Roman Catholics of Ireland maintained against the aristocracy of creed. Such is the struggle which the free people of color in Jamaica are now maintaining against the aristocracy of skin. Such, finally, is the struggle which the middle classes in England are maintaining against an aristocracy of mere locality, against an aristocracy the principle of which is to invest a hundred drunken pot-wallopers in one place, or the owner of a ruined hovel in another, with powers which are withheld from cities renowned to the furthest ends of the earth for the marvels of their wealth and of their industry.

But these great cities, says my honorable friend, the Member for the University of Oxford, are virtually, though not directly, represented. Are not the wishes of Manchester, he asks, as much consulted as those of any town which sends Members to Parliament? Now, Sir, I do not understand how a power which is salutary when exercised virtually can be noxious when exercised directly. If the wishes of Manchester have as much weight with us as they would have under a system which should give representatives to Manchester, how can there be any danger in giving representatives to Manchester? A virtual representative is, I presume, a man who acts as a direct representative would act: for surely it would be absurd to say that a man virtually represents the people of Manchester, who is in the habit of saying No, when a man directly representing the people of Manchester would say Aye. The utmost that can be expected from virtual representation is that it may be as good as direct representation. If so, why not grant direct representation to places which, as every body allows, ought, by some process or other, to be represented?

If it be said that there is an evil in change as change, I answer that there is also an evil in discontent as discontent. This, indeed, is the strongest part of our case. It is said that the system works well. I deny it. I deny that a system works well, which the people regard with aversion. We may say here, that it is a good system and a perfect system. But if any man were to say so to any six hundred and fifty-eight respectable farmers or shopkeepers, chosen by lot in any part of England, he would be hooted down, and laughed to scorn. Are these the feelings with which any part of the government ought to be regarded? Above all, are these the feelings with which the popular branch of the legislature ought to be regarded? It is almost as essential to the utility of a House of Commons, that it should possess the confidence of the people, as that it should deserve that confidence. Unfortunately, that which is in theory the popular part of our government, is in practice the unpopular part. Who wishes to dethrone the King? Who wishes to turn the Lords out of their House? Here and there a crazy radical, whom the boys in the street point at as he walks along. Who wishes to alter the constitution of this House? The whole people. It is natural that it should be so. The House of Commons is, in the language of Mr. Burke, a check, not on the people, but for the people. While that check is efficient, there is no reason to fear that the King or the nobles will oppress the people. But if that check requires checking, how is it to be checked? If the salt shall lose its savor, wherewith shall we season it? The distrust with which the nation regards this House may be unjust. But what then? Can you remove that distrust? That it exists cannot be denied. That it is an evil cannot be denied. That it is an increasing evil cannot be denied. One gentleman tells us that it has been produced by the late events in France and Belgium; another, that it is the effect of seditious works which have lately been published. If this feeling be of origin so recent, I have read history to little purpose. Sir, this alarming discontent is not the growth of a day or of a year. If there be any symptoms by which it is possible to distinguish the chronic diseases of the body politic from its passing inflammations, all those symptoms exist in the present case. The taint has been gradually becoming more extensive and more malignant, through the whole lifetime of two generations. We have tried anodynes. We have tried cruel operations.

What are we to try now? Who flatters himself that he can turn this feeling back? Does there remain any argument which escaped the comprehensive intellect of Mr. Burke, or the subtlety of Mr. Windham? Does there remain any species of coercion which was not tried by Mr. Pitt and by Lord Londonderry? We have had laws. We have had blood. New treasons have been created. The Press has been shackled. The Habeas Corpus Act has been suspended. Public meetings have been prohibited. The event has proved that these expedients were mere palliatives. You are at the end of your palliatives. The evil remains. It is more formidable than ever. What is to be done?

Under such circumstances, a great plan of reconciliation, prepared by the Ministers of the Crown, has been brought before us in a manner which gives additional lustre to a noble name, inseparably associated during two centuries with the dearest liberties of the English people. I will not say, that this plan is in all its details precisely such as I might wish it to be; but it is founded on a great and a sound principle. It takes away a vast power from a few. It distributes that power through the great mass of the middle order. Every man, therefore, who thinks as I think is bound to stand firmly by ministers who are resolved to stand or fall with this measure. Were I one of them, I would sooner, infinitely sooner, fall with such a measure than stand by any other means that ever supported a Cabinet.

My honorable friend, the Member for the University of Oxford, tells us, that if we pass this law, England will soon be a republic. The reformed House of Commons will, according to him, before it has sat ten years, depose the King, and expel the Lords from their House. Sir, if my honorable friend could prove this, he would have succeeded in bringing an argument for democracy, infinitely stronger than any that is to be found in the works of Paine. My honorable friend's proposition is in fact this: that our monarchical and aristocratical institutions have no hold on the public mind of England; that these institutions are regarded with aversion by a decided majority of the middle class. This, Sir, I say, is plainly deducible from his proposition; for he tells us that the representatives of the middle class will inevitably abolish royalty and nobility within ten years; and there is surely no reason to think that the representatives of the middle class will be more inclined to a democratic revolution than their constituents. Now, Sir, if I were convinced that the great body of the middle class in England look with aversion on monarchy and aristocracy, I should be forced, much against my will, to come to this conclusion, that monarchical and aristocratical institutions are unsuited to my country. Monarchy and aristocracy, valuable and useful as I think them, are still valuable and useful as means, and not as ends. The end of government is the happiness of the people: and I do not conceive that, in a country like this, the happiness of the people can be promoted by a form of government in which the middle classes place no confidence, and which exists only because the middle classes have no organ by which to make their sentiments known. But, Sir, I am fully convinced that the middle classes sincerely wish to uphold the Royal prerogatives and the constitutional rights of the Peers. What facts does my honorable friend produce in support of his opinion? One fact only; and that a fact which has absolutely nothing to do with the question. The effect of this Reform, he tells us, would be to make the House of Commons all-powerful. It was all-powerful once before, in the beginning of 1649. Then it cut off the head of the King, and abolished the House of Peers. Therefore, if it again has the supreme power, it will act in the same manner. Now, Sir, it was not the House of Commons that cut off the head of Charles the First; nor was the House of Commons then all-powerful. It had been greatly reduced in numbers by successive expulsions. It was under the absolute domination of the army. A majority of the House was willing to take the terms offered by the King. The soldiers turned out the majority; and the minority, not a sixth part of the whole House, passed those votes of which my honorable friend speaks, votes of which the middle classes disapproved then, and of which they disapprove still.

My honorable friend, and almost all the gentlemen who have taken the same side with him in this debate, have dwelt much on the utility of close and rotten boroughs. It is by means of such boroughs, they tell us, that the ablest men have been introduced into Parliament. It is true that many distinguished persons have represented places of this description. But, Sir, we must judge of a form of government by its general tendency, not by happy accidents. Every form of government has its happy accidents. Despotism has its happy accidents. Yet we are not disposed to abolish all constitutional checks, to place an absolute master over us, and to take our chance whether he may be a Caligula or a Marcus Aurelius. In whatever way the House of Commons may be chosen, some able men will be chosen in that way who would not be chosen in any other way. If there were a law that the hundred tallest men in England should be Members of Parliament, there would probably be some able men among those who would come into the House by virtue of this law. If the hundred persons whose names stand first in the alphabetical list of the Court Guide were made Members of Parliament, there would probably be able men among them. We read in ancient history, that a very able king was elected by the neighing of his horse: but we shall scarcely, I think, adopt this mode of election. In one of the most celebrated republics of antiquity, Athens, Senators and Magistrates were chosen by lot; and sometimes the lot fell fortunately. Once, for example, Socrates was in office. A cruel and unjust proposition was made by a demagogue. Socrates resisted it at the hazard of his own life. There is no event in

Grecian history more interesting than that memorable resistance. Yet who would have officers appointed by lot, because the accident of the lot may have given to a great and good man a power which he would probably never have attained in any other way? We must judge, as I said, by the general tendency of a system. No person can doubt that a House of Commons, chosen freely by the middle classes, will contain many very able men. I do not say, that precisely the same able men who would find their way into the present House of Commons will find their way into the reformed House: but that is not the question. No particular man is necessary to the state. We may depend on it that, if we provide the country with popular institutions, those institutions will provide it with great men.

There is another objection, which, I think, was first raised by the honorable and learned Member for Newport.[6] He tells us that the elective franchise is property; that to take it away from a man who has not been judicially convicted of malpractices is robbery; that no crime is proved against the voters in the closed boroughs; that no crime is even imputed to them in the preamble of the bill; and that therefore to disfranchise them without compensation would be an act of revolutionary tyranny. The honorable and learned gentleman has compared the conduct of the present Ministers to that of those odious tools of power, who, towards the close of the reign of Charles the Second, seized the charters of the Whig Corporations. Now, there was another precedent, which I wonder that he did not recollect, both because it is much more nearly in point than that to which he referred, and because my noble friend, the Paymaster of the Forces, had previously alluded to it. If the elective franchise is property, if to disfranchise voters without a crime proved, or a compensation given, be robbery, was there ever such an act of robbery as the disfranchising of the Irish forty-shilling freeholders? Was any pecuniary compensation given to them? Is it declared in the preamble of the bill which took away their franchise, that they had been convicted of any offence? Was any judicial inquiry instituted into their conduct? Were they even accused of any crime? Or if you say that it was a crime in the electors of Clare to vote for the honorable and learned gentleman who now represents the county of Waterford, was a Protestant freeholder in Louth to be punished for the crime of a Catholic freeholder in Clare? If the principle of the honorable and learned Member for Newport be sound, the franchise of the Irish peasant was property. That franchise the Ministers under whom the honorable and learned Member held office did not scruple to take away. Will he accuse those Ministers of robbery? If not, how can he bring such an accusation against their successors?

Every gentleman, I think, who has spoken from the other side of the

6. Mr. Horace Twiss.

House, has alluded to the opinions which some of His Majesty's Ministers formerly entertained on the subject of Reform. It would be officious in me, Sir, to undertake the defence of gentlemen who are so well able to defend themselves. I will only say that, in my opinion, the country will not think worse either of their capacity or of their patriotism, because they have shown that they can profit by experience, because they have learned to see the folly of delaying inevitable changes. There are others who ought to have learned the same lesson. I say, Sir, that there are those who, I should have thought, must have had enough to last them all their lives of that humiliation which follows obstinate and boastful resistance to changes rendered necessary by the progress of society, and by the development of the human mind. Is it possible that those persons can wish again to occupy a position which can neither be defended nor surrendered with honor? I well remember, Sir, a certain evening in the month of May, 1827. I had not then the honor of a seat in this House; but I was an attentive observer of its proceedings. The right honorable Baronet opposite,[7] of whom personally I desire to speak with that high respect which I feel for his talents and his character, but of whose public conduct I must speak with the sincerity required by my public duty, was then, as he is now, out of office. He had just resigned the seals of the Home Department, because he conceived that the recent ministerial arrangements had been too favorable to the Catholic claims. He rose to ask whether it was the intention of the new Cabinet to repeal the Test and Corporation Acts, and to reform the Parliament. He bound up, I well remember, those two questions together; and he declared that, if the Ministers should either attempt to repeal the Test and Corporation Acts, or bring forward a measure of Parliamentary Reform, he should think it his duty to oppose them to the utmost. Since that declaration was made four years have elapsed; and what is now the state of the three questions which then chiefly agitated the minds of men? What is become of the Test and Corporation Acts? They are repealed. By whom? By the right honorable Baronet. What has become of the Catholic disabilities? They are removed. By whom? By the right honorable Baronet. The question of Parliamentary Reform is still behind. But signs, of which it is impossible to misconceive the import, do most clearly indicate that, unless that question also be speedily settled, property, and order, and all the institutions of this great monarchy, will be exposed to fearful peril. Is it possible that gentlemen long versed in high political affairs cannot read these signs? Is it possible that they can really believe that the representative system of England, such as it now is, will last till the year 1860? If not, for what would they have us wait? Would they have us wait merely that we may show to all the world how little we

7. Sir Robert Peel.

have profited by our own recent experience? Would they have us wait, that we may once again hit the exact point where we can neither refuse with authority, nor concede with grace? Would they have us wait, that the numbers of the discontented party may become larger, its demands higher, its feelings more acrimonious, its organisation more complete? Would they have us wait till the whole tragi-comedy of 1827 has been acted over again; till they have been brought into office by a cry of "No Reform," to be reformers, as they were once before brought into office by a cry of "No Popery," to be emancipators? Have they obliterated from their minds—gladly, perhaps, would some among them obliterate from their minds—the transactions of that year? And have they forgotten all the transactions of the succeeding year? Have they forgotten how the spirit of liberty in Ireland, debarred from its natural outlet, found a vent by forbidden passages? Have they forgotten how we were forced to indulge the Catholics in all the license of rebels, merely because we chose to withhold from them the liberties of subjects? Do they wait for associations more formidable than that of the Corn Exchange, for contributions larger than the Rent, for agitators more violent than those who, three years ago, divided with the King and the Parliament the sovereignty of Ireland? Do they wait for that last and most dreadful paroxysm of popular rage, for that last and most cruel test of military fidelity? Let them wait, if their past experience shall induce them to think that any high honor or any exquisite pleasure is to be obtained by a policy like this. Let them wait, if this strange and fearful infatuation be indeed upon them, that they should not see with their eyes, or hear with their ears, or understand with their heart. But let us know our interest and our duty better. Turn where we may, within, around, the voice of great events is proclaiming to us, Reform, that you may preserve. Now, therefore, while everything at home and abroad forebodes ruin to those who persist in a hopeless struggle against the spirit of the age, now, while the crash of the proudest throne of the continent is still resounding in our ears, now, while the roof of a British palace affords an ignominious shelter to the exiled heir of forty kings, now, while we see on every side ancient institutions subverted, and great societies dissolved, now, while the heart of England is still sound, now, while old feelings and old associations retain a power and a charm which may too soon pass away, now, in this your accepted time, now, in this your day of salvation, take counsel, not of prejudice, not of party spirit, not of the ignominious pride of a fatal consistency, but of history, of reason, of the ages which are past, of the signs of this most portentous time. Pronounce in a manner worthy of the expectation with which this great debate has been anticipated, and of the long remembrance which it will leave behind. Renew the youth of the state. Save property, divided against itself. Save the multitude, endangered by its own

ungovernable passions. Save the aristocracy, endangered by its own unpopular power. Save the greatest, and fairest, and most highly civilized
community that ever existed, from calamities which may in a few days
sweep away all the rich heritage of so many ages of wisdom and glory. The
danger is terrible. The time is short. If this bill should be rejected, I pray to
God that none of those who concur in rejecting it may ever remember their
votes with unavailing remorse, amidst the wreck of laws, the confusion of
ranks, the spoliation of property, and the dissolution of social order.

4. W. J. Fox, Speech before the Anti–Corn Law League (28 September 1843)

The Corn Law, a protective tariff on imported grain (in English usage,
corn is the generic term for all varieties of grain), was passed in 1815 at
the conclusion of the Napoleonic Wars, by a Parliament made up largely
of landowners. The disruption of trade during the long period of hostilities had forced a vast expansion of the land under cultivation in England, and much of the land newly pressed into service was of poor
quality. Hence a high price had to be charged for its produce in order to
offset the landowner's large investment in converting and farming such
marginal soil. Without the Corn Law, the postwar influx of cheaper foreign grain into the English market would have dealt a heavy blow to
English agriculturists.

The Corn Law had been passed in 1815 over strong public protest.
Renewed several times (with slightly different provisions), it continued to
provoke public opposition until it was finally repealed in 1846, an event
regarded as a signal victory for economic liberalism in Britain. The campaign for repeal had been undertaken by an ad hoc organization called
the Anti–Corn Law League, founded in 1839 by two cotton manufacturers,
Richard Cobden and John Bright, representatives of the Manchester school
of political economy. The league collected campaign funds, published its
own newspaper, and put out an enormous quantity of written propaganda
in the form of tracts, handbills, and almanacs. Paid orators stumped the
country preaching the gospel of laissez-faire. Thus the league had pio-
neered a mode of successful extraparliamentary pressure on Parliament.
It formed the model for the banquet campaign for reform of the suffrage
undertaken by liberals in France in 1847.

The speech reprinted here was delivered at a meeting of the league in
the Covent Garden Theatre in London in 1843 by William J. Fox (1786–

From *Free Trade and Other Fundamental Doctrines of the Manchester School*, edited by
Francis W. Hirst (London and New York: Harper, 1903), pp. 168–72.

1864), whose effective speaking style had commended him to the league as one of its main orators. Of humble rural background, Fox was a Unitarian and editor of the *Monthly Repository,* the journal of the Unitarian Radicals. He was also a Benthamite and a friend of John Stuart Mill.

As historian Asa Briggs has written, the anti–Corn Law agitation helped popularize the "language of class" in nineteenth-century England. Fox's speech makes evident the class divisions that leaguers perceived in their country and the classes to which they were addressing their appeal for support.

In the able speeches of the mover and seconder of the address [Richard Cobden and John Bright, respectively] two points have been slightly passed over, or only incidentally mentioned, which I think tend very much to recommend that address to the adoption of the public, and the objects of its authors to their co-operation. One characteristic feature of the address is the plainness and frankness with which the plans of the League are told out. There are no claims of implicit confidence; there are no ambiguous promises; there is no endeavour to lead on the people towards results not specified; there is no saying, like a certain state physician, "Let me into office, give me the fee, and then you shall see my prescription"; but a succession of measures are distinctly marked out, all tending towards a definite point, which point gained, the objects of the League must needs be accomplished, and towards which a movement is made as distinct, and, I apprehend—as these measures in succession are realized—as resistless, as the great operations of nature. They conduct us towards a result which no administration can resist, which no law can stand, to that declaration of the will of the possessors of the political power of a great empire, which must be respected by all who aspire to administer its affairs, which cannot be resisted but in the dissolution of society, and before which any opposing power, any law, any institution even, however time-honoured, must pass away, as the leaves fall before the winds of autumn, or as snow vanishes in the sunshine of spring. And the men who propose this course of measures are plainly as honest as they are earnest in that for which they ask your cooperation. They make, themselves, the largest sacrifices that are made; and the very fact which has been thrown in their teeth, that they have an interest in this object, is their best justification. The interests of honest industry are surely one of the objects of the policy of a great empire. They have an interest in it; so have you; so have we all. Who that lives by eating bread has not an interest in the repeal of the bread tax? Who that is endeavouring to support himself and his family by commerce has not an interest in Free Trade? Who has not an interest in what advances the general prosperity of the country, even though his pursuits are artistical or intellectual, ministering to the spiritual rather than the material portions of our nature? For as one thrives will all thrive—they react the one upon the other—the starving do not encourage literature and art—they are bound together by the ties which Providence formed to uphold society; and it is because they and we have an interest in this matter that we are determined the question shall not drop until it is satisfactorily settled.

I say all classes have an interest in this matter; even they who are represented as the great opposing class—the landlord class. For what has made England the paradise of landowners but its being the workshop of the world? In the progress of manufacture, if machinery has enabled one man to do the work of two hundred, it has also employed two hundred, and two thousand, where one was employed; all bread eaters, coming to the landowner for his produce. And while the manufacturers of this country have been thus advancing in the last century, its growth of wheat has been tripled, and the rents of the farmers have been in many cases quadrupled. The landlords gain by railways enhancing the worth of their property; they gain by the rich and flourishing community arising around them; and if for a while they should have to make some slight sacrifice—if at first their rents should fall in the change—why, they will still be gaining that which gold could never buy. By the graceful concession they would be gaining the goodwill and gratitude of their fellow-countrymen; they would gain for themselves an exemption from the execration that pursues their class— from the infamy of their names in history—from the reprobation of their consciences, and the pollution of their souls.

The confidence which the Council expresses in the successful operations of the measures they trace out is, I think, a well-founded one. For when have recognized principles failed of meeting with success—when in the world's history? Some affect to sneer at abstract principles; but abstract good is the real, practical good, after all; the exceptions made to it are some little, dirty contrivances of those who would have trade free for others, but would reserve the monopoly for themselves—would have free trade as to what they buy, but restrictions as to what they sell; and who tell us that those principles are sound and excellent things in reference to all other commodities whatever, but that there is some one exception left—the exception of that in which the exceptor deals; and each in turn will tell you that Free Trade is the noblest thing in the world, except for corn, except for sugar, except for coffee, and except for this, that, and the other, till once, even in the House of Commons, it came to an exception of second-hand glass bottles. I say this is a principle recognized by all—recognized even by the Government in its measures of last year, however paltry their nature and limited their operation; recognized in their Canada Corn Bill; recognized in the repeal of the laws against the exportation of machinery, the last rag of that form of monopoly; and the repeal of the duties on imports must follow that of restriction on exports. A principle thus practically recognized by foes, as well as by friends, is certain of success. Thus was it that the great principle of Negro liberty was recognized, and thus eventually carried. And did not the recognition of a principle emancipate the Roman Catholics of Ireland? Ask Sir Robert Peel and the Duke of Wellington whether this was not the secret of the success of that measure.

I say this anticipation of triumph is well founded. For have we not the eternal power of truth? have we not the agency of a press that cannot be restricted in its advocacy of such principles? Have we not meetings like these—not only such meetings as these, but meetings held in the rural districts, where the opposing class is challenged to the combat? and have we not that power to which the address specially points, which with great propriety is introduced on such an occasion as this, that power which has ever been the cradle and is the bulwark of liberty, political and commercial—the power of great cities, the agency of civilization?—of great towns and cities, that first reared their towers as landmarks when the deluge of barbarism in the middle ages was beginning to subside; that in the civil wars of this country afforded the serf a refuge from his baronial oppressor, and gave him food and gave him freedom; towns and cities, that won the rudiments of representation, that formed our parliaments, that asserted the people's power of self-taxation, that gained one step after another in the progress of order and of human rights and enjoyments; where commerce throve, where the arts have flourished, where the poor serfs of the soil, that vainly struggled and shed their blood in the Jack Cade and Wat Tyler insurrections, at length had their emancipation achieved for them. In cities flourish luxuries and arts which make it life to live. Cities are the heralds of progress, as they have been the safeguards of the past; there congregated multitudes shout for justice, and demand that the oppressed shall be emancipated, raising a cry at the sight of wrong which reverberates from earth to heaven, and makes the oppressive class, however strong in station and in power, quail as before the thunder of the day of retribution.

And this is the second point in the address upon which I wish to fix your attention—the importance that it assigns to towns and cities. It looks to them as the machinery by which this great question is to be wrought out to its final, satisfactory, and triumphant decision. And well and rightly does it so, because it is in towns and cities that the wrong most deeply exists which it is the aim of the League in its noblest efforts to redress. It is in cities that the pressure is felt most extensively—that the iron enters most deeply into the soul. It is not merely in the expression and feeling of such an assemblage as this that I read the condemnation of the laws that uphold

monopoly; it is in what you know—it is in what leads you here. It is something, it is much to many here in this vast and brilliant assemblage, that
from day to day the pressure upon their circumstances is rendered more and
more hard by the artificial limitations of trade; it is something, it is much to
many here, that from time to time one hostile tariff after another makes its
appearance, shutting us out of markets on the Continent which had been
open; it is something, it is much to many here, that in the most frequented
thoroughfares of this great metropolis house after house should be shut up,
exhibiting a spectacle of desolation where once were thriving tradesmen
and enjoying families; it is something, it is much to many here, that the
pressure comes at each extremity, that the candle is burning at both ends—
on one side they are exhausted by paying to the relief of the poor, and on
the other side they are plundered by claims upon them for the income tax; it
is something, it is much to many here, that through every station, in every
rank of life, the pressure is felt—the demon seems to be omnipresent, and
they cannot escape his pestiferous influence. But even this is not the dead-
liest evil of the corn laws. Did one want to exhibit it in this great theatre, it
might be done; not by calling together such an audience as I now see here,
but by going into the by-places, the alleys, the dark courts, the garrets and
cellars of this metropolis, and by bringing thence their wretched and
famished inmates. Oh, we might crowd them here, boxes, pit, and galleries, with their shrunk and shrivelled forms, with their wan and pallid
cheeks, with their distressful looks, perhaps with dark and bitter passions
pictured in their countenances, and thus exhibit a scene that would appal
the stoutest heart, and melt the hardest; a scene that we would wish to bring
the prime minister of the country upon the stage to see; and we would say
to him, "There, delegate of majesty! leader of legislators, conservator of
institutions, look upon that mass of misery! That is what your laws and
power, if they did not create, have failed to prevent, have failed to cure or
mitigate." And supposing this to be done, could this scene be realized, we
know what would be said. We should be told, that "there has always been
poverty in the world; that there are numerous ills that laws can neither
make nor cure; that whatever is done, much distress must exist." He might
say, "It is the mysterious dispensation of Providence, and there we must
leave it." "Hypocrite, hypocrite!" I would say to him, "urge not that plea
yet; you have no right to it. Strike off every fetter upon industry; take the
last grain of the poison of monopoly out of the cup of poverty; give labour
its full rights; throw open the markets of the world to an industrious
people; and then, if after all there be poverty, you have earned your right to
qualify for the unenviable dignity of a blasphemer of Providence; but until
then, while any restriction whatever exists, while any impediment is raised
to the well-being of the many for the sordid profit of the few—till then you

cannot, you dare not, look this gaunt spectre of wretchedness in the face and exclaim, 'Thou canst not say I did it.'"

Why, the corn laws and the policy of our agricultural legislators hunt poverty and wretchedness from their own districts into ours. The landlord class call themselves feeders of the people. They speak of their ability, if properly encouraged and protected, to feed the nation. What feeds the people? Not the growing of corn, but the people being able to buy it. The people are no more fed, for all the wheat that is grown, than as if there were so many stones covering the rich valleys of the country. It is in the price required of the people who eat it; and if that is beyond the power of the multitude to give, the landlords become starvers instead of feeders of the people. Agriculture cannot support its own population; it is not in the course of nature that it should, for one man is vested with the ability to raise food for the many. Twenty-eight per cent. of the population are amply sufficient to cultivate the ground so as to yield food for the remainder of the hundred. How are the rest to be fed? By opening markets for the products of their industry, that they may obtain the means. In the natural growth of the population in the rural districts they find a superfluous population— that superfluity is continually on the increase. People talk much about machinery throwing hands out of employment; these very same people raise a cry of the evil results of corn-law repeal in throwing the cultivators of the ground out of employ. Why, are they not themselves throwing them out of employ every day? Have we not the Royal Agricultural Society and local agricultural societies all over the country, where premiums are offered of from £3 to £50, from £50 to £100, for the invention of machines to cheapen the tillage of the ground—to do that by mechanical ingenuity which had heretofore been wrought by human labour? Are there not machines for every process and operation?—machines for preparing and draining the ground for the reception of the seed, machines for ploughing and sowing, machines even for the splitting the beans that the cattle eat, machinery for reaping the produce, for thrashing the wheat, and for cutting the chaff—is there not machinery from the beginning to the end?—is there not mechanical power, chemical power, horse power, steam power?—and, what perverts it all, and lies at the back of all of the abuse, political power. These associations come forth with their splendid array of great names— some men who figure in one house and some who figure in another; some who are chiefly known as politicians, and others as warriors, until we find among them that great name whose judgment in machinery relates more to the sword than the plough, and who best understands the machinery by which battalions are mowed down, and the harvest of carnage is gathered in. And there is this remarkable difference between the employment of machinery in the one case and in the other, in which it has been so often assailed. When machinery is employed in manufacture, what is the natural result? Production is cheaper, goods, apparel of various kinds, are brought to market at a lower rate. The use of it is diffused more extensively in society; people have enjoyments and accommodation which they did not possess; the demand has increased, and this again reacts upon production; more hands are employed, and in the natural course of things there is found to be more work, more wages, and more enjoyment. But in the employment of agricultural machinery, the intention of the corn law is not to let those inventions affect the price—not to let them cheapen corn and to extend the enjoyment of wholesome food, but to keep up the price while the cost of production is cheapened, in order that the surplus may go into that great swamp of all, the receptacle of rent, still crying, "Give, give," and never satisfied.

Well, in this way there is more of the surplus population who go on in the natural course of wretchedness, who fall from one stage to another, in the agricultural districts than anywhere else. Up they troop to some great town; they come, men, women, and children; they toil their way along the hard roads, and then, without friends or help, they look around them, they ask for work, they ask for alms: they endeavour in vain to find that for which they are seeking, for monopoly has been there beforehand; having driven them out of the country, it bars the occasion for their employment in the towns, and so they are beaten and battered from pillar to post; they have, perhaps, to incur the frown of power by some irregular attempt to support themselves, for the police hunt and hound them for endeavouring to sell apples or lucifers in the streets; they are sent to the station-house, they are brought out of that to be committed to gaol; they go in beggars, they come out thieves; they pass through various stages of disease in the only factory into which they can get—in those great factories of typhus which abound in large towns. One union workhouse sends them to another, the overseers send them to the magistrates, and the magistrates send them back to the overseers; and at last, in this hopeless and heartless strife, they drop by the way. Death completes what monopoly began; and we, inhabitants of great towns, know that all this is passing around us, and we are quiet and acquiescing, and conscience never demands, "Are not you accessory to these murders?"

Wisely has the Council appealed to the great towns, for there is the power. What can the poor farmer do? His money is in his landlord's ground, and the man who has money in another man's ground must needs be a slave. His freedom is buried there with it, not, like the grain, to germinate, but only to rot and dissolve in corruption. It is where great bodies are congregated that they can stand by one another; where not the importance of the individual, but the importance of the many, is the great thing for all. And how independent are such places, if they but knew their position, of all that aristocracy is, or can do! Landlords! They built not this magnificent metropolis; they covered not these forty square miles with the great mass of human dwellings that spread over them; they crowd not our ports with shipping; they filled not your city with its monuments of science and art, with its institutions of literature and its temples of religion; they poured not that stream of commercial prosperity into the country which during the last century has made the grandeur of London; quadrupling its population, and showing that it has one heart with the entire community. They! Why, if they were to spend—if you could impose on them the laws which they would impose upon you, and they were bound to spend—in this metropolis all they received in their rents; if there were no toleration for French wines or foreign luxuries; if they were prohibited from storing and locking up in their remote galleries works of art, real or pretended, which they prize as property; if here, amongst the shopkeepers of London, they were bound to spend that which they had obtained by their rents—it would be wretched repayment to you for what you have forfeited by the absence of free trade. It is, as it were, to make war upon towns and cities, to cut off their supplies of food, to limit their resources, to levy upon them other taxation; for, in the vast spread of this metropolis, where there are nearly two millions of inhabitants, probably not less than six or eight millions sterling is wrung from your resources in different ways, not going into the pockets of the landlords, but being lost by the way, a great portion of it, in order that their extortion may keep up a veil on its horrid countenance, and have something of the show of legitimate taxation, instead of being apparent and downright plunder.

The time is opportune for the appeal which has been made to the inhabitants of this metropolis, and for the appeal to those among you who enjoy the franchise of the city of London. There will, in a very short period, be an opportunity for you to show decidedly that the principle of Free Trade is consecrated in your hearts and guides your votes. I trust the contest will be by no means a personal one, but one wholly of principle, and that no ambiguous pretensions, no praise of Free Trade, with certain qualifications and accommodations necessary to the hustings, will be tolerated for an instant; but that the plain and simple test will be the complete, total, and immediate abolition of the monopoly of food. I know not why one should hesitate to say, upon such an occasion as this, that the placards which I see round about this theatre express the feeling and preference that I think may be honestly entertained for Mr. Pattison as the representative of that great city.[1] . . . Here, then, I hope, will one of the first great electoral experi-

1. A vacancy in the City of London was occasioned by the death of Sir Matthew Wood: the candidates were Mr. Pattison and Mr. Thomas Baring. The former was elected by a majority of 165.

ments be tried, that not merely every member of the League, but every inhabitant of London, who can honourably influence the result of that election, should feel himself bound to do so, as amongst his earliest pledges of adherence to this great cause—the commencement of his answer to the appeal which has now been made to him for support. Other ways will soon open themselves; and I trust that its past backwardness will be amply redeemed by the metropolis in the readiness with which it will respond to the great call now made for its pecuniary liberality, and in the ardour which many will manifest in other modes of co-operating in this great work, showing that we look to yet higher principles and considerations than any that belong either to rural districts or to particular classes, and that we regard this as the common cause of humanity. And so it is; for Free-Trade principles are the dictates of Nature plainly written on the surface of land and ocean, so that the simplest may read them and imbibe their spirit. For that Power which stretched abroad the land, poured forth the ocean, and piled up the mountains; that Power which gave Western America its broad prairies, and reared the gigantic and boundless forests of the north; that Power which covered with rich vineyards the smiling hills of France, which wafts sweet odours from the "spicy shores of Araby the blest," which has endowed this country with its minerals and its insular advantages, and its people with their indomitable Saxon energy, with their skill, their hardihood, their perseverance, their enterprise;—that Power which doth all this, evidently designed it for the common good, for the reciprocal advantage of all; it intended that all should enrich all by the freest interchange, thus making the world no longer the patrimony of a class, but the heritage and the paradise of humanity.

5. 1846–47 Factory Legislation Debates

The following speeches are from the debates held in the House of Commons in 1846 and 1847 on the Ten Hours Bill, legislation introduced by Lord Ashley (Anthony Ashley Cooper) in 1833, but not passed until May 1847, to regulate working hours for adolescents and women. The bill, which followed the Factory Acts of 1833 and 1844, was a landmark in English social legislation, even if its practical implementation was often blocked by the obstruction of employers (especially by their use of the relay system) and unfavorable legal decisions. The debates that accompanied the bill illuminate the ambivalence it generated in prominent political circles.

Six speakers are represented here:

From *Parliamentary Debates*, 3d ser., vol. 86 (1846), cols. 1029–38, 1040, 1043–1044; vol. 89 (1847), cols. 487–91, 1074–81; vol. 90 (1847), cols. 768–74, 812–18.

John Fielden (1784–1849): one of the biggest cotton manufacturers in England and a leading advocate of factory reform. In 1836 he published a pamphlet titled "The Curse of the Factory System" and in 1846–47 replaced Lord Ashley, who had resigned his seat in early 1846 because of his position on the repeal of the Corn Laws, as parliamentary leader of the Ten Hour Movement.

Joseph Hume (1777–1855): a prominent Radical, in 1824, he helped repeal the Combination Acts on the principle that these laws, which made combinations among workmen illegal, interfered with individual liberty. He opposed the Ten Hours legislation for the same reason.

Joseph Brotherton (1783–1857): one of the few members of Parliament who had ever done manual labor. He had worked in the mills as a boy, had become a manufacturer, and then a pastor of an evangelical church. As a member of Parliament he was an active supporter of the reform.

James Graham (1792–1861): gentleman, baronet, and landowner. In the course of his career, Graham held several high offices (including the Admiralty and the Home Office) and refused others (including the governor-generalship of India.) As a Whig, he had helped draft the bill that reformed the British Parliament in 1832. His party politics at this period are not easily labeled: he found the Whigs too liberal and the Tories not liberal enough. He was in the same position, in this regard, as Sir Robert Peel, the final speaker, and like Peel had opposed Ashley's Ten Hours Bill.

Thomas Babington Macaulay: essayist and historian. (For more information see introduction to document 3.)

Sir Robert Peel (1788–1850): one of the most talented figures in English parliamentary history between Pitt and Gladstone. Peel rebuilt the Conservative party in the reformed Parliament, serving as prime minister from 1834 to 1835 and from 1841 to 1846. During his ministry, protectionism was abandoned in favor of free trade, but Peel's decision to complete the process by repealing the Corn Laws during the crisis wrought by the Irish famine of 1845 lost him the sympathy of his own party. After the repeal passed the House (with Whig support), Peel resigned as Prime Minister in 1846, eight months before he spoke in these debates. On the issue of factory reform, his father, a cotton manufacturer, had been extremely sympathetic, and Peel himself had supported earlier measures. He gives his reasons, however, for opposing the Ten Hours Bill.

John Fielden

Sir, I propose to bring in a Bill with regard to the hours of labour in factories, similar, as regards persons between thirteen and eighteen years of age, in its provisions to one which the late Sir Robert Peel proposed to the House nearly thirty-two years ago—that is, I propose to limit the labour of young persons between the ages of thirteen and eighteen to twelve hours a day, allowing two hours out of the twelve for meals—that is, to ten hours actual work per day for five days in the week, and eight hours on Saturdays; and I propose to carry out this alteration by restricting the hours of actual labour to sixty-three hours in the week until the 1st of May, 1848; and after that period to fifty-eight hours in the week; and I propose, further, that the same restrictions shall apply to females above eighteen years of age. My reason for proposing this measure is, that the time of working young persons and females in factories is far too long, has been very mischievous, and, if persevered in, will become the cause of great national evils. I ask for it, also, because the people employed in factories have wished for it, and have long petitioned the Legislature to concede it to them; and because the ministers of religion, medical practitioners, and indeed, all classes who have opportunities of observing the consequences of the present system, deprecate it as destructive of the moral and physical condition of a vast and most important class of the community. It is a question which involves the very existence of thousands who are, I am afraid, sacrificed annually for the want of those due and sufficient regulations without which the late Sir Robert Peel asserted that our improved machinery would become our bitterest curse. I will at once call the attention of the House to a document of authority on this subject, one which, I confess, startled me, though I have long been accustomed to fear the effects of the system we have been pursuing. I refer to "A Table of Deaths registered in 115 districts of England, during the quarter ending September 30, 1846"—that is, the autumn of the last year. . . .

Sir, I cannot quote these official reports without recalling to the attention of the House, that for many, many years, statements of a similar nature, though perhaps not so shocking in degree, have been brought before it by the late Mr. Sadler, by Mr. Oastler, and, more recently, by Lord Ashley; but always so strenuously denied by the manufacturing body that the Parliament had remained incredulous. You are now told, from authority, and in figures not to be disputed, how awful is the destruction of human life in our principal manufacturing towns; you are told distinctly that one of its chief causes is the "constant and unwholesome toil" of mothers, who are compelled to leave their offspring "long days alone to breathe sickly vapours soothed by opiates," "withholding nature's nutriment," to their destruction. I agree, Sir, with the Registrar General, that the "house and children of a labouring man can only be kept clean and healthy by the assiduous labour of a well-trained industrious wife." I agree with him, also, in his just but severe remark, that "this is overlooked in Lancashire, where the woman is often engaged in labour from home." Agreeing with him, and knowing well the truth of his remarks, I have framed this Bill, with the hope that this House will no longer overlook the fruitful cause of such wide-spread death as the Registrar General has recorded; but that it will sanction at once the restriction which I propose with regard to females, in order to stop this frightful state of things. I hear men talk very glibly of the "horrors of war"; and I believe there is in this country a "Peace-preservation Society," whose object is to show mankind that nations, to avoid such horrors, should always remain at peace. I applaud their efforts; but let me ask what are the "horrors of war," but a wholesale sacrifice of human life now and then occurring? They are "horrors," and I respect those who bestow the energy of their minds in endeavours to convince the world of their futility and wickedness; but when the Registrar General, in the document I have quoted, notifies to us the horrible sacrifice of human life that is annually perpetrated in our manufacturing towns, far exceeding the average sacrifice of life by war, I think we should give an earnest of our sincere desire to avoid such horrors by immediately setting to work, in every practical form, to effect the object at home. As to the young persons between thirteen and eighteen, whom I call children, no one, I should think, can, in the abstract, object to their labour being curtailed to ten hours per day. It is the most critical period of life; it was well ascertained that they have not now the opportunities of healthful recreation and of moral instruction that they absolutely require, and that their physical powers are, in many cases, destroyed. The only argument that I anticipate against it is "the tyrant's plea," the plea of necessity. I expect to hear that to reduce the hours of work of the child to such as is compatible with his strength and his necessary moral training, will indirectly curtail the hours of labour of the adult workman with whom the child performs his labour; that this is a legislative interference between master and man; and it is contrary to the principles of political economy. . . .

Sir, I think that a leading principle of political economy is, the care of the lives, the health, and the morals of the people; and it is upon the ground that the life, health, and morality of the young persons, and of women, are sacrificed by too long hours [of] work in our factories, that I ask leave to bring in this Bill. I must remind the House that, in 1833, it passed an Act for emancipating the black slaves of our West Indian colonies, in which a clause was inserted restricting the labour of the emancipated adult negro to forty-five hours in a week—a shorter period by thirteen hours than the English factory child claims at our hands, many of whom have to work in rooms of as high a temperature as that of the colonies. Sir, I wish to assure the House that the working people are now as anxious as ever for the abridgment of labour that this Bill would enact.

Joseph Hume

Some hon. Gentlemen—he did not think it was much to their credit—cast reflections upon the principles of political economy, not considering that it was by those principles that the best interests of the community were regulated. (Mr. FIELDEN: What are they?) His hon. Friend asked what these principles were? He would tell him. They were, that masters and men should be allowed to make what arrangement they pleased between themselves, both with regard to the length of hours and the rate of wages; and that Government should interfere as little as possible, except in every instance to remove prohibitions and protections. The only condition on which this right was acceded to was, that no man should carry it on to the injury of others. . . .

There was scarcely an interest in the kingdom, from the highest to the lowest, which had not sought and obtained protection. For 300 years laws had been passed, interfering with the labourer and with the employer, with this very view. But the evils arising from this practice had become so severe, and at the same time so obvious, that, by common consent, a great proportion of the laws so enacted, were repealed two or three and twenty years ago; and he could not help thinking that hon. Gentlemen who supported the present measure, were proceeding on a course likely to add to the evils which he was sure they were anxious to avoid. They professed their object to be the welfare of the labouring community. They thought they know better than the labourers themselves what were their interests. He repeated that any man who took upon himself to direct another in his ordinary affairs, told that other that he knew his affairs better than he himself did, and that he could manage them better. Now, he objected to that doctrine altogether. He held that the common sense of the working classes was capable of enabling them to take care of themselves; if it were not, let them be educated and better taught. He was an advocate for that species of education which should place them in the situation of being the best judges of their own interests; and he had yet to learn that this doctrine was not the true one. On every side he heard of their claims for universal suffrage—of the right of being represented in the House of Commons; yet these very men, who were the loudest in demanding the suffrage, which would enable them to take a part in deciding on the affairs of the nation, would appear, by this Bill, to say they were incapable of directing their own affairs; and, therefore, they desired the interference of legislation. This appeared to him one of the greatest contradictions it was possible to conceive. His hon. Friend (Mr. Fielden) on a former occasion, had presented to the House a petition signed by upwards of three millions of individuals, embracing a large proportion of the working classes of this country, in favour of a large extension of the suffrage; and he (Mr. Hume) had supported his hon. Friend on that occasion. He declared then, as he affirmed now, that he had too high an opinion of the intelligence of Englishmen belonging to the working classes, than to suppose that they were unworthy of the trust of sharing in the selection of representatives, as was generally thought. He, therefore, asked his hon. Friend (Mr. Fielden), when he came to address the House, to explain how it was that he now wished to introduce an Act of Parliament which should restrain the operations of the working classes, by laying down laws and regulations which were to prevent them from carrying on their labour as seemed to them best? . . .

The House must recollect that it was not a slight matter to interfere with fixed capital embarked in manufactures. It was well known that after defraying the expenses of individual labour and interest on capital, owners of mills had fixed expenses which they could not avoid. They had therefore to calculate, besides having the competition of the Continent and of America, what their expenses were—whether they could, after returning interest upon the capital employed, and paying adequate wages, obtain a proper and fair amount of profit. Mr. Senior had pointed this out in the clearest and most satisfactory manner. That gentleman might be a political economist; he was proud to call him his friend, and to say he concurred in his chief opinions. If hon. Members had not read Mr. Senior's pamphlet upon the state of our factories, and upon the hours of labour in them, he invited them to read it. If they did, they would find this result collected from impartial examination of a number of mills, that ten hours paid only the expenses of the "plant" and the wages of labour, and that if work stopped at ten hours, there would be no profit on the capital invested. (An Hon. MEMBER: How long has that calculation been made?) This calculation was made four years ago, but nothing had since occurred to diminish its accuracy. The surplus, then, whether it was one, one and one-half, or two hours, beyond ten hours, was the only time from which a remunerative return for capital could be made, without which it could not be expected that men would carry on business. If this view were correct, as he believed it was, for it was supported by the opinions and experience of practical men, he asked the House, and he asked his hon. Friend himself (Mr. Fielden), whether factories could be carried on if these hours were taken away upon which the profit of the manufacturer depended? . . .

He repeated that every interference which prevented men, whatever might be their talents, from employing their capital, and exercising their ingenuity under protection of the laws, in any manner they thought proper, was injurious and bad. In former days this was not the opinion of the Legislature; but twenty-five years ago it had fallen to his lot to submit to Parliament certain propositions affirming this principle, which the House of

Commons adopted and acted upon. These propositions, one of which he would read, embodied the sound and correct principles of political economy; and the innovations which had since taken place were violations of those great principles. In May, 1824, the House of Commons affirmed these principles, and thereby swept from the Statute-book sixty or seventy Acts of a restrictive character. After having relieved trade and emancipated commerce, were they to be so insane as again to place themselves under shackles and trammels? It would be madness, and he could not understand his friends who contended that such a policy was for the benefit of the people. The resolution he referred to was agreed to by a numerous Committee of that House, consisting of fifty-one Members. Among them were Mr. Huskisson, Mr. Sturges Bourne, Lord Stanley, Sir H. Parnell, and others of great weight and eminence. They agreed to this resolution:—

> It is the opinion of this Committee, that masters and workmen should be freed from all restrictions as regards the rate of wages and the hours of working, and that they be left at perfect liberty to make such agreements as they may mutually think proper; and that therefore all the statute laws that interfere in these particulars between masters and workmen should be repealed, and also that the common law which enacts that peaceable meetings of working men may be indictable for conspiracy should be altered.

The alterations in the law consequent upon this resolution had been most beneficial. They had been highly approved of by the working classes, as would be seen by his hon. Friend (Mr. Fielden), if he would examine the evidence taken before that Committee. He repeated, then, that hon. Gentlemen who wished to return to those laws were thereby alleging that the working classes were unable to see their own interests, and taking from them a discretion which they were capable of exercising. On these grounds, he felt very strongly against the present measure. He wished the Government and the Legislature to be consistent. If the resolution of 1824 were carried by a protection Parliament, what had taken place since? Had not the right hon. Baronet (Sir Robert Peel) introduced important measures upon the same principle? He was sorry the right hon. Baronet was not in his place, for he felt confident of his support; at all events, if he did not support his views, he would belie all the principles he had recently expressed, and stultify most of the acts of his life. Every Act the House had passed for the last three, four, or five years, had been to free industry, to emancipate capital, and relieve the mercantile interest from restriction: and it would be the height of injustice now, to say to men who were willing to work, "you should not work except for such time as we permit." One man might like to work for twelve hours; another man for less; another for more, that he might support his mother, or his father. Then why should the law interfere? Parliament had no right to interfere either with labour or capital; and for his part he was prepared to sweep away every restriction that now remained, and to let one general and uniform principle of perfect liberty pervade our legislation. Having stated these general principles, he asked hon. Gentlemen to give him an answer to the following points: were they desirous that England should maintain her manufacturing superiority? If so, were they disposed to give fair play to capital and industry in this country? Were they aware of what was going on in Belgium and Germany? Was there any restriction to ten hours there? Was there any restriction in the United States? In the factories at Lowell they worked, in summer, twelve hours; and he had read a report drawn up by a committee of the legislature of Massachusetts upon a petition praying for a restriction in the hours of labour. It was a most sensible report:—

"We cannot interfere," said the committee. "We admit the evil; we wish we could lessen the hours of labour to all classes; we wish that every man could maintain himself and his family by eight or nine hours of labour per day. But we find it cannot be done. Our manufacturers have competition to meet in neutral markets, and we must leave them to their own exertions."

The committee further stated, that the best means by which labour and capital could be employed, was to leave them free. If this principle were true in America, did it not hold good here? Undoubtedly, it did; it was more emphatically in force here. He begged to caution hon. Gentlemen against doing anything to drive capital from its proper employment, and prevent the exportation of cheap articles of manufacture—for it was upon their cheapness and their goodness that the extent of our exports depended— and every individual who interfered with these, to the extent of his interference did an injury to the class of people whose labour was interfered with—and when once they brought the population to ruin by this injudicious course of legislation, it would be too late to say, "We find we have inflicted an evil upon them, we must retrace our course."

Joseph Brotherton

In the year 1815, the mills in Manchester were working 78 or 79 hours a week, children of six years of age being sometimes employed 19 hours. Were not they left to the operation of the principle of political economy? If all men were men of humanity and justice, there would be no need of legislation; and if the people employed in manufactures were merely created to eat and drink, and work and die, the question might be argued on commercial principles, and on the abstract principles of political economy. But he (Mr. Brotherton) believed they were created for nobler objects; and it was important for statesmen to consider their physical and moral and social condition. . . .

When he was a boy, he experienced this wearisome toil himself; and he had witnessed delicate females compelled to stand at their work for many a long hour when they were ill able to do so; he recollected the feelings and sentiments he had at that time, and he resolved that, if ever he had the good fortune to be in a position in which he could be instrumental in shortening factory labour, he would endeavour to accomplish that end; and he was proud to say, that under other circumstances the feelings of his boyhood were still retained in his mature age. He knew that many most unjust charges had been made against the masters; and although he advocated the principle which he considered good for all classes, he never had identified himself with those who were in the habit of libelling men who were as humane and kind as any hon. Member of that House; but he was quite opposed to the system. Capital was so combined with labour, that the temptation to work long hours was too great for many to resist; and even the hon. Member for Oldham (Mr. Fielden) if he would act according to his humane feelings, rich as he was, would soon find himself in the *Gazette,* because if one mill worked two or three hours longer than another, it would be impossible for the latter to carry on a successful competition. He admitted that a material reduction of the hours of labour would, to a certain extent, increase the cost of production; but they ought to be governed by higher principles; and he contended that a reduction of the hours of labour would benefit not only the workmen but the masters themselves. . . .

He had always considered legislation necessary, and had supported every Bill which had been introduced; but the House had been so led away by the principles of political economy that it could not be convinced of their necessity. He was quite satisfied that the adoption of the present measure would advance the interest of all parties. He considered it a great mockery and a complete delusion to say to the working classes, "We wish to promote your physical and mental improvement—we will give you public parks and public institutions"—and yet, after keeping them immured twelve hours a day in factories, to expect them to cultivate their minds and become good subjects. He had seen females, some in an advanced state of pregnancy, and others in a condition which would melt the heart of a stone, compelled to perform this labour; and it was impossible, under the present system, that it should be otherwise. (Mr. BRIGHT: Not compelled to work.) They had no other choice; factory labour was not free labour. He implored the House not to negative the Bill.

Sir James Graham

Sir, I confess that I feel obliged for being allowed to follow the hon. Member (Mr. [Brotherton]) who has just sat down. I have listened, as I am sure the House has done, with infinite pleasure to the speech of the hon. Gentleman, who has mentioned one particular circumstance, which I confess, until I heard it from himself, I was not aware of—that at any period of his life, with his own hands, he had ministered to his own wants. I consider it a great honour that I now sit in this House on terms of perfect equality with the hon. Gentleman, who, by the speech he has just made, has proved that, even from the humblest classes of society in this country, a person can rise, by the influence of honest industry and unblemished character, to the highest station, the representative in Parliament of a free community. I must say the hon. Gentleman has given full effect to the feelings of his youth which he has described to us, and it is very honourable to him that he has done so; but, Sir, permit me to observe, that the success in life to which he owes his seat in this House, is owing to long hours of labour, and shows that by the careful employment of time most useful and honourable acquirements are compatible with long hours; and I cannot, therefore, see, when you fail by argument to convince the nation, why you should give way to the prejudices of the public. The hon. Gentleman has not, as appears to me, correctly stated the question at issue. He says, "Shall you compel women and children to work for twelve hours a day, or not?" Now, that does not appear to me to be the question; but the question is, shall you by indirect legislation restrain industrious men from working twelve hours a day for the purpose of earning their livelihood, though they are willing to undergo the fatigue? It is not with any feelings of pedantry that I make the observation, but I must, in passing, state, that should the House adopt the measure now before them, it will be a departure—a flagrant departure—from the strict rules of political economy—a science which in some quarters of this House appears to be treated almost with contempt, but it is a science which I have always considered as tending towards the benefit and general happiness of the nation; and I doubt if any legislation will be found safe if you depart from the great rules of that important science. Yet if I could satisfy my mind that this measure was conducive to the interests of the working classes, it is not a pedantic or rigid adherence to the rules of political science which would induce me to treat this question with that firm resistance which I am prepared to offer to the Bill now before the House. The hon. Gentleman has relied much on an observation which, I am bound to say, he thought conclusive in favour of this measure, but which, I grieve to add, did not carry conviction to my mind; he said, "Shall it be allowed that, to eat, to drink, to work, and to die, shall be the lot of a large portion of our fellow-countrymen?" But, alas! I grieve to say, the truth is, that not in this country only, but throughout the whole of this world of sorrow and of care, the lot of eating, drinking, working, and dying, must ever be the sum of human life among the masses of a large portion of the human family. It is grievous to admit this sad reality; but the question is, it being necessary that mankind must work for their subsistence, or in order to obtain their subsistence, should you help them to pass their lives as contentedly as possible by giving full scope to their energies? Or should you, by legislation, so interfere as to add to the wants and sufferings of their existence, and thereby embitter their lot?

Thomas Babington Macaulay

The first point which has been raised, and to which I wish to address myself, is a great question of principle, and which lies at the bottom of by far the greater portion of the discussion on this and former occasions. Is it, or is it not, a subject on which we should legislate? Is this one of those matters which the State may properly interfere to settle, or which it ought to leave to settle itself? I think it most important that there should be no mistake whatever upon this subject; that we should neither assume functions which do not properly belong to us, nor abdicate functions which, if they do properly belong to us, we are bound to exercise. I know not which of the two is the greatest pest to society—a patriarchal Government, or rather a meddling Government, which intrudes itself into every part of the system of human life, and thinks it can do everything for everybody better than anybody can do anything for himself; or, on the other hand, an easy, careless, *pococurante* Government, which suffers abuses, such as might be checked by an easy remedy, to exist under its sight, and to all complaint and all remonstrances answers only, "Oh, let things alone, let things take their course, let things find their level." I believe, if there is an important problem at all times, and especially at this time in politics, it is to ascertain where the line divides those cases with which the public authorities ought to interfere, from those with which they ought not. Formerly, I think, the general besetting sin of Governments was undoubtedly that of meddling. The magistrate pushed himself into everything. He interfered with matters on which, unless he possessed the powers and the wisdom of an angel, it was absolutely impossible for him to do any good. He was always attempting to correct some evil that was not within his sphere; and the consequence was, that he invariably augmented the evil he proposed to correct. He was shocked by the fear of scarcity, and so he made laws against forestalling and regrating, and created a famine; he was touched by the oppression practised upon borrowers, and so he made a law against usury; and the poor borrower, who might have got money at 10 per cent, could not possibly get it at 15 or at 20. Evils of this kind attracted the attention of some philosophical minds. They were exposed, and by the exposure inestimable service was rendered to society. I cannot, however, but fear some evils in the reaction, and I think I see some danger of very able and eminent men falling into the other extreme. I do not wish in the present debate to introduce questions not now before the House; but, by way of illustration, I would just say, that I do think it a very remarkable circumstance that we should have lived to see the settling of all the great communications of the Empire—a question always considered in every former age as strictly belonging to the province of the Government—abandoned by the Government to private speculation. Another instance of error on the same side I find in the way in which some Gentlemen, for whose judgment I have the highest respect, look on the question now before us. In the opinion of those gentlemen, such as the hon. Member for Sheffield and the hon. Member for Montrose, the question seems to resolve itself into the general principles of free trade; and they argue that you do not legislate to settle the price of gloves, but you leave that to find its own level—and so let this matter take its own course. You leave the hosier, they say, to manage his own business—to trust what customers he likes—to give long credit and make high charges, or to be content with swift returns and small profits; you own that he can judge better for himself than the State for him, and interference in such matters is legislating in the wrong direction. These Gentlemen say, that you departed from right principles when you legislated with respect to such a question as that now before the House; and that every step you take in the same direction is to go further and further in the wrong. With the greatest respect for those Gentlemen, I must confess I cannot see the matter in this point of view. I have laboured to submit my judgment to theirs, but I cannot do it, and must be guided by such light as I possess. I believe that I am as firmly attached as any Gentleman in this House to the principle of free trade properly stated, and I should state that principle in these terms: that it is not desirable the State should interfere with the contracts of persons of ripe age and sound mind, touching matters purely commercial. I am not aware of any exception to that principle; but you would fall into error if you apply it to transactions which are not purely commercial. Is there a single Gentleman so zealous for the principles of free trade as not to admit that he might consent to the restriction of commercial transactions when higher and other considerations are concerned? Take questions of police. For instance, you limit the number and regulate the fares of hackney coaches and hackney cabs. All the arguments in favour of free trade tell against such an interference. On a rainy day few cabs are to be met with on the stands, but there are plenty of persons possessed of cabs who would bring them out for hire on such occasions, if they were permitted to charge what fares they liked; but the Legislature interferes to prevent this. Can there then be a more striking instance of interference with the principles of free trade? In conformity with these principles, you should not regulate the charges for hackney carriages; but on good ground of police the State steps in and regulates the fares of public carriages in the metropolis. . . .

Take the question of lotteries. A man has an estate for which he wishes to get 20,000*l.*, and he issues 1,000 tickets at 20*l.* each, with the condition that the first ticket coming out of the wheel shall gain the estate. The Legislature interferes, and annuls the whole proceeding. But suppose the owner of the estate appeals to the principle of free trade—suppose he says, "What have you to do with this voluntary contract between me and other parties? You may think it a bad speculation—then don't take a ticket; but what right have you to prevent those men from doing so who are of ripe age and sound mind?" The answer is obvious; we interfere, because if we tolerated these things we should be giving encouragement to habits and qualities of mind incompatible with the virtue and morality of individuals in society. I hope I carry the House with me thus far, that the principle of non-interference is one that cannot be applied without great restrictions where the public health or the public morality is concerned. Then, I ask, is not the public health concerned in a question relating to the time of labour? Does any one who has examined the evidence, or opened his eyes in the world, or examined his own feelings, doubt that twelve hours a day of factory labour are more than are desirable for youths of thirteen? If so much labour be not desirable, then, I say, every argument on which interference can be justified calls on me to keep those youths from injuring their health by means of immoderate toil. Is this, or is it not, a question in which morality is concerned? Can any one doubt—certainly my Friends around me do not doubt—that education is a matter of the highest importance, as regards the virtue and happiness of the common people? For education we know that leisure is necessary. Do we believe that, after twelve hours have been taken from the day for factory labour, and after so much time as is necessary for refreshment and exercise has also been taken—do we believe that enough time will remain for that amount of education which it is desirable the people should have? I believe that we must answer that question in the negative. This I say, that all the principles on which you interfere to prohibit contracts of a nature which you believe to be prejudicial to public morality, justify me in endeavouring to prevent contracts like those which are now the subject of consideration. But there is another question. We are legislating here principally for the young. Now, I ask, whether it is not a rule universally adopted by all civilized society, in which anything like a body of law exists, that those who are of a tender age should be placed under the guardianship of the State? No one would say that a rich person under age should be permitted to sign away his property. We should cry out against such a proposition. And if any gentleman came forward and said, "What have you to do with the matter? Why do you pretend to know what is better for the man's benefit than he knows himself? Why do you interfere with a free contract between two persons?" The answer would be, that a boy of immature age cannot secure himself from injury, and the State is his guardian. But the property of the poor and young lies in his health and strength and skill—in the health both of his body and of his mind. To suffer him prematurely to impair that health by even his own consent, is greatly to depart from the first duty of a good guardian. These are the principles on which I hold that there is no objection to interference in this case. Where public health and public morality are concerned, I hold that the State may interfere, if, on the whole, such interference may appear advisable, even with the contracts of adults. Therefore interference, in such a case, would be justifiable, *a fortiori*, in reference to artisans under the adult age. This Bill does not propose to interfere with the labour of adult males. It may do so indirectly; though I certainly should, without hesitation, on the present occasion, vote against a proposition to interfere with adult males. ("Hear!") Yet, let me not be misunderstood. One would think I had uttered a most monstrous paradox. One would think that not a single Gentleman was aware of any society in which the labour of adults had been limited one day in seven. Pray, let me ask, with reference to this monstrous paradox, will Gentlemen name to me a single civilized State since the first dawn of history in which a certain time of rest and recreation has not been set apart, even for adults, by public authority, consecrated alike by law, religion, and morality? One would think this was an unheard-of paradox, and that the most horrible, portentous, monstrous results must follow if once you legislate to limit the labour of adults; but the moment we look at it rationally, we find ourselves in the midst of such restriction, that all this has been going on age after age, and without for a moment suspecting that it involves any dangerous consequences whatever. . . .

But, to come to the great argument which my hon. Friend and all those who have spoken on the same side of the question with him have relied most strongly upon. They have pleaded, and the subject is one which must be most gravely considered, the pernicious consequences which may result to the labouring classes themselves from this proposed interference. They say it is vain to think that you can take an hour off the labour of a man employed in a factory, without a reduction taking place in the remuneration which he receives for that labour—that there must be a diminution of wages if the hours of labour are shortened; that we may, by the adoption of this measure, sink the condition of our labouring classes lower than it is, and injure instead of improve them; and that we have here introduced a greater interference with labour than the safety of those who live by it would warrant. Now, I am far from denying that this argument deserves to be weighed with attention—that it is one of importance, and should induce us to act gradually and cautiously—and that we ought to feel our way well at every move; but I am at the same [time] firmly convinced that there must be some great flaw in this argument, in the straightforward way in which it is applied, as if it rested on some principle of arithmetic, or on some problem capable of demonstration. And the reason I think so is this. We have legislated in some such spirit as this before. We have shortened the hours of labour in some instances already. Thirty years ago, it was stated by the late Sir Robert Peel to be a common practice to make children of 8 years of age work fifteen hours a day in factories; and yet now we prevent all young persons under 18 years of age from working for more than twelve hours a day. What a change is this to have already made! Did not all the arguments that my hon. Friend has urged—did not all his demonstrations about the falling of wages, and the necessity of the protection of long hours against foreign competition—apply just as strongly against the reduction of the hours of labour that has already taken place, as it applies to the question of farther reduction? I observe that the same arguments which are now put forward against this measure were used against that former Bill. Any person who reads over those debates, will find that exactly the same admonitions were held out then as now; but have they been fulfilled? The same description which we have now listened to was then given of the ruin which must await the cotton trade if the Legislature did not interfere for its protection. But the House heeded not these alarms. It passed the measure, but the ruin has not followed. . . .

I do not at all doubt but that a person will, in a given number of hours, produce less than in a greater number of hours, or that in a given number of days he will produce less than in a greater number of days. I do not deny that a man will do a less quantity of work in eleven hours than in twelve hours, or a less quantity in twelve hours than in fifteen hours; but this I say, and believe, that a great society in which the children are made from an early age to begin to work for fifteen hours a day, will not produce so much in the course of a considerable space of time as a society where the hours of labour are much less. I look on men in a higher character. If we consider men simply in a commercial point of view, simply as a machine for productive labour, let us not forget what a piece of mechanism he is—how "fearfully and wonderfully made." If we have a fine horse, we do not use him exactly as a steam engine, and still less should we treat man so, more especially in his earlier years. The depressing labour that begins early in life, and is continued too long every day, enfeebles his body, enervates his mind, weakens his spirits, overpowers his understanding, and is incompatible with any good or useful degree of education. A state of society in which such a system prevails will inevitably and in no long space of time feel its baneful effects. It will find that the corporal and mental culture of the population cannot be neglected without producing results detrimental to its best interests, even in regard to the accumulation and creation of property. On the other hand, a day of rest regularly recurring every week, and hours of exercise, of leisure, of intellectual improvement recurring in every day, elevate the whole man—elevate him physically—elevate him intellectually—elevate him morally; and his elevation, physical, moral, and intellectual, again falls on the commercial prosperity of the country, which is advanced with it. . . .

Am I to believe that change which would clearly be found to improve the moral, physical, and intellectual character of the people, could possibly make them poorer? For my part, I look with no alarm upon the competition of those people with whose competition we are threatened.[1] I am told that we are in danger of being beaten out of the field by the people of Germany, who work seventeen hours a day, and who are in such a state that the public authorities complain that there is not one among them of stature sufficient to make a soldier. Sir, if ever the English nation is deprived of its commercial prosperity, it will be by no such race of dwarfs as these; it will be by some finer people than the English population—if ever such a people should arise. . . .

One single word, before I sit down, as to the question of time. My noble Friend near me seemed to think that the time was ill chosen. I must say that I am of a different opinion. We carried up on Monday to the House of Lords a Bill which, if our expectations are answered, will have the effect of raising the condition of the labouring classes, and of giving to the people of this country a very great advantage they have not hitherto possessed in their competition with foreign countries. It does seem to me that there could be no time more favourable for the transition we are now discussing, than the present. I must add, that I think it would be highly honourable to this House to make in one week, as far as is in our power, a reparation for two great errors of two different kinds; for, Sir, as lawgivers, we have errors of two different kinds to confess and repair. We have done that which we ought not to have done; we have left undone that which we ought to have done. We have regulated that which we ought to have left to regulate itself; we have left unregulated that which it was our especial business to

1. A previous speaker had reported, "in many foreign countries the hours of labour are seventy-eight hours or eighty-four hours a week; in Prussia seventy-two to ninety hours; in Austria eighty to ninety-two; in the Tyrol seventy-eight to eighty; in Saxony seventy-two; in Berne ninety-four; and we are proposing to reduce them in England to fifty-nine!"—ED.

have regulated. We have given to certain branches of industry a protection which was their bane. We have withheld from public health and from public morality a protection which it was our duty to have given. We have prevented the labourer from getting his loaf where he could get it cheapest, but we have not prevented him from prematurely destroying the health of his body and mind by inordinate toil. I hope and believe that we are approaching the end of a vicious system of interference, and of a vicious system of non-interference. We have just done what was in our power for the purpose of repairing the greatest of all the errors we have committed in the way of interference; and I hope we shall tonight, by giving an assent to the principle of this measure, take a step toward repairing another error—the error of neglect.

Sir Robert Peel

Sir, I will now address myself to the question actually before the House. I admit that it would be taking a narrow view, to argue it on what are generally understood to be the rigid principles of political economy. The Italian writers on political economy—and they are among the most distinguished writers on that science—charge the English economists with taking too restricted a view of the objects which it should embrace. They say that the English writers discuss only the means of acquiring and distributing wealth; whereas they regard political economy as a complex and comprehensive science which concerns, not only the wealth, but the morality and social welfare of the people. I will not say whether this charge of the Italian writers is well founded or not. I believe our political economists purposely and avowedly confine themselves to a single branch of a most extensive and diversified system of social policy, not claiming for that single branch exclusive or pre-eminent consideration. I am quite ready, however, to discuss this question on the extended ground assumed by the Italian writers. I will not confine my attention to the mere amount of material advantage to be derived from increased labour, or the mere pecuniary gain resulting from unfettered manufactures and extended commerce. I will take a far wider ground, and will give my vote against this Bill, from the sincere conviction that it is not for the benefit of the working classes—that it would not tend to the advancement of their intellectual culture, or of their social improvement, to impose a new restriction on the hours of labour. . . .

But what are your securities for the maintenance of manufacturing prosperity? There are three securities. You have capital, machinery, labour. I do not know why we should presume that we possess greater intellectual powers, or greater capacity for exertion than any other nation. Peace and the love of gain will sharpen their intellect and encourage their industry as well as ours. Look at the Germans who settle amongst us and carry on extensive trade—are they an inferior race? Will not the French also, and the Italians, be found to vie with us in all respects? Will not they be as desirous as we are to improve their skill, and to advance their interests? I wish not to detract from our native vigour of character, when I say that I think we are apt to rely too much upon our superiority. The three main securities for the maintenance of our manufacturing prosperity are, I repeat, capital, machinery, and labour. We may, I trust, safely calculate on the continuance of peace. But, peace continuing, what dependence can there be that the employment of English capital in foreign countries may not increase—that foreign countries may not see the policy of giving encouragement to such employment of it? Then, with regard to machinery, look at the increase of the quantity exported last year: there, at least, there was no decrease in our exports. (Lord G. BENTINCK: You permitted the export of machinery.) We did: and do you suppose that we authorized the exportation of machinery without some sufficient motive? There was no alternative left. There are some cases which laws cannot reach—some things which laws cannot prevent. . . .

There remains labour; and I advise you to direct your serious consideration to this point before you restrict it. I appeal to the noble Lord the Member for Lynn, who expected so much from the establishment of railways in Ireland—I appeal to him whether the more you extend the railway system, you do not lessen the impediments to locomotion, and increase the facilities, in time of peace, for skilled labourers to remove abroad, and there get higher wages for their labour? And observe, that not only are the physical impediments to traveling removed, but those prejudices against it which exist to a great extent in the English character. Working man read the accounts of the wages given in foreign countries; they learn also that they will be well received and heartily welcomed; they find that they can reach Rouen and other manufacturing towns in France or Belgium, in fourteen or fifteen hours: partly from curiosity, partly from the hope of gain, assured that they will be well treated, they are influenced by new motives, which did not operate when travelling was expensive, and when an impression prevailed that English workmen would be ill paid, and insulted, and treated as alien enemies in a foreign land. If this account be correct, look at our present position. You have no exclusive command over your own capital, over your own machinery, or over your own labour: in this state of things, you propose to place new legislative restrictions nominally upon the labour of women and children, but practically upon the labour of adult males. You say to the man, who, being in the possession of health, desires to labour—who, foreseeing the day when he will be incapacitated from labour by age or infirmity, wishes to provide some resource for the future—you say to this man, "You shan't work more than five days a week." You cut off, by law, two hours from that which constitutes his present working day. With the tendency there is, and must be, to equalise throughout Europe the advantages of capital, machinery, and labour, you inform the adult male operative, "It is not for your good that you should labour more than five days a week in your native country." Sir, I fear the consequences of such legislation. It may be said, that these are but prospective dangers, and that your linen, your silk, and your woollen manufactures have taken such root in the soil, that you cannot be dispossessed of your superiority. But other countries, in other times, have had the same superiority, have felt the same confidence in its continuance, and have had a bitter reverse of fortune, which may not, I hope, be in reserve for you.

But still there are higher considerations than those of wealth and commerce; and if you could convince me that the present measure would tend to the moral and intellectual improvement, to the general social welfare, of the labouring classes, I should be tempted to make the experiment; for I feel, that in improving the condition and elevating the character of those classes, we are advancing the first and highest interests. I feel that society is not safe unless we can do that. We are giving those classes intellectual improvement; but unless the general character of our legislation is to increase their comfort and improve their moral habits, their mere intellectual improvement will become a source of danger and not of strength. By every means, then—by the improvement of the sanitary condition of our towns—by substituting innocent recreation for vicious and sensual indulgence—we should do all in our power to increase the enjoyments and improve the character of the working classes. I firmly believe that the hopes of the future peace, happiness, and prosperity of this country, are closely interwoven with the improvement, religious as well as moral, of those classes. But, consistently with this persuasion, I oppose these restrictions on labour. Sir, the hon. Member for Salford (Mr. Brotherton), in a speech which did him much honour, was influenced by feelings in which I personally ought to, and do, participate. He says, the only question is, whether it is fit that women and children should work twelve hours a day. But is that the only question? If it be, then I am of opinion with him, that ten hours a day is enough for women and children to labour. Nay, I go farther than the hon. Member. If I am asked, whether I do not think eight hours a day sufficient labour for a girl of fourteen years of age, or for a mother with three or four children to attend to—if that is the question upon which the debate turns—then I am for eight hours, and not ten. But why do you hesitate about an Eight Hours Bill? Is it not because you strike a balance between the admitted advantages of additional leisure, and the evil that would arise from a reduction of wages? On what principle, except upon the principle to which I refer, do you give the preference to ten hours of labour over eight for a child or a mother? Sir, I do not deny the advantage of leisure; but I greatly doubt whether there be any better means of improving the condition of the labourer, and of elevating the character of the working classes, than to give them an increased command over the necessaries of life. You say that by this Bill you will not diminish wages. But will it not be a most marvellous event in legislation, if you provide by law that five days in the week shall be the maximum of labour in this country, and yet can induce the master to pay the same amount of wages? Notwithstanding the active competition of manufactures in America, France, Italy, and Germany, you expect that the masters in this country are to go on paying five days' work with six days' pay. But we are told that the mode of doing this will be by working the machinery so as to get twelve hours' work done in ten hours. I doubt whether you can do that; and I doubt, also, whether, if you can, you will thereby confer any advantage upon the workpeople. I doubt whether it is not for the advantage of adult women and children that they should continue working for twelve hours, rather than finish the same quantity of work in ten hours by a greater strain upon their bodily and mental faculties. . . .

It has been said by a high authority—and the remark is pregnant with truth—that in prosperous times the workman shares with his employer in the general prosperity, but that he does not benefit half so much by prosperity as he suffers from adversity. The owner of capital can bear up against temporary depression, for he can draw upon the gains accumulated in the time of prosperity. It is not so with him whose whole capital is labour. And it is to him, already labouring under disadvantage in this respect, that you are about to say, "You shall not lay by a surplus from your wages, in the vigour of life and while in the enjoyment of health, to meet the evil day by which you may before long be overtaken." You cannot over-estimate the importance to these men of a small saving—of the possession of some such sum as ten or twelve pounds. It may be to them the foundation of future independence. It may enable the father of a family—imitating the honourable example of the Member for Salford (Mr. Brotherton)—to gather that family around him and say, "From these small gains I will lay the foundation of a fortune, such as hundreds in Lancashire have acquired by their own industry and integrity." Why, I myself, could name at least ten individuals in Lancashire who, when I was a boy, were earning only 25s. or 30s. a week; and each of whom is now worth, it may be, from 50,000l. to 100,000l. But who is to answer for the result, if you paralyse the efforts of such men by your legislation—if you fetter their industry, and restrict their hours of labour, and by preventing them from profiting by the time of prosperity, drive them, when the hour of adversity shall come, to the poor law for a maintenance? Will not the labouring man go to a country in which no such restrictions do prevail? Will he not soon ask the price of a third-class fare to Dover, and transfer his skill and the vigour of his English character to some place where he could use them without restraint? The amount of weekly earnings is the great point on which the happiness and independence of a working man's family turns. I have here a book containing statements which have struck me forcibly, and which give an account of the appropriation of the wages of two families. In the first family the number of persons is nine, and the wages are 18*s.*; in the second the number of seven, and the wages are 9*s.* This is the way in which the weekly income is appropriated: In the first family the income of 18*s.* per week is laid out as follows:—Bread, 10*s.* 6*d.*; house-rent, 1*s.*; washing, 1*s.*; and fire, 1*s.*; making 13*s.* 6*d.*; this leaves for clothing, tea, sugar, and meat, 4*s.* 6*d.* extra. In the family of seven persons, having 9*s.* per week, the payments are, for bread, 5*s.* 6*d.*; rent, 1*s.*; fire, 1*s.*; washing, 9*d.*, making 8*s.* 3*d.*; there is left for clothing, for tea, sugar, and meat, not 4*s.* 6*d.* but 9*d.* only. Thus every shilling cut off from the income of such a family is attended with great diminution in their comforts. Intelligent men are asked in the volume before me how it is possible for a labouring man to maintain a family of four or five children upon 10*s.* a week? The question is put to clergymen and to persons engaged in agriculture, and here are the answers. Mr. Huxtable, a great agriculturist, being asked how a labouring man maintains a wife and four or five children upon 10*s.* a week, says that is a problem he cannot solve by any calculation, and that all attempts to solve it, so far as he has seen, are entire failures. The next person who is asked, says he cannot answer the question; that he was altogether at a loss to conceive how it was done, and that he was never satisfied with the explanation he received from labourers' wives upon this point. Let us reflect, then, what may be the consequence of reducing still further the wages of labour.

6. Samuel Smiles, *William Fairbairn*

Samuel Smiles (1812–1904) is today best remembered as a well-known author and popular moralist of the Victorian age. He began as a doctor, but, disappointed by the limited economic and intellectual opportunities open to him in a rural medical practice, he turned for a time to journalism and later to a longer career as a railroad executive. For many years he was the secretary of the South Eastern Railway.

Parallel with these various activities, and drawing on his experience in all of them, in his spare time Smiles established himself as one of

From Samuel Smiles, *Industrial Biography: Iron Workers and Tool Makers* (London: John Murray, 1863), pp. 314–16, 323–33.

England's most notable writers of popular inspirational books. In 1859 he published *Self-Help,* the first of a series of volumes stressing one main theme: that the continuing social progress of the nineteenth century could best be illustrated and validated by examining the biographies of men who had risen by their own efforts from humble origins to great achievements.

Given his own business experience and the contemporary enthusiasm for technological progress, it is not surprising that Smiles turned for his material to the lives of inventors and engineers, creating a new kind of "industrial biography." His essay on William Fairbairn (1787–1874) is an example of this genre of work. Fairbairn's life and career provided just the kind of personal saga that Smiles was eager to dramatize. It offered a striking contrast between humble and inauspicious beginnings and ultimate success over personal and professional difficulties. A poor but precocious Scots lad, Fairbairn was apprenticed to a millwright at fourteen, but soon set himself up as a free-lance inventor and produced in rapid succession a digging machine, a sausage maker, and a nail-making apparatus. In his thirties he produced cotton mill machinery, and later achieved great fame as a bridgebuilder and designer. Eventually he became one of the most accomplished civil engineers of his day. Toward the end of his life (in 1870) Fairbairn estimated that he had designed and built nearly one thousand bridges.

When William Fairbairn entered Manchester he was twenty-four years of age; and his hat still "covered his family." But, being now pretty well satiated with his "wanderschaft,"—as German tradesmen term their stage of travelling in search of trade experience,—he desired to settle, and, if fortune favoured him, to marry the object of his affections, to whom his heart still faithfully turned during all his wanderings. He succeeded in finding employment with Mr. Adam Parkinson, remaining with him for two years, working as a millwright, at good wages. Out of his earnings he saved sufficiently to furnish a two-roomed cottage comfortably; and there we find him fairly installed with his wife by the end of 1816. As in the case of most men of a thoughtful turn, marriage served not only to settle our engineer, but to stimulate him to more energetic action. He now began to aim at taking a higher position, and entertained the ambition of beginning business on his own account. One of his first efforts in this direction was the preparation of the design of a cast-iron bridge over the Irwell, at Blackfriars, for which a prize was offered. The attempt was unsuccessful, and a stone bridge was eventually decided on; but the effort made was creditable, and proved the beginning of many designs. The first job he executed on his own account was the erection of an iron conservatory and hothouse for Mr. J. Hulme, of Clayton, near Manchester; and he induced one of his shopmates, James Lillie, to join him in the undertaking. This proved the beginning of a business connection which lasted for a period of fifteen years, and laid the foundation of a partnership, the reputation of which, in connection with mill-work and the construction of iron machinery generally, eventually became known all over the civilized world.

Although the patterns for the conservatory were all made, and the castings were begun, the work was not proceeded with, in consequence of the notice given by a Birmingham firm that the plan after which it was proposed to construct it was an infringement of their patent. The young firm were consequently under the necessity of looking about them for other employment. And to be prepared for executing orders, they proceeded in the year 1817 to hire a small shed at a rent of 12s. a week, in which they set up a lathe of their own making, capable of turning shafts of from 3 to 6 inches in diameter; and they hired a strong Irishman to drive the wheel and assist at the heavy work. Their first job was the erection of a cullender, and their next a calico-polishing machine; but orders came in slowly, and James Lillie began to despair of success. His more hopeful partner strenuously urged him to perseverance, and so buoyed him up with hopes of orders, that he determined to go on a little longer. They then issued cards among the manufacturers, and made a tour of the principal firms, offering their services and soliciting work.

Amongst others, Mr. Fairbairn called upon the Messrs. Adam and George Murray, the large cotton-spinners, taking with him the designs of his iron bridge. Mr. Adam Murray received him kindly, heard his explanations, and invited him to call on the following day with his partner. The manufacturer must have been favourably impressed by this interview, for next day, when Fairbairn and Lillie called, he took them over his mill, and asked whether they felt themselves competent to renew with horizontal cross-shafts the whole of the work by which the mule-spinning machinery was turned. This was a formidable enterprise for a young firm without capital and almost without plant to undertake; but they had confidence in themselves, and boldly replied that they were willing and able to execute the work. On this, Mr. Murray said he would call and see them at their own workshop, to satisfy himself that they possessed the means of undertaking such an order. This proposal was by no means encouraging to the partners, who feared that when Mr. Murray spied "the nakedness of the land" in that quarter, he might repent him of his generous intentions. He paid his promised visit, and it is probable that he was more favourably impressed by the individual merits of the partners than by the excellence of their machine-tools—of which they had only one, the lathe which they had just made and set up; nevertheless he gave them the order, and they began with glad hearts and willing hands and minds to execute this their first contract. It may be sufficient to state that by working late and early—from 5 in the morning until 9 at night for a considerable period—they succeeded in completing the alterations within the time specified, and to Mr. Murray's entire satisfaction. The practical skill of the young men being thus proved, and their anxiety to execute the work entrusted to them to the best of their ability having excited the admiration of their employer, he took the opportunity of recommending them to his friends in the trade, and amongst others to Mr. John Kennedy, of the firm of MacConnel and Kennedy, then the largest spinners in the kingdom. . . .

To return to Mr. Fairbairn's career, and his progress as a millwright and engineer in Manchester. When he and his partner undertook the extensive alterations in Mr. Murray's factory, both were in a great measure unacquainted with the working of cotton-mills, having until then been occupied principally with corn-mills, and printing and bleaching works; so that an entirely new field was now opened to their united exertions. Sedulously improving their opportunities, the young partners not only thoroughly mastered the practical details of cotton-mill work, but they were very shortly enabled to introduce a series of improvements of the greatest importance in this branch of our national manufactures. Bringing their vigorous practical minds to bear on the subject, they at once saw that the gearing of even the best mills was of a very clumsy and imperfect character. They found the machinery driven by large square cast-iron shafts, on which huge wooden drums, some of them as much as four feet in diameter, revolved at the rate of about forty revolutions a minute; and the couplings were so badly fitted that they might be heard creaking and groaning a long way off. The speeds of the driving-shafts were mostly got up by a series of straps and counter drums, which not only crowded the rooms, but seriously obstructed the light where most required for conducting the delicate operations of the different machines. Another serious defect lay in the construction of the shafts, and in the mode of fixing the couplings, which were constantly giving way, so that a week seldom passed without one or more break-downs. The repairs were usually made on Sundays, which were the millwrights' hardest working days, to their own serious moral detriment; but when trade was good, every consideration was made to give way to the uninterrupted running of the mills during the rest of the week.

It occurred to Mr. Fairbairn that the defective arrangements thus briefly described, might be remedied by the introduction of lighter shafts driven at double or treble the velocity, smaller drums to drive the machinery, and the use of wrought-iron wherever practicable, because of its greater lightness and strength compared with wood. He also provided for the simplification

of the hangers and fixings by which the shafting was supported, and introduced the "half-lap coupling" so well known to millwrights and engineers.
His partner entered fully into his views; and the opportunity shortly presented itself of carrying them into effect in the large new mill erected in
1818, for the firm of MacConnel and Kennedy. The machinery of that concern proved a great improvement on all that had preceded it; and, to Messrs.
Fairbairn and Lillie's new system of gearing Mr. Kennedy added an original
invention of his own in a system of double speeds, with the object of giving
an increased quantity of twist in the finer descriptions of mule yarn.

The satisfactory execution of this important work at once placed the
firm of Fairbairn and Lillie in the very front rank of engineering millwrights. Mr. Kennedy's good word was of itself a passport to fame and
business, and as he was more than satisfied with the manner in which his
mill machinery had been planned and executed, he sounded their praises in
all quarters. Orders poured in upon them so rapidly, that they had difficulty
in keeping pace with the demands of the trade. They then removed from
their original shed to larger premises in Mather Street, where they erected
additional lathes and other tool-machines, and eventually a steam-engine.
They afterwards added a large cellar under an adjoining factory to their
premises; and from time to time provided new means of turning out work
with increased efficiency and despatch. In due course of time the firm
erected a factory of their own, fitted with the most improved machinery for
turning out millwork; and they went on from one contract to another, until
their reputation as engineers became widely celebrated. In 1826–27, they
supplied the water-wheels for the extensive cotton-mills belonging to
Kirkman Finlay and Company, at Catrine Bank in Ayrshire. These wheels
are even at this day regarded as among the most perfect hydraulic machines
in Europe. About the same time they supplied the mill gearing and water-
machinery for Messrs. Escher and Company's large works at Zurich,
among the largest cotton manufactories on the continent.

In the meanwhile the industry of Manchester and the neighbourhood,
through which the firm had risen and prospered, was not neglected, but
had the full benefit of the various improvements which they were introducing in mill machinery. In the course of a few years an entire revolution was
effected in the gearing. Ponderous masses of timber and cast-iron, with
their enormous bearings and couplings, gave place to slender rods of
wrought-iron and light frames or hooks by which they were suspended. In
like manner, lighter yet stronger wheels and pulleys were introduced, the
whole arrangements were improved, and, the workmanship being greatly
more accurate, friction was avoided, while the speed was increased from
about 40 to upwards of 300 revolutions a minute. The fly-wheel of the engine was also converted into a first motion by the formation of teeth on its

periphery, by which a considerable saving was effected both in cost and power.

These great improvements formed quite an era in the history of mill machinery; and exercised the most important influence on the development of the cotton, flax, silk, and other branches of manufacture. Mr. Fairbairn says the system introduced by his firm was at first strongly condemned by leading engineers, and it was with difficulty that he could overcome the force of their opposition; nor was it until a wheel of thirty tons weight for a pair of engines of 100-horse power each was erected and set to work, that their prognostications of failure entirely ceased. From that time the principles introduced by Mr. Fairbairn have been adopted wherever steam is employed as a motive power in mills.

Mr. Fairbairn and his partner had a hard uphill battle to fight while these improvements were being introduced; but energy and perseverance, guided by sound judgment, secured their usual reward, and the firm became known as one of the most thriving and enterprising in Manchester. Long years afterward, when addressing an assembly of working men, Mr. Fairbairn, while urging the necessity of labour and application as the only sure means of self-improvement, said, "I can tell you from experience, that there is no labour so sweet, none so consolatory, as that which is founded upon an honest, straightforward, and honourable ambition." The history of any prosperous business, however, so closely resembles every other, and its details are usually of so monotonous a character, that it is unnecessary for us to pursue this part of the subject; and we will content ourselves with briefly indicating the several further improvements introduced by Mr. Fairbairn in the mechanics of construction in the course of his long and useful career.

His improvements in water-wheels were of great value, especially as regarded the new form of bucket which he introduced with the object of facilitating the escape of the air as the water entered the bucket above, and its readmission as the water emptied itself out below. This arrangement enabled the water to act upon the wheel with the maximum of effect in all states of the river; and it so generally recommended itself, that it very soon became adopted in most water-mills both at home and abroad.[1]

His labours were not, however, confined to his own particular calling as a mill engineer, but were shortly directed to other equally important branches of the constructive art. Thus he was among the first to direct his attention to iron ship building as a special branch of business. In 1829, Mr. Houston, of Johnstown, near Paisley, launched a light boat on the Ardrossan Canal, for the purpose of ascertaining the speed at which it could

---

1. The subject will be found fully treated in Mr. Fairbairn's own work, *A Treatise on Mills and Mill-Work,* embodying the results of his large experience.

be towed by horses with two or three persons on board. To the surprise of Mr. Houston and the other gentlemen present, it was found that the labour the horses had to perform in towing the boat was much greater at six or seven, than at nine miles an hour. This anomaly was very puzzling to the experimenters, and at the request of the Council of the Forth and Clyde Canal, Mr. Fairbairn, who had already become extensively known as a scientific mechanic, was requested to visit Scotland and institute a series of experiments with light boats to determine the law of traction, and clear up, if possible, the apparent anomalies in Mr. Houston's experiments. This he did accordingly, and the results of his experiments were afterwards published. The trials extended over a series of years, and were conducted at a cost of several thousand pounds. The first experiments were made with vessels of wood, but they eventually led to the construction of iron vessels upon a large scale and on an entirely new principle of construction, with angle iron ribs and wrought-iron sheathing plates. The results proved most valuable, and had the effect of specially directing the attention of naval engineers to the employment of iron in ship-building.

Mr. Fairbairn himself fully recognised the value of the experiments, and proceeded to construct an iron vessel at his works at Manchester, in 1831, which went to sea the same year. Its success was such as to induce him to begin iron shipbuilding on a large scale, at the same time as the Messrs. Laird did at Birkenhead; and in 1835, Mr. Fairbairn established extensive works at Millwall, on the Thames,—afterwards occupied by Mr. Scott Russell, in whose yard the "Great Eastern" steamship was erected,— where in the course of some fourteen years he built upwards of a hundred and twenty iron ships, some of them above 2000 tons burden. It was in fact the first great iron ship-building yard in Britain, and led the way in a branch of business which has since become of first-rate magnitude and importance. Mr. Fairbairn was a most laborious experimenter in iron, and investigated in great detail the subject of its strength, the value of different kinds of riveted joints compared with the solid plate, and the distribution of the material throughout the structure, as well as the form of the vessel itself. It would indeed be difficult to over-estimate the value of his investigations on these points in the earlier stages of this now highly important branch of the national industry.

To facilitate the manufacture of his iron-sided ships, Mr. Fairbairn, about the year 1839, invented a machine for riveting boiler plates by steam-power. The usual method by which this process had before been executed was by hand-hammers, worked by men placed at each side of the plate to be riveted, acting simultaneously on both sides of the bolt. But this process was tedious and expensive, as well as clumsy and imperfect; and some more rapid and precise method of fixing the plates firmly together was urgently wanted. Mr. Fairbairn's machine completely supplied the want. By its means the rivet was driven into its place, and firmly fastened there by a couple of strokes of a hammer impelled by steam. Aided by the Jacquard punching-machine of Roberts, the riveting of plates of the largest size has thus become one of the simplest operations in iron-manufacturing.

The thorough knowledge which Mr. Fairbairn possessed of the strength of wrought-iron in the form of the hollow beam (which a wrought-iron ship really is) naturally led to his being consulted by the late Robert Stephenson as to the structures by means of which it was proposed to span the estuary of the Conway and the Straits of Menai; and the result was the Conway and Britannia Tubular Bridges, the history of which we have fully described elsewhere.[2] There is no reason to doubt that by far the largest share of the merit of working out the practical details of those structures, and thus realizing Robert Stephenson's magnificent idea of the tubular bridge, belongs to Mr. Fairbairn.

In all matters connected with the qualities and strength of iron, he came to be regarded as a first-rate authority, and his advice was often sought and highly valued. The elaborate experiments instituted by him as to the strength of iron of all kinds have formed the subject of various papers which he has read before the British Association, the Royal Society, and the Literary and Philosophical Society of Manchester. His practical inquiries as to the strength of boilers have led to his being frequently called upon to investigate the causes of boiler explosions, on which subject he has published many elaborate reports. The study of this subject led him to elucidate the law according to which the density of steam varies throughout an extensive range of pressures and atmospheres,—in singular confirmation of what had before been provisionally calculated from the mechanical theory of heat. His discovery of the true method of preventing the tendency of tubes to collapse, by dividing the flues of long boilers into short lengths by means of stiffening rings, arising out of the same investigation, was one of the valuable results of his minute study of the subject; and is calculated to be of essential value in the manufacturing districts by diminishing the chances of boiler explosions, and saving the lamentable loss of life which has during the last twenty years been occasioned by the malconstruction of boilers. Among Mr. Fairbairn's most recent inquiries are those conducted by him at the instance of the British government relative to the construction of iron-plated ships, his report of which has not yet been made public, most probably for weighty political reasons.

We might also refer to the practical improvements which Mr. Fairbairn

2. *Lives of the Engineers,* vol. 3, pp. 416–40. See also William Fairbairn, C.E., *An Account of the Construction of the Britannia and Conway Tubular Bridges,* 1849.

has been instrumental in introducing in the construction of buildings of various kinds by the use of iron. He has himself erected numerous iron structures, and pointed out the road which other manufacturers have readily followed. "I am one of those," said he, in his "Lecture on the Progress of Engineering," "who have great faith in iron walls and iron beams; and although I have both spoken and written much on the subject, I cannot too forcibly recommend it to public attention. It is now twenty years since I constructed an iron house, with the machinery of a corn-mill, for Halil Pasha, then Seraskier of the Turkish army at Constantinople. I believe it was the first iron house built in this country; and it was constructed at the works at Millwall, London, in 1839." [3]

Since then iron structures of all kinds have been erected: iron lighthouses, iron-and-crystal palaces, iron churches, and iron bridges. Iron roads have long been worked by iron locomotives; and before many years have passed a telegraph of iron wire will probably be found circling the globe. We now use iron roofs, iron bedsteads, iron ropes, and iron pavement; and even the famous "wooden walls of England" are rapidly becoming reconstructed of iron. In short, we are in the midst of what Mr. Worsaae has characterized as the Age of Iron.

At the celebration of the opening of the North Wales Railway at Bangor, almost within sight of his iron bridge across the Straits of Menai, Robert Stephenson said, "We are daily producing from the bowels of the earth a raw material, in its crude state apparently of no worth, but which, when converted into a locomotive engine, flies over bridges of the same material, with a speed exceeding that of the bird, advancing wealth and comfort throughout the country. Such are the powers of that all-civilizing instrument, Iron."

Iron indeed plays a highly important part in modern civilization. Out of

3. *Useful Information for Engineers,* 2d series, p. 225. The mere list of Mr. Fairbairn's writings would occupy considerable space; for, notwithstanding his great labours as an engineer, he has also been an industrious writer. His papers on Iron, read at different times before the British Association, the Royal Society, and the Literary and Philosophical Institution of Manchester, are of great value. The treatise on "Iron" in the *Encyclopaedia Britannica* is from his pen, and he has contributed a highly interesting paper to Dr. Scoffern's *Useful Metals and Their Alloys* on the Application of Iron to the purposes of Ordnance, Machinery, Bridges, and House and Ship Building. Another valuable but less-known contribution to Iron literature is his Report on Machinery in General, published in the *Reports on the Paris Universal Exhibition of 1855.* The experiments conducted by Mr. Fairbairn for the purpose of proving the excellent properties of iron for shipbuilding—the account of which was published in the *Transactions of the Royal Society*—eventually led to his further experiments to determine the strength and form of the Britannia and Conway Tubular Bridges, plate-girders, and other constructions, the result of which was to establish quite a new era in the history of bridge as well as ship building.

it are formed alike the sword and the ploughshare, the cannon and the printing-press; and while civilization continues partial and half-developed, as it still is, our liberties and our industry must necessarily in a great measure depend for their protection upon the excellence of our weapons of war as well as on the superiority of our instruments of peace. Hence the skill and ingenuity displayed in the invention of rifled guns and artillery, and iron-sided ships and batteries, the fabrication of which would be impossible but for the extraordinary development of the iron-manufacture, and the marvellous power and precision of our tool-making machines, as described in preceding chapters.

"Our strength, wealth, and commerce," said Mr. Cobden in the course of a recent debate in the House of Commons, "grow out of the skilled labour of the men working in metals. They are at the foundation of our manufacturing greatness; and in case you were attacked, they would at once be available, with their hard hands and skilled brains, to manufacture your muskets and your cannon, your shot and your shell. What has given us our Armstrongs, Whitworths, and Fairbairns, but the free industry of this country? If you can build three times more steam-engines than any other country, and have threefold the force of mechanics, to whom and to what do you owe that, but to the men who have trained them, and to those principles of commerce out of which the wealth of the country has grown? We who have some hand in doing that, are not ignorant that we have been and are increasing the strength of the country in proportion as we are raising up skilled artisans." [4]

The reader who has followed us up to this point will have observed that handicraft labour was the first stage of the development of human power, and that machinery has been its last and highest. The uncivilized man began with a stone for a hammer, and a splinter of flint for a chisel, each stage of his progress being marked by an improvement in his tools. Every machine calculated to save labour or increase production was a substantial addition to his power over the material resources of nature, enabling him to subjugate them more effectually to his wants and uses; and every extension of machinery has served to introduce new classes of the population to the enjoyment of its benefits. In early times the products of skilled industry were for the most part luxuries intended for the few, whereas now the most exquisite tools and engines are employed in producing articles of ordinary consumption for the great mass of the community. Machines with millions of fingers work for millions of purchasers—for the poor as well as the rich; and while the machinery thus used enriches its owners, it no less enriches the public with its products.

4. House of Commons Debate, 7 July 1862.

Much of the progress to which we have adverted has been the result of the skill and industry of our own time. "Indeed," says Mr. Fairbairn, "the mechanical operations of the present day could not have been accomplished at any cost thirty years ago; and what was then considered impossible is now performed with an exactitude that never fails to accomplish the end in view." For this we are mainly indebted to the almost creative power of modern machine-tools, and the facilities which they present for the production and reproduction of other machines. We also owe much to the mechanical agencies employed to drive them. Early inventors yoked wind and water to sails and wheels, and made them work machinery of various kinds; but modern inventors have availed themselves of the far more swift and powerful, yet docile force of steam, which has now laid upon it the heaviest share of the burden of toil, and indeed become the universal drudge. Coal, water, and a little oil, are all that the steam-engine, with its bowels of iron and heart of fire, needs to enable it to go on working night and day, without rest or sleep. Yoked to machinery of almost infinite variety, the results of vast ingenuity and labour, the Steam-engine pumps water, drives spindles, thrashes corn, prints books, hammers iron, ploughs land, saws timber, drives piles, impels ships, works railways, excavates docks; and, in a word, asserts an almost unbounded supremacy over the materials which enter into the daily use of mankind, for clothing, for labour, for defence, for household purposes, for locomotion, for food, or for instruction.

7. Two Articles from *The Economist* (1851)

The Great Exhibition, the first big international trade exhibition of the nineteenth century, was held in Hyde Park in London in 1851 under the presidency of the prince consort, Prince Albert. During the 141 days it was open, it was visited by more than 6 million people. The exhibition contained 13,907 exhibitors, 6,556 from countries outside of the British Empire. In its proud, even ostentatious, display of a series of new mechanical products for industry and agriculture—including a 31-ton locomotive; a hydraulic press that could lift 1,144 tons; hydraulic turbines and machine tools; steam threshers, reapers, and plows—the Exhibition was both an international symbol of competitive innovation and economic progress and an illustration of England's hegemony at midcentury as the premier industrial "workshop of the world."

The Crystal Palace was the center of the Great Exhibition of 1851. Designed by Sir Joseph Paxton (1801–65), it was the first monumental

From *The Economist* (London) 9 (1851): 4–6, 57–58.

edifice in Britain constructed solely from metal and glass. Occupying eighteen acres and built with thirty-four miles of iron piping and 900,000 square feet of plate glass, the building was 1,848 feet long and 456 feet wide. Since its modular parts were standardized and prefabricated, its actual construction required only twenty-two weeks. A contemporary commentator, Leigh Hunt, noted that the building was "neither crystal nor a palace. It was a bazaar, admirably constructed for its purpose and justly surprising those who beheld its interior." In 1854 it was moved to Sydenham, on the southern outskirts of London. It was destroyed by fire in 1936.

The two reprinted articles from *The Economist,* published in January 1851, on the eve of the exhibition's opening, suggest the enthusiasm, the pride, and the self-confidence of the mid-Victorian epoch in its financial, industrial, and moral attainments.

The Exhibition—The Crystal Palace

The last day of the year forms an epoch in the history of the Crystal Palace. It was to have been completed on that day, but the plans having been altered, more time was required, and probably a month must elapse before it can be handed over to the Commissioners, quite ready for the purposes for which it is destined. In the meantime, however, the things that are to be exhibited are beginning to arrive from India and other distant parts, and all the arrangements for giving satisfaction at once to exhibitors and the public seem in a fair way of being completed. The building is in such a state of forwardness—much of it being boarded round, and the floorings laid— that it was on Tuesday opened (by tickets) to a numerous company. The Society of Arts was invited to inspect the building. Professor Cowper, of King's College, gave, in a lecture, a description of it, illustrated by many models and drawings. He afterwards explained the many contrivances that have been invented, and are in use on the spot, to facilitate the work; and the great company present, consisting of thousands of persons, seemed all delighted with the wonders that they saw.

To attempt by words to vie with the pictorial representations of the enormous structure that now meet the eye in many illustrated publications, and in almost every engraver's and bookseller's shop, would be ridiculous. The form of the building, and the peculiarities of its structure; its long rows of light, graceful columns; its roof, that, like the sky, seems to have no supporters; its long galleries, that appear suspended in the air; the vast transept overarching the majestic trees, that were not allowed to be disturbed; are all long ago become familiar to the public, and will be known and remembered for years and ages throughout the land and throughout Europe as among the memorabilia of 1850. We have already said, and we can only repeat, that of all the marvels expected to be displayed in Hyde Park in 1851, none will be greater, if any be so great, as the Crystal Palace erected expressly for the Exhibition.

Many and untold benefits are expected from the gathering of all nations to do honour to the industrial arts; but benefits, perhaps unanticipated, have already begun to flow from the undertaking. The very conception immediately increased the friendly communication between distant and too-often hostile communities, and has doubtless had some influence on the minds of those who were lately sharpening their swords for war. It was impossible that their Majesties of Austria and Prussia and their advisers could for one moment recollect how much their contest would interfere with this great world fair—this pilgrimage of all nations to the shrine of peaceful industry—and how much it was, therefore, opposed to the opinions of the age and their own people, without feeling increased repugnance to begin a war that would mar so fair a prospect, and hand them down to posterity branded as the enemies of civilisation. The convocation of all nations to meet in London in 1851 has already had, in part, some of the best effects expected from it, and has contributed to dispose men's minds to peace, and to secure the political repose of nations.

In the early ages, when the labour necessary to procure subsistence was performed by slaves, and the work of slaughter was the only toil performed by free men, most kinds of useful industry were considered degraded and degrading. The proposed Exhibition marks the great fact, that useful industry has now wholly escaped from the contamination of slavery, and is raised to a post of honour. The parent of health, the source of subsistence and all that supports and adorns life, its statue henceforth will stand the highest in our mythology. The preparation for its elevation has already ennobled all workers. Not a man has been employed in getting things ready for the Exhibition, or in preparing the building, but must have felt additional dignity, from a conviction that the work of his hands was to be seen and admired by great multitudes of his fellow-creatures. The Exhibition is helping forward that great epoch in the history of industry of which the Crystal Palace is the splendid temple.

When Mr. Paxton explained, at the Society of Arts on November 13, the origin of the building, he said:—"When I consider the cheapness of glass and cast iron, and the great facility with which they can be used, I have no doubt but many structures similar to that of Darley will be attached to dwelling houses, where they may serve as sitting rooms, conservatories, waiting rooms, or omnibus rooms. I am now, in fact, engaged in making the design for a gentleman's house, to be covered wholly with glass; and when we consider that wherever lead is now used, glass may, with equal propriety, be substituted, I have every hope that it will be used for buildings of various conditions and character. Structures of the kind are also susceptible of the highest kind of ornamentation, as stained glass and general painting." The building at Darley referred to in this extract was a flat roof boarded conservatory, and the gentleman living at Darley, in a letter to Mr. Paxton, thus describes it:—"The use we chiefly make of it is as a sitting room, we find it so dry, light, and airy. While preparing the house for our residence during the last winter and spring, it was filled with all sorts of furniture, and books, pictures, &c., and a piano; nothing received any injury. Indeed, we selected it for being what it has proved, the most dry and airy part of the house. I cannot conceive its construction could be improved, so as to better answer the purposes for which you designed it." These two paragraphs tell us distinctly that the light and elegant, the cheerful and airy, the cheap and wholesome style of building of the Crystal Palace may be adopted for ordinary dwellings, and may be applied to improve the houses of the poor.

But it is doubtful, when Mr. Paxton made these remarks, whether he knew or foresaw all the rapid and cheap methods to which the necessity of building so vast a structure in so short a time has given rise. All the machinery for making gutters, sash bars, &c.— all the new contrivances for painting and glazing this huge building, may, and no doubt will, be applied to constructing common dwellings, and the result, from the competition between the workers in brick and iron, in glass and slate, will be great improvement in the form and reduction in the cost of buildings. As the ease and comfort of the increasing multitude will be more cheaply and better provided for, the land will be everywhere adorned with crystal palaces.

Connected as are all the works of the universe one with another—forming one whole, which we, for the convenience of our limited minds, break down into fractions—every future improvement in society will radiate in some unknown or known way from the Great Exhibition. To pretend to foresee all its consequences, is to claim the prerogatives of the Almighty; but we may surely yet humbly predict, as amongst them, the elevation in mental dignity and material well-being of the working multitude. It was observed when railways came into use that they would place all travellers on an equality. The poorest would be obliged to use them, and the rich would have nothing better. If crystal palaces can be erected cheaper than any other kind of dwelling, and if the richest can have no better houses, the poorest will have them also, and another step will be made by all towards reaching that high but equal level to which the natural development of society is rapidly leading. Living apart in their clubhouses, or gathering together in their *salons,* separate from the vulgar multitude, the opulent and great have neither means nor opportunity of spreading their refinements rapidly through all the subordinate classes. Railways and steamboats have contributed to bring all classes together, and make the manners that are most generally agreeable the most prevalent. A great improvement in this respect is obvious in all classes. The poor are not so rude, the rich not so arrogant as they were. The Exhibition will mingle them still more; dwellings of a common, but improved kind, will tend to the same end, and all will be raised and equalised.

If we do not mistake, a still grander lesson is in preparation. It was remarked by Professor Cowper, in his lecture, that an architect had seldom any occasion to resort to calculation to ascertain the strength of his materials. He piled brick on brick and stone on stone, without any idea of risk, or any thought of restricting himself to the smallest possible quantity of material. The engineer in iron, however, submits everything he uses to rigid calculation, and employs the smallest quantity of material by which he can get equal strength. He uses no columns carrying nothing; he puts up no solid beams where trellised rafters, at once lighter and stronger, will suffice; he has to erect a thing above the earth, and he considers how he can best overcome that gravity which in all materials makes them tend to fall to the earth. He studies therefore especially the curious problem of the influence of *form* in giving strength or overcoming gravity; and he has been eminently successful in showing that certain *forms,* be the materials what they may, are real powers; and, without other alteration in the weight, size, or character of the materials than a change in form, they become invested with very different attributes. The fact, indeed, has long been known; it has recently received a striking illustration at the Britannia Bridge; it has been, in a great variety of modes, illustrated in the course of building the Crystal Palace; and it teaches us—as form is a real power, capable of resisting and overcoming other powers—that quantity of materials (which has, for ages, been the great object of solicitude) may possibly become a matter of very secondary consideration. Other great powers or agents are at our command, such as magnetism, electricity, heat, and light; adding form to them, we have a dim perception of a coming time, when all the restraints and hindrances that we see and feel, shall be regarded as of trifling importance compared to the unseen, intangible powers around us, operating by which we are enabled to subdue all the visible material world.

On the whole, we may conclude that the Exhibition—which is both a sign of a prodigious improvement in the condition of man that has already come to pass, and a cause of continued improvement in the same direction—will probably be one of the most remarkable phenomena of the present year, as the conception of such a design is one of the most remarkable phenomena of the year and of the half century that has just elapsed.

The progress already made is the best justification of future hope. When we refer to a few only of the extraordinary improvements of the half century just elapsed—such as the 35 years' peace, so far as morals are concerned; such as the philanthropic and just conviction that the welfare of the multitude, not of one or two classes, is the proper object of social solicitude; the humane direction which the mind has received towards the abolition of slavery; the amelioration of all penal systems, and the doubts that have been generated of their utility; the advances in religious toleration, and in forbearing one with another: and such as the application of steam to locomotives on water and land, and the consequent vast extension of communication all over the world, so far as physics are concerned;—such as the invention and general introduction of gas; the use of railroads and electric telegraphs; the extended application of machinery to all the arts of life, almost putting an end to very severe injurious bodily toil, except in agriculture, in which, though the labourers are speedily doubled up with rheumatism, and become, from poverty and excessive labour in all kinds of weather, prematurely old, great improvements have nevertheless been made:—when we refer to a few events of this kind, we become convinced that the half century just elapsed is more full of wonders than any other record. Of that wonderful half century the Great Exhibition is both a fitting close and a fitting commencement of the new half century, which will, no doubt, surpass its predecessor as much as that surpassed all that went before it. Those who have lived through this wonderful era will lose all regret at not being suffered to witness the yet more wonderful things that are in store for their predecessors, in the bright hope that they will be the produce and the reward of the ingenuity and virtues they have been permitted to behold. All who have read, and can think, must now have full confidence that the "endless progression," ever increasing in rapidity, of which the poet sung, is the destined lot of the human race.

The First Half of the Nineteenth Century:
Progress of the Nation, and the Race

The close of one half-century and the commencement of another offer to us one of those resting-places in the march of time which, whenever they occur, at shorter or longer intervals, impressively summon us to the task of retrospect and reflection. "The poorest moment that passes over us is the conflux of two eternities;"—we are, it is true, at every moment standing on the narrow isthmus that divides the great ocean of duration—a ground that, even as we name it, is washed from beneath our feet;—but it is only at the termination of the longer epochs by which our life is told off into the past, that we fully feel this truth. At such times it is well to pause for a brief space amid the struggle and the race of life, to consider the rate of our progress and the direction of our course, to measure our distance from the starting-post in relation to the advantages with which we set out and the time we have spent upon the road, and to calculate, as far as may be, the probable rapidity of our future advance in a career to which there is no goal.

Too many of us are disposed to place our Golden Age in the Past: this is especially the tendency of the imaginative, the ignorant, the indolent, and the old. To such it is soothing to turn from the dry and disappointing labours of the present and the hot and dusty pathways of the actual world, and to speculate on that early spring-time of our Race in which Fancy, without toil or hindrance, can construct a Utopia of which History affords us no trace, and which Logic assures us could have had no existence. Another and a larger class are ever prone to seek a refuge from baffled exertions, disappointed hopes, and dissatisfied desires, in a distant Future in which all expectations, reasonable or unreasonable, are to have their fulfilment. But nearly everybody agrees by common consent to undervalue and abuse the present. We confess that we cannot share their disappointment, nor echo their complaints. We look upon the Past with respect and affection as a series of stepping-stones to that high and advanced position which we actually hold; and from the Future we hope for the realisation of those dreams, almost of perfectibility, which a comparison of the Past with the present entitles us to indulge in. But we see no reason to be discontented either with our rate of progress or with the actual stage which we have reached; and we think that man must be hard to please who, with due estimate of human powers and human aims, and a full knowledge of the facts which we propose concisely to recall to the recollection of our readers, can come to a different conclusion.

Economists are supposed to be, by nature and occupation, cold, arithmetical, and unenthusiastic. We shall not, we hope, do discredit to this character when we say that we consider it a happiness and a privilege to have had our lot cast in the first fifty years of this century. For not only has that period been rich beyond nearly all others in political events of thrilling interest and mighty moment, but in changes and incidents of moral and social significance it has had no parallel since the Christian era. It has witnessed the most tremendous war and the most enduring peace which we have known for centuries. It has beheld the splendid career and the sad retributive reverses of the greatest conqueror, scourge, and upsetter of old arrangements, since the days of Gengis-Khan, Attila, or Charlemagne. It has witnessed a leap forward in all the elements of material well-being such as neither scientific vision nor poetic fancy ever pictured. It is not too much to say that, in wealth, in the arts of life, in the discoveries of science and their application to the comfort, the health, the safety, and the capabilities of man, in public and private morality, in the diffusion if not in the advancement of knowledge, in the sense of social charity and justice, in religious freedom, and in political wisdom,—the period of the last fifty years has carried us forward faster and further than any other half-century in modern times. It stands at the head, *facile princeps,* unrivalled and unapproached, of all epochs of equal duration. Nay, more; it is scarcely too much to say that, in many of the particulars we have enumerated, it has witnessed a more rapid and astonishing progress than *all* the centuries which have preceded it. In several vital points the difference between the 18th and the 19th century, is greater than between the first and the 18th, as far as civilised Europe is concerned.

As we proceed we shall have occasion to justify this statement in several particulars; but if in the meantime it should seem too startling to any reader, we would ask him to compare Macaulay's celebrated picture of the state of England under the Stuarts with its condition at the close of the last century; and then to compare this last with its condition now;—and he will be amazed to find how nearly all those details of its astonishing advance which most bear upon the comforts and welfare of his daily life, are the produce of the last fifty years. The fact is, that the 18th and the last half of the 17th centuries, being a period of nearly incessant war or of perpetual internal strife, were not marked by any decided progress in the arts of civilisation, though during the latter portion of the time wealth appears to have increased faster than population, and comfort and plenty to have been, in consequence, more widely diffused. Compare the year 1800 with the year 1650, and we shall find the roads almost as bad everywhere, except near the metropolis; the streets nearly as ill-lighted and not much more safe at night; sanitary matters as much neglected; prisons only less pestilential and ill-arranged, the criminal law as sanguinary, vindictive, and inconsistent; bull and bear-bating nearly as favourite amusements, and intemperance among the higher classes almost as prevalent; locomotion scarcely more rapid or more pleasant, and the transmission of letters not much less tedious and not at all less costly.

But perhaps the best way of realising to our conceptions the actual progress of the last half-century would be to fancy ourselves suddenly transported back to the year 1800, with all our habits, expectations, requirements and standard of living formed upon the luxuries and appliances collected round us in the year 1850. In the first year of the century we should find ourselves eating bread at 1s 10-1/2d the quartern loaf, and those who could not afford this price driven to short commons, to entire abstinence, or to some miserable substitute. We should find ourselves grumbling at heavy taxes laid on nearly all the necessaries and luxuries of life—even upon salt; blaspheming at the high prices of coffee, tea, and sugar, which confined these articles, in any adequate abundance, to the rich and the easy classes of society; paying twofold for our linen shirts, threefold for our flannel petticoats, and above fivefold for our cotton handkerchiefs and stockings; receiving our newspapers seldom, poverty-stricken, and some days after date; receiving our Edinburgh letters in London a week after they were written, and paying thirteenpence halfpenny for them when delivered; exchanging the instantaneous telegraph for the slow and costly express by chaise and four; travelling with soreness and fatigue by the "old heavy," at the rate of seven miles an hour, instead of by the Great Western at fifty; and relapsing from the blaze of light which gas now pours along our streets, into a perilous and uncomfortable darkness made visible by a few wretched oil lamps scattered at distant intervals.

But these would by no means comprise the sum total, nor the worst part of the descent into barbarism. We should find our criminal law in a state worthy of Draco; executions taking place by the dozen; the stealing of five shillings punishable and punished as severely as rape or murder; slavery and the slave trade flourishing in their palmiest atrocity. We should find the liberty of the subject at the lowest ebb; freedom of discussion and writing always in fear and frequently in jeopardy; religious rights trampled under foot; Catholics, slaves and not citizens; Dissenters still disabled and despised. Parliament was unreformed; public jobbing flagrant and shameless; gentlemen drank a bottle where they now drink a glass, and measured their capacity by their cups; and the temperance medal was a thing undreamed of. Finally, the *people* in those days were little thought of, where they are now the main topic of discourse and statesmanship; steam-boats were unknown, and a voyage to America occupied eight weeks instead of ten days; and while in 1850, a population of nearly 30,000,000 paid 50,000,000 £ of taxes, in 1801 a population of 15,000,000 paid not less than 63,000,000 £.

8. Thomas Gisborne, *Enquiry into the Duties of the Female Sex*

Thomas Gisborne (1758–1846) was born into a gentry family in Staffordshire, where he remained all his life as a country clergyman. He was a member of the Evangelical movement, that movement within the Church of England for a more earnest religiosity than the nonchalant Christian "pagans" of the eighteenth century were alleged to have professed. (See documents 25 and 26 for a closer look at Evangelical doctrine, organiza-

From Gisborne, *An Enquiry into the Duties of the Female Sex* (London: Printed for T. Cadell and W. Davies in the Strand, 1797), pp. 272–75, 328–36, 357–60.

tion, and political activism. Document 26 includes a portrait of Gisborne by a contemporary.)

Evangelicals like Gisborne and Hannah More were particularly attentive to the role of religion in shaping individual conduct in ways that could minimize the social dislocations brought about by early industrialization in Britain. Thus More directed her Cheap Repository Tracts at the lower classes, urging them to accept their lot without complaint and to trust in God and in the good, paternal intentions of their betters. Similarly, Gisborne's *Enquiry into the Duties of the Female Sex* (and More's *Strictures on the Modern System of Female Education*) defined a new role for middle-class women in the face of rapid, often chaotic social and economic change. Recent historians such as Nancy Cott have described that role as presiding over a "cult of domesticity," and Gisborne's "On the Duties of Matrimonial Life," reprinted here from his *Enquiry,* well illustrates the meaning of that phrase.

Gisborne's *Enquiry* was a popular book, going through eight editions between 1797, the year of its publication, and 1810. Its author also had a reputation for being one of the best sermonizers of his era. In general, sermons were probably the chief vehicle for the propagation of the new conception of womanhood, which gained a foothold in middle-class culture during the period 1790–1830.

Are you then the mistress of a family? Fulfill the charge for which you are responsible. Attempt not to transfer your proper occupation to a favourite maid, however tried may be her fidelity and her skill. To confide implicitly in servants, is the way to render them undeserving of confidence. If they are already negligent or dishonest, your remissness encourages their faults, while it continues your own loss and inconvenience. If their integrity is unsullied, they are ignorant of the principles by which your expences ought to be regulated; and will act for you on other principles, which, if you knew them, you ought to disapprove. They know not the amount of your husband's income, or of his debts, or of his other incumbrances; nor, if they knew all these things, could they judge what part of his revenue may reasonably be expended in the departments with which they are concerned. They will not reflect that small degrees of waste and extravagance, when they could easily be guarded against, are criminal; nor will they suspect the magnitude of the sum to which small degrees of waste and extravagance, frequently repeated, will accumulate in the course of the year. They will consider the credit of your character as intrusted to them; and will conceive, that they uphold it by profusion. The larger your family is, the greater will be the annual portion of your expenditure, which will, by these means, be thrown away. And if your ample fortune inclines you to regard the sum as scarcely worth the little trouble which would have been required to prevent the loss; consider the extent of good which it might have accomplished, had it been employed in feeding the hungry and clothing the naked. Be regular in requiring, and punctual in examining, your weekly accounts. Be frugal without parsimony; save, that you may distribute. Study the comfort of all under your roof, even of the humblest inhabitant of the kitchen. Pinch not the inferior part of the family to provide against the cost of a day of splendor. Consider the welfare of the servants of your own sex as particularly committed to you. Encourage them in religion, and be active in furnishing them with the means of instruction. Let their number be fully adequate to the work which they have to perform; but let it not be swelled either from a love of parade, or from blind indulgence, to an extent which is needless. In those ranks of life where the mind is not accustomed to continued reflection, idleness is a never-failing source of folly and of vice. Forget not to indulge them at fit seasons with visits to their friends; nor grudge the pains of contriving opportunities for the indulgence. Let not one tyrannise over another. In hearing complaints, be patient; in inquiring into faults, be candid; in reproving, be temperate and unruffled. Let not your kindness to the meritorious terminate when they leave your house; but reward good conduct in them, and encourage it in others, by subsequent acts of benevolence adapted to their circumstances. Let it be your resolution, when called upon to describe the characters of servants who have quitted your family, to act conscientiously towards all the parties interested, neither aggravating nor disguising the truth. And never let any one of those whose qualifications are to be mentioned, nor of those who apply for the account, find you seduced from your purpose by partiality or by resentment. . . .

The habits of life which prevail in the metropolis, and particularly in fashionable families, are, in several respects, totally repugnant to the cultivation of affection and connubial happiness. The husband and the wife are systematically kept asunder. Separate establishments, separate sets of acquaintance, separate amusements, all conspire to render them first strangers, and afterwards indifferent to each other. If they find themselves brought together in mixed company, to be mutually cold, inattentive, and forbidding, is politeness. They who are inspired, or are supposed to be inspired, with the warmest attachment, are reciprocally to behave with a degree of repulsive unconcern, which, if exhibited towards a third person, would be construed as an affront. The truth is, that such unnatural maxims of behaviour have originated from cases in which, however blamable, they were not artificial. They have sprung from that indifference which was really felt. But those persons who are solicitous to preserve affection, will do well to cherish the outward manifestations of regard. If, on the one hand, it is possible to disgust by an ill-timed display of the familiarity of fondness; let it be remembered, on the other, that to disguise the natural feelings of the heart under the systematic restraints of assumed coldness, is offensive to every rational observer; at variance with simplicity and ingenuousness of character; and ultimately subversive of the tenderness of affection both in the party which practises the disguise, and in the person towards whom it is practised.

The influence of fashion, which of late has unhappily contributed in the metropolis to separate the husband and the wife, would have flowed in a more beneficial channel, had it been applied to draw closer the bands of domestic society. The wives of lawyers, of physicians, and of several other descriptions of men, are seldom allowed a large share of the company of their husbands. While the latter are occupied abroad by professional business, the former are left exposed to the temptations of a dissipated capital, temptations which borrow strength from the weariness of solitude at home. Hence, in addition to the common obligations which bind the consciences of married men to study the comfort and the welfare of their partners, the husband is under yet another tie to spend his leisure in the bosom of his family. Hence also the duty of the wife to render home, by the winning charms of her behaviour, attractive and delightful to her husband, derives additional force. Let her consider the numberless temptations to vice, to profusion, to idle amusement, with which he is encompassed. Let her remember with what various characters the business of his station renders him familiar; of whom some perhaps openly deride the principles of religion; others sap them by insidious machinations; others extenuate by their wit and talents the offensiveness of guilt; others add to the seducing example of gay wickedness the fascinations of rank and popularity. Is she desirous of his society? Would she confirm him in domestic habits? Would she fortify him against being allured into the haunts of luxury, riot, and profaneness? Let her conduct shew that home is dear to herself in his absence, still dearer when he is present. Let her unaffected mildness, her ingenuous tenderness, place before his mind a forcible contrast to the violence, the artifice, the unfeeling selfishness which he witnesses in his commerce with the world. Let the cheerful tranquillity of domestic pleasures stand in the place of trifling and turbulent festivity abroad. Let his house, as far as her endeavours can be effectual, be the abode of happiness; and he will have little temptation to bewilder himself in seeking for happiness under another roof.

There are motives of health or convenience which occasionally determine individuals, busied in mercantile concerns, rather to fix themselves at a country residence within a few miles of London than in the heart of the city; and thence to pay daily visits to their counting-houses in town. To the wives of persons thus circumstanced, the observations in the preceding paragraph may be addressed. It may indeed be said generally, that the turn of mind and the habits of life in the immediate neighbourhood of the capital are naturally become so far similar to those prevalent in St. James's-square, that almost every remark on moral duties, which is applicable to the latter situation, may be transferred to the former.

One of the duties which require to be expressly stated as incumbent on ladies who pass a large portion of the year in the metropolis, and especially on ladies of rank and influence, is the following; to endeavour to improve the general tone of social intercourse, and particularly in the article of amusements. Let them exchange the vast and promiscuous assemblages, which now crowd their suite of rooms from evening almost to day-break, for small and select parties, to which a virtuous character shall be a necessary introduction, and in which virtuous friendship and rational entertainment may be enjoyed. Let them discountenance the prevailing system of late hours, which undermine the constitution; and entail languor and idleness on that period of the day, which they who have not adopted the modern and destructive custom of late-rising know to be the most delightful and the most useful. Let them set up a standard against play, fashionable follies, and ensnaring customs; and unite the innocent pleasures of improving and entertaining society with the smallest possible expense of time, money, and domestic order. The benefits which might accrue to the youth of both sexes from the amelioration of the general state of meetings for purposes of conversation and amusement in polite circles are incalculable. The prospect of a happy settlement in life for individuals, their domestic conduct, their domestic comfort, the manners and habits of various classes of the community prone to imbibe the opinions and to copy the example of their immediate superiors; all these are circumstances which that amelioration would contribute to improve.

In the metropolis, the morals of servants are exposed to extraordinary dangers. By common temptations they are there beset more powerfully than in the country; and have also to contend with others peculiar to the capital. Yet it is, perhaps, in London that they receive the least attention from masters and mistresses of families. The proper inference to be drawn from these facts is obvious. Act conformably to it in all points. Let not your domestics of either sex be suffered to depend for a part of their emoluments on the perquisites of gaming. Let them be guarded to the utmost of your power against the irreparable mischiefs, which attend the practice of insuring in state lotteries.[1]

1. For some account of those mischiefs, see the "Treatise on the Police of the Metropolis," 2d ed., pp. 163–69.

Ladies who, being united to men occupied in the transactions of trade and business, find themselves resident in the city, often shew themselves extremely dissatisfied with their situation. Each wearies her husband with importunate earnestness that he would renounce the degrading profits of the counting-house and the shop, which he is now wealthy enough to despise; and exchange the ungenteel dulness of Lombard-street for the modish vicinity of the court. Affecting to look down on the polite world, deriding the barren rent-rolls of encumbered estates, apparent to their imaginations through the veil of superficial splendor; they are eager to ape the follies and to crowd into the society of the gilded swarm which they would seem to hold in contempt. Ladies of fashion in the mean time are exulting, at the other end of the town, that the hands of their husbands were never contaminated with the filthy gains of commerce; and delight in turning into ridicule the awkward efforts of the citizen's wife to rival the route and the public breakfast of the Peeress by expense void of propriety, and pomp destitute of taste. It is thus that pride and envy, displaying themselves under opposite forms, are equally conspicuous in both parties. . . .

When a large manufactory collects together, as is the case in cotton mills and some other instances, a number of women and children within its walls; or draws a concourse of poor families into its immediate vicinity, by the employment which it affords to the different parts of them; let the wife of the owner continually bear in mind that to their toil her opulence is owing. Let her remember that the obligations between the labourer and his employer are reciprocal. With cordial activity let her unite with her husband, in all ways compatible with the offices of her sex, to promote the comfort and welfare of his dependents by liberal charity adapted to their respective wants, and by all other means which personal inspection and inquiry may indicate as conducive to the preservation of their health, and the improvement of their moral and religious character. The assemblage of multitudes is highly unfavourable to virtue. The constant occupations of children in a manufactory, may easily be pushed to an extreme, that will leave neither time nor inclination for the acquisition of those principles of rectitude, which, if not impressed during childhood, are rarely gained afterwards. If such occupations are carried on in the contaminated atmosphere of crowded rooms, they sap the constitution in the years destined according to the course of nature for its complete establishment. These are evils which every person who has an interest in a manufactory is bound by the strongest ties of duty to prevent.

A similar obligation rests on the wives of tradesmen in general, in proportion to the ability and the opportunities which they possess of benefiting, in any of the methods which have been pointed out, the families of the workmen employed by the husbands. If a woman has herself the superintendence and management of the shop, let industry, punctuality, accuracy in keeping accounts, the scrupulousness of honesty shewing itself in a steady abhorrence of every manoeuvre to impose on the customer, and all other virtues of a commercial character which are reducible to practice in her situation, distinguish her conduct.[2] If her occupation be such as to occasion young women to be placed under her roof as assistants in her business, or for the purpose of acquiring the knowledge of it; let her behave to them with the kindness of a friend, and watch over their principles and moral behaviour with the solicitude of a mother.

9. J. S. Mill and Harriet Taylor, *Essays on Marriage and Divorce*

While Thomas Gisborne's view of the role of middle-class women (document 8) represents the prevailing nineteenth-century orthodoxy, the essays written by John Stuart Mill and Harriet Taylor in 1831 or 1832 represent a challenge to that orthodoxy and an early articulation of the liberal feminist demands that would be heard more loudly and clearly later in the century—for example, in Mill's own *The Subjection of Women* (1869). Indeed, in the text reprinted here, Mill refers dismissively to the chief tenets of the cult of domesticity as "vulgar talk."

The intellectual career of John Stuart Mill (1803–73) is virtually synonymous with the development of liberal theory in Britain during the nineteenth century. The son of James Mill, the Philosophical Radical leader who won Bentham over to that cause (see the introduction to documents 1 and 2), J. S. Mill had the principles of Benthamite utilitarianism inculcated in him from childhood. His *Autobiography* describes how this training led him to an intellectual and emotional impasse, necessitating a tempering of pure Benthamism with other intellectual traditions and a

2. It is said, by those who have sufficient opportunities of ascertaining the fact, to be no unfrequent practice among the wives of several descriptions of shopkeepers in London, knowingly to demand from persons who call to purchase articles for ready money, a price, when the husband is not present, greater than that which he would have asked. This overplus, if the article be bought, the wife conceals, and appropriates to her own use. If the customer demurs at the demand, and the husband chances to enter; the wife professes to have been mistaken, and apologises for the error. Thus detection is avoided. It is scarcely necessary to say, that the whole of the proceeding is gross dishonesty and falsehood on the part of the wife. If the husband has led her into temptation, by withholding from her an equitable supply of money for her proper expences, he also derives great blame. Does she then attempt to justify herself on this plea? As reasonably might she allege it in defence of forgery.

From John Stuart Mill and Harriet Taylor Mill, *Essays on Sex Equality,* edited by Alice Rossi (Chicago and London: University of Chicago Press, 1970), pp. 67–87.

nuancing of the "greatest happiness principle." These modifications of Benthamism are embodied in Mill's classic work *On Liberty* (1859).

In 1830 Mill, then a bachelor living in his parents' home, met Harriet Taylor (1807–58), then a young wife and the mother of young children. Both moved in the same intellectually avant-garde circles of the Philosophical Radicals and the Unitarian Radicals. Although their friendship appears to have remained a Platonic soul-union, it met with strong social disapproval. Harriet Taylor became increasingly estranged from her husband as her involvement with Mill intensified; but since divorce was simply out of the question in England at this date, the external forms of her marriage were maintained. Only after John Taylor's death in 1851 were Mill and Harriet Taylor married.

The issue, then, of the social conventions governing the lives of women and the relations between the sexes had been raised for Mill and Taylor by their own uncomfortable situation. The issue had been raised more formally as well in their intellectual milieu: both the Unitarians (whose number had, a generation before, included the early feminist Mary Wollstonecraft) and the Utilitarians had examined it in their journals in the 1820s and 1830s. Against this background, Mill prepared the essay reprinted here and Taylor supplied a brief comment on it, also included here. The essays remained in manuscript until publication in 1951.

The Essay by John Stuart Mill

She to whom my life is devoted has wished for written exposition of my opinions on the subject which, of all connected with human Institutions, is nearest to her happiness. Such as that exposition can be made without *her* to suggest and to decide, it is given in these pages: she, herself, has not refused to put into writing for *me*, what she has thought and felt on the same subject, and *there* I shall be taught, all perhaps which I have, and certainly all which I have not, found out for myself. In the investigation of truth, as in all else, "it is not good for man to be alone." And more than all, in what concerns the relations of Man with Woman, the law which is to be observed by both should surely be made by both; not, as hitherto, by the stronger only.

How easy would it be for either me or you, to resolve this question for ourselves alone. Its difficulties, for difficulties it has, are such as obstruct the avenues of all great questions which are to be decided for mankind at large, and therefore not for natures resembling each other, but for natures or at least characters tending to all the points of the moral compass. All popular morality is, as I once said to you, a compromise among conflicting natures; each renouncing a certain portion of what its own desires call for, in order to avoid the evils of a perpetual warfare with all the rest. That is the best popular morality, which attains this general pacification with the least sacrifice of the happiness of the higher natures; who are the greatest, indeed the only real, sufferers by the compromise; for *they* are called upon to give up what would really make them happy; while others are commonly required only to restrain desires the gratification of which would bring no real happiness. In the adjustment, moreover, of the compromise, the higher natures count only in proportion to their number, how small! and to the number of those whom they can influence: while the conditions of the compromise weigh heavily upon them in the state of their greater capacity of happiness, and its natural consequence, their keener sense of *want* and disappointment when the degree of happiness which they know would fall to their lot but for untoward external circumstances, is denied them.

By the higher natures I mean those characters who from the combination of natural and acquired advantages have the greatest capacity of feeling happiness, and of bestowing it. Of bestowing it in two ways: as being beautiful to contemplate, and therefore the natural objects of admiration and love; and also as being fitted, and induced, by their qualities of mind and heart, to promote by their actions, and by all that depends upon their will, the greatest possible happiness of all who are within the sphere of their influence.

If all persons were like these, or even would be guided by these, morality would be very different from what it must now be; or rather it would not exist at all as morality, since morality and inclination would coincide. If all resembled you, my lovely friend, it would be idle to prescribe rules for them: By following their own impulses under the guidance of their own judgment, they would find more happiness, and would confer more, than by obeying any moral principles or maxims whatever; since these cannot possibly be adapted beforehand to every peculiarity of circumstance which can be taken into account by a sound and vigorous intellect *worked* by a strong *will,* and guided by what Carlyle calls "an open loving heart." Where there exists a genuine and strong desire to do that which is most for the happiness of all, general rules are merely aids to prudence, in the choice of means; not peremptory obligations. Let but the desires be right, and the "imagination lofty and refined": and provided there be disdain of all false seeming, "to the pure all things are pure."

It is easy enough to settle to moral bearings of our question upon such characters. The highest natures are of course impassioned natures; to such, marriage is but one continued act of self-sacrifice where strong affection is not; every tie therefore which restrains them from seeking out and uniting themselves with some one whom they can perfectly love, is a yoke to which they cannot be subjected without oppression: and to such a person when found, they would, natural superstition apart, scorn to be united by any other tie than free and voluntary choice. If such natures have been healthily developed in other respects, they will have all other good and worthy feelings strong enough to prevent them from pursuing this happiness at the expense of greater suffering of others: and that is the limit of the forbearance which morality ought in such a case to enjoin.

But will the morality which suits the highest natures, in this matter, be also best for all inferior natures? My conviction is that it will: but this can be only a happy accident. All the difficulties of morality in any of its brands, grow out of the conflict which continually arises between the highest morality and even the best popular morality which the degree of development yet achieved by average human nature, will allow to exist.

If all, or even most persons, in the choice of a companion of the other sex, were led by any real aspiration towards, or sense of, the happiness which such companionship in its best shape is capable of giving to the best natures, there would never have been any reason why law or opinion should have set any limits to the most unbounded freedom of uniting and separating: nor is it probable that popular morality would ever, in a civilized or refined people, have imposed any restraint upon that freedom. But, as I once said to you, the law of marriage as it now exists, has been made *by* sensualists, and *for* sensualists and *to bind* sensualists. The aim and purpose of that law is either to tie up the sense, in the hope by so doing, of tying up the soul also, or else to tie up the sense because the soul is not cared about at all. Such purposes never could have entered into the minds of any to whom nature had given souls capable of the higher degrees of happiness: nor could such a law ever have existed but among persons to whose natures it was in some degree congenial, and therefore more suitable than at first sight may be supposed by those whose natures are widely different.

There can, I think, be no doubt that for a long time the indissolubility of marriage acted powerfully to elevate the social position of women. The state of things to which in almost all countries it succeeded, was one in which the power of repudiation existed on one side but not on both: in which the stronger might cast away the weaker, but the weaker could not fly from the stronger. To a woman of impassioned character, the difference between this and what now exists, is not worth much; for she would wish to be repudiated, rather than to remain united only because she could not be got rid of. But the aspirations of most women are less high. They would wish to retain any bond of union they have ever had with a man to whom they do not prefer any other, and for whom they have that inferior kind of affection which habits of intimacy frequently produce. Now, assuming what may be assumed of the greater number of men, that they are attracted to women solely by sensuality, or at best by transitory *taste;* it is not deniable, that the irrevocable vow gave to women, when the passing gust had blown over, a permanent hold upon the men who would otherwise have cast them off. Something, indeed *much,* of a community of interest, arose from the mere fact of being indissolubly united: the husband took an interest in the wife as being *his* wife, if he did not from any better feeling: it became essential to his respectability that his wife also should be respected; and commonly when the first revulsion of feeling produced by satiety, went off, the mere fact of continuing together if the woman had anything lovable in her and the man not wholly brutish, could hardly fail to raise up some feeling of regard and attachment. She obtained also, what is often far more precious to her, the certainty of not being separated from the children.

Now if this be all that human life *has* for women, it is little enough: and any woman who feels herself capable of great happiness, and whose aspirations have not been artificially checked, will claim to be set free from *only* this, to seek for more. But women in general, as I have already remarked, are more easily contented, and this I believe to be the cause of the general aversion of women to the idea of facilitating divorce. They have a habitual belief that their power over men is chiefly derived from men's sensuality; and that the same sensuality would go elsewhere in search of gratification, unless restrained by law and opinion. They on their part, mostly seek in marriage, a home, and the state or condition of a married woman, with the addition or not as it may happen, of a splendid establishment etc. etc. These things once obtained, the indissolubility of marriage renders them sure of keeping. And most women, either because these things give them all the happiness they are capable of, or from the artificial barriers which curb all spontaneous movements to seek their greatest felicity, are generally more anxious not to peril the good they have than to go in search of a greater. If marriage were dissoluble, they think they could not retain the position once acquired; or not without practicing upon the attention of men by those arts, disgusting in the extreme to any woman of simplicity, by which a cunning mistress sometimes established and retains her ascendancy.

These considerations are nothing to an impassioned character; but there is something in them, for the characters from which they emanate—is not that so? The only conclusion, however, which can be drawn from them, is one for which there would exist ample grounds even if the law of marriage as it now exists were perfection. This conclusion is, the absurdity and immorality of a state of society and opinion in which a woman is at all dependent for her social position upon the fact of her being or not being married.

Surely it is wrong, wrong in every way, and on every view of morality, even the vulgar view—that there should exist any motives to marriage except the happiness which two persons who love one another feel in associating their existence.

The means by which the condition of married women is rendered artificially desirable, are not any superiority of legal rights, for in that respect single women, especially if possessed of property, have the advantage: the civil disabilities are greatest in the case of the married woman. It is not law, but education and custom which make the difference. Women are so brought up, as not to be able to subsist in the mere physical sense, without a man to keep them: they are so brought up as not to be able to protect themselves against injury or insult, without some man on whom they have a special claim, to protect them: they are so brought up, as to have no vocation or useful office to fulfil in the world, remaining single; for all women who are educated to *be* married, and what little they are taught deserving the name useful, is chiefly what in the ordinary course of things will not come into actual use, unless nor until they are married. A single woman therefore is felt both by herself and others as a kind of excrescence on the surface of society, having no use or function or office there. She is not indeed precluded from useful and honorable exertion of various kinds: but a married woman is *presumed* to be a useful member of society unless there is evidence to the contrary; a single woman must establish what very few either women or men ever do establish, an *individual* claim.

All this, though not the less really absurd and immoral even under the law of marriage which now exists, evidently grows out of that law, and fits into the general state of society of which that law forms a part, nor could continue to exist if the law were changed, and marriage were not a contract at all, or were an easily dissoluble one: The indissolubility of marriage is the keystone of woman's present lot, and the whole comes down and must be reconstructed if that is removed.

And the truth is, that this question of marriage cannot properly be considered by itself alone. The question is not what marriage ought to be, but a far wider question, what woman ought to be. Settle that first, and the other will settle itself. Determine whether marriage is to be a relation between two equal beings, or between a superior and an inferior, between a protector and a dependent; and all other doubts will easily be resolved.

But in this question there is surely no difficulty. There is no natural inequality between the sexes; except perhaps in bodily strength; even that admits of doubt: and if bodily strength is to be the measure of superiority, mankind are no better than savages. Every step in the progress of civilization has tended to diminish the deference paid to bodily strength, until now when that quality confers scarcely any advantages except its natural ones:

the strong man has little or no power to employ his strength as a means of acquiring any other advantage over the weaker in body. Every step in the progress of civilization has similarly been marked by a nearer approach to equality in the condition of the sexes; and if they are still far from being equal, the hindrance is not now in the difference of physical strength, but in artificial feelings and prejudices.

If nature has not made men and women unequal, still less ought the law to make them so. It may be assumed, as one of those presuppositions which would almost be made weaker by anything so ridiculous as attempting to prove them, that men and women ought to be perfectly coequal: that a woman ought not to be dependent on a man, more than a man on a woman, except so far as their affections make them so, by a voluntary surrender, renewed and renewing at each instant by free and spontaneous choice.

But this perfect independence of each other for all save affection, cannot be, if there be dependence in pecuniary circumstances; a dependence which in the immense majority of cases must exist, if the woman be not capable, as well as the man, of gaining her own subsistence.

The first and indispensable step, therefore, towards the enfranchisement of woman, is that she be so educated, as not to be dependent either on her father or her husband for subsistence: a position which in nine cases out of ten, makes her either the plaything or the slave of the man who feeds her; and in the tenth case, only his humble friend. Let it not be said that she has an equivalent and compensating advantage in the exemption from toil: men think it base and servile in men to accept food as the price of dependence, and why do they not deem it so in women? solely because they do not desire that women should be their equals. Where there is strong affection, dependence is its own reward: but it must be voluntary dependence; and the more perfectly voluntary it is, the more exclusively each owes every thing to the other's affection and to nothing else,—the greater is the happiness. And where affection is not, the woman who will be dependent for the sake of a maintenance, proves herself as low-minded as a man in the like case— or *would* prove herself so if that resource were not too often the only one her education had not also taught her not to consider as degradation, that which is the essence of all prostitution, the act of delivering up her person for bread.

It does not follow that a woman should *actually* support herself because she should be *capable* of doing so: in the natural course of events she will *not*. It is not desirable to burthen the labour market with a double number of competitors. In a healthy state of things, the husband would be able by his single exertions to earn all that is necessary for both: and there would be no need that the wife should take part in the mere providing of what is required to *support* life: it will be for the happiness of both that her occupation should rather be to adorn and beautify it. Except in the class of actual day-labourers, that will be her natural task, if task it can be called, which will in so great a measure be accomplished rather by *being* than by *doing*.

We have all heard the vulgar talk that the proper employment of a wife are household superintendance, and the education of her children. As for household superintendance, if nothing be meant but merely seeing that servants do their duty, that is not an occupation; every woman that is capable of doing it at all can do it without devoting anything like half an hour every day to that purpose peculiarly. It is not like the duty of a head of an office, to whom his subordinates bring their work to be inspected when finished: the defects in the performance of household duties present *themselves* to inspection: skill in superintendance consists in knowing the right way of noticing a fault when it occurs, and giving reasonable advice and instruction how to avoid it: and more depends on establishing a good *system* at first, than upon a perpetual and studious watchfulness. But if it be meant that the mistress of a family shall herself do the work of servants, *that* is good and will naturally take place in the rank in which there do not exist the means of hiring servants; but nowhere else.

Then as to the education of children: if by that term be meant, instructing them in particular arts or particular branches of knowledge, it is absurd to impose that upon mothers: absurd in two ways: absurd to set one-half of the adult human race to perform each on a small scale, what a much smaller number of teachers would accomplish for all, by devoting themselves exclusively to it; and absurd to set all mothers doing that for which some persons must be fitter than others, and for which average mothers cannot possibly be *so* fit as persons trained to the profession. Here again, when the means do not exist for hiring teachers, the mother is the natural teacher: but no special provision needs to be made for that case. Whether she is to teach or not, it is desirable that she should *know;* because knowledge is desirable for its own sake; for its uses, for its pleasures, and for its beautifying influence when not cultivated to the neglect of other gifts. What she knows, she will be able to teach to her children if necessary: but to erect such teaching into her occupation whether she can better employ herself or not, is absurd.

The education which it *does* belong to mothers to give, and which if not imbibed from them is seldom obtained in any perfection at all, is the training of the affections: and through the affections, of the conscience, and the whole moral being. But *this* most precious, and most indispensable part of education, does not take up *time;* it is not a business, an occupation; and a mother does not accomplish it by sitting down with her child for one or two or three hours to a task. She effects it by being with the child; by making it happy, and therefore at peace with all things; by checking bad habits in the commencement and by loving the child and by making the child love her. It is not by particular effects, but imperceptibly and unconsciously that she makes her own character pass into the child; that she makes the child love what she loves, venerate what she venerates and imitate as far as a child can her example. These things cannot be done by a hired teacher; and they are better and greater than all the rest. But to impose upon mothers what hired teachers *can* do, is mere squandering of the glorious existence of a woman fit for a woman's highest destiny. With regard to such things, her part is to see that they are rightly done, not to do them.

The great occupation of woman should be to *beautify* life: to cultivate, for her own sake and that of those who surround her, all her faculties of mind, soul, and body; all her powers of enjoyment, and powers of giving enjoyment; and to diffuse beauty, elegance, and grace, everywhere. If in addition to this the activity of her nature demands more energetic and definite employment, there is never any lack of it in the world: If she loves, her natural impulse will be to associate her existence with him she loves, and to share *his* occupations; in which, if he loves her (with that affection of *equality* which alone deserves to be called love) she will naturally take as strong an interest, and be as thoroughly conversant, as the most perfect confidence on his side can make her.

Such will naturally be the occupations of a woman who has fulfilled what seems to be considered as the end of her existence and attained what is really its happiest state, by uniting herself to a man whom she loves. But whether so united or not, women will never be what they should be, nor their social position what it should be, until women, as universally as men, have the power of gaining their own livelihood: until, therefore, every girl's parents have either provided her with independent means of subsistence, or given her an education qualifying her to provide those means for herself. The only difference between the employments of women and those of men will be, that those which partake most of the beautiful, or which require delicacy and taste rather than muscular exertion, will naturally fall to the share of women: all branches of the fine arts in particular.

In considering, then, what is the best law of marriage, we are to suppose that women already are, what they would be in the best state of society; no less capable of existing independently and respectably without men, than men without women. Marriage, on whatever footing it might be placed, would be wholly a matter of choice, not, as for a woman it now is, something approaching to a matter of necessity; something, at least, which every woman is under strong artificial motives to desire, and which if she attain not, her life is considered to be a failure.

These suppositions being made: and it being no longer any advantage to a woman to be married, merely for the sake of being married: why should any woman cling to the indissolubility of marriage, as if it could be for the good of one party that it should continue when the other party desires that it should be dissolved?

It is not denied by anyone that there are numerous cases in which the happiness of both parties would be greatly promoted by a dissolution of marriage. We will add, that when the social position of the two sexes shall be perfectly equal, a divorce if it be for the happiness of either party, will be for the happiness of both. No one but a sensualist would desire to retain a merely animal connexion with a person of the other sex, unless perfectly assured of being preferred by that person, above all other persons in the world. This certainty never can be quite perfect under the law of marriage as it now exists: it would be nearly absolute, if the tie were merely voluntary.

Not only there are, but it is in vain to hope that there will not always be, innumerable cases, in which the first connexion formed will be one the dissolution of which if it *could be,* certainly would be and ought to be, effected: It has long ago been remarked that of all the more serious acts of the life of a human being, there is no one which is commonly performed with so little of forethought or consideration, as that which is irrevocable, and which is fuller of evil than any other acts of the being's whole life if it turn out ill. And this is not so astonishing as it seems: The imprudence, while the contract remains indissoluble, consists in marrying at all: If you do marry there is little wisdom shewn by a very anxious and careful deliberation beforehand: Marriage is really, what it has been sometimes called, a lottery: and whoever is in a state of mind to calculate chances calmly and value them correctly, is not at all likely to purchase a ticket. Those who marry after taking great pains about the matter, generally do but buy their disappointment dearer. Then the failures in marriage are such as are naturally incident to a first trial: the parties are inexperienced and cannot judge. Nor does this evil seem to be remediable. A woman is allowed to give herself away for life, at an age at which she is not allowed to dispose of the most inconsiderable landed estate: what then? if people are not to marry until they have learnt prudence, they will seldom marry before thirty: can this be expected, or is it to be desired? To direct the immature judgment, there is the advice of parents and guardians: a precious security! The only thing which a young girl can do, worse than marrying to please herself, is marrying to please any other person. However paradoxical it may sound to the ears of those who are reputed to have grown wise as wine grows good, by *keeping,* it is yet true, that A, an average person can better know what is for his own happiness, than B, an average person can know what is for A's happiness. Fathers and mothers as the world is constituted, do not judge more wisely than sons and daughters, they only judge differently: and the judgments of both being of the ordinary strength, or rather of the ordinary weakness, a person's own self has the advantage of a considerable greater number of *data* to judge from, and the further one of a stronger interest in the subject. . . .

The first choice, therefore, is made under very complicated disadvantages. By the facts of its being the *first* the parties are necessarily inexperienced in the particular matter: they are commonly young (especially the party who is in the greatest peril from a mistake) and therefore inexperienced in the knowledge and judgment of mankind and of themselves generally: and finally they have seldom had so much as an opportunity offered them of gaining any real knowledge of each other, since in nine cases out of ten they have never been once in each other's society completely unconstrained, or without consciously or unconsciously acting a part.

The chances therefore are many to one against the supposition that a person who requires, or is capable of, great happiness, will find that happiness in a first choice: and in a very large proportion of cases the first choice is such that if it cannot be recalled, it only embitters existence. The reasons, then, are most potent for allowing a subsequent change.

What there is to be said in favor of the indissolubility, superstition apart, resolves itself into this that it is highly desirable that changes should not be frequent, and desirable that the first choice should be, even if not compulsorily, yet very generally, persevered in: That consequently we ought to beware lest in giving facilities for retracting a bad choice, we hold out greater encouragement than at present for making such a choice as there will probably be occasion to retract.

It is proper to state as strongly as possible the arguments which may be advanced in support of this view in question.

Repeated trials for happiness, and repeated failures, have the most mischievous effects on all minds. The finer spirits are broken down, and disgusted with all things: their susceptibilities are deadened, or converted into sources of bitterness, and they lose the power of being ever *contented*. On the commoner natures the effects produced are not the less deplorable. Not only is their capacity for happiness worn out, but their morality is depraved: all refinement and delicacy of character is extinguished; all sense of any peculiar duties or of any peculiar sacredness attaching to the relation between the sexes is worn away: and such alliances come to be looked upon with the very same kind of feelings which are now connected with a passing intrigue.

Thus much as to the parties themselves: but besides the parties there are also to be considered their children: beings who are wholly dependent both for happiness and for excellence upon their parents: and who in all but the extreme causes of actual profligacy, or perpetual bickering and discussion, *must* be better cared for in both points if their parents remain together.

So much importance is due to this last consideration, that I am convinced, if marriages were easily dissoluble, two persons of opposite sexes who unite their destinies would generally, if they were wise, think it their duty to avoid having children until they had lived together for a considerable length of time, and found in each other a happiness adequate to their aspirations. If this principle of morality were observed, how many of the difficulties of the subject we are considering would be smoothed down! To be jointly the parents of a human being, should be the very last pledge of the deepest, holiest, and most desirable affection: for *that* is a tie which independently of convention, is indeed indissoluble: an additional and external tie, most precious where the souls are already indissolubly united, but simply burthensome while it appears possible to either that they should ever desire to separate.

It can hardly be anticipated, however, that such a course will be followed by any but those who to the greatest loftiness and delicacy of feeling, unite the power of the most deliberate reflexion. If the feelings be obtuse, the force of these considerations will not be felt; and if the judgment be weak or hasty, whether from inherent defect or inexperience, people will fancy themselves in love for their whole lives with a perfect being, when the case is far otherwise, and will suppose they risk nothing by creating a new relationship with that being, which can no longer be got rid of. It will therefore most commonly happen that when circumstances arise which induce the parents to separate, there will be children to suffer by the separation: nor do I see how this difficulty can be entirely got over, until the habits of society allow of a regulated community of living, among persons intimately acquainted, which would prevent the necessity of a total separation between the parents even when they had ceased to be connected by any nearer tie than mutual goodwill, and a common interest in their children.

There is yet another argument which may be urged against facility of divorce. It is this. Most persons have but a very moderate capacity of happiness; but no person ever finds this out without experience, very few even with experience: and most persons are constantly wreaking that discontent which has its source internally, upon outward things. Expecting therefore in marriages a far greater degree of happiness than they commonly find: and knowing not that the fault is in their own scanty capabilities of happiness—they fancy they should have been happier with some one else: or at all events the disappointment becomes associated in their minds with the being in whom they had placed their hopes—and so they dislike one another for a time—and during that time they would feel inclined to separate: but if they remain united, the feeling of disappointment after a time goes off, and they pass their lives together with fully as much happiness as they could find either singly or in any other union, without having undergone the wearing of repeated and unsuccessful experiments.

Such are the arguments for adhering to the indissolubility of the contract: and for such characters as compose the great majority of the human race, it is not deniable that these arguments have considerable weight.

That weight however is not so great as it appears. In all the above arguments it is tacitly assumed, that the choice lies between the absolute interdiction of divorce, and a state of things in which the parties would separate on the most passing feeling of dissatisfaction. Now this is not really the alternative. Were divorce ever so free, it would be resorted to under the same sense of moral responsibility and under the same restraints from opinion, as any other of the acts of our lives. . . . My belief is that—in a tolerably moral state of society, the first choice would almost always, especially where it had produced children, be adhered to, unless in case of such uncongeniality of disposition as rendered it positively uncomfortable to one or both of the parties to live together, or in case of a strong passion conceived by one of them for a third person. Now in either of these cases I can conceive no argument strong enough to convince me, that the first connexion ought to be forcibly preserved. . . .

The arguments, therefore, in favour of the indissolubility of marriage, are as nothing in comparison with the far more potent arguments for leaving this like the other relations voluntarily contracted by human beings, to depend for its continuance upon the wishes of the contracting parties. The strongest of all these arguments is that by no other means can the condition and character of women become what it ought to be.

When women are merely slaves, to give them a permanent hold upon their masters was a first step towards their evolution. That step is now complete: and in the progress of civilization, the time has come when women may aspire to something more than merely to find a protector. The position of a single woman has ceased to be dangerous and precarious; and the law, and general opinion, suffice without any more special guardianship, to shield her in ordinary circumstances from insult or inquiry: a woman in short is no longer a mere property, but a person who is counted not solely on her husband's or father's account but on her own. She is now ripe for equality. But it is absurd to talk of equality while marriage is an indissoluble tie. It was a change greatly for the better, from a state in which all the obligation was on the side of the weaker, all the rights on the side of the physically stronger, to even the present condition of an obligation nominally equal on both. But this nominal equality is not real equality. The stronger is always able to relieve himself wholly or in great measure, from as much of the obligation as he finds burthensome: the weaker cannot. The husband can ill-use his wife, neglect her, and seek other women, not perhaps altogether with impunity, but what are the penalties which opinion imposes on him compared with those which fall upon the wife who even with that provocation retaliates upon her husband? It is true perhaps that if divorce were permitted, opinion would with like injustice, try the wife who resorted to that remedy by a harder measure than the husband. But this would be of less consequence: Once separated she would be comparatively independent of opinion: but so long as she is forcibly united to one of those who *make* the opinion, she must to a great extent be its slave.

The Essay by Harriet Taylor

If I could be Providence for the world for a time, for the express purpose of raising the condition of women, I should come to you to know the *means*— the *purpose* would be to remove all interference with affection, or with anything which is, or which even might be supposed to be, demonstrative of affection. In the present state of women's mind, perfectly uneducated, and with whatever of timidity and dependence is natural to them increased a thousand fold by their habit of utter dependence, it would probably be mischievous to remove at once all restraints, they would buy themselves protectors at a dearer cost than even at present—but without raising their natures at all. It seems to me that once give women the desire to raise their social condition, and they have a power which in the present state of civilization and of men's characters, might be made of tremendous effect. Whether nature made a difference in the nature of men and women or not, it seems now that all men, with the exception of a few lofty minded, are sensualists more or less—women on the contrary are quite exempt from this trait, however it may appear otherwise in the cases of some. It seems strange that it should be so, unless it was meant to be a source of power in semi-civilized states such as the present—or it may not be so—it may be only that the habits of freedom and low indulgence on which boys grow up and the contrary notion of what is called purity in girls may have produced the appearance of different natures in the two sexes. As certain it is that there is equality in nothing now—all the pleasures such as they are being men's, and all the disagreeables and pains being women's, as that every pleasure would be infinitely heightened both in kind and degree by the perfect equality of the sexes. Women are educated for one single object, to gain their living by marrying—(some poor souls get it without the churchgoing. It's the same way—they do not seem to be a bit worse than their honoured sisters). To be married is the object of their existence and that object being gained they do really cease to exist as to anything worth calling life or any useful purpose. One observes very few marriages where there is any real sympathy between the parties. The woman knows what her power is and gains by it what she has been taught to consider "proper" to her state. The woman who would gain power by such means is unfit for power, still they do lose this power for paltry advantages and I am astonished it has never occurred to them to gain some large purpose; but their minds are degenerated by habits of dependance. I should think that 500 years hence none of the follies of their ancestors will so excite wonder and contempt as the fact of legislative restraints as to matters of feeling—or rather in the expression of feeling. When once the law undertakes to say which demonstration of feeling shall be given to which, it seems quite consistent not to legislate for *all*, and to say how many shall be seen and how many heard, and what kind and degree of feeling allows of shaking hands. The Turks' is the only consistent mode. I have no doubt that when the whole community is really educated, though the present laws of marriage were to continue they would be perfectly disregarded, because no one would marry. The wisest and perhaps the quickest means to do away with its evils is to be found in promoting education—as it is the means of all good—but meanwhile it is hard that those who suffer most from its evils and who are always the best people, should be left without remedy. Would not the best plan be divorce which could be attained by any *without any reason assigned,* and at small expence, but which could only be finally pronounced after a long period? not *less* time than two years should elapse between suing for divorce and permission to contract again—but what the decision will be must be certain at the moment of asking for it—unless during that time the suit should be withdrawn.

(I feel like a lawyer in talking of it only! O how absurd and little it all is!)

In the present system of habits and opinions, girls enter into what is called a contract perfectly ignorant of the conditions of it, and that they should be so is considered absolutely essential to their fitness for it!

But after all the one argument of the matter which I think might be said so as to strike both high and low natures is—who would wish to have the person without inclination? Whoever would take the benefit of a law of divorce must be those whose inclination is to separate and who on earth would wish another to remain with them against their inclination—I should think no one—people sophisticate about the matter now and will not believe that one *"really would wish to go"*! Suppose instead of calling it a "law of divorce" it were to be called "proof of affection"—they would like it better then.

At this present time, in this state of civilization, what evil could be caused by, first placing women on the most entire equality with men, as to all rights and privileges, civil and political, and then doing away with all laws whatever relating to marriage? Then if a woman had children she must take charge of them, women could not then have children without considering how to maintain them. Women would have no more reason to barter person for bread, or for anything else, than have men. Public offices being open to them alike, all occupations would be divided between the sexes in their natural arrangements. Fathers would provide for their daughters in the same manner as for their sons.

All the difficulties about divorce seem to be in the consideration for the children—but on this plan it would be the women's *interest* not to have children—now it is thought to be the woman's interest to have children as so many ties to the man who feeds her.

Love in its true and finest meaning, seems to be the way in which is manifested all that is highest best and beautiful in the nature of human beings—none but poets have approached to the perception of the beauty of the material world—still less of the spiritual—and hence never yet existed a poet, except by inspiration of that feeling which is the perception of beauty in all forms and by all means which are given us, as well as by *sight*. Are we not born with the *five* senses, merely as a foundation for others which we may make by them—and who extends and refines those material senses to the highest—into infinity—best fulfils the end of creation—that is only saying, *who enjoys most is most virtuous*. It is for *you*—the most worthy to be the apostle of all the highest virtues to teach such as may be taught, that the higher the *kind* of enjoyment, the *greater* the *degree*, perhaps there is but one class to whom this *can* be *taught*—the poetic nature struggling with superstition: you are fitted to be the saviour of such.

10. Victor Cousin, Speech on the Proposal to Reorganize the Medical Profession (4 June 1847)

Victor Cousin (1792–1867) is one of the best representatives of the dominant form of liberalism in early nineteenth-century France—the liberalism of the juste-milieu or golden mean. The official philosophy of the July Monarchy (1830–48), juste-milieu liberalism sought a political middle of the road for France. This ideal of "middlingness" was enshrined in the Charter (or constitution) of 1830, which established a parliamentary system with severely limited suffrage in which political power belonged to the propertied classes—the aristocracy and especially the upper bourgeoisie. Theorists of the juste-milieu, like Cousin and the historian and politician François Guizot, feared above all the kind of radicalization of a constitutional, parliamentary regime that had occurred in 1793 when the Jacobins took control of the revolution. Determined to

From *Enquêtes et documents relatifs a l'Enseignement Supérieur* (Paris: Ministère de l'Instruction Publique, 1884–1914), vol. 57, pp. 86, 93–100. Translated for this volume by Paula Wissing.

keep the July Monarchy stable and immune to radical tendencies, they made opposition to expansion of the suffrage an article of faith.

Born into a humble family, the young Cousin began climbing the social ladder with the aid of an acquired bourgeois protector—a man whose son he had defended from a bully. Cousin was sent to elite Paris schools and, proving his mettle there, embarked upon a career as a philosopher and professor of philosophy. His fortunes improved still further after the 1830 Revolution brought the July Monarchy to power. The new regime heaped bounties upon him: the title of peer of France, a professorship at the Sorbonne, membership in the Legion of Honor. Education became his special province. He sat on the council that supervised the entire state educational system and, during the year 1840, held the cabinet post of minister of public instruction.

In the speech reprinted here, Cousin responds to a proposal before the Chambers that the medical profession be reformed, primarily by ridding it of the so-called health officers. These were the second-class citizens of the medical world, practitioners who required less training for certification than did full-fledged doctors. The doctors themselves had launched the campaign for reform; they regarded the health officers as competing with them for patients and thereby lowering the fee scale. Cousin's speech before the Chamber of Peers clearly reveals the social attitudes that accompanied juste-milieu liberalism. It also provides insight into the problems of establishing the professions at a time when the groundwork was being laid for their ascendant position in modern Western society.

The agenda calls for . . . the discussion of the legislative proposal reported during the session of 6 May last year regarding the teaching and the practice of medicine. . . .

A peer [Mr. Victor Cousin], enrolled as the first to fight against the proposed legislation, is called to the rostrum. . . .

The noble peer now comes to the examination of a part of the legislation where the ministerial proposal and that of the commission seem to him contrary not only to the progress of science and the good organization of its teaching, but to the interest of society as a whole. He wishes to speak of the proposal to suppress the old and popular institution of the health officer. Health officers, it is said, are doomed. But why? Because of medical doctors, who think that they alone are capable of taking on the medical care of all of France. That is a generous ambition, if perhaps a somewhat foolhardy one; the speaker commends it and at the same time resists it. In his view the question of a second order of practitioners dominates the whole legislation. At stake are the fate of the secondary medical schools;

the true object of the medical faculties and the greatness of their subject matter; and the fate of the medical corps and of the health of a considerable part of the population.

The speaker defends the health officers in the interests of a people to whom the Government and the Chambers owe, not magnificent and chimerical promises, but real and effective aid. He defends them in the interest of the doctors themselves, in the interests of their course of study, which needs to be extended and strengthened, in the interest of their true dignity and of the rank that, in France and in Europe, belongs to French medicine. We must first, to prevent confusion, establish the precise nature of the question. We are no longer talking of the health officer described in the Law of the Year XI,[1] a law that organized things more or less haphazardly. This individual was hastily certified by juries of mediocre quality and was able to practice throughout the entire department in which he was named and, consequently, in the largest cities, even in Paris. Who today is defending the Law of the Year XI? Who is defending the medical juries? Who is defending unlimited practice for health officers? No one. Ever since Mr. Cuvier applied to this matter the range of good sense that characterized him, there has been no doubt concerning what a health officer can and should be. Above all else, the health officer must have studied for three years in schools especially created for the education of a second tier of doctors, with the help of a system of courses from which all scientific curiosity has been banished but where the areas of science needed for practical work are solidly taught. In the second place, each year the students of these schools must pass examinations in order to be promoted from one year to the next, as is done—or rather should be done—in the private secondary schools. And at the end of the entire course they must take a public examination where they are called upon to demonstrate all the knowledge a practitioner of medicine needs. This final and decisive examination should be entrusted to the professors of the secondary medical schools, just as the doctoral examinations are entrusted to university professors. It is even important that the presiding member of the examining board be a university professor, so that the State is assured, by competent, even severe judges, that the care of the public health never fall into undeserving hands. Finally,

---

1. The Law of 19 ventôse Year XI (1803), enacted during the Napoleonic Consulate, established the organization of the medical profession in France. It was urgently needed because the medical corporations, which had regulated that profession under the Old Regime, had been abolished during the Revolution. One of the innovative provisions of the law was the creation of a two-tiered system of medical practitioners, with the doctors (who held a doctorate in medicine from one of the medical faculties) on top and the less extensively trained health officers below. The 1847 attempt to revise the law failed; indeed the law remained intact until 1892.—ED.

as a third condition, the practitioners so educated must only practice in a limited area, while the medical doctor may practice freely throughout the nation.

And let us not believe that we are demeaning the public health officer by restricting him to the small towns and the countryside, unless we imagine also that the country priest and village schoolmaster are without value and dignity in the eyes of the State and religion. A health officer may practice only where medical doctors would not set up practice unless they had failed everywhere else—that is, because they were bad doctors. In this case the speaker refers to rural communes and small towns where the population does not exceed 6,000 inhabitants. This is the only health officer under discussion, the only one the speaker defends, and the only one who represents an attainable ideal. To attain that ideal, adding the salaries of professors in secondary medical schools to the State budget would be sufficient. These schools exist. They work. They were created by Mr. Cuvier. In 1840 the speaker tried hard to improve them, and several of his most illustrious colleagues at the Institute have authorized him to declare before the Chamber that three-year secondary schools with a good course of study can train practitioners completely prepared to meet the needs of the countryside and small town.

A doctor of medicine, on the other hand, must possess great knowledge and occupy a certain position in the world. He deals with men of the highest social condition and is often consulted by the judiciary and the State on points of forensic medicine and on complicated and delicate legal cases. This is why the minister proposes to increase the number of years of study needed to complete the medical doctorate. But would it not be strange if, at the same time that we were laboring to raise the profession to such a high plane, we were working to bring it down into the most humble communities? Thus the doctorate would henceforth require five years of study instead of four and, consequently, much more expense. And we would be requiring most of these doctors, so slowly trained, educated at such great expense, to resign themselves to practice in mere hamlets! In truth, the minister would cover France with Hippocrateses.

The speaker could ask for nothing better, if that were possible. But Hippocrateses are rare, and when they are found, it is in Athens and not in the village. The legislative proposal will not change human nature. We can be sure that, without exception, the villages would receive only the worst of the doctors. Think of the situation of a doctor who, unable to succeed elsewhere after many fruitless attempts, finds himself forced to practice in the country or in a very small town. What a comedown for a man who has spent several years among the bright lights and who has drunk from the cup of the most honored science. Here he is fallen among peasants, laborers, small merchants. Fate seems unkind to him, and instead of blaming his own lack of talent, he blames his plight on everyone else. Unhappy himself, he spreads and nourishes discontent all about him. Since he has, or believes he has, knowledge superior to his own social condition, that condition weighs heavily upon him. Concerned with surface appearances, he is disdainful. The life he leads hardly corresponds to the very natural dreams that are roused in any young soul by refined studies and too early exposure to the brilliant spectacle of city life. Our doctor trained in Strasbourg, Montpellier, or Paris,[2] when relegated to a poor commune, would resemble a degree holder of the Sorbonne who has become a village priest. Placed in a false situation, people are either sublime or detestable, and more frequently the latter.

The speaker knows of a country, and he does not say that this country is France, where great normal schools have been established at great expense to educate schoolmasters.[3] It was thought that something wonderful would be accomplished by raising to excessive heights the standards of literary and scientific instruction. The result: young people who are quite well educated, well versed in all the difficulties of grammar and mathematics. There is only one problem, which is that none of these young scholars has any desire to become a village schoolmaster. And if he is obliged to do so, he is far from bringing a spirit of peace and contentment to these humble functions. Most lacking is the spirit of self-abnegation, without which there can be no good teacher of the people. In place of such a person would it not be better to have a man with less education but with a command of the little he has to teach, who is satisfied with his condition (which the State should improve, if possible), but which even now is nearly adequate for him because he did not dream earlier on of another more brilliant, illusory one? In the same category as this modest schoolmaster, in the same category as this good country priest, the speaker likes to place a health officer born of parents too poor to aspire to the high and expensive instruction found in the medical faculties, a man whose fees for his entire course of study have not surpassed 200 francs, who has lived several years in a provincial town, leading there a life little different from the one that is awaiting him? This is a health officer who, it is true, is not a bachelor of arts or science, who knows neither mathematics, Greek, nor metaphysics, who is not in a position to read Hippocrates and Galen in the original any more than Thucydides, Demosthenes or Plato, who does not know the fine

2. Paris, Montpellier, and Strasbourg were the locations of the only medical faculties in France at this date. All doctorates in medicine were awarded by one of the three.—ED.

3. Despite his coyness here, Cousin is probably referring to France and in particular to the Guizot Law of 1833.—ED.

and elaborate parts of the most recent physiology, who is not versed in the history or philosophy of medicine, who has not learned things that he will later need to forget. Not the uncertain and hypothetical, but the incontestable and indispensable, this is the subject matter for the true country doctor. He is easily the confidant, the counselor, the consoler of the poor, because he is very nearly their companion. . . .

The Commission has justly felt one of the many inconsistencies of the ministerial proposal. It has understood that it was far too much both to impose the doctorate on all practitioners and to make the doctorate less accessible by raising the required expenses and demanding five instead of four years of study. Thus the Commission opposed the idea that the current number of years needed to be increased. The speaker applauds the Commission's good sense and spirit of equity but cannot help but inform it that it has not accorded a lofty enough meaning to the doctorate. Undoubtedly, if one does not want health officers, it is right to make the title of doctor more accessible; but if health officers, whose place cannot be taken by doctors, are maintained, one can easily raise the level of the doctorate. One can extend and fortify the courses and faculties according to the needs of science and the wishes of the most enlightened judges.

The speaker would like to make everyone aware of how an obscure and fearful problem is raised with the elimination of the health officers, and in what a dark night this proposal was conceived. Can doctors satisfy all the medical needs of France? That is the problem. To resolve it, first it is necessary to know what, in reality, these medical needs are, and the number of practitioners needed to serve them. This is in some way the crux of the matter, and it is indispensable to have the answer. We do not have it here. The exact number of practitioners needed for the medical service of the country every year has not been established. We do not even officially know how many doctors and health officers are practicing today. No statistics gathered by the State give accurate data on this matter. It was, however, very easy to ask the prefects to furnish the current number of doctors and health officers in each department.

What the Government ought to have done was attempted by the editor of a respected medical journal. With the help of his own correspondents, after much research and with considerable sacrifice, he tried to establish statistics on the medical personnel in France. This work testifies to the author's zeal but it is still of contestable value. Or at least, if the results are accepted by some, others reject them, and it would be desirable for the minister to verify them before citing them. The speaker would utilize them himself only after much hesitation. According to the statistics gathered by Mr. Lucas Championnière, there are nearly 20,000 practitioners in France, among whom 12,000 are doctors and 8,000 are health officers. We are reduced to supposing that this number of 20,000 is sufficient to satisfy the medical needs of France as a whole. We still need to know how many new personnel it would be necessary to add each year to maintain this number when the only practitioners would be doctors. Here the figures vary, for reasons that would fatigue the Chamber to hear. The most optimistic figures permit us to hope that, to close the gap created each year by retirement or death—which respects doctors no more than health officers and other men—among the 20,000, it would be necessary to increase the profession by 500 new doctors each year. In each of the past two years (1845 and 1846), just over 300 have joined the profession.

Where do we find the other 200? In the most fantastical of hypotheses. The proposed legislation assumes that the elimination of health officers should increase the number of doctors enough to bring the number of diplomas from 300 to 500 annually. Vain hope! People do not become health officers by choice, but by necessity, and because they are not rich enough to become bachelors of letters, bachelors of science, and doctors of medicine. But they will not become richer because they can no longer be health officers. The number of doctors, then, will increase very little. Each year this lack will grow, even with the aid of useful but inadequate scholarships. This need will grow. There is only one way to increase the number of doctors within the means offered by the current proposal and that is to make the doctoral examinations easier than they are today, even though it is common knowledge that they are already far from rigorous at Strasbourg and Montpellier. And yet today, without any great stoic effort it would be possible to introduce just severity into the examinations. For after all, one can say to the candidates who cannot give proof of all the required learning, "Become a health officer." But when we do not have that consolation and resource to offer unfortunate candidates, this support in the face of one's own weakness, even the firmest judges will lose courage, and many doctors will be created through indulgence and misunderstood humanitarianism.

The speaker does not, then, hesitate to say to the Minister, the Commission and the Chamber, "If you eliminate the institution of health officers, you inevitably do one of two things: either you do not assure the countryside and small towns of the practitioners that they need; or else, in order to prevent this danger, in order to distribute doctors everywhere, you diminish the worth of the doctorate and with it the worth of French medical science and of the whole medical corps." The speaker defies you to find a response to that alternative that would be reassuring to an assembly of practical people, an assembly of lawmakers. He will not carry this defense of health officers any further. Only, before stepping down from the rostrum he wishes to present in brief his opposition to a strange type of argument that he finds in the explanatory statement of the proposal. Here we read that the division of the medical corps into two classes goes against humanity, religion, the spirit of our institutions, and the nature of equality. What equality are we talking about? In what bill of rights have we found this right of all men to the same medical care? What is inhumane and godless about assuring the poor of adequate and reliable care rather than feeding them on hopes that cannot be realized? How can the spirit of our institutions be concerned that we have only one order of medical personnel and not two or even three?

The speaker had believed that it was possible to adopt and defend any opinion he pleased on this matter without its affecting his good standing as a Christian and a citizen. But we are now told that we are enemies of the people because we want to keep the people's doctors—the health officers—for the people and because we want the children of the people to be able, with little expense, good conduct, work and perseverance to rise in a few years to a modest but honorable profession; that we are aristocrats because we do not wish to make the practice of medicine and surgery the privilege of fortune and the monopoly of only one class of citizens! Where would this equalizing spirit lead the Minister if he were concerned with the result? He would thus also have to eliminate midwifery in order to have only one order of practitioners in the very dangerous art of abetting childbirth. If he deigns to keep the midwives in spite of his principles, he cannot give one reason in their favor that could not be used with respect to the health officer as well and which would not overturn his entire theory. Let him permit the speaker to say that the Minister is more of a republican in medicine than were the authors of the Law of the Year XI. But the Minister acts in vain. Whatever his passion for the unity and indivisibility of the medical profession, he will have a difficult time maintaining it absolutely. He will encounter an adversary before which the proudest can withdraw without shame: the nature of things. In reality, there has always been and necessarily always will be two orders of practitioners, even under the splendid mantle of the doctorate. Because a lower order is inevitable, reason advises us to accept it under its true name and through careful organization make it serve the greatest good of society. To strike the health officer down rather than raise him up, to proceed with an eye to destroying an entire profession rather than reforming it is not an enlightened, progressive or liberal measure; it is a revolutionary one.

The Minister says in his explanatory statement that if the elimination of a second tier of medical practitioners has unfortunate consequences, *one could always easily return to the original solution*. Is not this attitude rather astonishing? Laws are not experiments to be performed upon the people. One cannot ravage a nation's institutions with impunity. After carelessly destroying and blighting a modest but useful institution for the sake of a brilliant illusion, one is no longer the master who can turn around and bring it back to life when it is needed again. If there is the slightest doubt, let things well enough alone. Do not fling yourself into the unknown; improve what is already there. Do not destroy anything. Improve everything. That is the lawmaker's great art. Raise the level of the medical faculties even more by making the doctorate even more difficult. At the same time, strengthen and enliven the secondary schools of medicine by including them in the state budget and giving them a real purpose. Along with doctors truly worthy of the name, who can be presented, with justifiable pride, to France and all Europe, religiously maintain the people's doctors—not half doctors, but practitioners who are accomplished and complete in their own arena, endowed with an education that is solidly and admirably suited to the care of our dear compatriots in the small towns and countryside. The highest science will pardon you, and you will have accomplished a duty towards humanity. . . .

11. G. W. F. Hegel, on the Family, Civil Society, and the State

G. W. F. Hegel (1770–1831) was one of the most influential nineteenth-century European philosophers. As a student of Protestant theology in Tübingen in the years 1788–93, he greeted the revolutionary events on the other side of the Rhine with enthusiasm and joined a study group devoted to reading Rousseau. After more than two decades of humble employments (family tutor, instructor at the University of Jena, and rector of a gymnasium, or secondary school), Hegel was finally appointed to a chair in philosophy at the University of Heidelberg in 1816. Two years later he accepted the prestigious chair of philosophy at the University of Berlin in Prussia. Hegel remained at Berlin until his death, gathering disciples (his students included Ludwig Feuerbach [see document 27] and Karl Marx [see documents 19 and 43]) and serving as something of the official philosopher of the Prussian state.

Hegel's philosophy has always been regarded as notoriously difficult to understand. Even in his own day, Hegel had a reputation (endorsed by opponents and supporters alike) for obscurity of thought and awkwardness of expression. These difficulties are, however, part and parcel of the ambitious intellectual project that Hegel undertook. This project was the culmination of an Idealist movement in nineteenth-century German philosophy that began with J. G. Fichte and F. W. J. von Schelling.

From G. W. F. Hegel, *Hegel's Philosophy of Mind,* in the *Encyclopedia of the Philosophical Sciences,* translated by William Wallace (Oxford: Clarendon Press, 1894), pp. 119–54.

Hegel sought to produce an all-inclusive metaphysical system in which the rational transcendental principle, Mind or Spirit, first discovered its own internal structures, then found itself alienated in its encounter with the external world of finite, particular objects, and at length returned to itself by comprehending that it was actualized in the highest and most complex phenomena of the external world—that is, the state, history, and, finally, the three manifestations of so-called Absolute Spirit: art, religion and philosophy.

That Hegel cast his metaphysics as a "journey" of Spirit reflected his belief, inspired by Romanticism, that reality was not static but rather was in a continuous state of development or becoming. The dialectical method was designed to capture this flux. Although Hegel himself insisted upon the utter fluidity of the dialectic and resisted breaking it down into discrete stages, his subsequent commentators, trying to make his philosophy more readily comprehensible, found it useful to characterize the dialectic as a series of triads having the form thesis-antithesis-synthesis. According to this formulation, each thesis gradually generated its own negation (the antithesis), and the combination of the two in turn generated the synthesis. The synthesis was not achieved through a mutual annihilation of its two contradictory components but rather through a new conceptualization of their relationship, which preserved both by moving them to a higher plane where their contradiction was no longer felt. (Hegel gave the name *Aufhebung,* translated into English as sublation, to this crucial, preservative-and-progressive act of synthesis.) The synthesis, now a new thesis, then generated *its* own negation, and the process began again. The dialectical method, with its embracing of the creative potential of contradiction, was perhaps Hegel's most lasting intellectual contribution. A whole generation of thinkers, of whom Karl Marx is the most famous, retained Hegel's dialectical method while rejecting most of the content of his philosophy.

The selection reprinted here comes from the 1830 edition of the *Encyclopedia of the Philosophical Sciences,* a relatively concise overview of Hegel's whole system which he prepared, probably for pedagogical purposes, in 1817. The *Encyclopedia* is, not surprisingly, arranged triadically; our selection forms the last third of the middle section of the third and final part of the work as a whole. In this selection, the dialectic can be seen operating and unfolding through the "moments" of the family and civil society until it reaches a higher synthesis in the state. While there has been much scholarly debate about whether the late Hegel retained the political liberalism of his youth, the liberal elements of his political philosophy are evident here. And while many of those elements have their source in the French Enlightenment and revolutionary tradi-

tion, the conception of the state with which Hegel unifies them is peculiarly German and was destined to become a salient feature of nineteenth-
and twentieth-century German political thought.

The Moral Life, or Social Ethics [1]

§ 513

The moral life is the perfection of spirit objective—the truth of the subjective and objective spirit itself. The failure of the latter consists—partly in
having its freedom *immediately* in reality, in something external therefore,
in a thing—partly in the abstract universality of its goodness. The failure
of spirit subjective similarly consists in this, that it is, as against the universal, abstractly self-determinant in its inward individuality. When these two
imperfections are suppressed, subjective *freedom* exists as the covertly and
overtly *universal* rational will, which is sensible of itself and actively disposed in the consciousness of the individual subject, whilst its practical
operation and immediate universal *actuality* at the same time exist as
moral usage, manner and custom—where self-conscious *liberty* has become *nature*.

§ 514

The consciously free substance, in which the absolute 'ought' is no less an
'is', has actuality as the spirit of a nation. The abstract disruption of this
spirit singles it out into *persons,* whose independence it, however, controls
and entirely dominates from within. But the person, as an intelligent being,
feels that underlying essence to be his own very being—ceases when so
minded to be a mere accident of it—looks upon it as his absolute final aim.
In its actuality he sees not less an achieved present, than somewhat he
brings about by his action—yet somewhat which without all question *is*.
Thus, without any selective reflection, the person performs his duty as *his
own* and as something which *is;* and in this necessity *he* has himself and his
actual freedom.

§ 515

Because the substance is the absolute unity of individuality and universality of freedom, it follows that the actuality and action of each individual
to keep and to take care of his own being, while it is on one hand conditioned by the pre-supposed total in whose complex alone he exists, is on
the other a transition into a universal product.—The social disposition of
the individuals is their sense of the substance, and of the identity of all their

---

1. *Die Sittlichkeit.*

interests with the total; and that the other individuals mutually know each other and are actual only in this identity, is confidence (trust)—the genuine ethical temper.

§ 516

The relations between individuals in the several situations to which the substance is particularized form their *ethical duties*. The ethical personality, i.e. the subjectivity which is permeated by the substantial life, is *virtue*. In relation to the bare facts of external being, to *destiny,* virtue does not treat them as a mere negation, and is thus a quiet repose in itself: in relation to substantial objectivity, to the total of ethical actuality, it exists as confidence, as deliberate work for the community, and the capacity of sacrificing self thereto; whilst in relation to the incidental relations of social circumstance, it is in the first instance justice and then benevolence. In the latter sphere, and in its attitude to its own visible being and corporeity, the individuality expresses its special character, temperament, etc. as personal *virtues*.

§ 517

The ethical substance is:

(a) as 'immediate' or *natural* mind—the *Family*.

(b) The 'relative' totality of the 'relative' relations of the individuals as independent persons to one another in a formal universality—*Civil Society*.

(c) The self-conscious substance, as the mind developed to an organic actuality—the *Political Constitution*.

(a) The Family

§ 518

The ethical spirit, in its *immediacy,* contains the *natural* factor that the individual has its substantial existence in its natural universal, i.e. in its kind. This is the sexual tie, elevated, however, to a spiritual significance,—the unanimity of love and the temper of trust. In the shape of the family, mind appears as feeling.

§ 519

(1) The physical difference of sex thus appears at the same time as a difference of intellectual and moral type. With their exclusive individualities these personalities combine to form a *single person:* the subjective union of hearts, becoming a 'substantial' unity, makes this union an ethical tie— *Marriage*. The 'substantial' union of hearts makes marriage an indivisible

personal bond—monogamic marriage: the bodily conjunction is a sequel to the moral attachment. A further sequel is community of personal and private interests.

§ 520

(2) By the community in which the various members constituting the family stand in reference to property, that property of the one person (representing the family) acquires an ethical interest, as do also its industry, labour, and care for the future.

§ 521

The ethical principle which is conjoined with the natural generation of the children, and which was assumed to have primary importance in first forming the marriage union, is actually realized in the second or spiritual birth of the children—in educating them to independent personality.

§ 522

(3) The children, thus invested with independence, leave the concrete life and action of the family to which they primarily belong, acquire an existence of their own, destined, however, to found anew such an actual family. Marriage is of course broken up by the *natural* element contained in it, the death of husband and wife: but even their union of hearts, as it is a mere 'substantiality' of feeling, contains the germ of liability to chance and decay. In virtue of such fortuitousness, the members of the family take up to each other the status of persons; and it is thus that the family finds introduced into it for the first time the element, originally foreign to it, of *legal* regulation.

(b) Civil Society[2]

§ 523

As the substance, being an intelligent substance, particularizes itself abstractly into many persons (the family is only a single person), into families or individuals, who exist independent and free, as private persons, it loses its ethical character: for these persons as such have in their consciousness and as their aim not the absolute unity, but their own petty selves and particular interests. Thus arises the system of *atomistic:* by which the substance is reduced to a general system of adjustments to connect self-subsisting extremes and their particular interests. The developed totality of this connective system is the state as civil society, or *state external.*

2. *Die bürgerliche Gesellschaft.*

(α) The System of Wants[3]

§ 524

(α) The particularity of the persons includes in the first instance their wants. The possibility of satisfying these wants is here laid on the social fabric, the general stock from which all derive their satisfaction. In the condition of things in which this method of satisfaction by indirect adjustment is realized, immediate seizure (§ 488) of external objects as means thereto exists barely or not at all: the objects are already property. To acquire them is only possible by the intervention, on one hand, of the possessor's will, which as particular has in view the satisfaction of their variously defined interests; while, on the other hand, it is conditioned by the ever-continued production of fresh means of exchange by the exchangers' *own labour*. This instrument, by which the labour of all facilitates satisfaction of wants, constitutes the general stock.

§ 525

(β) The glimmer of universal principle in this particularity of wants is found in the way intellect creates differences in them, and thus causes an indefinite multiplication both of wants and of means for their different phases. Both are thus rendered more and more abstract. This 'morcellement' of their content by abstraction gives rise to the *division of labour*. The habit of this abstraction in enjoyment, information, learning, and demeanour constitutes training in this sphere, or nominal culture in general.

§ 526

The labour which thus becomes more abstract tends on one hand by its uniformity to make labour easier and to increase production—on another to limit each person to a single kind of technical skill, and thus produce more unconditional dependence on the social system. The skill itself becomes in this way mechanical, and gets the capability of letting the machine take the place of human labour.

§ 527

(γ) But the concrete division of the general stock—which is also a general business (of the whole society)—into particular masses determined by the factors of the notion—masses each of which possesses its own basis of subsistence, and a corresponding mode of labour, of needs, and of means for satisfying them, also of aims and interests, as well as of mental culture and habit—constitutes the difference of Estates (orders or ranks). Indi-

---

3. *Das System der Bedürfnisse.*

viduals apportion themselves to these according to natural talent, skill, option, and accident. As belonging to such a definite and stable sphere, they have their actual existence, which as existence is essentially a particular; and in it they have their social morality, which is *honesty,* their recognition and their *honour.*

Where civil society, and with it the State, exists, there arise the several estates in their difference: for the universal substance, as vital, *exists* only so far as it organically *particularizes* itself. The history of constitutions is the history of the growth of these estates, of the legal relationships of individuals to them, and of these estates to one another and to their centre.

§ 528

To the 'substantial', natural estate the fruitful soil and ground supply a natural and stable capital; its action gets direction and content through natural features, and its moral life is founded on faith and trust. The second, the 'reflected' estate has as its allotment the social capital, the medium created by the action of middlemen, of mere agents, and an ensemble of contingencies, where the individual has to depend on his subjective skill, talent, intelligence, and industry. The third, 'thinking' estate has for its business the general interests; like the second it has a subsistence procured by means of its own skill, and like the first a certain subsistence, certain, however, because guaranteed through the whole society.

(β) Administration of Justice [4]

§ 529

When matured through the operation of natural need and free option into a system of universal relationships and a regular course of external necessity, the principle of casual particularity gets that stable articulation which liberty requires in the shape of *formal right.* (1) The actualization which right gets in this sphere of mere practical intelligence is that it be brought to consciousness as the stable universal, that it be known and stated in its specificity with the voice of authority—the *Law.* [5]

The *positive* element in laws concerns only their form of *publicity* and *authority*—which makes it possible for them to be known by all in a customary and external way. Their content *per se* may be reasonable—or it may be unreasonable and so wrong. But when right, in the course of definite manifestation, is developed in detail, and its content analyses itself to gain definiteness, this analysis, because of the finitude of its materials, falls into the falsely infinite progress: the *final* definiteness, which is absolutely essential and causes a break in this progress of unreality, can in this

---

4. *Die Rechtspflege.*   5. *Gesetz.*

sphere of finitude be attained only in a way that savours of contingency and arbitrariness. Thus whether three years, ten thalers, or only 2 1/2, 2 3/4, 2 4/5 years, and so on *ad infinitum,* be the right and just thing, can by no means be decided on intelligible principles—and yet it should be decided. Hence, though of course only at the final points of deciding, on the side of external existence, the 'positive' principle naturally enters law as contingency and arbitrariness. This happens and has from of old happened in all legislations: the only thing wanted is clearly to be aware of it, and not be misled by the talk and the pretence as if the ideal of law were, or could be, to be, at *every* point, determined through reason or legal intelligence, on purely reasonable and intelligent grounds. It is a futile perfectionism to have such expectations and to make such requirements in the sphere of the finite.

There are some who look upon laws as an evil and a profanity, and who regard governing and being governed from natural love, hereditary divinity or nobility, by faith and trust, as the genuine order of life, while the reign of law is held an order of corruption and injustice. These people forget that the stars—and the cattle too—are governed and well governed too by laws;—laws, however, which are only internally in these objects, not *for them,* not as laws *set to* them:—whereas it is man's privilege to *know* his law. They forget therefore that he can truly obey only such known law— even as his law can only be a just law, as it is a *known* law;—though in other respects it must be in its essential contingency and caprice, or at least be mixed and polluted with such elements.

The same empty requirement of perfection is employed for an opposite thesis—viz. to support the opinion that a code is impossible or impracticable. In this case there comes in the additional absurdity of putting essential and universal provisions in one class with the particular detail. The finite material is definable on and on to the false infinite: but this advance is not, as in the mental images of space, a generation of new spatial characteristics of the same quality as those preceding them, but an advance into greater and ever greater speciality by the acumen of the analytic intellect, which discovers new distinctions, which again make new decisions necessary. To provisions of this sort one may give the name of *new* decisions or *new* laws; but in proportion to the gradual advance in specialization the interest and value of these provisions declines. They fall within the already subsisting 'substantial', general laws, like improvements on a floor or a door, within the house—which though something *new,* are not a new *house.* But there is a contrary case. If the legislation of a rude age began with single provisos, which go on by their very nature always increasing their number, there arises, with the advance in multitude, the need of a simpler code—the need, i.e. of embracing that lot of singulars in their general features. To find and be able to express these principles well beseems an intelligent and civilized nation. Such a gathering up of single rules into general forms, first really deserving the name of laws, has lately been begun in some directions by the English Minister Peel, who has by so doing gained the gratitude, even the admiration, of his countrymen.

§ 530

(2) The positive form of Laws—to be *promulgated and made known* as laws—is a condition of the *external obligation* to obey them; inasmuch as, being laws of strict right, they touch only the abstract will—itself at bottom external—not the moral or ethical will. The subjectivity to which the will has in this direction a right is here only that the laws be known. This subjective existence, is as existence of the absolute truth in this sphere of Right, at the same time an externally *objective* existence, as universal authority and necessity.

§ 531

(3) Legal forms get the necessity, to which objective existence determines itself, in the *judicial system*. Abstract right has to exhibit itself to the *court*—to the individualized right—as *proven:*—a process in which there may be a difference between what is abstractly right and what is provably right. The court takes cognisance and action in the interest of right as such, deprives the existence of right of its contingency, and in particular transforms this existence—as this exists as revenge—into *punishment* (§ 500).

§ 532

The function of judicial administration is only to actualize to necessity the abstract side of personal liberty in civil society. But this actualization rests at first on the particular subjectivity of the judge, since here as yet there is not found the necessary unity of it with right in the abstract. Conversely, the blind necessity of the system of wants is not lifted up into the consciousness of the universal, and worked from that point of view.

(γ) **Police and Corporation**[6]

§ 533

Judicial administration naturally has no concern with such part of actions and interests as belongs only to particularity, and leaves to chance not only the occurrence of crimes but also the care for public weal. In civil society the sole end is to satisfy want—and that, because it is man's want, in a uniform general way, so as to *secure* this satisfaction. But the machinery

---

6. *Die Polizei und die Corporation.*

of social necessity leaves in many ways a casualness about this satisfaction. This is due to the variability of the wants themselves, in which opinion and subjective good-pleasure play a great part. It results also from circumstances of locality, from the connections between nation and nation, from errors and deceptions which can be foisted upon single members of the social circulation and are capable of creating disorder in it—as also and especially from the unequal capacity of individuals to take advantage of that general stock. The onward march of this necessity also sacrifices the very particularities by which it is brought about, and does not itself contain the affirmative aim of securing the satisfaction of individuals. So far as concerns them, it *may* be far from beneficial: yet here the individuals are the morally justifiable end.

§ 534

To keep in view this general end, to ascertain the way in which the powers composing that social necessity act, and their variable ingredients, and to maintain that end in them and against them, is the work of an institution which assumes on *one* hand, to the concrete of civil society, the position of an external universality. Such an order acts with the power of an external state, which, in so far as it is rooted in the higher or substantial state, appears as state-'police'. On the *other* hand, in this sphere of particularity the only recognition of the aim of substantial universality and the only carrying of it out is restricted to the business of particular branches and interests. Thus we have the *corporation,* in which the particular citizen in his private capacity finds the securing of his stock, whilst at the same time he in it emerges from his single private interest, and has a conscious activity for a comparatively universal end, just as in his legal and professional duties he has his social morality.

(c) The State

§ 535

The State is the *self-conscious* ethical substance, the unification of the family principle with that of civil society. The same unity, which is in the family as a feeling of love, is its essence, receiving, however, at the same time through the second principle of conscious and spontaneously active volition the *form* of conscious universality. This universal principle, with all its evolution in detail, is the absolute aim and content of the knowing subject, which thus identifies itself in its volition with the system of reasonableness.

§ 536

The state is (α) its inward structure as a self-relating development—constitutional (inner-state) law: (β) a particular individual, and therefore in connection with other particular individuals—international (outer-state) law; (γ) but these particular minds are only stages in the general development of mind in its actuality: universal history.

(α) **Constitutional Law**[7]

§ 537

The essence of the state is the universal, self-originated, and self-developed—the reasonable spirit of will; but, as self-knowing and self-actualizing, sheer subjectivity, and—as an actuality—one individual. Its *work* generally— in relation to the extreme of individuality as the multitude of individuals—consists in a double function. First it maintains them as persons, thus making right a necessary actuality, then it promotes their welfare, which each originally takes care of for himself, but which has a thoroughly general side; it protects the family and guides civil society. Secondly, it carries back both, and the whole disposition and action of the individual—whose tendency is to become a centre of his own—into the life of the universal substance; and, in this direction, as a free power it interferes with those subordinate spheres and maintains them in substantial immanence.

§ 538

The laws express the special provisions for objective freedom. First, to the immediate agent, his independent self-will and particular interest, they are restrictions. But, secondly, they are an absolute final end and the universal work: hence they are a product of the 'functions' of the various orders which parcel themselves more and more out of the general particularizing, and are a fruit of all the acts and private concerns of individuals. Thirdly, they are the substance of the volition of individuals—which volition is thereby free—and of their disposition: being as such exhibited as current usage.

§ 539

As a living mind, the state only is as an organized whole, differentiated into particular agencies, which, proceeding from the one notion (though not known as notion) of the reasonable will, continually produce it as their result. The *constitution* is this articulation or organization of state-power. It provides for the reasonable will—in so far as it is in the individuals only *implicitly* the universal will—coming to a consciousness and an understanding of itself and being *found;* also for that will being put in actuality, through the action of the government and its several branches, and not left to perish, but protected both against *their* casual subjectivity and against

7. *Inneres Staatsrecht.*

that of the individuals. The constitution is existent *justice*—the actuality of liberty in the development of all its reasonable provisions.

Liberty and Equality are the simple rubrics into which is frequently concentrated what should form the fundamental principle, the final aim and result of the constitution. However true this is, the defect of these terms is their utter abstractness: if stuck to in this abstract form, they are principles which either prevent the rise of the concreteness of the state, i.e. its articulation into a constitution and a government in general, or destroy them. With the state there arises inequality, the difference of governing powers and of governed, magistracies, authorities, directories, etc. The principle of equality, logically carried out, rejects all differences, and thus allows no sort of political condition to exist. Liberty and equality are indeed the foundation of the state, but as the most abstract also the most superficial, and for that very reason naturally the most familiar. It is important therefore to study them closer.

As regards, first, Equality, the familiar proposition, All men are by nature equal, blunders by confusing the 'natural' with the 'notion'. It ought rather to read: *By nature* men are only unequal. But the *notion* of liberty, as it exists as such, without further specification and development, is abstract subjectivity, as a person capable of property (§ 488). This single abstract feature of personality constitutes the actual *equality* of human beings. But that this freedom should exist, that it should be *man* (and not as in Greece, Rome, etc. *some* men) that is recognized and legally regarded as a person, is so little *by nature,* that it is rather only a result and product of the consciousness of the deepest principle of mind, and of the universality and expansion of this consciousness. That the citizens are equal before the law contains a great truth, but which so expressed is a tautology: it only states that the legal status in general exists, that the laws rule. But, as regards the concrete, the citizens—besides their personality—are equal before the law only in these points when they are otherwise equal *outside the law.* Only that equality which (in whatever way it be) they, as it happens, otherwise have in property, age, physical strength, talent, skill, etc.—or even in crime, can and ought to make them deserve equal treatment before the law:—only it can make them—as regards taxation, military service, eligibility to office, etc.—punishment, etc.—equal in the concrete. The laws themselves, except in so far as they concern that narrow circle of personality, presuppose unequal conditions, and provide for the unequal legal duties and appurtenances resulting therefrom.

As regards Liberty, it is originally taken partly in a negative sense against arbitrary intolerance and lawless treatment, partly in the affirmative sense of subjective freedom; but this freedom is allowed great latitude both as regards the agent's self-will and action for his particular ends, and as regards his claim to have a personal intelligence and a personal share in general affairs. Formerly the legally defined rights, private as well as public rights of a nation, town, etc. were called its 'liberties'. Really, every genuine law is a liberty: it contains a reasonable principle of objective mind; in other words, it embodies a liberty. Nothing has become, on the contrary, more familiar than the idea that each must *restrict* his liberty in relation to the liberty of others: that the state is a condition of such reciprocal restriction, and that the laws are restrictions. To such habits of mind liberty is viewed as only casual good-pleasure and self-will. Hence it has also been said that 'modern' nations are only susceptible of equality, or of equality more than liberty: and that for no other reason than that, with an assumed definition of liberty (chiefly the participation of all in political affairs and actions), it was impossible to make ends meet in actuality— which is at once more reasonable and more powerful than abstract presuppositions. On the contrary, it should be said that it is just the great development and maturity of form in modern states which produces the supreme concrete inequality of individuals in actuality: while, through the deeper reasonableness of laws and the greater stability of the legal state, it gives rise to greater and more stable liberty, which it can without incompatibility allow. Even the superficial distinction of the words liberty and equality points to the fact that the former tends to inequality: whereas, on the contrary, the current notions of liberty only carry us back to equality. But the more we fortify liberty,—as security of property, as possibility for each to develop and make the best of his talents and good qualities, the more it gets taken for granted: and then the sense and appreciation of liberty especially turns in a *subjective* direction. By this is meant the liberty to attempt action on every side, and to throw oneself at pleasure in action for particular and for general intellectual interests, the removal of all checks on the individual particularity, as well as the inward liberty in which the subject has principles, has an insight and conviction of his own, and thus gains moral independence. But this liberty itself on one hand implies that supreme differentiation in which men are unequal and make themselves more unequal by education; and on another it only grows up under conditions of that objective liberty, and is and could grow to such height only in modern states. If, with this development of particularity, there be simultaneous and endless increase of the number of wants, and of the difficulty of satisfying them, of the lust of argument and the fancy of detecting faults, with its insatiate vanity, it is all but part of that indiscriminating relaxation of individuality in this sphere which generates all possible complications, and must deal with them as it can. Such a sphere is of course also the field of restrictions, because liberty is there under the taint of natural self-will and self-pleasing, and has therefore to restrict itself: and that, not merely with

regard to the naturalness, self-will and self-conceit, of others, but especially and essentially with regard to reasonable liberty.

The term political liberty, however, is often used to mean formal participation in the public affairs of state by the will and action even of those
individuals who otherwise find their chief function in the particular aims
and business of civil society. And it has in part become usual to give the
title constitution only to the side of the state which concerns such participation of these individuals in general affairs, and to regard a state, in which
this is not formally done, as a state without a constitution. On this use of
the term the only thing to remark is that by constitution must be understood
the determination of rights, i.e. of liberties in general, and the organization of the actualization of them; and that political freedom in the above
sense can in any case only constitute a part of it. Of it the following paragraphs will speak.

§ 540

The guarantee of a constitution (i.e. the necessity that the laws be reasonable, and their actualization secured) lies in the collective spirit of the
nation—especially in the specific way in which it is itself conscious of
its reason. (Religion is that consciousness in its absolute substantiality.)
But the guarantee lies also at the same time in the actual organization or
development of that principle in suitable institutions. The constitution presupposes that consciousness of the collective spirit, and conversely that
spirit presupposes the constitution: for the actual spirit only has a definite
consciousness of its principles, in so far as it has them actually existent
before it.

The question—To whom (to what authority and how organized) belongs
the power to make a constitution? is the same as the question, Who has to
make the spirit of a nation? Separate our idea of a constitution from that of
the collective spirit, as if the latter exists or has existed without a constitution, and your fancy only proves how superficially you have apprehended
the nexus between the spirit in its self-consciousness and in its actuality.
What is thus called 'making' a 'constitution', is—just because of this in-
separability—a thing that has never happened in history, just as little as the
making of a code of laws. A constitution only develops from the national
spirit identically with that spirit's own development, and runs through at
the same time with it the grades of formation and the alterations required
by its concept. It is the indwelling spirit and the history of the nation (and,
be it added, the history is only that spirit's history) by which constitutions
have been and are made.

§ 541

The really living totality—that which preserves, in other words continually produces the state in general and its constitution, is the *government*. The organization which natural necessity gives is seen in the rise of the family and of the 'estates' of civil society. The government is the *universal* part of the constitution, i.e. the part which intentionally aims at preserving those parts, but at the same time gets hold of and carries out those general aims of the whole which rise above the function of the family and of civil society. The organization of the government is likewise its differentiation into powers, as their peculiarities have a basis in principle; yet without that difference losing touch with the *actual unity* they have in the notion's subjectivity.

As the most obvious categories of the notion are those of *universality* and *individuality,* and their relationship that of *subsumption* of individual under universal, it has come about that in the state the legislative and executive power have been so distinguished as to make the former *exist* apart as the absolute superior, and to subdivide the latter again into administrative (government) power and judicial power, according as the laws are applied to public or private affairs. The *division* of these powers has been treated as *the* condition of political equilibrium, meaning by division their *independence* one of another in existence—subject always, however, to the above mentioned subsumption of the powers of the individual under the power of the general. The theory of such 'division' unmistakably implies the elements of the notion, but so combined by 'understanding' as to result in an absurd collocation, instead of the self-redintegration of the living spirit. The one essential canon to make liberty deep and real is to give every business belonging to the general interests of the state a separate organization wherever they are essentially distinct. Such real division must be: for liberty is only deep when it is differentiated in all its fullness and these differences manifested in existence. But to make the business of legislation an independent power—to make it the first power, with the further proviso that all citizens shall have part therein, and the government be merely executive and dependent, presupposes ignorance that the true idea, and therefore the living and spiritual actuality, is the self-redintegrating notion, in other words, the subjectivity which contains in it universality as only one of its moments. (A mistake still greater, if it goes with the fancy that the constitution and the fundamental laws were still one day to make— in a state of society, which includes an already existing development of differences.) Individuality is the first and supreme principle which makes itself felt through the state's organization. Only through the government, and by its embracing in itself the particular businesses (including the abstract legislative business, which taken apart is also particular), is the state *one*. These, as always, are the terms on which the different elements essentially and alone truly stand towards each other in the logic of 'reason', as opposed to the external footing they stand on in 'understanding', which never gets beyond subsuming the individual and particular under the universal. What disorganizes the unity of logical reason, equally disorganizes actuality.

§ 542

In the government—regarded as organic totality—the sovereign power (principate) is (a) *subjectivity* as the *infinite* self-unity of the notion in its development;—the all-sustaining, all-decreeing will of the state, its highest peak and all-pervasive unity. In the perfect form of the state, in which each and every element of the notion has reached free existence, this subjectivity is not a so-called 'moral person', or a decree issuing from a majority (forms in which the unity of the decreeing will has not an *actual* existence), but an actual individual—the will of a decreeing individual,—*monarchy*. The monarchical constitution is therefore the constitution of developed reason: all other constitutions belong to lower grades of the development and realization of reason.

The unification of all concrete state-powers into one existence, as in the patriarchal society—or, as in a democratic constitution, the participation of all in all affairs—impugns the principle of the division of powers, i.e. the developed liberty of the constituent factors of the Idea. But no whit less must the division (the working out of these factors each to a free totality) be reduced to 'ideal' unity, i.e. to *subjectivity*. The mature differentiation or realization of the Idea means, essentially, that this subjectivity should grow to be a *real* 'moment', an *actual* existence; and this actuality is not otherwise than as the individuality of the monarch—the subjectivity of abstract and final decision existent in *one* person. All those forms of collective decreeing and willing—a common will which shall be the sum and the resultant (on aristocratic or democratic principles) of the atomistic of single wills, have on them the mark of the unreality of an abstraction. Two points only are all-important, first to see the necessity of each of the notional factors, and secondly the form in which it is actualized. It is only the nature of the speculative notion which can really give light on the matter. That subjectivity—being the 'moment' which emphasizes the need of abstract deciding in general—partly leads on to the proviso that the name of the monarch appear as the bond and sanction under which everything is done in the government;—partly, being simple self-relation, has attached to it the characteristic of *immediacy,* and then of *nature*—whereby the destination of individuals for the dignity of the princely power is fixed by inheritance.

§ 543

(b) In the *particular* government-power there emerges, first, the division of state-business into its branches (otherwise defined), legislative power, administration of justice or judicial power, administration and police, and its consequent distribution between particular boards or offices, which having their business appointed by law, to that end and for that reason, possess independence of action, without at the same time ceasing to stand under higher supervision. Secondly, too, there arises the participation of *several* in state-business, who together constitute the 'general order' (§ 528) in so far as they take on themselves the charge of universal ends as the essential function of their particular life;—the further condition for being able to take individually part in this business being a certain training, aptitude, and skill for such ends.

§ 544

The estates-collegium or provincial council is an institution by which all such as belong to civil society in general, and are to that degree private persons, participate in the governmental power, especially in legislation— viz. such legislation as concerns the universal scope of those interests which do not, like peace and war, involve the, as it were, personal interference and action of the State as one man, and therefore do not belong specially to the province of the sovereign power. By virtue of this participation subjective liberty and conceit, with their general opinion, can show themselves palpably efficacious and enjoy the satisfaction of feeling themselves to count for something.

The division of constitutions into democracy, aristocracy and monarchy, is still the most definite statement of their difference in relation to sovereignty. They must at the same time be regarded as necessary structures in the part of development—in short, in the history of the State. Hence it is superficial and absurd to represent them as an object of *choice*. The pure forms—necessary to the process of evolution—are, in so far as they are finite and in course of change, conjoined both with forms of their degeneration—such as ochlocracy, etc., and with earlier transition-forms. These two forms are not to be confused with those legitimate structures. Thus, it may be—if we look only to the fact that the will of one individual stands at the head of the state—oriental despotism is included under the vague name monarchy—as also feudal monarchy, to which indeed even the favourite name of 'constitutional monarchy' cannot be refused. The true difference of these forms from genuine monarchy depends on the true value of those principles of right which are in vogue and have the actuality and guarantee in the state-power. These principles are those expounded earlier, liberty of property, and above all personal liberty, civil society, with its industry and its communities, and the regulated efficiency of the particular bureaux in subordination to the laws.

The question which is most discussed is in what sense we are to understand the participation of private persons in state affairs. For it is as private persons that the members of bodies of estates are primarily to be taken, be they treated as mere individuals, or as representatives of a number of people or of the nation. The aggregate of private persons is often spoken of as the *nation:* but as such an aggregate it is *vulgus,* not *populus:* and in this direction it is the one sole aim of the state that a nation should *not* come to existence, to power and action, *as such an aggregate.* Such a condition of a nation is a condition of lawlessness, demoralization, brutishness: in it the nation would only be a shapeless, wild, blind force, like that of the stormy, elemental sea, which, however, is not self-destructive, as the nation—a spiritual element—would be. Yet such a condition may be often heard described as that of true freedom. If there is to be any sense in embarking upon the question of the participation of private persons in public affairs, it is not a brutish mass, but an already organized nation—one in which a governmental power exists—which should be presupposed. The desirability of such participation, however, is not to be put in the superiority of particular intelligence, which private persons are supposed to have over state officials—the contrary must be the case—nor in the superiority of their goodwill for the general best. The members of civil society as such are rather people who find their nearest duty in their private interest and (as especially in the feudal society) in the interest of their privileged corporation. Take the case of *England* which, because private persons have a predominant share in public affairs, has been regarded as having the freest of all constitutions. Experience shows that that country—as compared with the other civilized states of Europe—is the most backward in civil and criminal legislation, in the law and liberty of property, in arrangements for art and science, and that objective freedom or rational right is rather *sacrificed* to formal right and particular private interest; and that this happens even in the institutions and possessions supposed to be dedicated to religion. The desirability of private persons taking part in public affairs is partly to be put in their concrete, and therefore more urgent, sense of general wants. But the true motive is the right of the collective spirit to appear as an *externally universal* will, acting with orderly and express efficacy for the public concerns. By this satisfaction of this right it gets its own life quickened, and at the same time breathes fresh life in the administrative officials; who thus have it brought home to them that not merely have they to enforce duties but also to have regard to rights. Private citizens are in the state the incomparably greater number, and form the multitude of such as are recognized as persons. Hence the will-reason exhibits its existence in them as a preponderating majority of freemen, or in its 'reflectional' universality, which has its actuality vouchsafed it as a participation in the sovereignty. But it has already been noted as a 'moment' of civil society (§§ 527, 534) that the individuals rise from external into substantial universality, and form a *particular* kind—the Estates: and it is not in the inorganic form of mere individuals as such (after the *democratic* fashion of election), but as organic factors, as estates, that they enter upon that participation. In the state a power or agency must never appear and act as a formless, inorganic shape, i.e. basing itself on the principle of multeity and mere numbers.

Assemblies of Estates have been wrongly designated as the *legislative power,* so far as they form only one branch of that power—a branch in which the special government-officials have an *ex officio* share, while the sovereign power has the privilege of final decision. In a civilized state, moreover, legislation can only be a further modification of existing laws, and so-called new laws can only deal with minutiae of detail and particularities (cf. § 529 note), the main drift of which has been already prepared or preliminarily settled by the practice of the law-courts. The so-called *financial law,* in so far as it requires the assent of the estates, is really a government affair: it is only improperly called a law, in the general sense of embracing a wide, indeed the whole, range of the external means of government. The finances deal with what in their nature are only particular needs, ever newly recurring, even if they touch on the sum total of such needs. If the main part of the requirement were—as it very likely is—regarded as permanent, the provision for it would have more the nature of a law: but to be a law it would have to be made once for all, and not to be made yearly, or every few years, afresh. The part which varies according to time and circumstances concerns in reality the smallest part of the amount, and the provisions with regard to it have even less the character of a law: and yet it is and may be only this slight variable part which is matter of dispute, and can be subjected to a varying yearly estimate. It is this last then which falsely bears the high-sounding names of the *'Grant'* of the *Budget,* i.e. of the whole of the finances. A law for one year and made each year has even to the plain man something palpably absurd: for he distinguishes the essential and developed universal, as content of a true law, from the reflectional universality which only externally embraces what in its nature is many. To give the name of a law to the annual fixing of financial requirements only serves—with the presupposed separation of legislative from executive—to keep up the illusion of that separation having real existence, and to conceal the fact that the legislative power, when it makes a decree about finance, is really engaged with strict executive business. But the importance attached to the power of from time to time granting 'supply', on the ground that the assembly of estates possesses in it a *check* on the government, and thus a guarantee against injustice and violence—this importance is in one way rather plausible than real. The financial measures necessary for the state's subsistence cannot be made conditional on any other circumstances, nor can the state's subsistence be put yearly in doubt. It would be a parallel absurdity if the government were, e.g., to grant and arrange the judicial institutions always for a limited time merely; and thus, by the threat of suspending the activity of such an institution and the fear of a consequent state of brigandage, reserve for itself a means of coercing private individuals. Then again, the pictures of a condition of affairs, in which it might be useful and necessary to have in hand means of compulsion, are partly based on the false conception of a contract between rulers and ruled, and partly presuppose the possibility of such a divergence in spirit between these two parties as would make constitution and government quite out of the question. If we suppose the empty possibility of getting *help* by such compulsive means brought into existence, such help would rather be the derangement and dissolution of the state, in which there would no longer be a government, but only parties, and the violence and oppression of one party would only be helped away by the other. To fit together the several parts of the state into a constitution after the fashion of mere understanding—i.e. to adjust within it the machinery of a balance of powers external to each other—is to contravene the fundamental idea of what a state is.

§ 545

The final aspect of the state is to appear in immediate actuality as a single nation marked by physical conditions. As a single individual it is exclusive against other like individuals. In their mutual relations, waywardness and chance have a place; for each person in the aggregate is autonomous: the universal of law is only postulated between them, and not actually existent. This independence of a central authority reduces disputes between them to terms of mutual violence, a *state of war,* to meet which the general estate in the community assumes the particular function of maintaining the state's independence against other states, and becomes the estate of bravery.

§ 546

This state of war shows the omnipotence of the state in its individuality—an individuality that goes even to abstract negativity. Country and fatherland then appear as the power by which the particular independence of individuals and their absorption in the external existence of possession and in natural life is convicted of its own nullity—as the power which procures the maintenance of the general substance by the patriotic sacrifice on the part of these individuals of this natural and particular existence—so making nugatory the nugatoriness that confronts it.

(β) External Public Law [8]

§ 547

In the state of war the independence of States is at stake. In one case the result may be the mutual recognition of free national individualities (§ 430): and by peace-conventions supposed to be for ever, both this general recognition, and the special claims of nations on one another, are settled and fixed. External state-rights rest partly on these positive treaties, but to that extent contain only rights falling short of true actuality (§ 545): partly so-called *international* law, the general principle of which is its presupposed recognition by the several States. It thus restricts their otherwise unchecked action against one another in such a way that the possibility of peace is left; and distinguishes individuals as private persons (nonbelligerents) from the state. In general, international law rests on social usage.

(γ) Universal History [9]

§ 548

As the mind of a special nation is actual and its liberty is under natural conditions, it admits on this nature-side the influence of geographical and climatic qualities. It is in time; and as regards its range and scope, has essentially a *particular* principle on the lines of which it must run through a development of its consciousness and its actuality. It has, in short, a history of its own. But as a restricted mind its independence is something secondary; it passes into universal world-history, the events of which exhibit the dialectic of the several national minds—the judgement of the world.

§ 549

This movement is the path of liberation for the spiritual substance, the deed by which the absolute final aim of the world is realized in it, and the merely implicit mind achieves consciousness and self-consciousness. It is thus the revelation and actuality of its essential and completed essence, whereby it becomes to the outward eye a universal spirit—a world-mind. As this development is in time and in real existence, as it is a history, its several

8. *Das aüssere Staatsrecht.*   9. *Die Weltgeschichte.*

stages and steps are the national minds, each of which, as single and en-
dued by nature with a specific character, is appointed to occupy only one
grade, and accomplish one task in the whole deed.

The presupposition that history has an essential and actual end, from
the principles of which certain characteristic results logically flow, is called
an *a priori* view of it, and philosophy is reproached with *a priori* history-
writing. On this point, and on history-writing in general, this note must go
into further detail. That history, and above all universal history, is founded
on an essential and actual aim, which actually is and will be realized in it—
the plan of Providence; that, in short, there is Reason in history, must be
decided on strictly philosophical ground, and thus shown to be essentially
and in fact necessary. To presuppose such aim is blameworthy only when
the assumed conceptions or thoughts are arbitrarily adopted, and when a
determined attempt is made to force events and actions into conformity
with such conceptions. For such *a priori* methods of treatment at the
present day, however, those are chiefly to blame who profess to be purely
historical, and who at the same time take opportunity expressly to raise
their voice against the habit of philosophizing, first in general, and then in
history. Philosophy is to them a troublesome neighbour: for it is an enemy
of all arbitrariness and hasty suggestions. Such *a priori* history-writing has
sometimes burst out in quarters where one would least have expected it,
especially on the philological side, and in Germany more than in France
and England, where the art of historical writing has gone through a process
of purification to a firmer and maturer character. Fictions, like that of a
primitive age and its primitive people, possessed from the first of the true
knowledge of God and all the sciences—of sacerdotal races—and, when
we come to minutiae, of a Roman epic, supposed to be the source of the
legends which pass current for the history of ancient Rome, etc., have
taken the place of the pragmatizing which detected psychological motives
and associations. There is a wide circle of persons who seem to consider it
incumbent on a *learned* and *ingenious* historian drawing from the original
sources to concoct such baseless fancies, and form bold combinations of
them from a learned rubbish-heap of out-of-the-way and trivial facts, in
defiance of the best-accredited history.

Setting aside this subjective treatment of history, we find what is properly the opposite view forbidding us to import into history an *objective
purpose*. This is after all synonymous with what *seems* to be the still more
legitimate demand that the historian should proceed with *impartiality*. This
is a requirement often and especially made on the *history of philosophy:*
where it is insisted there should be no prepossession in favour of an idea or
opinion, just as a judge should have no special sympathy for one of the
contending parties. In the case of the judge it is at the same time assumed

that he would administer his office ill and foolishly, if he had not an interest, and an exclusive interest in justice, if he had not that for his aim and one sole aim, or if he declined to judge at all. This requirement which we may make upon the judge may be called *partiality* for justice; and there is no difficulty here in distinguishing it from *subjective* partiality. But in speaking of the impartiality required from the historian, this self-satisfied insipid chatter lets the distinction disappear, and rejects both kinds of interest. It demands that the historian shall bring with him no definite aim and view by which he may sort out, state, and criticize events, but shall narrate them exactly in the casual mode he finds them, in their incoherent and unintelligent particularity. Now it is at least admitted that a history must have an object, e.g. Rome and its fortunes, or the Decline of the grandeur of the Roman empire. But little reflection is needed to discover that this is the presupposed end which lies at the basis of the events themselves, as of the critical examination into their comparative importance, i.e. their nearer or more remote relation to it. A history without such aim and such criticism would be only an imbecile mental divagation, not as good as a fairy tale, for even children expect a *motif* in their stories, a purpose at least dimly surmiseable with which events and actions are put in relation.

In the existence of a *nation* the substantial aim is to be a state and preserve itself as such. A nation with no state formation (a *mere nation*), has, strictly speaking, no history—like the nations which existed before the rise of states and others which still exist in a condition of savagery. What happens to a nation, and takes place within it, has its essential significance in relation to the state: whereas the mere particularities of individuals are at the greatest distance from the true object of history. It is true that the general spirit of an age leaves its imprint in the character of its celebrated individuals, and even their particularities are but the very distant and the dim media through which the collective light still plays in fainter colours. Ay, even such singularities as a petty occurrence, a word, express not a subjective particularity, but an age, a nation, a civilization, in striking portraiture and brevity; and to select such trifles shows the hand of a historian of genius. But, on the other hand, the main mass of singularities is a futile and useless mass, by the painstaking accumulation of which the objects of real historical value are overwhelmed and obscured. The essential characteristic of the spirit and its age is always contained in the great events. It was a correct instinct which sought to banish such portraiture of the particular and the gleaning of insignificant traits, into the *Novel* (as in the celebrated romances of Walter Scott, etc.). Where the picture presents an unessential aspect of life it is certainly in good taste to conjoin it with an unessential material, such as the romance tales from private events and subjective passions. But to take the individual pettinesses of an age and of the persons in it, and, in the interest of so-called truth, weave them into the picture of general interests, is not only against taste and judgement, but violates the principles of objective truth. The only truth for mind is the substantial and underlying essence, and not the trivialities of external existence and contingency. It is therefore completely indifferent whether such insignificances are duly vouched for by documents, or, as in the romance, invented to suit the character and ascribed to this or that name and circumstances.

The point of interest of *Biography*—to say a word on that here—appears to run directly counter to any universal scope and aim. But biography too has for its background the historical world, with which the individual is intimately bound up: even purely personal originality, the freak of humour, etc. suggests by allusion that central reality and has its interest heightened by the suggestion. The mere play of sentiment, on the contrary, has another ground and interest than history.

The requirement of impartiality addressed to the history of philosophy (and also, we may add, to the history of religion, first in general, and secondly, to church history) generally implies an even more decided bar against presupposition of any objective aim. As the State was already called the point to which in political history criticism had to refer all events, so here the *'Truth'* must be the object to which the several deeds and events of the spirit would have to be referred. What is actually done is rather to make the contrary presupposition. Histories with such an object as religion or philosophy are understood to have only subjective aims for their theme, i.e. only opinions and mere ideas, not an essential and realized object like the truth. And that with the mere excuse that there is no truth. On this assumption the sympathy with truth appears as only a partiality of the usual sort, a partiality for opinion and mere ideas, which all alike have no stuff in them and are all treated as indifferent. In that way historical truth means but correctness—an accurate report of externals, without critical treatment save as regards this correctness—admitting, in this case, only qualitative and quantitative judgements, no judgements of necessity or notion (cf. notes to §§ 172 and 175). But, really, if Rome or the German empire, etc. are an actual and genuine object of political history, and the aim to which the phenomena are to be related and by which they are to be judged; then in universal history the genuine spirit, the consciousness of it, and of its essence, is even in a higher degree a true and actual object and theme, and an aim to which all other phenomena are essentially and actually subservient. Only therefore through their relationship to it, i.e. through the judgement in which they are subsumed under it, while it inheres in them, have they their value and even their existence. It is the spirit which not merely broods *over* history as over the waters but lives in it and is alone its principle of movement: and in the path of that spirit, liberty, i.e. a development determined by the notion of spirit, is the guiding principle and only its notion its final aim, i.e. truth. For Spirit is consciousness. Such a doctrine—or in other words that Reason is in history—will be partly at least a plausible faith, partly it is a cognition of philosophy.

§ 550

This liberation of mind, in which it proceeds to come to itself and to realize its truth, and the business of so doing, is the supreme right, the absolute Law. The self-consciousness of a particular nation is a vehicle for the contemporary development of the collective spirit in its actual existence: it is the objective actuality in which that spirit for the time invests its will. Against this absolute will the other particular natural minds have no rights: *that* nation dominates the world: but yet the universal will steps onward over its property for the time being, as over a special grade, and then delivers it over to its chance and doom.

§ 551

To such extent as this business of actuality appears as an action, and therefore as a work of *individuals,* these individuals, as regards the substantial issue of their labour, are *instruments,* and their subjectivity, which is what is peculiar to them, is the empty form of activity. What they personally have gained therefore through the individual share they took in the substantial business (prepared and appointed independently of them) is a formal universality or subjective mental idea—*Fame,* which is their reward.

§ 552

The national spirit contains nature-necessity, and stands in external existence (§ 483): the ethical substance, potentially infinite, is actually a particular and limited substance (§§ 549, 550); on its subjective side it labours under contingency, in the shape of its unreflective natural usages, and its content is presented to it as something *existing* in time and tied to an external nature and external world. The spirit, however (which *thinks* in this moral organism) overrides and absorbs within itself the finitude attaching to it as national spirit in its state and the state's temporal interests, in the system of laws and usages. It rises to apprehend itself in its essentiality. Such apprehension, however, still has the immanent limitedness of the national spirit. But the spirit which thinks in universal history, stripping off at the same time those limitations of the several national minds and its own temporal restrictions, lays hold of its concrete universality, and rises to apprehend the absolute mind, as the eternally actual truth in which the contemplative reason enjoys freedom, while the necessity of nature and the

necessity of history are only ministrant to its revelation and the vessels of
its honour.

12. Documents on the Status of German Jewry and the Debate over Jewish Emancipation

The process called, in the nineteenth century, Jewish emancipation—the
granting to the Jews of citizenship, or full equality before the law—was
part of the universalistic program of political liberalism. It was firmly
identified as such when, after some initial hesitation, the French Constituent Assembly decided in January 1790 that the preservation of the
founding principles of the revolution required extending the "rights of
man and the citizen" to the Jews within French borders. (In fact, this
ambivalent decree referred only to those highly acculturated Jews of
Spanish and Portuguese origin who had been living in France since the
sixteenth century. A new decree of September 1791 finally embraced all
French Jews, including the relatively recent, Yiddish-speaking immigrants from eastern Europe.)

As exporter of the revolution abroad, Napoleon insisted upon Jewish
emancipation in the countries conquered by his armies. But these externally imposed measures were generally rescinded after 1815, though
Jewish emancipation did remain in place in Prussia (where it had been
granted by the Prussian king, not compelled by a foreign occupying power)
and in France itself. Hence after 1815 the so-called Jewish question became an intensely debated subject in many German states.

The first document in this section is an instance of that debate. The
exchange between Heinrich Paulus (1761–1851), professor of oriental
languages and theology at the University of Heidelberg, and the young
Jewish jurist Gabriel Riesser (1806–63) was occasioned by the publication in 1831 of Paulus's book *Die jüdische Nationalabsonderung nach
Ursprung, Folgen und Verbesserungsmitteln* (The segregation of the Jewish nation with respect to its origin, consequences, and correctives),
which is the source of the statement by him reprinted here. Riesser,
whose reply to Paulus appeared later that same year and is excerpted
here, had decided to devote himself to the cause of Jewish emancipation
after the legal restrictions against Jews had debarred him from obtaining a
university lectureship in jurisprudence and even from practicing as a no-
tary in his native city of Hamburg.

The second document, a letter from Abraham Mendelssohn to his
daughter Fanny in 1820 at the time of her confirmation into the Lutheran
church, reflects another response of German Jews to a hostile and restric-

tive social environment. Abraham Mendelssohn (1776–1835) was the son of Moses Mendelssohn, the major Enlightenment philosopher of the German Jewish community and probably the model for the title character in G. E. Lessing's plea for religious toleration, *Nathan the Wise*. As expressed here, Abraham Mendelssohn's own conception of religion is strongly marked by Enlightenment ideals. Fanny Mendelssohn (1805–47), a pianist and an accomplished composer in her own right, was the sister of the celebrated composer Felix Mendelssohn (1809–47), who, like Fanny, was baptized into the Lutheran church in 1816.

Heinrich Paulus and Gabriel Riesser, The Paulus-Riesser Debate

PROFESSOR HEINRICH PAULUS: The main point is this. . . . As long as the Jews believe that their continued existence as Jews must be in accordance with the Rabbinic-Mosaic spirit, no nation could grant them civil rights. Civil rights [are to be denied the Jews] because they apparently wish to remain a nation apart, for they conceive of their religious objectives in such a way that they perforce remain a nation apart from those nations which have provided them with shelter. . . . One cannot seek or obtain civil rights from any nation if one wishes to continue to belong to a different nation and believes one should persist in this adherence. Clearly, granting civil rights presupposes that [the recipient] belongs to the nation which grants these rights and not to any other nation. Jewry, however, dispersed over the entire earth, aspires to preserve through [endogamous] marriage customs and its many particularistic and exclusive laws its nationhood and apartness.

Therefore, it is only possible to grant the Jews (as one specific association in our society) no more than the status of "tolerated residents" or at best that of "protected residents." And notwithstanding their egregious religion, they should have no reason or desire to insist upon their own national identity. This renunciation must be emphatic and tangible. The Jews must demonstrate that they belong solely to the country of their residence and accept the national identity of that country. They must demonstrate that they no longer consider themselves as members of a necessarily separate, self-sufficient people of God.

DR. GABRIEL RIESSER: To be sure, the Jews were once a nation. But they

---

ceased to be one some two thousand years ago as have most other nations whose descendants constitute the states of present-day Europe. [When the Jews ceased to be a nation], they were dispersed throughout all the provinces of the Roman Empire and were subject to the same legal provisions that applied to other peoples subjugated by the Romans. After the Peregrinic reforms[1] they enjoyed equal rights as Roman citizens. Their creed was not an obstacle here. Although Roman law did preserve the purity of the Roman cult, it is known that the rule of conduct in and out of Rome allowed non-Romans the rights to preserve their own cult, and did not see this as a basis for the exclusion of non-Romans from civil rights.

The charge that our forefathers immigrated here centuries or millennia ago is as fiendish as it is absurd. We are not immigrants; we are native born. And, since that is the case, we have no claim to a home someplace else. We are either German or we are homeless. Does someone seriously wish to use our original, foreign descent against us? Does someone with that civilized status revert back to the barbarous principle of indigenous rights? . . .

Religion has its creed; the state its laws. The confession of a creed constitutes a religious affiliation; obedience to laws determines citizenship in a state. The confusion of these principles leads to misunderstanding, thoughtlessness and falsehood. . . . There is only one baptism that can initiate one into a nationality, and that is the baptism of blood in the common struggle for a fatherland and for freedom. "Your blood was mixed with ours on the battlefield," this was that cry which put an end to the last feeble stirrings of intolerance and antipathy in France.[2] The German Jews also have earned this valid claim to nationality. The Jews in Germany fulfill their military obligations in all instances. They did so even before the Wars of Liberation. They have fought both as conscripts and volunteers in proportionate numbers within the ranks of the German forces. . . .

We the Jews of Germany might indeed enjoy a degree of freedom. But we conceive of freedom differently. We struggle and strive with all of our might to obtain a higher freedom than that which we presently enjoy; we

1. The reference is to the *Constitutio Antoniniana* of 212 C.E. This decree extended Roman citizenship to all free inhabitants of the empire, thus obliterating the distinction between Romans and provincials, between conquerors and conquered, between urban and rural dwellers, and between those who possessed Graeco-Roman culture and those who did not. Promulgated by Caracalla, emperor from 211 to 217 C.E., this legislation culminated a process initiated by Julius Caesar.

2. Even prior to their emancipation, the Jews of France—especially in Bordeaux and Paris—volunteered for the various militias formed during the revolution. This fact was raised and regarded favorably during the debates in the National Assembly concerning the eligibility of Jews for citizenship.

are committed to struggle and to strive [to obtain this freedom] until the very last breath of our lives—this is what we believe makes us worthy to be *German* and to be called *German*. The vigorous tones of the German language and the songs of German poets ignite and nurture the holy fire of freedom in our breast. The breath of freedom which wafts over Germany awakens our dormant hopes for freedom, of which many happy prospects have already been fulfilled. We wish to belong to the German fatherland. We can, and should, and may be required by the German state [to do] all that it justly requires of its citizens. We will readily sacrifice everything for this state: not, however, belief and loyalty, truth and honor, for Germany's heroes and Germany's sages have not taught us that one becomes a German through such sacrifices.

Abraham Mendelssohn, Letter to His Daughter (1820)[1]

My dear Daughter,

You have taken an important step, and in sending you my best wishes for the day and for your future happiness, I have it at heart to speak seriously to you on subjects hitherto not touched upon.

Does God exist? What is God? Is He a part of ourselves, and does He continue to live after the other part has ceased to be? And where? And how? All this I do not know, and therefore I have never taught you anything about it. But I know that there exists in me and in you and in all human beings an everlasting inclination towards all that is good, true, and right, and a conscience which warns and guides us when we go astray. I know it, I believe it, I live in this faith, and this is my religion. This I could not teach you, and nobody can learn it; but everybody has it who does not intentionally and knowingly cast it away. The example of your mother, the best and noblest of mothers, whose whole life is devotion, love and charity, is like a bond to me that you will *not* cast it away. You have grown up under her guidance, ever intuitively receiving and adopting what alone gives real worth to mankind. Your mother has been, and is, and I trust will long remain to you, to your sister and brothers, and to all of us, a providential leading star on our path of life. When you look at her and turn over in your thoughts all the immeasurable good she has lavished upon you by her constant self-sacrificing devotion as long as you live, and when that reflection makes your heart and eyes overflow with gratitude, love, and veneration, then you feel God and are godly.

This is all I can tell you about religion, all I know about it; but this will

From S. Hensel, *The Mendelssohn Family (1729–1847)*, in *Letters and Journals*, vol. 1, 2d revised edition, translated by C. Klingemann (New York, 1882), pp. 79–80.

remain true, as long as one man will exist in the creation, as it has been true since the first man was created.

The outward form of religion your teacher has given you is historical, and changeable like all human ordinances. Some thousands of years ago the Jewish form was the reigning one, then the heathen form, and now it is the Christian. We, your mother and I, were born and brought up by our parents as Jews, and without being obliged to change the form of our religion have been able to follow the divine instinct in us and in our conscience. We have educated you and your brothers and sister in the Christian faith, because it is the creed of most civilized people, and contains nothing that can lead you away from what is good, and much that guides you to love, obedience, tolerance, and resignation, even if it offered nothing but the example of its Founder, understood by so few, and followed by still fewer.

By pronouncing your confession of faith you have fulfilled the claims of *society* on you, and obtained the *name* of a Christian. Now *be* what your duty as a human being demands of you, *true, faithful, good;* obedient and devoted till death to your mother, and I may also say to your father, unremittingly attentive to the voice of your conscience, which may be suppressed but never silenced, and you will gain the highest happiness that is to be found on earth, harmony and contentedness with yourself.

I embrace you with fatherly tenderness, and hope always to find in you a daughter worthy of your, of our, mother. Farewell, and remember my words.

2
The Social Question, Utopian Visions, and the Upheaval at Midcentury

13. Charles Fourier, on the Phalanstery

Charles Fourier (1772–1837), critic of laissez-faire and creator of an alternate, socialist blueprint for the organization of work, was the only son of a successful cloth merchant in Besançon. He was expected to take charge of the family firm when he came of age. But his tastes since childhood had run to music and poetry; he has recounted (perhaps apocryphally) that at the age of seven, he swore an oath, as ardent as Hannibal's against Rome, vowing "an eternal hatred of commerce." Fourier sought in a variety of ways to elude his fate, but he eventually succumbed to a career as a traveling salesman. He abandoned this work only in the last decade of his life when, supported by friends and family, he devoted all his time to his writing.

Fourier liked to point out that his central insight, like that of Isaac Newton, had come to him via an apple. In his case the critical apple was that ordered by a fellow diner in a Paris restaurant in 1798. It cost the man fourteen sous, and Fourier realized to his horror that more than a hundred apples of superior quality and size could be had in Normandy for the same price. At that moment, he later noted, "I began to suspect that the economic system was fundamentally disordered." The analogy with Newton was hardly accidental. A careful reader of Fourier's social theory will recognize the "Newtonianism" of his method and vocabulary.

Fourier published a half-dozen treatises between 1808 and 1836 articulating various aspects of his theory. Having had a spotty formal education, he was largely self-taught, which helps account for his strongly personal, idiosyncratic style of expression. His plan for society and the economy focused upon an artificially constructed community of some 1,600 or 2,000 individuals which he called a phalanstery. He firmly be-

From *Socialist Thought: A Documentary History* (New York: Doubleday, 1964), pp. 129–51. Reprinted by permission of the editors, Albert Fried and Ronald Sanders.

lieved that once a single phalanstery had been founded, the wisdom of the experiment would be apparent to all and the model would be widely copied. To this end, Fourier placed, in his 1823 *Traité de l'association domestique agricole,* a tactful "advertisement" for such a founder, who would need only ten thousand francs to spare. No one showed up. Ever hopeful, Fourier made a practice of being at home in Paris each day between the hours of noon and one o'clock in order to receive the wished-for benefactor. But at the time of Fourier's death, such a person had still not arrived. Fourier did, however, succeed in attracting a small group of French followers, including some adherents of Saint-Simonianism (see document 14), and his ideas caught on in other countries as well. From the 1830s through the 1850s, phalansteries were established in France, the United States (where the most famous was Brook Farm), and even in Rumania.

Marx and Engels classified Fourier among the "utopian socialists," and that label has tended to stick. To others, the whimsical quality of Fourier's thought has made him seem something of a genial madman. But recent commentators have taken seriously Fourier's acute awareness of the psychological exactions of work in industrial society.

The initials at the end of each selection refer, with the volume and page numbers, to the works of Fourier as follows:

QM—*Théorie des quatre mouvements,* 2d edition, 1841.
NM—*Le nouveau monde industriel et sociétaire,* 3d edition, 1848.
UU—*Théorie de l'unité universelle,* 4 vols., 2d edition, 1838.
FI—*La fausse industrie,* 2 vols., 1835–36.
Man.—*Manuscrits de Fourier,* 1851.

Of the Role of the Passions

All those philosophical whims called duties have no relation whatever to Nature; duty proceeds from men, Attraction proceeds from God; now, if we desire to know the designs of God, we must study Attraction, Nature only, without any regard to duty, which varies with every age, while the nature of the passions has been and will remain invariable among all nations of men. (QM 107)

The learned world is wholly imbued with a doctrine termed MORALITY, which is a mortal enemy of passional attraction.

Morality teaches man to be at war with himself, to resist his passions, to repress them, to believe that God was incapable of organizing our souls, our passions wisely; that he needed the teachings of Plato and Seneca in order to know how to distribute characteristics and instincts. Imbued with these prejudices regarding the impotence of God, the learned world was not qualified to estimate the natural impulses or passional attractions, which morality proscribes and relegates to the rank of vices.

It is true that these impulses entice us only to evil, if we yield to them individually; but we must calculate their effect upon a body of about two thousand persons socially combined, and not upon families or isolated individuals: this is what the learned world has not thought of; in studying it, it would have recognized that as soon as the number of associates (*sociétaires*) has reached 1600, the natural impulses, termed attractions, tend to form series of contrasting groups, in which everything incites to industry, become attractive, and to virtue, become lucrative. (NM 125)

The passions, believed to be the enemies of concord, in reality conduce to that unity from which we deem them so far removed. But outside of the mechanism termed *"exalted," emulatory, interlocked Series,* they are but unchained tigers, incomprehensible enigmas. It is this which has caused philosophers to say that we ought to repress them; an opinion doubly absurd inasmuch as we can only repress our passions by *violence* or *absorbing replacement,* which replacement is no repression. On the other hand, should they be efficiently repressed, the civilized order would rapidly decline and relapse into the nomad state, where the passions would still be malevolent as with us. The virtue of shepherds is as doubtful as that of their apologists, and our utopia-makers, by thus attributing virtues to imaginary peoples, only succeed in proving the impossibility of introducing virtue into civilization. (UU 3:33)

We are quite familiar with the five *sensitive* passions tending to Luxury,[1] the four *affective* ones tending to Groups; it only remains for us to learn about the three *distributive* ones whose combined impulse produces *Series,* a social method of which the secret has been lost since the age of primitive mankind, who were unable to maintain the Series more than about 300 years. (QM 118)

The four *affective* passions tending to form the four groups of friendship, love, ambition, paternity or consanguinity are familiar enough; but no analyses, or parallels, or scales have been made of them.

The three others, termed distributive, are totally misunderstod, and bear only the title of VICES, although they are infinitely precious; for these three possess the property of forming and directing the series of groups, the mainspring of social harmony. Since these series are not formed in the civilized order, the three distributive passions cause disorder only. Let us define them. (UU 1:145)

1. Fourier means by this the five senses.

10th. THE CABALIST is the passion that, like love, has the property of confounding ranks, drawing superiors and inferiors closer to each other. Everyone must recall occasions when he has been strongly drawn into some path followed with complete success.

For instance: electoral cabal to elect a certain candidate; cabal on 'Change in the stock-jobbing game; cabal of two pairs of lovers, planning a *partie carrée* without the father's knowledge; a family cabal to secure a desirable match. If these intrigues are crowned with success, the participants become friends; in spite of some anxiety, they have passed happy moments together while conducting the intrigue; the emotions it arouses are necessities of the soul.

Far removed from the insipid calm whose charms are extolled by morality, the cabalistic spirit is the true destination of man. Plotting doubles his resources, enlarges his faculties. Compare the tone of a formal social gathering, its moral, stilted, languishing jargon, with the tone of these same people united in a cabal: they will appear transformed to you; you will admire their terseness, their animation, the quick play of ideas, the alertness of action, of decision; in a word, the rapidity of the spiritual or material motion. This fine development of the human faculties is the fruit of the cabalist or tenth passion, which constantly prevails in the labors and the reunions of a passionate series.

As it always results in some measure of success, and as its groups are all precious to each other, the attraction of the cabals becomes a potent bond of friendship between all the sectaries (*sectaires*), even the most unequal. (UU 4:339)

The general perfection of industry will spring, then, from the passion which is most condemned by the philosophers; the cabalist or dissident, which has never been able to obtain among us the rank of a passion, notwithstanding that it is so strongly rooted even in the philosophers themselves, who are the greatest intriguers in the social world.

The cabalist is a favorite passion of women; they are excessively fond of intrigue, the rivalries and all the greater and lesser flights of a cabal. It is a proof of their eminent fitness for the new social order, where cabals without number will be needed in every series, periodical schisms, in order to maintain a movement of coming and going among the sectaries of the different groups. . . .

12th. THE COMPOSITE.—This passion requires in every action a composite allurement or pleasure of the senses and of the soul, and consequently the blind enthusiasm which is born only of the mingling of the two kinds of pleasure. These conditions are but little compatible with civilized labor, which, far from offering any allurement either to the senses or the soul, is only a double torment even in the most vaunted of work-shops, such as the spinning factories of England where the people, even the children, work fifteen hours a day, under the lash, in premises devoid of air.

The composite is the most beautiful of the twelve passions, the one which enhances the value of all the others. A love is not beautiful unless it is a composite love, combining the charm of the senses and of the soul. It becomes trifling or deception if it limits itself to one of these springs. An ambition is not vehement unless it brings into play the two springs, glory and interest. It is then that it becomes capable of brilliant efforts.

The *composite* commands so great a respect, that all are agreed in despising people inclined to simple pleasure. Let a man provide himself with fine viands, fine wines, with the intention of enjoying them alone, of giving himself up to gormandizing by himself, and he exposes himself to well-merited gibes. But if this man gathers a select company in his house, where one may enjoy at the same time the pleasure of the senses by good cheer, and the pleasure of the soul by companionship, he will be lauded, because these banquets will be a composite and not a simple pleasure.

If general opinion despises simple material pleasure, the same is true as well of simple spiritual pleasure, of gatherings where there is neither refreshment, nor dancing, nor love, nor anything for the senses, where one enjoys oneself only in imagination. Such a gathering, devoid of the *composite* or pleasure of the senses and the soul, becomes insipid to its participants, and it is not long before it "grows bored and dissolves."

11th. THE PAPILLONNE [butterfly] or *Alternating*. Although eleventh according to rank, it should be examined after the twelfth, because it serves as a link between the other two, the tenth and the twelfth. If the sessions of the series were meant to be prolonged twelve or fifteen hours like those of civilized workmen, who, from morning till night, *stupefy themselves* by being engaged in insipid duties without any diversion, God would have given us a taste for monotony, an abhorrence of variety. But as the sessions of the series are to be very short, and the enthusiasm inspired by the composite is incapable of being prolonged beyond an hour and a half, God, in conformity to this industrial order, had to endow us with the passion of *papillonnage*, the craving for periodic variety in the phases of life, and for frequent variety in our occupations. Instead of working twelve hours with a scant intermission for a poor, dull dinner, the associative state will never extend its sessions of labor beyond an hour and a half or at most two; besides, it will diffuse a host of pleasures, reunions of the two sexes terminating in a repast, from which one will proceed to new diversions, with different company and cabals.

Without this hypothesis of associative labor, arranged in the order I have described, it would be impossible to conceive for what purpose God should have given us three passions so antagonistic to the monotony experienced in civilization, and so unreasonable that, in the existing state, they have not even been accorded the rank of passions, but are termed only vices.

A series, on the contrary, could not be organized without the permanent co-operation of these three passions. They are bound to intervene constantly and simultaneously in the serial play of intrigue. Hence it comes that these three passions could not be discerned until the invention of the serial mechanism, and that up to that time they had to be regarded as vices. When the social order for which God has destined us shall be known in detail, it will be seen that these pretended vices, *the Cabalist, the Papillonne, the Composite,* become there three pledges of virtue and riches; that God did indeed know how to create passions such as are demanded by social unity; that He would have been wrong to change them in order to please Seneca and Plato; that on the contrary human reason ought to strive to discover a social condition which shall be in affinity with these passions. No moral theory will ever change them, and, in accordance with the rules of the duality of tendency, they will intervene for ever to lead us TO EVIL in the disjointed state or social limbo, and TO GOOD in the *regime* of association or serial labor. (UU 3:405–11)

The seven "affective" and "distributive" passions depend more upon the spirit than upon matter; they rank as PRIMITIVES. Their combined action engenders a collective passion or one formed by the union of the other seven, as white is formed by the union of the seven colors of a ray of light; I shall call this thirteenth passion *Harmonism* or *Unityism.* . . .

Unityism is the inclination of the individual to reconcile his own happiness with that of all surrounding him, and of all human kind, to-day so odious. It is an unbounded philanthropy, a universal good-will, which can only be developed when the entire human race shall be rich, free, and just. (QM 121)

I shall, in order to dispose others to share my confidence, explain the object of one of these impulses, accounted as vicious.

I select a propensity which is the most general and the most thwarted by education: it is the gluttony of children, their fondness for dainties, in opposition to the advice of the pedagogues who counsel them to like bread, to eat more bread than their allowance.

Nature, then, is very clumsy to endow children with tastes so opposed to sound doctrines! every child regards a breakfast of dry bread as a punishment; he would wish for sugared cream, sweetened milk—food and pastry, marmalades and stewed fruit, raw and preserved fruit, lemonades and orangeades, mild white wines. Let us observe closely these tastes which prevail among all children; on this point a great case is to be adjudged: the question to be determined is who is wrong, God or morality?

God, dispenser of attraction, gives all children a liking for dainties: it was in his power to give them a liking for dry bread and water; it would have suited the views of morality; why then does he knowingly militate against sound civilized doctrines? Let us explain these motives.

God has given children a liking for substances which will be the least costly in the associative state. When the entire globe shall be populated and cultivated, enjoying free-trade, exempt from all duties, the sweet viands mentioned above will be much less expensive than bread; the abundant edibles will be fruit, milk-foods, and sugar, but not bread, whose price will be greatly raised, because the labor incident to the growing of grain and the daily making of bread is wearisome and little attractive; these kinds of labor would have to be paid much higher than that in orchards or confectioneries.

And as it is fitting that the food and maintenance of children should involve less expense than those of their parents, God has acted judiciously in attracting them to those sweetmeats and dainties which will be cheaper than bread as soon as we shall have entered upon the associative state. Then the sound moral doctrines will be found to be altogether erroneous concerning the nourishment of children, as well as upon all other points which oppose attraction. It will be recognized *that God did well what he did,* that he was right in attracting children to milk-foods, fruit, and sweet pastries; and that, instead of foolishly losing three thousand years in declaiming against God's wisest work, against the distribution of tastes and passionate attractions, it would have been better to study its aim, by reckoning with all those impulses combined, which morality insults singly, under the pretext that they are hurtful to the civilized and barbarous orders; this is true, but God did not create the passions for the civilized and barbarous orders. If he had wished to maintain these two forms of society exclusively, he would have given children a fondness for dry bread, and to the parents a love of poverty, since that is the lot of the immense majority of mankind in civilization and barbarism. (NM 23)

In the civilized state, love of eating does not ally itself to industry because the *laboring* producer does not enjoy the commodities which he has cultivated or manufactured. This passion therefore becomes an attribute of the idle; and through that alone it would be vicious, were it not so already by the outlay and the excesses which it occasions.

In the associative state love of eating plays an entirely opposite *rôle;* it is no longer a reward of idleness but of industry; because there the poorest tiller of the soil participates in the consumption of choice commodities. Moreover, its only influence will be to preserve us from excess, by dint of variety, and to stimulate us to work by allying the intrigues of consumption to those of production, preparation, and distribution. Production being the most important of the four, let us first state the principle which must guide it; it is the generalization of epicurism. In point of fact:

If the whole human race could be raised to a high degree of gastronomic refinement, even in regard to the most ordinary kinds of food, such as cabbages and radishes, and everyone be given a competence which would allow him to refuse all edibles which are mediocre in quality or treatment, the result would be that every cultivated country would, after a few years, be covered with delicious productions; for there would be no sale for mediocre ones, such as bitter melons, bitter peaches, which certain kinds of soil yield, upon which neither melons nor peaches would be cultivated; every district would confine itself to productions which its soil is capable of raising to perfection; it would fetch earth for spots where the soil is poor, or perhaps convert them into forests, artificial meadows, or whatever else might yield products of good quality. It is not that the passionate Series do not consume ordinary eatables and stuffs; but they desire, even in ordinary things such as beans and coarse cloth, the most perfect quality possible, in conformity to the proportions which Nature has established in industrial attraction.

The principle which must be our starting-point is, *that a general perfection in industry will be attained by the universal demands and refinement of the consumers, regarding food and clothing, furniture and amusements.* (NM 253)

My theory confines itself to *utilizing the passions now condemned, just as Nature has given them to us and without in any way changing them.* That is the whole mystery, the whole secret of the calculus of passionate Attraction. There is no arguing there whether God was right or wrong in giving mankind these or those passions; the associative order avails itself of them without changing them, and as God has given them to us. (UU 4 : 157)

Its mechanism produces co-incidence in every respect between individual interest and collective interest, in civilization always divergent.

It makes use of men as they are, utilizing the discords arising from antipathies, and other motives accounted vicious, and vindicating the Creator from the reproach of a lacuna in providence, in the matter of general unity and individual foresight.

Finally, it in nowise disturbs the established order, limiting itself to trial on a small scale, which will incite to imitation by the double allurement of quadruple proceeds and attractive industry. (FI 497)

Of Education

There is no problem upon which people have gone more astray than upon public instruction and its methods. Nature has, in this branch of social politics, taken a malign pleasure in all ages in confounding our theories and their exponents, from the time of the disgrace incurred by Seneca, the instructor of Nero, to that of the failures of Condillac and Rousseau, of whom the first fashioned only a political idiot and the second did not dare to undertake the education of his own children. (UU 4:1)

It will be observed that in Harmony the only paternal function of the father is to yield to his natural impulse, to spoil the child, to humor all his whims.

The child will be sufficiently reproved and rallied by his peers. When an infant or little child has in the course of the day passed through half a dozen such groups and undergone their jokes, he is thoroughly imbued with a sense of his insufficiency, and quite disposed to listen to the advice of the patriarchs and venerables who are good enough to offer him instruction.

It will, after that, be of little consequence that the parents at the child's bed-time indulge themselves in spoiling him, telling him that he has been treated too severely, that he is really very charming, very clever; these effusions will only skim the surface, they will not convince. The impression has been made. He is humbled by the railleries of seven or eight groups of little ones which he has visited during the day. In vain will it be for the father and mother to tell him that the children who have repulsed him are barbarians, enemies of social intercourse, of gentleness and kindliness; all these parental platitudes will have no effect, and the child on returning to the infantile seristeries the following day will remember only the affronts of the day before; it is he who in reality will cure the father of the habit of SPOILING, by redoubling his efforts and proving that he is conscious of his inferiority. (UU 4:33)

Nature endows every child with a great number of instincts in industry, about thirty, of which some are primary or guiding and lead to those that are secondary.

The point is to discover first of all the primary instincts: the child will seize this bait as soon as it is presented to him; accordingly, as soon as he is able to walk, to leave the infant seristery, the male and female nurses in whose charge he is placed hasten to conduct him to all the workshops and all the industrial reunions which are close by; and as he finds everywhere diminutive tools, an industry in miniature, in which little tots of from two and a half to three years already engage, with whom he is anxious to associate, to rummage about, to handle things, at the end of a fortnight one may discern what are the workshops that attract him, what his industrial instincts.

The phalanx containing an exceedingly great variety of occupations, it is impossible that the child in passing from one to the other should not find opportunities of satisfying several of his dominant instincts; these will exhibit themselves at the sight of the little tools manipulated by other children a few months older than himself.

According to civilized parents and teachers, *children are little idlers;*

nothing is more erroneous; children are already at two and three years of age very industrious, but we must know the springs which Nature wishes to put in action to attract them to industry *in the passionate series and not in civilization*.

The dominant tastes in all children are:

1. *Rummaging* or inclination to handle everything, examine everything, look through everything, to constantly change occupations.
2. Industrial *commotion*, taste for noisy occupations.
3. *Aping* or imitative mania.
4. Industrial *miniature*, a taste for miniature workshops.
5. *Progressive attraction* of the weak toward the strong.

There are many others; I limit myself to naming these five first, which are very familiar to the civilized. Let us examine the method to be followed in order to apply them to industry at an early age.

The male and female nurses will first exploit the mania for rummaging so dominant in a child of two. He wants to peer into every place, to handle and examine everything he sees. He is consequently obliged to be kept apart, in a bare room, otherwise he would destroy everything.

This propensity to handle everything is a bait to industry; to draw him to it, he will be conducted to the little workshops; there he will see children only two and a half and three years old using little tools, little hammers. He will wish to exercise his imitative mania, termed APING; he will be given some tools, but he will want to be admitted among the children of twenty-six and twenty-seven months who know how to work, and who will repel him.

He will persist if the work coincides with any of his instincts; the nurse or the patriarch will teach him some portion of the work, and he will very soon succeed in making himself useful in some trifling things which will serve him as an introduction; let us examine this effect in regard to an inconsiderable kind of labor, within the reach of the smallest children,—the shelling and sorting of green peas. This work which with us would occupy the hands of people of thirty, will be consigned to children of two, three, four years of age: the hall is provided with inclined tables containing a number of hollows; two little ones are seated at the raised side; they take the peas out of the shell, the inclination of the table causes the grains to roll towards the lower side where three tots are placed of twenty-five, thirty, thirty-five months, charged with the task of sorting, and furnished with special implements.

The thing to be done is to separate the smallest peas for the sweetened ragout, the medium ones for the bacon ragout, and the largest for the soup. The child of thirty-five months first selects the little ones which are the most difficult to pick out; she sends all the large and medium ones to the next hollow, where the child of thirty months shoves those that seem large to the third hollow, returns the little ones to the first, and drops the medium grains into the basket. The infant of twenty-five months, placed at the third hollow, has an easy task; he returns some medium grains to the second, and gathers the large ones into his basket.

It is in this third rank that the infant *débutant* will be placed; he will mingle proudly with the others in throwing the large grains into the basket; it is very trifling work, but he will feel as if he had accomplished as much as his companions; he will grow enthusiastic and be seized by a spirit of emulation, and at the third *séance* he will be able to replace the infant of twenty-five months, to send back the grains of the second size into the second compartment, and to gather up only the largest ones, which are easily distinguished. (NM 181)

The Phalanstery

The announcement does, I acknowledge, sound very improbable, of a method for combining three hundred families unequal in fortune, and rewarding each person,—man, woman, child—according to the three properties, *capital, labor, talent.* More than one reader will credit himself with humor when he remarks: "Let the author try to associate but three families, to reconcile three households in the same dwelling to social union, to arrangements of purchases and expenses, to perfect harmony in passions, character, and authority; when he shall have succeeded in reconciling three mistresses of associated households, we shall believe that he can succeed with thirty and with three hundred."

I have already replied to an argument which it is well to reproduce (for repetition will frequently be necessary here); I have observed *that as economy can spring only from large combinations, God had to create a social theory applicable to large masses and not to three or four families.* (UU 2:29)

If social experiments have miscarried, it is because some fatality has impelled all speculators to work with bodies of poor people whom they subjected to a *monastic-industrial* discipline, chief obstacle to the working of the series. Here, as in everything else, it is ever SIMPLISM (*simplisme*) which misleads the civilized, obstinately sticking to experiments with combinations of the poor; they cannot elevate themselves to the conception of a trial with combinations of the rich. They are veritable Lemming rats (migrating rats of Lapland), preferring drowning in a pond to deviating from the route which they have decided upon. (UU 3:156)

It is necessary for a company of 1,500 to 1,600 persons to have a stretch of land comprising a good square league, say a surface of six million square *toises* (do not let us forget that a third of that would suffice for the simple mode).

The land should be provided with a fine stream of water; it should be intersected by hills, and adapted to varied cultivation; it should be contiguous to a forest, and not far removed from a large city, but sufficiently so to escape intruders.

The experimental Phalanx standing alone, and without the support of neighboring phalanxes, will, in consequence of this isolation, have so many gaps in attraction, and so many passional calms to dread in its workings, that it will be necessary to provide it with the aid of a good location fitted for a variety of functions. A flat country such as Antwerp, Leipsic, Orleans, would be totally unsuitable, and would cause many Series to fail, owing to the uniformity of the land surface. It will, therefore, be necessary to select a diversified region, like the surroundings of Lausanne, or, at the very least, a fine valley provided with a stream of water and a forest, like the valley of Brussels or of Halle. A fine location near Paris would be the stretch of country lying between Poissy and Confleurs, Poissy and Meulan.

A company will be collected consisting of from 1,500 to 1,600 persons of graduated degrees of fortune, age, character, of theoretical and practical knowledge; care will be taken to secure the greatest amount of variety possible, for the greater the number of variations either in the passions or the faculties or the members, the easier will it be to make them harmonize in a short space of time.

In this district devoted to experiment, there ought to be combined every species of practicable cultivation, including that in conservatories and hot-houses; in addition, there ought to be at least three accessory factories, to be used in winter and on rainy days; furthermore, various practical branches of science and the arts, independent of the schools.

Above all, it will be necessary to fix the valuation of the capital invested in shares; lands, materials, flocks, implements, etc. This point ought, it seems, to be among the first to receive attention; I think it best to dismiss it here. I shall limit myself to remarking that all these investments in transferable shares and stock-coupons will be represented.

A great difficulty to be overcome in the experimental Phalanx will be the formation of the ties of high mechanism or collective bonds of the Series, before the close of the first season. It will be necessary to accomplish the passional union of the mass of the members; to lead them to collective and individual devotion to the maintenance of the Phalanx, and, especially, to perfect harmony regarding the division of the profits, according to the three factors, *Capital, Labor, Talent.*

This difficulty will be greater in northern than in southern countries, owing to the difference between devoting eight months and five months to agricultural labor. (UU 3:427, 429)

Let us proceed with the details of composition.

At least seven-eighths of the members ought to be cultivators and manu-facturers; the remainder will consist of capitalists, scholars, and artists.

The Phalanx would be badly graded and difficult to balance, if among its capitalists there were several having 100,000 francs, several 50,000 francs, without intermediate fortunes. In such a case it would be necessary to seek to procure intermediate fortunes of 60,000, 70,000, 80,000, 90,000 francs. The Phalanx best graduated in every respect raises social harmony and profits to the highest degree. (UU 3:431)

Attractive Labor

In the civilized mechanism we find everywhere composite unhappiness in-stead of composite charm. Let us judge of it by the case of labor. It is, says the Scripture very justly, a punishment of man: Adam and his issue are con-demned to earn their bread by the sweat of their brow. That, already, is an affliction; but this labor, this ungrateful labor upon which depends the earning of our miserable bread, we cannot even get it! a laborer lacks the labor upon which his maintenance depends,—he asks in vain for a tribula-tion! He suffers a second, that of obtaining work at times whose fruit is his master's and not his, or of being employed in duties to which he is entirely unaccustomed. . . . The civilized laborer suffers a third affliction through the maladies with which he is generally stricken by the excess of labor demanded by his master. . . . He suffers a fifth affliction, that of being de-spised and treated as a beggar because he lacks those necessaries which he consents to purchase by the anguish of repugnant labor. He suffers, finally, a sixth affliction, in that he will obtain neither advancement nor sufficient wages, and that to the vexation of present suffering is added the perspec-tive of future suffering, and of being sent to the gallows should he demand that labor which he may lack to-morrow. (Man. 208)

Labor, nevertheless, forms the delight of various creatures, such as beavers, bees, wasps, ants, which are entirely at liberty to prefer inertia: but God has provided them with a social mechanism which attracts to in-dustry, and causes happiness to be found in industry. Why should he not have accorded us the same favor as these animals? What a difference be-tween their industrial condition and ours! A Russian, an Algerian, work from fear of the lash or the bastinado; an Englishman, a Frenchman, from fear of the famine which stalks close to his poor household; the Greeks and the Romans, whose freedom has been vaunted to us, worked as slaves, and from fear of punishment, like the negroes in the colonies to-day. (UU 2:249)

Associative labor, in order to exert a strong attraction upon people, will have to differ in every particular from the repulsive conditions which render it so odious in the existing state of things. It is necessary, in order that it become attractive, that associative labor fulfil the following seven conditions:

1. That every laborer be a partner, remunerated by dividends and not by wages.
2. That every one, man, woman, or child, be remunerated in proportion to the three faculties, *capital, labor,* and *talent.*
3. That the industrial sessions be varied about eight times a day, it being impossible to sustain enthusiasm longer than an hour and a half or two hours in the exercise of agricultural or manufacturing labor.
4. That they be carried on by bands of friends, united spontaneously, interested and stimulated by very active rivalries.
5. That the workshops and husbandry offer the laborer the allurements of elegance and cleanliness.
6. That the division of labor be carried to the last degree, so that each sex and age may devote itself to duties that are suited to it.
7. That in this distribution, each one, man, woman, or child, be in full enjoyment of the right to labor or the right to engage in such branch of labor as they may please to select, provided they give proof of integrity and ability.

X^2 Finally, that, in this new order, people possess a guarantee of well-being, of a minimum sufficient for the present and the future, and that this guarantee free them from all uneasiness concerning themselves and their families.

We find all these properties combined in the associative mechanism, whose discovery I make public. (UU 2:15)

In order to attain happiness, it is necessary to introduce it into the labors which engage the greater part of our lives. Life is a long torment to one who pursues occupations without attraction. Morality teaches us to love work: let it know, then, how to render work lovable, and, first of all, let it introduce luxury into husbandry and the workshop. If the arrangements are poor, repulsive, how arouse industrial attraction?

In work, as in pleasure, variety is evidently the desire of nature. Any enjoyment prolonged, without interruption, beyond two hours, conduces to satiety, to abuse, blunts our faculties, and exhausts pleasure. A repast of four hours will not pass off without excess; an opera of four hours will end by cloying the spectator. Periodical variety is a necessity of the body and of

---

2. The sign X, in the language of Fourier, serves to designate that which is "pivotal," that is to say, fundamental, in enumeration.

the soul, a necessity in all nature; even the soil requires alteration of seeds, and seed alteration of soil. The stomach will soon reject the best dish if it be offered every day, and the soul will be blunted in the exercise of any virtue if it be not relieved by some other virtue.

If there is need of variety in pleasure after indulging in it for two hours, so much the more does labor require this diversity, which is continual in the associative state, and is guaranteed to the poor as well as the rich. (UU 1:147)

The chief source of light-heartedness among Harmonians is the frequent change of sessions. Life is a perpetual torment to our workmen, who are obliged to spend twelve, and frequently fifteen, consecutive hours in some tedious labor. Even ministers are not exempt; we find some of them complain of having passed an entire day in the stupefying task of affixing signatures to thousands of official vouchers. Such wearisome duties are unknown in the associative order; the Harmonians, who devote an hour, an hour and a half, or at most two hours, to the different sessions, and who, in these short sessions, are sustained by cabalistic impulses and by friendly union with selected associates, cannot fail to bring and to find cheerfulness everywhere. . . .

The radical evil of our industrial system is the employment of the laborer in a single occupation, which runs the risk of coming to a stand-still. The fifty thousand workmen of Lyons who are beggars to-day (besides fifty thousand women and children), would be scattered over two or three hundred phalanxes, which would make silk their principal article of manufacture, and which would not be thrown out by a year or two of stagnation in that branch of industry. If at the end of that time their factory should fail completely, they would start one of a different kind, without having stopped work, without ever making their daily subsistence dependent upon a continuation or suspension of outside orders. (FI)

In a progressive series all the groups acquire so much the more skill in that their work is greatly subdivided, and that every member engages only in the kind in which he professes to excel. The heads of the Series, spurred on to study by rivalry, bring to their work the knowledge of a student of the first rank. The subordinates are inspired with an ardor which laughs at all obstacles, and with a fanaticism for the maintenance of the honor of the Series against rival districts. In the heat of action they accomplish what seems humanly impossible, like the French grenadiers who scaled the rocks of Mahon, and who, upon the day following, were unable, in cold blood, to clamber up the rock which they had assailed under the fire of the enemy. Such are the progressive Series in their work; every obstacle vanished before the intense pride which dominates them; they would grow angry at the word *impossible,* and the most daunting kinds of labor, such as

managing the soil, are to them the lightest of sports. If we could to-day
behold an organized district, behold at early dawn thirty industrial groups
issue in state from the palace of the Phalanx, and spread themselves over
the fields and the workshops, waving their banners with cries of triumph
and impatience, we should think we were gazing at bands of madmen intent upon putting the neighboring districts to fire and sword. Such will be
the athletes who will take the place of our mercenary and languid workmen, and who will succeed in making ambrosia and nectar grow upon a
soil which yields only briers and tares to the feeble hands of the civilized.
(QM 244)

14. The Trial of the Saint-Simonians in the Court of Assizes of Paris (27–28 August 1832)

Saint-Simonianism was one of the several varieties of French socialism
propagated during the 1830s and 1840s. It drew its inspiration from
Claude-Henri de Rouvroy, Comte de Saint-Simon (1760–1825), a scion
of the old nobility whose ideas verged upon but stopped short of socialism. Saint-Simon's thought had a strong technocratic strain. Opposed
to a system of laissez-faire, he believed that both the management of the
economy and the government of the state should be placed in the hands
of experts in finance and engineering. Thus in his famous Parable, he
contrasted hypothetically the consequences to France of the death of all
her nobles and administrative officials—these would be quite minimal,
he said—with the truly disastrous consequences of the death of all her
scientists, artisans, industrialists, and bankers. Toward the end of his life,
Saint-Simon became preoccupied with the need to found a new religion
suitable to the industrial age. The same unlikely combination of technocratic and moral-religious themes can be found in the work of his
disciples.

Saint-Simon's disciples emerged upon the scene and articulated their
doctrine in a series of public lectures in Paris in 1828–29. As the doctrine developed over the next few years, it added to the characteristic
themes of the mentor a commitment to better the lot of the working class,
a strong condemnation of private property and inheritance, and a call to
renovate the relations between men and women and to raise the status of
women in society. In addition to its lectures in Paris, the group published

From *Religion Saint-Simonienne: Procès en la Cour d'Assises de la Seine, les 27 et
28 août 1832* (Paris: Librairie Saint-Simonienne, 1832), pp. 53–57, 60–64, 73-76, 161–
70. Translated for this volume by Paula Wissing.

a newspaper and sent missions to the French provinces and Belgium. The doctrine became known to the entire European intelligentsia. Among its sympathizers outside of France in the early 1830s were the Englishmen J. S. Mill and Thomas Carlyle and a group called Young Germany, which included the poet Heinrich Heine.

Chief among the French Saint-Simonians was Barthélemy Prosper Enfantin (1796–1864), an engineer by training who exercised an almost charismatic power over the group. Under Enfantin's direction, they repaired to Ménilmontant, outside Paris, early in 1832 and lived there in communitarian fashion.

That the French government brought the Saint-Simonians to trial in 1832 says as much about the attitudes of the leaders of the July Monarchy as it docs about the attitudes of the Saint-Simonians themselves. The mentalities of both accuser and accused are illuminated in the selections from the trial reprinted here.

The court found the Saint-Simonians guilty as charged and sentenced the leaders to a year's imprisonment. This interruption of their activities weakened the momentum and solidarity of the group. Upon his release from prison, Enfantin led a pilgrimage to Egypt to search (unsuccessfully) for the Female Messiah—that is, his necessary female counterpart in the priestly couple that was to guide the Saint-Simonian religion. Taking another tack, Michel Chevalier (1806–79) became interested in the development of the French railroads and in 1840 was named professor of political economy at the Collège de France. In light of Chevalier's testimony at the trial (see pp. 181–84), it is not surprising to learn that he and other Saint-Simonians made their most lasting contributions as economic advisers to the Second Empire, pioneering the new banking and credit system that aided France's notable industrial spurt in the 1860s and floating the loan for the building of the Suez Canal. This seeming metamorphosis of Saint-Simonianism from a plan for socialism in the 1830s to a support for capitalism some three decades later was not entirely a metamorphosis at all.

Speech by the Prosecuting Attorney

The Prosecutor begins his speech as follows:

The Saint-Simonians have placed themselves outside of society; they have wanted to put themselves beyond the law. Today justice brings these men before you, and, it should be said, we are almost embarrassed by the way in which we must present this case.

The accused are brought before you for having formed an unauthorized association;[1] they are brought before you for having spoken against public morality and good conduct. We could restrict ourselves to saying, "They are accused of forming an illegal association; they admit it." We could restrict ourselves to saying to you, "They have published writings that attack public morality; read their writings." However, gentlemen, by doing so we would perhaps fail to satisfy all that this indictment demands. Why, in fact, was the authorization not given? Wasn't their association merely ridiculous? That is what you would like to know. It is because there was danger along with ridiculousness that justice has pursued them.

For some time the name of Saint-Simon has resounded. He has been made into a man almost divine. There was a desire to make of him something more than the propagator of a doctrine. Who was this Saint-Simon?

Saint-Simon is not a man of the distant past. He is our contemporary. We look in the books setting forth his doctrines, in the books written by the accused, and we discover that Saint-Simon belonged to an illustrious family, which he claimed dated back to the most renowned origins. At first he followed the military calling, and, back when liberty seemed to flower for us, he took part in the American war. It is said that at that time Saint-Simon had his valet awaken him each morning with the phrase, "Wake up, Count, you have great things to do." Was that a way of doing great things? Was it pride or simply a way to substitute bombast for true grandeur? It is for the wisdom of men to decide. Whatever the case, Saint-Simon, after fighting with courage, returned to France, and the books written by the people who appear before you today tell us that he was then involved in speculations concerning the sale of *émigrés'* goods. At first he was successful and made a great deal of money, but soon paper currency[2] brought about his ruin.

Ruined, Saint-Simon became an agitator. He wrote several works containing ideas of high moral tone. At that time, however, he was impoverished and attempted suicide. He did not succeed; the shot he directed at himself was not a mortal one and he was revived. It was then, say the Saint-Simonian writers, that, wounded, he dreamed and came to perfect his doctrine. He said that property was divided in an unworthy fashion. What is an inheritance law that apportions wealth unequally and not according to

1. A provision of the French penal code stipulated that associations of more than twenty persons be allowed to meet only with the prior approval of the government. The rigor with which the July Monarchy enforced this provision indicates its strong fear of subversive political movements—in other words, of the revival of the radical movements of the French Revolution.—ED.

2. The reference is to the *assignats,* the paper currency issued during the French Revolution. Within several years, its value had become severely inflated.—ED.

merit! It was necessary to reform the world. Property must be divided according to talent, and the patriarchal management of wealth and of inheritance must be replaced by a general administration. There must be in other words a sort of managerial church which does not restrict itself to governing things spiritual but administers all temporal property and distributes revenue. It was a dream, a dream like many others. He fell asleep in this dream.

Saint-Simon was our contemporary. He was called before the Court of Assizes, where his doctrine was attacked.

The legacy of Saint-Simon's ideas was entrusted to a number of men, who tried to revive them. Olinde Rodrigues, who had lived closely with him, was best acquainted with the heart of Saint-Simon's thought. Olinde Rodrigues and Enfantin had been joined in a partnership where they had made some money. They founded a journal called the *Producteur.* They wanted to disseminate Saint-Simon's ideas among us, but the journal was unsuccessful.

In 1830, despite the *Producteur*'s lack of success, one began to hear talk of the Saint-Simonian religion, of this *conjecture.* . . . That term may seem severe, but it is precise.

A newspaper, the *Globe,* purchased by the Saint-Simonians, spread their doctrines among the public, and there was a hall where people came to hear the new morality being preached.

The authorities, gentlemen, thought that this morality was dangerous, that it tended to sow in the bosom of society the seeds of all kinds of corruption. The authorities investigated the effects of these doctrines and saw that they militated against good conduct, that they tended to stir up trouble, to destroy the principles upon which society is based. Thus, gentlemen, the authorities decided to act. The Saint-Simonians protested that they were being persecuted. You will see whether it was persecution or rather a measure needed to protect society, and you will see up to what point special doctrines, even special clothing, can be permitted.

The Saint-Simonians held meetings of more than twenty people on rue Taitbout and in Ménilmontant. What was behind these gatherings? What was their goal?

Before you is a man, Enfantin. Judge him as a man. He was formerly a student at the Ecole Polytechnique, where he acquired skills. Like all citizens, he could have utilized his acquired knowledge for the benefit of his country. Well, gentlemen, for the Saint-Simonians, Enfantin is no longer a man. Enfantin is the Father. He is the supreme Father, the Father of all. Not only that, he is the living law of humanity! And this statement comes from the mouths of the Saint-Simonians, from Enfantin's own mouth. You will see just how far these superstitions go. You are going to judge by the writings before you how Father Enfantin is described by those around him and by himself.

Here is a speech delivered during a religious ceremony. We read in the *Globe* of 5 December, "You are the living law of humanity, undoubtedly imperfect (Father Enfantin lacked a wife); in you I love God's highest manifestation in humanity."

Here are expressions used by the preachers in Ménilmontant: "You feel the movements of the external world, the storms of humanity, . . . you foresee events."

If it were misguided youths who spoke this way, you would hardly be astonished. But Father Enfantin says of himself, "I told you that I was not your president, nor even a teacher, I am not even a priest. . . . I am the FATHER of humanity. . . . If someone protests against the authority that I assume, let him withdraw. . . ."

In a time when men are tormented by a vain desire for fame, there are those who divulge extraordinary pretensions. But where, gentlemen, can we see someone in whom this thirst for fame has prompted such prodigious language?

What is the goal of the Saint-Simonian family? Why are there so many apostles?

We have spoken of the group from a financial standpoint. A Saint-Simonian apostle, however high his position, is a man, and this apostle must live. Among these apostles we see a lawyer giving up his practice, a doctor giving up medicine, a speculator on the market giving up his speculating. . . . These occupations offer a living, but doctrine does not.

In a piece addressed to the supreme father we see that the cost of maintaining the apostles for a period of nine months came to 72,000 francs.

The Saint-Simonians had used every possible means to spread their doctrines, but these means led to expenses. They had a house on rue Monsigny. They had handsome drawing rooms where they entertained many people. For that they needed money. To get money they asked it of everyone. Then they asked for more in other ways. . . .

And now to make you appreciate the Saint-Simonian morality, we could cite the objections that arose against the chiefs of the doctrine, we could speak of the complaints lodged by fathers of children. Young men renounced the father that nature had given them to take on another, to recognize Father Enfantin! We could tell you of men who abjured their own brothers to embrace Saint-Simonian brothers.

The Saint-Simonians form a group. This group aims to meet on certain days in numbers of more than twenty to concern itself with religious and political matters. They have said, "We profess a religion; the law protects all religions; we must be protected like the others." But religion is the worship of God in a thousand different forms. It is faith in a future that everyone can imagine in different ways according to his own faith. It is religious ceremonies that can accompany this worship—and not all religious ceremonies can be tolerated. But the distinctive character of every religion, gentlemen, is that it takes no action concerning the material world, that it restricts itself to reigning in the spiritual domain. Would you call religion a doctrine whose goal is to exercise a constant action on secular society, especially if it claimed to disorganize it? Would you call religion the deed of men who pool their fortunes, who give themselves a leader, and who act against the social order? No, undoubtedly you will say that these men are beyond all religion. The law is not intended to reach down into private consciences but to protect and facilitate the expression of each individual's religious sentiments. Yet at the same time the law was not intended to permit associations that take religion as their pretext, that concern themselves with the temporal world and attack society itself.

There is a great association, gentlemen. It is the country as a whole. All of us—citizens, judges, soldiers—we form a vast association comprising the whole country. We are associated under the authority of the law. This association has a goal, that of its preservation. It would neglect its future if it did not see to its own preservation. Now, if a smaller society says we will work with all our strength, all our power to destroy the great society, we will work toward this by setting up a leader, by obeying his orders—if a private society organizes this way, if, by proclaiming its principles of disorganization and corruption and by its obstinacy in spreading them, it tends to compromise us with foreign ministries, if it works openly for the destruction of the social order, the great society must repulse and dissolve it because the great society, which needs to survive, must prevent upheavals and repel whatever attacks it. Those of us who form the great society come to you asking for the dissolution of the lesser one.

Look in their writings to see if they attack society.

They attack private property. They attack the legal position of women. They proclaim themselves to be the workers' political party.

When did they call themselves the workers' political party? During the trouble in Lyons.[3] They said then that the disturbances in that city were

3. Lyons, in southeastern France, was the largest industrial town on the Continent during the early nineteenth century. It was a one-industry town, a producer of silk; but it was not, until the introduction of power-driven silk looms late in the century, a factory town. After a long period of falling wages, the Lyons silk workers staged an uprising in 1831 and again in 1834, events that naturally alarmed the government of the July Monarchy and that Friedrich Engels later called the first proletarian revolution. The Saint-Simonians had sent a mission to Lyons in 1830 to proselytize among the silk workers, and they often claimed (surely inaccurately) to be responsible for the uprising.—Ed.

the result of the workers' political party. "All theories of constitutional equilibrium fell under the bullets of Lyons. Society is going to be concerned with this new form of politics which we have initiated. A year from now," they said, "both French politics and European politics will be Saint-Simonian politics."

Let us see how they seek to influence the people.

At a time of danger for the country, at a time when each individual had an obligation to fulfill his role as citizen, at a time when juries sat in the public square to reestablish order, at a time when the sanctuary of justice was closed, when the canon sounded and blood flowed,[4] the Saint-Simonians were engaged in making an impact on the people. They sought whatever external means, whatever trickery they could find to succeed in making an effect. They were concerned with their clothing![5]

When you were carrying out your duties as a citizen, they were renouncing theirs! What was the one they called FATHER doing at that time? He distributed the various districts of Paris among his disciples. Each one had a faubourg under his control, with the order to mingle with the people, and he was dismissed if he failed to act. . . . (Astonishment among the accused apostles.) Gentlemen, I speak from your books. (The Prosecutor holds up a pamphlet called "Ménilmontant Retreat," 6 June.) We have a society, we have a social order. Good or bad, we must preserve it. (Murmurs from the audience.) We say that we members of the great family must fight any private association that has agents in the neighborhoods to attack this family.

Now we are going to accuse the Saint-Simonians of professing immorality.

The sentiment of public morality is in your hearts, gentlemen. You know what it requires, you know what it permits you to say and what it orders you to keep silent about.

Before coming to the reading of the indicted writings, perhaps we should ask ourselves what the moral doctrine of the Saint-Simonians is.

Here it is in brief:

Women are exploited because they have an inferior station in society; it must be raised.

4. The prosecutor is referring to the events in Paris on 5–6 June 1832, when the funeral of a general who had led the republican armies during the revolutionary era became the occasion for a republican insurrection in several parts of the capital.—Ed.

5. After the establishment of their community at Ménilmontant, the Saint-Simonians adopted a brightly colored costume consisting of white trousers, a red vest, a blue-violet tunic, and a variety of sashes and headdresses. Each of the colors carried symbolic meaning. The red, for example, symbolized labor and, by extension, the Saint-Simonians' commitment to the working class. The Saint-Simonians appeared at their trial wearing these outfits.—Ed.

In all times the principles of good and evil have been recognized. In religion there has been an attempt to personify these two principles. God has been recognized as the good and Satan as the evil. In the Christian religion these two principles have been recognized. The principle of good is the spirit; that of evil is the flesh.

But the Saint-Simonian religion is a religion of progress. It is thus nec-esssary to rehabilitate the flesh. To accomplish this, it is not necessary to keep the flesh from yielding but only to eradicate the idea that the short-comings of the flesh are transgressions. Man is put in the world to be happy; God would not have created him for anything else. Now, if the ma-terial part of man demands satisfaction, man would not be happy if this material part were not satisfied.

But how will it be satisfied?

The world is composed of people who are constant and others who are fickle, who love change. By current morality, how is it possible to satisfy those who love change? It is thus necessary to establish a morality that sat-isfies both the man of stable affection and the man of changeable affection. There are two great types of these affections, found in Othello and in Don Juan: Othello, the man of deep affection, and Don Juan, the man of fleeting affections. Othello and Don Juan are blameworthy men, however, because both of them are exaggerated. Both overdo their passion.

You will say that we are exaggerating the Saint-Simonian principles to support our case. No, gentlemen, we are toning them down. Our modesty prevents us from repeating all that they have said and printed. . . .

Statement Made by Michel Chevalier

MICHEL CHEVALIER: I come now to the events of the 5th and 6th of June.[6] We [Saint-Simonians] did in fact intervene in these events, and I wish to thank the Prosecutor for giving me the opportunity to speak about it here.

The government had put Paris in a state of siege, and that in turn put the government itself in a delicate position. The FATHER decided that the time was ripe for me to approach the chancellor to tell him how our policy could provide the government with an honorable way of extricating itself from the difficult situation it had gotten itself into, a way that would be ad-vantageous for everyone. . . . I explained to the chancellor that the gov-ernment . . . must quickly take the initiative concerning highly charged questions of material interest and property, questions that needed to be ap-proached with the greatest wisdom. For if the first persons to raise these

---

6. See note 4.—ED.

questions were angry men, as were found in the opposition, they would be likely to make matters more acute and increase the government's difficulties still more.

The Judge, interrupting him: The Court refuses to hear your theories.

MICHEL CHEVALIER: We are here because of theories.

The FATHER: I ask you to tell us, your Honor, why we are here before the jury. We are here because of theories of morality and we must respond to the prosecutor's attacks.

Judge: You have been responding for eight hours.

The FATHER: As many hours for our defense, as months of accusations, defamation, hearings.

MICHEL CHEVALIER: If the Prosecuting Attorney will retract his assertion that our doctrines are dangerous to public order, I will immediately drop the subject. But as long as he persists in this accusation, we are within our rights in maintaining that we are and have been the most solid support of the true order in France.

The FATHER: The course of action with respect to the chancellor was taken; it is not an invention. It is not a dream.

MICHEL CHEVALIER: I raised the question of amortization with the chancellor. (The Judge stirs.) You know, gentlemen, that among taxes there is one that particularly riles the populace. One of its complaints against the imperial regime was this tax. It was to the cries of "No more conscription, no more combined excises [on salt, tobacco, and liquor]" that the Restoration was accomplished in France. I recalled to the chancellor that we had indicated in the *Globe* the practical way to eliminate this odious tax by abolishing the onerous fiction of amortization without raising the people's charges by one centime. I will omit the details I presented on this question.

The tolls (the Judge stirs in his seat), tolls are taxes hated by the working classes living in the cities. It is a tax with a poor basis, for tolls are collected by internal customs houses; moreover, their revenue is slight. For the whole of France this revenue amounts to only 40 million francs of which 25 million comes from Paris. The elimination of the toll barriers would be a really sterling political act. A government that decided upon it would be blessed by the Parisian populace. It would earn the name of father, or at least friend, of the people, a title few governments have obtained today. The revenue from amortization comes to about 90 million francs; this sum would be sufficient to replace the tolls for two years, and there would still be 10 million francs left to pay indemnities to the tollhouse employees, for we want everyone to live. The policy that does not fear to create victims is a bad one. Try this for two years, I said. You will do well by it. (Signs of impatience from the Judge.)

Gentlemen, it seems that it was not possible to follow this advice, for instead of being eliminated, the tolls have just been increased.

I also spoke to him of the horrible scenes of the Vendée.[7] (Exclamation from the Judge, "When will you come to the end of this?") You will never get to the end of this, I told him, as far as the soldiers are concerned. Here you are, dealing with poor and ignorant people who mistrust you. Give them a sense of well-being; flood them with the light of knowledge; win their confidence with favors. And for that here is what you must do.

Then I outlined a financial and industrial project which, by increasing the state's investment in stock to a sum of 358 thousand francs, we could obtain 50 million, which would be spread throughout the Vendée in agricultural improvements and communications centers. I showed him how there would soon be increased income well above these 358 thousand francs.

In a word, I told him, today you have dictatorial power; it is not a question of how you came to this power. The fact is that you have it. Take advantage of it to endow France in the most expeditious way with a multitude of invaluable improvements. I will tell you about a few more of them. (Signs of impatience from the Judge.)

Then I explained to him how, with a sum of four to five million, it would be possible to pay for the education of five hundred young men who each year would bring to industry knowledge gained at the Ecole Polytechnique, the School of Mines, Bridges, and Roads, the School of Forestry, trade schools, manufacturing schools, etc.

The Judge, who consulted the lawyers: You wish to establish a complete system of political economy, after your fashion. I insist that the court can no longer hear you.

MICHEL CHEVALIER: I intended to say here that these elements, which many take to be a policy of disorganization and which have been presented to you as such, have in them elements of order and prosperity.

The Judge: The court has said it will no longer hear you.

---

7. This region in the west of France was one of the chief loci of counterrevolutionary activity during the 1790s. The government of the July Monarchy feared the Vendéens' continued support of the House of Bourbon and their disloyalty to the new regime.—ED.

The FATHER: That is enough, Michel. The jury must have gotten an idea of the distance that lies between our policy and one of disorder from this brief discussion.

MICHEL CHEVALIER takes his seat. . . .

Testimony of Mr. Lambert

I go on to the moral order.

The FATHER and some of my brothers are under accusation for speaking bold words on the liberation of women.

First, I say that the obvious sign of your moral incapacity to appreciate these words is that only men are in this courtroom. There are no women here.

(The Judge and lawyers smile.)

It is doubtless unfortunate that serious men find cause for amusement in the observation I just made. But this laughter, in this chamber, is proof of the urgency of our intervention in the world. This laughter requires me to develop an idea that I believed obvious yet which provoked this mirth.

What is the accusation of immorality based on? On the future of the relationships between men and *women*. Your society keeps women from shedding light on the question themselves. It is a man's conscience that ultimately will decide upon it!

It is the conscience of a *small* number of *men* that will judge the terms of a *universal* morality, of a morality whose aim is to rule over the whole globe, to direct and develop the feelings, thoughts, and acts of *men* and *women!* And these men live in a society where the morality consists of openly condemning all actions that *happen* outside a law henceforth too narrow; in a society that neither foresees these actions nor reckons with them but strikes them down instead; in a society where practice belies theory every day.

Here we have two men confronting each other over the issue of morality! One of them, the Prosecuting Attorney, arm of the male priesthood, confines himself to making accusations and blushes for the accused. The other, our FATHER, states that his word awaits the assent of women. Where is the morality? Where is the respect for women? Where is the true modesty?

The absence of women in this assembly has seemed strange, and this is why I return to it in another manner.

The FATHER, who felt how much their presence was linked to this cause had upon arriving in the courtroom asked for two women to serve as counsel for the defense. The Court, which had never seen such a thing in the memory of the judges, . . . the Court responded as if to a blasphemy. . . .

What, two women for counsel! But!—Yes, two women for counsel, in a trial concerning the woman question. Can you explain their absence from any judicial intervention in or healing of the ills of society? For my part, I ingenuously admit, I believe that if on this occasion the world must hear a judgment of immorality, it applies better to this blasphemous negation of the moral power of women than to ourselves, who loudly proclaim the sanctity of women's emancipation. . . .

Excerpt from Enfantin's *The Father's Word* at the General Gathering of the Family, 19 November 1831 [One of the pamphlets submitted as evidence by the prosecution]

Throughout our discussions one question has especially disturbed us. It disturbs us now and should continue to do so. It is the question of the LIB- ERATION OF WOMEN.

I told you that I had been the first to feel and to express the need for this liberation. I add that in point of fact I was the only one of the two of us (Bazard and myself) who was in a position to call women to the new life. This feeling led me to state that once we were engaged in the foundation of a new MORAL ORDER, any man who claimed to impose a LAW on women was not a Saint-Simonian; that the Saint-Simonian's only position with re- gard to women was to declare his incapacity to JUDGE her for as long as she herself did not feel liberated enough to reveal freely everything she feels, everything she desires, everything she wishes for the future.

It was thus necessary to provoke the LIBERATION OF WOMEN.

The terms used to make this provocation were spread among you in such a disordered manner that it is essential now that I present them to you myself.

MAN and WOMAN form the SOCIAL INDIVIDUAL. This is our highest faith concerning the relations between the two sexes. It is the basis for the MO- RALITY of the future. Man's *exploitation* of woman still exists, and it is here that we find the need for our mission.

This exploitation, this subordination, which in the future will go against nature, produces *lies* and fraud on the one hand and *violence* and brutal passions on the other. Such are the vices that must be stopped.

The man who comes forth imbued with the faith to LIBERATE WOMEN is therefore forced to put himself in such a position that no woman will blush to confess her life to him, or to reveal what she is, what she wants, what she desires. This man must act in such a way that nothing in his own person offers the symbol of Christian disapproval. By Christian disapproval I mean the exclusion of women from the temple, from politics: her inferior position with respect to men. That is the position in which I had to place

myself. Moreover, I had to present myself to women by rejecting with
equal force the Christian anathema against them, the anathema against the
flesh. That is what I did. In declaring my own thoughts about the future of
women, I had to express my opinion in such a way that men listening to it
would not adopt it. If men had adopted it, if the LAW that I, a man, introduced had been accepted by men, this LAW made without women would
have been imposed upon them. They would then still remain in a state of
inferiority and slavery. But just as I ought to have foreseen it, my LAW was
rejected by men, and we await the women who, with men, will find the
FINAL LAW under which men and women will unite and live in *holy
equality*.

In a moment, when I come to the ideas about women that I introduced,
you shall consider the goal that guided them and see them as an EXTREME
CASE, set at some remove from the Christian law. This is so that women
may dare and be able to come forth to speak freely, in the space separating
these ideas from current ones.

You know that all our teachings about the past and the principal ways in
which we order historical facts can be reduced to the following: humanity
first developed *materially*, then *spiritually*. One day humanity must find
harmony between these two developments, *spirit* and *matter*.

When humanity was subservient to the law of the FLESH, the law of
blood, its leaders were *violent*, the followers *slaves*. When SPIRIT tried to
resist FLESH and defeat it through Christianity, it had recourse to *lies*, miracles, and Jesuitism. Today *violence* and *lies* must cease; for Christian *ecstasy* and pagan *exaltation* have made the *flesh* and *spirit* enemies and have
consequently destined FLESH to *violence* and SPIRIT to *lies*. Now this war,
this struggle, this hostile arrangement must disappear and give way to the
LAW OF LOVE, which will satisfy both flesh and spirit, industry and science, worship and dogma, practice and theory. The entire social problem
of the future, then, consists of understanding how *sensual* and *intellectual
appetites* can be directed, ordered, combined, and separated during each
period of human civilization according to humanity's progressive needs.
Thus the PRIEST must decide to inspire and direct his *two* distinct *natures*—enemies up until now—to direct them in a shared love of a common destiny. This he must do by ceaselessly narrowing the gap between
them and by working with all his strength, wisdom, and love so that this
union gives rise to a struggle, a DUEL.

This is the politics, this is the government of the future. It consists in
establishing the relation between theoretician and practitioner, men of
spirit and men of flesh, in such a way that the duel between them that
existed in the past exists no longer, in such a way that this duel gives way to
HARMONY.

You may feel, by the words I have been using, that this is the same problem as that of MEN and WOMEN. Harmony must be established between men and women. As their relations have up to now been either *false* or *violent,* this falseness and violence must vanish. But, by keeping to the terms of flesh and spirit, science and industry, dogma and worship—metaphysical, historical, and political terms—I do not make myself FELT. Therefore let us employ a new form.

There are people of DEEP AFFECTION, affections that last, that time only strengthens. There are others of ARDENT AFFECTION, feelings that are rapid, transitory yet powerful, and that time puts to a painful, often unbearable test.

Heretofore each time these two types of affection have encountered one another, they have scorned, rebuffed, alienated and defiled each other. How, in the future, can those of deep affection—not love those of ardent affection (which would be for each a union of pain and sacrifice)—but do each other justice, respect each other, consider each other equally useful to the development of humanity? That is the question that concerns us.

Now I say that in the world there are three types of relations: those based on *intimacy, propriety* (or convention), and RELIGION. Relations that will exist between those of deep affection are based on *intimacy,* just as those that exist between people of ardent affection. The relations between people of different natures are what I call relations of propriety. Finally, the union of these two natures around a PRIEST, who understands them both, who feels both one and the other, who ennobles both of them, forms RELIGION. The *temple,* seen from a moral perspective, is thus divided into three parts—just like the City and humanity—corresponding to these three facets of life: *ardent affection, profound affection,* and CALM or PRIESTLY AFFECTION, which is able to comprehend them both.

Meanwhile I need to return to what I just said about the past. We have already noted in many ways that the future is distinguished from the last organic period,[8] Christianity, by *industrial* development in particular. This is why we said, in those other terms, that our mission consists of the *rehabilitation* of the *flesh.* You should remember, then, that up until now, on every question we have examined, whether philosophical or political, you have always found yourselves to be Christian, Christian without knowing

8. In the Saint-Simonian philosophy of history, progress occurred through the alternation of organic periods and critical periods. The former were characterized by the predominance of feeling over reason and hence by social cohesion and harmony. The latter were characterized by relentless rational criticism of existing institutions and hence by social fragmentation. The critical period ushered in by the Enlightenment and culminating in the French Revolution was seen as continuing into the early decades of the nineteenth century. The Saint-Simonians regarded their own doctrine as laying the foundation for the next, organic period.—ED.

it, Christian even when you were criticizing Christianity. And this is why you must expect, now that it comes to a MORAL question—the *rehabilitation of flesh* seen from a MORAL standpoint—you must expect to have found and still find yourselves Christians. Remember then, before all these words that can call forth the future, remember to refrain from any anticipated rejection. Make an effort to free yourselves, children of Saint-Simon, from the still-living influence of Christian anathema. This anathema still weighs upon our world, no matter what one says of the state of demoralization in which three hundred years of criticism have plunged us and of the disorder in our time of PHYSICAL appetites. This world of immorality nonetheless maintains CHRISTIAN MORAL LAW as the ruling force behind its judgments. It is according to this morality that the world praises and blames even though otherwise it does not follow it. Such morality is the last, mystical homage to ancient virtue. It is a fiction good for this world, but one which should not worry us too much in our daring and holy quest for the NEW MORAL LAW, for ultimate law of humanity. . . .

15. Flora Tristan, *The Workers' Union* (1843)

One of the relatively few women to contribute to the ferment of radical ideas in France in the 1830s and 1840s, Flora Tristan (1803–44) can be best described as an early socialist-feminist. Her most striking and innovative formulation was her equation of women and proletarians as society's two groups of "pariahs." Neither group, she contended, could be liberated if the other were not liberated as well.

Tristan's unusual, even exotic background may help explain the unusual role she carved out for herself: she was the child of a French woman and a Peruvian aristocrat. Since her parents' marriage in Spain had never been sanctioned by French law, she was technically illegitimate; having no legal right to her father's inheritance (he died when she was four), she was forced to learn a trade in order to support herself. Tristan availed herself of the time-honored path of female upward social mobility: she married her employer. But he consistently brutalized her and, after bearing him three children in four years, she abandoned him. She never returned or remarried.

For many years, Tristan traveled and wrote. A long sojourn in Peru

From *Before Marx: Socialism and Communism in France, 1830–1848*, edited by Paul E. Corcoran (New York: St. Martin's Press, 1983), pp. 117–24. © Paul E. Corcoran 1983 and reprinted by permission of St. Martin's Press Inc. and Macmillan, London and Basingstoke. Tristan's footnotes translated for this volume by Jan Goldstein from Flora Tristan, *Union ouvrière,* 3d edition (Paris and Lyons, 1844), pp. 44–46, 50, 54–59.

produced a travel diary, published under the title *Peregrinations of a Pariah* (1838). A trip to Britain produced a series of reports on social conditions across the Channel, *Promenades in London* (1840). Tristan's last book, *The Workers' Union* (1843), the source of our selections, marked her entrance into political activism—that is, her attempt to unify the proletariat. Having suffered from ill health for some time, Tristan died at the age of forty-one, a year after the book was completed.

Tristan was very much a part of the radical political culture of her day. Her Paris apartment served as a meeting place for socialists of all stripes. She was familiar with the ideas of the Saint-Simonians (see document 14), knew Fourier personally (see document 13), and had met Robert Owen; to launch her campaign for the workers' union, she took a *tour de France* in the style of a compagnon (see document 16).

To Working Men and Working Women

Listen to me. For twenty-five years, the most intelligent and devoted of men have dedicated their lives to the defence of our holy cause. In their writings, speeches, reports, memoirs, investigations and statistics, they have pointed out, affirmed and demonstrated to the Government and to the wealthy that the working class is, in the present state of things, materially and morally placed in an intolerable condition of poverty and suffering. They have shown that, from this state of abandonment and neglect, it necessarily follows that the greater part of workers, embittered by misfortune, brutalised by ignorance and exhausting work, were becoming dangerous to society. They have proved to the Government and to the wealthy that not only justice and humanity imposed the duty of coming to the aid of the working classes by a law permitting the organisation of labour, but that even general interest and security imperiously recommended this measure. But even so, for twenty-five years, many eloquent voices have been unable to awaken the solicitude of the Government concerning the dangers courted by society in the face of seven to eight million workers exasperated by neglect and despair, among whom a great number find themselves torn between suicide . . . or theft!

Workers, what remains to be said in defence of your cause? For twenty-five years, hasn't everything been said and said again, to the saturation point, about all these forms? There is nothing more to say, nothing more to write, because your unhappy condition is well known to *all*. Only one thing remains to be done: *to act in pursuance of the rights inscribed in the Charter.*

Now, the day has come when it is necessary to *act*. It is to you, *to you alone,* that it falls to act in the interest of your own cause. That way lies your life . . . or your death from that horrible end which kills at every instant: *poverty* and *hunger!*

Worker, wait no longer for the intervention promised to you for twenty-five years. Experience and the facts tell you well enough that the Government *cannot* and *does not want* to be bothered with your kind in the matter of amelioration. On you alone it depends, if you firmly desire it, to get out of the labyrinth of miseries, injuries and abasement in which you languish. Do you want to assure your children the benefit of a good vocational education and for yourselves the assurance of repose in your old age? You can do so.

Your action, on your own behalf, is not armed revolt, a riot in public places, arson or pillage. No. Because destruction, instead of remedying your ills, would only make them worse. The riots in Lyon and Paris have attested to that. Your action, on your own behalf, must only be legal, legitimate and avowed before God and men. It is the *Universal Union of Working Men and Women.*

Workers, your condition in present society is miserable and distressing. In good health, you do not have a *right to work.* Sick, infirm, wounded or old, you do not have a *right to hospital.* Lacking everything, you do not even have a *right to beg,* because mendicancy is prohibited by law. This precarious position plunges you into that savage state where man, living in the forest, is obliged each morning to dream up means by which he might procure his nourishment for the day. Such an existence is veritable torture. The plight of an animal which feeds in a sty is a thousand times preferable to yours. It is sure of *eating tomorrow.* Its master keeps straw and hay in the barn, just for an animal, for the winter. The lot of the bee, in a tree trunk, is a thousand times preferable to yours. The life of the ant, which works in summer in order to live tranquilly in the winter, is a thousand times preferable to yours. Workers, you are unhappy, yes, undoubtedly. But from whence comes the principal cause of your ills? If a bee and an ant, instead of working in concert with other bees and ants to furnish the common abode for the winter, decided to separate themselves and work alone, they too would die of cold and hunger in their solitary corner. So why do you remain in isolation? Divided, you are weak and fall, crushed underfoot by all sorts of misery! *Union makes power.* You have numbers in your favour, and numbers mean a great deal.

I come now to propose to you a *general union* irrespective of trade among working men and women living in the same kingdom—a union which would have as its goal to *constitute the working class* and to build several Palaces of the Workers' Union distributed equally throughout all of France. There children of both sexes would be raised, from six to eighteen years of age, and infirm or injured workers and the elderly would be admitted. Listen to the numbers speak, and you will have an idea of what can be done with the *Union*.

There are about five million working men and two million working women in France. If only these seven million workers would unite in thought and deed, with a view to a great common task, to the profit of *all men* and *all women*, and each contributed two francs a year to it, at the end of a single year the Workers' Union would possess the enormous sum of *fourteen million francs*.

You might well say: How are we to *unite* for this great task? By location and the rivalry between trades we are dispersed, often even enemies at war one against another. And a two franc annual fee is a great deal for poor daily labourers!

To these two objections I reply: To *unite* for the realisation of a great task is not necessarily to associate. Footsoldiers and seamen who, through a deduction from their pay, contribute an equal share to a common fund to care for 3,000 soldiers and seamen at the Hotel des Invalides are not by that fact *associated* amongst themselves. They have no need of knowing each other or of being sympathetic in opinions, tastes, and character. It is enough to know that the whole military, from one end of France to the other, pay the same subscription, assuring to the wounded, the infirm and the aged their entry *by right* to the Hotel des Invalides.

As for the amount, I ask you, what worker, even among the *poorest*, would not be able, by economising a little, to come up with a two franc annual subscription, so as to assure him of a retirement in his old age. Why consider your neighbours, the unhappy Irish, *the poorest people in all the world*, the people who eat *only potatoes*, and then only every other day! And such a people (they number only seven million souls) have found the means to pay nearly two million in rents to a single man (O'Connell), and for *twelve years* running at that! And you French people, *the richest in all the world*, cannot find the means to build large, healthy, comfortable palaces to care for your children, your wounded and your aged? Oh, this would be a veritable shame, an eternal shame indicting your egoism, carelessness and lack of intelligence! Yes, yes, if the Irish workers, going barefoot and *hollow bellied*, have given, *for twelve years*, a two-million franc honorarium to their defender, O'Connell, you are much more able to give fourteen million a year to house and nourish your *brave veterans of labour*, and to train *apprentices*.

Two francs a year! Who amongst you does not pay, for your *little individual associations* such as trade-guilds, mutual benefits and others, or even your little bad habits, such as tobacco, coffee, brandy, etc., ten to twenty times this amount? Two francs apiece is a small sum to scrape together and each, in giving this *pittance,* produces a total of *fourteen million.* See what wealth you possess solely *through your numbers?* But, to enjoy this wealth, the numbers must *unite,* form a *whole,* a *unity.*

Workers, put aside all your petty rivalries of trade and, outside of your particular associations, form one compact, solid, indissoluble Union. To-morrow, immediately, may all hearts be lifted up spontaneously in a single, unique idea: Union! May the cry of *union* resound throughout France, and in one year, if you steadfastly desire it, *the Workers' Union will be established.* In two years you will have fourteen million francs of your own in the bank to build a palace worthy of the great labouring people. . . .

Yes, it falls to you champions of labour to raise the first voice to honour *the only truly honourable thing,* Labour. It is to the producers, still despised by those who exploit you, that the task falls of building the first palace for the retirement of your aged workers. It remains to you workers, who built the palaces of kings and the rich, the temples of God, the homes and sanctuaries where all humanity finds shelter, finally to construct a refuge where you may die in peace—never having had a place to rest your head except in hospital, *if there was room.* To work then! To work! Workers, reflect carefully upon the efforts I have made to tempt you in order to wrest you away from poverty. Oh, if you do not respond to this call for Union, if, through egoism or carelessness, you refuse to Unite yourselves, what else can be done to save you?

Brothers, a distressing thought wounds the heart of all those who write for the poor people, who are so forsaken, so overburdened with labour from childhood, that three-quarters of them *do not know how to read* and the other quarter *haven't the time to read.* Thus, to write a book for the people is to throw a drop of water in the ocean. So I know that if I were limiting myself to putting my proposal for a Universal Union on paper, as magnificent as it is, the proposal would be a dead letter, as it has been with so many other plans already proposed. I understand that, my book published, I have another work to accomplish, which is to go myself, proposal for union in hand, from city to city, from one end of France to another, to speak to the workers *who do not know how to read* and to *those who haven't the time to read.* I tell myself that the moment has come to act. And for those who really love the workers, who want to devote themselves, body and soul, to their cause, a wonderful mission is there to fulfil. Such a person must follow the example of the first apostles of Christ. These men, braving persecution and fatigue, took up a beggar's sack and staff and went from country to country preaching the New Law—*brotherhood in God, union in God.* And so why, as a woman who has faith and strength, should I not go, the same as the apostles, from city to city, announcing the Good News to the workers and preaching to them *brotherhood in humanity, union in humanity?*

In the legislative assembly, in the Christian pulpit, in the assemblies of the world, in theatres and especially in the courts of law, people often speak *about workers;* but no one as yet has tried to speak *to the workers.* It is a direction that must be explored. God tells me that it will succeed. That is why I set upon this new path with confidence.—Yes, I will go find them in their workshops, in their garrets and even in their cabarets, if necessary, and there, face to face with their misery, I will move them to tears about their plights and force them, *in spite of themselves,* to leave this horrible poverty which degrades them and kills them. . . .

Why I Mention Women

Workers, my brothers, I work for you with love because you represent the *hardiest,* most *numerous* and the most *useful* part of humanity. With this in mind I find my own satisfaction in serving your cause. I earnestly beg you to read this chapter carefully and with the greatest attention. You must be persuaded by it, because it is in your own *material interests* to understand fully *why* I always mention women by using the feminine *ouvrières* and *toutes.*

For anyone whose intelligence is illumined by the rays of divine love and the love of humanity it is easy to grasp the logical sequence of the relations which exist between causes and effects. For such a person, all philosophy, all religion comes down to two questions. The first: How *may* and how *ought* we to love God and serve him *with a view to the universal well-being of all men and women making up humanity?* The second: How may and how ought we to love and treat woman *with a view to the universal well-being of all men and women making up humanity?*

I do not believe this is the place to respond to these two questions. Later, if workers show any interest in it, I will gladly discuss with them, metaphysically and philosophically, questions of the highest order. But, for the moment, it suffices here to adopt these two questions, *as the formal declaration of an absolute principle. . . .*

To the present time, woman has counted for nothing in human societies. And what is the result? That the priest, the legislator and the philosopher have treated her as the *true pariah.* Woman (that is, half of humanity) has been placed *outside the Church,* outside the *law,* outside of *society.* [1]

---

1. Aristotle, less tenderhearted than Plato, asked this question without answering it: Do women have souls? . . . Thus . . . woman [might have been] acknowledged to belong to the kingdom of the brute beasts, and that being the case, man, the master and lord, would have been obliged to cohabit with a brute beast! The very thought makes one shudder and freeze in horror! Besides, things being the way they are, it would have been a source of deep sadness for the wisest of the wise to think that they descended from the female race. For if they are really convinced that woman is as stupid as they claim, what shame for them to have been conceived in the womb of such a creature, to have suckled her milk and remained under her tutelage for a

For her there can be no office in the Church, no representation before the law, no position in the State. The priest says to her: "Woman, you are temptation, sin, evil. You represent the flesh, which is to say corruption and decay. Weep for your condition, throw ashes upon yourself, close yourself up in a cloister and there mortify your heart, which is made for love, and your womb, which is made for motherhood. And when you have mutilated your heart and body offer them, all bloody and dessicated, to your God for the remission of *original sin* committed by your mother, Eve." Then the lawmaker says to her: "Woman, by yourself you are nothing as an active member of the body of humanity. You may not hope to find a seat at the banquet of society. If you wish to live, you must serve as an *annex* to your lord and master, man. Therefore, young girl, you will obey your father. Wife, you will obey your husband. Widow and old woman, you will not even be taken into account." Finally, the wise philosopher says to her: "Woman, it has been confirmed by science that, due to your makeup, you are *inferior* to man. Now, you have no intelligence, no comprehension of higher questions, no grasp of ideas, no capacity at all for the so-called exact science, no aptitude for serious works. Finally, you are weak in body and spirit, cowardly and superstitious. In a word, you are only a capricious

---

good part of their lives! Oh, it is very likely that if these sages had been able to put woman outside nature, as they put her outside the Church, the law and society, they would have spared themselves the shame of descending from her. But fortunately, above the wisdom of the sages, there is a law of God.

All the prophets, with the exception of Jesus, have treated woman with an inexplicable injustice, scorn, and harshness. Moses has his God say, "I will multiply your pain in childbearing; in pain shall you bring forth children, yet your desire shall be for your husband, and he shall rule over you" (Gen. 3:16). The author of Ecclesiastes has pushed the pride of the male sex as far as saying, "Better a vicious man than a virtuous woman."

Mohammad says in the name of his God, "Men are superior to women because of the qualities by which God has raised the latter above the former, and because men use their riches to provide women with dowries. You will reprimand those women whose disobedience you fear; you will relegate them to separate beds, you will beat them; but as soon as they obey you, do pick quarrels with them" (Koran, 4:58). . . . Provisions of the [Napoleonic] Civil Code:

215. A woman cannot appear in court without the permission of her husband. . . .

37. Those signing birth, marriage and death certificates in the capacity of legal witnesses must be of the male sex.

"One (the man) must be active and strong, the other (the woman) must be passive and weak," J.-J. Rousseau, *Emile*.

Rousseau's formula is reproduced in the Civil Code:

213. The husband owes protection to his wife; the wife owes obedience to her husband.

child, wilful and frivolous. During the first ten or fifteen years of your life you are sweet *little doll*, but full of defects and vices. This is why, woman, that man must be *your master* and have complete authority over you."

For the six thousand years the world has existed, this is how the wisest of sages have judged the *female race*.

Such a terrible condemnation, repeated for six thousand years, would naturally influence the masses, because the sanction of time carries much authority with the common people. However, what ought to make us hope that this judgement might be appealed is that in the same way, for six thousand years, the wisest of sages have delivered a judgement no less terrible upon another race of humanity: the Proletarians. Prior to 1789, what was the proletarian in French society?—A *villain*, a *churl*, to be treated as a *beast sentenced to hard labour*. Then came the 1789 Revolution and all of a sudden the wisest of sages were proclaiming that the *plebeians* be named *people*, that villains and churls be called *citizens*. Finally, they openly proclaimed in the National Assembly the *rights of man*.

The proletarian, that self-same poor worker regarded heretofore as a *brute*, was quite surprised to learn that the *contemptuous treatment and loss of his rights had caused the misfortunes of the world*. Oh, he was well and truly *surprised to learn that he was now going to enjoy his civil, political and social rights*, and that finally he was to become the *equal* of his ancient lord and master! His surprise grew when he was informed that he possessed an intellect of absolutely the *same quality* as that of a crown prince. What a change! Meanwhile no time was lost in realising that this *second* judgement handed down upon the *proletarian race* was much more exact than the first. Scarcely had it been proclaimed that the proletarians were *capable* of all kinds of civil, military and social offices, than generals such as Charlemagne were said to have come from their ranks, and neither Henry IV nor Louis XIV were able to recruit officers from the ranks of their own proud and brilliant nobility. Then, as if by magic, intellectuals, artists, poets, writers, men of State and financiers cropped up by the dozen from the ranks of the proletarians, bringing to France a lustre she had never known. Military glory crowned them with a halo; scientific discoveries enriched them; the arts embellished them. Their commerce grew in immense proportions, and in less than thirty years the wealth of the land *tripled*. A demonstration with facts is unanswerable. Indeed the world today concedes that men are born alike, with faculties more or less equal, and that the only thing which should concern us is to *seek to develop all the faculties of the individual with a view to the general welfare*.

What happened for the proletarians, it must be agreed, augurs well for women when their 1789 is sounded. Following simple logic, it is evident that wealth will indefinitely hasten the day when women (one-half of humankind) are called upon to bring their store of intelligence, strength and talents to bear upon social progress. This is as simple to comprehend as two being the *double* of one. But, alas, we are not there yet, and while awaiting this happy '89, let us take note of what is happening in 1843.

The Church claims that woman is *evil*. The lawmaker finds that *by herself, she is nothing, and should enjoy no rights*. The wise philosopher suggests that by her *makeup she lacks intelligence*. One would conclude that here is a poor creature disinherited by God; men and society in consequence have treated her precisely in that way. I know nothing so powerful as the compelling, inevitable logic which flows from a received principle or an hypothesis representing it. The inferiority of woman, once proclaimed and postulated as a *principle*,[2] leads to disastrous consequences *for the universal well-being of all humanity, both men and women.* . . .

In the life of workers, the woman is all-important. She is their unique providence. Lacking her, they lack everything. You hear it said that "it is the woman who makes or destroys a home," and that the exactness of that truth is why it has become a proverb. However, what education, training, direction and moral or physical development do these women of the people receive? None. As a child, she is left to the mercy of a mother and grandmother, who themselves received no education. The former, as is only natural, will be brutal and mean, beating and mistreating her for no reason, the latter weak and careless, giving in to a girl's every whim. (In this, as in all of my arguments, I speak in general terms. Of course, I admit to numerous exceptions.) The poor child will be raised amidst the most shocking contradictions: one day irritated by abuse and injustice, the next day cosseted and spoiled by no less pernicious indulgences.

Instead of sending her to school, they are kept at home in preference to their brothers, because better use can be made of daughters around the house: minding the children, running errands, tending the soup, etc. At

2. In truth, from time to time, some intelligent and sensitive men . . . have cried out against the barbarity and absurdity of such an order of things, energetically protesting against such an iniquitous condemnation. Here is what Fourier says, among other things: "In the course of my research on the best mode of association, I found much more reason among women than among men, for several times women gave me fresh ideas that furnished me with very unexpected solutions to problems. Several times I have been indebted to women of the class called quick-witted (the mind which grasps things promptly and immediately presents its own ideas with exactitude) for solutions to problems that had racked my brain. Men were never able to offer me help of this kind. Why isn't this aptitude for fresh, unprejudiced ideas found among men? Because their minds have been enslaved by the biased philosophy that is imbued in them in school. They leave school with their heads stuffed with principles contrary to nature and are no longer able to envision a new idea on their own. If disagreement, no matter how little, is expressed with Plato or Seneca, they rise in insurrection and cry anathema . . ." (*La fausse industrie*, p. 326).

twelve, they are placed in an apprenticeship, where they continue to be exploited by their master and often mistreated as badly as by her parents. Nothing sours the character, hardens the heart and renders one mean-spirited so much as the continual suffering endured during an unjust and brutal upbringing. From the start, injustice wounds, afflicts and makes us desperate. Then, as it continues, we become irritated, exasperated and, dreaming only of a means of avenging ourselves, we end up becoming, ourselves, hard, unjust and mean. Such is the normal state of a poor twenty year-old girl. Then she will marry, without love, simply because one must marry to escape the tyranny of one's parents. What happens then? I suppose she has children, and in her turn she will become incapable of raising her own children properly, being as brutal to them as her mother and grandmother were toward her.

Working class wives, I beg you to pay close attention. In pointing out here *the realities* of your ignorance and inability to raise your children, I have no intention at all of making the least accusation *against you and your nature*. No, it is society that I accuse for allowing you to be so *uncultivated*—you, wives and mothers, who have so much need, on the contrary, of being trained and developed so that in turn you may *train and develop men, as children, confided to your care*.

Working class wives are, in general brutal, mean and hard. This is true, but what is the source of this state of affairs which so badly conforms to the gentle, good, sensitive and generous nature of woman?

Poor working women! They have so many subjects of vexation. First the husband. (One must confess that few working class households are happy.) Having received more instruction, being *the head by law* and also *by money,* which they bring home,[3] the husband believes himself to be (as he

3. It must be noted that in all the trades carried on by both men and women, the female worker is paid half the daily wage of the male worker, and the same is true if she does piece-work. Since we are unable even to imagine such a flagrant injustice, the first thought that comes to mind is the following: Because of his muscular strength, the man must doubtless do twice the work of the woman. Ah well, dear reader! it is quite the reverse. In all the trades requiring manual dexterity, women do almost twice the work of men. For example, typesetting in a printing shop (in truth, women make many errors, but that is because of their lack of education); or refastening the threads in a cotton or silk spinning factory; in short, in all trades that require a certain lightness of touch, women excel. A printer said to me one day with a naïveté that is entirely characteristic, "It is very just that they are paid half as much, since they go *faster* than the men; they would earn too much if they were paid at the same rate." Yes, they are paid not for the work they do, but for the few expenses they have as a result of the privations they impose upon themselves. Workers, you have not yet caught a glimpse of the disastrous consequences that would result for you if a similar injustice were perpetrated on your mothers, sisters, wives, and daughters. What has happened? The entrepreneurs, seeing women work more quickly for half the pay, dismiss workers from their workshops every day and replace them with women. And the men cross their arms and die of hunger in the streets!

is in fact) superior to his wife who brings home a small wage for her day's work and in the home is no more than a very humble servant.

It follows that the husband treats his wife, at the very least, with much disdain. The poor wife, who finds herself humiliated by every word and glance from her husband, secretly or overtly rebels, depending upon her personality. Here is the origin of violent, wounding scenes which end up leading to a state of constant irritation between the *master* and the *servant* (or one might even say *slave,* because the wife is, as it were, the husband's *property*). The condition becomes so painful that the husband, instead of staying home to talk with his wife, cannot wait to get away. Because he has nowhere else to go, he goes to the cabaret to drink *cheap wine* with *other husbands* who are just as miserable as he is, in the hope of *drowning their sorrows.* [4]

That is how the factory owners in England have operated. And once on that path, they discharge women to replace them with twelve-year-old children. Half-pay economy! Finally, only children of seven or eight years are getting hired. Let one injustice slip by and you can be sure that it will engender thousands more.

4. Why do workers go to taverns? Egoism has struck the upper classes, the ruling classes, blind. They do not understand that their wealth, happiness, and security depend upon the moral, intellectual, and material improvement of the working class. They abandon the worker to poverty and ignorance, thinking, as the old maxim goes, that a rude, uncultured people is that much easier to muzzle. That was well and good before the Declaration of the Rights of Man, but since then it has become a gross anachronism and a serious error. Besides, they ought at least be consistent: if they believe that it is a good and well-informed policy to let the poor class remain in its rude condition, then why recriminate incessantly against their vices? The rich accuse the workers of being lazy, debauched, and drunk, and to support their accusations, they exclaim: "If the workers are miserable, it is their fault alone. Go to the edges of the town, enter the taverns, and you will find them filled with workers who are there to drink and waste time." I believe that if the workers, instead of going to a tavern, met seven to a room (the maximum number permitted by the laws of September) to instruct one another about their common rights and to consider the steps to take to make those rights worth something legally, the rich would be more unhappy than they are to see the taverns packed.

In the present state of things, the tavern is the TEMPLE of the worker; it is the only place he can go. He believes nothing in church; he understands nothing at the theater. That is why the taverns are always full. In Paris, three-fourths of the workers do not even have a home; they sleep in barracks-style lodgings; the married ones live in cramped and airless attics, so that they are forced to get out to stretch their legs and revive their lungs. You do not want to educate the people. You forbid them from meeting for fear that they will educate themselves, that they will talk about politics or social doctrines; you do not want them to read, to write, to use their minds, for fear that they will revolt. But what then do you want them to do? If you prohibit everything mental, it is clear that all that remains is resort to the tavern. Poor workers! Weighed down with all sorts of troubles and sorrows either at home or with their boss, or because of the repugnant forced labor to which they are condemned, their nervous system becomes so irritated that they sometimes almost go mad. In that state, they have no other refuge than the tavern to escape from their suffering. So they go there and drink cheap wine, that execrable medicine—but at least it has the virtue of numbing them.

This means of distraction compounds the problem. The wife who waits for pay-day on Sunday to keep her family alive for the next week despairs in seeing her husband spend the greater part of it at the cabaret. Then her irritation is carried to the limit, her brutality and meanness redoubled. One must see these working class households close at hand (especially the worst) to form an idea of the unhappiness experienced by the husband, and the suffering of the wife. From reproaches and insults, they pass to blows, and finally to tears, discouragement and despair.[5]

In the face of such facts, there are people in the world called virtuous and religious who, comfortably ensconced in their houses, drink good bordeaux, vintage chablis, top quality champagne in abundance with each meal—and then ramble on moralistically about the drunkenness, debauchery, and intemperance of the working class! . . .

5. In support of the point I am arguing here about the brutality of women of the people as well as their excellent nature, I will cite an incident that occurred in the city of Bordeaux while I was there in 1827. Among the vegetable sellers with open-air stalls in the marketplace was one feared by all the others for her insolence, wickedness, and brutality. Her husband was a street sweeper, gathering up mud and garbage. One evening he came home and supper was not ready. A domestic quarrel broke out. From verbal insults the husband progressed to blows, and he struck his wife. At that moment, she was cutting up soup ingredients with a large kitchen knife, and, exasperated with anger, she turned on her husband with knife in hand and pierced his heart. He fell dead. She was taken to prison.

Seeing her husband dead, this brutal, wicked woman was seized with such pain and remorse that, despite her crime, she inspired universal compassion and respect. It was easy to establish that the husband had provoked her, that the murder was carried out in a fit of anger without premeditation. Her sorrow was such that they feared for her life, and since she was nursing a four-month-old infant, the judge, trying to calm her, assured her that she would be acquitted. But imagine everyone's surprise when, hearing these words, the woman cried out, "Me, acquitted? Oh, Your Honor, how dare you say that. If a wretch like me is acquitted, there will no longer be any justice on earth."

They tried to reason with her and to make her understand that she was not a criminal because she had not *thought* of committing the murder. "Oh, what does the thought matter?" she kept repeating, "if there is a brutality inside me which brings me, one time, to maim one of my children, another time to kill my husband? Aren't I a dangerous person, unfit to live in society?" Finally, when she was convinced that she would be acquitted, this rough uneducated woman made a resolution worthy of the strongest men of the Roman republic. She declared that she would take justice into her own hands and starve herself to death. And with such strength, such dignity did she carry out this terrible death sentence she had pronounced on herself! Her mother, her family, her seven children came in tears to plead with her to agree to live for their sake. She handed her little infant over to her mother saying, "Teach my children to be glad they lost such a mother, for, in a moment of brutality, I might have killed them, as I killed their father." Judges, priests, women of the market, and many townspeople went before her to entreat her to act in her own favor. Her resolve was unshakable. Then another approach was tried: cakes, fruit, dairy products, wine, meats were brought to her room. They went so far as to roast a chicken and to bring it to her piping hot so that the smell would entice her to eat. "Everything you are doing is useless," she repeated with calm and dignity. "A woman who is brutal enough to kill the father of her seven children ought to die. And I will die." She suffered horrible torment without complaining, and on the seventh day, she expired.

The burning disappointments caused by her husband are followed in turn by pregnancies, sickness, the lack of work and poverty—a poverty which is always there at the door like the head of Medusa. . . .

Amongst the misfortunes which populate the houses of prostitution . . . and the unfortunates who groan in prisons, how many there are who can say: "If only we had a mother *capable of raising us properly,* certainly we should not be here."

I repeat, a woman is everything in the life of a worker. As a mother, she influences him during his childhood. It is from her, and uniquely from her, that he draws his first notion of that science which is so important to acquire, the science of life which teaches us to live befittingly to ourselves and others, according to the condition in which our fate has placed us. As a lover, she has influence over him during his youth, and what a powerful influence may be exercised by a pretty and beloved girl! As wife, she has an influence over him for three-quarters of his life. Finally, as a daughter, she has an influence over him in his old age.

It is noteworthy that the position of a worker is very different from that of an idler. If a child of the rich has a mother incapable of raising him, he can be pensioned elsewhere, or given a governess. If a rich young man hasn't a mistress, he may busy his heart and imagination in the study of the arts or sciences. If a rich man has no spouse, he never lacks for contact with the world's distractions. When old, and he has no daughter, he finds several old friends or young nephews who gladly consent to play cards with him, while the worker, to whom all these pleasures are forbidden, has for all joys and consolation only the society of women in the family, his companions in misfortune.

It follows from this situation that it is of the greatest importance, for the *intellectual, moral, and material* amelioration of the working class that working class women receive, from infancy, a rational, solid and proper education in order to develop all of their good propensities. Then they can become skilful workers in their trade, good mothers to their families, capable of raising and guiding their children, becoming, as *La Presse* put it, *their natural and free tutors for school lessons.* They can also serve as *moralising agents* for men over whom they have an influence from birth till death.

Do you begin to understand—you men who cry scandal before deigning to examine the question—why I lay claim to *woman's rights?* Why I want to see her placed on a footing of *absolute equality* with man, so that she might benefit from the *legal right obtaining to every creature at birth?*

I protest for women's rights because I am convinced that all the world's misfortunes derive from this scornful ignorance shown to this very day toward the natural and imprescriptible rights of the female person. I speak out for the rights of women because I am convinced that it is the *unique means by which she can take charge of her own education.* And upon the woman's education depends that of man in general, and *particularly the man of the people.* I claim certain rights for woman because there lies the sole means of obtaining her rehabilitation before the Church, the law and society. This prior rehabilitation must occur so that *the workers themselves may be rehabilitated.*

Workers, as things now stand you know what takes place in your homes. You, man, *having the right* of master over your wife, do you and she live with a contented heart? Are you happy? No, no. It is easy to see that despite your right, you are neither *content* nor *happy.* Between the master and the slave, one can only be fatigued by the weight of the chain that ties them together. Where this absence of liberty is felt so keenly, happiness could never exist. . . .

The husband, knowing that his wife had *rights equal to his,* would no longer treat her with disdain, the contempt one shows to inferiors. On the contrary, he would treat her with that respect and deference that one accords *to equals.* As his contempt is no longer a constant irritation and, once the cause of the problem is destroyed, his wife will no longer show herself to be brutal, wily, crabby, hot tempered, exasperating or mean. Being no longer regarded in the home as the *husband's servant,* but rather the *associate, friend and companion* of the man, naturally she will take an interest in the association and will do all that she can to make the little household prosper. . . .

In the conditions I have just outlined, the household, instead of being a cause of ruin for the worker, would be on the contrary a cause of well-being. Who knows but that love and a contented heart might triple or quadruple the strength of a man? We have already seen this in rare examples. It has happened that a worker, adoring his family and taking the lead in giving an education to his children, to attain this noble aim, did the work that three *unmarried men* could not have done. . . .

Workers, this hastily sketched picture of the position the proletarian class would enjoy if women were recognised as the *equal of men* ought to make you reflect *on the evil which exists* and *the good which might be.* This should provide you with great determination.

Workers, if you do not have the power to abrogate ancient laws and make new ones—and without a doubt you cannot—you do have the power to protest against the injustice and absurdity of laws which hinder the progress of humanity and make you suffer—you, most of all. It is even your *sacred duty* to protest energetically in thought, speech and writing against all the laws which oppress you. Thus it is important that you endeavour to understand this point: the law which *enslaves the woman* and *deprives her of education* oppresses you *proletarian men.*

16. Agricol Perdiguier, *Memoirs of a Compagnon*

Compagnonnage was a traditional form of craftsmen's association in France, dating back at least to the sixteenth century. Unlike the craft guilds, which included the three ranks of masters, journeymen, and apprentices (and in which discipline was enforced by the masters), compagnonnage was composed of journeymen only. And unlike the craft guilds, which were officially sanctioned by the royal government and then abolished during the French Revolution, compagnonnage had always been a technically illegal and hence clandestine organization; thus, ironically, it was able to survive the revolution. It continued to flourish during the first half of the nineteenth century.

The activities of compagnonnage centered upon the *tour de France*. This was the six or seven years spent by the young journeyman in moving from city to city, perfecting the skills of his craft by laboring in and learning the techniques of different workshops.

Agricol Perdiguier, born near Avignon in the south of France in 1805, learned the rudiments of the carpenter's trade as an apprentice to his father and then joined a society of compagnons in 1823. In 1839 he published his *Livre du compagnonnage,* which revealed the secret customs and rituals of compagnonnage to the public for the first time. The book also called for the reform of compagnonnage, especially for an end to the hostilities between its rival sects, and expressed Perdiguier's hope that, thus modified, compagnonnage might become the general mode of working-class organization in France. The book brought its author to the attention of the Paris literati, many of whom had in the 1830s and 1840s strong popular sympathies. Among this group, Perdiguier's closest tie was to George Sand, with whom he was to correspond for the rest of his life. Sand subsidized Perdiguier's campaign for the reform of compagnonnage, and he in turn provided her with background information for her novel *Le compagnon du tour de France* (1841).

The 1848 Revolution brought Perdiguier into political life. He was elected as a deputy first to the Constituent and then to the Legislative Assembly of the Second Republic. Following the Bonpartist coup, he was proscribed for his radicalism and went into exile in Belgium and Switzerland. It was during this period of exile that he wrote and published his autobiographical *Mémoires d'un compagnon* (1854–55). Perdiguier returned to France in 1855 and resumed his career as a writer on

From Agricol Perdiguier, *Mémoires d'un compagnon* (Moulins: Cahiers du Centre, 1914), pp. 54–67, 246–48. Translated for this volume by Paula Wissing.

the social question, though without regaining the influence he had enjoyed in the more favorable ideological climate of the 1830s and 1840s.
He died in Paris in 1875.

In the selections from his *Mémoires* reprinted here, Perdiguier describes his life immediately before and after his initiation into compagnonnage. His description of the compagnons' strike procedures is also
included.

My Stay in Avignon—Mr. D . . .—Work

To return to the matter of my work. I said earlier that I had acceded to my
father's will, that I had entered his workshop, that I sought to become a
carpenter. I repeat, Father lacked patience, he was too strict. I was sensitive. I did not want to displease him. Thus I would have preferred to
plunge an awl into my own flesh, to wound myself, rather than to spoil
the smallest piece of wood. Finally I succeeded in making mortises and
tenons well; in using the saw with some skill, as well as shears, joining
planes and other planes. I made a casement window by myself. That was
something. . . .

On Easter Sunday, one of my father's friends, a Mr. D . . . , who was a
master carpenter in Avignon, came to see us in Morières. That was in
1822. I was a little over sixteen. Mr. D . . . took me aside and asked me to
come work in his shop. I answered that I would like to if my father approved. They spoke together and consent was given. I was left free to decide for myself. The next morning I left Morières for Avignon.

Mr. D . . . gave me food and lodging, nothing else, not the slightest bit
of encouragement. He had me get up before five o'clock every morning,
winter and summer, and work until eight or nine o'clock at night. We ate
our meals in an instant. During the day, whether he was there or not, I used
my time as best I could. On Sunday I straightened up the shop, the attic,
where bits of wood were stored, and I was hardly ever free before ten or
noon. I was shy, very sensitive. I was in despair for fear of being scolded.

I slept on the fourth floor; Mr. D . . . slept below. He woke me in the
morning by banging some kind of stick against the ceiling. That way he
didn't have to get out of bed. One night he knocked. I got up. But I was still
tired, very sleepy. I looked out the window. They were closing Mr. M's
apothecary shop across the way. I didn't understand a thing. I got dressed
and went to work.

It was eleven at night. I had to stay up all night and then all day the
following day. They did not fear to use my strength, nor to exhaust it.

Mr. D . . . gave me wood to saw or plane. Then he blocked out the design. I made mortises and tenons; I planed dados, rabbets, and mouldings. He took the trouble or pleasure of assembling them. It was my job to fasten, to plane, and to finish. In this way we made windows, doors, storefronts, and other pieces. Often he had me make crates for Mr. Poncet to pack his silk. It was rough, unpleasing work for the workman, but very lucrative for the master.

I had been at Mr. D . . .'s for six months, and he had never given me a cent for my Sundays. I was seventeen at that time. I deserved better.

I told my father that I could not stay in such a place; that his friend never had me lay anything out or assemble it. I told him I still had not seen a cent and that I wanted to leave Mr. D . . . My father advised me to stay, adding that he would give me ten sous on Sundays. It was not much, but enough for me. I curbed my impatience.

Since Mr. D . . . persisted in not letting me lay out or assemble anything, and in giving me nothing on Sunday, I resolved not to stay there any longer. I asked my father to tell him, which my father did. Moreover, even though he had no agreement either oral or written with Mr. D . . . , he told him that if he thought that I had not earned my keep, he was ready to settle up with him. Mr. D . . . answered that I had earned my way. I should say so. He could have said that I had made him some profit. I left that shop on Easter. I had worked there a year to the day.

As for money, Mr. D . . . finally paid me. On New Year's Day 1823 I received 1.50 francs from him as a gift, I am pleased to say. But the sum total of his gifts and his encouragement during the twelve months I worked there was limited to that. And nevertheless, during peak times he had me work throughout the night. It was simple stinginess on his part.

Mr. D . . . did not behave as a friend but rather as a selfish master who speculates and intentionally keeps a young man ignorant of his trade in order to exploit him even longer. When I started with him I knew how to work with tools. He had me do what I already knew how to do, nothing more. If I made any progress in his shop, it was without his knowledge, without any help from anyone, and as the natural result of constant practice.

Nevertheless, when I left, I was extremely careful not to offend him. My father did the same for his part. All our efforts were in vain. Mr. D . . . was very cool. He went even further, as we shall see.

Several days after leaving his house I met him in the street and said, doffing my cap, "Good day, Mr. D . . ." He stared and passed without answering. I was hurt by this rebuff. A few weeks later, I met him a second time. Again I greeted him. Mr. D . . . looked at me again and kept the same silence. I had done my duty, and more. I was not about to take respect and submission any further. I stopped greeting him after that day. His conduct toward my father was also extremely ill willed.

Ten years later, after some travel, a long absence and my return to Avignon, I met this man near Mr. Poncet's house. I was with Antoine Rochetin, a stonecutter, called Sapeur, or The Flame, and he can recall the scene. I said to the master carpenter, "Good day, Mr. D . . . , how are you?" He blushed ever so red; he answered rudely, accusing my father, complaining of him and me, doubtless wrongly. This stubborn and inexplicable ill will, this behavior the likes of which I had never seen, gave me a profound distaste for this man. I said nothing to his unreasonable words, which lacked any spirit of justice or honesty. I shrugged and went off with a sneer. Afterward, he could complain about me, about us, and lie, slander, or gossip. It fits his hateful nature. He is not capable of anything else. But let us stop here and limit ourselves to pitying this spiteful, lying devil, whose name should no longer sully these pages.

Mr. Poussin—*Gavots*—*Dévorants*—Work

Leaving Mr. D . . . I went to work for Mr. Poussin, another friend of my father's. My first boss employed *dévorants*, with whom I became well acquainted and who took me several times to their *mère*. The second boss employed *gavots*. The least intelligent of these looked on me with ill will. They took me for an aspirant to their Society or for an *esponton*, I imagine, and for that reason their welcome was more than chilly.[1]

Mr. Poussin employed me on a daily basis. He fed me and housed me and besides that gave me ten sous a day. That was three francs every Sunday! An enormous sum! What riches all of a sudden. I was delighted. I was overwhelmed. My happiness knew no bounds. Later I took rooms and went to eat at the inn like the other journeymen.

For Mr. Poussin I made windows, shutters, doors, and fan windows. . . .

Mr. D . . . never taught me to lay out or assemble; I never had any theoretical or practical training. Nevertheless I did all the work that was given to me [by Mr. Poussin] without any trouble. I was able to understand without effort the plans the master gave me to follow. I did my work without interference or help from anyone.

I have a story to tell, at the risk of making myself look foolish. I was making a fan window for a mezzanine. I was assembling the curved part of the design, which was made of excessively burled wood. While assembling

1. This paragraph introduces some of the special terminology, or slang, of compagnonnage. *Dévorants* (or *dévoirants*) and *gavots* were two rival sects of compagnons. Later in these selections, Perdiguier will also identify the first of these as Compagnons of Duty and the second as Compagnons of the Duty of Liberty. The *mère* (mother) is the name given to the inn where all the compagnons belonging to a certain trade would congregate and receive food and lodging when they arrived in a given town. An *esponton* is a craftsman who attempts to operate outside the institutional structure of compagnonnage.—ED.

I was a little too forceful with the tenon. I struck it very, very gently with my mallet. In spite of my care, the mortise broke, and the curved piece split in two. It was no longer good for anything. I was hurt, humiliated, outraged. Truly I broke down and cried. I did not want to eat or drink. I wanted to punish my belly for the clumsiness of my hands. Mr. Poussin arrived, amiably scolded me on my weakness for despairing over such a little thing, cheered me up with his good words, gave me more wood. And, my word, my courage and my appetite returned.

Mr. Poussin and Mr. Brunet had the contract for the work at Notre-Dame-des-Dons, which was being restored at the time and which, taking the place of Saint-Agricol, was to become the archiepiscopal church of Avignon. Workers were placed in the choir and nave to build the stalls, the wainscotting, and to do other jobs. My boss had me do the frame of a large door leading from the choir into the sacristy and, in the sacristy, a buffet with sliding shelves. I also made the cope cupboard, which was about ten feet long and five feet deep, with accordion doors opening to the left and right. . . .

The compagnons who, like myself, worked in the church, assured me that this job was worth at least one hundred francs for the workmanship. They encouraged me to hold out for this price and have it appraised if the bourgeois wanted to give me less. The latter offered me only seventy-five francs. I refused. There was a friendly appraisal made by Mr. Poussin's partner, Mr. Brunet, and a compagnon who worked for both of them. The price was raised to eighty francs, which I accepted. After this little dispute I left Mr. Poussin, but we remained friends. He always looked upon me with kindness and never stopped making me welcome. Our good relations lasted as long as he lived, that is, twenty-nine years. Now that he is dead, they have continued with his children. What a difference between him and my first boss.

Compagnonnage—Different Societies

While I worked for Mr. D . . . I was in daily contact with the *dévorants,* or Compagnons of Duty, and had I begun my tour of France after leaving that workshop I would have been a zealous member of their Society. Mr. Poussin employed *gavots,* or Compagnons of the Duty of Liberty. My ideas were to change as a result of my contact with them. However, during my early days the members and adherents of this new Society were far from friendly to me.

I came from a workshop of *dévorants!* It was thought that I must be a little aspiring *dévorant,* or an *esponton*—that is, a loose person who aspires to complete independence and who flees all of the Societies. I was young, I could only be a bad workman. From this line of reasoning came the inclination, especially on the part of some of the apprentices, to make fun of me. There were three of them, two of whom, Louiset and Pinçu, were a few years older than I. The other one was my age. My first day at the shop, I made a mallet I needed and sawed some wood. I was mockingly praised for my skill. I understood what was going on and said nothing. But when I finished the first four windows that the boss had given me to do, they softened and became polite. When I had assembled my first four sets of blinds and they saw the crosspieces and slats join perfectly even before I had fastened them, I received sincere and unanimous congratulations. The two apprentices who had finished their apprenticeship and considered themselves my superiors understood that they were mistaken and became very different toward me; they became my friends. I remember with pleasure Louiset from Orgon, Pinçu from Carpentras, and Ravoust from Barbentane. I would be happy to see all of them again.

Here I want to mention something. When I was only on my first windows, and when they did not yet appreciate my worth as a workman, a compagnon called Vivarais permitted himself to do the following: My frames were made of wood. One of them was laid out on two sawhorses, the frame in the casement. Clamps were fixed on the upper crosspiece and the sill. I was going to drill holes with the brace and then fasten the hardware: I turned away for a minute. Vivarais arrived, loosened the clamps, and walked off with them. I complained to Mr. Poussin of this carelessness. He went to find him and told him firmly, "Vivarais, return those clamps that you just took right now."

"What! You prefer an *esponton* to a *compagnon?*"

"I prefer what is fair to everything else."

"Well then, I'm leaving."

"Leave whenever you want."

The clamps were returned to me. Vivarais left instantly, outraged that, in his words, an *esponton* had been preferred to a *compagnon.*

I tell this story to show how an ignorant fellow with any old title believes himself superior to other men and lords it over them like a great *seigneur.* He would willingly say to the people, "Down on your knees, peasant!"

I quickly made myself liked at the shop.

All the compagnons were nice, gentle, helpful, and obliging to me. These *gavots,* whom their enemies had painted so black and frightening and whose very name made me tremble, seemed charming, delightful people. They took me for walks with them on Sunday, they took me to their *mère* on several occasions, and I was always well received. With great pleasure I saw young men from all over France live together like brothers and help and mutually sustain one another. I was very much struck by the peacefulness, honesty, and respect that reigned in this house.

At the *mère* of the aspirants I had noticed more gaiety, which meant more noise and more obscene stories. Everyone used the *tu* form and joked together. The character of this new house was different. No use of the *tu* or suggestive words, but something great, fraternal, and sublime. This attracted me. It won me over. I was already half-*gavot*.

Mr. Ponson—I Am Hired

Two excellent workmen, Carcassonne le Coeur-Aimable (the Kind-Hearted) and Provençal la Justesse (Justice), both fine men, advised me when I left Mr. Poussin to hire myself out and become a member of the Society of Compagnons of the Duty of Liberty. I readily agreed, asking them only to have me placed with Mr. Ponson, a long-standing friend of my father of whom I had often heard and whom I had seen only once at our house in Morières. They spoke of me to the head compagnon, Languedoc la Douceur (Sweetness).[2] He answered that he could grant my request.

When he received the order to hire me from the chief of the Society, the roll keeper, or compagnon in attendance,[3] took me with him and we went before the bourgeois, at his shop on Amphoux Street. With all three of us present and with our hats off, Mr. Ponson took five francs out of his pocket and put them in the roll keeper's hand. The latter offered them to me saying, "Here are five francs that the bourgeois advances to you; I hope that you will earn them." I answered that I would certainly earn more. That is the hiring ceremony. It is the same for the compagnon as for the newly initiated—in that Society at least. Once I had been hired, Mr. Ponson, who I thought did not know me, said to me familiarly, "Well now, don't do like your father did. Back then, he was supposed to leave with me to make his tour of France; he made me wait a week, then ten days, then two weeks, and the waiting period always began again. Finally I left by myself; and your father never left the area. You must travel." I answered Mr. Ponson that that was exactly my thinking. "So much the better," he answered.

For Mr. Ponson I made walnut wardrobes with doors with ornamental trim and hand-carved moldings. I carved stars, hearts, and other decorations on the large rails above and below. I was doing piecework. My earnings were not much on these jobs, but they were enough. I ate at the *mère*, and slept there, too.

---

2. As part of their initiation, all compagnons assumed a new name, the first part of which indicated their native town or region. Perdiguier's own assumed name was Avignonnais-la-Vertu (Virtue from Avignon).—ED.

3. The *rouleur*, or roll keeper, was an officer of the Society of Compagnons. One of his main responsibilities was to meet the compagnons newly arrived at the *mère* and find employment for them in the local workshops.—ED.

Drawing School—My Entry into Compagnonnage

There was a compagnon who, every night after work and for a low monthly fee, gave his brothers drawing lessons. His name was Lyonnais l'Ami du Trait (Friend of the Stroke). I wanted to take advantage of this good opportunity. I built myself a stand and some T-squares. My father bought me India ink, paints, brushes, a pencil, and a compass. I made drawings from side views of moldings, of the five orders of architecture. I had facility, taste, and passion. I wanted to learn. I made the best use of my time.

Let us talk of compagnonnage, which was to occupy a part of my life. On the first Sunday of every month, the compagnons of all societies gathered in a general assembly to collect money to meet the expenses common to all. I had been hired. I was to be introduced to my brothers during the meeting.

The roll keeper had passed by the shops on Saturday and requested each member of the Society to be at the *mère* the next day. On Sunday at the appointed time, first the compagnons, then the affiliates had to go up to the room. I stayed by myself downstairs. The roll keeper came to take me by the hand and brought me upstairs with him. He knocked in a certain way on a door that immediately opened and brought me into the assembly room in the midst of a circle of men. They were standing, calm, silent, properly dressed, decorated with blue and white ribbons . . . I was stunned, startled, embarrassed. He had me cross the room and presented me to the presiding compagnon with the words, "Here is a young man who seeks to be admitted into the Society." "Do you seek," the leader asked me, "to become part of the Society?" "Yes." "Do you know what Society this is?" "It is the Society of Compagnons." "That is true, but there are several societies; that of the Compagnons of Duty, or *dévorants;* that of the Compagnons of the Duty of Liberty, or *gavots.* Which of the two do you wish to join?" That of the Compagnons of the Duty of Liberty." "They are both good, and if you have gotten the wrong address you may leave." "It's indeed the one here I wish to join."

After this dialogue the first compagnon ordered the secretary to read me the rules to which all members of the Society without exception must adhere. He read them aloud. These rules state that all must contribute to the expenses of the Society, that members must be polite to one another and not use the *tu* form, or call each other by nicknames; that members must be respectful to the mother, father, sisters, and brothers,[4] and toward all mem-

---

4. We call sisters and brothers the sons and daughters of the father and mother, as well as their servants of both sexes. The Compagnons of Duty give these titles to the children of the house, but not to hired servants [Perdiguier's note].

bers of the Society, both compagnons and affiliates; that they must be clean, well mannered; that during the week they must not come to the *mère* in shirt-sleeves or in their aprons and on Sunday must wear a tie and gaiters. In a word, all my duties and rights were spelled out there.

When the reading was over, the first compagnon said to me, "Can you obey these rules?" "Yes," I replied. He added that, if I did not feel capable of observing them, I was always free to leave.

What I had understood I approved, and I promised to abide by it. The first compagnon proclaimed me an affiliate. The roll keeper showed me to the place reserved for me. As the newest in the Society, I was to be the last in line. Then the business turned to the interests of the Society. Each member paid his small dues. Common expenses were met by each in equal portions.

A little later I attended a party. It was a dance for Saint Anne, held on the election of a head compagnon, and like the others, I voted. This is all very fine. I will speak of it elsewhere. . . .

A Theft at the *Mère*—The Grenoble Rule

I used to draw at the *mère* until eleven every night, and I slept there. One morning a fellow from Languedoc complained that four of his shirts had been stolen. The members of the local club[5] were upset and advised him to tell the head compagnon. He did this immediately. An inquiry was begun. A binder named Saint-Brieuc, a little old drunk who was very learned, very nice, and who was attracted by the wine at the *mère* and thereby became our friend, came up with some useful information. From his windows, across from ours, he saw Orange, a young affiliate, enter the little courtyard below us. Orange undressed and put on shirt after shirt. This seemed *funny* (that was his word) to Saint-Brieuc. This declaration had great weight.

The head compagnon, the roll keeper, and others followed Orange's trail, went through the second-hand clothing shops. The shirts were found in one of them.

The compagnons and affiliates were immediately ordered to return to the *mère*. An assembly took place. Orange was introduced. Accused, he tried to defend himself. He was easily confused. He confessed the whole thing.

They made him undergo the Grenoble Rule, although not in its strictest

5. The French is *chambrée* and refers to a type of men's drinking club that was widespread in the south of France. The *chambrée* tended to become the main locus of political discussion for the artisans or peasants who composed it.—Ed.

form. They made him kneel in the middle of the room; they shouted insults at him; they made him swear never to boast of having belonged to the Society of Compagnons of the Duty of Liberty. Then they sent him off with a kick in the pants.

Orange did not recognize the compagnons' right to punish him in any way. He complained to the authorities. The heads of the Society were called before the king's prosecutor. Forced to tell the truth, they denounced the one who had denounced them. A hearing took place. Orange was arrested, judged, and condemned. He spent a year in prison.

Compagnons do not denounce thieves; they judge them, punish them in their ancient way, and then banish them, covered with shame, from their Societies. Orange wanted revenge; he got himself doubly punished.

An Aspirant from Nantes—Quarrels among the Compagnons

At this time a man from Nantes, an aspirant to the Society of Carpenters of Duty, came to our *mère* and asked the head compagnon permission to be admitted among us as an affiliate. These changes between one Society and another can be made, as long as one has not yet been admitted as a full compagnon. Our head called the roll taker and sent him to the *dévorants* to inquire about the newcomer's situation and bring his receipt if it was paid up. That formality out of the way, the Nantais could join our Society.

The *dévorants* had affirmed that the Nantais left no debts. However, they left doubts about his character and his conduct. The newcomer said they spoke this way out of ill will because he was leaving them.

Relations between the two societies turned sour. Fights broke out.

At night the two enemy parties patrolled the streets and spied on and skirmished with each other. The *gavots* stopped in front of the *mère* of the locksmiths of the *devoir*, . . . Mr. Vidal's. The man from Nantes, a real firebrand, went in. He was detained inside. The compagnons outside broke the windows and frames, laid siege to the house, and were working to break the door down when the police arrived. The Nantais and others were arrested and thrown into prison.

The *gavots* had destroyed the *dévorants'* property. The following evening, *dévorants* of all trades—carpenters, locksmiths, stonecutters, wheelwrights, farriers, tanners, tinsmiths, and others—all took turns wreaking havoc against the *gavots*. The latter, expecting a formidable attack, had opened a huge trapdoor on the ground floor of the *mère* in the hopes of dousing the lights when the assailants arrived and pitching them into the cellars.

The cobblers, although Compagnons of Duty, had come to give the *gavots* a hand. They reinforced their house and prepared themselves for the defense. Each had vowed to mix his blood with that of the enemy. All were on the lookout, on the alert, jumping up at the slightest noise. They heard some footsteps, then more: it's the *dévorants!* They are here. . . . The footsteps stop in front of the door. Will the fight start? . . . No, they continue, then return, then leave again.

The authorities, aware of the situation, had sent their agents: soldiers who were moving through the streets dispersing the compagnons and removing the chances of a fight.

Some arrests took place. Both *gavots* and *dévorants* were put into prison. There was a trial. Several were sentenced to six months.

The societies did not abandon their prisoners; they regarded them, as is their habit, as heroes or martyrs and made it possible for them to enjoy all the amenities possible while under lock and key.

What courage! What bravery! What devotion blindly and foolishly wasted, not in the interests of all but for their common destruction.

The man from Nantes, the original cause of these fights, these injurious sentences, soon revealed his bad character and dishonesty. The *gavots,* who know him well, but too late, sent this false brother away with curses. He was far from being worth what he had cost!

Prelude to the Tour of France—The Canopy

I was an affiliate; I went to all the meetings; I scrupulously paid my dues. All that I had seen, except for the hatred and violence, had pleased me. At last, I wished to begin my tour of France. My father was not opposed, but he had a portable walnut canopy to make for the church in Morières and wanted me to undertake the project. The trip would come afterward.

This canopy, which had four fluted columns, four brackets decorated with acanthus leaves, a plume gouged at the top and all set on the simplest of pedestals—I made all by myself. I was both woodworker and sculptor, and in the village I was said to have created a masterpiece. This canopy is of little value, not a work of art or science at all, but I was only eighteen when I made it. That was enough for that age. The piece still exists. I saw it in 1850. It was perfectly preserved, and the inhabitants of the town of Morières made quite a fuss over it. They never see it without thinking of their little Agricol, who is now no longer young and lives in exile.

Tour of France—The Trip from Avignon to Marseilles

The moment of my departure was approaching. At this time the compagnons were often fighting, and to set out to make one's tour of France was almost like going off to war. Thus my mother worried and advised me to go to confession before starting out on such a dangerous expedition.

Up to that time I wore only a short vest. My father had a suit made for me, as well as some shirts and other clothes; he bought me a trunk to carry it all and gave me 30 francs and 6 coins of 100 sous each, the largest amount of money I had ever had up to then. On the third day after Easter, that is, 20 April 1824, I put my trunk on the coach and, carrying a small bundle suspended on a stick over my shoulder, I set out on foot for Avignon. I was with a compagnon named Jargea, surnamed Vivarais Palme de la Gloire (Palm of Glory), who, like myself, was headed toward Marseilles. The compagnons, according to custom, bid us farewell with songs. Then they embraced us and left us alone to go on our way. . . .

On the Compagnons' Strikes

In that year (1827) there was a strike in Nîmes. Several of our compagnons were imprisoned. We had to help them as we had helped out our brothers in Blois, with collections taken up in every town.

Competition is something that comes naturally. Each master wants to work and, to obtain preference, he offers to produce and to deliver goods at a lower price than his fellows. Cheap prices lead to even cheaper prices. But when the masters are running businesses that make little money, when they fear losing what they have, when in fact they may lose it, what do they do? They lower the cost of the manufacture—the workman's wages. This wage sags, then falls from one year to the next, all as the completely natural result of man's mercantile tendency.

The workingman, when he works for a very low wage, when he does not know how to make ends meet, cannot lay any part of his too-heavy burden on anyone else, since he cannot lower proportionately the price of meat, bread, or rent. Since he wants to live as an honest man, to honor his obligations, what does he do? He goes on strike.

No other way exists for him to obtain justice, to increase wages, to balance his wage with his necessary expenses.

The most intelligent, active, and devoted workmen, the best willed among them, and often heads of different societies of the corporation will act in concert, draft a price list, assess the value of each type of job done in the trade and confer with the masters.

If the latter wish to discuss the complaints, the two parties negotiate and debate their respective interests, together establishing the wage, either by day or by piece, and everything is worked out amicably, as in a family. If the masters do not want to listen or are too demanding, the compagnons say the word, and both *gavots* and *dévorants* halt work. The shops are emptied. The bosses have no more workers. All labor is suspended.

It sometimes happens that, tired of the struggle, the masters accept the workmen's claims, agree formally to the new rates, and then good order is restored immediately. Other times, they call the law to their aid; they set traps for the leaders of the strike and cause them to be arrested, convicted, and imprisoned as leaders of a coalition.

In Nîmes, three Compagnons of Duty and the same number of Compagnons of the Duty of Liberty had been put into prison as a reward for their devotion to their brothers. For that reason we took up our collections in Châlons, as elsewhere; for that reason the help of all the compagnons on the tour of France was enlisted.

Why, leaders of government, do you imprison men who seek to live by honest work? When their wages are not enough, when these men can no longer feed themselves, should they harm the innkeeper, the landlord, or any good-hearted man to whom they are obliged, and become dishonest? Or would it be better if they were honest but never could satisfy their hunger, if they ruined their health, their physical constitution, if they became an impoverished, malnourished race incapable of serving the country and defending it when needed? These are two extremes that you cannot accept, which I am sure you reject with equal force.

Thus workers must be honest and be able to maintain themselves.

Well then! Let them strike. Let them reach an understanding to raise their shrinking salary. Let it be possible for them to sell the labor of their hands, of their minds, their only merchandise, their only resource, for a decent price. Have a care for these men, who are your brothers, who devote themselves to useful work and whose unhealthy existence forms the reality on which more fortunate lives are based. Compare the lives of the one to those of the others! What would society be without the worker? Would there be rich and powerful men? Would there be grandees, princes, or kings? Or even a shadow of civilization or prosperity or ease anywhere?

If, however, their strikes are violent, if the workers mistreat any boss or any fellow worker who refuses to stop working, then pursue them, condemn them, punish them for their acts of violence. But allow them the freedom to debate the price of their sweat, their blood, their lives. Let them live by their work.

Ah! Does not society feed everyone: robbers, beggars, prostitutes, the meanest and vilest people? Yes, it feeds them all, either in prison, in the hospital, or in infamous places. Others roam free and are parasites, violating or tricking society and living off of it. Since society feeds all, why not encourage the honest rather than the dishonest? In work rather than laziness? In a calm and dignified situation instead of through filth and rebellion? With what one spends on prison, what a fine society we could have.

Let the workingman and workingwoman protect themselves; let them debate their own interests. Raise the wage that is not enough to feed them. Allow them to live by work and in virtue, that they may help their parents, bring up their sons and daughters, that they may raise themselves up, grow greater and greater. . . . Be Christian not in name only but in reality. Let a foretaste of paradise come down on earth. . . . Think of the people, think of the workers. . . . Leaders . . . do not govern for yourself any more, but for them, with the intent of ensuring their welfare, and you will see no more civil wars or revolutions. And you, like us, will live in peace and security. You will be calmer, happier, in the bosom of your family; the clouds of the future disperse, hearts will be more serene, and from the height of his eternal throne God will bless all his children. . . .

17. 1848 in France

Unlike the French Revolution that began in 1789, the one inaugurated in February 1848 turned its attention almost immediately to the special problems of the urban worker. Indeed the widely shared conviction that the new republic, based on universal suffrage, would be able to minister simultaneously to the needs of diverse social groups was the salient feature of the first few months of the new regime's existence, later prompting the historian George Duveaux to characterize the mood of that period as "lyrical illusion."

The following documents, drawn from both printed and archival sources, illustrate the rapid dispelling of that "lyrical illusion" as the concrete policies adopted by the republic began to foster dissent and conflict. The conflict pitted propertyless workers against property owners; it also pitted Paris against the provinces. The issues addressed by the documents are the measures taken by the provisional government to end the insecurity of the workers' lot—that is, the formation of the Luxembourg Commission and especially of the national workshops; the 45 percent surcharge on direct taxation, which was designed to keep the new regime solvent and which fell most heavily on landowners; and the provincial perception of the ideological foundations of the republic. All these issues contributed to the explosion of the so-called June Days of 1848, and all figure in Tocqueville's interpretation of the revolution (document 18).

The Luxembourg Commission

Whereas the Revolution brought about by the people should be to the people's benefit;

From *1848 in France*, edited by Roger Price (London: Thames and Hudson, 1975), pp. 69, 88–89, 101–4. Copyright © 1975 by Thames and Hudson Ltd. Used by permission of the publishers, Cornell University Press and Thames and Hudson Ltd.

Whereas the time has come to put an end to the workers' long and iniq-uitous sufferings;

Whereas the question of work is of supreme importance;

Whereas there is no problem that is greater or more worthy of a Repub-lican government's concern;

Whereas it is pre-eminently for France to study keenly to resolve a prob-lem manifested in this day and age in all the industrial nations of Europe;

Whereas means must be found without the least delay to guarantee to the people the proper fruits of their toil;

The provisional government of the Republic decrees that:

A standing committee, to be called the Government Committee for the Workers, shall be appointed with the express and specific task of concern-ing itself with the workers' problems.

To demonstrate what importance the provisional government of the Re-public attaches to the solution of this major problem, it nominates as Chairman of the Government Committee for the Workers one of its own members, M. Louis Blanc, and, as vice-chairman, another of its members, M. Albert, who is himself a worker.

Workers will be invited to join the committee.

The committee will sit in the Luxembourg palace.

Government decision of 28 February 1848; published in *Le Moniteur,*
29 February 1848.

Effects of the Forty-Five-Centime Tax

The decree relative to the forty-five-centime tax had, above all, a disastrous effect on the country folk. In the Charente, where the land is parcelled out in small lots and where the rural population itself owns most of the land, nearly everybody has been hit hard by this surtax.

The emissaries who came at election time and who went about the coun-tryside preaching communistic and other socially subversive doctrines did more than strengthen a little the hand of the enemies of the Republic.

Report (undated) from the prefect of the Charente for the *Rapport de la commission d'enquête sur l'insurrection qui a éclaté dans la journée du 23 juin sur les événements du 15 mai* (commission of inquiry on the insurrection).

Everywhere the tax is having the worst possible effect on the Republican cause. Either they all refuse to pay up or else they simply cannot raise the money.

Report from the Jura by M. Mereaux, delegate of the Club of Clubs
(Archives nationales C.938).

That measure prevented the horrors of bankruptcy. But it was killing the Republic, for it made it hated in the countryside without making it any more popular in the towns.

Odilon Barrot, *Mémoires posthumes*.

Fear of Socialism and Communism

The rumour was put about that our delegate was going to preach female emancipation, St-Simonism and communism. He was pelted with stones and garbage.

Report from Vitré (Ille-et-Vilaine) by M. Peu, delegate of the Club of Clubs, 14 April 1848 (Archives nationales C.938).

Nobody appreciates the sublime virtues of abnegation and self-sacrifice. The bourgeois are scared by the phantom of communism and they terrify the ill-informed peasants by talking about it. The bankers and capitalists have ridiculous fears. . . . The worker himself seems for the most part not to be aware of the consequences of the solemn act he is about to perform. In Paris, people feel strong, happy and proud; in the provinces, it is as if people had leaden cloaks about their shoulders.

There are things about which it is best not to speak outside Paris. If you want to irritate the man you are talking to, lose his respect or perhaps expose yourself to a worse risk, mention the name of Robespierre or else introduce into your conversation the words communism, fourièrism, or even socialism.

Report from Ruffec (Charente) by M. Prat, delegate of the Club of Clubs, 10 April 1848 (Archives nationales C.938).

National Workshops

The Government View

The national workshops, their numbers swollen by poverty and laziness, became every day a heavier burden, a less productive element in society and a greater menace to public order. They were only a makeshift to ensure good order and to provide a primitive form of public relief for the poor, which became necessary in the days following the Revolution, when the people had to be fed. And it had not been merely a question of feeding them; they had to be kept busy, too, if disorder was not to result from their unemployment.

Alphonse de Lamartine, *Histoire de la révolution de 1848*.

The Conservative View

The national workshops—set up not as casual places of shelter, but as the permanent refuges which society owes to the unemployed—allowed the workers to demand from the masters inflated wages. The worker, protected by the state against the ill-effects of unemployment, could put the master out of business by his demands, and there was almost no way of avoiding that.

The national workshops received a growing population. The men were supported during their strikes by the government, which paid them for doing nothing. They were encouraged by speeches that were hostile to the masters. The men's solidarity in their strikes was confirmed, and they became more and more hostile to the employers. As this system developed the alarm increased in industry and commerce. The workers' poverty helped swell what the employers regarded as the army of anarchy.

From *Le Constitutionnel*, 22 June 1848.

The maintaining of national workshops offered temptations to idleness which it was necessary to get rid of. These workshops had been represented, immediately after the February Revolution, as a provisional resource imposed by imperious necessity. [But] we found ourselves . . . faced by an agglomeration of a hundred thousand . . . paid by the state for fictitious work, and become, clandestinely at first, openly afterward, a dangerous army of socialism. To bring the evil to light and to endeavour to remedy it seemed to the Labour committee the first thing they had to do.

Count de Falloux, *Mémoires*.

Decision to Run Them Down

At Citizen Garnier-Pagès' proposal, the commission resolves that the registers of workers for the national workshops shall be closed; that lists shall be opened for workers aged between eighteen and twenty-five years who are willing to sign on for an engagement in the army. Those who refuse to do so will be sent back to their home districts.

Decision of the executive commission of the government, 13 May 1848; not published in *Le Moniteur* until 22 June. (Restrictions on entry into the national workshops, however, started immediately.)

The Commission decides on the following measures relative to the national workshops:

All the workers who have been in Paris for less than six months are to be sent away from the capital with marching orders. . . .

Labour exchanges are to be opened where employers will be able to come and ask for workers. Those workers who refuse jobs in particular industries will immediately be sent away from the national workshops.

Decision of the executive commission of the government, 23 May 1848; not published in *Le Moniteur* until 4 June.

The commission of executive power decides that, within five days, the workers in the national workshops aged between eighteen and twenty-five must accept a two-year engagement in the army or, if they refuse, be excluded from the workshops.

Decision of the executive commission of the government, 16 June 1848; published in *Le Moniteur* 22 June.

The Measures Seen as Provocative

. . . More effort could have been made, in our view, to prepare opinion for the announcement; more prudence could have been shown. Because the announcement was sudden and because there was a lack of reassuring comment, there is a danger of jeopardizing this decision which has been staved off for so long.

It is plain that the assistance provided for the workers will be cut off only when they have found alternative means of livelihood. Doubtless the government has other measures up its sleeve. It should have announced them, or, at least, have given some hint. It is regrettable that these precautions were not taken to allay all the workers' anxieties about this and to avoid creating alarm.

This new decision by the government could not have been presented in a more unfortunate fashion, and indeed there are already reports of disquiet in the national workshops.

From *Le Constitutionnel*, 23 June 1848.

Workers' Reactions to the Threatened Closures

Addressed to Minister Goudchaux: "Are you really the man who was the first finance minister of the Republic, of the Republic won at the cost of blood thanks to the workers' courage, of this Republic whose first vow was to provide bread every day for all its children by proclaiming the universal right to work? Work, who will give it to us if not the state at a time when industry has everywhere closed its workshops, shops and factories? Yesterday martyrs for the Republic out on the barricades, today its defenders in the ranks of the national guard, the workers might consider it owed them something. . . .

"Why do the national workshops so rouse your reprobation? You are not asking for their reform, but for their total abolition. But what is to be done with this mass of 110,000 workers who are waiting each day for their modest pay, for the means of existence for themselves and their families? Are they to be left a prey to the evil influences of hunger and of the excesses that follow in the wake of despair?"

> Poster signed *Les membres du bureau provisoire du Club de l'Union des Brigadiers des Ateliers nationaux;* dated 20 June 1848 (Archives nationales C.930).

We are not people asking for charity. The Republic promised work to provide a livelihood for all its children. . . . So give us work so that we may live like free men. . . .

Do not forget, Monarchists, that it was not so that we could remain your slaves that we brought about a third revolution. We fought your social system, the sole cause of the disorder and poverty that devours and swallows contemporary society.

> *Réponse des ouvriers à Dupin:* signed by the workers of the nineteenth brigade of the national workshops; undated (Archives nationales C.930).

I live in the faubourg; by trade I am a cabinet-maker and I am enrolled in the national workshops, waiting for trade to pick up again.

I went into the workshops when I could no longer find bread elsewhere. Since then people have said we were given charity there. But when I went in I did not think that I was becoming a beggar. I believed that my brothers who were rich were giving me a little of what they had to spare simply because I was their brother.

I admit that I have not worked very hard in the national workshops, but then I have done what I could. I am too old now to change my trade easily—that is one explanation. But there is another: the fact is that, in the national workshops, there was absolutely nothing to do.

> Letter to the editor of the newspaper *L'Aimable Fabourien,* appearing in the issue of 4 June 1848 (Archives nationales C.930).

18. Alexis de Tocqueville, *Recollections*

Alexis de Tocqueville (1805–59) was the scion of a French noble family in Normandy. His father, Hervé de Tocqueville, had been a prisoner in Paris in 1794 during the Reign of Terror and was only saved from the guillotine by the 9th of Thermidor. During the Restoration his father served as a prefect of several departments, including the Moselle and Seine-et-Oise. Educated first by private tutors and then at Paris in the law,

From *The Recollections of Alexis de Tocqueville,* translated by Alexander Teixeira de Mattos (New York: Macmillan, 1896), pp. 3–6, 9–16, 79–101, 187–90, 204–5, 211–12.

Tocqueville was appointed to a lower magistracy in 1827. Although in 1830 he swore allegiance to the new Orleanist king, Louis-Philippe, he did so with considerable unease and in spite of the opposition of his Legitimist family. In 1831–32 he traveled (with Gustave de Beaumont) in the United States and published his *Democracy in America* in 1835–40, justly celebrated as one of the most insightful and intelligent commentaries ever produced on American society. In 1839 Tocqueville became a member of the French Chamber of Deputies, where he joined the small liberal opposition against the regime of Louis-Philippe, but remained isolated from the chief liberal leaders. In the Chamber he took a special interest in laws for prison reform and for the abolition of slavery.

During the Revolution of 1848 Tocqueville's political fortunes oscillated between extraordinary success and deep humiliation. Elected to the Constituent Assembly in April 1848, he was named a member of the committee charged with drafting the new constitution, but his advice was usually ignored. In June 1849 Tocqueville was appointed minister of foreign affairs in the ministry of Odilon Barrot, a position he was forced to resign in October by the new president of the Second Republic, Louis Bonaparte. He continued as an interested, if embittered, bystander to the ministerial politics of the revolution until the coup d'état of Bonaparte in December 1851, at which point Tocqueville retired from public life.

The *Souvenirs* (from which our selections are taken) are the product of a period of reflection and writing by Tocqueville in 1850–51. He forbade their publication during his lifetime; they were only printed long after his death by his grandnephew, in 1893.

Origin and Character of These Recollections—General Aspect of the Period Preceding the Revolution of 1848—Preliminary Symptoms of the Revolution

Removed for a time from the scene of public life, I am constrained, in the midst of my solitude, to turn my thoughts upon myself, or rather to reflect upon contemporary events in which I have taken part or acted as a witness. And it seems to me that the best use I can make of my leisure is to retrace these events, to portray the men who took part in them under my eyes, and thus to seize and engrave, if I can, upon my memory the confused features which compose the disturbed physiognomy of my time.

In taking this resolve I have taken another, to which I shall be no less true: these recollections shall be a relaxation of the mind rather than a contribution to literature. I write them for myself alone. They shall be a mirror in which I will amuse myself in contemplating my contemporaries and myself; not a picture painted for the public. My most intimate friends shall not see them, for I wish to retain the liberty of depicting them as I shall depict myself, without flattery. I wish to arrive truly at the secret motives which have caused them, and me, and others to act; and, when discovered, to reveal them here. In a word, I wish this expression of my recollections to be a sincere one; and to effect this, it is essential that it should remain absolutely secret.

I intend that my recollections shall not go farther back than the Revolution of 1848, nor extend to a later date than the 30th of October 1849, the day upon which I resigned my office. It is only within these limits that the events which I propose to relate have any importance, or that my position has enabled me to observe them well.

My life was passed, although in a comparatively secluded fashion, in the midst of the parliamentary world of the closing years of the Monarchy of July. Nevertheless, it would be no easy task for me to recall distinctly the events of a period so little removed from the present, and yet leaving so confused a trace in my memory. The thread of my recollections is lost amid the whirl of minor incidents, of paltry ideas, of petty passions, of personal views and contradictory opinions in which the life of public men was at that time spent. All that remains vivid in my mind is the general aspect of the period; for I often regarded it with a curiosity mingled with dread, and I clearly discerned the special features by which it was characterized.

Our history from 1789 to 1830, if viewed from a distance and as a whole, affords as it were the picture of a struggle to the death between the Ancien Régime, its traditions, memories, hopes, and men, as represented by the aristocracy, and New France under the leadership of the middle class. The year 1830 closed the first period of our revolutions, or rather of our revolution: for there is but one, which has remained always the same in the face of varying fortunes, of which our fathers witnessed the commencement, and of which we, in all probability, shall not live to behold the end. In 1830 the triumph of the middle class had been definite and so thorough that all political power, every franchise, every prerogative, and the whole government was confined and, as it were, heaped up within the narrow limits of this one class, to the statutory exclusion of all beneath them and the actual exclusion of all above. Not only did it thus alone rule society, but it may be said to have formed it. It ensconced itself in every vacant place, prodigiously augmented the number of places, and accustomed itself to live almost as much upon the Treasury as upon its own industry.

No sooner had the Revolution of 1830 become an accomplished fact, than there ensued a great lull in political passion, a sort of general subsidence, accompanied by a rapid increase in the public wealth. The particular spirit of the middle class became the general spirit of the government; it ruled the latter's foreign policy as well as affairs at home: an active, industrious spirit, often dishonourable, generally sober, occasionally reckless through vanity or egoism, but timid by temperament, moderate in all things, except in its love of ease and comfort, and wholly undistinguished. It was a spirit which, mingled with that of the people or of the aristocracy, can do wonders; but which, by itself, will never produce more than a government shorn of both virtue and greatness. Master of everything in a manner that no aristocracy had ever been or may ever hope to be, the middle class, when called upon to assume the government, took it up as a trade; it entrenched itself behind its power, and before long, in their egoism, each of its members thought much more of his private business than of public affairs, and of his personal enjoyment than of the greatness of the nation.

Posterity, which sees none but the more dazzling crimes, and which loses sight, in general, of mere vices, will never, perhaps, know to what extent the government of that day, towards its close, assumed the ways of a trading company, which conducts all its transactions with a view to the profits accruing to the shareholders. These vices were due to the natural instincts of the dominant class, to the absoluteness of its power, and also to the character of the time. Possibly also King Louis-Philippe had contributed to their growth. . . .

In this political world thus constituted and conducted, what was most wanting, particularly towards the end, was political life itself. It could neither come into being nor be maintained within the legal circle which the Constitution had traced for it: the old aristocracy was vanquished, the people excluded. As all business was discussed among members of one class, in the interest and in the spirit of that class, there was no battlefield for contending parties to meet upon. This singular homogeneity of position, of interests, and consequently of views, reigning in what M. Guizot had once called the legal country, deprived the parliamentary debates of all originality, of all reality, and therefore of all genuine passion. I have spent ten years of my life in the company of truly great minds, who were in a constant state of agitation without succeeding in heating themselves, and who spent all their perspicacity in vain endeavours to find subjects upon which they could seriously disagree.

On the other hand, the preponderating influence which King Louis-Philippe had acquired in public affairs, which never permitted the politicians to stray very far from that Prince's ideas, lest they should at the same time be removed from power, reduced the different colours of parties to the merest shades, and debates to the splitting of straws. I doubt whether any parliament (not excepting the Constituent Assembly, I mean the true one, that of 1789) ever contained more varied and brilliant talents than did ours during the closing years of the Monarchy of July. Nevertheless, I am able to declare that these great orators were tired to death of listening to one another, and, what was worse, the whole country was tired of listening to them. It grew unconsciously accustomed to look upon the debates in the Chambers as exercises of the intellect rather than as serious discussions, and upon all the differences between the various parliamentary parties— the majority, the left centre, or the dynastic opposition—as domestic quarrels between children of one family trying to trick one another. A few glaring instances of corruption, discovered by accident, led it to presuppose a number of hidden cases, and convinced it that the whole of the governing class was corrupt; whence it conceived for the latter a silent contempt, which was generally taken for confiding and contented submission.

The country was at that time divided into two unequal parts, or rather zones: in the upper, which alone was intended to contain the whole of the nation's political life, there reigned nothing but languor, impotence, stagnation, and boredom; in the lower, on the contrary, political life began to make itself manifest by means of feverish and irregular signs, of which the attentive observer was easily able to seize the meaning.

I was one of these observers; and although I was far from imagining that the catastrophe was so near at hand and fated to be so terrible, I felt a distrust springing up and insensibly growing in my mind, and the idea taking root more and more that we were making strides towards a fresh revolution. This denoted a great change in my thoughts; since the general appeasement and flatness that followed the Revolution of July had led me to believe for a long time that I was destined to spend my life amid an enervated and peaceful society. Indeed, anyone who had only examined the inside of the governmental fabric would have had the same conviction. Everything there seemed combined to produce with the machinery of liberty a preponderance of royal power which verged upon despotism; and, in fact, this result was produced almost without effort by the regular and tranquil movement of the machine. King Louis-Philippe was persuaded that, so long as he did not himself lay hand upon that fine instrument, and allowed it to work according to rule, he was safe from all peril. His only occupation was to keep it in order, and to make it work according to his own views, forgetful of society, upon which this ingenious piece of mechanism rested; he resembled the man who refused to believe that his house was on fire, because he had the key in his pocket. I had neither the same interests nor the same cares, and this permitted me to see through the mechanism of institutions and the agglomeration of petty every-day facts, and to observe the state of morals and opinions in the country. There I clearly beheld the appearance of several of the portents that usually denote the approach of revolutions, and I began to believe that in 1830 I had taken for the end of the play what was nothing more than the end of an act.

A short unpublished document which I composed at the time, and a speech which I delivered early in 1848, will bear witness to these preoccupations of my mind.

A number of my friends in Parliament met together in October 1847, to decide upon the policy to be adopted during the ensuing session. It was agreed that we should issue a programme in the form of a manifesto, and the task of drawing it up was deputed to me. Later, the idea of this publication was abandoned, but I had already written the document. I have discovered it among my papers, and I give the following extracts. After commenting on the symptoms of languor in Parliament, I continued:

. . . The time will come when the country will find itself once again divided between two great parties. The French Revolution, which abolished all privileges and destroyed all exclusive rights, has allowed one to remain, that of landed property. Let not the landlords deceive themselves as to the strength of their position, nor think that the rights of property form an insurmountable barrier because they have not as yet been surmounted; for our times are unlike any others. When the rights of property were merely the origin and commencement of a number of other rights, they were easily defended, or rather, they were never attacked; they then formed the surrounding wall of society, of which all other rights were the outposts; no blows reached them; no serious attempt was ever made to touch them. But to-day, when the rights of property are nothing more than the last remnants of an overthrown aristocratic world, when they alone are left intact, isolated privileges amid the universal levelling of society; when they are no longer protected behind a number of still more controversible and odious rights, the case is altered, and they alone are left daily to resist the direct and unceasing shock of democratic opinion. . . .

. . . Before long, the political struggle will be restricted to those who have and those who have not; property will form the great field of battle; and the principal political questions will turn upon the more or less important modifications to be introduced into the rights of landlords. We shall then have once more among us great public agitations and great political parties.

How is it that these premonitory symptoms escape the general view? Can anyone believe that it is by accident, through some passing whim of the human brain, that we see appearing on every side these curious doctrines, bearing different titles, but all characterized in their essence by their denial of the rights of property, and all tending, at least, to limit, diminish, and weaken the exercise of these rights? Who can fail here to recognise the final symptom of the old democratic disease of the time, whose crisis would seem to be at hand?

I was still more urgent and explicit in the speech which I delivered in the Chamber of Deputies on the 29th of January 1848, and which appeared in the *Moniteur* of the 30th.

I quote the principal passages:

. . . I am told that there is no danger because there are no riots; I am told that, because there is no visible disorder on the surface of society, there is no revolution at hand.

Gentlemen, permit me to say that I believe you are deceived. True, there is no actual disorder; but it has entered deeply into men's minds. See what is passing in the breasts of the working classes, who, I grant, are at present quiet. No doubt they are not disturbed by political passion, properly so-called, to the same extent that they have been; but can you not see that their passions, instead of political, have become social? Do you not see that there are gradually forming in their breasts opinions and ideas which are destined not only to upset this or that law, ministry, or even form of government, but society itself, until it totters upon the foundations on which it rests today? Do you not listen to what they say to themselves each day? Do you not hear them repeating unceasingly that all that is above them is incapable and unworthy of governing them; that the present distribution of goods throughout the world is unjust; that property rests on a foundation which is not an equitable foundation? And do you not realize that when such opinions take root, when they spread in an almost universal manner, when they sink deeply into the masses, they are bound to bring with them sooner or later, I know not when nor how, a most formidable revolution?

This, gentlemen, is my profound conviction: I believe that we are at this moment sleeping on a volcano. I am profoundly convinced of it. . . .

. . . I was saying just now that this evil would, sooner or later, I know not how nor whence it will come, bring with it a most serious revolution: be assured that that is so.

When I come to investigate what, at different times, in different periods, among different peoples, has been the effective cause that has brought about the downfall of the governing classes, I perceive this or that event, man, or accidental or superficial cause; but, believe me, the real reason, the effective reason which causes men to lose their power is, that they have become unworthy to retain it.

Think, gentlemen, of the old Monarchy: it was stronger than you are, stronger in its origin; it was able to lean more than you do upon ancient customs, ancient habits, ancient beliefs; it was stronger than you are, and yet it has fallen to dust. And why did it fall? Do you think it was by some particular mischance? Do you think it was by the act of some man, by the deficit, the oath in the Tennis Court, La Fayette, Mirabeau? No, gentlemen; there was another reason: the class that was then the governing class had become, through its indifference, its selfishness and its vices, incapable and unworthy of governing the country.

That was the true reason.

Well, gentlemen, if it is right to have this patriotic prejudice at all times, how much more is it not right to have it in our own? Do you not feel, by some intuitive instinct which is not capable of analysis, but which is undeniable, that the earth is quaking once again in Europe? Do you not feel . . . what shall I say? . . . as it were a gale of revolution in the air? This gale, no one knows whence it springs, whence it blows, nor, believe me, whom it will carry with it; and it is in such times as these that you remain calm before the degradation of public morality—for the expression is not too strong.

I speak without bitterness; I am even addressing you without any party spirit; I am attacking men against whom I feel no vindictiveness. But I am obliged to communicate to my country my firm and decided conviction. Well then, my firm and decided conviction is this: that public morality is being degraded, and that the degradation of public morality will shortly, very shortly, perhaps, bring down upon you a new revolution. Is the life of kings held by stronger threads? Are these more difficult to snap than those of other men? Can you say to-day that you are certain of to-morrow? Do you know what may happen in France a year hence, or even a month or a day hence? You do not know; but what you must know is that the tempest is looming on the horizon, that it is coming towards us. Will you allow it to take you by surprise?

Gentlemen, I implore you not to do so. I do not ask you, I implore you. I would gladly throw myself on my knees before you, so strongly do I believe in the reality and the seriousness of the danger, so convinced am I that my warnings are no empty rhetoric. Yes, the danger is great. Allay it while there is yet time; correct the evil by efficacious remedies, by attacking it not in its symptoms but in itself.

Legislative changes have been spoken of. I am greatly disposed to think that these changes are not only very useful, but necessary; thus, I believe in the need of electoral reform, in the urgency of parliamentary reform; but I am not, gentlemen, so mad as not to know that no laws can affect the destinies of nations. No, it is not the mechanism of laws that produces great events, gentlemen, but the inner spirit of the government. Keep the laws as they are, if you wish. I think you would be very wrong to do so; but keep them. Keep the men, too, if it gives you any pleasure. I raise no objection so far as I am concerned. But, in God's name, change the spirit of the government; for, I repeat, that spirit will lead you to the abyss. . . .[1]

My Explanation of the 24th of February, and My Views as to Its Effects upon the Future

And so the Monarchy of July was fallen, fallen without a struggle, and before rather than beneath the blows of the victors, who were as astonished

---

1. Tocqueville delivered this speech in the Chamber of Deputies on 27 January 1848, in the debate on the Address in response to the Speech from the Throne.—ED.

at their triumph as were the vanquished at their defeat. I have often, since the Revolution of February, heard M. Guizot and even M. Molé and M. Thiers declare that this event should only be attributed to a surprise and regarded as a mere accident, a bold and lucky stroke and nothing more. I have always felt tempted to answer them in the words which Molière's Misanthrope uses to Oronte:

Pour en juger ainsi, vous avez vos raisons;

for these three men had conducted the affairs of France, under the guidance of King Louis-Philippe, during eighteen years, and it was difficult for them to admit that it was the King's bad government which had prepared the catastrophe which hurled him from the Throne.

As for me, I have not the same motives for forming an opinion, and I could hardly persuade myself to be of theirs. I am not prepared to say that accidents played no part in the Revolution of February: on the contrary, they played a great one; but they were not the only thing.

I have come across men of letters, who have written history without taking part in public affairs, and politicians, who have only concerned themselves with producing events without thinking of describing them. I have observed that the first are always inclined to find general causes, whereas the others, living in the midst of disconnected daily facts, are prone to imagine that everything is attributable to particular incidents, and that the wires which they pull are the same that move the world. It is to be presumed that both are equally deceived.

For my part, I detest these absolute systems, which represent all the events of history as depending upon great first causes linked by the chain of fatality, and which, as it were, suppress men from the history of the human race. They seem narrow, to my mind, under their pretence of broadness, and false beneath their air of mathematical exactness. I believe (*pace* the writers who have invented these sublime theories in order to feed their vanity and facilitate their work) that many important historical facts can only be explained by accidental circumstances, and that many others remain totally inexplicable. Moreover, chance, or rather that tangle of secondary causes which we call chance, for want of the knowledge how to unravel it, plays a great part in all that happens on the world's stage; although I firmly believe that chance does nothing that has not been prepared beforehand. Antecedent facts, the nature of institutions, the cast of minds and the state of morals are the materials of which are composed those impromptus which astonish and alarm us.

The Revolution of February, in common with all other great events of this class, sprang from general causes, impregnated, if I am permitted the expression, by accidents; and it would be as superficial a judgment to ascribe it necessarily to the former or exclusively to the latter.

The industrial revolution which, during the past thirty years, had turned Paris into the principal manufacturing city of France and attracted within its walls an entire new population of workmen (to whom the works of the fortifications had added another population of labourers at present deprived of work) tended more and more to inflame this multitude. Add to this the democratic disease of envy, which was silently permeating it; the economical and political theories which were beginning to make their way and which strove to prove that human misery was the work of laws and not of Providence, and that poverty could be suppressed by changing the conditions of society; the contempt into which the governing class, and especially the men who led it, had fallen, a contempt so general and so profound that it paralyzed the resistance even of those who were most interested in maintaining the power that was being overthrown; the centralization which reduced the whole revolutionary movement to the overmastering of Paris and the seizing of the machinery of government; and lastly, the mobility of all things, institutions, ideas, men and customs, in a fluctuating state of society which had, in less than sixty years, undergone the shock of seven great revolutions, without numbering a multitude of smaller, secondary upheavals. These were the general causes without which the Revolution of February would have been impossible. The principal accidents which led to it were the passions of the dynastic Opposition, which brought about a riot in proposing a reform; the suppression of this riot, first over-violent, and then abandoned; the sudden disappearance of the old Ministry, unexpectedly snapping the threads of power, which the new ministers, in their confusion, were unable either to seize upon or to reunite; the mistakes and disorder of mind of these ministers, so powerless to reestablish that which they had been strong enough to overthrow; the vacillation of the generals; the absence of the only Princes who possessed either personal energy or popularity; and above all, the senile imbecility of King Louis-Philippe, his weakness, which no one could have foreseen, and which still remains almost incredible, after the event has proved it.

I have sometimes asked myself what could have produced this sudden and unprecedented depression in the King's mind. Louis-Philippe had spent his life in the midst of revolutions, and certainly lacked neither experience, courage, nor readiness of mind, although these qualities all failed him so completely on that day. In my opinion, his weakness was due to his excessive surprise; he was overwhelmed with consternation before he had grasped the meaning of things. The Revolution of February was *unforeseen* by all, but by him more than any other; he had been prepared for it by no warning from the outside, for since many years his mind had withdrawn into that sort of haughty solitude into which in the end the intellect almost always settles down of princes who have long lived happily, and who, mistaking luck for genius, refuse to listen to anything, because they think that there is nothing left for them to learn from anybody. Besides, Louis-Philippe had been deceived, as I have already said that his ministers were, by the misleading light cast by antecedent facts upon present times. One might draw a strange picture of all the errors which have thus been begotten, one by the other, without resembling each other. We see Charles I. driven to tyranny and violence at the sight of the progress which the spirit of opposition had made in England during the gentle reign of his father; Louis XVI. determined to suffer everything because Charles I. had perished by refusing to endure anything; Charles X. provoking the Revolution, because he had with his own eyes beheld the weakness of Louis XVI.; and lastly, Louis-Philippe, who had more perspicacity than any of them, imagining that, in order to remain on the Throne, all he had to do was to observe the letter of the law while violating its spirit, and that, provided he himself kept within the bounds of the Charter, the nation would never exceed them. To warp the spirit of the Constitution without changing the letter; to set the vices of the country in opposition to each other; gently to drown revolutionary passion in the love of material enjoyment: such was the idea of his whole life. Little by little, it had become, not his leading, but his sole idea. He had wrapped himself in it, he had lived in it; and when he suddenly saw that it was a false idea, he became like a man who is awakened in the night by an earthquake, and who, feeling his house crumbling in the darkness, and the very ground seeming to yawn beneath his feet, remains distracted amid this unforeseen and universal ruin.

I am arguing very much at my ease to-day concerning the causes that brought about the events of the 24th of February; but on the afternoon of that day I had many other things in my head: I was thinking of the events themselves, and sought less for what had produced them than for what was to follow.

I returned slowly home. I explained in a few words to Madame de Toqueville what I had seen, and sat down in a corner to think. I cannot remember ever feeling my soul so full of sadness. It was the second revolution I had seen accomplish itself, before my eyes, within seventeen years! . . .

I had spent the best days of my youth amid a society which seemed to increase in greatness and prosperity as it increased in liberty; I had conceived the idea of a balanced, regulated liberty, held in check by religion, custom and law; the attractions of this liberty had touched me; it had become the passion of my life; I felt that I could never be consoled for its loss, and that I must renounce all hope of its recovery.

I had gained too much experience of mankind to be able to content myself with empty words; I knew that, if one great revolution is able to establish liberty in a country, a number of succeeding revolutions make all regular liberty impossible for very many years.

I could not yet know what would issue from this last revolution, but I was already convinced that it could give birth to nothing that would satisfy me; and I foresaw that, whatever might be the lot reserved for our posterity, our own fate was to drag on our lives miserably amid alternate reactions of licence and oppression.

I began to pass in review the history of our last sixty years, and I smiled bitterly when I thought of the illusions formed at the conclusion of each period in this long revolution; the theories on which these illusions had been fed; the sapient dreams of our historians, and all the ingenious and deceptive systems by the aid of which it had been endeavoured to explain a present which was still incorrectly seen, and a future which was not seen at all.

The Constitutional Monarchy had succeeded the Ancien Régime; the Republic, the Monarchy; the Empire, the Republic; the Restoration, the Empire; and then came the Monarchy of July. After each of these successive changes it was said that the French Revolution, having accomplished what was presumptuously called its work, was finished; this had been said and it had been believed. Alas! I myself had hoped it under the Restoration, and again after the fall of the Government of the Restoration; and here is the French Revolution beginning over again, for it is still the same one. As we go on, its end seems farther off and shrouded in greater darkness. Shall we ever—as we are assured by other prophets, perhaps as delusive as their predecessors—shall we ever attain a more complete and more far-reaching social transformation than our fathers foresaw and desired, and than we ourselves are able to foresee; or are we not destined simply to end in a condition of intermittent anarchy, the well-known chronic and incurable complaint of old races? As for me, I am unable to say; I do not know when this long voyage will be ended; I am weary of seeing the shore in each successive mirage, and I often ask myself whether the *terra firma* we are seeking does really exist, and whether we are not doomed to rove upon the seas for ever.

I spent the rest of the day with Ampère, who was my colleague at the Institute, and one of my best friends. He came to discover what had become of me in the affray, and to ask himself to dinner. I wished at first to relieve myself by making him share my vexation; but I soon perceived that his impression was not the same as mine, and that he looked differently upon the revolution which was in progress. Ampère was a man of intelligence and, better still, a man full of heart, gentle in manner, and reliable. His good-nature caused him to be liked; and he was popular because of his versatile, witty, amusing, good-humoured conversation, in which he made many remarks that were at once entertaining and agreeable to hear, but too shallow to remember. Unfortunately, he was inclined to carry the *esprit* of the salons into literature and the *esprit* of literature into politics. What I call literary *esprit* in politics consists in seeking for what is novel and ingenious rather than for what is true; in preferring the showy to the useful; in showing one's self very sensible to the playing and elocution of the actors, without regard to the results of the play; and, lastly, in judging by impressions rather than reasons. I need not say that this eccentricity exists among others besides Academicians. To tell the truth, the whole nation is a little inclined that way, and the French Public very often takes a man-of-letters' view of politics. Ampère held the fallen Government in great contempt, and its last actions had irritated him greatly. Moreover, he had witnessed many instances of courage, disinterestedness, and even generosity among the insurgents; and he had been bitten by the popular excitement.

I saw that he not only did not enter into my view, but that he was disposed to take quite an opposite one. Seeing this, I was suddenly impelled to turn against Ampère all the feelings of indignation, grief and anger that had acccumulating in my heart since the morning; and I spoke to him with a violence of language which I have often since recalled with a certain shame, and which none but a friendship so sincere as his could have excused. I remember saying to him, *inter alia:*

> You understand nothing of what is happening; you are judging like a poet or a Paris cockney. You call this the triumph of liberty, when it is its final defeat. I tell you that the people which you so artlessly admire has just succeeded in proving that it is unfit and unworthy to live a life of freedom. Show me what experience has taught it! Where are the new virtues it has gained, the old vices it has laid aside? No, I tell you, it is always the same, as impatient, as thoughtless, as contemptuous of law and order, as easily led and as cowardly in the presence of danger as its fathers were before it. Time has altered it in no way, and has left it as frivolous in serious matters as it used to be in trifles.

After much vociferation we both ended by appealing to the future, that enlightened and upright judge who always, alas! arrives too late.

Paris on the Morrow of the 24th of February and the Next Days— The Socialistic Character of the New Revolution

The night passed without accidents, although not until the morning did the streets cease to resound with cries and gun-shots; but these were sounds of triumph, not of combat. So soon as it was light, I went out to observe the appearance of the town, and to discover what had become of my two young nephews, who were being educated at the Little Seminary. The Little Seminary was in the Rue de Madame, at the back of the Luxembourg, so that I had to cross a great part of the town to reach it.

I found the streets quiet, and even half deserted, as they usually are in Paris on a Sunday morning, when the rich are still asleep and the poor are resting. From time to time, along the walls, one met the victors of the preceding day; but they were filled with wine rather than political ardour, and were, for the most part, making for their homes without taking heed of the passers-by. A few shops were open, and one caught sight of the frightened, but still more astonished, shopkeepers, who reminded one of spectators witnessing the end of a play which they did not quite understand. What one saw most of in the streets deserted by the people, was soldiers; some walking singly, others in little groups, all unarmed, and crossing the city on their roads home. The defeat these men had just sustained had left a very vivid and lasting impression of shame and anger upon them. This was noticed later, but was not apparent at the time: the pleasure of finding themselves at liberty seemed to absorb every other feeling in these lads; they walked with a careless air, with a light and easy gait.

The Little Seminary had not been attacked nor even insulted. My nephews, however, were not there; they had been sent home the evening before to their maternal grandmother. Accordingly, I turned back, taking the Rue du Bac, to find out what had become of Lamoricière, who was then living in that street; and it was only after recognizing me that the servants admitted that their master was at home, and consented to take me to him.

I found this singular person, whom I shall have occasion to mention more than once, stretched upon his bed, and reduced to a state of immobility very much opposed to his character or taste. His head was half broken open; his arms pierced with bayonet-thrusts; all his limbs bruised and powerless. For the rest, he was the same as ever, with his bright intelligence and his indomitable heart. He told me of all that happened to him the day before, and of the thousand dangers which he had only escaped by miracle. I strongly advised him to rest until he was cured, and even long after, so as not uselessly to endanger his person and his reputation in the chaos about to ensue: good advice, undoubtedly, to give to a man so enamoured of action and so accustomed to act that, after doing what is necessary and useful, he is always ready to undertake the injurious and dangerous, rather than do nothing; but no more effective than all those counsels which go against nature.

I spent the whole afternoon in walking about Paris. Two things in particular struck me: the first was, I will not say the mainly, but the uniquely and exclusively popular character of the revolution that had just taken place; the omnipotence it had given to the people properly so-called—that is to say, the classes who work with their hands—over all others. The second was the comparative absence of malignant passion, or, as a matter of fact, of any keen passion—an absence which at once made it clear that the lower orders had suddenly become masters of Paris.

Although the working classes had often played the leading part in the events of the First Revolution, they had never been the sole leaders and masters of the State, either *de facto* or *de jure;* it is doubtful whether the Convention contained a single man of the people; it was composed of *bourgeois* and men of letters. The war between the Mountain and the Girondists was conducted on both sides by members of the middle class, and the triumph of the former never brought power down into the hands of the people alone. The Revolution of July was effected by the people, but the middle class had stirred it up and led it, and secured the principal fruits of it. The Revolution of February, on the contrary, seemed to be made entirely outside the *bourgeoisie* and against it.

In this great concussion, the two parties of which the social body in France is mainly composed had, in a way, been thrown more completely asunder, and the mass of the people, which had stood alone, remained in sole possession of power. Nothing more novel had been known in our annals. Similar revolutions had taken place, it is true, in other countries and other days; for the history of our own times, however new and unexpected it may seem, always belongs at bottom to the old history of humanity, and what we call new facts are oftenest nothing more than facts forgotten. Florence, in particular, towards the close of the middle ages, had presented on a small scale a spectacle analogous to ours; the noble classes had first been succeeded by the burgher classes, and then one day the latter were, in their turn, expelled from the government, and a *gonfalonier* was seen marching barefoot at the head of the people, and thus leading the Republic. But in Florence this popular revolution was the result of transient and special causes, while with us it was brought about by causes very permanent and of a kind so general that, after stirring up France, it was to be expected that it would excite all the rest of Europe. This time it was not only a question of the triumph of a party; the aim was to establish a social science, a philosophy, I might almost say a religion, fit to be learned and followed by all mankind. This was the really new portion of the old picture.

Throughout this day, I did not see in Paris a single one of the former agents of the public authority: not a soldier, not a gendarme, not a policeman; the National Guard itself had disappeared. The people alone bore arms, guarded the public buildings, watched, gave orders, punished; it was an extraordinary and terrible thing to see in the sole hands of those who possessed nothing all this immense town, so full of riches, or rather this great nation: for, thanks to centralization, he who reigns in Paris governs France. Hence the affright of all the other classes was extreme; I doubt whether at any period of the Revolution it had been so great, and I should say that it was only to be compared to that which the civilized cities of the

Roman Empire must have experienced when they suddenly found themselves in the power of the Goths and Vandals. As nothing like this had ever
been seen before, many people expected acts of unexampled violence. For
my part I did not once partake of these fears. What I saw led me to predict
strange disturbances in the near future—singular crises. But I never believed that the rich would be pillaged; I knew the men of the people in Paris
too well not to know that their first movements in times of revolution are
usually generous, and that they are best pleased to spend the days immediately following their triumph in boasting of their victory, laying down the
law, and playing at being great men. During that time it generally happens
that some government or other is set up, the police returns to its post, and
the judge to his bench; and when at last our great men consent to step down
to the better known and more vulgar ground of petty and malicious human
passion, they are no longer able to do so, and are reduced to live simply
like honest men. Besides, we have spent so many years in insurrections
that there has arisen among us a kind of morality peculiar to times of disorder, and a special code for days of rebellion. According to these exceptional laws, murder is tolerated and havoc permitted, but theft is strenuously forbidden; although this, whatever one may say, does not prevent a
good deal of robbery from occurring upon those days, for the simple reason that society in a state of rebellion cannot be different from that at any
other time, and it will always contain a number of rascals who, as far as
they are concerned, scorn the morality of the main body, and despise its
point of honour when they are unobserved. What reassured me still more
was the reflection that the victors had been as much surprised by success as
their adversaries were by defeat: their passions had not had time to take fire
and become intensified in the struggle; the Government had fallen un-
defended by others, or even by itself. It had long been attacked, or at
least keenly censured, by the very men who at heart most deeply regretted
its fall.

For a year past the dynastic Opposition and the republican Opposition
had been living in fallacious intimacy, acting in the same way from different motives. The misunderstanding which had facilitated the revolution
tended to mitigate its aftereffects. Now that the Monarchy had disappeared,
the battle-field seemed empty; the people no longer clearly saw what enemies remained for them to pursue and strike down; the former objects of
their anger, themselves, were no longer there; the clergy had never been
completely reconciled to the new dynasty, and witnessed its ruin without
regret; the old nobility were delighted at it, whatever the ultimate consequences might be: the first had suffered through the system of intolerance
of the middle classes, the second through their pride: both either despised
or feared their government.

For the first time in sixty years, the priests, the old aristocracy and the people met in a common sentiment—a feeling of revenge, it is true, and not of affection; but even that is a great thing in politics, where a community of hatred is almost always the foundation of friendships. The real, the only vanquished were the middle class; but even this had little to fear. Its reign had been exclusive rather than oppressive; corrupt, but not violent; it was despised rather than hated. Moreover, the middle class never forms a compact body in the heart of the nation, a part very distinct from the whole; it always participates a little with all the others, and in some places merges into them. This absence of homogeneity and of exact limits makes the government of the middle class weak and uncertain, but it also makes it intangible, and, as it were, invisible to those who desire to strike it when it is no longer governing.

From all these united causes proceeded that languor of the people which had struck me as much as its omnipotence, a languor which was the more discernible, in that it contrasted strangely with the turgid energy of the language used and the terrible recollections which it evoked. The lukewarm passions of the time were made to speak in the bombastic periods of '93, and one heard cited at every moment the name and example of the illustrious ruffians whom no one possessed either the energy or even a sincere desire to resemble.

It was the Socialistic theories which I have already described as the philosophy of the Revolution of February that later kindled genuine passion, embittered jealousy, and ended by stirring up war between the classes. If the actions at the commencement were less disorderly than might have been feared, on the very morrow of the Revolution there was displayed an extraordinary agitation, an unequalled disorder, in the ideas of the people.

From the 25th of February onwards, a thousand strange systems came issuing pell-mell from the minds of innovators, and spread among the troubled minds of the crowd. Everything still remained standing except Royalty and Parliament; yet it seemed as though the shock of the Revolution had reduced society itself to dust, and as though a competition had been opened for the new form that was to be given to the edifice about to be erected in its place. Everyone came forward with a plan of his own: this one printed it in the papers, that other on the placards with which the walls were soon covered, a third proclaimed his loud-mouthed in the open air. One aimed at destroying inequality of fortune, another inequality of education, a third undertook to do away with the oldest of all inequalities, that between man and woman. Specifics were offered against poverty, and remedies for the disease of work which has tortured humanity since the first days of its existence.

These theories were of very varied natures, often opposed and sometimes hostile to one another; but all of them, aiming lower than the government and striving to reach society itself, on which government rests, adopted the common name of Socialism.

Socialism will always remain the essential characteristic and the most redoubtable remembrance of the Revolution of February. The Republic will only appear to the on-looker to have come upon the scene as a means, not as an end.

It does not come within the scope of these Recollections that I should seek for the causes which gave a socialistic character to the Revolution of February, and I will content myself with saying that the discovery of this new facet of the French Revolution was not of a nature to cause so great surprise as it did. Had it not long been perceived that the people had continually been improving and raising its condition, that its importance, its education, its desires, its power had been constantly increasing? Its prosperity had also grown greater, but less rapidly, and was approaching the limit which it hardly ever passes in old societies, where there are many men and but few places. How should the poor and humbler and yet powerful classes not have dreamt of issuing from their poverty and inferiority by means of their power, especially in an epoch when our view into another world has become dimmer, and the miseries of this world become more visible and seem more intolerable? They had been working to this end for the last sixty years. The people had first endeavoured to help itself by changing every political institution, but after each change it found that its lot was in no way improved, or was only improving with a slowness quite incompatible with the eagerness of its desire. Inevitably, it must sooner or later discover that that which held it fixed in its position was not the constitution of the government but the unalterable laws that constitute society itself; and it was natural that it should be brought to ask itself if it had not both the power and the right to alter those laws, as it had altered all the rest. And to speak more specially of property, which is, as it were, the foundation of our social order—all the privileges which covered it and which, so to speak, concealed the privilege of property having been destroyed, and the latter remaining the principal obstacle to equality among men, and appearing to be the only sign of inequality—was it not necessary, I will not say that it should be abolished in its turn, but at least that the thought of abolishing it should occur to the minds of those who did not enjoy it?

This natural restlessness in the minds of the people, this inevitable perturbation of its thoughts and its desires, these needs, these instincts of the crowd formed in a certain sense the fabric upon which the political innovators embroidered so many monstrous and grotesque figures. Their work may be regarded as ludicrous, but the material on which they worked is the most serious that it is possible for philosophers and statesmen to contemplate.

Will Socialism remain buried in the disdain with which the Socialists of

1848 are so justly covered? I put the question without making any reply. I do not doubt that the laws concerning the constitution of our modern society will in the long run undergo modification: they have already done so in many of their principal parts. But will they ever be destroyed and replaced by others? It seems to me to be impracticable. I say no more, because—the more I study the former condition of the world and see the world of our own day in greater detail, the more I consider the prodigious variety to be met with not only in laws, but in the principles of law, and the different forms even now taken and retained, whatever one may say, by the rights of property on this earth—the more I am tempted to believe that what we call necessary institutions are often no more than institutions to which we have grown accustomed, and that in matters of social constitution the field of possibilities is much more extensive than men living in their various societies are ready to imagine.

The Days of June

I come at last to the insurrection of June, the most extensive and the most singular that has occurred in our history, and perhaps in any other: the most extensive, because, during four days, more than a hundred thousand men were engaged in it; the most singular, because the insurgents fought without a war-cry, without leaders, without flags, and yet with a marvellous harmony and an amount of military experience that astonished the oldest officers.

What distinguished it also, among all the events of this kind which have succeeded one another in France for sixty years, is that it did not aim at changing the form of government, but at altering the order of society. It was not, strictly speaking, a political struggle, in the sense which until then we had given to the word, but a combat of class against class, a sort of Servile War. It represented the facts of the Revolution of February in the same manner as the theories of Socialism represented its ideas; or rather it issued naturally from these ideas, as a son does from his mother. We behold in it nothing more than a blind and rude, but powerful, effort on the part of the workmen to escape from the necessities of their condition, which had been depicted to them as one of unlawful oppression, and to open up by main force a road towards that imaginary comfort with which they had been deluded. It was this mixture of greed and false theory which first gave birth to the insurrection and then made it so formidable. These poor people had been told that the wealth of the rich was in some way the produce of a theft practised upon themselves. They had been assured that the inequality of fortunes was as opposed to morality and the welfare of society as it was to nature. Prompted by their needs and their passions, many had believed this obscure and erroneous notion of right, which, mingled with brute force, imparted to the latter an energy, a tenacity and a power which it would never have possessed unaided.

It must also be observed that this formidable insurrection was not the enterprise of a certain number of conspirators, but the revolt of one whole section of the population against another. Women took part in it as well as men. While the latter fought, the former prepared and carried ammunition; and when at last the time had come to surrender, the women were the last to yield. These women went to battle with, as it were, a housewifely ardour: they looked to victory for the comfort of their husbands and the education of their children. They took pleasure in this war as they might have taken pleasure in a lottery.

As to the strategic science displayed by this multitude, the warlike na ture of the French, their long experience of insurrections, and particularly the military education which the majority of the men of the people in turn receive, suffice to explain it. Half of the Paris workmen have served in our armies, and they are always glad to take up arms again. Generally speaking, old soldiers abound in our riots. On the 24th of February, when Lamoricière was surrounded by his foes, he twice owed his life to insurgents who had fought under him in Africa, men in whom the recollection of their military life had been stronger than the fury of civil war.

As we know it, it was the closing of the national workshops that occasioned the rising. Dreading to disband this formidable soldiery at one stroke, the Government had tried to disperse it by sending part of the workmen into the country. They refused to leave. On the 22nd of June, they marched through Paris in troops, singing in cadence, in a monotonous chant, "We won't be sent away, we won't be sent away. . . ." Their delegates waited upon the members of the Committee of the Executive Power with a series of arrogant demands, and on meeting with a refusal, withdrew with the announcement that next day they would have recourse to arms. Everything, indeed, tended to show that the long-expected crisis had come.

When this news reached the Assembly it caused the greatest alarm. Nevertheless, the Assembly did not interrupt its order of the day; it continued the discussion of a commercial act, and even listened to it, despite its excited condition; true, it was a very important question and a very eminent orator was speaking. The Government had proposed to acquire all the railways by purchase. Montalembert opposed it; his case was good, but his speech was excellent; I do not think I ever heard him speak so well before or since. As a matter of fact, I thought as he did, this time; but I believe that, even in the eyes of his adversaries, he surpassed himself. He made a vigorous attack without being as peevish and outrageous as usual. A certain fear tempered his natural insolence, and set a limit to his paradoxical and querulous humour; for, like so many other men of words, he had more temerity of language than stoutness of heart.

The sitting concluded without any question as to what was occurring outside, and the Assembly adjourned. . . .

. . . [I] returned to the Assembly. I found them discussing a decree to proclaim Paris in a state of siege, to abolish the powers of the Executive Commission, and to replace it by a military dictatorship under General Cavaignac.

The Assembly knew precisely that this was what it wanted. The thing was easily done: it was urgent, and yet it was not done. Each moment some little incident, some trivial motion interrupted and turned aside the current of the general wish; for assemblies are very liable to that sort of nightmare in which an unknown and invisible force seems always at the last moment to interpose between the will and the deed and to prevent the one from influencing the other. Who would have thought that it was Bastide who should eventually induce the Assembly to make up its mind? Yet he it was.

I had heard him say—and it was very true—speaking of himself, that he was never able to remember more than the first fifteen words of a speech. But I have sometimes observed that men who do not know how to speak produce a greater impression, under certain circumstances, than the finest orators. They bring forward but a single idea, that of the moment, clothed in a single phrase, and somehow they lay it down in the rostrum like an inscription written in big letters, which everybody perceives, and in which each instantly recognizes his own particular thought. Bastide, then, displayed his long, honest, melancholy face in the tribune, and said, with a mournful air: "Citizens, in the name of the country, I beseech you to vote as quickly as possible. We are told that perhaps within an hour the Hôtel de Ville will be taken."

These few words put an end to debate, and the decree was voted in the twinkling of an eye.

I protested against the clause proclaiming Paris in a state of siege; I did so by instinct rather than reflection. I have such a contempt and so great a natural horror for military despotism that these feelings came rising tumultuously in my breast when I heard a state of siege suggested, and even dominated those prompted by our peril. In this I made a mistake in which I fortunately found few to imitate me.

The friends of the Executive Commission have asserted in very bitter terms that their adversaries and the partisans of General Cavaignac spread ominous rumours on purpose to precipitate the vote. If the latter did really resort to this trick, I gladly pardon them, for the measures they caused to be taken were indispensable to the safety of the country. . . .

I observed that when the National Guards were told that Paris was in a state of siege, they were pleased, and when one added that the Executive Commission was overthrown, they cheered. Never were people so delighted to be relieved of their liberty and their government. And yet this was what Lamartine's popularity had come to in less than two months.

When we had done speaking, the men surrounded us; they asked us if we were quite sure that the Executive Commission had ceased to act; we had to show them the decree to satisfy them.

Particularly remarkable was the firm attitude of these men. We had come to encourage them, and it was rather they who encouraged us. "Hold on at the National Assembly," they cried, "and we'll hold on here. Courage! no transactions with the insurgents! We'll put an end to the revolt: all will end well." I had never seen the National Guard so resolute before, nor do I think that we could rely upon finding it so again; for its courage was prompted by necessity and despair, and proceeded from circumstances which are not likely to recur.

Paris on that day reminded me of a city of antiquity whose citizens defended the walls like heroes, because they knew that if the city were taken they themselves would be dragged into slavery. As we turned our steps back towards the Assembly, Goudchaux left us. "Now that we have done our errand," said he, clenching his teeth, and in an accent half Gascon and half Alsatian, "I want to go and fight a bit." He said this with such a martial air, so little in harmony with his pacific appearance, that I could not help smiling.

He did, in fact, go and fight, as I heard the next day, and so well that he might have had his little paunch pierced in two or three places, had fate so willed it. I returned from my round convinced that we should come out victorious; and what I saw on nearing the Assembly confirmed my opinion.

Thousands of men were hastening to our aid from every part of France, and entering the city by all the roads not commanded by the insurgents. Thanks to the railroads, some had already come from fifty leagues' distance, although the fighting had only begun the night before. On the next and the subsequent days, they came from distances of a hundred and two hundred leagues. These men belonged indiscriminately to every class of society; among them were many peasants, many shopkeepers, many landlords and nobles, all mingled together in the same ranks. They were armed in an irregular and insufficient manner, but they rushed into Paris with unequalled ardour: a spectacle as strange and unprecedented in our revolutionary annals as that offered by the insurrection itself. It was evident from that moment that we should end by gaining the day, for the insurgents received no reinforcements, whereas we had all France for reserves. . . .

19. Karl Marx, *The Eighteenth Brumaire of Louis Bonaparte*

Karl Marx was born in 1818 in Trier (Rhineland), the son of a prosperous Jewish lawyer who had converted to Protestantism. After academic studies (chiefly devoted to philosophy and history) and a brief period of journalistic activity (most notably as the editor of the *Rheinische Zeitung*), Marx went abroad to Paris and Brussels between 1843 and 1848. In Paris Marx established contacts with leaders of various contemporary French socialist and communist movements, especially those influenced by Saint-Simon and Fourier, and undertook an intensive study of the history of the French Revolution of 1789. Not only did Marx become acquainted with other German émigrés, such as Heinrich Heine and Georg Herwegh, he also associated with revolutionary anarchists such as Mikhail Bakunin and Pierre-Joseph Proudhon, the latter soon to become the target of Marx's acerbic *The Poverty of Philosophy* (1847).

The Revolution of 1848 brought Marx back to Germany; after the revolution's collapse in 1849 he went into exile in London, where he lived until his death in 1883. Supported financially by Friedrich Engels (whom he had first met in Paris in 1842) and other friends, Marx devoted all his energies to furthering socialist revolutionary activities on an international scale: as a social philosopher; as the leading member of the International Workingmen's Association (the First International, 1864–74); as a brilliant historian of class struggles and civil wars (*The Eighteenth Brumaire of Louis Bonaparte; The Class Struggles in France 1848–1850; The Civil War in France*, etc.); and above all as a student of the history and theory of modern capitalism (*A Contribution to the Critique of Political Economy*, 1859; *Capital*, vol. 1, 1867; vols. 2 and 3 posthumously published by Engels in 1885 and 1894).

Marx's treatise on Louis Bonaparte was written between December 1851 and March 1852 and first published in German in New York in May 1852. Along with Tocqueville's *Souvenirs*, the *Eighteenth Brumaire* is one of the most incisive contemporary analyses of the Revolution of 1848 in France. The selections presented here are taken from the first, second, third, and seventh chapters of that book. The translation is based on the 1869 edition of the work, but where Marx's later revisions of the original 1852 version are of special interest, they have been noted in the footnotes.

From *Karl Marx and Frederick Engels: Collected Works*, vol. 2, *1851–53* (New York: International Publishers, 1979), pp. 103–12, 119–20, 123–24, 127–31, 184–97. Some footnotes deleted.

I

Hegel remarks somewhere that all facts and personages of great importance in world history occur, as it were, twice. He forgot to add: the first
time as tragedy, the second as farce.[1] Caussidière for Danton, Louis Blanc
for Robespierre, the Montagne of 1848 to 1851[2] for the Montagne of 1793
to 1795, the Nephew for the Uncle. And the same caricature occurs in the
circumstances attending the second edition of the eighteenth Brumaire!

Men make their own history, but they do not make it just as they please;
they do not make it under circumstances chosen by themselves, but under
circumstances directly encountered, given and transmitted from the past.
The tradition of all the dead generations weighs like a nightmare on the
brain of the living. And just when they seem engaged in revolutionising
themselves and things, in creating something that has never yet existed,
precisely in such periods of revolutionary crisis they anxiously conjure up
the spirits of the past to their service and borrow from them names, battle-
cries and costumes in order to present the new scene of world history in
this time-honoured disguise and this borrowed language. Thus Luther
donned the mask of the Apostle Paul, the revolution of 1789 to 1814
draped itself alternately as the Roman Republic and the Roman Empire,
and the revolution of 1848 knew nothing better to do than to parody, now
1789, now the revolutionary tradition of 1793 to 1795. In like manner a
beginner who has learnt a new language always translates it back into his
mother tongue, but he has assimilated the spirit of the new language and
can freely express himself in it only when he finds his way in it without
recalling the old and forgets his native tongue in the use of the new.

Consideration of this world-historical necromancy reveals at once a salient difference. Camille Desmoulins, Danton, Robespierre, Saint-Just,
Napoleon, the heroes as well as the parties and the masses of the old

1. Hegel expressed this idea in his work *Vorlesungen über die Philosophie der Geschichte*
(its first edition came out in Berlin in 1837). In the third part of this work, at the end of
Section 2, entitled "Rom vom zweiten punischen Krieg bis zum Kaiserthum," Hegel wrote in
particular that "A coup d'état is sanctioned as it were in the opinion of people if it is repeated.
Thus, Napoleon was defeated twice and twice the Bourbons were driven out. Through repetition, what at the beginning seemed to be merely accidental and possible becomes real and
established." Hegel also repeatedly expressed the idea that in the process of dialectical development there is bound to be a transition from the stage of formation and efflorescence to that
of disintegration and ruin (see, in particular, G. W. F. Hegel, *Grundlinien der Philosophie des
Rechts,* Th. 3, Abt. 3, §347).

2. *Montagne* (the Mountain)—representatives in the Constituent and subsequently in the
Legislative Assembly of a bloc of democrats and petty-bourgeois socialists grouped round the
newspaper *La Réforme.* They called themselves Montagnards or the Mountain by analogy
with the Montagnards in the Convention of 1792–94.

French Revolution, performed the task of their time in Roman costume and with Roman phrases, the task of unchaining and setting up modern *bourgeois* society. The first ones knocked the feudal basis to pieces and mowed off the feudal heads which had grown on it. The other created inside France the conditions under which free competition could first be developed, parcelled landed property exploited and the unchained industrial productive forces of the nation employed; and beyond the French borders he everywhere swept the feudal institutions away, so far as was necessary to furnish bourgeois society in France with a suitable up-to-date environment on the European Continent. The new social formation once established, the antediluvian Colossi disappeared and with them resurrected Romanity—the Brutuses, Gracchi, Publicolas, the tribunes, the senators, and Caesar himself. Bourgeois society in its sober reality had begotten its true interpreters and mouthpieces in the Says, Cousins, Royer-Collards, Benjamin Constants and Guizots; its real commanders sat behind the counter, and the hogheaded Louis XVIII was its political chief. Wholly absorbed in the production of wealth and in peaceful competitive struggle, it no longer comprehended that ghosts from the days of Rome had watched over its cradle. But unheroic as bourgeois society is, it nevertheless took heroism, sacrifice, terror, civil war and battles of peoples to bring it into being. And in the classically austere traditions of the Roman Republic its gladiators found the ideals and the art forms, the self-deceptions that they needed in order to conceal from themselves the bourgeois limitations of the content of their struggles and to maintain their passion on the high plane of great historical tragedy. Similarly, at another stage of development, a century earlier, Cromwell and the English people had borrowed speech, passions and illusions from the Old Testament for their bourgeois revolution. When the real aim had been achieved, when the bourgeois transformation of English society had been accomplished, Locke supplanted Habakkuk.

Thus the resurrection of the dead in those revolutions served the purpose of glorifying the new struggles, not of parodying the old; of magnifying the given task in imagination, not of fleeing from its solution in reality; of finding once more the spirit of revolution, not of making its ghost walk about again.

From 1848 to 1851 only the ghost of the old revolution walked about, from Marrast, the *républicain en gants jaunes,*[3] who disguised himself as the old Bailly, down to the adventurer who hides his commonplace repulsive features under the iron death mask of Napoleon. An entire people, which had imagined that by means of a revolution it had imparted to itself an accelerated power of motion, suddenly finds itself set back into a de-

3. Republican in yellow gloves.

funct epoch and, in order that no doubt as to the relapse may be possible, the old dates arise again, the old chronology, the old names, the old edicts, which had long become a subject of antiquarian erudition, and the old myrmidons of the law, who had seemed long decayed. The nation feels like that mad Englishman in Bedlam who fancies that he lives in the times of the ancient Pharaohs and daily bemoans the hard labour that he must perform in the Ethiopian mines as a gold digger, immured in this subterranean prison, a dimly burning lamp fastened to his head, the overseer of the slaves behind him with a long whip, and at the exits a confused welter of barbarian mercenaries, who understand neither the forced labourers in the mines nor one another, since they speak no common language. "And all this is expected of me," sighs the mad Englishman, "of me, a freeborn Briton, in order to make gold for the old Pharaohs." "In order to pay the debts of the Bonaparte family," sighs the French nation. The Englishman, so long as he was in his right mind, could not get rid of the fixed idea of making gold. The French, so long as they were engaged in revolution, could not get rid of the memory of Napoleon, as the election of December 10[4] proved. They hankered to return from the perils of revolution to the fleshpots of Egypt, and December 2, 1851 was the answer. They have not only a caricature of the old Napoleon, they have the old Napoleon himself, caricatured as he must appear in the middle of the nineteenth century.

The social revolution of the nineteenth century cannot draw its poetry from the past, but only from the future. It cannot begin with itself before it has stripped off all superstition about the past. Earlier revolutions required recollections of past world history in order to dull themselves to their own content. In order to arrive at its own content, the revolution of the nineteenth century must let the dead bury their dead. There the words went beyond the content; here the content goes beyond the words.

The February revolution was a surprise attack, a *taking* of the old society *unawares,* and the people proclaimed this unexpected *coup de main* as a deed of historic importance, ushering in the new epoch. On December 2 the February revolution is conjured away by a cardsharper's trick, and what seems overthrown is no longer the monarchy but the liberal concessions that were wrung from it by centuries of struggle. Instead of *society* having conquered a new content for itself, it seems that the *state* only returned to its oldest form, to the shamelessly simple domination of the sabre and the cowl. This is the answer to the *coup de main* of February 1848, given by the *coup de tête* of December 1851. Easy come, easy go. Meanwhile the intervening time has not passed by unused. During the years

---

4. On December 10, 1848 Louis Bonaparte was elected President of the French Republic by a majority vote.

1848 to 1851 French society made up, and that by an abbreviated because revolutionary method, for the studies and experiences which, in a regular, so to speak, textbook course of development, would have had to precede the February revolution, if it was to be more than a ruffling of the surface. Society now seems to have fallen back behind its point of departure; it has in truth first to create for itself the revolutionary point of departure, the situation, the relations, the conditions under which alone modern revolution becomes serious.

Bourgeois revolutions, like those of the eighteenth century, storm swiftly from success to success, their dramatic effects outdo each other, men and things seem set in sparkling brilliants, ecstasy is the everyday spirit, but they are short-lived, soon they have attained their zenith, and a long crapulent depression seizes society before it learns soberly to assimilate the results of its storm-and-stress period. On the other hand, proletarian revolutions, like those of the nineteenth century, criticise themselves constantly, interrupt themselves continually in their own course, come back to the apparently accomplished in order to begin it afresh, deride with unmerciful thoroughness the inadequacies, weaknesses and paltrinesses of their first attempts, seem to throw down their adversary only in order that he may draw new strength from the earth and rise again, more gigantic, before them, and recoil again and again from the indefinite prodigiousness of their own aims, until a situation has been created which makes all turning back impossible, and the conditions themselves cry out:

> Hic Rhodus, hic salta!
> Here is the rose, here dance![5]

. . . Let us recapitulate in general outline the phases that the French Revolution went through from February 24, 1848 to December 1851.

Three main periods are unmistakable: *the February period;* May 4, 1848 to May 28, 1849: *the period of the constitution of the republic* or *of the Constituent National Assembly;* May 28, 1849 to December 2, 1851: *the period of the constitutional republic* or *of the Legislative National Assembly.*

The *first period,* from February 24, or the overthrow of Louis Philippe, to May 4, 1848, the meeting of the Constituent Assembly, the *February period* proper, may be described as the *prologue* to the revolution. Its char-

---

5. *Hic Rhodus, hic salta!* ("Here is Rhodes, leap here!"—meaning: here is the main point, now show us what you can do!)—words addressed to a swaggerer (in a fable by Aesop, "The Boasting Traveller") who claimed that he had made tremendous leaps in Rhodes.

Here is the rose, here dance!—a paraphrase of the preceding quotation (in Greek Rhodes, the name of an island, also means "rose") used by Hegel in the preface to his work *Grundlinien der Philosophie des Rechts.*

acter was officially expressed in the fact that the government improvised by it declared itself that it was *provisional* and, like the government, everything that was mooted, attempted or enunciated during this period proclaimed itself to be only *provisional*. Nothing and nobody ventured to lay claim to the right of existence and of real action. All the elements that had prepared or determined the revolution, the dynastic opposition,[6] the republican bourgeoisie, the democratic-republican petty bourgeoisie and the Social-Democratic workers, provisionally found their place in the February *government*.

It could not be otherwise. The February days originally aimed at an electoral reform, by which the circle of the politically privileged among the possessing class itself was to be widened and the exclusive domination of the finance aristocracy overthrown. When it came to the actual conflict, however, when the people mounted the barricades, the National Guard maintained a passive attitude, the army offered no serious resistance and the monarchy ran away, the republic appeared to be a matter of course. Every party construed it in its own way. Having secured it arms in hand, the proletariat impressed its stamp upon it and proclaimed it to be a *social republic*. There was thus indicated the general content of the modern revolution, a content which was in most singular contradiction to everything that, with the material available, with the degree of education attained by the masses, under the given circumstances and relations, could be immediately realised in practice. On the other hand, the claims of all the remaining elements that had collaborated in the February revolution were recognised by the lion's share that they obtained in the government. In no period do we, therefore, find a more confused mixture of high-flown phrases and actual uncertainty and clumsiness, of more enthusiastic striving for innovation and more thorough domination of the old routine, of more apparent harmony of the whole of society and more profound estrangement of its elements. While the Paris proletariat still revelled in the vision of the wide prospects that had opened before it and indulged in earnest discussions on social problems, the old forces of society had grouped themselves, rallied, reflected and found unexpected support in the mass of the nation, the peasants and petty bourgeois, who all at once stormed on to the political stage, after the barriers of the July monarchy had fallen.

The *second period,* from May 4, 1848 to the end of May 1849, is the period of the *constitution,* the *foundation, of the bourgeois republic.* Di-

6. The *dynastic opposition*—an opposition group in the French Chamber of Deputies during the July monarchy (1830–48). The group, headed by Odilon Barrot, expressed the views of the liberal industrial and commercial bourgeoisie and favoured a moderate electoral reform, which they regarded as a means of preventing a revolution and preserving the Orleans dynasty.

rectly after the February days not only had the dynastic opposition been surprised by the republicans and the republicans by the Socialists, but all France by Paris. The National Assembly, which met on May 4, 1848, had emerged from the national elections and represented the nation. It was a living protest against the aspirations of the February days and was to reduce the results of the revolution to the bourgeois scale. In vain the Paris proletariat, which immediately grasped the character of this National Assembly, attempted on May 15, a few days after it met, forcibly to negate its existence, to dissolve it, to disintegrate again into its constituent parts the organic form in which the proletariat was threatened by the reacting spirit of the nation.[7] As is known, May 15 had no other result save that of removing Blanqui and his comrades, that is, the real leaders of the proletarian party,[8] from the public stage for the entire duration of the cycle we are considering.

The *bourgeois monarchy* of Louis Philippe can be followed only by a *bourgeois republic,* that is to say, whereas a limited section of the bourgeoisie ruled in the name of the king, the whole of the bourgeoisie will now rule on behalf of the people. The demands of the Paris proletariat are utopian nonsense, to which an end must be put. To this declaration of the Constituent National Assembly the Paris proletariat replied with the *June insurrection,* the most colossal event in the history of European civil wars. The bourgeois republic triumphed. On its side stood the finance aristocracy, the industrial bourgeoisie, the middle class, the petty bourgeois, the army, the lumpenproletariat organised as the Mobile Guard,[9] the intellec-

7. On April 16, 1848 a peaceful procession of Paris workers marched towards the Town Hall to present a petition to the Provisional Government for "organisation of labour" and "abolition of the exploitation of man by man." The workers encountered battalions of the bourgeois national guard and were forced to retreat.

On May 15, 1848 Paris workers led by Blanqui, Barbès and others took revolutionary action against the anti-labour and anti-democratic policy of the bourgeois Constituent Assembly which had opened on May 4. The participants in the mass demonstraton forced their way into the Assembly, demanded the formation of a Ministry of Labour and presented a number of other demands. An attempt was made to form a revolutionary government. National guards from the bourgeois quarters and regular troops succeeded, however, in restoring the power of the Constituent Assembly. The leaders of the movement were arrested and put on trial.

8. The 1852 edition has: "the real leaders of the proletarian party, the revolutionary Communists."

9. The *Mobile Guard* was set up by a decree of the Provisional Government on February 25, 1848 with the secret aim of fighting the revolutionary masses. Its armed units consisted mainly of lumpenproletarians and were used to crush the June uprising of the Paris workers. Subsequently, it was disbanded on the insistence of the Bonapartists, who feared that in the event of a conflict between President Bonaparte and the republicans the Mobile Guard would side with the latter.

For Marx's description of the Mobile Guard see his work *The Class Struggles in France, 1848 to 1850.*

tuals, the clergy and the rural population. On the side of the Paris proletariat stood none but itself. More than 3,000 insurgents were butchered after the victory, and 15,000 were deported without trial. With this defeat the proletariat recedes into the *background* of the revolutionary stage. It attempts to press forward again on every occasion, as soon as the movement appears to make a fresh start, but with ever decreased expenditure of strength and always slighter results. As soon as one of the social strata situated above it gets into revolutionary ferment, the proletariat enters into an alliance with it and so shares all the defeats that the different parties suffer, one after another. But these subsequent blows become the weaker, the greater the surface of society over which they are distributed. The more important leaders of the proletariat in the Assembly and in the press successively fall victim to the courts, and ever more equivocal figures come to head it. In part it throws itself into *doctrinaire experiments, exchange banks and workers' associations, hence into a movement in which it renounces the revolutionising of the old world by means of the latter's own great, combined resources, and seeks, rather, to achieve its salvation behind society's back, in private fashion, within its limited conditions of existence, and hence necessarily suffers shipwreck.* It seems to be unable either to rediscover revolutionary greatness in itself or to win new energy from the connections newly entered into, until *all classes* with which it contended in June themselves lie prostrate beside it. But at least it succumbs with the honours of the great, world-historic struggle; not only France, but all Europe trembles at the June earthquake, while the ensuing defeats of the upper classes are so cheaply bought that they require barefaced exaggeration by the victorious party to be able to pass for events at all, and become the more ignominious the further the defeated party is from the proletarian party.

The defeat of the June insurgents, to be sure, had indeed prepared and levelled the ground on which the bourgeois republic could be founded and built up, but it had shown at the same time that in Europe the questions at issue are other than that of "republic or monarchy." It had revealed that here *bourgeois republic* signifies the unlimited despotism of one class over other classes. It had proved that in countries with an old civilisation, with a developed formation of classes, with modern conditions of production and with an intellectual consciousness in which all traditional ideas have been dissolved by the work of centuries, *the republic* signifies *in general only the political form of the revolutionising of bourgeois society* and not its *conservative form of life,* as, for example, in the United States of North America, where, though classes already exist, they have not yet become fixed, but continually change and interchange their component elements in constant flux, where the modern means of production, instead of coinciding with a stagnant surplus population, rather compensate for the relative deficiency of heads and hands, and where, finally, the feverish, youthful movement of material production, which has to make a new world its own, has left neither time nor opportunity for abolishing the old spirit world.

During the June days all classes and parties had united in the *Party of Order* against the proletarian class as the *Party of Anarchy,* of socialism, of communism. They had "saved" society from *"the enemies of society."* They had given out the watch-words of the old society, *"property, family, religion, order,"* to their army as passwords and had proclaimed to the counter-revolutionary crusaders: "By this sign thou shalt conquer!" [10] From this moment, as soon as one of the numerous parties which had gathered under this sign against the June insurgents seeks to hold the revolutionary battlefield in its own class interest, it goes down before the cry: "Property, family, religion, order." Society is saved just as often as the circle of its rulers contracts, as a more exclusive interest is maintained against a wider one. Every demand of the simplest bourgeois financial reform, of the most ordinary liberalism, of the most formal republicanism, of the most shallow democracy, is simultaneously castigated as an "attempt on society" and stigmatised as "socialism." And, finally, the high priests of "religion and order" themselves are driven with kicks from their Pythian tripods, hauled out of their beds in the darkness of night, put in prison-vans, thrown into dungeons or sent into exile; their temple is razed to the ground, their mouths are sealed, their pens broken, their law torn to pieces in the name of religion, of property, of the family, of order. Bourgeois fanatics for order are shot down on their balconies by mobs of drunken soldiers, their domestic sanctuaries profaned, their houses bombarded for amusement—in the name of property, of the family, of religion and of order. Finally, the scum of bourgeois society forms the *holy phalanx of order* and the hero Krapülinski [11] installs himself in the Tuileries as the *"saviour of society."*

II

. . . I have discussed elsewhere the significance of the election of December 10. I will not revert to it here. It is sufficient to remark here that it was a *reaction of the peasants,* who had to pay the cost of the February revolution, against the remaining classes of the nation, a *reaction of the country against the town.* It met with great approval in the army, for which the republicans of the *National* had provided neither glory nor additional

10. An allusion to a legend according to which the Roman Emperor Constantine (274–337) on the eve of a battle against his rival Maxentius in 312 saw in the sky the sign of the Cross and over it the words: "By this sign thou shalt conquer!" With this legend the Church links Constantine's "conversion" from the persecution of Christianity to its protection.

11. *Krapülinski*—one of the main characters in Heine's poem "Zwei Ritter" (*Romanzero*). Here Marx alludes to Louis Bonaparte.

pay, among the big bourgeoisie, who hailed Bonaparte as a bridge to the monarchy, and among the proletarians and petty bourgeois, who hailed him as a scourge for Cavaignac. I shall have an opportunity later of going more closely into the relationship of the peasants to the French Revolution.

The period from December 20, 1848 [12] until the dissolution of the Constituent Assembly, in May 1849, comprises the history of the downfall of the bourgeois republicans. After having founded a republic for the bourgeoisie, driven the revolutionary proletariat out of the field and reduced the democratic petty bourgeoisie to silence for the time being, they are themselves thrust aside by the mass of the bourgeoisie, which justly impounds this republic as *its property*. This bourgeois mass was, however, *royalist*. One section of it, the big landowners, had ruled during the *Restoration* and was accordingly *Legitimist*. The other, the finance aristocracy and big industrialists, had ruled during the July monarchy and was consequently *Orleanist*. The high dignitaries of the army, the university, the church, the bar, the Academy and of the press were to be found on either side, though in various proportions. Here, in the bourgeois republic, which bore neither the name *Bourbon* nor the name *Orleans,* but the name *Capital,* they had found the form of state in which they could rule *conjointly*. The June insurrection had already united them in the "Party of Order." Now it was necessary, in the first place, to remove the coterie of bourgeois republicans who still occupied the seats of the National Assembly. Just as brutal as these pure republicans had been in their misuse of physical force against the people, just as cowardly, mealy-mouthed, spiritless, broken and incapable of fighting were they now in their retreat, when it was a question of maintaining their republicanism and their legislative rights against the executive power and the royalists. I need not relate here the ignominious story of their dissolution. It was a fading-away, not a going-under. Their history has come to an end forever, and, both inside and outside the Assembly, they figure in the following period only as memories, memories that seem to regain life whenever the mere name of Republic is once more the issue and as often as the revolutionary conflict threatens to sink down to the lowest level. I may remark in passing that the journal which gave its name to this party, the *National,* was converted to socialism in the following period. . . .

III

On May 28, 1849 the Legislative National Assembly met. On December 2, 1851 it was dispersed. This period covers the span of life of the *constitutional or parliamentary republic*.

---

12. The day of the expiry of Cavaignac's powers and of Louis Bonaparte's accession to the presidency.

In the first French Revolution the rule of the *Constitutionalists* is followed by the rule of the *Girondins* and the rule of the *Girondins* by the rule of the *Jacobins*. Each of these parties relies on the more progressive party for support. As soon as it has brought the revolution far enough to be unable to follow it further, still less to go ahead of it, it is thrust aside by the bolder ally that stands behind it and sent to the guillotine. The revolution thus moves along an ascending line.

It is the reverse with the revolution of 1848. The proletarian party appears as an appendage of the petty-bourgeois-democratic party. It is betrayed and dropped by the latter on April 16, May 15, and in the June days. The democratic party, in its turn, leans on the shoulders of the bourgeois-republican party. The bourgeois republicans no sooner believe themselves well established than they shake off the troublesome comrade and support themselves on the shoulders of the Party of Order. The Party of Order hunches its shoulders, lets the bourgeois republicans tumble and throws itself on the shoulders of armed force. It fancies it is still sitting on its shoulders when, one fine morning, it perceives that the shoulders have turned into bayonets. Each party kicks back at the one behind, which presses upon it, and leans against the one in front, which pushes backwards. No wonder that in this ridiculous posture it loses its balance and, having made the inevitable grimaces, collapses with curious capers. The revolution thus moves in a descending line. It finds itself in this state of retrogressive motion before the last February barricade has been cleared away and the first revolutionary authority constituted. . . .

Before we pursue parliamentary history further, some remarks are necessary to avoid common misconceptions regarding the whole character of the epoch that lies before us. Looked at with the eyes of democrats, the period of the Legislative National Assembly is concerned with what the period of the Constituent Assembly was concerned with: the simple struggle between republicans and royalists. The movement itself, however, they sum up in the one shibboleth: *"reaction"*—night, in which all cats are grey and which permits them to reel off their night watchman's commonplaces. And, to be sure, at first sight the Party of Order reveals a tangled knot of different royalist factions, which not only intrigue against each other—each seeking to elevate its own pretender to the throne and exclude the pretender of the opposing faction—but also all unite in common hatred of, and common attacks on, the "republic." In opposition to this royalist conspiracy the Montagne, for its part, appears as the representative of the "republic." The Party of Order appears to be perpetually engaged in a "reaction," directed against press, association and the like, neither more nor less than in Prussia, and which, as in Prussia, is carried out in the form of brutal police intervention by the bureaucracy, the gendarmerie and the law courts. The "Montagne," for its part, is just as continually occupied in warding off these attacks and thus defending the "eternal rights of man" as every so-called people's party has done, more or less, for a century and a half. If one looks at the situation and the parties more closely, however, this superficial appearance, which veils the *class struggle* and the peculiar physiognomy of this period, disappears.

Legitimists and Orleanists, as we have said, formed the two great factions of the Party of Order. Was what held these factions fast to their pretenders and kept them apart from one another nothing but lily and tricolour, House of Bourbon and House of Orleans, different shades of royalism, was it their royalist faith at all? Under the Bourbons, *big landed property* had governed, with its priests and lackeys; under the Orleans, high finance, large-scale industry, large-scale trade, that is, *capital,* with its retinue of lawyers, professors and smooth-tongued orators. The Legitimate monarchy was merely the political expression of the hereditary rule of the lords of the soil, as the July monarchy was only the political expression of the usurped rule of the bourgeois parvenus. What kept the two factions apart, therefore, was not any so-called principles, it was their material conditions of existence, two different kinds of property, it was the old contrast between town and country, the rivalry between capital and landed property. That at the same time old memories, personal enmities, fears and hopes, prejudices and illusions, sympathies and antipathies, convictions, articles of faith and principles bound them to one or the other royal house, who is there that denies this? Upon the different forms of property, upon the social conditions of existence, rises an entire superstructure of different and distinctly formed sentiments, illusions, modes of thought and views of life. The entire class creates and forms them out of its material foundations and out of the corresponding social relations. The single individual, to whom they are transmitted through tradition and upbringing, may imagine that they form the real motives and the starting-point of his activity. While Orleanists and Legitimists, while each faction sought to make itself and the other believe that it was loyalty to their two royal houses which separated them, facts later proved that it was rather their divided interests which forbade the unification of the two royal houses. And as in private life one differentiates between what a man thinks and says of himself and what he really is and does, so in historical struggles one must still more distinguish the language and the imaginary aspirations of parties from their real organism and their real interests, their conception of themselves from their reality. Orleanists and Legitimists found themselves side by side in the republic, with the same claims. If each side wished to effect the *restoration* of its *own* royal house against the other, that merely signified that each of the *two great interests* into which the *bourgeoisie* is split—landed property and capital—sought to restore its own supremacy and the subordination of the other. We speak of two interests of the bourgeoisie, for large landed property, despite its feudal coquetry and pride of race, has been rendered thoroughly bourgeois by the development of modern society. Thus the Tories in England long imagined that they were enthusiastic about monarchy, the church and the beauties of the old English Constitution, until the day of danger wrung from them the confession that they are enthusiastic only about *rent*. . . .

As against the coalitioned bourgeoisie, a coalition between petty bourgeois and workers had been formed, the so-called *Social-Democratic* party. The petty bourgeois saw themselves badly rewarded after the June days of 1848, their material interests imperilled and the democratic guarantees which were to ensure the implementation of these interests called in question by the counter-revolution. Accordingly, they came closer to the workers. On the other hand, their parliamentary representation, the *Montagne,* thrust aside during the dictatorship of the bourgeois republicans, had in the last half of the life of the Constituent Assembly reconquered its lost popularity through the struggle with Bonaparte and the royalist ministers. It had concluded an alliance with the socialist leaders. In February 1849, banquets celebrated the reconciliation. A joint programme was drafted, joint election committees were set up and joint candidates put forward. The revolutionary point was broken off from the social demands of the proletariat and a democratic turn given to them; the purely political form was stripped from the democratic claims of the petty bourgeoisie and their socialist point turned outward. Thus arose *Social-Democracy.* The new *Montagne,* the result of this combination, contained, apart from some working-class supernumeraries and some members of the socialist sects, the same elements as the old Montagne, only numerically stronger. However, in the course of development, it had changed with the class that it represented. The peculiar character of Social-Democracy is epitomised in the fact that democratic-republican institutions are demanded as a means, not of superseding two extremes, capital and wage labour, but of weakening their antagonism and transforming it into harmony. However different the means proposed for the attainment of this end may be, however much it may be embellished with more or less revolutionary notions, the content remains the same. This content is the reformation of society in a democratic way, but a reformation within the bounds of the petty bourgeoisie. Only one must not form the narrow-minded notion that the petty bourgeoisie, on principle, wishes to enforce an egoistic class interest. Rather, it believes that the *special* conditions of its emancipation are the *general* conditions within which alone modern society can be saved and the class struggle avoided. Just as little must one imagine that the democratic representatives are indeed all shopkeepers or enthusiastic supporters of shopkeepers. In their education and individual position they may be as far apart from them as heaven from earth. What makes them representatives of the petty bourgeoisie is the fact that in their minds they do not get beyond the limits which the latter do not get beyond in life, that they are consequently driven, theoretically, to the same problems and solutions to which material interest and social position drive the latter in practice. This is, in general, the relationship between the *political* and *literary representatives* of a class and the class they represent. . . .

VII

. . . Why did the Paris proletariat not rise in revolt after December 2?[13]

The overthrow of the bourgeoisie had as yet been only decreed: the decree had not been carried out. Any serious insurrection of the proletariat would at once have put fresh life into the bourgeoisie, would have reconciled it with the army and ensured a second June defeat for the workers.

On December 4 the proletariat was incited by bourgeois and *épicier* to fight. On the evening of that day several legions of the National Guard promised to appear, armed and uniformed, on the scene of battle. For the bourgeois and the *épicier* had got wind of the fact that in one of his decrees of December 2 Bonaparte abolished the secret ballot and enjoined them to record their "yes" or "no" in the official registers after their names. The resistance of December 4 intimidated Bonaparte. During the night he caused placards to be posted on all the street corners of Paris, announcing the restoration of the secret ballot. The bourgeois and the *épicier* believed that they had gained their end. Those who failed to appear next morning were the bourgeois and the *épicier*.

By a *coup de main* during the night of December 1 to 2, Bonaparte had robbed the Paris proletariat of its leaders, the barricade commanders. An army without officers, averse to fighting under the banner of the Montagnards because of the memories of June 1848 and 1849 and May 1850, it left to its vanguard, the secret societies, the task of saving the insurrectionary honour of Paris, which the bourgeoisie had so unresistingly surrendered to the soldiery that, later on, Bonaparte could sneeringly give as his motive for disarming the National Guard — his fear that its arms would be turned against itself by the anarchists!

"*C'est le triomphe complet et définitif du socialisme!*" Thus Guizot characterised December 2. But if the overthrow of the parliamentary republic contains within itself the germ of the triumph of the proletarian revolution, its immediate and palpable result was *the victory of Bonaparte over parliament, of the executive power over the legislative power, of force without words over the force of words*. In parliament the nation made its

13. In the 1852 edition this paragraph reads as follows: "Why did the proletariat not rescue the bourgeoisie? Implied in this is the question: Why did the Paris proletariat not rise in revolt after December 2?"

general will the law, that is, it made the law of the ruling class its general will. Before the executive power it renounces all will of its own and submits to the superior command of an alien will, to authority. The executive power, in contrast to the legislative power, expresses the heteronomy of a nation, in contrast to its autonomy. France, therefore, seems to have escaped the despotism of a class only to fall back beneath the despotism of an individual, and, what is more, beneath the authority of an individual without authority. The struggle seems to be settled in such a way that all classes, equally impotent and equally mute, fall on their knees before the rifle butt.

But the revolution is thorough. It is still journeying through purgatory. It does its work methodically. By December 2, 1851 it had completed one half of its preparatory work; it is now completing the other half. First it perfected the parliamentary power, in order to be able to overthrow it. Now that it has attained this, it perfects the *executive power,* reduces it to its purest expression, isolates it, sets it up against itself as the sole target, in order to concentrate all its forces of destruction against it. And when it has done this second half of its preliminary work, Europe will leap from its seat and exultantly exclaim: Well burrowed, old mole!

This executive power with its enormous bureaucratic and military organisation, with its extensive and artificial state machinery, with a host of officials numbering half a million, besides an army of another half million, this appalling parasitic body, which enmeshes the body of French society like a net and chokes all its pores, sprang up in the days of the absolute monarchy, with the decay of the feudal system, which it helped to hasten. The seignorial privileges of the landowners and towns became transformed into so many attributes of the state power, the feudal dignitaries into paid officials and the motley pattern of conflicting medieval plenary powers into the regulated plan of a state authority whose work is divided and centralised as in a factory. The first French Revolution, with its task of breaking all separate local, territorial, urban and provincial powers in order to create the civil unity of the nation, was bound to develop what the absolute monarchy had begun: the centralisation, but at the same time the extent, the attributes and the agents of governmental power. Napoleon perfected this state machinery. The Legitimist monarchy and the July monarchy added nothing but a greater division of labour, growing in the same measure as the division of labour within bourgeois society created new groups of interests, and, therefore, new material for state administration. Every *common* interest was straightway severed from society, counterposed to it as a higher, *general* interest, snatched from the activity of society's members themselves and made an object of government activity, whether it was a bridge, a schoolhouse and the communal property of a village community, or the railways, the national wealth and the national university of France. Finally, in its struggle against the revolution, the parliamentary republic found itself compelled to strengthen, along with the repressive measures, the resources and centralisation of governmental power. All revolutions perfected this machine instead of breaking it. The parties that contended in turn for domination regarded the possession of this huge state edifice as the principal spoils of the victor.

But under the absolute monarchy, during the first revolution, under Napoleon, bureaucracy was only the means of preparing the class rule of the bourgeoisie. Under the Restoration, under Louis Philippe, under the parliamentary republic, it was the instrument of the ruling class, however much it strove for power of its own.

Only under the second Bonaparte does the state seem to have made itself completely independent.[14] As against civil society, the state machine has consolidated its position so thoroughly that the chief of the Society of December 10 suffices for its head, a casual adventurer from abroad, raised up as leader by a drunken soldiery, which he has bought with liquor and sausages, and which he must continually ply with more sausage. Hence the downcast despair, the feeling of most dreadful humiliation and degradation that oppresses the breast of France and makes her catch her breath. She feels dishonoured.

And yet the state power is not suspended in mid air. Bonaparte represents a class, and the most numerous class of French society at that, the *small-holding peasantry*.

Just as the Bourbons were the dynasty of big landed property and just as the Orleans were the dynasty of money, so the Bonapartes are the dynasty of the peasants, that is, the mass of the French people. Not the Bonaparte who submitted to the bourgeois parliament, but the Bonaparte who dispersed the bourgeois parliament is the chosen man of the peasantry. For three years the towns had succeeded in falsifying the meaning of the election of December 10 and in cheating the peasants out of the restoration of the empire. The election of December 10, 1848 has been consummated only by the coup d'état of December 2, 1851.

The small-holding peasants form a vast mass, the members of which live in similar conditions but without entering into manifold relations with one another. Their mode of production isolates them from one another instead of bringing them into mutual intercourse. The isolation is increased by France's bad means of communication and by the poverty of the peasants. Their field of production, the smallholding, admits of no division of

14. In the 1852 edition this sentence reads thus: "Only under the second Bonaparte does the state seem to have made itself independent of society and subjected it." The text went on as follows: "The independence of the executive power emerges into the open when its chief no longer requires genius, its army no longer requires glory, and its bureaucracy no longer requires moral authority in order to justify itself."

labour in its cultivation, no application of science and, therefore, no diversity of development, no variety of talent, no wealth of social relationships. Each individual peasant family is almost self-sufficient; it itself directly produces the major part of its consumption and thus acquires its means of life more through exchange with nature than in intercourse with society. A smallholding, a peasant and his family; alongside them another smallholding, another peasant and another family. A few score of these make up a village, and a few score of villages make up a department. In this way, the great mass of the French nation is formed by simple addition of homologous magnitudes, much as potatoes in a sack form a sack of potatoes. Insofar as millions of families live under economic conditions of existence that separate their mode of life, their interests and their culture from those of the other classes, and put them in hostile opposition to the latter, they form a class. Insofar as there is merely a local interconnection among these small-holding peasants, and the identity of their interests begets no community, no national bond and no political organisation among them, they do not form a class. They are consequently incapable of enforcing their class interests in their own name, whether through a parliament or through a convention. They cannot represent themselves, they must be represented. Their representative must at the same time appear as their master, as an authority over them, as an unlimited governmental power that protects them against the other classes and sends them rain and sunshine from above. The political influence of the small-holding peasants, therefore, finds its final expression in the executive power subordinating society to itself.

Historical tradition gave rise to the belief of the French peasants in the miracle that a man named Napoleon would bring all the glory back to them. And an individual turned up who gives himself out as the man because he bears the name of Napoleon, as a result of the *Code Napoléon,* which lays down that *la recherche de la paternité est interdite*. After a vagabondage of twenty years and after a series of grotesque adventures, the legend finds fulfilment and the man becomes Emperor of the French. The fixed idea of the Nephew was realised, because it coincided with the fixed idea of the most numerous class of the French people.

But, it may be objected, what about the peasant risings in half of France,[15] the raids on the peasants by the army, the mass incarceration and transportation of peasants?

15. This refers to the participation of peasants in the republican uprisings in France in late 1851 in protest against the Bonapartist coup d'état. These uprisings, involving mainly artisans and workers of small towns and settlements, local peasants, tradesmen and intellectuals, embraced nearly twenty departments in south-east, south-west and central France. Lacking unity and centralisation they were fairly quickly suppressed by police and troops.

Since Louis XIV, France has experienced no similar persecution of the peasants "for demagogic practices." [16]

But let there be no misunderstanding. The Bonaparte dynasty represents not the revolutionary, but the conservative peasant; not the peasant that strikes out beyond the condition of his social existence, the smallholding, but rather the peasant who wants to consolidate this holding; not the country folk who, linked up with the towns, want to overthrow the old order through their own energies, but on the contrary those who, in stupefied seclusion within this old order, want to see themselves and their smallholdings saved and favoured by the ghost of the empire. It represents not the enlightenment, but the superstition of the peasant; not his judgment, but his prejudice; not his future, but his past; not his modern Cévennes, but his modern Vendée. [17]

The three years' rigorous rule of the parliamentary republic had freed a part of the French peasants from the Napoleonic illusion and had revolutionised them, even if only superficially; but the bourgeoisie violently repressed them whenever they set themselves in motion. Under the parliamentary republic the modern and the traditional consciousness of the French peasant contended for mastery. This progress took the form of an incessant struggle between the schoolmasters and the priests. The bourgeoisie struck down the schoolmasters. For the first time the peasants made efforts to behave independently in the face of the activity of the government. This was shown in the continual conflict between the *maires* and the prefects. The bourgeoisie deposed the *maires*. Finally, during the period of the parliamentary republic, the peasants of different localities rose against their own offspring, the army. The bourgeoisie punished them with states of siege and punitive expeditions. And this same bourgeoisie now cries out about the stupidity of the masses, the *vile multitude,* that has betrayed it to Bonaparte. It has itself forcibly strengthened the imperial sentiments of the peasant class, it conserved the conditions that form the birthplace of this

16. Here Marx compares the Bonapartist authorities' reprisals against the participants in the republican movement, including peasants, with the persecution of the so-called demagogues in Germany in the 1820s and 1830s.

Demagogues in Germany were participants in the opposition movement of intellectuals. The name became current after the Karlsbad Conference of Ministers of the German States in August 1819, which adopted a special decision against the intrigues of "demagogues."

17. *Cévennes*—a mountain region in the Languedoc Province of France where an uprising of peasants, known as the uprising of "Camisards" (*camise* in old French means shirt) took place between 1702 and 1705. The uprising, which began in protest against the persecution of Protestants, assumed an openly anti-feudal character.

Vendée—a department in Western France; during the French Revolution of 1789–94 a centre of a royalist revolt in which the mass of the local peasantry took part. The name "Vendée" came to denote counter-revolutionary activity.

peasant religion. The bourgeoisie, to be sure, is bound to fear the stupidity of the masses as long as they remain conservative, and the insight of the masses as soon as they become revolutionary.

In the risings after the coup d'état, a part of the French peasants protested, arms in hand, against their own vote of December 10, 1848. The school they had gone through since 1848 had sharpened their wits. But they had made themselves over to the underworld of history; history held them to their word, and the majority was still so prejudiced that in precisely the reddest departments the peasant population voted openly for Bonaparte. In its view, the National Assembly had hindered his progress. He had now merely broken the fetters that the towns had imposed on the will of the countryside. In some parts the peasants even entertained the grotesque notion of a convention side by side with Napoleon.

After the first revolution had transformed the peasants from semi-villeins into freeholders, Napoleon confirmed and regulated the conditions on which they could exploit undisturbed the soil of France which had only just fallen to their lot and slake their youthful passion for property. But what is now causing the ruin of the French peasant is his smallholding itself, the division of the land, the form of property which Napoleon consolidated in France. It is precisely the material conditions which made the French feudal peasant a small-holding peasant and Napoleon an emperor. Two generations have sufficed to produce the inevitable result: progressive deterioration of agriculture, progressive indebtedness of the agriculturist. The "Napoleonic" form of property, which at the beginning of the nineteenth century was the condition for the liberation and enrichment of the French country folk, has developed in the course of this century into the law of their enslavement and pauperisation. And precisely this law is the first of the *"idées napoléoniennes"* which the second Bonaparte has to uphold. If he still shares with the peasants the illusion that the cause of their ruin is to be sought, not in this small-holding property itself, but outside it, in the influence of secondary circumstances, his experiments will burst like soap bubbles when they come in contact with the relations of production.

The economic development of small-holding property has radically changed the relation of the peasants to the other classes of society. Under Napoleon, the fragmentation of the land in the countryside supplemented free competition and the beginning of big industry in the towns.[18] The peasant class was the ubiquitous protest against the landed aristocracy

18. The 1852 edition further has: "Even the advantages given to the peasant class were in the interest of the new bourgeois order. This newly created class was the all-round extension of the bourgeois regime beyond the gates of the towns, its realisation on a national scale."

which had just been overthrown.[19] The roots that small-holding property struck in French soil deprived feudalism of all nutriment. Its landmarks formed the natural fortifications of the bourgeoisie against any *coup de main* on the part of its old overlords. But in the course of the nineteenth century the feudal lords were replaced by urban usurers; the feudal obligation that went with the land was replaced by the mortgage; aristocratic landed property was replaced by bourgeois capital. The smallholding of the peasant is now only the pretext that allows the capitalist to draw profits, interest and rent from the soil, while leaving it to the tiller of the soil himself to see how he can extract his wages. The mortgage debt burdening the soil of France imposes on the French peasantry payment of an amount of interest equal to the annual interest on the entire British national debt. Small-holding property, in this enslavement by capital to which its development inevitably pushes forward, has transformed the mass of the French nation into troglodytes. Sixteen million peasants (including women and children) dwell in hovels, a large number of which have but one opening, others only two and the most favoured only three. And windows are to a house what the five senses are to the head. The bourgeois order, which at the beginning of the century set the state to stand guard over the newly arisen smallholding and manured it with laurels, has become a vampire that sucks out its blood and brains and throws them into the alchemist's cauldron of capital. The *Code Napoléon* is now nothing but a *codex* of distraints, forced sales and compulsory auctions. To the four million (including children, etc.) officially recognised paupers, vagabonds, criminals and prostitutes in France must be added five million who hover on the margin of existence and either have their haunts in the countryside itself or, with their rags and their children, continually desert the countryside for the towns and the towns for the countryside. The interests of the peasants, therefore, are no longer, as under Napoleon, in accord with, but in opposition to the interests of the bourgeoisie, to capital. Hence the peasants find their natural ally and leader in the *urban proletariat*, whose task is the overthrow of the bourgeois order. But *strong and unlimited government*— and this is the second *"idée napoléonienne,"* which the second Napoleon has to carry out—is called upon to defend this "material" order by force. This *"ordre matériel"* also serves as the catchword in all of Bonaparte's proclamations against the rebellious peasants.

Besides the mortgage which capital imposes on it, the smallholding is burdened by *taxes*. Taxes are the source of life for the bureaucracy, the army, the priests and the court, in short, for the whole apparatus of the

19. The 1852 edition further has: "If it was favoured most of all, it was also suited most of all as a point of attack for the restoration of feudalism."

executive power. Strong government and heavy taxes are identical. By its very nature, small-holding property forms a suitable basis for an all-powerful and innumerable bureaucracy. It creates a uniform level of relationships and persons over the whole surface of the land. Hence it also permits of uniform action from a supreme centre on all points of this uniform mass. It annihilates the aristocratic intermediate grades between the mass of the people and the state power. On all sides, therefore, it calls forth the direct interference of this state power and the interposition of its immediate organs. Finally, it produces an unemployed surplus population for which there is no place either on the land or in the towns, and which accordingly reaches out for state offices as a sort of respectable alms, and provokes the creation of state posts.[20] By the new markets which he opened at the point of the bayonet, by the plundering of the Continent, Napoleon repaid the compulsory taxes with interest. These taxes were a spur to the industry of the peasant, whereas now they rob his industry of its last resources and complete his inability to resist pauperism. And an enormous bureaucracy, well-braided and well-fed, is the *"idée napoléonienne"* which is most congenial of all to the second Bonaparte. How could it be otherwise, seeing that alongside the actual classes of society he is forced to create an artificial caste, for which the maintenance of his regime becomes a bread-and-butter question? Accordingly, one of his first financial operations was the raising of officials' salaries to their old level and the creation of new sinecures.

Another *"idée napoléonienne"* is the domination of the *priests* as an instrument of government. But while in its accord with society, in its dependence on natural forces and its submission to the authority which protected it from above, the smallholding that had newly come into being was naturally religious, the smallholding that is ruined by debts, at odds with society and authority, and driven beyond its own limitations naturally becomes irreligious. Heaven was quite a pleasing accession to the narrow strip of land just won, especially as it makes the weather; it becomes an insult as soon as it is thrust forward as substitute for the smallholding. The priest then appears as only the anointed bloodhound of the earthly police—another *"idée napoléonienne."*[21] On the next occasion, the expedition

20. The 1852 edition has: "Under Napoleon this numerous government personnel was not only directly productive in that it provided for the new peasantry, by state coercion, in the form of public works, etc., what the bourgeoisie was still unable to provide with the resources of private industry. The state taxes were an essential means of coercion for maintaining exchange between town and country. Otherwise the smallholder would, in peasant self-complacency, have broken off the connection with the towns as was the case of Norway and in part of Switzerland."

21. In the 1852 edition this sentence reads as follows: "The priest then appears as only the anointed bloodhound of the earthly police—another *'idée napoléonienne'*—whose duty under the second Bonaparte is not, as under Napoleon, to watch the enemies of the peasant regime in the towns, but Bonaparte's enemies in the country."

against Rome will take place in France itself, but in a sense opposite to that of M. de Montalembert.[22]

Lastly, the culminating point of the *"idées napoléoniennes"* is the preponderance of the *army*. The army was the *point d'honneur* of the smallholding peasants, it was they themselves transformed into heroes, defending their new possessions against the outer world, glorifying their recently won nationhood, plundering and revolutionising the world. The uniform was their own state dress; war was their poetry; the smallholding, extended and rounded off in imagination, was their fatherland, and patriotism the ideal form of their sense of property. But the enemies against whom the French peasant has now to defend his property are not the Cossacks; they are the *huissiers*[23] and the tax collectors. The smallholding lies no longer in the so-called fatherland, but in the register of mortgages. The army itself is no longer the flower of the peasant youth; it is the swamp-flower of the peasant lumpenproletariat. It consists in large measure of *remplaçants,* of substitutes, just as the second Bonaparte is himself only a *remplaçant,* the substitute for Napoleon. It now performs its deeds of valour by hunting down the peasants like chamois, and in organised drives, by doing *gendarme* duty, and if the internal contradictions of his system chase the chief of the Society of December 10 over the French border, his army, after some acts of brigandage, will reap, not laurels, but thrashings.

One sees: all *"idées napoléoniennes" are ideas of the undeveloped smallholding in the freshness of its youth;* for the smallholding that has outlived its day they are an absurdity. They are only the hallucinations of its death struggle, words that are transformed into phrases, spirits transformed into ghosts. But the parody of the empire was necessary to free the mass of the French nation from the weight of tradition and to work out in pure form the opposition between the state power and society. With the progressive undermining of small-holding property, the state structure erected upon it collapses. The centralisation of the state that modern society requires arises only on the ruins of the military-bureaucratic government machinery which was forged in opposition to feudalism.[24]

The condition of the French peasants provides us with the answer to the

22. This refers to a speech by Montalembert, leader of the Legitimists, in the Legislative Assembly on May 22, 1850, in which he urged them to "wage a serious war against socialism."

23. Bailiffs.

24. Instead of the last two sentences, the 1852 edition has: "The demolition of the state machine will not endanger centralisation. Bureaucracy is only the low and brutal form of a centralisation that is still afflicted with its opposite, with feudalism. When he is disappointed in the Napoleonic Restoration, the French peasant will part with his belief in his smallholding, the entire state edifice erected on this smallholding will fall to the ground and *the proletarian revolution will obtain that chorus without which its solo becomes a swan song in all peasant countries."*

riddle of the *general elections of December 20 and 21,* which bore the second Bonaparte up Mount Sinai, not to receive laws, but to give them.[25]

Manifestly, the bourgeoisie had now no choice but to elect Bonaparte. When the puritans at the Council of Constance complained of the dissolute lives of the popes and wailed about the necessity of moral reform, Cardinal Pierre d'Ailly thundered at them: "Only the devil in person can still save the Catholic Church, and you ask for angels." In like manner, after the coup d'état, the French bourgeoisie cried: Only the chief of the Society of December 10 can still save bourgeois society! Only theft can still save property; only perjury, religion; bastardy, the family; disorder, order!

As the executive authority which has made itself an independent power, Bonaparte feels it to be his mission to safeguard "bourgeois order." But the strength of this bourgeois order lies in the middle class. He looks on himself, therefore, as the representative of the middle class and issues decrees in this sense. Nevertheless, he is somebody solely due to the fact that he has broken the political power of this middle class and daily breaks it anew. Consequently, he looks on himself as the adversary of the political and literary power of the middle class. But by protecting its material power, he generates its political power anew. The cause must accordingly be kept alive; but the effect, where it manifests itself, must be done away with. But this cannot pass off without slight confusions of cause and effect, since in their interaction both lose their distinguishing features. New decrees that obliterate the border line. As against the bourgeoisie, Bonaparte looks on himself, at the same time, as the representative of the peasants and of the people in general, who wants to make the lower classes of the people happy within the framework of bourgeois society. New decrees that cheat the "true Socialists"[26] of their statecraft in advance. But, above all, Bonaparte looks on himself as the chief of the Society of December 10, as the representative

25. In the 1852 edition: "but to give and execute them." Then follows this passage: "Of course in those fateful days the French nation committed a mortal sin against democracy, which daily prays on its knees: Holy Universal Suffrage, plead for us! The believers in Universal Suffrage are naturally unwilling to dispense with the miraculous power which has worked such great things with them, which has transformed Bonaparte II into a Napoleon, a Saul into a Paul and a Simon into a Peter. The popular spirit speaks to them through the ballot box as the God of the Prophet Ezekiel spoke to the dry bones: *'Haec dicit dominus deus ossibus suis: Ecce, ego intromittam in vos spiritum et vivetis.' 'Thus saith the Lord God unto these bones: Behold, I will cause breath to enter into you, and ye shall live'"* [Ezekiel 37:5].

26. The reference is to German or "true socialism" which was widespread in Germany in the 1840s, mostly among petty-bourgeois intellectuals. The "true socialists"—Karl Grün, Moses Hess, Hermann Kriege—substituted the sentimental preaching of love and brotherhood for the ideas of socialism and denied the need for a bourgeois-democratic revolution in Germany. Marx and Engels criticised this trend in the following works: *The German Ideology, Circular Against Kriege, German Socialism in Verse and Prose* and *Manifesto of the Communist Party.*

of the lumpenproletariat, to which he himself, his entourage, his government and his army belong, and whose prime consideration is to benefit itself and draw California lottery prizes from the state treasury. And he vindicates his position as chief of the Society of December 10 with decrees, without decrees and despite decrees.

This contradictory task of the man explains the contradictions of his government, the confused, blind to-ing and fro-ing which seeks now to win, now to humiliate first one class and then another and arrays all of them uniformly against him, whose practical uncertainty forms a highly comical contrast to the imperious, categorical style of the government decrees, a style which is faithfully copied from the uncle.

Industry and trade, hence the business affairs of the middle class, are to prosper in hothouse fashion under the strong government. The grant of innumerable railway concessions. But the Bonapartist lumpenproletariat is to enrich itself. The initiated play *tripotage* on the *bourse* with the railway concessions. But no capital is forthcoming for the railways. Obligation of the Bank to make advances on railway shares. But, at the same time, the Bank is to be exploited for personal ends and therefore must be cajoled. Release of the Bank from the obligation to publish its report weekly. Leonine agreement of the Bank with the government. The people are to be given employment. Initiation of public works. But the public works increase the obligations of the people in respect of taxes. Hence reduction of the taxes by an onslaught on the *rentiers,* by conversion of the five per cent bonds to four-and-a-half per cent. But, once more, the middle class must receive a *douceur.* Therefore doubling of the wine tax for the people, who buy it *en détail,* and halving of the wine tax for the middle class, who drink it *en gros.* Dissolution of the actual workers' associations, but promises of miracles of association in the future. The peasants are to be helped. Mortgage banks that expedite their getting into debt and accelerate the concentration of property. But these banks are to be used to make money out of the confiscated estates of the House of Orleans. No capitalist wants to agree to this condition, which is not in the decree, and the mortgage bank remains a mere decree, etc., etc.

Bonaparte would like to appear as the patriarchal benefactor of all classes. But he cannot give to one class without taking from another. Just as at the time of the Fronde it was said of the Duke of Guise that he was the most *obligeant* man in France because he had turned all his estates into his partisans' obligations to him, so Bonaparte would fain be the most *obligeant* man in France and turn all the property, all the labour of France into a personal obligation to himself. He would like to steal the whole of France in order to be able to make a present of her to France or, rather, in order to be able to buy France anew with French money, for as the chief of the Society of December 10 he must needs buy what ought to belong to him. And all the state institutions, the Senate, the Council of State, the legislative body, the Legion of Honour, the soldiers' medals, the wash-houses, the public works, the railways, the *état-major* of the National Guard excluding privates, and the confiscated estates of the House of Orleans—all become parts of the institution of purchase. Every place in the army and in the government machine becomes a means of purchase. But the most important feature of this process, whereby France is taken in order to be given back, is the percentages that find their way into the pockets of the head and the members of the Society of December 10 during the transaction. . . .

Driven by the contradictory demands of his situation and being at the same time, like a conjurer, under the necessity of keeping the public gaze fixed on himself, as Napoleon's substitute, by springing constant surprises, that is to say, under the necessity of executing a coup d'état *en miniature* every day, Bonaparte throws the entire bourgeois economy into confusion, violates everything that seemed inviolable to the revolution of 1848, makes some tolerant of revolution, others desirous of revolution, and produces actual anarchy in the name of order, while at the same time stripping its halo from the entire state machine, profanes it and makes it at once loathsome and ridiculous. The cult of the Holy Coat of Trier[27] he duplicates in Paris with the cult of the Napoleonic imperial mantle. But when the imperial mantle finally falls on the shoulders of Louis Bonaparte, the bronze statue of Napoleon will crash from the top of the Vendôme Column.[28]

20. Louis Napoleon, Speech to the Bordeaux Chamber of Commerce (1852)

Louis Napoleon (1808–73) was the nephew of Napoleon I. Upon the death of the latter's son in 1832, Louis Napoleon assumed the role of dynastic pretender, hoping to capitalize upon the cult of Napoleon that had been flourishing under the rather lackluster July Monarchy. In 1836, and again in 1840, he attempted to provoke insurrection among French

27. The *Holy Coat of Trier*—a relic exhibited in the Catholic Cathedral at Trier, allegedly a garment of Christ of which he was stripped at his crucifixion. Generations of pilgrims came to venerate it.

28. The *Vendôme Column* was erected in Paris between 1806 and 1810 in tribute to the military victories of Napoleon I. It was made of bronze from captured enemy guns and crowned by a statue of Napoleon; the statue was removed during the Restoration but reerected in 1833. In the spring of 1871, by order of the Paris Commune, the Vendôme Column was destroyed as a symbol of militarism.

From *Moniteur universel*, 12 October 1852. Translated for this volume by Paula Wissing.

troops with the intent of staging a coup d'état; both times he failed utterly and ended up in exile. The more sedentary life of exile bore fruit in his book *Napoleonic Ideas* (1839), which persuasively reformulated the Bonapartist legacy in terms more suitable to a new era, deemphasizing its military ethos and stressing instead its social, industrial, and commercial aims. "One of the cleverest pieces of political sales talk produced in the nineteenth century," the historian David Thomson has called it.

The Second Republic provided Louis Napoleon with his long-awaited opportunity, and Karl Marx's *Eighteenth Brumaire* (document 19) offers a caustic analysis of the socioeconomic factors responsible for his victory in the presidential elections of 1849 and for the ease with which he was able to replace constitutionalism with dictatorship through his coup d'état of 2 December 1851.

The document reprinted here takes us from Marx's portrait of Louis Napoleon in 1851 to the politician as presented in his own words less than a year later. The early part of 1852 had been spent consolidating the coup, in part by putting down insurrections by supporters of the republic. In the fall, the prince-president (as he was called) embarked upon a tour of south and central France, boldly visiting those departments that had been the scene of strong resistance to his takeover. Everywhere he was greeted with enthusiasm and with pomp and circumstance; no seditious murmurs were heard. The climax of the trip was his visit to the Atlantic port of Bordeaux. At a banquet in his honor given by the chamber of commerce—to mark the launching of a new ship called the *Louis-Napoleon* which featured an enormous bust of the prince on its prow—he made his momentous announcement: the restoration of the empire. The content of the speech, as well as Napoleon III's subsequent policies, explains why the nineteenth-century critic Sainte-Beuve called this second modern emperor of the French "Saint-Simon on horseback." (See introduction to document 14.)

Gentlemen:

The invitation extended to me by the chamber of commerce and commercial court of Bordeaux, which I eagerly accepted, allows me the opportunity to thank your great city for its warm welcome and magnificent hospitality, and it is with pleasure, now that I am near the end of my journey, that I share with you the impressions I gained from it.

As you know the goal of this trip for me was to acquaint myself with our beautiful southern provinces and to study their needs. It also produced a much more important result, however.

In fact, and I say this with a frankness that is as far removed from pride as it is from false modesty, never has a people expressed so directly, spontaneously, and unanimously the will to liberate itself from worries about the future by consolidating in one hand a power that is favorable to its interests. This is because they know now both the false hopes that have been used to lull them and the dangers that threaten them. They know that in 1852, society was foundering because each party saw in the prospect of a total shipwreck the consolation that it would be the one to plant its flag on the debris that would float to the top. They are grateful to me for saving the ship by flying the flag of France.

Disabused of absurd theories, the people have acquired the conviction that the so-called reformers were only dreamers, for there was always an inconsistency or disproportion between their means and the promised ends.

Today France surrounds me with warm support precisely because I do not belong to the family of ideologues. In order to do good for the country it is not necessary to apply new systems, but to provide confidence in the present, security in the future. It is for this reason that France seems to desire to return to the empire.

Nevertheless, there is a fear that I must address. In a spirit of mistrust, some people say to themselves that empire means war. I say that empire means peace.

The empire is peace because France desires peace, and when France is satisfied, the world is calm. Glory is bequeathed by right of inheritance, but war is not. Have the princes who justly prided themselves on being the grandsons of Louis XIV begun fighting his battles again? War is not waged for pleasure but of necessity. And, during these times of transition where everywhere, alongside so many elements of prosperity, breed so many causes of death, one can truthfully say: Woe to him who first in Europe would give the signal for a confrontation whose consequences would be incalculable!

I agree, however, that I, like the emperor, have many conquests to make. Like him I want to win the conciliation of dissenting parties and bring back into the course of the great popular river the divergent streams that are now being lost without profit to anyone.

I want to win for religion, morality, and affluence that still great portion of the population who, in the midst of a nation of faith and belief, barely know the precepts of Christ, and who, in the bosom of the most fertile land on earth, can hardly attain life's most basic necessities.

We have vast wastelands to clear, roads to build, harbors to dredge, rivers to open to navigation, canals to finish, a railway system to complete. We have, across the sea from Marseilles, a vast kingdom to assimilate into France. Our great western ports are there to provide a link to the American continent, yet these communications are still lacking in rapidity. Finally, everywhere are ruins to tear down, false gods to lay low, and truths to bring to triumph.

That is how I would understand the empire, if the empire should be re-established. These are the conquests I am planning, and all of you around me who seek, as I do, the good of our country, you are my soldiers.

21. Heinrich von Gagern, Speech to the Frankfurt National Assembly on German Unity (26 October 1848)

Heinrich von Gagern (1799–1880) was the son of a Liberal statesman from Hesse. As a young officer in a Bavarian unit he fought with Allied forces against Napoleon, participating in the Battle of Waterloo. He studied law at the Universities of Heidelberg and Jena, where he became a leader in the *Burschenschaft* (or student association) movement as well as an enthusiastic supporter of German unification in a liberal constitutional mode. Elected to the Diet of Hesse-Darmstadt in 1832, Gagern resigned his position as a state civil servant in 1833 because of his liberal political views. Although he left the Hessian Parliament in 1836, he became, as a wealthy landowner and regional notable, an influential and articulate Liberal opinion-maker during the later Vormärz.

With the Revolutions of 1848, Gagern was launched into national politics. In early March he was given charge of the State Ministry in Hesse and also participated in the *Vorparlament* (or Preparliament) that met in Frankfurt to organize a German legislative assembly. Following the spring elections to that body, Gagern became the president of the Frankfurt Parliament in May 1848, a post he held until his appointment as federal minister-president in December. Gagern's December 1848 formal program for the unification of Germany—a closer federal state under Prussian leadership, which would stand in a looser political relationship with Hapsburg Austria—is anticipated by his famous speech of 26 October 1848 arguing for the unification of Germany and for a special constitutional relationship of that nation to an Austria that contained both German and non-German peoples.

Although the unification of Germany in 1866–71 under Bismarck seemed to violate Gagern's hopes for a continuing role of Austria in Germany, Gagern's Liberal federalist solution to the problem of Austro-German relations was vaguely similar, in structure, if not in ethos, to that finally proposed by Bismarck in 1879. True, Austria's relationship with Germany after 1879 was that of alliance partner rather than constitutional member, but Bismarck himself could justify this alliance as implementing "Gagernesque dreams." Gagern's linkage of liberalism and nationalism

From *Stenographischer Bericht über die Verhandlungen der deutschen constituierenden Nationalversammlung zu Frankfurt am Main*, edited by Franz Wizard, vol. 4 (Leipzig, 1848), pp. 2896–2900. Translated for this volume by William Kunze.

was closer to the praxis of Mazzini, however, than to that of Bismarck, and it was this that marked Gagern as a classic representative of the failed German Revolution of 1848.

The German nation has fallen into humiliation, and we must seek the means to raise it up again. In order to secure it against repeated downfall we want to formulate these means into the principles of our future constitution. It is natural to ask oneself first: What were the main reasons for our humiliation in our previous state of affairs? What were the obstacles that prevented our nation from rising to the power it deserves?

Foremost among these reasons was the relationship of the mixed states, that relationship in which, under one sovereign, German and non-German states were united under one government in a political union. The resolution of this situation is the first great difficulty confronting us in the deliberations over the constitution which the nation awaits with expectation. With respect to the mixed states created by the Federal Act, there is a crucial distinction to be made: (1) whether the German-speaking area is subordinate and connected to a primarily non-German-speaking area; or (2) whether the German-speaking area is predominant, with non-German regions being subordinate to it. The first relationship is one that has brought about the saddest consequences, and under which no national policy could exist, much less be achieved harmoniously. It was this condition that caused us to be scorned even by inferior nations and that harmed our own interests. This was the relationship that Luxemburg and Limburg had to Holland, and Holstein to Denmark. These conditions must be changed. No national life can be maintained in such incongruous political relationships. I doubt whether Paragraphs 2 and 3[1] will directly resolve these conditions because, as was correctly noted from this rostrum today, there are international legal conditions that must be first taken into account and settled.

Within Germany, however, there have existed and still do exist other confused, unclear relationships, connections between non-German subordinate regions and dominant German areas. Prussia abolished one of these hybrid relationships by uniting to the German Confederation the most important of those parts of its monarchy that, according to the Federal Act,

---

1. The Constitutional Committee of the Frankfurt Parliament had proposed as part of the draft constitution for the German federal state that:

Paragraph 2: "No part of the German empire may be united in one state with non-German territories" [majority version].

Paragraph 3: "If a German territory has the same head of state as a non-German territory, the relationship between the two territories is to be arranged according to the principles of a purely personal union." —ED.

had not belonged to the Confederation. Even though Prussia did not have a separate policy with regard to those provinces that formerly did not belong to the Confederation—for these provinces were just as German as any others—still their formal union to the Confederation greatly simplified our national relations, and one can say that we have been merged together! Austria is a different situation. It may seem unclear which is the principal nationality within the Austrian complex of states, but there is no doubt that the German element, although in the minority in terms of population, is the most influential in this monarchy and must become even more so. Therefore, Gentlemen, I cannot agree with the opinion that Austria ought to be compelled to separate politically from the states that have until now been joined with it in one political union, thereby dissolving the monarchy. The implementation of Paragraphs 2 and 3 would entail this separation of the German-Austrian from the non-German provinces as well as the dissolution of the Austrian monarchy. There is no doubt about that, no matter how much one tries to gloss over this question. And, yes, I do call it evading the question if one says, as is often said even here: "We do not desire dissolution, we want to hold Austria together, but we want to do it through a personal union, which is sufficient to maintain Austria intact." I thought this question had been settled. But since so little attention has been paid to the arguments that have already been so decisively developed; since even men with great experience and skill in political matters have asserted that a personal union would assure the lasting cohesion of Austria; and since they have asked why I see "dissolution" in "personal union"; therefore I must answer that they seem not to have taken into account the full interrelated effects of Paragraphs 2 and 3 as they are presented in the constitutional draft.

Paragraph 2 forbids a common political life. It orders that the German and non-German—which until now have been united in one state separate, the non-German to be left to itself, to an independent political or at least national life. But with this kind of independent political life it is obvious that any lasting agreement on political aims between one constitutional state and another, through the means of a personal union, would be purely fortuitous. Because the majorities in the various states united by a mere personal union might have different political goals, the different executive authorities might be obliged to follow different lines or directions, and even to adopt positions hostile to each other.

Let us examine what would happen to Austria if Paragraphs 2 and 3 went into effect there, for I must immediately call your attention to the alternative. It is not enough to say that we want to establish Paragraphs 2 and 3 as law here, but then wait and let events determine whether they are carried out. I believe that if we declare that something should or should not be, that we deem it to correspond to the interests of the Fatherland, and that it should be thus and not otherwise, that we must also agree in advance on the means with which to make it effective—we should not leave the conclusion hanging in the air. We are called upon to present a constitution to the nation, to the entire German people. But with this task we have also taken on the obligation to take into account the circumstances and facts that must be considered if we want to make the constitution viable. What would the consequences of the implementation of Paragraphs 2 and 3 be for Austria? We would draw the German-Austrian provinces into the German federal state and sever them from the non-German regions and provinces of Austria. These remaining parts of Austria would not then form a unified state; they would, by the nature of things, fall apart as soon as their common center of gravity, which lies in the German hereditary lands, was stripped from them. This topic has been sufficiently developed by other speakers, and I can proceed to other points.

Galicia, as well as Hungary (the way has already been paved by the constitution of this country), perhaps even the lands adjoining Hungary, and Italy would become independently organized. Now I ask you, Gentlemen, if we vote for paragraphs that lead to such results, are we meeting our natural obligations or are we not in fact, as has been said today, indulging ourselves by disregarding the circumstances that must be taken into account? It seems to me that at a time when civil war is breaking out in a member state of the Confederation, when the fire is blazing, we have an obligation not to throw more wood on the fire. We will be acting in the spirit of confederation if we help to extinguish the flames and if we do not act as if the continued existence of the Austrian monarchy is in question. We must indicate instead our conviction that the Austrian monarchy, whose continuance as a political unit is of vital interest for the entire Fatherland, will endure as a powerful empire, strengthened by freedom, closely united with Germany in pursuit of our great national mission. We must act in this manner or we are not fulfilling our duty as a good neighbor, much less as a national ally. If we accepted Paragraphs 2 and 3 in their present form and without reservation, as is suggested, and if we forced Austria to comply, we would dismember a great empire and leave its non-German sections without any connection, uncertain what would become of them, uncertain what role these areas would play in relation to the family of European nations or what influences would gain control over them. In the making of constitutions, other nations would consider it their primary duty to leave no doubt about the possession of even one village. Should we, then, want to frivolously estrange an entire seed crop of the future, a rich prospect for future national development that has been connected to us until now, and abandon it to chance?

I believe, Gentlemen, that this can be neither our intention nor our task. But this would be the consequence if we applied Paragraphs 2 and 3 to Austria and tried to force the dynasty into a mere personal union with the individual sections. That would only constitute a "dynastic union," a complaint erroneously made against the Pragmatic Sanction, which however is something entirely different. If states have nothing else in common aside from personal union, then they might as well have nothing in common and each go its own way. Those who advocate personal union also feel this way: they really only have complete separation in mind. Someone mentioned Sweden and Norway, but there they have already been trying for some time to create something that would make the bond between the two more advantageous, something like Austria's Pragmatic Sanction. Either this will come about, or someday a separation will become more probable; things cannot remain as they are now. If the relation of personal union is applied to Austria, we will see in the future four Austrian envoys, four Austrian armies, everything in fours. Should we then hurl such chaotic conditions upon a Europe that has already been undermined in so many ways? By doing so we would violate the obligation of a great nation in the family of European peoples, if it claims its rank as the result of an upheaval, which so fundamentally reorganizes its relationships and has such unpredictable effects. Our first duty is not to disappoint the hopes and right of the peoples to a secure peace with freedom, that is, not to sow the seeds of the new revolutions that would potentially lie within such chaotic conditions. This would hold true for those non-German provinces of Austria that have not made any demand at all to become independent states, such as Dalmatia and the coast, Croatia, and even Galicia. It has been said, it is true, that all of these provinces are only bound to Austria by bayonets, but this has never been proved. The opinion of some people   that there is no other possibil ity, that every nation and group of people must deem its government to be its enemy and must always carry within itself the urge toward revolution and sedition—is only the exaggerated opinion of a few. Many of those provinces, content with their situation, have not expressed any conception of political or even national independence. With the application of Articles 2 and 3 in the Austrian states and their unavoidable consequences, we violate our first obligation toward Europe, for we offer no guarantee for the continuance of peaceful relations. Instead, we abolish the hopes for peace and thereby take up an action that, far from preserving international law, actually damages the international order.

I ask further: Is it in our own national interest to abandon the non-German provinces of Austria to themselves and to chance? I conceive the mission of the German people to be that of a great world power. Some might scoff at that and cynically and disparagingly deny any such national calling. I believe in it and would lose the pride I feel in belonging to my people if I had to abandon my belief in such a higher destiny. Our task is not fulfilled merely by the creation of a constitution that is designed for the narrow limits of our current political circumstances. Nor is it fulfilled by admitting into the constitution a principle of unity which detaches us from those upon whom that unitary power depends, or which, while other nations are expanding their power and influence, condemns us to warm ourselves by our hearths, in seclusion, so long as our neighbors leave us in peace and freedom.

What sort of unity should we strive for, then? To live up to the destiny that has set our sights on the East, to take those peoples along the Danube who have neither a calling nor a claim to independence, and set them like satellites into our planetary system. The rights of nationalities are often referred to. I grant these rights in their full measure where they exist, for example in Italy. That is why I am convinced that, in the general interest of the nation, the troubles in Italy will only be solved when Austria removes itself from Lombardy. For our national development we must maintain a secure position on the Adriatic Sea. We must use all the power of our national unity to secure the borders necessary to maintain that position, and insofar as we limit ourselves to that, we are not violating nationality rights. Let the Italians, like us, put their affairs in order and unite, and we will gladly join them in cheers when this Italian Federation is formed and when it presents, along with the guarantee of independence, the guarantee of peaceful future relations.

The question of what will become of Galicia has thrown a haze over the circumstances of Poland. We will not raise the demand that we want to include Galicia in our national development. But the time has not yet come to leave it to itself: for the moment, we wish to see it remain joined to Austria. Given the hostile position the peasantry has adopted against the nobility, if Galicia became independent it might become a focus of revolution and provide occasion for a war with Russia. If war became a political necessity, we would fight it with all the energy of the reborn might of our people, but we do not deliberately want to provoke it. This is what would happen, however, if Galicia were to become independent at present. The circumstances would be similar to those that led to the destruction of the Free State of Cracow, only more intense. Hungary enjoys constitutional autonomy from Austria, and the questions that were raised on one or the other side during the recent disturbances will be settled in the old spirit of brotherhood if the Magyars do not themselves violate the rights of the nationalities. In the other non-German provinces of Austria, there exists neither the right to, the conditions for, nor the claim to independent national development. Tearing off provinces, especially the southern ones, would probably only play into the hands of foreign influences and foreign power, to our own immense disadvantage.

Two groups are currently pressing for the acceptance of Paragraphs 2 and 3, although for different reasons. One group wants to dissolve the Austrian monarchy into its parts. I have explained why I do not want this dissolution and why I believe it is counter to German interests. The other says: We do not believe in this dissolution; it will not take place because the personal union is sufficient to hold Austria together. I have already answered this question too. The political dissolution of the state in fact means complete dissolution. But Austria must not annul the political unity between its German and non-German provinces; and we must not make the unreasonable demand of Austria that it commit such a crime against its provinces, which have the constitutional right to maintain the advantages they have gained through this political union. Every constitutional state has the obligation of self-preservation. The Austrian government would fail in its first duty if it dissolved its political connections with the provinces, which do not yet have any idea of what form their future could take after separation from the monarchy as a whole. Thus I believe, Gentlemen, that we must search for a relationship whereby Austria will not be forced to detach its German from its non-German provinces but will nevertheless be able to remain in the closest association with Germany. The question is then as follows: Is it in Germany's interest that Germany as a whole be shaped into such a loose union that Austria can belong to the Reich under the same conditions as the rest of the German states without having to separate her German and non-German provinces? Or is it not more in the overall interest of the nation, as much of Austria as of the rest of Germany, that the rest of the German states at least join together more firmly with each other—even if Austria, on account of her non-German provinces, cannot enter into this close federation under the same conditions—but that a close federal connection nevertheless be maintained between Austria and the remainder of Germany?

The concepts "federal state" and "confederation of states" are vague, for one can imagine federative relationships which lie between these two and form bridges between them. Why have closer ties for so long not arisen within the union created by the Federal Act in Germany? Because no common interests existed, because people deliberately kept their interests apart and cultivated particularism in the extreme. When did the need for and consciousness of unity begin to develop to such a high degree in Germany? From the moment when common national interests united a large part of Germany and made it impossible for these more closely allied states to maintain such separate policies, that is, from the beginning and development of the Customs Union. Let us consider the possibility of merging the material interests of Austria with those of the rest of Germany. We could unite Austria to us in this manner without having to separate (if we could) the German provinces from the non-German. Associations that lie between a "federal state" and a "confederation of states" can be created in this manner.

But again, are we capable of enforcing the separation of Austria, that is, the separation of the German from the non-German provinces? And if we cannot do that, dare we think of Austria as removed, severed from the rest of Germany? We cannot enforce and do not want the former, and we must not have the latter. Whatever may be said from the other side about the views of the Austrians on this question, I believe that the majority of Austrians desire that the political cohesion of their Empire continue, as the Tyroleans have just recently said in their proclamation. One can be of many opinions on this question; one can hold different views. Each man will obtain his point of view from his own experiences and from the sources of knowledge at his command. The Austrians want to be with Germany but also to maintain Austria intact—to make both unions possible. But that does not mean that we should set aside the indispensable task facing the rest of Germany, that of establishing unity in a federal state, while Austria maintains her position in the world with and beside us.

It has been said that if German Austria joins with Germany in a federal state, non-German Austria will be left to a dubious fate, for then the united German people could carry out its destiny in the East even more energetically. This logic eludes me. If we dissolve the political connection that exists between the German and non-German provinces, new ties with a united Germany will not soon be formed. The close relations that have existed for centuries among the Austrian provinces and between the dynasty and the non-German provinces, once torn apart, will not soon be replaced by new ones. A general German government, a distant national authority, would not command the means that are available to the Austrian government—because of custom and Austria's real connection to those provinces—for exercising beneficial influence. Decades would go by before the national authority could appropriate this legacy under such changed circumstances, and we can ill afford for such a long time to do without the influence in the East that comes from Austria's position in the world. The Eastern Question—for whose solution Austria's world position and, through Austria, Germany's too can and must be of great influence—stands in the background at the moment. When the internal political state of affairs of the European powers are put in order again, it will quickly come to the fore again. Germany will not be made stronger if it is more closely united with the German provinces of Austria but has been separated from the non-German ones and deprived of Austria's multiple connections to the lands of the southern Danube. But we will be in a strong and powerful position in terms of this question if Austria, detached from Italy, shares one policy with Germany, if the political interests of the two are united. It has been said, in fact on this [the right] side, that Germany must adhere to its own national policy and must therefore renounce the Austrian policy and Austria itself if the latter, with its German provinces, will not separate itself from the non-German provinces. I ask, in reply, what national policy can Germany have if we do not take part in Austria's mission to spread German culture, language, and morals along the Danube as far as the Black Sea? These regions, so thinly populated and with such varied nationalities, but so promising, have a civilization already accustomed to depending on German civilization. They long for the protection and increased influence of German Austria, and they would open up a rich market for German industry. And what prospects would not arise if, behind the unified might of Austria—which would be called upon to exercise its power first—the rest of Germany stood like a wedge, unified, using its power to press its interests? Emigrants who now sail to the West will turn to the Danubian lands, for freedom will be and already is there too. Why should not those who wish to emigrate prefer to erect their homes on the banks of the nearby Danube rather than in distant America? As soon as the way is opened to us, the acquisition of free property is made easy, and German protection, progress, and influence are secured in these areas, they can profit from their labor and capital among friendly races that have been familiar with German customs and language for centuries. How much more quickly then will German culture spread and enable us to take and maintain the rank due us in the company of European nations!

If we retreat from this mission of spreading German culture along the Danube—which we do if we undermine the political connections of German Austria to the eastern Danubian lands or harbor the fear that the Slavic element will win the upper hand over the German in Austria if the monarchy should continue to be united—if we do not accept this mission for Germany in league with Austria, then others will seize it. If we do not strengthen our influence along the Danube, the Russians are notoriously ready to organize theirs. They will get the better of us until we come to our senses and allow Austria the freedom to maintain and cultivate its long-standing political and neighborly relations with the Danubian lands. In the light of this, I am not in favor of postponing the decision on the relationship between Austria and the rest of Germany. I believe that we must bring the matter to a head straightaway and recognize that Austria cannot for the present enter into the kind of closer union desired by the rest of Germany. The majority of Austrians will not accept the political separation of the German provinces from the non-German as a condition for entering into a

closer federation. In addition, it is just as little in the German national interest to bring about this division, and with it the dissolution of the Austrian monarchy and the abandonment of its historical calling, which must
be fulfilled in the closest alliance with Germany. I have therefore formulated a proposal in conformity with this view, which I have the honor of
presenting to the noble Assembly:

"Austria remains, with consideration of its constitutional connection
with non-German regions and provinces, in steadfast and indissoluble federation with the rest of Germany.

"The organic provisions for this federal relationship, which are made
necessary by the new circumstances, will be the contents of a separate Act
of Federation."

I will allow myself a few words in defense of this motion. As this proposal is formulated it should go after Paragraph 1, that is, it must be inserted between Paragraphs 1 and 2. I am of the opinion that the subsequent
statements, from Paragraph 2 on, are in part not applicable to Austria, although I nevertheless wish to see these provisions maintained for the union
to be entered into by the rest of Germany. It has been said that it is against
our mandate to found or to permit a double federal structure. We are called
to create unity as far as it is advantageous under the given circumstances;
any further we cannot go. But if we accept paragraphs that we can foresee
will not satisfy Austria and which will force her to sever herself from Germany, no longer to belong to the German Reich at all—then, Gentlemen,
we have not created unity but have torn it asunder. And I oppose this rup-
turing of unity.

The question of the future place of Austria within and in relation to Germany has been linked to that of the future head, or the holder of power in
the future Reich. Months ago I publicly expressed my thoughts on this
question, and I would consider it premature and inappropriate to read
aloud now what I expressed about this matter at the beginning of our revolution. I have not wanted to prejudice the decision on the question in any
way through my amendment. I am, to be sure, of the opinion that a single
unitary head belongs at the top of the federal union; this already excludes
the idea of Prussian hegemony. For the leadership of all of Germany, Austria included, we must fashion a broader arrangement. This would be, of
course, a very important and difficult question, one that awaits its solution
in the future. We would have to create an organism within which a central
leadership would supervise the common interests of all of Germany in co-
operation with the united representatives of all the German lands.

In my proposal I have also not expressed an opinion as to whether the
organic provisions for the wider federal arrangement, which will have to be
newly created, should be made part of the constitution. I would want them

to be part of the constitution. But since such an arrangement has hitherto lain outside the purview of the committee, I did not want my proposal, even if it found approval, to anticipate the views of the committee with respect to this matter. The more closely Austria can be united with the rest of Germany without thereby annulling the political unity of its provinces, and the more room we can leave to the non-German provinces to enable them too to form a closer federal relationship with Germany, the more completely will we have fulfilled our task. The federal union remains our goal; transitions are necessary on the way to achieving that goal. We cannot avoid these transitions without destroying, without doing the opposite of what we should do—which is to create unity of interests. The formula of unity captured in the constitution should be only the appropriate expression of this unity of interests, the means to an end, not an end in itself. Since we are called to create this unity, we must beware of choosing formulas so narrow that they force our national interests, against their nature, into a straitjacket. Let us instead pull the door wide open so that we do not impede entrance into the German family and into its great and hospitable house.

22. Macaulay on Jefferson in the 1850s: A Letter to H. S. Randall

For information about T. B. Macaulay, see document 3. Henry Stephens Randall (1811–76) was a New York lawyer who authored *The Life of Thomas Jefferson*, published in 1858.

Holly Lodge, Kensington, London, May 23d, 1857

Dear Sir,—The four volumes of the "Colonial History of New York" reached me safely. I assure you that I shall value them highly. They contain much to interest an English as well as an American reader. Pray accept my thanks, and convey them to the regents of the university.

You are surprised to learn that I have not a high opinion of Mr. Jefferson, and I am surprised at your surprise. I am certain that I never wrote a line, and that I never, in Parliament, in conversation, or even on the hustings—a place where it is the fashion to court the populace—uttered a word indicating an opinion that the supreme authority in a state ought to be intrusted to the majority of citizens told by the head; in other words, to the poorest and most ignorant part of society. I have long been convinced that institutions

From G. Otto Trevelyan, *The Life and Letters of Lord Macaulay,* Enlarged and Complete Edition, vol. 2 (New York: Harper and Brothers, 1908), pp. 451–54.

purely democratic must, sooner or later, destroy liberty or civilization, or both. In Europe, where the population is dense, the effect of such institutions would be almost instantaneous. What happened lately in France is an example. In 1848 a pure democracy was established there. During a short time there was reason to expect a general spoliation, a national bankruptcy, a new partition of the soil, a maximum of prices, a ruinous load of taxation laid on the rich for the purpose of supporting the poor in idleness. Such a system would, in twenty years, have made France as poor and barbarous as the France of the Carlovingians. Happily, the danger was averted; and now there is a despotism, a silent tribune, an enslaved press. Liberty is gone, but civilization has been saved. I have not the smallest doubt that if we had a purely democratic government here the effect would be the same. Either the poor would plunder the rich, and civilization would perish; or order and prosperity would be saved by a strong military government, and liberty would perish. You may think that your country enjoys an exemption from these evils. I will frankly own to you that I am of a very different opinion. Your fate I believe to be certain, though it is deferred by a physical cause. As long as you have a boundless extent of fertile and unoccupied land, your laboring population will be far more at ease than the laboring population of the Old World, and, while that is the case, the Jefferson politics may continue to exist without causing any fatal calamity. But the time will come when New England will be as thickly peopled as old England. Wages will be as low, and will fluctuate as much with you as with us. You will have your Manchesters and Birminghams, and in those Manchesters and Birminghams hundreds of thousands of artisans will assuredly be sometimes out of work. Then your institutions will be fairly brought to the test. Distress everywhere makes the laborer mutinous and discontented, and inclines him to listen with eagerness to agitators who tell him that it is a monstrous iniquity that one man should have a million, while another can not get a full meal. In bad years there is plenty of grumbling here, and sometimes a little rioting. But it matters little. For here the sufferers are not the rulers. The supreme power is in the hands of a class, numerous indeed, but select; of an educated class; of a class which is, and knows itself to be, deeply interested in the security of property and the maintenance of order. Accordingly, the malcontents are firmly yet gently restrained. The bad time is got over without robbing the wealthy to relieve the indigent. The springs of national prosperity soon begin to flow again: work is plentiful, wages rise, and all is tranquillity and cheerfulness. I have seen England pass three or four times through such critical seasons as I have described. Through such seasons the United States will have to pass in the course of the next century, if not of this. How will you pass through them? I heartily wish you a good deliverance. But my reason and my wishes are at war, and I can not help foreboding the worst. It is quite plain that your Government will never be able to restrain a distressed and discontented majority. For with you the majority is the Government, and has the rich, who are always a minority, absolutely at its mercy. The day will come when in the State of New York a multitude of people, none of whom has had more than half a breakfast, or expects to have more than half a dinner, will choose a Legislature. Is it possible to doubt what sort of a Legislature will be chosen? On one side is a statesman preaching patience, respect for vested rights, strict observance of public faith. On the other is a demagogue ranting about the tyranny of capitalists and usurers, and asking why any body should be permitted to drink Champagne and to ride in a carriage, while thousands of honest folks are in want of necessaries. Which of the two candidates is likely to be preferred by a working-man who hears his children cry for more bread? I seriously apprehend that you will, in some such season of adversity as I have described, do things which will prevent prosperity from returning; that you will act like people who should in a year of scarcity devour all the seed-corn, and thus make the next year a year not of scarcity, but of absolute famine. There will be, I fear, spoliation. The spoliation will increase the distress. The distress will produce fresh spoliation. There is nothing to stop you. Your Constitution is all sail and no anchor. As I said before, when a society has entered on this downward progress, either civilization or liberty must perish. Either some Caesar or Napoleon will seize the reins of government with a strong hand, or your republic will be as fearfully plundered and laid waste by barbarians in the twentieth century as the Roman Empire was in the fifth; with this difference, that the Huns and Vandals who ravaged the Roman Empire came from without, and that your Huns and Vandals will have been engendered within your own country by your own institutions.

Thinking thus, of course I can not reckon Jefferson among the benefactors of mankind. I readily admit that his intentions were good, and his abilities considerable. Odious stories have been circulated about his private life; but I do not know on what evidence those stories rest, and I think it probable that they are false, or monstrously exaggerated. I have no doubt that I shall derive both pleasure and information from your account of him.

I have the honor to be, dear sir, your faithful servant,

T. B. Macaulay.

23. Giuseppe Mazzini, *Duties to Country*

Giuseppe Mazzini (1805–72) was one of the great fighters for Italian independence and unity. Born in Genoa, Mazzini studied law at a local university, while involving himself in the conspiracies of the Carbonari secret society. Arrested in 1830 because of his radical republicanism, Mazzini was forced to spend most of his life as an emigrant in France, Switzerland, and England, continuing from abroad his efforts to foment revolutions in Italy. His lifelong goal was a unitary Italy, free of foreign meddling, possessing a republican constitution. In 1831 and 1834 respectively he organized the movements of Young Italy (*La Giovine Italia*) and Young Europe (*La Giovine Europa*) for "men believing in a future of liberty, equality and fraternity of all mankind." For the revolutionary years of 1848–49 he returned to Italy, where, together with Garibaldi, he directed the affairs of the Republican regime at Rome. After its failure he went back to London where, with other revolutionary émigrés (Arnold Ruge of Germany and Alexandre Ledru-Rollin from France), he formed another society, the Central Democratic Committee for Europe. He lived in London and Switzerland until he returned to Italy two years before his death (the latter event characteristically involved a failed attempt to provoke a republican insurrection that would sweep from Sicily to Rome).

Mazzini was a prolific writer, as is witnessed by his thousands of letters and by the 94-volume edition of his collected works published between 1906 and 1943. The following selection, which first appeared in February 1859, is from a collection of Mazzini's essays published in 1860 as *The Duties of Man*, in which Mazzini spoke "as my heart dictates to me, of the most sacred things we know—of God, of Humanity, of the Fatherland, of the Family."

Your first Duties—first, at least, in importance—are, as I have told you, to Humanity. You are *men* before you are *citizens* or *fathers*. If you do not embrace the whole human family in your love, if you do not confess your faith in its unity—consequent on the unity of God—and in the brotherhood of the Peoples who are appointed to reduce that unity to fact—if wherever one of your fellow-men groans, wherever the dignity of human nature is violated by falsehood or tyranny, you are not prompt, being able, to succour that wretched one, or do not feel yourself called, being able, to fight for the purpose of relieving the deceived or oppressed—you disobey your law of life, or do not comprehend the religion which will bless the future. . . .

From Joseph Mazzini, *The Duties of Man and Other Essays* (London: J. M. Dent, 1907), pp. 51, 53–59.

Without Country you have neither name, token, voice, nor rights, no admission as brothers into the fellowship of the Peoples. You are the bastards of Humanity. Soldiers without a banner, Israelites among the nations, you will find neither faith nor protection; none will be sureties for you. Do not beguile yourselves with the hope of emancipation from unjust social conditions if you do not first conquer a Country for yourselves; where there is no Country there is no common agreement to which you can appeal; the egoism of self-interest rules alone, and he who has the upper hand keeps it, since there is no common safeguard for the interests of all. Do not be led away by the idea of improving your material conditions without first solving the national question. You cannot do it. Your industrial associations and mutual help societies are useful as a means of educating and disciplining yourselves; as an economic fact they will remain barren until you have an Italy. The economic problem demands, first and foremost, an increase of capital and production; and while your Country is dismembered into separate fragments—while shut off by the barrier of customs and artificial difficulties of every sort, you have only restricted markets open to you— you cannot hope for this increase. Today—do not delude yourselves—you are not the working-class of Italy; you are only fractions of that class; powerless, unequal to the great task which you propose to yourselves. Your emancipation can have no practical beginning until a National Government, understanding the signs of the times, shall, seated in Rome, formulate a Declaration of Principles to be the guide for Italian progress, and shall insert into it these words, *Labour is sacred, and is the source of the wealth of Italy.*

Do not be led astray, then, by hopes of material progress which in your present conditions can only be illusions. Your Country alone, the vast and rich Italian Country, which stretches from the Alps to the farthest limit of Sicily, can fulfil these hopes. You cannot obtain your *rights* except by obeying the commands of *Duty*. Be worthy of them, and you will have them. O my Brothers! love your Country. Our Country is our home, the home which God has given us, placing therein a numerous family which we love and are loved by, and with which we have a more intimate and quicker communion of feeling and thought than with others; a family which by its concentration upon a given spot, and by the homogeneous nature of its elements, is destined for a special kind of activity. Our Country is our field of labour; the products of our activity must go forth from it for the benefit of the whole earth; but the instruments of labour which we can use best and most effectively exist in it, and we may not reject them without being unfaithful to God's purpose and diminishing our strength. In labouring according to true principles for our Country we are labouring for Humanity; our Country is the fulcrum of the lever which we have to wield for the common good. If we give up this fulcrum we run the risk of becoming useless to our Country and to Humanity. Before *associating* ourselves with the Nations which compose Humanity we must exist as a Nation. There can be no association except among equals; and you have no recognised collective existence.

Humanity is a great army moving to the conquest of unknown lands, against powerful and wary enemies. The Peoples are the different corps and divisions of that army. Each has a post entrusted to it; each a special operation to perform; and the common victory depends on the exactness with which the different operations are carried out. Do not disturb the order of the battle. Do not abandon the banner which God has given you. Wherever you may be, into the midst of whatever people circumstances may have driven you, fight for the liberty of that people if the moment calls for it; but fight as Italians, so that the blood which you shed may win honour and love, not for you only, but for your Country. And may the constant thought of your soul be for Italy, may all the acts of your life be worthy of her, and may the standard beneath which you range yourselves to work for Humanity be Italy's. Do not say *I;* say *we.* Be every one of you an incarnation of your Country, and feel himself and make himself responsible for his fellow-countrymen; let each one of you learn to act in such a way that in him men shall respect and love his Country.

Your Country is one and indivisible. As the members of a family cannot rejoice at the common table if one of their number is far away, snatched from the affection of his brothers, so you should have no joy or repose as long as a portion of the territory upon which your language is spoken is separated from the Nation.

Your Country is the token of the mission which God has given you to fulfil in Humanity. The faculties, the strength of *all* its sons should be united for the accomplishment of this mission. A certain number of common duties and rights belong to every man who answers to the *Who are you?* of the other peoples, *I am an Italian.* Those duties and those rights cannot be represented except by one *single* authority resulting from your votes. A Country must have, then, a single government. The politicians who call themselves federalists, and who would make Italy into a brotherhood of different states, would dismember the Country, not understanding the idea of Unity. The States into which Italy is divided today are not the creation of our own people; they are the result of the ambitions and calculations of princes or of foreign conquerors, and serve no purpose but to flatter the vanity of local aristocracies for which a narrower sphere than a great Country is necessary. What you, the people, have created, beautified, and consecrated with your affections, with your joys, with your sorrows, and with your blood, is the City and the Commune, not the Province or the

State. In the City, in the Commune, where your fathers sleep and where your children will live, where you exercise your faculties and your personal rights, you live out your lives as *individuals*. It is of your City that each of you can say what the Venetians say of theirs: *Venezia la xe nostra: l'avemo fatta nu.* [1] In your City you have need of *liberty* as in your Country you have need of *association*. The Liberty of the Commune and the Unity of the Country—let that, then, be your faith. Do not say Rome and Tuscany, Rome and Lombardy, Rome and Sicily; say Rome and Florence, Rome and Siena, Rome and Leghorn, and so through all the Communes of Italy. Rome for all that represents Italian life; your Commune for whatever represents the *individual* life. All the other divisions are artificial, and are not confirmed by your national tradition.

A Country is a fellowship of free and equal men bound together in a brotherly concord of labour towards a single end. You must make it and maintain it such. A Country is not an aggregation, it is an *association*. There is no true Country without a uniform right. There is no true Country where the uniformity of that right is violated by the existence of caste, privilege, and inequality—where the powers and faculties of a large number of individuals are suppressed or dormant—where there is no common principle accepted, recognised, and developed by all. In such a state of things there can be no Nation, no People, but only a multitude, a fortuitous agglomeration of men whom circumstances have brought together and different circumstances will separate. In the name of your love for your Country you must combat without truce the existence of every privilege, every inequality, upon the soil which has given you birth. One privilege only is lawful—the privilege of Genius when Genius reveals itself in brotherhood with Virtue; but it is a privilege conceded by God and not by men, and when you acknowledge it and follow its inspirations, you acknowledge it freely by the exercise of your own reason and your own choice. Whatever privilege claims your submission in virtue of force or heredity, or any right which is not a common right, is a usurpation and a tyranny, and you ought to combat it and annihilate it. Your country should be your Temple. God at the summit, a People of equals at the base. Do not accept any other formula, any other moral law, if you do not want to dishonour your Country and yourselves. Let the secondary laws for the gradual regulation of your existence be the progressive application of this supreme law.

And in order that they should be so, it is necessary that *all* should contribute to the making of them. The laws made by one fraction of the citizens only can never by the nature of things and men do otherwise than reflect the thoughts and aspirations and desires of that fraction; they repre-

---

1. Venice is our own: we have made her.

sent, not the whole country, but a third, a fourth part, a class, a zone of the country. The law must express the general aspiration, promote the good of all, respond to a beat of the nation's heart. The whole nation therefore should be, directly or indirectly, the legislator. By yielding this mission to a few men, you put the egoism of one class in the place of the Country, which is the union of *all* the classes.

A Country is not a mere territory; the particular territory is only its foundation. The Country is the idea which rises upon that foundation; it is the sentiment of love, the sense of fellowship which binds together all the sons of that territory. So long as a single one of your brothers is not represented by his own vote in the development of the national life—so long as a single one vegetates uneducated among the educated—so long as a single one able and willing to work languishes in poverty for want of work—you have not got a Country such as it ought to be, the Country of all and for all. *Votes, education, work* are the three main pillars of the nation; do not rest until your hands have solidly erected them.

And when they have been erected—when you have secured for every one of you food for both body and soul—when freely united, entwining your right hands like brothers round a beloved mother, you advance in beautiful and holy concord towards the development of your faculties and the fulfilment of the Italian mission—remember that that mission is the moral unity of Europe; remember the immense duties which it imposes upon you. Italy is the only land that has twice uttered the great word of unification to the disjoined nations. Twice Rome has been the metropolis, the temple, of the European world; the first time when our conquering eagles traversed the known world from end to end and prepared it for union by introducing civilised institutions; the second time when, after the Northern conquerors had themselves been subdued by the potency of Nature, of great memories and of religious inspiration, the genius of Italy incarnated itself in the Papacy and undertook the solemn mission—abandoned four centuries ago—of preaching the union of souls to the peoples of the Christian world. Today a third mission is dawning for our Italy; as much vaster than those of old as the Italian People, the free and united Country which you are going to found, will be greater and more powerful than Caesars or Popes. The presentiment of this mission agitates Europe and keeps the eye and the thought of the nations chained to Italy.

Your duties to your Country are proportioned to the loftiness of this mission. You have to keep it pure from egoism, uncontaminated by falsehood and by the arts of that political Jesuitism which they call diplomacy.

The government of the country will be based through your labours upon the worship of principles, not upon the idolatrous worship of interests and of opportunity. There are countries in Europe where Liberty is sacred within, but is systematically violated without; peoples who say, *Truth is one thing, utility another: theory is one thing, practice another.* Those countries will have inevitably to expiate their guilt in long isolation, oppression, and anarchy. But you know the mission of our Country, and will pursue another path. Through you Italy will have, with one only God in the heavens, one only truth, one only faith, one only rule of political life upon earth. Upon the edifice, sublimer than Capitol or Vatican, which the people of Italy will raise, you will plant the banner of Liberty and of Association, so that it shines in the sight of all the nations, nor will you lower it ever for terror of despots or lust for the gains of a day. You will have boldness as you have faith. You will speak out aloud to the world, and to those who call themselves the lords of the world, the thought which thrills in the heart of Italy. You will never deny the sister nations. The life of the Country shall grow through you in beauty and in strength, free from servile fears and the hesitations of doubt, keeping as its *foundation* the people, as its *rule* the consequences of its principles logically deduced and energetically applied, as its *strength* the strength of all, as its *outcome* the amelioration of all, as its *end* the fulfilment of the mission which God has given it. And because you will be ready to die for Humanity, the life of your Country will be immortal.

3
Religion and Liberal Culture

24. Friedrich Schleiermacher, *On Religion: Speeches to Its Cultured Despisers*

Friedrich Daniel Ernst Schleiermacher (1768–1834) was one of the most influential theologians of modern times. He has been called the "father of modern theology" in the nineteenth- and early twentieth-century German Liberal Protestant tradition. Indeed, for many intellectuals in nineteenth-century Germany, Schleiermacher's thought was as momentous, in the realm of theology and church history, as that of Hegel, his colleague at the University of Berlin between 1818 and 1831, in philosophy and social theory.

Born in Breslau to a family of Reformed ministers, Schleiermacher studied at the University of Halle, where he was especially influenced by the work of Plato, Aristotle, and Kant. He passed his theological examination in 1790 and, after service as a private tutor, was appointed a Reformed chaplain at the Charité Hospital in Berlin in 1796. While in Berlin Schleiermacher was influenced by the circle of friends around Friedrich von Schlegel and was thus introduced to the world of German Romanticism. In 1804 he was called to an associate professorship in theology at Halle, but abandoned this post in the aftermath of the French occupation of the town in 1806. He returned to Berlin, first as a preacher at the Trinity Church and after 1810 as professor in the theological faculty of the new University of Berlin. His stirring sermons against Napoleon and for the liberation of Prussia formed a major component of the early literature of German nationalism. Indeed, given his liberal beliefs on nationalism and constitutionalism, Schleiermacher was held in suspicion by Prussian ruling circles after the defeat of Napoleon in 1815. As a theologian he was prolific in his publications, producing by the time

From Friedrich Schleiermacher, *On Religion: Speeches to Its Cultured Despisers,* translated by John Oman (New York: Harper Torchbook Edition, 1958), pp. 8–11, 39–40, 51–55, 124–28, 226–27, 252–53.

of his death a corpus that runs to thirty volumes. The work of later German liberal theologians such as Adolf von Harnack and Ernst Troeltsch, as well as cultural critics such as Wilhelm Dilthey, cannot be comprehended without an awareness of Schleiermacher.

In 1799 Schleiermacher published his *Reden über Religion* (On Religion: Speeches to Its Cultured Despisers), which attempted to win back the educated German *Bürgertum* to an activist Christianity by defining religion in individualist, romantic sense as an intuitive "feeling of absolute dependence" and as a "feeling and intuition of the infinite." Religious faith was both prior to its dogmatic representations—to question dogma was not to abandon faith—and was an essential and natural part of the individual's own humanity. Religion was an autonomous intuitive force in life, anterior to the results of knowledge and to the prescriptive codes of morality. Schleiermacher's work has been seen as an effort to synthesize the two nominally hostile movements of Enlightenment rationalism and German romanticism. His greatest accomplishment may have been his success in preserving an independent role for religious consciousness in the German Idealist tradition.

Permit me to speak of myself. You know that what is spoken at the instigation of piety cannot be pride, for piety is always full of humility. Piety was the mother's womb, in whose sacred darkness my young life was nourished and was prepared for a world still sealed for it. In it my spirit breathed ere it had yet found its own place in knowledge and experience. It helped me as I began to sift the faith of my fathers and to cleanse thought and feeling from the rubbish of antiquity. When the God and the immortality of my childhood vanished from my doubting eyes it remained to me. Without design of mine it guided me into active life. It showed me how, with my endowments and defects, I should keep myself holy in an undivided existence, and through it alone I have learnt friendship and love. In respect of other human excellences, before your judgment-seat, ye wise and understanding of the people, I know it is small proof of possession to be able to speak of their value. They can be known from description, from observation of others, or, as all virtues are known, from the ancient and general traditions of their nature. But religion is of such a sort and is so rare, that whoever utters anything of it, must necessarily have had it, for nowhere could he have heard it. Of all that I praise, all that I feel to be the true work of religion, you would find little even in the sacred books. To the man who has not himself experienced it, it would only be an annoyance and a folly.

Finally, if I am thus impelled to speak of religion and to deliver my testimony, to whom should I turn if not to the sons of Germany? Where else is an audience for my speech? It is not blind predilection for my native soil or for my fellows in government and language, that makes me speak thus, but the deep conviction that you alone are capable, as well as worthy, of having awakened in you the sense for holy and divine things. Those proud Islanders whom many unduly honour, know no watchword but *gain* and *enjoyment*. Their zeal for knowledge is only a sham fight, their worldly wisdom a false jewel, skilfully and deceptively composed, and their sacred freedom itself too often and too easily serves self-interest. They are never in earnest with anything that goes beyond palpable utility. All knowledge they have robbed of life and use only as dead wood to make masts and helms for the life's voyage in pursuit of gain. Similarly they know nothing of religion, save that all preach devotion to ancient usages and defend its institutions, regarding them as a protection wisely cherished by the constitution against the natural enemy of the state.

For other reasons I turn from the French. On them, one who honours religion can hardly endure to look, for in every act and almost in every word, they tread its holiest ordinances under foot. The barbarous indifference of the millions of the people, and the witty frivolity with which individual brilliant spirits behold the sublimest fact of history that is not only taking place before their eyes, but has them all in its grasp, and determines every movement of their lives, witnesses clearly enough how little they are capable of a holy awe or a true adoration. What does religion more abhor than the unbridled arrogance with which the rulers of the people bid defiance to the eternal laws of the world? What does it inculcate more strongly than that discreet and lowly moderation of which aught, even the slightest feeling, does not seem to be suggested to them? What is more sacred to it than that lofty Nemesis, of whose most terrible dealings in the intoxication of infatuation they have no understanding? Where varied punishments that formerly only needed to light on single families to fill whole peoples with awe before the heavenly Being and to dedicate to eternal Fate the works of the poets for centuries, are a thousandfold renewed in vain, how ludicrously would a single lonely voice resound unheard and unnoticed.

Only in my native land is that happy clime which refuses no fruit entirely. There you find, though it be only scattered, all that adorns humanity. Somewhere, in individuals at least, all that grows attains its most beautiful form. Neither wise moderation, nor quiet contemplation is wanting; there, therefore, religion must find a refuge from the coarse barbarism and the cold worldly mind of the age. . . .

It is true that religion is essentially contemplative. You would never call anyone pious who went about in impervious stupidity, whose sense is not open for the life of the world. But this contemplation is not turned, as your knowledge of nature is, to the existence of a finite thing, combined with and opposed to another finite thing. It has not even, like your knowledge of God—if for once I might use an old expression—to do with the nature of the first cause, in itself and in its relation to every other cause and operation. The contemplation of the pious is the immediate consciousness of the universal existence of all finite things, in and through the Infinite, and of all temporal things in and through the Eternal. Religion is to seek this and find it in all that lives and moves, in all growth and change, in all doing and suffering. It is to have life and to know life in immediate feeling, only as such an existence in the Infinite and Eternal. Where this is found religion is satisfied, where it hides itself there is for her unrest and anguish, extremity and death. Wherefore it is a life in the infinite nature of the Whole, in the One and in the All, in God, having and possessing all things in God, and God in all. Yet religion is not knowledge and science, either of the world or of God. Without being knowledge, it recognizes knowledge and science. In itself it is an affection, a revelation of the Infinite in the finite, God being seen in it and it in God. . . .

Wherefore, you will find every truly learned man devout and pious. Where you see science without religion, be sure it is transferred, learned up from another. It is sickly, if indeed it is not that empty appearance which serves necessity and is no knowledge at all. And what else do you take this deduction and weaving together of ideas to be, which neither live nor correspond to any living thing? Or in ethics, what else is this wretched uniformity that thinks it can grasp the highest human life in a single dead formula? The former arises because there is no fundamental feeling of that living nature which everywhere presents variety and individuality, and the latter because the sense fails to give infinity to the finite by determining its nature and boundaries only from the Infinite. Hence the dominion of the mere notion; hence the mechanical erections of your systems instead of an organic structure; hence the vain juggling with analytical formulas, in which, whether categorical or hypothetical, life will not be fettered. Science is not your calling, if you despise religion and fear to surrender yourself to reverence and aspiration for the primordial. Either science must become as low as your life, or it must be separated and stand alone, a division that precludes success. If man is not one with the Eternal in the unity of intuition and feeling which is immediate, he remains, in the unity of consciousness which is derived, for ever apart. . . .

Music is one great whole; it is a special, a self-contained revelation of the world. Yet the music of each people is a whole by itself, which again is divided into different characteristic forms, till we come to the genius and style of the individual. Each actual instance of this inner revelation in the individual contains all these unities. Yet while nothing is possible for a musician, except in and through the unity of the music of his people, and the unity of music generally, he presents it in the charm of sound with all the pleasure and joyousness of boundless caprice, according as his life stirs in him, and the world influences him. In the same way, despite the necessary elements in its structure, religion is, in its individual manifestations whereby it displays itself immediately in life, from nothing farther removed than from all semblance of compulsion or limitation. In life, the necessary element is taken up, taken up into freedom. Each emotion appears as the free self-determination of this very disposition, and mirrors one passing moment of the world.

It would be impious to demand here something held in constraint, something limited and determined from without. If anything of this kind lies in your conception of system then you must set it quite aside. A system of perceptions and feelings you may yourselves see to be somewhat marvellous. Suppose now you feel something. Is there not at the same time an accompanying feeling or thought—make your own choice—that you would have to feel in accordance with this feeling, and not otherwise were but this or that object, which does not now move you, to be present? But for this immediate association your feeling would be at an end, and a cold calculating and refining would take its place. Wherefore it is plainly an error to assert that it belongs to religion, to be conscious of the connection of its separate manifestations, not only to have it within, and to develop it from within, but to see it described and to comprehend it from without, and it is presumption to consider that, without it, piety is poverty-stricken. The truly pious are not disturbed in the simplicity of their way, for they give little heed to all the so-called religious systems that have been erected in consequence of this view.

Poor enough they are too, far inferior to the theories about music, defective though they be. Among those systematizers there is less than anywhere, a devout watching and listening to discover in their own hearts what they are to describe. They would rather reckon with symbols, and complete a designation which is about as accidental as the designation of the stars. It is purely arbitrary and never sufficient, for something new that should be included, is always being discovered, and a system, anything permanent and secure, anything corresponding to nature, and not the result of caprice and tradition, is not to be found in it. The designation, let the forms of religion be ever so inward and self-dependent, must be from without. Thousands might be moved religiously in the same way, and yet each, led, not so much by disposition, as by external circumstances, might designate his feeling by different symbols. Furthermore, those systematizers are less anxious to present the details of religion than to subordinate them one to the other, and to deduce them from a higher. Nothing is of less importance to religion, for it knows nothing of deducing and connecting. There is no single fact in it that can be called original and chief. Its facts are one and all immediate. Without dependence on any other, each exists for itself. True, a special type of religion is constituted by one definite kind and manner of feeling, but it is mere perversion to call it a principle, and to treat it as if the rest could be deduced from it. This distinct form of a religion is found, in the same way, in every single element of religion. Each expression of feeling bears on it immediately this peculiar impress. It cannot show itself without it, nor be comprehended without it. Everything is to be found immediately and not proved from something else. Generals, which include particulars, combination and connection belong to another sphere, if they rest on reality, or they are merely a work of phantasy and caprice. Every man may have his own regulation and his own rubrics. What is essential can neither gain nor lose thereby. Consequently, the man who truly knows the nature of his religion, will give a very subordinate place to all apparent connection of details, and will not sacrifice the smallest for the sake of it.

By taking the opposite course, the marvellous thought has arisen of a universality of one religion, of one single form which is true, and in respect of which all others are false. Were it not that misunderstanding must be guarded against, I would say that it is only by such deducing and connecting that such a comparison as true and false, which is not peculiarly appropriate to religion, has ever been reached. It only applies where we have to do with ideas. Elsewhere the negative laws of your logic are not in place. All is immediately true in religion, for except immediately how could anything arise? But that only is immediate which has not yet passed through the stage of idea, but has grown up purely in the feeling. All that is religious is good, for it is only religious as it expresses a common higher life. But the whole circumference of religion is infinite, and is not to be comprehended under one form, but only under the sum total of all forms. It is infinite, not merely because any single religious organization has a limited horizon, and, not being able to embrace all, cannot believe that there is nothing beyond; but more particularly, because everyone is a person by himself, and is only to be moved in his own way, so that for everyone the elements of religion have most characteristic differences. Religion is infinite, not only because something new is ever being produced in time, by the endless relations both active and passive between different minds and the same limited matter; not only because the capacity for religion is never perfected, but is ever being developed anew, is ever being more beautifully reproduced, is ever entering deeper into the nature of man; but religion is infinite on all sides. As the knowledge of its eternal truth and infallibility accompanies knowledge, the consciousness of this infinity accompanies religion. It is the very feeling of religion, and must therefore accompany everyone that really has religion. He must be conscious that his religion is only part of the whole; that about the same circumstances there may be views and sentiments quite different from his, yet just as pious; and that there may be perceptions and feelings belonging to other modifications of religion, for which the sense may entirely fail him.

You see how immediately this beautiful modesty, this friendly, attractive forbearance springs from the nature of religion. How unjustly, therefore, do you reproach religion with loving persecution, with being malignant, with overturning society, and making blood flow like water. Blame those who corrupt religion, who flood it with an army of formulas and definitions, and seek to cast it into the fetters of a so-called system. What is it in religion about which men have quarrelled and made parties and kindled wars? About definitions, the practical sometimes, the theoretical always, both of which belong elsewhere. Philosophy, indeed, seeks to bring those who would know to a common knowledge. Yet even philosophy leaves room for variety, and the more readily the better it understands itself. But religion does not, even once, desire to bring those who believe and feel to one belief and one feeling. Its endeavour is to open in those who are not yet capable of religious emotions, the sense for the unity of the original source of life. But just because each seer is a new priest, a new mediator, a new organ, he flees with repugnance the bald uniformity which would again destroy this divine abundance. . . .

Man is born with the religious capacity as with every other. If only his sense for the profoundest depths of his own nature is not crushed out, if only all fellowship between himself and the Primal Source is not quite shut off, religion would, after its own fashion, infallibly be developed. But in our time, alas! that is exactly what, in very large measure, does happen. With pain I see daily how the rage for calculating and explaining suppresses the sense. I see how all things unite to bind man to the finite, and to a very small portion of the finite, that the infinite may as far as possible vanish from his eyes.

Who hinders the prosperity of religion? Not you, not the doubters and scoffers. Even though you were all of one mind to have no religion, you would not disturb Nature in her purpose of producing piety from the depths of the soul, for your influence could only later find prepared soil. Nor, as is supposed, do the immoral most hinder the prosperity of religion, for it is quite a different power to which their endeavours are opposed. But the discreet and practical men of today are, in the present state of the world, the foes of religion, and their great preponderance is the cause why it plays such a poor and insignificant role, for from tender childhood they maltreat man, crushing out his higher aspirations. . . .

In proportion as man must busy himself in a narrow way with a single object, to rescue the universality of the sense an impulse awakes in everyone to allow the dominating activity and all its kindred to rest, and to open all organs to the influence of all impressions. By a secret and most helpful sympathy this impulse is strongest when the general life reveals itself most clearly in our own breasts and in the surrounding world. But to yield to this impulse in comfortable inactivity cannot be permitted, for, from the middle-class standpoint, it would be laziness and idling. In everything there must be design and aim; somewhat has always to be performed, and if the spirit can no more serve, the body must be exercised. Work and play, but no quiet, submissive contemplation!

But most of all, men are taught to analyze and explain. By this explaining they are completely cheated of their sense, for, as it is conducted, it is absolutely opposed to any perceptive sense. *Sense* of its own accord seeks objects for itself, it advances to meet them and it offers to embrace them. It communicates something to them which distinguishes them as its possession, its work.

It will find and be found. But this *explaining* knows nothing of this living acquisition, of this illuminating truth, of the true spirit of discovery in childlike intuition. But from first to last, objects are to be transcribed accurately in thought as something simply given. They are, God be thanked, for all men ever the same, and who knows how long already they have been docketed in good order with all their qualities defined. Take them, then, only as life brings them, and understand that and nothing more. But to seek for yourselves and to wish to have living intercourse with things is eccentric and high-flown. It is a vain endeavour, availing nothing in human life, where things are only to be seen and handled as they have already presented themselves.

Fruitful in human life this endeavour is not, except that, without it, an active life, resting on true inward culture, is not to be found. The sense strives to comprehend the undivided impress of something whole; it will perceive what each thing is and how it is; it will know everything in its peculiar character. But that is not what they mean by understanding. What and how are too remote for them, around whence and to what end, they eternally circle. They seek to grasp nothing in and for itself, but only in special aspects, and therefore, not as a whole, but only piecemeal. To inquire or thoroughly examine whether the object they would understand is a whole, would lead them too far. Were this their desire, they could hardly escape so utterly without religion.

But all must be used for some excellent purpose, wherefore they dissever and anatomize. This is how they deal with what exists chiefly for the highest satisfaction of the sense, with what, in their despite, is a whole in itself, I mean with all that is art in nature and in the works of man. Before it can operate they annihilate it by explaining it in detail. Having first by decomposition robbed it of its character as art, they would teach and impress this or that lesson from the fragments.

You must grant that this is the practice of our people of understanding, and you must confess that a superabundance of sense is necessary if anything is to escape this hostile treatment. On that account alone the number must be small who are capable of such a contemplation of any object as might awake in them religion. . . .

The charge that everyone who allows himself to be embraced in a positive religion, can only be an imitator of those who have given it currency and cannot develop himself individually, is baseless. This judgment no more applies here, than it would to the state or to society. It seems to us morbid or quixotic for any one to maintain that he has no room in any existing institution, and that he must exclude himself from society. We are convinced that every healthy person will, in common with many, have a great national character. Just because he is rooted in it and influenced by it, he can develop his individuality with the greatest precision and beauty. Similarly, in religion only morbid aberration so cuts off a man from a life in fellowship with those among whom nature has placed him, that he belongs to no great whole. Somewhere, on a great scale, everyone will find exhibited or will himself exhibit what for him is the middle-point of religion. To every such common sphere we ascribe a boundless activity that goes into detail, in virtue of which all individual characteristics issue from its bosom. Thus understood, the church is with right called the common mother of us all.

To take the nearest example, think of Christianity as a definite individual form of the highest order. First there is in our time the well known outward division, so definite and pronounced. Under each section there is then a mass of different views and schools. Each exhibits a characteristic development, and has a founder and adherents, yet the last and most personal development of religiousness remains for each individual, and so much is it one with his nature that no one can fully acquire it but himself. And the more a man, by his whole nature, has a claim to belong to you, ye cultured, the more religion must reach this stage in him, for his higher feeling, gradually developing and uniting with other educated capacities, must be a characteristic product. . . .

In all ways the Deity is to be contemplated and worshipped. Varied types of religion are possible, both in proximity and in combination, and if it is necessary that every type be actualized at one time or another, it is to be desired that, at all times, there should be a dim sense of many religions. The great moments must be few in which all things agree to ensure to one among them a wide-extended and enduring life, in which the same view is developed unanimously and irresistibly in a great body, and many persons are deeply affected by the same impression of the divine. Yet what may not be looked for from a time that is so manifestly the border land between two different orders of things? If only the intense crisis were past, such a moment might arrive. Even now a prophetic soul, such as the fiery spirits of our time have, turning its thoughts to creative genius, might perhaps indicate the point that is to be for the future generations the centre for their fellowship with the Deity. But however it be, and however long such a moment may still linger, new developments of religion, whether under Christianity or alongside of it, must come and that soon, even though for a long time they are only discernible in isolated and fleeting manifestations. Out of nothing a new creation always comes forth, and in all living men in whom the intellectual life has power and fulness, religion is almost nothing. From some one of the countless occasions it will be developed in many and take new shape in new ground. Were but the time of caution and timidity past! Religion hates loneliness, and in youth especially, which for all things is the time of love, it wastes away in a consuming longing. When it is developed in you, when you are conscious of the first traces of its life, enter at once into the one indivisible fellowship of the saints, which embraces all religions and in which alone any can prosper. Do you think that because the saints are scattered and far apart, you must speak to unsanctified ears? You ask what language is secret enough—is it speech, writing, deed, or quiet copying of the Spirit? All ways, I answer, and you see that I have not shunned the loudest. In them all sacred things remain secret and hidden from the profane. They may gnaw at the shell as they are able, but to worship the God that is in you, do not refuse us.

25. William Wilberforce, *A Practical View of the Prevailing Religious System of Professed Christians in the Higher and Middle Classes, Contrasted with Real Christianity*

Evangelicalism

The religious revival called Evangelicalism—which, unlike its early eighteenth-century predecessor, Methodism, stayed within the confines of the Anglican church—made a deep impression on nineteenth-century English

From William Wilberforce, *A Practical View of the Prevailing Religious System of Professed Christians in the Higher and Middle Classes, Contrasted with Real Christianity* (London and New York: Leavitt, Lord and Co., 1835), pp. 125–35, 142–43, 152–53.

manners, morals, and politics. Document 8 presented the influential Evangelical ideal of domesticity and womanhood. The following two documents deal, respectively, with the religious doctrine of Evangelicalism and the informal organization of its leaders.

William Wilberforce (1759–1833) converted to Evangelical Christianity in 1785, largely through the proselytizing efforts of one of his former teachers at Cambridge. Already an M.P. since 1780, he now became close friends with William Pitt and assumed the role of main spokesman for Evangelical causes, especially the abolition of slavery, in the House of Commons. Although he had been a supporter of liberal political reform in the 1780s, the experience of the French Revolution turned his politics in an increasingly conservative direction, and it is not surprising that he declared, a few months before his death, that he regarded the Great Reform of 1832 as too radical a measure. Wilberforce's tract, *A Practical View of the Prevailing Religious System of Professed Christians in the Higher and Middle Classes, Contrasted with Real Christianity,* was published in 1797, the same year that its energetic author founded both the Society for the Reformation of Manners and the Committee for the Abolition of the Slave Trade. The book went through five editions in the first six months. The selections are taken from chapter 4, "On the Prevailing Inadequate Conceptions concerning the Nature and Strictness of Practical Christianity."

The group of like-minded and zealous Evangelicals that formed around Wilberforce was originally known as the Saints, but after Wilberforce's purchase of a property at Clapham, it acquired the name of Clapham sect. James Stephen (1789–1859), the son of one of the original members of the group (another James Stephen [1758–1832]), took on the role of Clapham's historian, describing in a chapter of his *Essays in Ecclesiastical Biography* (1849) the characters of individual Claphamites and the quality of their interactions with one another and with their families. This second James Stephen inherited the Evangelical creed and outlook from his father. It was he who drafted the abolition bill that passed in 1833, and he subsequently accepted the post of undersecretary for colonial affairs in the hope of directly influencing the slavery situation.

As the historian Noel Annan has pointed out, Clapham served as the source of an English "intellectual aristocracy" that began to form at the beginning of the nineteenth century and lasted into the next century. These intellectuals were upper middle class and, unlike the more radical and iconoclastic intelligentsias on the Continent, were infused with evangelical principles and committed to gradual reform of institutions. They held influential positions in the civil service and as editors and writers for periodicals and publishing houses. And, perhaps most striking, they were linked by ties of intermarriage and perpetuated their kind through several generations. Thus, to cite some of the figures who appear in the following selection, the Claphamite Zachary Macaulay was the father of Thomas Babington Macaulay (see documents 3 and 22); the Claphamite James Stephen was the grandfather of the men of letters Leslie Stephen and James Fitzjames Stephen and the great-grandfather of novelist Virginia Woolf (see vol. 9, document 27.)

Having endeavored to establish the strictness, and to ascertain the essential character of true practical Christianity, let us investigate more in detail the practical system of the bulk of professed Christians among ourselves.[1]

It was formerly remarked, that the whole subject of religion was often viewed from such a distance as to be seen only in the gross. We now, it is to be feared, shall find too much cause for believing that those who approach nearer, and do discover in Christianity somewhat of a distinct form, yet come not close enough to discern her peculiar conformation.

A very erroneous notion prevails concerning the true nature of religion. Religion, agreeably to what has been already stated, may be considered as the implantation of a vigorous and active principle; it is seated in the heart, where its authority is recognized as supreme, whence by degrees it expels whatever is opposed to it, and where it gradually brings all the affections and desires under its complete control.

But though the heart be its special residence, every endeavor and pursuit must acknowledge its presence; and whatever does not, or will not, or cannot receive its sacred stamp, is to be condemned, and is to be at once abstained from or abandoned. It is like the principle of vitality, which communicates its influence to the smallest and remotest fibres of the frame. But the notion of religion entertained by many among us seems altogether different. They begin, indeed, in submission to her clear prohibitions, by fencing off from the field of human action a certain district, which, though it in many parts bears fruits on which they cast a longing eye, they cannot but confess to be forbidden ground. They next assign to religion a portion according to their circumstances and views, in which however she is to possess merely a qualified jurisdiction, and having so done, they conceive that without hinderance they have a right to range at will over the spacious re-

1. It will be remembered by the reader, that it is not the object of this work to animadvert on the vices, defects, and erroneous opinions of the times, except as they are received into the prevailing religious system, or are tolerated by it, and are not thought sufficient to prevent a man from being esteemed, on the whole, a very tolerable Christian. [Wilberforce's note]

mainder. Religion can claim only a stated proportion of their thoughts, and time, and fortune, and influence; the rest they think is now their own, to do what they will with; they have paid their tithes—say rather, their composition; the demands of the Church are satisfied, and they may surely be permitted to enjoy what she has left without molestation or interference.

It is scarcely possible to state too strongly the mischief which results from this fundamental error. At the same time its consequences are so natural and obvious, that one would think it scarcely possible not to foresee that they must infallibly follow. The greatest part of human actions is considered as indifferent. If men are not chargeable with gross vices, and are decent in the discharge of their religious duties; if they do not stray into the forbidden ground, what more can be expected from them? Instead of keeping at a distance from *all sin,* in which alone consists our safety, they will be apt not to care how near they approach what they conceive to be the boundary line; if they have not actually passed it, there is no harm done, it is no trespass. Thus the free and active spirit of religion is checked. She must keep to her prescribed confines, and every attempt to extend them will be resisted.

This is not all. Since whatever can be gained from her allotment, or whatever can be taken in from the forbidden ground, will be so much of addition to that land where men may roam at large, free from restraint or molestation, they will of course be constantly pressing upon the limits of the religious allotment on the one hand, and on the other will be removing back a little farther and farther the fence which abridges them on the side of the forbidden ground. The space she occupies diminishes till it is scarcely discernible; whilst, her spirit extinguished and her force destroyed, she is little more than the nominal possessor even of the contracted limits to which she has been avowedly reduced.

This is but too faithful a representation of the general state of things among ourselves. The promotion of the glory of God, and the possession of his favor, are no longer recognized as the objects of our highest regard, and most strenuous endeavors; as furnishing to us a vigorous, habitual, and universal principle of action. We set up for ourselves: we are become our own masters. The sense of continual service is irksome and galling to us; and we rejoice in being emancipated from it. Thus the very tenure and condition by which life and all its possessions are held, undergo a total change. Whatever we have is regarded rather as a property than as a trust; or if there still exists the remembrance of some paramount claim, we are satisfied with an occasional acknowledgment, as of a nominal right.

Hence it is that so little sense of responsibility seems attached to the possession of high rank, or splendid abilities, or affluent fortunes, or other means or instruments of usefulness. The instructive admonitions, "Give an account of thy stewardship"—"Occupy till I come," are forgotten. Or if it be acknowledged by some men of larger views than ordinary, that reference is to be had to some principle superior to that of our own gratification, it is, at best, to the good of society, or to the welfare of our families: and even then the obligations resulting from these relations are seldom enforced on us by any higher sanctions than those of family comfort, and of worldly interest or estimation. Beside, what multitudes of persons are there, people without families, in private stations, or of a retired turn, to whom they are scarcely held to apply! and what multitudes of cases to which it would be thought unnecessary scrupulosity to extend them! Accordingly we find, in fact, that the generality of mankind among the higher order, in the formation of their schemes, in the selection of their studies, in the choice of their place of residence, in the employment and distribution of their time, in their thoughts, conversation and amusements, are considered as being at liberty, if there be no actual vice, to consult their own gratification.

Thus the generous and wakeful spirit of Christian benevolence, seeking and finding everywhere occasions for its exercise, is exploded, and a system of *decent selfishness* is avowedly established in its stead; a system scarcely more to be abjured for its impiety, than to be abhorred for its cold insensibility to the opportunities of diffusing happiness. "Have we no families, or are they provided for? Are we wealthy and bred to no profession? Are we young and lively, and in the gayety and vigor of youth? Surely we may be allowed to take our pleasure. We neglect no duty, we live in no vice, we do nobody any harm, and have a right to amuse ourselves. We have nothing better to do; we wish we had; our time hangs heavy on our hands for want of it."

But no man has a right to be idle. Not to speak of that great work which we all have to accomplish, and surely the whole attention of a short and precarious life is not more than an eternal interest may well require; where is it that, in such a world as this, health, and leisure, and affluence may not find some ignorance to instruct, some wrong to redress, some want to supply, some misery to alleviate? Shall ambition and avarice never sleep? Shall they never want objects on which to fasten? Shall they be so observant to discover, so acute to discern, so eager, so patient to pursue, and shall the benevolence of Christians want employment?

Yet thus life rolls away with too many of us, in a course of "shapeless idleness." Its recreations constitute its chief business. Watering-places, the sports of the field, cards! never-failing cards! the assembly, the theatre, all contribute their aid; amusements are multiplied, and combined, and varied, "to fill up the void of a listless and languid life"; and by the regulated use of these different resources, there is often a kind of sober settled plan of domestic dissipation, in which, with all imaginable decency, year after year wears away in unprofitable vacancy. Even old age often finds us pacing in the same round of amusements which our early youth had tracked out. Meanwhile, being conscious that we are not giving in to any flagrant vice, and it may be, that we are not neglecting the offices of religion, we persuade ourselves that we need not be uneasy. In the main, we do not fall below the general standard of morals of the class and station to which we belong; we may therefore allow ourselves to glide down the stream without apprehension of the consequences.

Some, of a character often hardly to be distinguished from the class we have been just describing, take up with sensual pleasures. The chief happiness of their lives consists in one species or another of animal gratification; and these persons perhaps will be found to compose a large proportion. It belongs not to our purpose to speak of the grossly and scandalously profligate, who renounce all pretensions to the name of Christians; but of those who, maintaining a certain decency of character, and perhaps being tolerably observant of the forms of religion, may yet be not improperly termed sober sensualists. These, though less impetuous and more measured, are not less stanch and steady than the professed votaries of licentious pleasure, in the pursuit of their favorite objects. "Mortify the flesh, with its affections and lusts," is the Christian *precept;* but a soft luxurious course of habitual indulgence is the *practice* of the bulk of modern Christians: and that constant moderation, that wholesome discipline of restraint and self-denial, which are requisite to prevent the unperceived encroachments of the inferior appetites, seem altogether as disused as the exploded austerities of monkish superstition. . . .

As there is a sober sensuality, so is there also a sober avarice, and a sober ambition. The commercial and the professional world compose the chief sphere of their influence. They are often recognised and openly avowed as just master principles of action. But where this is not the case, they assume such plausible shapes, are called by such specious names, and urge such powerful pleas, that they are received with cordiality, and suffered to gather strength without suspicion. The seducing considerations of diligence in our callings, of success in our profession, of making handsome provisions for our children, beguile our better judgments. "We rise early, and late take rest, and eat the bread of carefulness." In our few intervals of leisure, our exhausted spirits require refreshment; the serious concerns of our immortal souls are matters of speculation too grave and gloomy to answer the purpose, and we fly to something that may better deserve the name of relaxation, till we are again summoned to the daily labors of our employment.

Meanwhile religion scarcely occurs to our thoughts; and when some secret misgivings begin to be felt on this head, company soon drowns, amusements dissipate, or habitual occupations insensibly displace or smother the rising apprehension. Professional and commercial men often quiet their consciences by the plea, that their business leaves them no time to think on these serious subjects at present. "Men of leisure they confess should consider them; they themselves will do it hereafter when they retire; meanwhile they are usefully, or at least innocently employed." Thus business and pleasure fill up our time, and the "one thing needful" is forgotten. Respected by others, and secretly applauding ourselves, perhaps congratulating ourselves that we are not like such a one who is a spendthrift or a mere man of pleasure, or such another who is a notorious miser, the true principle of action is no less wanting in us, and personal advancement or the acquisition of wealth is the object of our supreme desires and predominant pursuit. . . .

It is indeed a most lamentable consequence of the practice of regarding religion as a compilation of statutes, and not as an internal principle, that it soon comes to be considered as being conversant about external actions, rather than about habits of mind. This sentiment sometimes has even the hardiness to insinuate and maintain itself under the guise of extraordinary concern for practical religion; but it soon discovers the falsehood of this pretension, and betrays its real nature. The expedient indeed of attaining to superiority in practice, by not wasting any of the attention on the internal principles from which alone practice can flow, is about as reasonable, and will answer about as well, as the economy of the architect who should account it mere prodigality to expend any of his materials in laying foundations, from an idea that they might be more usefully applied to the raising of the superstructure. We know what would be the fate of such an edifice. . . .

The nature and uses, and proper employments of a Christian Sabbath, have been pointed out more particularly, not only because the day will be found, when thus employed, eminently conducive, through the Divine blessing, to the maintenance of the religious principle in activity and vigor; but also because we must all have had occasion often to remark, that many persons, of the graver and more decent sort, seem not seldom to be nearly destitute of religious resources. The Sunday is with them, to say the best of it, a heavy day; and that larger part of it, which is not claimed by the public offices of the church, dully drawls on in comfortless vacuity, or without improvements, is trifled away in vain and unprofitable discourse. Not to speak of those who, by their more daring profanation of this sacred season, openly violate the laws and insult the religion of their country, how little do many seem to enter into the spirit of the institution who are not wholly inattentive to its exterior decorums! How glad are they to qualify the rigor of their religious labors! How hard do they plead against being compelled to devote the whole of the day to religion, claiming to themselves no small merit for giving up to it a part, and purchasing therefore, as they hope, a right to spend the remainder more agreeably! How dextrously do they avail themselves of any plausible plea for introducing some week-day employment into the Sunday, whilst they have not the same propensity to introduce any of the Sunday's peculiar employment into the rest of the week! How often do they find excuses for taking journeys, writing letters, balancing accounts; or, in short, doing something which, by a little management, might probably have been anticipated, or which, without any material inconvenience, might be postponed! Even business itself is recreation, compared with religion, and from the drudgery of this day of sacred rest they fly for relief to their ordinary occupations.

Others again, who would consider business as a profanation, and who still hold out against the encroachments of the card-table, get over much of the day, and gladly seek for an innocent resource in the social circle or in family visits, where it is not even pretended that the conversation turns on such topics as might render it in any way conducive to religious instruction or improvement. Their families, meanwhile, are neglected, their servants robbed of Christian privileges, and their example quoted by others, who cannot see that they are themselves less religiously employed, while playing an innocent game at cards or relaxing in the concert-room.

26. James Stephen, "The Clapham Sect"

Though living amidst the throes of Empires, and the fall of Dynasties, men are not merely warriors and politicians. Even in such times they buy and sell, build and plant, marry and are given in marriage. And thus it happened, that during the war with revolutionary France, Henry Thornton, the then representative in Parliament of the borough of Southwark, having become a husband, became also the owner of a spacious mansion on the confines of the villa-cinctured common of Clapham.

It is difficult to consider the suburban retirement of a wealthy banker aesthetically (as the Germans have it); but, in this instance, the intervention of William Pitt imparted some dignity to an occurrence otherwise so unpoetical. He dismissed for a moment his budgets and his subsidies, for the amusement of planning an oval saloon, to be added to this newly purchased residence. It arose at his bidding, and yet remains, perhaps, a soli-

From James Stephen, *Essays in Ecclesiastical Biography,* 5th edition (London: Longmans, Green, Reader and Dyer, 1867), chap. 10, pp. 523–33, 535–43, 546–52, 579, 581–84.

tary monument of the architectural skill of that imperial mind. Lofty and symmetrical, it was curiously wainscoted with books on every side, except where it opened on a far-extended lawn, reposing beneath the giant arms of aged elms and massive tulip-trees.

Few of the designs of the great Minister were equally successful. Ere many years had elapsed, the chamber he had thus projected became the scene of enjoyments which, amidst his proudest triumphs, he might well have envied, and witnessed the growth of projects more majestic than any which ever engaged the deliberations of his Cabinet. For there, at the close of each succeeding day, drew together a group of playful children, and with them a knot of legislators, rehearsing, in sport or earnestly, some approaching debate; or travellers from distant lands; or circumnavigators of the worlds of literature and science; or the Pastor of the neighbouring Church, whose look announced him as the channel through which benedictions passed to earth from heaven; and, not seldom, a youth who listened, while he seemed to read the book spread out before him. There also was still a matronly presence, controlling, animating, and harmonising the elements of this little world, by a kindly spell, of which none can trace the working, though the charm was confessed by all. Dissolved in endless discourse, or rather in audible soliloquy, flowing from springs deep and inexhaustible, the lord of this well-peopled enclosure rejoiced over it with a contagious joy. In a few paces, indeed, he might traverse the whole extent of that patriarchal dominion. But within those narrow precincts were his Porch, his Studio, his Judgment-Seat, his Oratory, and "the Church that was in his house,"—the reduced, but not imperfect, resemblance of that innumerable Company which his catholic spirit embraced and loved, under all the varying forms which conceal their union from each other and from the world. Discord never agitated that tranquil home; lassitude never brooded over it. Those demons quailed at the aspect of a man in whose heart peace had found a resting-place, though his intellect was incapable of repose.

Henry was the third son of John Thornton, a merchant, renowned in his generation for a munificence more than princely, and commended to the reverence of posterity by the letters and the poetry of Cowper. The father was one of those rare men in whom the desire to relieve distress assumes the form of a master passion; and, if faith be due to tradition, he indulged it with a disdain, alternately ludicrous and sublime, of the good advice which the eccentric have to undergo from the judicious. Conscious of no aims but such as might invite the scrutiny of God and man, he pursued them after his own fearless fashion—yielding to every honest impulse, relishing a frolic when it fell in his way, choosing his associates in scorn of mere worldly precepts, and worshipping with any fellow-Christian whose heart beat in unison with his own, however inharmonious might be some of the articles of their respective creeds.

His son was the heir of his benevolence, but not of his peculiarities. If Lavater had been summoned to divine the occupation of Henry Thornton, he would probably have assigned to him the highest rank among the Judges of his native land. Brows capacious and serene, a scrutinising eye, and lips slightly separated, as of one who listens and prepares to speak, were the true interpreters of the informing mind within. It was a countenance on which were graven the traces of an industry alike quiet and persevering, of a self-possession unassailable by any strong excitement, and of an understanding keen to detect and comprehensive to reconcile distinctions. The judicial, like the poetical nature, is a birthright; and by that imprescriptible title he possessed it. Forensic debates were indeed beyond his province; but even in Westminster Hall, the noblest of her temples, Themis had no more devoted worshipper. To investigate the great controversies of his own and of all former times, was the chosen employment: to pronounce sentence in them, the dear delight of his leisure hours.

Nothing which fell within the range of his observation escaped this curious inquiry. His own duties, motives, and habits, the characters of those whom he loved best, the intellectual resources and powers of his various friends and companions, the prepossessions, hereditary or conventional, to which he or they were subject, the maxims of society, the dogmas of the Church, the problems which were engaging the attention of Parliament or of political economists, and those which affected his own commercial enterprises—all passed in review before him, and were all in their turn adjudicated with the grave impartiality which the Keeper of the Great Seal is expected to exhibit. . . .

Having inherited an estate, which, though not splendid, was enough for the support of his commercial credit, he adjudged that it ought never to be increased by accumulation, nor diminished by sumptuousness; and he lived and died in the rigid practice of this decision. In the division of his income between himself and the poor, the share he originally assigned to them was nearly six-sevenths of the whole; and, as appeared after his death, from accounts kept with the most minute commercial accuracy, the amount expended by him in one of his earlier years for the relief of distress, considerably exceeded nine thousand pounds. When he had become the head of a family, he reviewed this decree, and thenceforward regarded himself as trustee for the miserable, to the extent only of one-third of his whole expenditure. The same faithful record showed that the smallest annual payment ever paid by him on this account amounted to two thousand pounds. As a legislator, he had condemned the unequal pressure of the direct taxes on the rich and the poor; but instead of solacing his defeat with the narcotic of virtuous indignation, combined with discreet parsimony, he silently raised his own contribution to the level of his censure. Tidings of the commercial failure of a near kinsman embarked him at once on an inquiry—how far he was obliged to indemnify those who might have given credit to his relative, in a reliance, however unauthorised, on his own resources; and again the coffers of the banker were unlocked by the astuteness of the casuist. . . .

And yet, for more than thirty years, he was a member of the unreformed parliament, representing there that people, so few and singular, who dare to think, and speak, and act for themselves. He never gave one party vote, was never claimed as an adherent by any of the contending factions of his times, and, of course, neither won nor sought the favour of any. An impartial arbiter, whose suffrage was the honourable reward of superior reason, he sat apart and aloft, in a position which, though it provoked a splenetic sarcasm from Burke, commanded the respect even of those whom it rebuked.

To the great Whig doctrines of Peace, Reform, Economy, and Toleration, he lent all the authority of his name, and occasionally the aid of his voice. But he was an infrequent and unimpressive speaker, and sought to influence the measures of his day rather by the use of his pen, than by any participation in his rhetoric. His writings, moral, religious, and political, were voluminous, though destitute of any such mutual dependence as to unite them into one comprehensive system; or of any such graces of execution as to obtain for them permanent acceptance. But in a domestic liturgy composed for the use of his own family, and made public after his death, he encountered, with as much success as can attend it, the difficulty of finding thoughts and language meet to be addressed by the ephemeral dwellers on the earth to Him who inhabiteth eternity. It is simple, grave, weighty, and reverential; and forms a clear, though a faint and subdued, echo of the voice in which the Deity has revealed his sovereign will to man. That will he habitually studied, adored, and laboured to adopt. Yet his piety was reserved and unobtrusive. Like the life-blood throbbing in every pulse and visiting every fibre, it was the latent though perennial source of his mental health and energy.

A peace, perfect and unbroken, seemed to possess him. His tribute of pain and sorrow was paid with a submission so tranquil, as sometimes to assume the appearance of a morbid insensibility. But his affections, unimpaired by lawless indulgence, and constant to their proper objects, were subject to a control to be acquired by no feebler discipline. Ills from without assailed him, not as the gloomy ministers of vengeance, but as the necessary exercise of virtues not otherwise to be called into activity. They came as the salutary lessons of a father, not as the penal inflictions of a judge. Nor did the Father, to whom he so meekly bowed, see fit to lay on him those griefs, under the pressure of which the bravest stagger. He never witnessed the irruption of death into his domestic paradise, nor the rending asunder by sin, the parent of death, of the bonds of love and reverence which united to each other the inmates of that happy home—a home happy in his presence from whose lips no morose, or angry, or impatient word ever fell; on whose brow no cloud of anxiety or discontent was ever seen to rest. Surrounded to his latest hours by those whom it had been his chief delight to bless and to instruct, he bequeathed to them the recollection of a wise, a good, and a happy man; that so, if in future life a wider acquaintance with the world should chill the heart with the scepticism so often engendered by such knowledge, they might be reassured in the belief that human virtue is no vain illusion; but that, nurtured by the dews of heaven, it may expand into fertility and beauty, even in those fat places of the earth which romance disowns, and on which no poet's eye will condescend to rest.

A goodly heritage! yet to have transmitted it (if that were all) would, it must be confessed, be an insufficient title to a place amongst memorable men. Nor, except for what he accomplished as the associate of others, could that claim be reasonably preferred on behalf of Henry Thornton. Apart, and sustained only by his own resources, he would neither have undertaken, nor conceived, the more noble of those benevolent designs to which his life was devoted. Affectionate, but passionless—with a fine and indeed a fastidious taste, but destitute of all creative imagination—gifted rather with fortitude to endure calamity, than with courage to exult in the struggle with danger—a lover of mankind, but not an enthusiast in the cause of our common humanity—his serene and perspicacious spirit was never haunted by the visions, nor borne away by the resistless impulses, of which heroic natures, and they alone, are conscious. Well qualified to impart to the highest energies of others a wise direction, and inflexible perseverance, he had to borrow from them the glowing temperament which hopes against hope, and is wise in despite of prudence. He had not far or long to seek for such an alliance. . . .

Of Mr. Wilberforce we have had occasion to write so recently, and so much at large, that though the Agamemnon of the host we celebrate—the very sun of the Claphamic system—we pause not now to describe him. His fair demesne was conterminous with that of Mr. Thornton; nor lacked there sunny banks, or sheltered shrubberies, where, in each change of season, they revolved the captivity under which man was groaning, and projected schemes for his deliverance. And although such conclaves might scarcely be convened except in the presence of these two, yet were they rarely held without the aid of others, especially of such as could readily find their way thither from the other quarters of the sacred village.

Yet to that village would not seldom resort guests from more rural abodes which in that age, ignorant of iron railways, were regarded as sequestered dwellings in remote districts of our island. Among them not the least frequent, or welcome, or honoured visitor, was one who descended to the table-land of Clapham Common from that loftier table-land, once covered by the ancient forest of Needwood. It is furrowed by several sloping valleys, each forming the bed of a rapid brook, which chafes and twists itself round the roots of oaks so venerable as to have sheltered the deer beneath their branches in the time of the Heptarchy. In later times a keeper's lodge, which takes its name from the adjacent village of Yoxall, was erected for the protection of the game at the confluence of two of these rivulets; for the bolts of "Guy of good Gisborne" had not rarely stricken down the noblest bucks as they came to slake their thirst at those running waters. In the reign of George II, a family, deriving their name from the same "Gisborne," had added Yoxall Lodge to their large possessions, and pursued the sports of the forest with scarcely less ardour than the bold outlaw himself. But this hereditary passion for the chase did not descend to Thomas Gisborne,[1] the second of the race among the modern proprietors of Yoxall Lodge. Though fortune had given him wealth, and nature had endowed him with a figure as graceful and as elastic as that of the deer which peeped out on his mansion from the neighbouring hollies, and though his spirit was brave and joyous, yet his stout heart and masculine intellect were wedded to a feminine soul. Though he never feared the face or the understanding of mortal man, he shrank with a kind of virgin sensitiveness from the coarse familiarities of the field and of the world. Though gay, even to uproar, in the morning of life, and in his interior circle, he appeared beyond those narrow precincts, like a man driven by constitutional shyness into silence and seclusion. When, therefore, the freeholders of his native county proposed to send him as their representative to the House of Commons, he turned away with aversion from such a plunge into the miry waters of parliamentary strife, and from such an exile from the glades and the forest banks over which he rejoiced. He was not a man to be cajoled out of his own happiness by any concert of his neighbours' tongues, and escaped the importunities of the electors of Derbyshire by taking sanctuary in the Church. In early manhood he became one of her ministers, and sheltered himself, for the rest of his days, among the "patrician trees" and the "plebeian underwood" of his forest, from the conflicts of the aristocracy and commonalty of the Palace of Westminster.

Though secluded, he was not solitary. A daughter of the ancient family of Babington became the companion of his retirement, during a period of almost sixty years; staying her steps upon his arm, imbibing wisdom from

1. The author of document 8.—ED.

his lips, gathering hope and courage from his eye, and rendering to him such a homage, or rather such a worship, as to draw from the object of it a raillery so playful, so tender, and so full of meaning, that perhaps it ultimately enhanced the affectionate error which, for the moment, it rebuked. . . .

It was the populous village in which Mr. Gisborne ministered as a country clergyman. Among its poor inhabitants he seemed to remember nothing except that they were his flock, and he their pastor. Happy in his books, his pencil, his writings, and his home, he never was so happy as when, sitting by the poor man's hearth, he chatted with him about crops and village politics, or with the goodwife about her children, her chickens, and her bees, and then gently deposited, in hearts softened by his kindness, some prolific seeds of a more than human wisdom.

From the lodge in the centre of the forest, to the fold thus settled on the slopes of it, there was happily a distance of three miles, which became to Mr. Gisborne a species of enlarged though most secluded Study, where, from day to day, he revolved that series of publications to which he was indebted throughout many years for an extensive influence and celebrity. That fame is now dying away. The thoughts of his times were widely dissimilar from those of the present generation. A more impassioned poetry, a severer philosophy, and a theology far more inquisitive and adventurous, are consigning to a premature oblivion many of his books, which his contemporaries hailed with delight, and with predictions of enduring renown. Nor were those predictions uttered without much apparent reason. For Mr. Gisborne contributed largely to the formation of the national mind on subjects of the highest importance to the national character. He was the expositor of the "Evangelical" system to those cultivated or fastidious readers, who were intolerant of the ruder style of his less refined brethren. He addressed them as a poet, as a moralist, as a natural philosopher, and as a divine. . . . His literary fame, if it shall indeed endure the competitions of a later age, must rest on his sermons. They were regarded by his contemporaries as models in a style of composition in which the English language has scarcely a single specimen of excellence. Except one or two discourses of South, and as many of Robert Hall, we have absolutely nothing to put in competition with the pulpit oratory of France. We possess, indeed, many homiletical essays of exuberant power, wealth, and eloquence, but scarcely an attempt attesting even the consciousness of what constitutes the perfection of a homily. Mr. Gisborne approached more nearly than any Anglican clergyman of his time towards the ideal of that much neglected art. . . .

During a period of more than fifty years, an intimacy the most confiding and affectionate united Thomas Gisborne to William Wilberforce. The member for Yorkshire made Yoxall Lodge his country residence, and the Staffordshire divine had his suburban sojourn at the house of his friend at

Clapham. Among the sectaries of that village he took his share in labour and in deliberation, whether the abolition of the slave trade, the diffusion of Christianity, the war against vice and ignorance, or the advancement of evangelical theology, was the object of the passing day. Yet, when he was engaged in these public duties, they who know him best would perceive that their publicity was painful, and their seeming ostentation offensive to him. When seated at the cabinet held in the library of Henry Thornton, it was obvious that the heart of Thomas Gisborne was still turning to his parish, and that his imagination was far away in the recesses of his forest. It had been the cradle of his childhood; and there, at the age of eighty-seven, his body was committed to the grave in the fulness of that sure and certain hope which had thrown her bright hues over every passage of his protracted residence on earth. . . .

It is not permitted to any coterie altogether to escape the spirit of coterie. Clapham Common, of course, thought itself the best of all possible commons. Such, at least, was the opinion of the less eminent of those who were entitled to house-bote and dinner-bote there. If the common was attacked, the whole homage was in a flame. If it was laughed at, there could be no remaining sense of decency amongst men. The commoners admired in each other the reflection of their own looks, and the echo of their own voices. A critical race, they drew many of their canons of criticism from books and talk of their own parentage; and for those on the outside of the pale, there might be, now and then, some failure of charity. Their festivities were not exhilarating. New faces, new topics, and a less liberal expenditure of wisdom immediately after dinner, would have improved them. . . .

They were the sons, by natural or spiritual birth, of men who, in the earlier days of Methodism, had shaken off the lethargy in which, till then, the Church of England had been entranced—of men, by whose agency the great evangelic doctrine of faith, emerging in its primeval splendour, had not only overpowered the contrary heresies, but had perhaps obscured some kindred truths. This earlier generation of the evangelic school had been too ingenuous, and too confident in the divine reality of their cause, to heed much what hostility they might awaken. They had been content to pass for fools, in a world whose boasted wisdom they accounted folly. In their once central and all-pervading idea, they had found an influence hardly less than magical. They had esteemed it impossible to inculcate too emphatically, or too widely, that truth which Paul had proclaimed indifferently to the idolaters of Ephesus, the revellers of Corinth, the sophists of Athens, and the debauched citizens of sanguinary Rome.

Their sons adopted the same creed with equal sincerity and undiminished earnestness, but with a far keener sense of the hindrances opposed to the indiscriminate and rude exhibition of it. Absolute as was the faith of

Mr. Wilberforce and his associates, it was not possible that the system called "Evangelical" should be asserted by them in the blunt and uncompromising tone of their immediate predecessors. A more elaborate education, greater familiarity with the world and with human affairs, a deeper insight into science and history, with a far nicer discernment of mere conventional proprieties, had opened to them a range of thought, and had brought them into relations with society, of which their fathers were comparatively destitute. . . .

And such were they whom the second generation of the Evangelical party acknowledged as their secular chiefs. They fell on days much unlike those which we, their children, have known—days less softened by the charities and courtesies, but less enervated by the frivolities of life. Since the fall of the Roman republic, there had not arisen within the bosom, and armed with the weapons, of civilisation itself, a power so full of menace to the civilised world as that which then overshadowed Europe. In the deep seriousness of that dark era, they of whom we speak looked back for analogies to that remote conflict of the nations, and drew evil auguries from the event of the wars which, from Sylla to Octavius, had dyed the earth with the blood of its inhabitants, to establish at length a military despotism—ruthless, godless, and abominable. But they also reverted to the advent, even in that age of lust and cruelty, of a power destined to wage successful war, not with any external or earthly potentate, but with the secret and internal spring of all this wretchedness and wrong—the power of love, incarnate though divine—of love exercised in toils and sufferings, and at length yielding up life itself, that from that sacrifice might germinate the seeds of a new and enduring life—the vital principle of man's social existence, of his individual strength, and of his immortal hopes.

And as, in that first age of Christianity, truth, and with it heavenly consolation, had been diffused, not alone or chiefly by the lifeless text, but by living messengers proclaiming and illustrating the renovating energy of the message intrusted to them; so to those who, at the commencement of this century, were anxiously watching the convulsions of their own age, it appeared that the sorrows of mankind would be best assuaged, and the march of evil most effectually stayed, by a humble imitation of that inspired example. They therefore formed themselves into a confederacy, carefully organised and fearlessly avowed, to send forth into all lands, but above all into their own, the two witnesses of the Church—Scripture and Tradition;—Scripture, to be interpreted by its divine Author to the devout worshippers—Tradition, not of doctrinal tenets, but of that unextinguishable zeal, which, first kindled in the apostolic times, has never since wanted either altars to receive, or attendant ministers to feed and propagate the flame. Bibles, schools, missionaries, the circulation of evangelical books, and the training of evangelical clergymen, the possession of well-attended pulpits, war through the press, and war in parliament, against every form of injustice which either law or custom sanctioned—such were the forces by which they hoped to extend the kingdom of light, and to resist the tyranny with which the earth was threatened.

Nor was it difficult to distinguish or to grapple with their antagonists. The slave trade was then brooding like a pestilence over Africa; that monster iniquity which fairly outstripped all abhorrence, and baffled all exaggeration—converting one quarter of this fair earth into the nearest possible resemblance of what we conceive of hell, reversing every law of Christ, and openly defying the vengeance of God. . . .

At the distance of a few bow-shots from the house of Henry Thornton, was the happy home in which dwelt Granville Sharpe; at once the abiding guest and the bosom friend of his more wealthy brothers. A critic, with the soul of a churchwarden, might indeed fasten on certain metes and bounds, hostile to the parochial claims of the family of Sharpe; but in the wider ken and more liberal judgment of the historian, the dignity of a true Claphamite is not to be refused to one whose evening walk and morning contemplations led him so easily and so often within the hallowed precincts. . . .

The grandson of an Archbishop of York, the son of an Archdeacon of Northumberland, the brother of a Prebendary of Durham, Granville Sharpe, descending to the rank from which Isaac Walton rose, was apprenticed to a linen-draper of the name of Halsey, a Quaker, who kept his shop on Tower Hill. When the Quaker died, the indentures were transferred to a Presbyterian of the same craft. When the Presbyterian retired, they were made over to an Irish Papist. When the Papist quitted the trade, they passed to a fourth master, whom the apprentice reports to have had no religion at all. At one time a Socinian took up his abode at the draper's, and assaulted the faith of the young apprentice in the mysteries of the Trinity and the Atonement. Then a Jew came to lodge there, and contested with him the truth of Christianity itself. But blow from what quarter it might, the storm of controversy did but the more endear to him the shelter of his native nest, built for him by his forefathers, like that of the swallow of the Psalmist, in the courts and by the altar of his God. He studied Greek to wrestle with the Socinian—he acquired Hebrew to refute the Israelite—he learned to love the Quaker, to be kind to the Presbyterian, to pity the Atheist, and to endure even the Roman Catholic. Charity (so he judged) was nurtured in his bosom by these early polemics, and the affectionate spirit which warmed to the last the current of his maturer thoughts, grew up, as he believed, within him, while alternately measuring crapes and muslins, and defending the faith against infidels and heretics.

The cares of the mercer's shop engaged no less than seven years of a life destined to be held in grateful remembrance as long as the language or the history of his native land shall be cultivated among men. The next eighteen were consumed in the equally obscure employment of a clerk in the office of Ordnance. . . . The Ordnance clerk sat at his desk with a soul as distended as that of a Paladin bestriding his warhorse; and encountered with his pen such giants, hydras, and discourteous knights, as infested the world in the eighteenth century. . . . He laboured long, and with good success, to defeat an unjust grant made by the Treasury to Sir James Lowther of the Forest of Inglewood, and the manor and castle of Carlisle. He waged a less fortunate war against the theatrical practice of either sex appearing in the habiliments of the other. He moved all the powers of his age, political and intellectual, to abolish the impressment of seamen. . . . Presenting himself to the then Secretary of State, Lord Dartmouth, he denounced, with prophetic solemnity, the guilt of despoiling and exterminating in the Charib war that miserable remnant of the aboriginal race of the Antilles. As a citizen of London, he came to the rescue of Crosby, the Lord Mayor, in his struggle with the House of Commons. As a citizen of the world, he called on earth and heaven to stay the plagues of slavery and the slave-trade, and advocated the independence of America with such ardour as to sacrifice to it his own. Orders had reached his office to ship munitions of war to the revolted colonies. If his hand had entered the account of such a cargo, it would have contracted in his eyes the stain of innocent blood. To avoid that pollution he resigned his place, and his means of subsistence, at a period of life when he could no longer hope to find any other lucrative employment. But he had brothers who loved and supported him; and his release from the fatigues of a subordinate office left him free to obey the impulses of his own brave spirit, as the avenger of the oppressed.

While yet a chronicler of gunpowder and small arms, a negro, abandoned to disease, had asked of him an alms. Silver and gold he had none, but such as he had he gave him. He procured for the poor sufferer medical aid, and watched over him with affectionate care until his health was restored. The patient, once more become sleek and strong, was an object on which Barbadian eyes could not look without cupidity; and one Lisle, his former master, brought an action against Granville Sharpe for the illegal detention of his slave. Three of the infallible doctors of the Church of Westminster—Yorke, Talbot, and Mansfield—favoured the claim; and Blackstone, the great expositor of her traditions, hastened, at their bidding, to retract a heresy on this article of the faith into which his uninstructed reason had fallen. Not such the reverence paid by the hard-working clerk to the inward light which God had vouchsafed to him. He conned his entries indeed, and transcribed his minutes all day long, just as if nothing had happened; but throughout two succesive years he betook himself to his solitary chamber, there, night by night, to explore the original sources of the Law of England, in the hope that so he might be able to correct the authoritative dogmas of Chancellors and Judges. His inquiries closed with the firm conviction that, on this subject at least, these most learned persons were but shallow pretenders to learning. In three successive cases he struggled against them with various and doubtful success; when fortune, or, be it rather said, when Providence, threw in his way the negro Somerset.

For the vindication of the freedom of that man, followed a debate, ever memorable in legal history for the ability with which it was conducted;—for the first introduction to Westminster Hall of Francis Hargrave;—for the audacious assertion then made by Dunning, of the maxim, that a new brief will absolve an advocate from the disgrace of publicly retracting an avowal, however solemn, of any principle however sacred;—for the reluctant abandonment by Lord Mansfield of a long-cherished judicial error;—and for the recognition of a rule of law of such importance, as almost to justify the poets and rhetoricians in their subsequent embellishments of it;—but above all memorable for the magnanimity of the prosecutor, who, though poor and dependent and immersed in the duties of a toilsome calling, supplied the money, the leisure, perseverance, and the learning, required for this great controversy—who, wholly forgetting himself in his object, had studiously concealed his connection with it, lest, perchance, a name so lowly should prejudice a cause so momentous—who, denying himself even the indulgence of attending the argument he had provoked, had circulated his own researches in the name, and as the work, of a plagiarist who had republished them—and who, mean as was his education, and humble as were his pursuits, had proved his superiority as a Jurist, on one main branch of the law of England, to some of the most illustrious Judges by whom that law had been administered.

Never was abolitionist more scathless than Granville Sharpe by the reproach to which their tribe had been exposed, of insensibility to all human sorrows, unless the hair of the sufferer be thick as wool, and the skin as black as ebony. His African client may indeed have usurped a larger share of his attachment than the others; and of his countless schemes of beneficence, that which he loved the best was the settlement at Sierra Leone of a free colony, to serve as a *point-d'appui* in the future campaigns against the slave trade. But he may be quoted as an experimental proof of the infinite divisibility of the kindly affections. Much he wrote, and much he laboured, to conciliate Great Britain and America; much to promote the diffusion of the Holy Scriptures; much to interpret the prophecies contained in them; much to refute the errors of the Socinians; much to sustain the cause of Grattan and the Irish volunteers; much to recommend reform in Parliament; and much, it must be added, (for what is a man in his best estate?) to dissuade the emancipation of the Catholics. Many also were the benevolent societies which he formed or fostered; and his publications, who can number? Their common aim was to advance the highest interests of mankind; but to none of them, with perhaps one exception, could the praise either of learning or of originality be justly given. For he possessed rather a great soul than a great understanding; and was less admirable for the extent of his resources, than for the earnest affection and the quiet energy with which he employed them. . . .

Thirty-seven years have rolled away since these men met at Clapham, in joy and thanksgiving, and mutual gratulation, over the abolition of the African slave trade.[2] It was still either the dwelling-place, or the haunt, of almost every one of the more eminent supporters of that measure; and it may be that they exulted beyond the limits of sober reason in the prospects which that success had opened to them. Time has brought to light more than they knew or believed of the inveteracy of the evil; and of the impotency of law in a protracted contest with avarice. But time has also ascertained, that throughout the period assigned for the birth and death of a whole generation of mankind, there has been no proof, or reasonable suspicion, of so much as a single evasion of this law in any one of the transatlantic British colonies. Time has shown that to that law we may now confidently ascribe the deliverance of our own land from this blood-guiltiness for ever. Time has ascertained that the solemn practical assertion then made of the great principles of justice, was to be prolific of consequences, direct and indirect, of boundless magnitude. Time has enlisted on our side all the powers and all the suffrages of the earth; so that no one any longer attempts to erase the brand of murder from the brow of the slave trader. Above all, time has shown that, in the extinction of the slave trade, was involved, by slow but inevitable steps, the extinction of the slavery which it had created and sustained. This, also, was a result of which, as far as human agency is concerned, the mainsprings are to be found among that sect to which, having first given a name, we would now build up a monument.

It is with a trembling hand that we inscribe on that monument the name of Zachary Macaulay. . . . To [those whom he honoured with his intimacy] he appeared a man possessed by one idea, and animated by one master passion—an idea so comprehensive, as to impart a profound interest to all which indicated its influence over him—a passion so benevolent, that the coldest heart could not withhold some sympathy from him who was the

2. Depending on the date Stephen wrote this essay, he could be referring to 1806, the adoption of a bill prohibiting British merchants from providing slaves to foreign colonies; 1807, the adoption of a bill prohibiting all slave trading by British vessels as well as importation of slaves into British colonies; or 1811, the adoption of a bill designed to insure enforcement of the previous two by defining the prohibited activities as criminal offenses.—ED.

subject of it. Trained in the hardy habits of Scotland in ancient times, he had received from his father much instruction in theology, with some Latin and a little Greek, when not employed in cultivating his father's glebe at Cardross, on the northern bank of the Clyde. While yet a boy, he had watched as the iron entered into the soul of the slaves, whose labours he was sent to superintend in Jamaica; and, abandoning with abhorrence a pursuit which had promised him early wealth and distinction, he pondered the question—how shall the earth be delivered from this curse? Turning to Sierra Leone, he braved for many years the deadly climate, that he might aid in the erection and in the defence of what was then the one city of refuge for the Negro race; and as he saw the slave trade crushing to the dust the adjacent tribes of Africa, he again pondered the question—how shall the earth be delivered from this curse?

That God had called him into being to wage war with this gigantic evil, became his immutable conviction. During forty successive years, he was ever burdened with this thought. It was the subject of his visions by day, and of his dreams by night. To give them reality, he laboured as men labour for the honours of a profession, or for the subsistence of their children. The rising sun ever found him at his task. He went abroad but to advance it. His commerce, his studies, his friendships, his controversies, even his discourses in the bosom of his family, were all bent to the promotion of it. He edited voluminous periodical works; but whether theology, literature, or politics were the text, the design was still the same—to train the public mind to a detestation of the slave trade and of slavery. He attached himself to most of the religious and philanthropic societies of his age, that he might enlist them as associates, more or less declared, in his holy war. To multiply such allies, he called into existence one great association, and contributed largely to the establishment of another. In that service he sacrificed all that men may lawfully sacrifice   health, fortune, repose, favour, and celebrity. He died a poor man, though wealth was within his reach. He pursued the contest to the end, though oppressed by such pains of body as strained to their utmost tension the self-sustaining powers of the soul. . . .

Throughout the slave trade abolition war, the other chiefs who hailed him as the earliest, and as among the mightiest of their host, kept their communications open by encamping in immediate vicinity to each other. Even to Lord Brougham[3] the same station may, with poetical truth at least, be assigned by the Homer who shall hereafter sing these battles; for though, at that period, his London domicile was in the walks of the Inner Temple,

3. Henry Brougham (1778–1868), an important Whig politician for some three decades and a member of the cabinet at the time of the passage of the 1832 Reform Bill. He was an early and constant supporter of the antislavery agitation and had formed an alliance with Wilberforce on this issue by 1806.—ED.

yet might he not seldom be encountered in the less inviting walks which led
him to the suburban councils of his brethren in command. There he formed
or cemented attachments, of which no subsequent elevation of rank, or intoxicating triumph of genius, or agony of political strife, have ever rendered
him forgetful. Of one of those denizens of Clapham he has published a
sketch, of which we avail ourselves, not as subscribing altogether to the
accuracy of it, but as we can thus fill up, from the hand of so great a Master, a part of our canvas which must have otherwise remained blank and
colourless.

> Mr. Stephen was a person of great natural talents, which, if accidental
> circumstances had permitted him fully to cultivate, and early enough
> to bring into play upon the best scene of political exertion—the House
> of Commons—would have placed him high in the first rank of English
> orators. For he had, in an eminent degree, that strenuous firmness of
> purpose and glowing ardour of soul, which lies at the root of all elo-
> quence; he was gifted with great industry, a retentive memory, an in-
> genuity which was rather apt to err by excess than by defect. His
> imagination was, besides, lively and powerful; little, certainly, under
> the chastening discipline of severe taste, but often enabling him to
> embody his own feelings and recollections with great distinctness of
> outline and strength of colouring. He enjoyed, moreover, great natural
> strength of constitution, and had as much courage as falls to the lot of
> most men. But having passed the most active part of his life in one of
> the West Indian colonies, where he followed the profession of a barri-
> ster, and having, after his return, addicted himself to the practice of a
> court which affords no scope at all for oratorical display, it happened
> to him, as it has to many other men of natural genius for rhetorical
> pursuits, that he neither gained the correct taste which the habit of
> frequenting refined society, and above all, addressing a refined au-
> ditory, can alone bestow, nor acquired the power of condensation,
> which is sure to be lost altogether by those who address hearers com-
> pelled to listen, like judges and juries, instead of having to retain them
> by closeness of reasoning, or felicity of illustration. . . . It must have
> struck all who heard him, when, early in 1808, he entered Parliament
> under the auspices of Mr. Perceval,[4] that whatever defects he had,
> arose entirely from accidental circumstances, and not at all from in-
> trinsic imperfections; nor could any one doubt that his late entrance
> upon parliamentary life, and his vehemence of temperament, alone
> kept him from the front rank of debaters, if not of eloquence itself.
> With Mr. Perceval his friendship had been long and intimate. To this
> the similarity of their religious character mainly contributed; for Mr.

4. Spencer Perceval (1762–1812), an influential statesman with strong Evangelical sympathies and prime minister from 1809 until his death.—ED.

Stephen was a distinguished member of the evangelical party, to which
the minister manifestly leant without belonging to it; and he was one
whose pious sentiments and devotional habits occupied a very marked
place in his whole scheme of life. . . . Of all subjects, that of the
slave trade and slavery most engrossed his mind. His experience in the
West Indies, his religious feelings, and his near connection with Mr.
Wilberforce, whose sister he married, all contributed to give this great
question a peculiarly sacred aspect in his eyes; nor could he either
avoid mixing it up with almost all other discussions, or prevent his
views of its various relations from influencing his sentiments on other
matters of political discussion.

The author of the preceding portrait enjoyed the happiness denied to the
subject of it, not merely of witnessing, but of largely participating in, the
last great act by which the labours borne by them in common, during so
many preceding years, were consummated. . . .[5]

What is a party, political or religious, without a Review? A bell swing-
ing without a clapper. What is any society of men, if not recruited from the
rising generation? A hive of neutral bees. Reviewless, Clapham had
scarcely been known beyond her own Common. Youthless, her memory
had never descended to the present age. At once rapt into future times, and
thoughtful of her own, she addressed the world on the first day of each
successive month through the columns of the "Christian Observer"; and
employed the pen of him on whom her hopes most fondly rested, to confer splendour and celebrity on pages not otherwise very alluring. To Mr.
Macaulay was assigned the arduous post of Editor. He and his chief contributors enjoyed the advantage, permitted, alas! to how few of their tribe,
of living in the same village, and meeting daily in the same walks or at the
same table, and lightening, by the common counsel, the cares of that
feudal sovereignty. . . .

And thus closes, though it be far from exhausted, our chronicle of the
worthies of Clapham, of whom it may be said, as it was said of those of
whom the world was not worthy, "These all died in faith." With but very
few exceptions, they had all partaken largely of those sorrows which probe
the inmost heart, and exercise its fortitude to the utmost. But sweet, and
not less wise than sweet, is the song in which George Herbert teaches, that
when the Creator had bestowed every other gift on his new creature man,
he reserved Rest to himself, that so the wearied heart in search of that last
highest blessing, might cheerfully return to Him who made it. They died in

5. The Abolition Act of 1833, by which slaves in the British colonies were set free (after a
transitional period of apprenticeship to their masters) and slave owners compensated out of
the British Treasury.—ED.

the faith that for their descendants, at no remote period, was reserved an epoch glorious, though probably awful, beyond all former example. It was a belief derived from the intimations, as they understood them, of the prophets of Israel; but it was also gathered from sources which to many will seem better entitled to such confidence.

Revolving the great dramatic action of which this earth has been the scene, they perceived that it was made up of a protracted conflict between light and darkness. They saw that, on the one side, science and religion— on the other, war and superstition—had been the great agents on this wide theatre. They traced a general movement of events towards the final triumph of good over evil; but observed that this tendency was the result of an all-controlling Providence, which had almost invariably employed the bad passions of man as the reluctant instruments of the Divine mercy—sending forth a long succession of conquerors, barbarous or civilised, as missionaries of woe, to prepare the way for the heralds of peace. They saw, or thought they saw, this economy of things drawing to its close. Civilization and, in name at least, Christianity, had at length possessed the far greater and nobler regions of the globe. Goths and Vandals were now the foremost amongst the nations. Even the Scythians had become members of a vast and potent monarchy. The Arabs had again taken refuge in their deserts. If Genghis or Timour should reappear, their power would be broken against the British empire of Hindostan. The mightiest of warriors had triumphed and had failed; as if to prove how impregnable had become the barriers of the European world against such aggressions. On every side the same truth was proclaimed, that military subjugation was no longer to be the purifying chastisement of Christendom.

But the religion of Christ was conquering and to conquer. Courting and exulting in the light, it had made a strict alliance with philosophy—the only faith which could ever endure such an association. Amidst the imbecility and dotage of every other form of belief and worship, it alone flourished in perennial youth and indomitable vigour. If anything in futurity could be certain, it was the ultimate and not very remote dominion, over the whole earth, of the faith professed by every nation which retained either wisdom to investigate, or energy to act, or wealth to negotiate, or power to interpose in the questions which most deeply affect the entire race of man. If any duty was most especially incumbent on those who exercised an influence in the national councils of England, it was that of contributing, as best they might, to speed onwards the approaching catastrophe of human affairs—the great consummation whence is to arise that new era with which creation travails and is in birth, which poets have sung and prophets foretold, and which shall justify to the world, and perhaps to other worlds, all that Christians believe of the sacrifice, surpassing thought and language, made for the deliverance and the exaltation of mankind.

When such thoughts as these force themselves on the German mind, it forthwith soars towards the unapproachable, and indites the unutterable. When the practical Englishman is the subject of them, he betakes himself to form societies, to collect subscriptions, to circulate books, to send forth teachers, to build platforms, and to afflict his neighbours by an eloquence of which one is tempted to wish that it were really unutterable. Such was the effect of these bright anticipations on the Clapham mind—an effect perceptible in many much better things, but, among the rest, in much equivocal oratory, and in at least one great effort of architecture.

Midway between the Abbey of Westminster and the Church of the Knights Templars, twin columns, emulating those of Hercules, fling their long shadows across the strait through which the far-resounding Strand pours the full current of human existence into the deep recesses of Exeter Hall. Borne on that impetuous tide, the mediterranean waters lift up their voice in a ceaseless swell of exulting or pathetic declamation. The changeful strain rises with the civilisation of Africa, or becomes plaintive over the wrongs of chimney-boys, or peals anathemas against the successors of Peter, or in rich diapason calls on the Protestant Churches to wake and evangelise the world. . . .

It is a prophetical age. We have Nominalists who, from the monosyllable "Church," educe a long line of shadowy forms, hereafter to arise and reign on Episcopal or patriarchal thrones—and Realists, who foresee the moral regeneration of the land by means of union workhouses, of emigrant ships, or of mechanics' institutes—and Mediaevals, who promise the return of Astraea in the persons of Bede and Barnard *redivivi*—and Mr. Carlyle, who offers most eloquent vows for the reappearance of the heroes who are to set all things right—and profound interpreters of the Apocalypse, who discover the woes impending over England in chastisement of the impiety which moved Lord Melbourne to introduce Mr. Owen to the Queen of England. In the midst of all these predictions, Exeter Hall also prophesies. As to the events which are coming upon us, she adopts the theory of her Claphamic progenitor. In reducing that theory to practice, she is almost as much a Socialist as Mr. Owen himself. The moral regeneration which she foretells is to be brought about neither by church, by workhouse, by monk, by hero, nor by the purifying of St. James's. She believes in the continually decreasing power of individual, and the as constantly augmenting power of associated, minds. She looks on the age as characterised by a nearer approach than was ever known before to intellectual equality. But Exeter Hall is no croaker. Her temperament is as sanguine as her eloquence. Enumerate to her the long list of illustrious men who, while scarcely beyond their boyhood, had, at the commencement of this century, reached the highest eminence in every path to distinction; and point out to her the impossibility of selecting now, from those who have yet to complete their fortieth summer, any four names, the loss of which would be deplored by any art, or science, or calling in use amongst us;—and, in despite of Oxford, and Young England, and Mr. Carlyle, Exeter Hall makes answer— "So much the better. The sense of separate weakness is the secret of collective strength." Ours is the age of societies. For the redress of every oppression that is done under the sun, there is a public meeting. For the cure of every sorrow by which our land or our race can be visited, there are patrons, vice-presidents, and secretaries. For the diffusion of every blessing of which mankind can partake in common, there is a committee. That confederacy which, when pent up within the narrow limits of Clapham, jocose men invidiously called a "Sect," is now spreading through the habitable globe. The day is not distant when it will assume the form, and be hailed by the glorious title, of "The Universal Church."

Happy and animating hopes! Who would destroy them if he could? Long may they warm many an honest bosom, and quicken into activity many an otherwise sluggish temper! The true Claphamite will know how to separate the pure ore of truth from the dross of nonsense to which the prophets of his time give utterance. He will find sympathy for most, and indulgence for all, of the schemes of benevolence which surround him. Like the founders of his sect, he will rejoice in the progress and prospects of their cause; nor will he abandon his creed, however unpopular it may be made by the presumption, or however ridiculous by the follies, of some of the weaker brethren by whom it has been adopted.

27. Ludwig Feuerbach, *The Essence of Christianity*

The son of a professor of jurisprudence, Ludwig Feuerbach (1804–72) was a young man of intense Protestant religiosity when he went to the University of Berlin in 1824–25, attended all of Hegel's (see document 11) lectures, and was won over to Hegelianism. He called his contact with Hegel the "turning point" of his "whole life"; indeed it marked a sharp rupture with his earlier beliefs. By the late 1830s, he had affiliated himself with a loosely knit circle of Young or Left Hegelians (including David Friedrich Strauss, Bruno Bauer, Arnold Ruge and, later, Karl Marx) who interpreted Hegel's dialectic march of spirit through history to mean that existing Western cultural and institutional forms—and, in particular, Christianity—would soon be superseded. Of the members of the group, it was Feuerbach who received the greatest public recognition in the 1840s, the result of the publication of his controversial *The Essence*

From Ludwig Feuerbach, *The Essence of Christianity,* translated by George Eliot (New York: Harper Torchbook, 1958), chap. 1, pp. 1–6, 11–14, 20–23, 25–32.

of Christianity (1841), which boldly and enthusiastically announced the imminent arrival of a new, post-Christian era. The book was soon translated into all major languages. (The English edition, from which this selection is reprinted, was translated in 1854 by Marian Evans, who later, under the name George Eliot, became one of the major English novelists of the nineteenth century. A French translation appeared in 1864.)

Whereas Hegel had defined alienation as the encounter of rational spirit with the external world of finite, particular phenomena, Feuerbach located alienation in the experience of traditional religious belief, especially in man's relationship with God. According to this latter conception, alienated man could be restored to himself when he unmasked the true nature of theology, understanding that it was, as Feuerbach sometimes expressed it in condensed form, covert "anthropology." Some of the main lines of his argument, couched in Hegelian terminology, appear in this selection from *The Essence of Christianity.*

Feuerbach refused to write on political subjects, believing that the demise of Christianity was the first item on the agenda and the necessary prerequisite to any effective political action. Nonetheless he served, reluctantly, in the Frankfurt Assembly (see document 21) and was deeply depressed by the abortive outcome of the revolutions of 1848. "Europe is in prison," he observed gloomily.

In addition to its role in the religious debate of the period, *The Essence of Christianity* had exercised an important, intellectually formative influence on Karl Marx. Marx came to regard Feuerbach's concept of alienation as inadequate, as not going far enough; it was through writing a set of "Theses on Feuerbach" in 1845 that Marx hammered out the rudiments of his own philosophical position by criticizing that of his fellow Young Hegelian.

Introduction

§ 1. The Essential Nature of Man

Religion has its basis in the essential difference between man and the brute—the brutes have no religion. It is true that the old uncritical writers on natural history attributed to the elephant, among other laudable qualities, the virtue of religiousness; but the religion of elephants belongs to the realm of fable. Cuvier, one of the greatest authorities on the animal kingdom, assigns, on the strength of his personal observations, no higher grade of intelligence to the elephant than to the dog.

But what is this essential difference between man and the brute? The most simple, general, and also the most popular answer to this question is—consciousness:—but consciousness in the strict sense; for the consciousness implied in the feeling of self as an individual, in discrimination by the senses, in the perception and even judgment of outward things according to definite sensible signs, cannot be denied to the brutes. Consciousness in the strictest sense is present only in a being to whom his species, his essential nature, is an object of thought. The brute is indeed conscious of himself as an individual—and he has accordingly the feeling of self as the common centre of successive sensations—but not as a species: hence, he is without that consciousness which in its nature, as in its name, is akin to science. Where there is this higher consciousness there is a capability of science. Science is the cognisance of species. In practical life we have to do with individuals; in science, with species. But only a being to whom his own species, his own nature, is an object of thought, can make the essential nature of other things or beings an object of thought.

Hence the brute has only a simple, man a twofold life: in the brute, the inner life is one with the outer; man has both an inner and an outer life. The inner life of man is the life which has relation to his species, to his general, as distinguished from his individual, nature. Man thinks—that is, he converses with himself. The brute can exercise no function which has relation to its species without another individual external to itself; but man can perform the functions of thought and speech, which strictly imply such a relation, apart from another individual. Man is himself at once I and thou; he can put himself in the place of another, for this reason, that to him his species, his essential nature, and not merely his individuality, is an object of thought.

Religion being identical with the distinctive characteristic of man, is then identical with self-consciousness—with the consciousness which man has of his nature. But religion, expressed generally, is consciousness of the infinite; thus it is and can be nothing else than the consciousness which man has of his own—not finite and limited, but infinite nature. A really finite being has not even the faintest adumbration, still less consciousness, of an infinite being, for the limit of the nature is also the limit of the consciousness. The consciousness of the caterpillar, whose life is confined to a particular species of plant, does not extend itself beyond this narrow domain. It does, indeed, discriminate between this plant and other plants, but more it knows not. A consciousness so limited, but on account of that very limitation so infallible, we do not call consciousness, but instinct. Consciousness, in the strict or proper sense, is identical with consciousness of the infinite; a limited consciousness is no consciousness; consciousness is essentially infinite in its nature. The consciousness of the infinite is nothing else than the consciousness of the infinity of the consciousness; or, in the consciousness of the infinite, the conscious subject has for his object the infinity of his own nature.

What, then, *is* the nature of man, of which he is conscious, or what constitutes the specific distinction, the proper humanity of man?[1] Reason, Will, Affection. To a complete man belong the power of thought, the power of will, the power of affection. The power of thought is the light of the intellect, the power of will is energy of character, the power of affection is love. Reason, love, force of will, are perfections—the perfections of the human being—nay, more, they are absolute perfections of being. To will, to love, to think, are the highest powers, are the absolute nature of man as man, and the basis of his existence. Man exists to think, to love, to will. Now that which is the end, the ultimate aim, is also the true basis and principle of a being. But what is the end of reason? Reason. Of love? Love. Of will? Freedom of the will. We think for the sake of thinking; love for the sake of loving; will for the sake of willing—*i.e.*, that we may be free. True existence is thinking, loving, willing existence. That alone is true, perfect, divine, which exists for its own sake. But such is love, such is reason, such is will. The divine trinity in man, above the individual man, is the unity of reason, love, will. Reason, Will, Love, are not powers which man possesses, for he is nothing without them, he is what he is only by them; they are the constituent elements of his nature, which he neither has nor makes, the animating, determining, governing powers—divine, absolute powers—to which he can oppose no resistance. . . .

Man is nothing without an object. The great models of humanity, such men as reveal to us what man is capable of, have attested the truth of this proposition by their lives. They had only one dominant passion—the realisation of the aim which was the essential object of their activity. But the object to which a subject essentially, necessarily relates, is nothing else than this subject's own, but objective, nature. If it be an object common to several individuals of the same species, but under various conditions, it is still, at least as to the form under which it presents itself to each of them according to their respective modifications, their own, but objective, nature.

Thus the Sun is the common object of the planets, but it is an object to Mercury, to Venus, to Saturn, to Uranus, under other conditions than to the Earth. Each planet has its own sun. The Sun which lights and warms Uranus has no physical (only an astronomical, scientific) existence for the Earth; and not only does the Sun appear different, but it really is *another* sun on Uranus than on the Earth. The relation of the Sun to the Earth is therefore at the same time a relation of the Earth to itself, or to its own nature, for the measure of the size and of the intensity of light which the Sun possesses as the object of the Earth is the measure of the distance

1. The obtuse Materialist says: "Man is distinguished from the brute *only* by consciousness—he is an animal with consciousness superadded;" not reflecting, that in a being which awakes to consciousness, there takes place a qualitative change, a differentiation of the entire nature.

which determines the peculiar nature of the Earth. Hence each planet has in its sun the mirror of its own nature.

In the object which he contemplates, therefore, man becomes acquainted with himself; consciousness of the objective is the self-consciousness of man. We know the man by the object, by his conception of what is external to himself; in it his nature becomes evident; this object is his manifested nature, his true objective *ego*. And this is true not merely of spiritual, but also of sensuous objects. Even the objects which are the most remote from man, *because* they are objects to him, and to the extent to which they are so, are revelations of human nature. . . . That he sees [the moon, the sun, the stars], and so sees them, is an evidence of his own nature. The animal is sensible only of the beam which immediately affects life; while man perceives the ray, to him physically indifferent, of the remotest star. Man alone has purely intellectual, disinterested joys and passions; the eye of man alone keeps theoretic festivals. The eye which looks into the starry heavens, which gazes at that light, alike useless and harmless, having nothing in common with the earth and its necessities—this eye sees in that light its own nature, its own origin. The eye is heavenly in its nature. Hence man elevates himself above the earth only with the eye; hence theory begins with the contemplation of the heavens. The first philosophers were astronomers. It is the heavens that admonish man of his destination, and remind him that he is destined not merely to action, but also to contemplation.

The *absolute* to man is his own nature. The power of the object over him is therefore the power of his own nature. Thus the power of the object of feeling is the power of feeling itself; the power of the object of the intellect is the power of the intellect itself; the power of the object of the will is the power of the will itself. The man who is affected by musical sounds is governed by feeling; by the feeling, that is, which finds its corresponding element in musical sounds. But it is not melody as such, it is only melody pregnant with meaning and emotion, which has power over feeling. Feeling is only acted on by that which conveys feeling, *i.e.*, by itself, its own nature. Thus also the will; thus, and infinitely more, the intellect. Whatever kind of object, therefore, we are at any time conscious of, we are always at the same time conscious of our own nature; we can affirm nothing without affirming ourselves. And since to will, to feel, to think, are perfections, essences, realities, it is impossible that intellect, feeling, and will should feel or perceive themselves as limited, finite powers, *i.e.*, as worthless, as nothing. For finiteness and nothingness are identical; finiteness is only a euphemism for nothingness. Finiteness is the metaphysical, the theoretical—nothingness the pathological, practical expression. . . .

Consciousness is self-verification, self-affirmation, self-love, joy in one's own perfection. Consciousness is the characteristic mark of a perfect nature; it exists only in a self-sufficing, complete being. Even human vanity attests this truth. A man looks in the glass; he has complacency in his appearance. This complacency is a necessary, involuntary consequence of the completeness, the beauty of his form. A beautiful form is satisfied in itself; it has necessarily joy in itself—in self-contemplation. This complacency becomes vanity only when a man piques himself on his form as being his individual form, not when he admires it as a specimen of human beauty in general. . . .

Man cannot get beyond his true nature. He may indeed by means of the imagination conceive individuals of another so-called higher kind, but he can never get loose from his species, his nature; the conditions of being, the positive final predicates which he gives to these other individuals, are always determinations or qualities drawn from his own nature—qualities in which he in truth only images and projects himself. There may certainly be thinking beings besides men on the other planets of our solar system. But by the supposition of such beings we do not change our standing point—we extend our conceptions *quantitatively* not *qualitatively*. For as surely as on the other planets there are the same laws of motion, so surely are there the same laws of perception and thought as here. In fact, we people the other planets, not that we may place there different beings from ourselves, but *more* beings of our own or of a similar nature.

§ 2. The Essence of Religion Considered Generally

What we have hitherto been maintaining generally, even with regard to sensational impressions, of the relation between subject and object, applies especially to the relation between the subject and the religious object.

In the perceptions of the senses consciousness of the object is distinguishable from consciousness of self; but in religion, consciousness of the object and self-consciousness coincide. The object of the senses is out of man, the religious object is within him, and therefore as little forsakes him as his self-consciousness or his conscience; it is the intimate, the closest object. "God," says Augustine, for example, "is nearer, more related to us, and therefore more easily known by us, than sensible, corporeal things." The object of the senses is in itself indifferent—independent of the disposition or of the judgment; but the object of religion is a selected object; the most excellent, the first, the supreme being; it essentially presupposes a critical judgment, a discrimination between the divine and the non-divine, between that which is worthy of adoration and that which is not worthy. And here may be applied, without any limitation, the proposition: the object of any subject is nothing else than the subject's own nature taken objectively. Such as are a man's thoughts and dispositions, such is his God; so much worth as a man has, so much and no more has his God. Consciousness of God is self-consciousness, knowledge of God is self-knowledge. By his God thou knowest the man, and by the man his God; the two are identical. Whatever is God to a man, that is his heart and soul; and conversely, God is the manifested inward nature, the expressed self of a man,— religion the solemn unveiling of a man's hidden treasures, the revelation of his intimate thoughts, the open confession of his love-secrets.

But when religion—consciousness of God—is designated as the self-consciousness of man, this is not to be understood as affirming that the religious man is directly aware of this identity; for, on the contrary, ignorance of it is fundamental to the peculiar nature of religion. To preclude this misconception, it is better to say, religion is man's earliest and also indirect form of self-knowledge. Hence, religion everywhere precedes philosophy, as in the history of the race, so also in that of the individual. Man first of all sees his nature as if *out of* himself, before he finds it in himself. His own nature is in the first instance contemplated by him as that of another being. Religion is the childlike condition of humanity; but the child sees his nature—man—out of himself; in childhood a man is an object to himself, under the form of another man. Hence the historical progress of religion consists in this: that what by an earlier religion was regarded as objective, is now recognised as subjective; that is, what was formerly contemplated and worshipped as God is now perceived to be something *human*. What was at first religion becomes at a later period idolatry; man is seen to have adored his own nature. Man has given objectivity to himself, but has not recognised the object as his own nature: a later religion takes this forward step; every advance in religion is therefore a deeper self-knowledge. But every particular religion, while it pronounces its predecessors idolatrous, excepts itself—and necessarily so, otherwise it would no longer be religion—from the fate, the common nature of all religions: it imputes only to other religions what is the fault, if fault it be, of religion in general. Because it has a different object, a different tenor, because it has transcended the ideas of preceding religions, it erroneously supposes itself exalted above the necessary eternal laws which constitute the essence of religion—it fancies its object, its ideas, to be superhuman. But the essence of religion, thus hidden from the religious, is evident to the thinker, by whom religion is viewed objectively, which it cannot be by its votaries. And it is our task to show that the antithesis of divine and human is altogether illusory, that it is nothing else than the antithesis between the human nature in general and the human individual; that, consequently, the object and contents of the Christian religion are altogether human.

Religion, at least the Christian, is the relation of man to himself, or more correctly to his own nature (*i.e.*, his subjective nature); but a relation to it, viewed as a nature apart from his own. The divine being is nothing else than the human being, or, rather, the human nature purified, freed from the limits of the individual man, made objective—*i.e.*, contemplated and revered as another, a distinct being. All the attributes of the divine nature are, therefore attributes of the human nature.

In relation to the attributes, the predicates, of the Divine Being, this is admitted without hesitation, but by no means in relation to the subject of these predicates. The negation of the subject is held to be irreligion, nay, atheism; though not so the negation of the predicates. But that which has no predicates or qualities, has no effect upon me; that which has no effect upon me has no existence for me. To deny all the qualities of a being is equivalent to denying the being himself. A being without qualities is one which cannot become an object to the mind, and such a being is virtually non-existent. Where man deprives God of all qualities, God is no longer anything more to him than a negative being. To the truly religious man, God is not a being without qualities, because to him he is a positive, real being. The theory that God cannot be defined, and consequently cannot be known by man, is therefore the offspring of recent times, a product of modern unbelief. . . .

The identity of the subject and predicate is clearly evidenced by the progressive development of religion, which is identical with the progressive development of human culture. So long as man is in a mere state of nature, so long is his god a mere nature-god—a personification of some natural force. Where man inhabits houses, he also encloses his gods in temples. The temple is only a manifestation of the value which man attaches to beautiful buildings. Temples in honour of religion are in truth temples in honour of architecture. With the emerging of man from a state of savagery and wildness to one of culture, with the distinction between what is fitting for man and what is not fitting, arises simultaneously the distinction between that which is fitting and that which is not fitting for God. God is the idea of majesty, of the highest dignity; the religious sentiment is the sentiment of supreme fitness. The later more cultured artists of Greece were the first to embody in the statues of the gods the ideas of dignity, of spiritual grandeur, of imperturbable repose and serenity. But why were these qualities in their view attributes, predicates of God? Because they were in themselves regarded by the Greeks as divinities. Why did those artists exclude all disgusting and low passions? Because they perceived them to be unbecoming, unworthy, unhuman, and consequently ungodlike. The Homeric gods eat and drink;—that implies eating and drinking is a divine pleasure. Physical strength is an attribute of the Homeric gods: Zeus is the strongest of the gods. Why? Because physical strength, in and by itself, was regarded as something glorious, divine. To the ancient Germans the highest virtues were those of the warrior; therefore their supreme god was the god of war, Odin,—war, "the original or oldest law." Not the attribute of the divinity, but the divineness or deity of the attribute, is the first true Divine Being. Thus what theology and philosophy have held to be God, the Absolute, the Infinite, is not God; but that which they have held not to be God is God: namely, the attribute, the quality, whatever has reality. Hence he alone is the true atheist to whom the predicates of the Divine Being,—for example, love, wisdom, justice,—are nothing; not he to whom merely the subject of these predicates is nothing. And in no wise is the negation of the subject necessarily also a negation of the predicates considered in themselves. These have an intrinsic, independent reality; they force their recognition upon man by their very nature; they are self-evident truths to him; they prove, they attest themselves. It does not follow that goodness, justice, wisdom, are chimaeras because the existence of God is a chimaera, nor truths because this is a truth. The idea of God is dependent on the idea of justice, of benevolence; a God who is not benevolent, not just, not wise, is no God; but the converse does not hold. The fact is not that a quality is divine because God has it, but that God has it because it is in itself divine: because without it God would be a defective being. Justice, wisdom, in general every quality which constitutes the divinity of God, is determined and known by itself independently, but the idea of God is determined by the qualities which have thus been previously judged to be worthy of the divine nature; only in the case in which I identify God and justice, in which I think of God immediately as the reality of the idea of justice, is the idea of God self-determined. But if God as a subject is the determined, while the quality, the predicate, is the determining, then in truth the rank of the godhead is due not to the subject, but to the predicate.

Not until several, and those contradictory, attributes are united in one being, and this being is conceived as personal—the personality being thus brought into especial prominence—not until then is the origin of religion lost sight of, is it forgotten that what the activity of the reflective power has converted into a predicate distinguishable or separable from the subject, was originally the true subject. Thus the Greeks and Romans deified accidents as substances; virtues, states of mind, passions, as independent beings. Man, especially the religious man, is to himself the measure of all things, of all reality. Whatever strongly impresses a man, whatever produces an unusual effect on his mind, if it be only a peculiar, inexplicable sound or note, he personifies as a divine being. Religion embraces all the objects of the world: everything existing has been an object of religious reverence; in the nature and consciousness of religion there is nothing else than what lies in the nature of man and in his consciousness of himself and of the world. Religion has no material exclusively its own. In Rome even the passions of fear and terror had their temples. The Christians also made mental phenomena into independent beings, their own feelings into qualities of things, the passions which governed them into powers which governed the world, in short, predicates of their own nature, whether recognised as such or not, into independent subjective existences. Devils, cobolds, witches, ghosts, angels, were sacred truths as long as the religious spirit held undivided sway over mankind.

In order to banish from the mind the identity of the divine and human predicates, and the consequent identity of the divine and human nature, recourse is had to the idea that God, as the absolute, real Being, has an infinite fulness of various predicates, of which we here know only a part, and those such as are analogous to our own; while the rest, by virtue of which God must thus have quite a different nature from the human or that which is analogous to the human, we shall only know in the future—that is, after death. But an infinite plenitude or multitude of predicates which are really different, so different that the one does not immediately involve the other, is realised only in an infinite plenitude or multitude of different beings, or individuals. Thus the human nature presents an infinite abundance of different predicates, and for that very reason it presents an infinite abundance of different individuals. Each new man is a new predicate, a new phasis of humanity. As many as are the men, so many are the powers, the properties of humanity. It is true that there are the same elements in every individual, but under such various conditions and modifications that they appear new and peculiar. The mystery of the inexhaustible fulness of the divine predicates is therefore nothing else than the mystery of human nature considered as an infinitely varied, infinitely modifiable, but, consequently, phenomenal being. . . .

Now, when it is shown that what the subject is lies entirely in the attributes of the subject; that is, that the predicate is the true subject; it is also proved that if the divine predicates are attributes of the human nature, the subject of those predicates is also of the human nature. But the divine predicates are partly general, partly personal. The general predicates are the metaphysical, but these serve only as external points of support to religion; they are not the characteristic definitions of religion. It is the personal predicates alone which constitute the essence of religion—in which the Divine Being is the object of religion. Such are, for example, that God is a Person, that he is the moral Lawgiver, the Father of mankind, the Holy One, the Just, the Good, the Merciful. It is, however, at once clear, or it will at least be clear in the sequel, with regard to these and other definitions, that, especially as applied to a personality, they are purely human definitions, and that consequently man in religion—in his relation to God— is in relation to his own nature; for to the religious sentiment these predicates are not mere conceptions, mere images, which man forms of God, to be distinguished from that which God is in himself, but truths, facts, realities. Religion knows nothing of anthropomorphisms; to it they are not anthropomorphisms. It is the very essence of religion, that to it these definitions express the nature of God. They are pronounced to be images only by the understanding, which reflects on religion, and which while defending them yet before its own tribunal denies them. But to the religious sentiment God is a real Father, real Love and Mercy; for to it he is a real, living, personal being, and therefore his attributes are also living and personal. Nay, the definitions which are the most sufficing to the religious sentiment are precisely those which give the most offence to the understanding, and which in the process of reflection on religion it denies. Religion is essentially emotion; hence, objectively also, emotion is to it necessarily of a divine nature. Even anger appears to it an emotion not unworthy of God, provided only there be a religious motive at the foundation of this anger.

But here it is also essential to observe, and this phenomenon is an extremely remarkable one, characterising the very core of religion, that in proportion as the divine subject is in reality human, the greater is the apparent difference between God and man; that is, the more, by reflection on religion, by theology, is the identity of the divine and human denied, and the human, considered as such, is depreciated. The reason of this is, that as what is positive in the conception of the divine being can only be human, the conception of man, as an object of consciousness, can only be negative. To enrich God, man must become poor; that God may be all, man must be nothing. But he desires to be nothing in himself, because what he takes from himself is not lost to him, since it is preserved in God. Man has his being in God; why then should he have it in himself? Where is the necessity of positing the same thing twice, of having it twice? What man withdraws from himself, what he renounces in himself, he only enjoys in an incomparably higher and fuller measure in God.

The monks made a vow of chastity to God; they mortified the sexual passion in themselves, but therefore they had in heaven, in the Virgin Mary, the image of woman—an image of love. They could the more easily dispense with real woman in proportion as an ideal woman was an object of love to them. The greater the importance they attached to the denial of sensuality, the greater the importance of the heavenly virgin for them: she was to them in the place of Christ, in the stead of God. The more the sensual tendencies are renounced, the more sensual is the God to whom they are sacrificed. For whatever is made an offering to God has an especial value attached to it; in it God is supposed to have especial pleasure. That which is the highest in the estimation of man is naturally the highest in the estimation of his God; what pleases man pleases God also. The Hebrews did not offer to Jehovah unclean, ill-conditioned animals; on the contrary, those which they most highly prized, which they themselves ate, were also the food of God (*Cibus Dei,* Lev. 3: 2). Wherever, therefore, the denial of the sensual delights is made a special offering, a sacrifice well-pleasing to God, there the highest value is attached to the senses, and the sensuality which has been renounced is unconsciously restored, in the fact that God takes the place of the material delights which have been renounced. The nun weds herself to God; she has a heavenly bridegroom, the monk a heavenly bride. But the heavenly virgin is only a sensible presentation of a general truth, having relation to the essence of religion. Man denies as to himself only what he attributes to God. Religion abstracts from man, from the world; but it can only abstract from the limitations, from the phenomena; in short, from the negative, not from the essence, the positive, of the world and humanity: hence, in the very abstraction and negation it must recover that from which it abstracts, or believes itself to abstract. And thus, in reality, whatever religion consciously denies—always supposing that what is denied by it is something essential, true, and consequently incapable of being ultimately denied—it unconsciously restores in God. Thus, in religion man denies his reason; of himself he knows nothing of God, his thoughts are only worldly, earthly; he can only believe what God reveals to him. But on this account the thoughts of God are human, earthly thoughts: like man, he has plans in his mind, he accommodates himself to circumstances and grades of intelligence, like a tutor with his pupils; he calculates closely the effect of his gifts and revelations; he observes man in all his doings; he knows all things, even the most earthly, the commonest, the most trivial. In brief, man in relation to God denies his own knowledge, his own thoughts, that he may place them in God. Man gives up his personality; but in return, God, the Almighty, infinite, unlimited being, is a person; he denies human dignity, the human *ego;* but in return God is to him a selfish, egotistical being, who in all things seeks only himself, his own honour, his own ends; he represents God as simply seeking the satisfaction of his own selfishness, while yet he frowns on that of every other being; his God is the very luxury of egoism. Religion further denies goodness as a quality of human nature; man is wicked, corrupt, incapable of good; but, on the other hand, God is only good—the Good Being. Man's nature demands as an object goodness, personified as God; but is it not hereby declared that goodness is an essential tendency of man? If my heart is wicked, my understanding perverted, how can I perceive and feel the holy to be holy, the good to be good? Could I perceive the beauty of a fine picture if my mind were aesthetically an absolute piece of perversion? Though I may not be a painter, though I may not have the power of producing what is beautiful myself, I must yet have aesthetic feeling, aesthetic comprehension, since I perceive the beauty that is presented to me externally. Either goodness does not exist at all for man, or, if it does exist, therein is revealed to the individual man the holiness and goodness of human nature. That which is absolutely opposed to my nature, to which I am united by no bond of sympathy, is not even conceivable or perceptible by me. The holy is in opposition to me only as regards the modifications of my personality, but as regards my fundamental nature it is in unity with me. The holy is a reproach to my sinfulness; in it I recognise myself as a sinner; but in so doing, while I blame myself, I acknowledge what I am not, but ought to be, and what, for that very reason, I, according to my destination, can be; for an "ought" which has no corresponding capability does not affect me, is a ludicrous chimaera without any true relation to my mental constitution. But when I acknowledge goodness as my destination, as my law, I acknowledge it, whether consciously or unconsciously, as my own nature. Another nature than my own, one different in quality, cannot touch me. I can perceive sin as sin, only when I perceive it to be a contradiction of myself with myself—that is, of my personality with my fundamental nature. As a contradiction of the absolute, considered as another being, the feeling of sin is inexplicable, unmeaning. . . .

As with the doctrine of the radical corruption of human nature, so is it with the identical doctrine, that man can do nothing good, *i.e.*, in truth, nothing of himself—by his own strength. For the denial of human strength and spontaneous moral activity to be true, the moral activity of God must also be denied; and we must say, with the Oriental nihilist or pantheist: the Divine being is absolutely without will or action, indifferent, knowing nothing of the discrimination between evil and good. But he who defines God as an active being, and not only so, but as morally active and morally critical,—as a being who loves, works, and rewards good, punishes, rejects, and condemns evil,—he who thus defines God only in appearance denies human activity, in fact, making it the highest, the most real activity. He who makes God act humanly, declares human activity to be divine; he says: A god who is not active, and not morally or humanly active, is no god; and thus he makes the idea of the Godhead dependent on the idea of activity, that is, of human activity, for a higher he knows not.

Man—this is the mystery of religion—projects his being into objectivity,[2] and then again makes himself an object to this projected image of himself thus converted into a subject; he thinks of himself, is an object to himself, but as the object of an object, of another being than himself. Thus here. Man is an object to God. That man is good or evil is not indifferent to

---

2. The religious, the original mode in which man becomes objective to himself, is (as is clearly enough explained in this work) to be distinguished from the mode in which this occurs in reflection and speculation; the latter is voluntary, the former involuntary.

God; no! He has a lively, profound interest in man's being good; he wills
that man should be good, happy—for without goodness there is no happiness. Thus the religious man virtually retracts the nothingness of human
activity, by making his dispositions and actions an object to God, by
making man the end of God—for that which is an object to the mind is an
end in action; by making the divine activity a means of human salvation.
God acts, that man may be good and happy. Thus man, while he is apparently humiliated to the lowest degree, is in truth exalted to the highest.
Thus, in and through God, man has in view himself alone. It is true that
man places the aim of his action in God, but God has no other aim of action
than the moral and eternal salvation of man: thus man has in fact no other
aim than himself. The divine activity is not distinct from the human.

How could the divine activity work on me as its object, nay, work in me,
if it were essentially different from me; how could it have a human aim, the
aim of ameliorating and blessing man, if it were not itself human? Does not
the purpose determine the nature of the act? When man makes his moral
improvement an aim to himself, he has divine resolutions, divine projects;
but also, when God seeks the salvation of man, he has human ends and a
human mode of activity corresponding to these ends. Thus in God man has
only his own activity as an object. But for the very reason that he regards
his own activity as objective, goodness only as an object, he necessarily
receives the impulse, the motive not from himself, but from this object. He
contemplates his nature as external to himself, and this nature as goodness;
thus it is self-evident, it is mere tautology to say that the impulse to good
comes only from thence where he places the good.

God is the highest subjectivity of man abstracted from himself; hence
man can do nothing of himself, all goodness comes from God. The more
subjective God is, the more completely does man divest himself of his subjectivity, because God is, *per se*, his relinquished self, the possession of
which he however again vindicates to himself. As the action of the arteries
drives the blood into the extremities, and the action of the veins brings it
back again, as life in general consists in a perpetual systole and diastole; so
is it in religion. In the religious systole man propels his own nature from
himself, he throws himself outward; in the religious diastole he receives the
rejected nature into his heart again. God alone is the being who acts of
himself,—this is the force of repulsion in religion; God is the being who
acts in me, with me, through me, upon me, for me, is the principle of my
salvation, of my good dispositions and actions, consequently my own good
principle and nature,—this is the force of attraction in religion.

The course of religious development which has been generally indicated
consists specifically in this, that man abstracts more and more from God,
and attributes more and more to himself. This is especially apparent in the
belief in revelation. That which to a later age or a cultured people is given

by nature or reason, is to an earlier age, or to a yet uncultured people, given by God. Every tendency of man, however natural—even the impulse to cleanliness, was conceived by the Israelites as a positive divine ordinance. From this example we again see that God is lowered, is conceived more entirely on the type of ordinary humanity, in proportion as man detracts from himself. How can the self-humiliation of man go further than when he disclaims the capability of fulfilling spontaneously the requirements of common decency? The Christian religion, on the other hand, distinguished the impulses and passions of man according to their quality, their character; it represented only good emotions, good dispositions, good thoughts, as revelations, operations—that is, as dispositions, feelings, thoughts,—of God; for what God reveals is a quality of God himself: that of which the heart is full overflows the lips; as is the effect such is the cause; as the revelation, such the being who reveals himself. A God who reveals himself in good dispositions is a God whose essential attribute is only moral perfection. The Christian religion distinguishes inward moral purity from external physical purity; the Israelites identified the two. In relation to the Israelitish religion, the Christian religion is one of criticism and freedom. The Israelite trusted himself to do nothing except what was commanded by God; he was without will even in external things; the authority of religion extended itself even to his food. The Christian religion, on the other hand, in all these external things made man dependent on himself, *i.e.,* placed in man what the Israelite placed out of himself in God. Israel is the most complete presentation of Positivism in religion. In relation to the Israelite, the Christian is an *esprit fort,* a free-thinker. Thus do things change. What yesterday was still religion is no longer such to-day; and what to-day is atheism, tomorrow will be religion.

28. Ernest Renan, *The Life of Jesus*

Ernest Renan

For Ernest Renan (1823–92), as for many other nineteenth-century intellectuals, a crisis of faith was a pivotal life event. Renan's occurred when he was in his early twenties. He had been educated since his boyhood in ecclesiastical seminaries in the Breton town of Tréguier, had always excelled in his courses, and planned to take a degree in philology before entering the priesthood. It was through philology that doubt entered his

From Ernest Renan, *The Life of Jesus* (Boston: Roberts Brothers, 1896), pp. 11–18, 20–35. Translated from the French.

mental universe. His study of ancient Hebrew made him aware of the textual discrepancies in the Bible—for example, that the grammar of the Pentateuch actually postdated the time of Moses. Such errors in a revealed text must, he believed, incriminate the whole. In 1845, after struggling between his deep emotional attraction to Catholic religiosity and his intellectual convictions, he left the seminary. He soon came to embrace the scientific ideal with something of the same fervor he had once brought to Catholicism.

Renan's scholarly outpouring was prodigious. He wrote both philological works, such as *A General History of the Semitic Languages* (1847), and works of cultural criticism such as *The Future of Science* (inspired by the 1848 Revolution but not published until 1890), which attempted to reconcile democracy with the fact that the progress of knowledge would always be in the hands of a scientific elite. He held a major academic post only once, and then very briefly. Appointed to the chair of Hebrew at the prestigious Collège de France in 1862, he declared in his inaugural lecture that Jesus Christ was "an incomparable man" and was promptly removed by the minister of education.

Renan's *Life of Jesus* is one of the best known examples of the so-called historical criticism of the Bible. Renan began the project while on an archaeological mission in Syria to gather ancient Phoenician inscriptions, and the resulting book is suffused with his first-hand impressions of what he calls "the East." Published in 1863, the book received the condemnation of the church, and, in part because of the public controversy surrounding it, enjoyed a commercial success unprecedented for a scholarly work. New editions of five thousand copies sold out within a week. The thirteenth edition, for which Renan prepared a new preface, appeared in 1867. A selection from that preface, in which Renan discusses the method and aims of his biography of Jesus, is reprinted here.

The second selection, document 29, comes from *The Intellectual and Moral Reform of France* (1871), Renan's analysis of and response to the French defeat in the Franco-Prussian War. The pages reprinted here focus upon the relationship between religion and science (Renan's perennial theme) in the national cultures of France and Germany.

The twelve earlier editions of this work differ from one another only in trifling changes. The present edition, on the contrary, has been revised and corrected with the greatest care. During the four years since the book appeared, I have laboured incessantly to improve it. The numerous criticisms to which it has given rise have rendered the task in certain respects an easy one. I have read all those which contain anything important. I believe I can conscientiously affirm that not once have the outrage and the calumny which have been imported into them hindered me from deriving profit from the just observations which those criticisms might contain. I have weighed everything, tested everything. If in certain cases people should wonder why I have not answered fully the censures which have been made with such extreme assurance, and as if the errors alleged had been proved, it is not that I did not know of these censures, but that it was impossible for me to accept them. In such cases I have generally added in a note the texts or the considerations which have kept me from changing my opinion, or else by some slight change of expression I have endeavoured to show wherein lay the error of my critics. These notes, though very brief and doing little more than point out the original sources, are still enough to show the intelligent reader the reasonings that have guided me in the composition of my text.

To answer in detail all the charges that have been brought against me, it would have been necessary for me to triple or quadruple this volume. I should have had to repeat things which have already been well said, even in French. I must have gone into religious controversy,—a thing that I absolutely forbid myself to do. I should have had to speak of myself, a thing I never do. I write in order to put my ideas before those who seek the truth. As for those persons who in the interest of their belief must have it that I am an ignoramus, a lying spirit, or a man of bad faith, I make no attempt to modify their opinion. If that opinion is necessary for the peace of mind of certain pious people, I should feel a genuine scruple at disabusing them.

The controversy, moreover, if I had entered upon it, must have led me very often to points quite outside historical criticism. The objections made against me have come from two opposing parties. One set has been addressed to me by free-thinkers, who do not believe in the supernatural,[1] nor, consequently, in the inspiration of the sacred books; or else by theologians of the liberal Protestant school, who have come to take such broad doctrinal views that the rationalist can readily arrive at an understanding with them. These adversaries and I find ourselves on common ground; we start with the same principles; we can discuss according to the rules followed in all questions of history, philology, and archaeology. As to the refutations of my book (and these are much the most numerous) which have been made by orthodox theologians, both Catholic and Protestant, who believe in the supernatural and in the sacred character of the books of the Old and New Testaments, they all involve a fundamental misapprehension. If

---

1. By this word I always mean the *special* supernatural act, miracle, or the divine intervention for a particular end; not the general supernatural force, the hidden Soul of the Universe, the ideal, source, and final cause of all movements in the system of things.

the miracle has any reality, this book is but a tissue of errors. If the Gospels are inspired books, and true consequently to the letter, from beginning to end, I have been wholly in the wrong in not contenting myself with piecing together the broken fragments of the four texts, as the Harmonists do, sure of constructing thus an *ensemble* at once most redundant and most contradictory. If, on the contrary, miracle is a thing inadmissible, then I am right in regarding the books which contain miraculous tales as history mixed with fiction, as legends full of inaccuracies, errors, and systematic shifts. If the Gospels are like other books, I am right in treating them in the same manner as the student of Greek, Arabian, or Hindoo lore treats the legendary documents which he studies. Criticism knows no infallible texts; its first principle is to admit the possibility of error in the text which it examines. Far from being accused of scepticism, I ought to be classed with the moderate critics, since, instead of rejecting in the lump documents damaged by so much alloy, I try to get something historical out of them by cautious modifications of the story.

And let no one assert that to put the question in such a manner implies that we take for granted beforehand what is to be proved in detail,—namely, that the miracles related by the Gospels had no reality; that the Gospels are not books written by help of the Divinity. Those two negations do not with us result from our method of criticism; they are anterior to it. They are the outcome of an experience which has never been belied. Miracles are things which never happen. Only credulous people think they see them: you cannot cite a single one which has taken place in presence of witnesses competent to give a clear account of it. No special intervention of the Divinity, whether in the composition of a book, or in any event whatever, has been proved. In the very fact that one admits the supernatural, he is so far outside the province of science; he accepts an explanation which is non-scientific, an explanation which is set aside by the astronomer, the physicist, the chemist, the geologist, the physiologist,—one which the historian also must set aside. We reject the supernatural for the same reason that we reject the existence of centaurs and hippogriffs; and this reason is, that nobody has ever seen them. It is not because it has been proved to me beforehand that the evangelists do not merit absolute credence, that I reject the miracles which they relate. It is because they tell of miracles that I say, "The Gospels are legends; they may contain history, but certainly all that they set forth is not historical."

It is hence impossible that the orthodox believer and the rationalist, who denies the supernatural, can help each other much in such discussions. In the eyes of theologians, the Gospels and the contents of the Bible in general are books like no others,—books more historic than the best of histories, inasmuch as they contain no error. To the rationalist, on the contrary, the Gospels are texts to which his very business is to apply the ordinary rules of criticism. We are in this respect like Arabic scholars in presence of the Koran and the *hadith;* like Hindoo students in presence of the Vedas and the Buddhist books. Do our Arabic scholars regard the Koran as infallible? Do we accuse them of falsifying history when they relate the origins of Islamism differently from the Mussulman theologians? Do our Orientalists hold the legendary life of Buddha [*Lalitavistara*] to be an authentic biography?

How can we come to an understanding when we set out from opposite principles? All rules of criticism assume that a document subjected to examination has but a relative value; that it may be in error, and corrected by some better document. A classical scholar, persuaded that all books bequeathed to us from the past are the work of men, does not hesitate to challenge the texts when they contradict one another; when they set forth absurd statements, or those formally disproved by documents of greater authority. The orthodox believer, on the contrary, sure in advance that his sacred books do not contain an error or a contradiction, is party to the most violent tactics, to expedients the most desperate, to get out of difficulties. Orthodox exegesis is, in this way, a tissue of subtilties. A single forced interpretation may be true; but a thousand such subtilties at once cannot be true. If there were in Tacitus or Polybius errors so pronounced as those committed by Luke regarding Quirinius and Theudas, we should say that Tacitus and Polybius were wrong. Reasonings which we would not allow if the question were one of Greek or Latin literature—hypotheses which a Boissonade, or even a Rollin, would never think of—are held to be plausible when one sets himself to defend a sacred writer.

Hence it is the orthodox apologist that is guilty of bad logic when he reproaches the rationalist with falsifying history, because he does not accept word for word the documents which orthodoxy holds to be sacred. Because a fact is written down, it does not follow that it is true. The miracles of Mahomet are down in writing, as well as those of Jesus; and certainly the Arabian biographies of Mahomet—that of Ibn-Hashim, for example—have a much more historical character than the Gospels. Do we on this account admit the miracles of Mahomet? We follow Ibn-Hashim, with more or less confidence, when we have no reasons to differ from him. But when he relates to us things perfectly incredible, we make no difficulty about abandoning him. Certainly, if we had four lives of Buddha, partly fabulous, and as irreconcilable with one another as the four Gospels, and if a scholar essayed to relieve the four Buddhist narratives of their contradictions, we should not accuse that scholar of charging the texts with falsehood. It might be well should he attempt to reconcile discordant passages, or seek a compromise, a sort of neutral tale, a narrative to contain nothing impossible, in which opposing testimony should be balanced and treated with as little violence as possible. If, after that, the Buddhists believed in a lie, in the falsification of history, we should have a right to say to them: "The question here is not one of history; and if we must at times discard your texts, it is the fault of those texts which contain things impossible of belief, and which, moreover, contradict one another."

At the bottom of all discussion on such matters is the question of the supernatural. If miracle and the inspiration of certain books are actual facts, our method is false and wrong. If miracle and the inspiration of such books are beliefs without reality, our method is the right one. Now, the question of the supernatural is settled for us with absolute certainty by this simple reason, that there is no room for belief in a thing of which the world can offer no experimental test. We do not believe in a miracle, just as we do not believe in ghosts, in the devil, in sorcery, or in astrology. Have we any need to refute step by step the long reasonings of astrology in order to deny that the stars influence human events? No. For this the purely negative evidence is enough—quite as convincing as the best direct proof—that such an influence has never been established.

God forbid that we should be unmindful of the services which theologians have rendered to science! Investigation and verification of the texts which serve as authorities for this history have often been the work of orthodox theologians. The labour of criticism has been the task of liberal theologians. But there is one thing that a theologian can never be,—I mean, an historian. History is essentially disinterested. The historian has but one care,—art and truth. These two are inseparable: art guards the secret of the laws most closely related to truth. The theologian has an interest,—his dogma. Minimise that dogma as much as you will; it is still, to the artist and the critic, an insupportable burden. The orthodox theologian may be compared to a caged bird: every movement natural to it is forbidden. The liberal theologian is a bird, some of whose wing-feathers have been clipped. You think him master of himself; and in fact he is so until the moment he seeks to take his flight. Then it is seen that he is not completely the child of the air. Let us say it boldly: critical studies relating to the origin of Christianity will not have said their last word until they are cultivated in a purely secular and unprofessional spirit, after the method of Greek, Arabic, or Sanscrit scholars,—men strangers to all theology, who think neither of edifying nor of scandalising nor of defending nor of refuting dogmas.

Day and night, I presume to say, I have reflected on these questions, which ought to be discussed without any other prejudices than those that make the very essence of reason itself. The weightiest of all, unquestionably, is that of the historic value of the Fourth Gospel. Those who have never changed their view on such problems give room for the belief that they have not comprehended the whole difficulty. We may range the opinions on this Gospel into four classes, of which the following is the abridged expression:—

First opinion: "The Fourth Gospel was written by the Apostle John, the son of Zebedee. The statements contained in that Gospel are all true; the discourses which the author puts into the mouth of Jesus were actually spoken by Jesus." This is the orthodox opinion. From the point of view of rational criticism, it is wholly untenable.

Second opinion: "The Fourth Gospel is in substance by the Apostle John, although it may have been revised and retouched by his disciples. The facts related in this Gospel are direct traditions in regard to Jesus. The discourses are often free compositions, expressing only the manner in which the author conceived the mind of Jesus." This is the opinion of Ewald, and in some respects that of Lücke, Weisse, and Reuss. It is the opinion which I adopted in the first edition of this work.

Third opinion: "The Fourth Gospel is not the work of the Apostle John. It was attributed to him by some disciple of his about the year 100. The discourses are almost entirely fictitious; but the narrative parts contain valuable traditions, ascending in part to the Apostle John." This is the opinion of Weizsäcker and of Michael Nicolas. It is the opinion which I now hold.

Fourth opinion: "The Fourth Gospel is in no sense the work of the Apostle John. Neither the facts nor the discourses reported in it are historical. It is a work of the imagination, and in part allegorical, which came to birth about the year 150; and the author's purpose in it is not to recount the actual life of Jesus, but to propagate the idea which he has himself formed of Jesus." Such is, with some variations, the opinion of Baur, Schwegler, Strauss, Zeller, Volkmar, Hilgenfeld, Schenkel, Scholten, and Réville.

I cannot quite fall in with this radical party. I am still convinced that the Fourth Gospel has a real connection with the Apostle John, and that it was written about the end of the first century. I confess, however, that in certain passages of my first edition I leaned too much in the direction of authenticity. The convincing force of some arguments upon which I then insisted seems to me diminished. I no longer believe that Saint Justin put the Fourth Gospel on the same footing with the Synoptics among the "Memoirs of the Apostles." The existence of "John the Elder," a personage distinct from the Apostle John, appears to me now very problematical. The opinion that John, the son of Zebedee, wrote the work,—an hypothesis which I have never fully admitted, but for which, at moments, I felt a certain weakness,—is here discarded as improbable. Finally, I acknowledge that I was wrong in my hostility to the hypothesis of a spurious writing, ascribed to an apostle at the end of the apostolic age. The Second Epistle of Peter, the authenticity of which no one can reasonably maintain, is an example of a work, much less important no doubt than the Fourth Gospel, forged under such conditions. Moreover, this is not for the moment the capital question. The essential thing is to know what use it is fit to make of the the Fourth Gospel when one essays to write the Life of Jesus. I persist in believing that this Gospel has a substantial value equal to that of the Synoptics, and even sometimes superior. . . .

The course I have taken in discarding bibliography has often been wrongly interpreted. I believe I have plainly enough declared what I owe to the masters of German learning in general, and to each of them in particular, to prevent my silence from being taxed with ingratitude. Bibliography is useful only when it is complete. Now, the German genius has displayed such activity in the field of evangelical criticism that if I had cited all the works bearing on the questions treated in this book, I should have tripled the bulk of the notes and changed the character of my work. One cannot do everything at once. I have therefore kept to the rule of only admitting citations at first hand. . . .

The fabric of the narrative has been little changed. Certain too strong expressions as to the communistic temper which was of the essence of Christianity at its birth have been softened down. Among those holding personal relations with Jesus I have admitted some whose names do not figure in the Gospels, but who are known to us through trustworthy evidence. That which relates to the name of Peter has been modified. I have also adopted another hypothesis in regard to Levi, son of Alpheus, and his relations with the Apostle Matthew. As to Lazarus, I unhesitatingly adopt now the ingenious hypothesis of Strauss, Baur, Zeller, and Scholten, according to which the pious beggar of Luke's parable and the person restored to life by Jesus are one and the same. It will nevertheless be seen how I still make him a real person by identifying him with Simon the Leper. I adopt likewise the hypothesis of Strauss in respect of various discourses ascribed to Jesus during his last days, which appear to be quotations from writings current in the first century. The textual discussion as to the duration of the public life of Jesus has been brought to greater precision. The topography of Bethphage and Dalmanutha has been modified. The question as to Golgotha has been taken up anew, following the investigations of M. Vogüé. A person well versed in the history of botany has taught me to distinguish, in the orchards of Galilee, between trees which grew there eighteen hundred years ago and those which were not transplanted there till later. Some facts have also been communicated to me in regard to the potion administered to the crucified; and to these I have given a place. In general, in the account of the last hours of Jesus, I have toned down some phraseology which might have too much the look of history. It is here that Strauss's favorite explanations best meet the case, since here motives of symbol and dogma may be seen at every step.

I have said, and I repeat, that if in writing the Life of Jesus one should confine himself to setting forth those matters only which are certain, he must limit himself to a few lines. Jesus existed. He was from Nazareth in Galilee. There was charm in his preaching, and he left profound sayings deeply graven in the memory of his hearers. His two chief disciples were Cephas (Peter) and John the son of Zebedee. He excited the hatred of the orthodox Jews, who succeeded in having him put to death by Pontius Pilate, then procurator of Judaea. He was crucified outside the gate of the city. It was shortly after believed that he had been restored to life. This is what we should know for certain, even if the Gospels did not exist or were false, through authentic texts of incontestable date, such as the evidently genuine epistles of Saint Paul, the Epistle to the Hebrews, the Apocalypse, and other texts accepted by all. Beyond that, it is permissible to doubt. What was his family? What in particular was his affinity to that James, "the Lord's brother," who after his death plays an important part? Had he actual relations with John the Baptist, and did the most celebrated of his disciples belong to the school of the Baptist before they belonged to his? What were his ideas of the messiahship? Did he regard himself as the Messiah? What were his apocalyptic ideas? Did he believe that he would appear as the Son of Man in the clouds? Did he imagine that he wrought miracles? Were any attributed to him during his life? Did his legend grow up round himself, and had he cognisance of it? What was his moral character? What were his ideas regarding the admission of Gentiles into the Kingdom of God? Was he a pure Jew, like James, or did he break with Judaism, as the most active party in his Church did afterward? In what order of growth was his thought subsequently wrought out? Those who seek only the indubitable in history must keep silent upon all that. In respect of these questions the Gospels are not much to be relied on, seeing that they often furnish arguments for two opposite opinions, the aspect of Jesus being modified in them according to the dogmatic view of the narrator. For my part I think that in such cases it is allowable to make conjectures, provided that they are presented as such. The texts, not being historic, give no certainty; but they give something. We should not follow them with blind confidence; we should not reject their testimony with unjust disdain. We must strive to divine what they conceal, without being ever quite certain of having found it.

It is singular that on almost all these points it is the liberal school of theology that offers the most sceptical solutions. The more sensible defenders of Christianity have come to consider it advantageous to leave a gap in the historical circumstances bearing upon the birth of Christianity. Miracles and messianic prophecies, formerly the bases of the Christian apology, have come to be its embarrassment: the aim now is to put them aside. If we hearken to the partisans of this theology, among whom I could cite many eminent critics and noble thinkers, Jesus never pretended to perform a miracle; he did not believe himself to be the Messiah; he had no thought of the apocalyptic discourses which have been imputed to him touching the final catastrophe. That Papias, so clinging to tradition, so zealous to gather up the words of Jesus, was an enthusiastic millenarian; that Mark, the oldest and most authentic of the Gospel writers, is almost exclusively taken up with miracles,—matters little. The part assigned to Jesus is in this way so dwarfed that we should find it hard to tell what it was. His condemnation to death can on such an hypothesis no more be accounted for than the fortune which made him the chief of a messianic and an apocalyptic movement. Was it on account of his moral precepts or the Sermon on the Mount that Jesus was crucified? Certainly not. These maxims had for a long time been the current coin of the synagogues. No one has ever been put to death for repeating them. If Jesus was put to death at all, it was for saying something more than that. A learned man, who has taken part in these discussions, wrote me lately: "As in former times it was necessary to prove at all hazards that Jesus was God, so the Protestant theologians of our day must needs prove, not only that he was a mere man, but also that he always regarded himself as such. People persist in representing him as a man of clear intelligence, as the especially practical man; they transform him into the image and according to the spirit of modern theology. I believe with you that this is not doing justice to historical truth, but is neglecting an essential side of it." . . .

Pure history must construct its edifice out of two kinds of materials,— so to speak, out of two factors: first, the general state of the human mind in a given age and country; second, the particular incidents which, combining with general causes, determined the course of events. To explain history by incidental facts is as false as to explain it by principles purely philosophic. The two explanations ought mutually to sustain and complete each other. The history of Jesus and of the apostles must, before all, be a history constructed out of a vast mixture of ideas and sentiments. Nor would even that be sufficient. A thousand chances, a thousand whims, a thousand trifles, are mingled in the ideas and sentiments. To trace at this day the exact details of these chances, whims, and trifles is impossible; what legend tells us of them may be true, but it may also not be true. In my opinion, the best course to hold is to keep as close as we can to the original narratives, while we discard impossibilities, put an interrogation-mark at every point, and offer as conjectures the various ways in which the event may have taken place. I am not quite sure that the conversion of Paul came about as we have it related in the Acts; but it took place in a manner not widely different from that, for Paul himself tells us that he had a vision of the risen Jesus, which gave an entirely new direction to his life. I am not sure whether the narrative of the Acts as to the descent of the Holy Spirit on the day of Pentecost is quite historic; but the ideas which went abroad as to the baptism of fire lead me to believe that a scene took place in the apostolic circle in which thunder played a part, as at Sinai. The visions of the risen Jesus were in like manner occasioned by chance circumstances, interpreted by vivid and already preoccupied imaginations.

If liberal theologians repudiate explanations of this kind, it is because they do not wish to bring Christianity under the laws common to other religious movements; because also, perhaps, they do not sufficiently understand the theory of spiritual life. There is no religious movement in which such deceptions do not play a great part. It may even be said that they make the standing condition of certain communities, such as the Protestant pietists, the Mormons, and Catholic convents. In these little excited worlds it is not rare that conversions are the result of some incident in which the stricken soul sees the finger of God. These incidents, which always have in them something puerile, are kept hid by the believers; it is a secret between Heaven and them. Chance is nothing to a cold or indifferent soul; to a soul possessed, it is a sign from God. To say that it was an outward incident which changed Paul or Ignatius Loyola through and through, or rather which gave a new turn to their activity, is certainly inexact. It is the interior movement of these strong natures that prepares a way for the thunderclap, yet the thunderclap itself was determined by an exterior cause. All these phenomena, moreover, have to do with a moral condition which is no longer our own. In a multitude of their acts the ancients were governed by dreams they had had the night before, by inferences drawn from the object that happened first to strike their sight, or by sounds which they believed they heard. The flight of birds, currents of the air, slight nervous attacks, have determined the fate of the world. This we must say, that our judgment may be honest and impartial; and when documents fairly accurate tell us stories of this kind, we must beware how we pass them over in silence. In history there are but few details which are certain; details, nevertheless, possess always some significance. The historian's talent consists in making a true picture out of features that are of themselves but half true. . . .

The first task of the historian is to sketch well the environment in which the events he recounts took place. Now, the history of religious beginnings transports us into a world of women and children, of heads hot or dizzied. These facts, placed before minds of a positive order, are absurd and unintelligible: this is why countries such as England, ponderously rational, find it impossible to comprehend anything about them. The thing that lacks in the arguments, once so famous, of Sherlock or Gilbert West upon the resurrection, of Lyttelton upon the conversion of Saint Paul, is not the reasoning process,—that is a triumph of solidity; it is the just appreciation of the difference in environment. Every religious effort we are clearly acquainted with exhibits a prodigious mixture of the sublime and the ridiculous. Read those narratives of primitive Saint Simonism, written with admirable candour by the surviving adepts.[2] By the side of repulsive exhibitions, tasteless declamations, what charm, what sincerity, when the man or the woman of the people enters upon the scene, bearing the artless confession of a soul which opens to the first gentle ray that has struck it! There is more than one example of beautiful, durable things which have been founded upon strange puerilities. It were needless to seek for any proportion between the conflagration and the spark that lights it. The devotion of Salette is one of the great religious events of our age.[3] These cathedrals, so noble, of Chartres or Laon, were reared upon illusions of the same sort. . . . We could instance movements, absolutely sincere, which have sprung up about impostors. The discovery of the holy lance at Antioch, in which the fraud was so patent, decided the fortune of the Crusades. . . .

Let us guard against applying our scrupulous distinctions, our reasonings of cool and clear heads, to the appreciation of these extraordinary events, which are at once so much above and beneath us. One would make Jesus a sage, one a philosopher, one a patriot, one a good man, one a moralist, one a saint. He was not any one of these. He was a charmer. Let us not make the past in our own image. Let us not believe that Asia is Europe. With us, for example, the madman is a creature outside the common rule; we torture him so as to make him re-enter it: the horrible methods of the old mad-houses were the result of scholastic and Cartesian logic. In the East, the lunatic is a privileged being; he enters the highest councils without any one daring to stop him; he is listened to, he is consulted. He is a being believed to be nearer to God, inasmuch as, his individual reason being extinguished, he is believed to be a partaker in the divine reason. . . .

Troubled consciences cannot have the clearness of good sense. Now, it is only troubled consciences that lay foundations with power. I have tried to draw a picture in which the colours should be blended as they are in nature, which should be a likeness of humanity,—that is to say, at once

2. *Oeuvres de Saint-Simon et d'Enfantin* (Paris: Dentu, 1865–66).

3. That of Lourdes seems to be taking equal proportions. [The nineteenth century saw a resurgence of popular Catholic religiosity in France in the form of pilgrimages to shrines where the Virgin Mary was alleged to have appeared and to continue to dispense miraculous healing powers. The most famous of these shrines were at La Salette and Lourdes, small mountain villages where in 1846 and 1858 respectively the apparition was made to shepherd children. The Lourdes miracle cult ultimately proved to be the more popular and long lasting.—Ed.]

grand and puerile, in which one should see the divine instinct threading its way with safety through a thousand peculiarities. If the picture had been without shadow, this would have been the proof that it was false. The condition of the written proofs does not permit us to say in what cases the illusion was conscious of itself. All that we can say is, that sometimes it was so. One cannot lead for years the life of a wonder-worker without being often cornered,—without having one's hand forced by the public. The man who has a legend in his lifetime is led tyrannically by his legend. One begins by artlessness, credulity, absolute innocence,—one ends in all sorts of embarrassments; and, in order to sustain the divine power which is at fault, he gets out of these embarrassments by the most desperate expedients. When one is pushed to the wall, must he leave the work of God to perish because God is slow to show himself? Did not Joan of Arc more than once make her Voices speak in response to the need of the moment? If the account of the secret revelation which she made to King Charles VII. has any reality,—which it is difficult to deny,—it must be that this innocent girl gave out as supernatural intuition what she had heard in confidence. An exposition of religious history which does not throw some cross-light upon suggestions of this sort, is by that very fact argued to be incomplete.

Every true or probable or possible circumstance must then have place in my narration, together with its shade of probability. In such a history it was necessary to speak not only of what actually took place, but also of that which may probably have taken place. The impartiality with which I treated my subject forbade me to reject a supposition, even a painful one; for undoubtedly there was much to shock in the way things came to pass. From beginning to end I have applied the same process in an inflexible manner. I have spoken the good impressions which the texts have suggested to me; I must not, therefore, be silent as to the bad. I have wished that my book might keep its value even in the day when people should come to regard a certain amount of fraud as an element inseparable from religious history. It was necessary to make my hero noble and charming,— for undeniably he was so; and that, too, in spite of actions which in our days would be judged unfavorably. I have been praised for attempting to construct a narrative living, human, and possible. Would my work have deserved these praises if it had pictured the origins of Christianity as absolutely spotless? That would have been to admit the greatest of miracles; and the result of this would have been a picture lifeless to the last degree. I do not say that in lack of faults I ought to have invented some. . . .

The same difficulty presents itself, moreover, in the history of the Apostles. This history is admirable in its way; but what can be more shocking than the "speaking with tongues," which is attested by unexceptionable texts of Paul? Liberal theologians admit that the disappearance of the body of Jesus was one of the grounds for the belief in the resurrection. What does that signify, but that the Christian conscience at that moment was two-sided; that one-half of that conscience gave birth to the illusion of the other half? If the same disciples had taken away the body, and then spread themselves over the city crying, "He is risen!" the imposture would have been called by the right name. But, no doubt, it was not the same persons who did the two things. For belief in a miracle to be accepted, it is indeed necessary that some one be responsible for the first rumour which is spread abroad; but, ordinarily, this is not the principal actor. His part is limited to making no protest against the reputation which has been given him. Even if he did protest, it would be useless; popular opinion would prove stronger than he. . . . Fraud shared among many grows unconscious of itself; or, rather, it ceases to be fraud, and becomes misapprehension. Nobody in that case deceives deliberately; everybody deceives innocently. Formerly it was taken for granted that every legend implies deceivers and deceived; in our opinion, all the parties to a legend are at once deceived and deceivers. A miracle, in other words, presupposes three conditions: first, general credulity; second, a little complaisance on the part of some; third, tacit acquiescence in the principal actor. Let us not, through reaction against the brutal explanations of the eighteenth century, fall into the trap of hypotheses which imply effects without cause. Legend does not spring up of itself; outside help brings it to the birth. The points it rests on are often extremely slight. It is the popular imagination that makes the snowball; there was, however, an original nucleus. The two persons who composed the two genealogies of Jesus, knew quite well that the lists were not of any great authenticity. The apocryphal books, the alleged apocalypses of Daniel, Enoch, and Esdras, proceed from persons of strong convictions; but the authors of these works knew well they were neither Daniel, Enoch, nor Esdras. . . . We should say the same of the author of the Fourth Gospel, surely a person of first-rate importance. Drive the illusion of religious history out of one door, and it re-enters by another. In fine, one can hardly mention a great event of the past which took place in an entirely defensible manner. Shall we cease to be Frenchmen because France was founded by centuries of perfidy? Shall we refuse to profit by the benefits of the Revolution because the Revolution committed crimes without number? . . .

Science alone is pure, for science has nothing to do with practice: it does not touch men; the Propaganda takes no heed of it. Its duty is to prove, not to persuade or to convert. He who has discovered a theorem publishes its demonstration for those who can understand it. He does not go up into a pulpit; he does not gesticulate; he has no recourse to oratorical artifices to get it adopted by those who do not perceive its truth. Enthusiasm, certainly, has its good faith, but it is the good faith of a child; it is not the deep reflective good faith of the critical scholar. The ignorant yield only to bad reasonings. If Laplace had had to gain the multitude over to his system of the world, he could not have limited himself to mathematical demonstrations. M. Littré, in writing the Life of a man whom he regards as his master, could push candour so far as to leave nothing unsaid, however it might lower him in general esteem. That is without example in religious history. Science alone seeks after pure truth. She alone offers good reasons for truth, and carries a severe criticism into the employment of her means of conviction. This is no doubt the reason why, till now, she has had no influence on the people. In the future, perhaps, when people are better instructed, as we are led to hope they may be, they will yield only to good formal proofs. But it would not be fair to judge the great men of the past on such grounds. There are natures that resign themselves to impotence,— that accept humanity, with all its weaknesses, such as it is. Many great things could not have been accomplished without lies or without violence. If to-morrow the incarnate ideal were to come and offer itself to men to govern them, it would find itself confronted by folly, which wishes to be deceived; by self-will, which insists on being beaten down. The only one without reproach is the contemplative man, who aims simply to find the truth, without caring either to make it triumph or to apply it to facts.

Ethics is not history. To paint and to relate is not to approve. The naturalist who describes the transformations of a chrysalis neither blames nor praises it. He does not tax it with ingratitude because it abandons its shroud; he does not regard it as rash because it unfolds its wings; he does not accuse it of folly because it aspires to soar into space. One may be the passionate friend of the true and the beautiful, and yet show himself indulgent to the simple ignorance of the people. The ideal alone is spotless. Our happiness has cost our fathers torrents of tears and rivers of blood. In order that pious souls may taste at the foot of the altar the inward consolation which gives them life, it has needed centuries of tyrannical restraint, the mysteries of sacerdotal polity, a rod of iron, fires of martyrdom. The respect due to every great institution demands no sacrifice of historical good faith. Formerly, to be a good Frenchman, it was necessary to believe in Clovis's dove, in the national antiquities of the Treasure of Saint Denis, in the virtues of the oriflamme, in the supernatural mission of Joan of Arc; it was necessary to believe that France was the first of nations, that French royalty was superior to all other royalties, that God had a predilection for that crown wholly unique, and was constantly engaged in protecting it. To-day we know that God protects equally all kingdoms, all empires, all republics; we own that many kings of France have been contemptible men; we recognise that the French character has its faults; we frankly admire a multitude of things which come from abroad. Are we on that account worse Frenchmen? We can say, on the contrary, that we are better patriots; since, instead of being blind to our faults, we seek to correct them, and in place of maligning the foreigner, seek to imitate the good there is in him. In like manner we are Christians. He who speaks with irreverence of mediaeval royalty, of Louis XIV., of the Revolution, of the Empire, commits an act of bad taste. He who does not speak gently of Christianity and of the Church of which he forms a part makes himself guilty of ingratitude. But filial gratitude ought not to be carried to the length of closing our eyes to the truth. One is not wanting in respect to a government when he points out that it has not succeeded in satisfying the conflicting needs that are in man; or to a religion, in saying that it is not free from the formidable objections which science raises against all supernatural belief. Responding to certain social demands and not to certain others, governments fall by the very causes that have founded them and made their strength. Responding to the aspirations of the heart despite the protests of reason, religions crumble away in turn, because no force hitherto has succeeded in stifling reason.

Disastrous to Reason the day when she should stifle religion! Our planet, believe me, is toiling at some mighty task. Do not pronounce rashly upon the inutility of such and such of its parts; do not say that it is needful to suppress this wheelwork, which seems only to thwart the play of the others. Nature, which has endowed the animal with an infallible instinct, has put into humanity nothing deceptive. From his organs you may fearlessly infer his destiny. *Est Deus in nobis.* Religions are false when they attempt to prove the infinite, to define it, to incarnate it (if I may so speak); but they are true when they affirm it. The greatest errors they import into that affirmation are nothing compared to the value of the truth which they proclaim. The simplest of the simple, provided he practise heart-worship, is more enlightened as to the reality of things than the materialist who thinks he explains everything by chance or by finite causes.

29. Ernest Renan, *The Intellectual and Moral Reform of France* (1871)

In the conflict which has just ended, the inferiority of France was mainly intellectual; what we lacked was not heart, but head. Public education is of paramount importance; French intelligence is enfeebled and must be fortified. Our greatest error is to believe that man is born already educated. The German, it is true, believes too much in teaching; he becomes a ped-

From *France: Empire and Republic, 1850–1940*, edited and translated by David Thomson (New York: Harper and Row, 1968), pp. 229–34. Copyright © 1968 by David Thomson. Reprinted by permission of Harper and Row, Publishers, Inc.

ant. But we do not believe in it enough. Lack of faith in science is a grave failing in France; our military and political inferiority has no other cause. We are too distrustful of what reflection and informed cooperation can achieve. Our system of education needs radical reform; almost everything the First Empire did in this direction is bad. Public education cannot be given directly by the central authority. A Ministry of Public Education will always be a very mediocre education machine.

Primary schooling is the most difficult to organize. We envy the superiority of Germany in this respect; but it is not philosophical to want the fruit without the trunk and roots. In Germany, popular education came from Protestantism. Lutheranism made religion consist of reading a book, and later reduced Christian dogma to an intangible quintessence, thereby giving unusual importance to the schoolhouse; the illiterate have been almost driven away from Christianity, they are sometimes refused Holy Communion. Catholicism, on the other hand, made salvation depend on sacraments and supernatural beliefs, and so regards the school as of secondary importance. To excommunicate somebody who can neither read nor write seems to us impious. Since the school is not the annex to the Church, it is the Church's rival. The *curé* is suspicious of it, tries to keep it as poor as possible, and even prohibits it if it is not entirely clerical. And without the collaboration and good will of the *curé*, the village school will never flourish. We may well hope that Catholicism will reform itself and relax its old-fashioned rules! A *curé*, a Catholic pastor, could do so much, offering every village the model of a well-ordered family, looking after the school, almost a schoolmaster himself, giving to the education of the peasant the time that he spends in tedious repetition of his breviary! In truth, Church and school are equally necessary; a nation can no more do without one than the other. When Church and school oppose each other, everything goes badly.

We touch here on the problem which underlies all others. France wanted to remain Catholic, and is experiencing the consequences. Catholicism is too hieratic to provide intellectual and moral nourishment for the population. It permits transcendent mysticism to flourish side by side with ignorance. It has no moral effectiveness. It has a fatal influence on the development of the brain. A pupil of the Jesuits will never be an officer capable of opposing a Prussian officer; a pupil from the Catholic elementary schools will never be able to engage in a scientific war with improved weapons. The Catholic nations which do not reform themselves will always inevitably be beaten by the Protestant nations. Supernatural beliefs are like poison which kills if the dose is too strong. Protestantism does put a certain amount in its brew; but the proportion is small and therefore beneficial. The Middle Ages had created two controllers of the life of the spirit, the

Church and the University. The Protestant countries have kept these two foundations; they created liberty in the Church and liberty in the University so that these countries can have Established Churches and official education, together with full liberty of conscience and education. The rest of us have had to have separation of the Church in order to obtain liberty; the Jesuits had long ago reduced our universities to a secondary role. And so our efforts have been feeble, for they are not linked to any tradition or to any institution of the past.

A liberal, such as we are, is in an acute dilemma; for it is our first principle that in anything affecting liberty of conscience the State has no right of interference. Faith, like all exquisite things, is sensitive; at the least touch it complains of violence. We should aim at liberal reform of Catholicism, without State intervention. Let the Church admit two categories of believers, those who hold to the letter, and those who believe in the spirit. At a certain level of rational culture, belief in the supernatural becomes for many an impossibility; do not force them to wear a cope of lead. Do not interfere with what we teach or what we write, and we will not compete with you for the people; do not dispute our place in the university and the academy, and we will leave you in sole possession of the village school. The human spirit is a ladder where every rung is necessary. What is right at one level is not right at another; what is harmful for one is not so for another. Keep for the people their religious education, but leave us free. There is no powerful development of the brain without liberty; moral energy is the result not of any particular doctrine, but of the race and the vigor of its education. There has been enough talk of the decadence of Germany, presented as a hotbed of enervating errors and dangerous subtleties. It was killed, they said, by sophism, Protestantism, materialism, pantheism and fatalism. I would not swear to it that M. de Moltke does not confess to one of these errors; but one must concede that it does not prevent him from being a very good staff officer. Let us renounce these fatuous rantings. Liberty of thought allied to the highest culture, far from weakening a country, is one condition for the full development of the intelligence. No one particular solution strengthens the mind; what does strengthen it is discussion and liberty. It could be said that for the educated man there is no bad doctrine. For him every doctrine is a striving toward the truth, a useful exercise for the health of the mind. You want to keep your young men in a sort of intellectual gynaeceum; you will make limited men of them. If you want to turn out good scientists, and serious, dedicated officers, you must have an education open to everything, without narrowing dogma. Intellectual and military superiority will henceforth belong to the nation which thinks freely. Everything which exercises the brain is salutary. Furthermore, liberty of thought in the universities has the advantage that the free thinker is content to reason unhampered from his chair, among people with the same point of view as himself, and is therefore not tempted to make propaganda among other people of high or low degree. The German universities offer a very curious example in this respect.

Our secondary education, although open to criticism, is the best part of our system of teaching. Good pupils from a Paris lycée are better than young Germans in their talent for writing, the art of composition. They are better prepared to be lawyers or journalists; but they do not know enough facts. We must persuade ourselves to let science rank much higher than what we in France call *"lettres."*

Teaching ought to be mainly scientific; the result of education ought to be that the young man knows as much as possible of what the human mind has discovered about the reality of the universe. When I say scientific, I do not mean practical or professional; the State should not concern itself with occupational training, but it should take care that the education it gives is not limited to empty rhetoric, which does not strengthen the intelligence. We in this country esteem only brilliant gifts, talent, wit, genius. In Germany these gifts are rare, perhaps because they are not highly thought of. There are few good writers. Journalism and public speaking are not so brilliant as here. But brainpower, learning, balanced judgment, are much more widely spread, and result in a level of intellectual culture superior to anything that has yet been achieved in any nation.

It is in higher education that a reform is most urgent. The special schools thought up by the Revolution, the puny faculties created by the Empire, in no way replace the fine, great system of autonomous, rival universities, a system Paris created in the Middle Ages and which Europe has kept, except for France, in fact, which introduced it about 1200. By returning to this system we should not be imitating anyone, but merely renewing our own tradition. There must be created in France five or six universities, independent from one another, independent of the towns where they are established, and independent of the clergy. At the same time the special schools must be abolished: the Polytechnic, the *École Normale,* etc.—useless institutions if you possess a good system of universities and which impede the development of the universities. These schools skim the cream off the university students with disastrous consequences. The university teaches everything, prepares for everything, and within its walls all branches of the human mind touch and embrace. Beside the universities there must and should be schools of instruction; there must not be closed State schools in competition with the universities. There are complaints that the Faculties of Letters and Science have no diligent students. Is this surprising? Those who ought to be there are at the *École Normale,* or the Polytechnic, where they receive the same teaching, but without experiencing anything of the healthy interplay and community spirit created by a university.

Without prejudice, naturally, to the University of Paris and those great foundations which are unique, such as the *Collège de France,* and which are proper to Paris, universities set up in provincial towns seem to me to provide the best method of reawakening the French spirit. They would be schools founded on serious study, honesty and patriotism. Real liberty of thought would develop, which does not flourish without hard work. They would also effect a healthy change in the spirit of youth. They would encourage respect; they would adopt the idea of the importance of science. One factor which gives much cause for reflection is this: it is recognized that our schools are centers of irresponsible democratic thought and disbelief, tending to frivolous popular propaganda. It is quite the opposite in Germany, where the universities are centers of the aristocratic spirit, reactionary (as we would say), and almost feudal centers of free thought, but not of indiscreet proselytism. What is the reason for this difference? It is because in German universities liberty of discussion is absolute. Rationalism has very little bearing on democracy. Reflection teaches that reason is not the simple expression of the ideas and wishes of the masses, but the result of the apperceptions of a small number of privileged individuals. Far from being inclined to hand over the public administration to the whims of the mob, a generation which has been trained in this way will jealously preserve the privilege of reason, and will be hard-working, studious, and not very revolutionary. Science will be a title of nobility for this generation, which will not renounce it easily and which will even defend it with some ruthlessness. Young men educated to a sense of their own superiority will revolt if they count for no more than one, like just anybody. Filled with the just pride which is bestowed by awareness of knowing the truth of which the common herd is ignorant, they will not wish to be the interpreters of the superficial thoughts of the crowd. The universities will thus be nurseries of aristocrats. In that case, the sort of antipathy which the French conservative party entertains toward the highest culture of the mind will appear as the most inconceivable nonsense and the gravest of mistakes.

It goes without saying that beside these universities endowed by the State, open to all opinions knowledgeably presented, complete latitude will be left for the establishment of free universities. I believe that these free universities will produce but very mediocre results; whenever liberty really exists within the universtiy, liberty outside the university is of little consequence, but by permitting them to be set up you would have a clean conscience and you would silence those naïve people who always tend to believe that they would perform wonders if it were not for the tyranny of the State. It is quite probable that the most fervent Catholics, like Ozanam, for example, would prefer the wide range of the State universities, where everything goes on in the open, to these little universities behind closed doors founded by their own sect. In any case, they would have the choice. What could these Catholics most ready to rise against State monopoly complain about in such an arrangement? Nobody would be excluded from university chairs because of his opinions. Catholics would be appointed like everybody else.

The system of *Privatdocent* would further permit all doctrines to be expounded independently of the endowed chairs. Finally, the free universities would remove the last remaining excuse for recriminations. It would be the opposite of our French system, which proceeds by the exclusion of brilliant people. We think that we have done enough for impartiality if, when we have dismissed or refused to appoint a freethinker, we dismiss or refuse to appoint a Catholic. In Germany they set them face to face; instead of serving only mediocrity, their system serves the emulation and awakening of intelligence. By distinguishing the degrees carefully and the right to exercise a profession, as they do in Germany, by laying down that the university does not train doctors or lawyers, but makes men fit to become doctors or lawyers, some of the difficulties would be removed which certain people object to in the conferring of degrees by the State. In such a system the State does not reward certain scientific or literary opinions; in the highest social interests, and for the benefit of all kinds of opinion, it opens up great fields, vast arenas, where different feelings can be expressed and debated among themselves and can vie for the approbation of the young people who attend these discussions, and who are already matured by deep thought.

30. The Politics of Anticlericalism: Speeches by Jules Ferry, Léon Gambetta, and Paul Bert

The Politics of Anticlericalism in the Early Third Republic

The French Third Republic was declared on 4 September 1870, a few days after the Prussians decisively defeated the French at the Battle of Sedan, bringing obloquy upon the imperial government of Napoleon III, which had been prosecuting the war. For the next six or seven years, however, the Third Republic was a republic in name only, as monarchists worked behind the scenes to use this moment of acute political instability to their own ends. The decisive turning point—the so-called republicanization of the republic—occurred only in 1877–79, as a result of a

From *Les fondateurs de la Troisième République*, edited by Pierre Barral (Paris: A. Colin, 1968), pp. 168–70, 173–76, 200–202. Translated for this volume by Paula Wissing.

complex political drama including an attempted monarchist coup and a number of bitterly contested national elections.

Once they were firmly in control of the state, the republicans' main immediate agenda was a negative one: diminishing the official role of the Catholic church in the national culture, especially in the public educational system. A series of laws embodied this policy: one of 9 August 1879 set up state normal schools to train primary schoolteachers of both sexes; one of 21 December 1880 established state secondary schools for girls, thus wresting away a population that had been traditionally taught almost exclusively by nuns; and one, the most famous, of 28 March 1882 made facilities for "laic" primary instruction obligatory in every village and town. (The terms *laïque* and *laïcité* gained currency during this period and denoted the secularization of civil society and the strict division between the religious and civil spheres.) Other laic laws, not related to education, were those authorizing divorce, permitting businesses to remain open on Sundays, and abolishing public prayers at the opening of parliamentary sessions.

Document 30 is composed of speeches and a ministerial circular by three of the most prominent republican politicians of the era, all exponents of the ideology of anticlericalism. Jules Ferry (1832–93), a lawyer by training, served in the cabinet almost without interruption from 1879 to 1885, twice as prime minister. His name is associated both with the establishment of the laic state school system and with the acquisition of French colonies in Africa and especially Indochina. Léon Gambetta was the most charismatic of the group, a fiery orator whose famous "Le cléricalisme, voilà l'ennemi" functioned as a battle cry. Gambetta was responsible for the declaration of the republic in 1870, and he served as prime minister from the end of 1881 until his premature death the next year. That his burial was entirely a civil ceremony—without priests and without prayers—shocked many contemporaries and was intended in part to inculcate by example the spirit of republican anticlericalism. Paul Bert (1833–86) was an eminent physiologist who combined a scientific and a political career. He served as minister of education in Gambetta's cabinet and wrote a widely disseminated pedagogical manual, *Civic Instruction in the Schools.*

Document 31 offers a glimpse at what the laicization of the school system, by laws made in Paris, meant in the French provinces. The new schoolteachers, trained in the new normal schools and staffing the compulsory primary schools, functioned as missionaries of secularization and republicanization in the towns and villages to which they were sent; they often met with strong and protracted resistance from the local religious authorities. The teachers' autobiographical sketches in document 31 were among those solicited during the school year 1911–12 by the Ministry of Public Education.

Jules Ferry, *The State Must Be Secular*

Given before the Chamber of Deputies, 3 June 1876

I pronounce the words *secular state* without any trepidation, even though, for some of our honorable colleagues they would seem to have a certain radical, anarchist, or revolutionary flavor. Yet I am not saying anything new, revolutionary, or anarchist when I maintain that the state must be secular, that the totality of society is necessarily represented by secular organizations.

What, exactly, is this principle? It is a doctrine that [the Catholic church] prides itself on having introduced into the world: the doctrine of the separation of temporal and spiritual power. Yes, Christianity introduced the doctrine of the separation of these two domains, the realm of the state and that of conscience, the temporal and the spiritual. It was successful, after centuries of struggle, in the midst of full-blown paganism. However, there is one reproach we could make against the church in this matter. After taking four or five centuries to introduce this doctrine, the church has then spent seven or eight centuries vehemently attacking it. (Applause from the left.)

Gentlemen, what was the key accomplishment, the major concern, the great passion and service of the French Revolution? To have built this secular state, to have succeeded in making the social organisms of society exclusively secular, to have taken away from the clergy its political organization and role as a cadre within the state—that, precisely, is the French Revolution in its full reality. Well now, we do not presume to convert the honorable members seated on this side of the Chamber [i.e., on the right] to the doctrines of the revolution. We only wish it to be well understood that we do not deviate from these doctrines. Convinced that the first concern, the first duty of a democratic government is to maintain incessant, powerful, vigilant and efficient control over public education, we insist that this control belong to no authority other than the state. We cannot admit, we will never admit, and this country of France will never admit that the State can be anything but a secular one. ("Very good! Very good!" from the left and center left.)

Léon Gambetta, *Clericalism, That Is the Enemy*

Given before the Chamber of Deputies, 4 May 1877

While some people do not have the right of association, barely even have the right of public assembly, others have every option, privilege, and meeting place at their disposal. They have every freedom to seek, receive, transmit or admit members into their societies or to dissolve them; they may disguise themselves, or take on all sorts of corporate anonymity or enter into partnerships. They are the only ones in France who are privileged to be above the law, which they carelessly violate, thereby offering to the world the painful spectacle of a state placed under tutelage almost by its own consent. (Bravos and prolonged applause from the left and some seats on the right.)

We have come to the point where we ask ourselves if the state is not now part of the church,

From the left: "That's it. Very good."

Mr. Gambetta: . . . contrary to the truth of those principles that maintain that the church must be part of the state.

From the left: "Very good! Very good!"

Mr. Gambetta: Gentlemen, if we do not find a speedy remedy against this invasive spirit that touches all and neglects nothing—for it is thanks to this spirit that, at home, in the workshops, the fields, everywhere, this opinion has spread: this certainty that ultramontanism, or clericalism, is all-powerful to protect the material interests of those who form its clientele— If, I say, we do not adopt a quick solution to resist this spirit of invasiveness and corruption, clericalism will attain the dual goal it has set for itself: the conquest of the state and the leadership of the masses.

From the left: "Well said! Well said!"

Mr. Gambetta: That is the predicament we are in!

Now, are we truly innovators when we have just said, not in the name of our republican ideas—that would be our duty—, nor in the name of French democracy—that would be our mission—but in the name of the indefeasible rights of societies that wish to remain free and self-governing. . . . Are we innovators when we say that it is time to make the churches, whatever they are, respect the laws and time to reintegrate the churches into the subordinate, inferior positions that they should hold in our society? (Vigorous applause from the left and from several seats in the center.)

. . . You feel then, you admit that there is one thing in this country that inspires as much loathing as the Old Regime, that is repulsive to the peasants of France (noisy interruptions from the right) . . . and that is the domination of clericalism? (Bravos and applause from the left and the center.)

You are right, and it is for that reason that I say it from the height of this rostrum, so it becomes precisely your condemnation before the tribunal of universal suffrage! (Noises from the right.) And I am only translating the innermost feelings of the people of France when I say of clericalism what my friend Peyrat said one day, "Clericalism? That is the enemy!" (Acclamations and prolonged applause from the left and center. The speaker, descending from the podium, receives the congratulations of a great number of his colleagues.)

Paul Bert, *Civic Education*

Speech of 21 March 1880, Le Havre

Yes, it is necessary for the child to be familiar with his country's political organization and learn at the same time a few ideas about its social organization. . . . But there is more to it. The child must not only be acquainted with the state of society but love it as well, so that if necessary, when he is grown, he may devote himself to it, or defend it. They tell a story about Louis XV's tutor, who took the child out onto the balcony one day and, showing him the crowd assembled in the square, said to him, "Sire, this entire people is yours!" I think that Louis XV loved that social body. Well, to make the child love the milieu in which he will live the teacher has only to say to him, "No one commands you except the law! Here no one is master except for the nation. You are a part of that nation, and, if there are 10 million electors, you partake, for your 10 millionth, of the same advantages as your fellow citizens, and you partake of the same rights."

But when the instructor has said that to the child, he must go further still. He must make him aware of the superiority of the democratic regime over the monarchy. The child must be made to understand how the first is the reign of equality, the second that of privilege. The first is the regime of rights, the other that of arbitrary power. Teach the child that man must count on only his own development and improvement, that he has nothing to gain from the capricious favors or the indulgences of those above him, that it is through labor that he becomes the master of his fate, for the democratic state is based on equality and justice, and must accord to everyone the share and place attained by his own merit. (Very vigorous applause.)

He must also say to the child—and this is of considerable importance—that under the monarchy he who suffers has recourse only to charity, while in the democratic state, along with charity—not supplanting it but cooperating with it—is solidarity. That is, alongside the duty morality imposes on each individual is the duty imposed on society itself by its policy to come to the aid of those who suffer. And concerning all these advantages of the democratic regime, the teacher must show the child how far we are from the realization of all its promises, how our present social condition displays imperfections. For the child will thus learn how to be patient about a passing misfortune and at the same time how to work to make it disappear when he is called upon to vote! (New burst of applause.)

How do we achieve this? By doing what we were just doing, by comparing for the child the social condition preceding the revolution with the one that followed it. There is nothing more fruitful, more instructive, and I would say even more necessary than this astonishing contrast. We have the right, the duty, to make it.

Does this mean to say that we would like to have politics introduced into the schools?

Yes and no.

No, if we understand by politics that the child must know what happens every day in the houses of government, who is minister today and who will be minister tomorrow. Yes, if you call politics the teaching of this truth: that this social condition in which he lives and which one day he will have the duty of preserving dates from the revolution. The introduction of the love of the principles of '89 into public education is a law of social defense, in the true meaning of the word. For since the Bonapartist party has lost its leaders, and consequently no longer has any reason for being, France is cleanly divided between the sons of the revolution and the fomenters of the counterrevolution. Well! We want it, the country wants it, the millions of votes that have given us the power have at the same time given us the order to act so that the principles of the Revolution triumph over its adversaries. (Applause.)

Jules Ferry, *Letter to Teachers* (17 November 1883)

The law of 28 March[1] is marked by two tendencies that complement without contradicting each other: on the one hand, the law excludes the teaching of any particular dogma from the required program; on the other, it accords moral and civic education the highest rank. Religious instruction belongs to the home and the church; moral instruction belongs to the

1. The so-called Ferry Law of 28 March 1882 made primary education mandatory and specified that its content be wholly secular in nature. The law also stipulated that the primary school curriculum include "moral and civic instruction."—ED.

school. The legislator thus did not intend to undertake a purely negative project. Undoubtedly, his first goal was to separate school and church, to assure the freedom of conscience for both masters and pupils, to distinguish at last between two domains that have been for too long confused: that of beliefs, which are personal, free, and variable; and that of knowledge, which is common and indispensable to all, consensual. But there is something else in the law of 28 March. It is a declaration of our will to found our own national education and base it on those notions of duty and right that the lawmaker does not hesitate to place among the first truths no one can fail to know. For this keystone of education, it is upon you, gentlemen, that the public powers have counted.

By dispensing you from religious instruction, we have no thoughts of freeing you from the teaching of morals. That would be removing the dignity of your profession. On the contrary, it seemed completely natural that the teacher, while teaching children to read and write, teach them as well the elementary rules of the moral life, which are no less universally accepted than those of grammar and mathematics.

. . . You do not, strictly speaking, have to teach anything new, anything that is not already as familiar to you as it is to all good people. And when we speak to you of your mission and apostolate, you should not misunderstand us. You are not the apostles of a new gospel. The legislator did not wish to transform you into philosophers or makeshift theologians. He asks of you what one may ask of any man of heart and sense. It is impossible for you to see all these children who gather around you every day to listen to your lessons, who observe your conduct and are inspired by your example, at the age when the mind awakens, the heart opens, the memory becomes enriched, without your having the idea of taking advantage of this docility and this confidence for purposes of moral instruction. You cannot help but give, along with what is strictly speaking, scholarly knowledge, the very principles of morality—by which I mean that good, simple, and ancient morality that we received from our parents and that in our relationships in life we all pride ourselves on following without troubling to examine its philosophical basis.

You are the auxiliary and, in some respects, the substitute for the father of the family. Speak then to his son as you would wish one to speak to your own: with force and authority every time it is a question of an incontestable truth, of a matter of common morality: with the greatest reserve the moment you risk touching upon a religious feeling of which you are not the judge.

If at times you are at a loss to know exactly how far you may go in your moral teaching, here is a practical rule for you to follow. The moment you are planning to propose any precept or maxim to your students, ask your-

self if you know of any good man who could be offended by what you are
going to say. Ask yourself if any family man present in your class and hearing you could with good faith refuse to assent to what you say. If the answer
is yes, refrain from saying it. If not, speak boldly, for what you are going to
communicate to the child is not your own wisdom, but that of the human
race. It is one of the ideas of a universal order that centuries of human
civilization have bequeathed us. However narrow this circle of action may
seem, make it a point of honor never to leave it. Remain within its boundaries rather than overstepping them. You can never be too scrupulous about
touching that delicate and sacred thing that is a child's conscience. But,
once you are thus loyally confined to the humble and secure role of every-
day morality, what do we ask of you? Speeches? Wise explanations? Brilliant exposés, scholarly teaching? No! Family and society ask you to help
raise their children, to make honest people of them. That is to say that they
expect not words but acts, not another course added to the program but a
completely practical service that you can render to the country more as a
man than as a teacher.

31. French Schoolteachers' Testimonies from the Early Third Republic

Haute-Vienne

October, 1899. I have been appointed to a village forty miles from my family. My chief is an old, sweet-faced sister still in the service in spite of the
laicization of the department. She received me with a great deal of cordiality and animation, looked at me from behind her spectacles, and declared, "We shall get on well together, I can see that." Sister Mélanie, her
companion, is faded and as colorless as a tapestry figure.

My room, a closet about as big as a handkerchief, is hung in blue paper
covered with birds chasing each other. My classroom is long and narrow,
very low, with a worm-eaten, shaky door which opens out on a sunken
path. The desks are old and shaky, too, but my enthusiasm is great, and my
aspirations are boundless. *Monday.* I have eighty-five pupils. Later on
others will be coming along, who are now picking potatoes. I feel be-
wildered in the face of this crowd of little people. I have passed the day
organizing my classes and getting things under way. The principal came
into my classroom this morning, made the sign of the cross, and all the

From *France: Empire and Republic, 1850–1940,* edited and translated by David Thomson (New York: Harper and Row, 1968), pp. 239–43. Copyright © 1968 by David Thomson.
Reprinted by permission of Harper and Row, Publishers, Inc.

pupils chanted prayers for a half-hour. What could one do? And this morning Sister Mélanie, coming in stealthily, took a seat at the farther end of my classroom, gave me a friendly little nod, and started the little ones on syllable exercises. Now I understand the words of the academy inspector when he gave me this "position of responsibility," "You will need patience and tact, Mademoiselle."

Rhône

I am the only teacher in a little village near Lyons. Rising at six in the morning, I put my little home in order. I have a clean, attractive apartment which the municipality has fitted out above the classroom. There are four bright airy rooms, with fireplaces, running water in the kitchen sink, and electricity everywhere. In short, I have all the modern conveniences, as well as a new school that looks like a little villa, with beds of roses on either side of the entrance door and flowering shrubs around the playground.

Rhône

In the eyes of the peasant and the working man the teacher, correctly dressed and decently lodged, is a lady, almost an aristocrat. It should surely be a simple matter to keep children in a brilliantly lighted, well-ventilated room that is heated in winter and kept cool in summer! To have one rest day a week besides Sunday, to have holidays at Christmas and Easter and two long months of liberty in August and September—is not that an enviable existence? So a latent but real jealousy springs up among these workers, who have no idea of the exhausting labors of the school teachers.

Vienne

This is a country of large landholders. The town provides my lodging and my property is not negotiable: woods that thrive under the open sky, meadows where the grass touches the knees of the cattle, red-soil lands where the crops form green rivers. I have no *métayers* to call me "our gentleman," as in the olden times. I am far away, and that is a great objection. My mother came to see us. Her *coif* was not like those in this part of the country. These are important matters, things that help establish a reputation. Finally I have no horse and carriage, and since I read late into the night I am judged eccentric.

Haute Loire

We must please everybody, and especially the good electors of Monsieur the Mayor; if not, look out for trouble! Please everybody, but how, especially when politics are involved?

Monsieur the Mayor comes into the school as if it were his own house, or rather as if it were a barn, to drag the teacher off to the town hall, while the pupils dance in the classroom. Another day he sends the teacher to the next hamlet for an entire afternoon in order the help the tax collector, who is allotting the firewood in the forest. Meanwhile the children, who have been set at liberty, gambol in the village streets, in the fields, or in the woods.

A small farmer said to me one day in speaking of his son, "I should like to make a teacher out of him but for the fact that he would have to be everybody's dog."

Vendée

The task is hard for us teachers in the Vendean country, where the priest and the squire are in league against us and our teaching. Think of being awakened with a start in the night by abusive noises made under your windows according to orders, of reading each morning on your door odious anonymous posters pasted there during your sleep. In the classroom itself you encounter the ill-will of the children, their apathy, and their indolence. Are you obliged to scold for careless work, for a lesson half learned, for vulgar language? The child sneers and says half aloud, "I will go over to the good sisters."

Mayenne

From the moment of my arrival at B————, I turned my attention to making myself popular with the children and to winning the hearts of the mothers. The population sought to make things hard for me. I was spied upon, and the children were questioned to see if I had not been guilty of intolerance. The *curé* organized the campaign. He gave orders to close the doors in my face when I made my first round of visits. He used every means to make life unbearable for me and to keep me shut up at home. But I was not long in gaining a real influence over this community, and ever since I have been guarding it as a treasure. Established as it is in the popular confidence, my school is, so to speak, invulnerable. The violent attacks on the "schoolbooks" slipped by unnoticed. Not a single mother listened to the belligerent suggestions so freely made.

Sarthe

My financial situation would be precarious enough if I were not secretary of the town council and treasurer of the savings bank. At forty-one years of age, with a salary of 1800 francs, I am grouped in the teachers of the third class.[1] I have four children, and truly we should be in misery but for my outside work. In fact, the teacher is a government employee who cannot earn his living at teaching. He is obliged to resort to other work in order to keep his family alive.

Lot-et-Garonne

While adding a small sum to his slender income, the schoolmaster who serves as town clerk unquestionably increases his prestige in the community. Though he be ever so little conversant with his duties, he nevertheless quickly becomes indispensable to the village, and the mayor and the other inhabitants of the locality consult him daily.

Corrèze

One teacher founded consecutively a savings bank, a school lunchroom, a school pharmacy, a museum, a library, a society for the prevention of cruelty to animals, a temperance society, an alumni association, a loan fund for farmers, a farmers' syndicate, a mutual fire-insurance society, and a cattle-insurance society. Another teacher is the confidant of the peasants.

The peasant, surrounded by sharpers who prey upon his weakness and ignorance, is glad to have somebody in whom to confide. He becomes devoted body and soul to the schoolmaster who can win his affection. He makes the schoolmaster his counselor, his secretary, his confidant. Of all the compensations in my career, this was one of the greatest and most satisfactory. The good teacher has nothing to fear from pupils or parents; on the contrary, he derives his strength from them.

32. Edmund Gosse, *Father and Son*

Edmund Gosse's *Father and Son* (1907) is an autobiographical account of its author's childhood and adolescent relationship with his father; it is the latter who is the main object of our concern here.

1. I.e., who have served the State for at least ten years.

From Edmund Gosse, *Father and Son: A Study of Two Temperaments* (Boston: Houghton Mifflin, 1965), chap. 5, pp. 74–81, 84–87.

Philip Gosse (1810–88) was a naturalist, devoted to the collection of zoological specimens and to the microscopic examination of animalcules. He established his scientific reputation with *The Birds of Jamaica* (1847), the result of an expedition to the Caribbean sponsored by the British Museum. He then turned his attention to the field that was to become his speciality, marine fauna, publishing *A Naturalist's Rambles on the Devonshire Coast* (1853). Having been able to keep marine animals alive in captivity for almost a year, a feat unprecedented at the time, he is credited with the invention of the aquarium, the subject (and title) of a book he published in 1854. Two years later he was elected fellow of the Royal Society in recognition of his scientific achievements.

In addition to being a scientist, Gosse was a rigorous Calvinist, a member of a sect called the Plymouth Brethren, which eschewed all priests, rituals and festivals, focusing exclusively upon the reading and exposition of Scripture. Chapter 5 of *Father and Son*, partially reprinted here, describes the conflict between Philip Gosse's two passions—the scientific and the religious—in 1857, the year he learned that Charles Darwin and A. R. Wallace were preparing to make a joint preliminary announcement of their theory of evolution. (Darwin's great book, *The Origin of Species*, would appear two years later.) Determined to reconcile Scripture with scientific discovery, the indefatigable Gosse senior produced *Omphalos* in a matter of weeks, articulating a conception of "prochronic time"—that is, a temporal dimension extending backward that may never have transpired in historical time. Prochronic time was, said Gosse, etched upon all living things as a mark of the divine conception of the cyclical nature of life. In the divine mind, each living thing must necessarily have ancestors as well as progeny. Thus the growth rings of a tree, for example, might not all represent years actually endured by that particular tree; some might be markers of the divine plan, according that tree, like every other, an existence in prochronic time. Gosse was thoroughly satisfied with this solution to his intellectual dilemma; but, as his son recounts below, the response of contemporary reviewers of the book was far from laudatory.

If Philip Gosse failed to persuade his contemporaries that seeming discrepancies between religious truth and scientific truth could be easily rectified, he failed to transmit either of his twin passions to his only child: the creed of Edmund Gosse, a poet, literary critic, and translator, was agnosticism and aestheticism.

It was . . . with my Father, that I became accustomed to make the laborious and exquisite journeys down to the sea and back again. His work as a naturalist eventually took him, laden with implements, to the rock-pools on the shore, and I was in attendance as an acolyte. But our earliest winter in South Devon was darkened for us both by disappointments, the cause of which lay, at the time, far out of my reach. In the spirit of my Father were then running with furious velocity, two hostile streams of influence. I was standing, just now, thinking of these things, where the Cascine ends in the wooded point which is carved out sharply by the lion-coloured swirl of the Arno on the one side and by the pure flow of the Mugnone on the other. The rivers meet, and run parallel, but there comes a moment when the one or the other must conquer, and it is the yellow vehemence that drowns the purer tide.

So, through my Father's brain, in that year of scientific crisis, 1857, there rushed two kinds of thought, each absorbing, each convincing, yet totally irreconcilable. There is a peculiar agony in the paradox that truth has two forms, each of them indisputable, yet each antagonistic to the other. It was this discovery, that there were two theories of physical life, each of which was true, but the truth of each incompatible with the truth of the other, which shook the spirit of my Father with perturbation. It was not, really, a paradox, it was a fallacy, if he could only have known it, but he allowed the turbid volume of superstition to drown the delicate stream of reason. He took one step in the service of truth, and then he drew back in an agony, and accepted the servitude of error.

This was the great moment in the history of thought when the theory of the mutability of species was preparing to throw a flood of light upon all departments of human speculation and action. It was becoming necessary to stand emphatically in one army or the other. Lyell was surrounding himself with disciples, who were making strides in the direction of discovery. Darwin had long been collecting facts with regard to the variation of animals and plants. Hooker[1] and Wallace,[2] Asa Gray[3] and even Agassiz,[4] each in his own sphere, were coming closer and closer to a perception of that secret which was first to reveal itself clearly to the patient and humble genius of Darwin. In the year before, in 1856, Darwin, under pressure from Lyell, had begun that modest statement of the new revelation, that "abstract of an essay," which developed so mightily into "The Origin of Spe-

1. Sir Joseph Hooker, English botanist and close friend of Darwin.
2. A. R. Wallace, English biologist and co-discoverer with Darwin of the principle and theory of evolution.
3. American botanist; sometimes a critic, but more often a defender, of Darwin's ideas.
4. Jean L. R. Agassiz, Swiss-American naturalist and geologist. Agassiz ultimately rejected Darwin's ideas. On more than one occasion he held public debate on the subject with his Harvard colleague Gray.

cies." Wollaston's[5] "Variation of Species" had just appeared, and had been a nine days' wonder in the wilderness.

On the other side, the reactionaries, although never dreaming of the fate which hung over them, had not been idle. In 1857 the astounding question had for the first time been propounded with contumely, "What, then, did we come from an orangoutang?" The famous "Vestiges of Creation" had been supplying a sugar-and-water panacea for those who could not escape from the trend of evidence, and who yet clung to revelation. Owen[6] was encouraging reaction by resisting, with all the strength of his prestige, the theory of the mutability of species.

In this period of intellectual ferment, as when a great political revolution is being planned, many possible adherents were confidentially tested with hints and encouraged to reveal their bias in a whisper. It was the notion of Lyell, himself a great mover of men, that before the doctrine of natural selection was given to a world which would be sure to lift up at it a howl of execration, a certain body-guard of sound and experienced naturalists, expert in the description of species, should be privately made aware of its tenour. Among those who were thus initiated, or approached with a view towards possible illumination, was my Father. He was spoken to by Hooker, and later on by Darwin, after meetings of the Royal Society in the summer of 1857.

My Father's attitude towards the theory of natural selection was critical in his career, and, oddly enough, it exercised an immense influence on my own experience as a child. Let it be admitted at once, mournful as the admission is, that every instinct in his intelligence went out at first to greet the new light. It had hardly done so, when a recollection of the opening chapter of Genesis checked it at the outset. He consulted with Carpenter,[7] a great investigator, but one who was fully as incapable as himself of remodelling his ideas with regard to the old, accepted hypotheses. They both determined, on various grounds, to have nothing to do with the terrible theory, but to hold steadily to the law of the fixity of species. It was exactly at this juncture that we left London, and the slight and occasional, but always extremely salutary personal intercourse with men of scientific leading which my Father had enjoyed at the British Museum and at the Royal Society came to an end. His next act was to burn his ships, down to the last beam and log out of which a raft could have been made. By a strange act of wilfulness, he closed the doors upon himself for ever.

5. English entomologist and conchologist.
6. Sir Richard Owen, the greatest comparative anatomist of the day.
7. W. B. Carpenter, English physiologist.

My Father had never admired Sir Charles Lyell. I think that the famous "Lord Chancellor manner" of the geologist intimidated him, and we undervalue the intelligence of those whose conversation puts us at a disadvantage. For Darwin and Hooker, on the other hand, he had a profound esteem, and I know not whether this had anything to do with the fact that he chose, for his impetuous experiment in reaction, the field of geology, rather than that of zoology or botany. Lyell had been threatening to publish a book on the geological history of Man, which was to be a bomb-shell flung into the camp of the catastrophists. My Father, after long reflection, prepared a theory of his own, which, as he fondly hoped, would take the wind out of Lyell's sails, and justify geology to godly readers of "Genesis." It was, very briefly, that there had been no gradual modification of the surface of the earth, or slow development of organic forms, but that when the catastrophic act of creation took place, the world presented, instantly, the structural appearance of a planet on which life had long existed.

The theory, coarsely enough, and to my Father's great indignation, was defined by a hasty press as being this—that God hid the fossils in the rocks in order to tempt geologists into infidelity. In truth, it was the logical and inevitable conclusion of accepting, literally, the doctrine of a sudden act of creation; it emphasised the fact that any breach in the circular course of nature could be conceived only on the supposition that the object created bore false witness to past processes, which had never taken place. For instance, Adam would certainly possess hair and teeth and bones in a condition which it must have taken many years to accomplish, yet he was created full-grown yesterday. He would certainly—though Sir Thomas Browne denied it—display an *omphalos*, yet no umbilical cord had ever attached him to a mother.

Never was a book cast upon the waters with greater anticipations of success than was this curious, this obstinate, this fanatical volume. My Father lived in a fever of suspense, waiting for the tremendous issue. This "Omphalos" [8] of his, he thought, was to bring all the turmoil of scientific speculation to a close, fling geology into the arms of Scripture, and make the lion eat grass with the lamb. It was not surprising, he admitted, that there had been experienced an ever-increasing discord between the facts which geology brings to light and the direct statements of the early chapters of "Genesis." Nobody was to blame for that. My Father, and my Father alone, possessed the secret of the enigma; he alone held the key which could smoothly open the lock of geological mystery. He offered it, with a glowing gesture, to atheists and Christians alike. This was to be the universal panacea; this the system of intellectual therapeutics which could not but

8. The Greek word for "navel" or "umbilical."

heal all the maladies of the age. But alas! atheists and Christians alike looked at it and laughed, and threw it away.

In the course of that dismal winter, as the post began to bring in private letters, few and chilly, and public reviews, many and scornful, my Father looked in vain for the approval of the churches, and in vain for the acquiescence of the scientific societies, and in vain for the gratitude of those "thousands of thinking persons," which he had rashly assured himself of receiving. As his reconciliation of Scripture statements and geological deductions was welcomed nowhere; as Darwin continued silent, and the youthful Huxley was scornful, and even Charles Kingsley, from whom my Father had expected the most instant appreciation, wrote that he could not "give up the painful and slow conclusion of five and twenty years' study of geology, and believe that God has written on the rocks one enormous and superfluous lie,"—as all this happened or failed to happen, a gloom, cold and dismal, descended upon our morning tea cups. It was what the poets mean by an "inspissated" gloom; it thickened day by day, as hope and self-confidence evaporated in thin clouds of disappointment. My Father was not prepared for such a fate. He had been the spoiled darling of the public, the constant favourite of the press, and now, like the dark angels of old,

> so huge a rout
> Encumbered him with ruin.[9]

He could not recover from amazement at having offended everybody by an enterprise which had been undertaken in the cause of universal reconciliation.

During that grim season, my Father was no lively companion, and circumstance after circumstance combined to drive him further from humanity. He missed more than ever the sympathetic ear of my Mother; there was present to support him nothing of that artful, female casuistry which insinuates into the wounded consciousness of a man the conviction that, after all, he is right and all the rest of the world is wrong. My Father used to tramp in solitude round and round the red ploughed field which was going to be his lawn, or sheltering himself from the thin Devonian rain, pace up and down the still-naked verandah, where blossoming creepers were to be. And I think that there was added to his chagrin with all his fellow mortals a first tincture of that heresy which was to attack him later on. It was now that, I fancy, he began, in his depression, to be angry with God. How much devotion had he given, how many sacrifices had he made, only to be left storming round this red morass with no one in all the world to care for him except one pale-faced child with its cheek pressed to the window!

9. John Milton, *Paradise Lost,* VI, 873–74.

After one or two brilliant excursions to the sea, winter, in its dampest, muddiest, most languid form, had fallen upon us and shut us in. It was a dreary winter for the wifeless man and the motherless boy. We had come into the house, in precipitate abandonment to that supposed answer to prayer, a great deal too soon. In order to rake together the lump sum for buying it, my Father had denuded himself of almost everything, and our sticks of chairs and tables filled but two or three rooms. Half the little house, or "villa" as we called it, was not papered, two-thirds were not furnished. The workmen were still finishing the outside when we arrived, and in that connection I recall a little incident which exhibits my Father's morbid delicacy of conscience. He was accustomed, in his brighter moments— and this was before the publication of his "Omphalos"—occasionally to sing loud Dorsetshire songs of his early days, in a strange, broad Wessex lingo that I loved. One October afternoon he and I were sitting on the verandah, and my father was singing; just round the corner, out of sight, two carpenters were putting up the framework of a greenhouse. In a pause, one of them said to his fellow: "He can zing a zong, zo well's another, though he be a minister." My Father, who was holding my hand loosely, clutched it, and looking up, I saw his eyes darken. He never sang a secular song again during the whole of his life.

Later in the year, and after his literary misfortune, his conscience became more troublesome than ever. I think he considered the failure of his attempt at the reconciliation of science with religion to have been intended by God as a punishment for something he had done or left undone. In those brooding tramps round and round the garden, his soul was on its knees searching the corners of his conscience for some sin of omission or commission, and one by one every pleasure, every recreation, every trifle scraped out of the dust of past experience, was magnified into a huge offence. He thought that the smallest evidence of levity, the least unbending to human instinct, might be seized by those around him as evidence of inconsistency, and might lead the weaker brethren into offence. The incident of the carpenters and the comic song is typical of a condition of mind which now possessed my Father, in which act after act became taboo, not because each was sinful in itself, but because it might lead others into sin. . . .

Of our dealings with the "Saints," a fresh assortment of whom met us on our arrival in Devonshire, I shall speak presently. My Father's austerity of behaviour was, I think, perpetually accentuated by his fear of doing anything to offend the consciences of these persons, whom he supposed, no doubt, to be more sensitive than they really were. He was fond of saying that "a very little stain upon the conscience makes a wide breach in our communion with God," and he counted possible errors of conduct by hundreds and by thousands. It was in this winter that his attention was particularly drawn to the festival of Christmas, which, apparently, he had scarcely noticed in London.

On the subject of all feasts of the Church he held views of an almost grotesque peculiarity. He looked upon each of them as nugatory and worthless, but the keeping of Christmas appeared to him by far the most hateful, and nothing less than an act of idolatry. "The very word is Popish," he used to exclaim, "Christ's Mass!" pursing up his lips with the gesture of one who tastes assafoetida by accident. Then he would adduce the antiquity of the so-called feast, adapted from horrible heathen rites, and itself a soiled relic of the abominable Yule-Tide. He would denounce the horrors of Christmas until it almost made me blush to look at a hollyberry.

On Christmas Day of this year 1857 our villa saw a very unusual sight. My Father had given strictest charge that no difference whatever was to be made in our meals on that day; the dinner was to be neither more copious than usual nor less so. He was obeyed, but the servants, secretly rebellious, made a small plum-pudding for themselves. . . . Early in the afternoon, the maids,—of whom we were now advanced to keeping two,—kindly remarked that "the poor dear child ought to have a bit, anyhow," and wheedled me into the kitchen, where I ate a slice of plum-pudding. Shortly I began to feel that pain inside which in my frail state was inevitable, and my conscience smote me violently. At length I could bear my spiritual anguish no longer, and bursting into the study I called out: "Oh! Papa, Papa, I have eaten of flesh offered to idols!" It took some time, between my sobs, to explain what had happened. Then my Father sternly said: "Where is the accursed thing?" I explained that as much as was left of it was still on the kitchen table. He took me by the hand, and ran with me into the midst of the startled servants, seized what remained of the pudding, and with the plate in one hand and me still tight in the other, ran till we reached the dust-heap, when he flung the idolatrous confectionery on to the middle of the ashes, and then raked it deep down into the mass. The suddenness, the violence, the velocity of this extraordinary act made an impression on my memory which nothing will ever efface.

The key is lost by which I might unlock the perverse malady from which my Father's conscience seemed to suffer during the whole of this melancholy winter. But I think that a dislocation of his intellectual system had a great deal to do with it. Up to this point in his career, he had, as we have seen, nourished the delusion that science and revelation could be mutually justified, that some sort of compromise was possible. With great and ever greater distinctness, his investigations had shown him that in all departments of organic nature there are visible the evidences of slow modification of forms, of the type developed by the pressure and practice of aeons. This conviction had been borne in upon him until it was positively irresistible. Where was his place, then, as a sincere and accurate observer? Manifestly, it was with Darwin, Wallace and Hooker. But did not the second chapter of "Genesis" say that in six days the heavens and earth were finished, and the host of them, and that on the seventh day God ended his work which he had made?

Here was a dilemma! Geology certainly *seemed* to be true, but the Bible, which was God's word, *was* true. If the Bible said that all things in Heaven and Earth were created in six days, created in six days they were,—in six literal days of twenty-four hours each. The evidences of spontaneous variation of form, acting, over an immense space of time, upon ever-modifying organic structures, *seemed* overwhelming, but they must either be brought into line with the six-day labour of creation, or they must be rejected. I have already shown how my Father worked out the ingenious "Omphalos" theory in order to justify himself as a strictly scientific observer who was also a humble slave of revelation. But the old convention and the new rebellion would alike have none of his compromise.

To a mind so acute and at the same time so narrow as that of my Father—a mind which is all logical and positive without breadth, without suppleness and without imagination—to be subjected to a check of this kind is agony. It has not the relief of a smaller nature, which escapes from the dilemma by some foggy formula; nor the resolution of a larger nature to take to it wings and surmount the obstacle. My Father, although half suffocated by the emotion of being lifted, as it were, on the great biological wave, never dreamed of letting go his clutch of the ancient tradition, but hung there, strained and buffeted. It is extraordinary that he—an "honest hodman of science," as Huxley once called him—should not have been content to allow others, whose horizons were wider than his could be, to pursue those purely intellectual surveys for which he had no species of aptitude. As a collector of facts and marshaller of observations, he had not a rival in that age; his very absence of imagination aided him in this work. But he was more an attorney than a philosopher, and he lacked that sublime humility which is the crown of genius. For, this obstinate persuasion that he alone knew the mind of God, that he alone could interpret the designs of the Creator, what did it result from if not from a congenital lack of that highest modesty which replies "I do not know" even to the questions which Faith, with menacing finger, insists on having most positively answered?

33. Leo XIII, *Rerum Novarum*

Pope Leo XIII (Vincenzo Gioacchino Pecci) was born in Carpineto, Italy, in March 1810. After his ordination to the priesthood in 1837, Pecci was assigned to the city of Benevento in the Kingdom of Naples as apostolic delegate. From 1838 until his election to the papacy in 1878, Pecci occupied a series of important diplomatic, episcopal, and curial administrative positions. In the conclave of 1878, Pecci was the candidate of the moderates in the Curia, who saw his pontificate as a transitional (and brief) one.

Against such expectations, however, Leo XIII ruled for over twenty-five years (he died in July 1903) and was responsible for many noteworthy accomplishments. He reopened channels of communication between the Vatican and the anti-Catholic regime of Bismarck in Germany and eventually saw the end of the *Kulturkampf*. Leo XIII was also instrumental in encouraging a greater sense of realism among French Catholics concerning their acceptance (if only the very grudging acceptance) of the Third Republic. The Thomistic revival in Catholic philosophy, the effects of which have endured within the late-twentieth-century church, was a third major feature of his reign. Among his most notable doctrinal statements was the encyclical *Rerum Novarum* (on the condition of the working classes), issued on 15 May 1891, selections of which appear below. The encyclical provided a moderate, non-Marxist statement of the social rights and obligations of the working classes. In its broad formulations, the encyclical reflected an intense debate over the social question within the Catholic church in the 1870s and 1880s. The pope and his curial advisors sought to acknowledge as many views as possible; his subtle mix of voluntarism and etatism, of capitalism and corporatism, was successful in offering something to almost every faction in the church, while alienating, at least publicly, very few. *Rerum Novarum* proved important in inspiring the policies of the new Christian Democratic and labor union movements that emerged in Europe after 1890 and, in the *longue durée*, in legitimating the admixture of conservatism and liberalism so characteristic of post-1945 European Center-Right party politics.

Introduction: The Worsened Condition of the Workers

1. The nations of the world have for long been disturbed by the lust for revolution and it was to be expected that once eagerness for change had

From Leo XIII, *Rerum Novarum*, translated by Joseph Kirwan (London: Catholic Truth Society, 1983).

been aroused it would spread from the field of politics into the related sphere of economics.

The coming of new industrial growth with the application of new techniques; of changed relationships between employers and employed; of immense wealth for a small number and deepest poverty for the multitude; of greater self-reliance and closer collaboration of the workers among themselves; and, finally, of a worsening of morals; from all of these changes has come an explosive struggle. The desperate anxiety which has seized upon men's minds shows how much is at stake. In learned circles, in business meetings, in popular assemblies, in legislative bodies, in councils of government, everywhere men meet there is deep concern about what is happening. No question is of more pressing importance at the present time, none more strongly grips the attention of mankind.

And so, venerable brethren, just as on former occasions when, for the sake of the Church and the common weal, we thought it opportune to address to you letters on political power, human liberty, the Christian constitution of states, and other matters of a similar kind, so also now we find ourselves drawn to write in like manner about the condition of the workers. . . .

2. . . . it is clearly universally agreed that the interests of the people at the bottom of the social scale must be consulted promptly, as befits their plight. For the most part, they are tossed about helplessly and disastrously in conditions of pitiable and utterly undeserved misery. The old working men's guilds were abolished in the last century and no other means of protection was provided in their place. At the same time, all trace of the religion of our fathers was stripped from government and the law. And so it comes about that working men are now left isolated and helpless, betrayed to the inhumanity of employers and the unbridled greed of competitors. Voracious usury makes matters worse, an evil condemned frequently by the Church but nevertheless still practised in deceptive ways by avaricious men. In addition to all this, the hiring of labour and the management of industry and trade have become concentrated into the hands of a few, so that a tiny group of extravagantly rich men have been able to lay upon a great multitude of unpropertied workers a yoke little better than that of slavery itself.

I. The False Remedy: Socialism

3. While inciting the needy to envy the wealthy owners of the means of production, the socialists argue that the remedy for this evil is the abolition of private property. Individual possessions should become common property, they say, to be administered either by local authorities or by central

government. In this transference of property from the private to the public sphere they claim to have found a cure for present ills which will lead to an equitable distribution of capital and income. Their device is ill-adapted to its purpose. It will not end the conflict; it will do harm to the working class; and it is, moreover, greatly unjust. It will do violence to lawful owners, divert government from its proper tasks and cause utter confusion in the state.

4. It is easy to see that anyone who does anything of any kind for pay does it primarily to get something as his own, something that belongs to him and to nobody else. He hires out his strength and skill to get possession of what he must have to satisfy his human needs. In working for a wage he works also for a full and perfect right to use his earnings as seems good to him. If, therefore, a man spends less on consumption and uses what he saves to buy a farm, that farm is his wage in another form, as much at his disposal as was the wage itself. It is precisely in this power of disposal that ownership consists, whether the property be in real estate or in movable goods. It follows that when socialists endeavour to transfer privately owned goods into common ownership they worsen the condition of all wage-earners. By taking away from them freedom to dispose of their wages they rob them of all hope and opportunity of increasing their possessions and bettering their condition.

5. What is even more serious is that the remedy proposed is plainly unjust, since to possess property privately as his own is a right which a man receives from nature.

In this consideration is to be found one of the greatest differences between man and the rest of the animal creation. Brute beasts do not govern themselves. They are guided and controlled by two natural instincts: one keeps them on the alert, ready to display their strength and capacity for action, the other stimulates and at the same time regulates their individual desires. By one instinct they are led to protect their own lives, by the other to propagate their species. Both purposes are served by the use of things which lie ready to hand, a condition which prevents any further development since it is only by their senses and what their senses perceive that they are moved. Man's nature is very different. At least as much as the rest of the animal creation he has full and perfect possession of animal faculties and therefore also of the enjoyment of material things. But even at its highest level, animal nature cannot set bounds to human nature, so far inferior is the one to the other. The animal nature is made to answer the call of the human nature and be obedient to it. What is most remarkable about us and distinguishes us, what classifies man as man and sets him apart from the brute creation, is the possession of mind or reason. It is because he is the only animal possessed of reason that there must be attributed to man the right not only to use things as all animals do, but also to have and to hold them in settled and permanent possession; and that applies not only to goods which are used up in their using, but also to goods which continue to give service over time.

6. This becomes even clearer when we make a deeper study of human nature in itself. Man's ability to understand an indefinitely large number of objects enables him to link the present with the future. Since he also has mastery over his own acts, he can govern himself by his own foresight and judgment, subject always to the eternal law, the guidance of God whose providence extends to all things. It follows that he has freedom to choose whatever course of action he judges to be in his own best interest, not only for the passing moment but also into the future. And from that it follows that it is right and proper for a man to have ownership, not only of the fruits of the earth, but also of the earth itself, because of his awareness that the earth is the source from which his future needs will be supplied. Because his needs are forever recurring—satisfied today, they are as pressing tomorrow—nature must have given to man access to a stable source of supply, one that is always at his disposition and on which he might expect to draw perennially. It is only the earth with its fruitfulness which can satisfy this requirement of permanency.

There is no case for introducing the providence of the state. Man is older than the state. Before any state came into existence, man had already received from nature the right to make provision for his life and livelihood.

7. An objection to private ownership cannot be based upon the fact that God has given the earth to the whole human race for them to use and enjoy. In giving the earth to mankind in general he does not intend that all should exercise dominion over it indiscriminately. It is because he does not assign any part of it to anyone in particular, but leaves this question to be settled by man's industry and established national customs, that he is said to have given it in general. Besides, however it is distributed among individuals, the earth does not cease to serve the needs which are common to all men. There is no one who does not feed upon the produce of the fields. People without capital supply labour. Thus it may truly be said that the universal means of providing the necessities and comforts of life consists in labour, whether it is applied to a man's own land or in some type of industry, earning a wage which can have no other source than the manifold fruits of the earth, for which it is exchanged. . . .

8. It is amazing that some people dissent from arguments as powerful as these and seek to resurrect bad opinions long since outworn. Enjoyment only of the different products of the soil is all they are willing to concede to a private person. They flatly deny the existence of any right of freehold possession, whether of the land on which a man has built or of a farm

which he has cultivated. They do not see that in making these denials they defraud a man of part of the produce of his labour. For the soil which is cultivated with toil and skill is greatly changed in condition: the wilderness is made productive, the infertile fruitful. That which has improved the soil becomes so completely mingled with it as to inhere in it and become to a large extent utterly inseparable from it. Does justice allow any man to seize and enjoy something which another man has stained with his sweat? As effects follow their cause, so is it right for the fruit of labour to belong to those who have given their labour. It is with good reason, then, that the common opinion of mankind has found no merit in the dissenting opinions of a few. Making a close study of nature, men have found in nature's law the basis for a distribution of goods and for private ownership and have been fully convinced that these are in the highest degree in conformity with the nature of man and with peace and tranquillity. Practice has sanctioned this conclusion throughout the ages. It is confirmed and enforced by the civil laws, which, when they are just, receive their binding force from the natural law. . . .

9. The importance of rights of this kind which inhere in individual human beings is much better understood when they are looked at in the light of their connexion with and appropriateness to the obligations imposed on men by their family relationships. It is indisputable that everyone is completely free to choose between following Christ's counsel on virginity or committing himself to the bonds of matrimony when he decides upon a state of life. No human law can take away the original natural right of a man to marry or in any way impose limits on the principal purpose of marriage ordained by God's authority from the beginning: "Increase and multiply" (Gen. 1:28). And so we have the family, the society of the household, which, small though it is, is a true society and older than any state; one therefore which must have its own rights and duties which depend not at all upon the state. Thus, the right of ownership, which we have seen to be given by nature to individual persons, must belong also to a man in his capacity of head of a family. That right is all the stronger inasmuch as the human personality is further developed in the family group.

10. A most sacred law of nature ordains that the head of a family should provide for the necessities and comforts of the children he has begotten. That same nature leads him to want to provide for his children—who recall and in some sense extend his personality—a reasonable degree of protection against ill-fortune in life's uncertain course. This he can do only by leaving income yielding property to his children as his heirs. As we have said, the family is a true society equally with the state and, like the state, it possesses its own source of government, the authority of the father. Provided that it stays within the bounds set for it by its own special purpose,

the family has for this reason at least equal rights with the state to choose and employ whatever is necessary for its rightful life and liberty. We say, at least equal rights. Inasmuch as the domestic household precedes the state, both as an idea and as a fact, it must also have prior rights and duties which are more immediately grounded in nature. Detestation of political society would quickly take the place of desire for it if citizens, families, found that when they entered upon it their rights were rendered less secure and they were hindered rather than helped.

11. It follows that to want to see the state's power arbitrarily at work within the intimacy of households is to make a great and pernicious mistake. Of course, when a family happens to be in a state of great distress, helpless and utterly unable to escape from its predicament, it is right that its pressing need be met by public aid. After all, every family is a part of the state. Similarly, when within a family there is grave dispute about mutual rights, it is for the public authority to insist upon each party giving to the other its due. In doing this the state does not rob citizens of their rights, but rather strengthens them and supports them as it should. However, rulers must stop at this point. Nature does not permit them to go further. Its origin being where human life itself begins, a father's authority is such that it can be neither abolished nor absorbed by the state. "Children are something of the father" and in some sense an extension of his personality. Strictly speaking, it is not of themselves but by virtue of the family into which they are born that children enter into and partake in civil society. And precisely because "children are naturally something of their father . . . they are held under the care of their parents until they acquire the use of free will" (St Thomas, *S. Theol.* II-II, Q. 10, art. 12). Thus, when socialists set aside parental care and put that of the state in its place they offend against natural justice and dissolve the bonds of family life.

12. The harm goes further than injustice. Exceedingly great disturbance and upset would afflict all classes. Close behind would come hard and hateful servitude for the citizens. The door would be thrown open to mutual envy, detraction and dissension. All incentive for individuals to exercise their ingenuity and skill would be removed and the very founts of wealth dry up. The dream of equality would become a reality of equal want and degradation for all. None would be spared. From this it is plain to see that the socialist doctrine of common ownership ought to be altogether repudiated. It harms those it is meant to help; it denies to individuals their rights; it throws the administration of public affairs into disorder; it disturbs the peace. The conclusion is inescapable. All who set out to improve the conditions of the masses must start from the fundamental principle that private possessions must be held inviolate. That being established, let us proceed to an explanation of where the sought-for remedy is to be found.

II. The True Remedy: Concerted Measures

A. The Action of the Church

13. We approach this matter with confidence, as we are fully entitled to do, since no good solution to the problem can be found without recourse to religion and the Church. Since the care of religion and of those matters for which the Church has responsibility falls principally to us, continued silence on our part would be seen as neglect of duty. Undoubtedly, there is need for others besides ourselves to bend their efforts to the cause: members of governments, employers and wealthy owners of the means of production, and finally those whose cause we are pleading, the people without property. Nevertheless, we do not hesitate to insist that whatever men may choose to do will be in vain if they leave out the Church. Evidently it is the Church which draws from the Gospel teaching strong enough to end the conflict or, at the very least, make it less bitter; and she it is who tries by her injunctions not merely to inform men's minds, but also to guide the life and morals of every one of them. She has highly efficient organizations which promote better conditions for the unpropertied; she urges all classes to work together in thought and action to produce the best possible solution to the difficulties of the workers; she argues that the state ought to apply its administrative and legislative authority to the same end, to the extent that the situation requires.

14. The first point to be made is that men must put up with the human predicament: in civil society it is not possible for those at the bottom to be equal with those at the top. Socialists are violently opposed to this, but they struggle in vain against the nature of things. The differences which exist naturally between men are great and many. There is no equality in talent, or skill, or health, or strength, and these unavoidable differences lead of themselves to inequalities of fortune. This is clearly of advantage both to individuals and to society. A community needs to have within it different capacities for action and a variety of services at its disposal; and men are most impelled to supply these by the differences of their condition.

As regards manual work, even in the state of innocence men would not have been wholly idle; but what they would then have chosen freely for the pleasure it gave them became, after the Fall, something to which necessity compelled them to submit, in painful atonement for their sin. "Accursed be the soil because of you. With suffering shall you get your food from it every day of your life" (Gen. 3:17). In like manner, men may not look for an end to their bitter legacy in this life. The burden of the ill-effects of sin lies heavily on them, harsh and difficult to bear. There is no escape for any man to the end of his days. To suffer and endure is the lot of men; and whatever means they use and however much they try, no art, no force can free their society from this painful condition. Anyone who claims to be able to rid the common people of all pain and sorrow and to bring them peace and a life of never-ending pleasure lies outrageously. . . .

15. In the subject under discussion it is a great mistake to imagine that class is spontaneously hostile to class, as if nature had matched together the wealthy owners of the means of production and the unpropertied workers to persist stubbornly in laying wildly about each other. This picture is so far removed from truth and reason as to be directly contrary to both. Just as the different parts of the body unite to form a whole so well proportioned as to be called symmetrical, so also nature has decreed that in the state these twin classes should correspond to each other in concord and create an equilibrium. Each stands entirely in need of the other: there can be no capital without labour, nor labour without capital. Concord begets order and beauty, whereas a continuation of conflict leads inevitably to barbarity and wild confusion. Christian institutions are possessed of marvellous and many-sided strength which enables them to put an end to conflict and to cut away its roots.

16. By constantly recalling both parties to the duties they owe each other, and especially to their obligations in justice, the teaching of religion, of which the Church is the interpreter and guardian, is immensely well qualified to bring together the wealthy owners of the means of production and the men without property. Among the obligations of justice which bind the unpropertied worker are: to fulfil faithfully and completely whatever contract of employment he has freely and justly made; to do no damage to the property nor harm to the persons of his employers; to refrain from the use of force in defence of his interests and from inciting civil discord; to avoid the company of men of evil principles who use artful promises of great results to raise extravagant hopes which can end only in vain regrets and heavy loss. For his part, the rich employer must not treat his workers as though they were his slaves, but must reverence them as men who are his equals in personal dignity and made the more noble by their Christian calling. Both natural reason and Christian philosophy agree that it does not shame a man to engage in a profitable occupation. Rather does it do him credit, for it provides him with an honourable means of livelihood. What is truly shameful and inhuman is to misuse men as instruments for gain and to value them only as so much mere energy and strength. There is an obligation to keep in view the religious needs of unpropertied men and the good of their souls. Employers must see to it, therefore, that the worker has time for his religious duties; that he is not exposed to morally corrupting influences and occasions of sin; and that he is not seduced from his domestic duties and a wise use of his earnings. Furthermore, employers must not

impose tasks which overtax a man's strength or are of a kind which is un-
fitted to a worker's age and sex.

17. However, among the major duties of employers the most important
is to give to each and every man what is just. Of course, there are many
matters to be kept in mind when a just standard of wages is being considered; but wealthy owners of the means of production and employers must
never forget that both divine and human law forbid them to squeeze the
poor and wretched for the sake of gain or to profit from the helplessness of
others. To defraud a man of the wage which is his due is to commit a griev-
ously sinful act which cries out to heaven for vengeance. "Labourers
mowed your fields, and you cheated them—listen to the wages that you
kept back, calling out; realize that the cries of the reapers have reached the
ears of the Lord of hosts" (James 5:4). Lastly, the wealthy owners of the
means of production must take scrupulous care not to harm in any way
the savings of the unpropertied, whether by force, or fraud, or usurious
dealings; and this the more so both because their poverty makes them ill-
equipped to counter injustice and because what few possessions they have
should be held the more sacred the scantier they are. . . .

18. . . . Therefore, the wealthy are warned that wealth brings neither
freedom from sorrow nor help towards the happiness of eternity, to which
indeed it is more of an obstacle (Matt. 19:23–24). Let the rich owners of
the means of production tremble at the exceptional threats of Jesus Christ
(Luke 6:24–25): God will demand the strictest accounting for the use they
make of their possessions.

19. Most excellent and of the greatest importance is the teaching on the
use to be made of wealth which philosophy discovers incompletely but the
Church gives clearly and perfectly. Moreover, she does this in such a way
as to influence men's conduct as well as inform their minds. The fundamental point of this teaching is that the rightful possession of riches is to be
distinguished from their rightful use. As has just been established, to own
goods privately is a natural right of man; and to exercise that right, particularly in society, is not only good but entirely necessary. . . . And if the
question be asked, "How must possessions be used?" the Church replies
without hesitation: "No man is entitled to manage things merely for himself, he must do so in the interests of all, so that he is ready to share them
with others in the case of necessity." . . .

This teaching can be summarized thus: whoever has been generously
supplied by God with either corporal and external goods or those of the
spirit, possesses them for this purpose—to apply them equally to his own
perfection and, in his role as a steward of divine providence, to the benefit
of others. "Let him who has a talent, therefore, be careful not to hide it;
let him who enjoys abundance watch lest he fail in generosity to the poor;

let him who possesses the skills of management be particularly careful to share them and their benefits with his neighbour" (St Gregory the Great, *Evang. Hom.* IX, n. 7).

20. As for the poor, the Church teaches insistently that God sees no disgrace in poverty, nor cause for shame in having to work for a living. Christ our Lord confirmed this by his way of life, when for our salvation he who "was rich became poor for our sake" (2 Cor. 8:9). He chose to be seen and thought of as the son of a carpenter, despite his being the Son of God and very God himself; and having done so, made no objection to spending a large part of his life at the carpenter's trade. "Surely, this is the carpenter, the son of Mary?" (Mark 8:3). . . . Knowledge of all this cannot but lower the pride of the well-to-do and lift up the heart of the poor man who is full of misery, turning the one to fellowship and the other to moderation in his desires. Thus, the separation which pride tends to create will be lessened in extent and it will not be difficult for the two classes willingly to join themselves together in bonds of friendship.

21. However, if they obey Christian teaching it will be the bond of brotherly love rather than of friendship that will unite them. They will then feel and understand the obvious truth that all men have the same Father, who is God the Creator; that all reach out for the same final good, who is God himself, who alone can bring absolutely perfect happiness to both men and angels; that by the action of Jesus Christ all alike are redeemed and re-established in the dignity of sons of God, so that all might be bound together in fraternal love, brothers to one another as they are to Christ our Lord, "the first born among many brothers." The same benefits of nature and gifts of divine grace belong in common to the whole human race, without distinction, and only those who are unworthy will be disinherited. "If we are children we are heirs as well: heirs of God and co-heirs with Christ" (Rom. 8:17).

Such is the scheme of rights and duties which Christian philosophy teaches. Where this teaching flourishes will not all strife quickly end?

22. Not content with merely pointing out the way to set things right, the Church herself takes reform in hand. She commits herself entirely to educating men by her teaching and forming them by her discipline, and by the work of her bishops and priests she seeks to spread the life-giving waters of her doctrine to the furthest possible extent. . . .

23. It must not be thought that the Church's great concern with the care of souls leads her to neglect the affairs of this earthly and mortal life. She wants expressly to see the unpropertied workers emerge from their great poverty and better their condition; and what she wants, she works for. That she calls men to virtue and forms them in its practice is no small help of itself in that direction. Complete adherence to the code of Christian morals

leads directly of itself to greater prosperity. It joins men with God, the ground and fount of all good things; it restrains an excessive appetite for material possessions and a thirst for pleasure, the twin plagues which often make even the rich man unhappy. . . .

24. In addition to this, moreover, the Church takes direct action to bring prosperity to the unpropertied by founding and fostering institutions which she knows will be conducive to their escape from poverty; and in this she has always been successful enough to wring praise even from her enemies. . . . Thus there came gradually into existence an inheritance which the Church has looked after with scrupulous care as the property of the poor. She has always tried to collect funds to help them so as to spare them the humiliation of begging. Acting as the mother of the rich owners of the means of production and of the poor alike and drawing upon the great fount of love which she everywhere creates, the Church has founded congregations of religious and many other useful institutions which have done their work so well that there is hardly any kind of need for which help is not provided. There are many today who follow the example of the heathens of old and find fault with the Church for showing such great charity. They argue that state welfare benefits should be provided instead. But there is no human device which can take the place of this Christian charity, which thinks of nothing other than to bring help where it is needed. . . .

25. However, it is not to be doubted that to do what needs to be done calls for everything that lies within men's powers. It is necessary for all who have a part to play to work and strain to do their share. As with the providence which governs the world so also here, we see that effects which depend upon a number of causes come about only when all are at work together.

B. The Action of the State

The next step to take, therefore, is to ask what part of the remedy is to be looked for from the action of the state, it being understood that in this context "state" does not refer to such examples as we find in practice in this country or in that, but to that which sound reasoning congruent with nature and the lessons of divine wisdom show to be good. All of this has been clearly explained in encyclicals on the Christian constitution of states.

26. The first task of rulers is to make use of the whole system of laws and institutions to give assistance both generally and to particular classes. Statesmanship consists in making the structure and administrative functioning of the state conduce of themselves to public and private prosperity. Bringing this about is the particular function of those who govern. The prosperity of a state is best served where there are sound morals, well-ordered family life, regard for religion and justice, moderate taxes equi-

tably levied, growing industry and trade, a flourishing agriculture, and other provisions of a like kind which it is generally agreed will contribute to the greater well-being and happiness of the citizens. By these means rulers can benefit other classes and at the same time be of the greatest help to the unpropertied. It is fully within their right to act thus and since by virtue of its office the state ought to care for the common good they are not to be accused of excessive interference. The greater the abundance of opportunities which arise out of this general care, the less will be the need to try other measures to help the workers.

27. But there is another aspect to be considered which is of very great importance in this connection. The one purpose for which the state exists is common to the highest and the lowest within it. By nature, the right of the unpropertied men to citizenship is equal to that of the wealthy owners of the means of production, for they through their families are among the true and living parts which go to form the body of the state. Indeed, it can be added, in every actual state they are greatly in the majority. Since it would be utterly absurd to care for one section of citizens and neglect another, it is evident that the public authority ought to take proper care to safeguard the lives and well-being of the unpropertied class. To fail in this would be to violate justice which bids us give to every man his due. As St Thomas has wisely said: "As a part and the whole are identical in a sense, so too in a sense that which is of the whole is also of a part" (*S. Theol.* II-II, Q. 61, art. 1, ad. 2). Consequently, not the least nor the lightest of the duties which fall to rulers in their regard for the common good, but that which comes first of all, is to keep inviolate the justice which is called distributive by caring impartially for each and every class of citizen.

However much it is necessary for all citizens without exception to make some contribution to the common good, which of itself benefits every individual, each enjoying his share, it is not possible for everyone to contribute in the same way or to an equal extent. For a state to exist at all, or even be thought possible, there have to be differences of degree among its citizens and these will persist however much forms of government may change. It will always be necessary to find people who will devote themselves to public affairs, make the laws, dispense justice, and by their counsel and authority administer affairs of state and the conduct of war. Such people have a leading part to play and ought to be accorded pre-eminence in every state. Anyone can see that their labours make an immediate and invaluable contribution to the common good. Then there are those who are engaged in some kind of business. These do not serve the state in the same way and to the same extent and, valuable though their service is, it is less direct. Lastly, although it is obvious that the social good is principally a moral good, since it ought to be of such a kind that in enjoyment of it men are made better, nevertheless a characteristic of a well constituted state is an abundance of material goods, "the use of which is necessary to virtuous action" (St. Thomas, *De Regimine Principum,* I, xv). Such goods cannot be provided without the highly productive, skilled and painstaking labour of the unpropertied workers who are employed in farms and factories. So great is their vigour and efficiency in this regard that it may truly be said that it is only by the labour of working-men that states grow rich. Equity requires of the state, therefore, that it have particular regard for the unpropertied workers, so that those who bring so much of advantage to the community should themselves be well housed and clothed, enjoy greater comfort and suffer less hardship. Whence it follows that measures ought to be supported which are seen in some way to offer an improvement of the condition of the workers. . . .

28. We have said already that the state has no authority to swallow up either the individual or the family. To the extent that the common good is not endangered or any person hurt, justice requires full freedom of action for both. . . . Since the power to rule originates in God and might be termed a participation in his supreme authority, the example to be followed is that of God's dominion which cares like a father for each individual creature as much as for the whole universe. . . .

29. The maintenance of peace and order is of as much importance to the public as to private good. Its requirements are: the regulation of family life in accordance with God's commands and the law of nature; respect for and the fostering of religion; insistence upon the integrity of public and private morals and on the sanctity of justice, so that no one shall hurt another with impunity; care for young citizens so that they can grow up strong enough to serve and, if need be, defend the state. Wherefore, should it happen that a strike or a lock-out threatens disorder; or the natural ties of the family are weakened among the unpropertied; or the practice of religion among the workers is harmed because time is not allowed to them for its observance; or the integrity of morality is endangered in the factories by indiscriminate mixing of the sexes or other evil practices which create occasions of sin; or the employing class imposes unjust burdens on the working class or afflicts them with conditions inconsistent with the dignity of the human person; or too great a burden of work damages health or has insufficient regard for sex and age; in all such cases it is plainly true that, within certain limits, the force and authority of the·law must be brought to bear. The facts of each particular case determine the limits to the application of the law; but evidently, the law must not be asked to do more nor to proceed further than is necessary to put right what is wrong or to avert what threatens.

Rights must be held sacred wherever they exist. The public authority

must enable every individual to maintain his right by providing for the prevention and punishment of transgressions. Where the protection of private
rights is concerned, special regard must be had for the poor and weak.
Rich people can use their wealth to protect themselves and have less need
of the state's protection; but the mass of the poor have nothing of their own
with which to defend themselves and have to depend above all upon the
protection of the state. Because the wage-earners are numbered among the
multitude of the poor, the state owes them particular care and protection.

30. Particular attention must now be given to certain very important
matters. At the head of the list is the duty to use the strength and protection
of the law to safeguard private possessions. At the present time, when
greed is rampant, it is of the greatest importance to keep the masses in the
way of duty. It is permissible for people to try to better themselves provided that in doing so they commit no injustice, but neither justice nor reasons of public advantage permit them to take what belongs to others and to
pounce upon the fortunes of others in the name of some foolish uniformity.
Of course, the great majority of the workers prefer to improve their condition by honest work without inflicting injury on any one; nevertheless,
there are not a few who, steeped in false opinions and eager for revolution,
seek by every means to foment trouble and urge others on to violence. The
public authority should intervene to put a brake on the activities of rabble-
rousers and thus protect workers from bad influences and legitimate owners
of property from the risk of plunder.

31. Hours that are too long, work that is too heavy, wages said to be too
low, these are reasons usually given by workers when they go on strike.
These stoppages are a frequent cause of serious inconvenience, hurt employers and employed alike, do harm to trade and damage the general public interest, bringing violence and disorder close and endangering peace.
Everybody should be seeking a remedy. Much the best and most efficacious
course is for the law to intervene in good time before trouble starts, to prevent it from erupting by removing the causes of conflict between employers
and workers.

32. There are many matters of a like kind in which the worker needs the
protection of the state. His spiritual good comes first. Good and desirable
though this mortal life is in itself, it is not the ultimate end for which we are
born. It is only the way and the means by which, through knowledge of the
truth and love of the good, we reach the perfection of the life of the soul. It
is upon the soul that is impressed the divine image and likeness and it is in
it that resides the sovereignty by virtue of which man is commanded to rule
over the whole of the lower creation and to use all the earth and the sea for
his own needs. "Be fruitful, multiply, fill the earth and conquer it. Be masters of the fish of the sea, the birds of heaven and all the living animals on

earth" (Gen. 1:28). In this respect all men are equal. There is here no difference between rich and poor, between masters and servants, between rulers and ruled: "all belong to the same Lord" (Rom. 10:12). Nor may anyone violate with impunity the dignity of man, whom God himself treats "with great reverence," or to impede progress to that perfection which corresponds with the eternal life in heaven.

It follows that no man has the power freely to consent to treatment not in accordance with his nature and to deliver his soul into slavery. . . .

33. As regards protection of this world's goods, the first task is to save the wretched workers from the brutality of those who make use of human beings as mere instruments for the unrestrained acquisition of wealth. It is evident that neither justice nor common humanity permits some men to impose upon others such a heavy burden of labour as will stupefy their minds and exhaust their bodies. A man's ability to work is limited, as is his nature, and there is a point beyond which he cannot go. He can develop his strength by training and use, but only if he obeys the rule of limited spells and frequent periods of rest. Care must be taken, therefore, not to lengthen the working day beyond a man's capacity. How much time there must be for rest depends upon the type of work, the circumstances of time and place and, particularly, the health of the workers. There must be appropriately shorter hours of work in occupations, such as mining for coal and quarrying iron and the like, where the burden of labour is particularly heavy and also injurious to health. Account should be taken also of the seasons of the year, for often what can be done easily at one time becomes quite impossible or extremely difficult at another. Finally, it is unjust to ask of a woman or a child work which is well within the capacity of a strong and healthy adult man. Great care must be taken always to prevent the employment of children in factories until they are sufficiently mature in mind and body and character. Calls which are made too early upon the strength of youth can beat it down, like new-grown grass too tender to be trodden, and quite destroy all possibility of education. It is equally true that certain types of work are less suitable for women, who are adapted rather to domestic tasks. It is these which best safeguard their womanly virtue and most correspond to the bringing-up of children and the well-being of the family. The general rule is that the greater the burden of labour the greater must be the provision for rest and recuperation: what work has taken away, rest from work must restore. In any contract made between employers and employed there is always the explicit or implicit condition that opportunities must be provided for both rest and recuperation. Any other agreement would be unjust, for there is a duty never to ask on one side, nor promise on the other, neglect of the duties which a man owes either to God or to himself.

34. The subject we now approach is of equally great importance. It is

one which must be properly understood if we are not to offend against one party or the other. It is argued that, given that the scale of wages is decided by free agreement, it would appear that the employer fulfils the contract by paying the wage agreed upon, that nothing further is due from him and that injustice will be done only if the employer does not pay the full price or the worker does not perform the whole of his task. In these cases and not otherwise it would be right for the political authority to intervene and require each party to give to the other his due. This is an argument which a balanced judgment can neither entirely agree with nor easily accept. It does not take every consideration into account; and there is one consideration of the greatest importance which is omitted altogether. This is that to work is to exert oneself to obtain those things which are necessary for the various requirements of life and most of all for life itself. "With sweat on your brow shall you eat your bread" (Gen. 3:9). Thus, human work has stamped upon it by nature, as it were, two marks peculiar to it. First, it is *personal*, because the force acting adheres to the person acting; and therefore it belongs entirely to the worker and is intended for his advantage. Second, it is *necessary*, because a man needs the results of his work to maintain himself in accordance with a command of nature itself which he must take particular care to obey. Were we to confine our attention to the personal aspect, we could take it for granted that the worker is free to agree to any rate of pay, however small. Since he works of his own free will, he is free to offer his work for a small payment, or for none at all. But this position changes radically when to the personal we join the necessary aspect of labour, as we must. For although they can be separated in theory, in practice the two are inseparable. The reality is that it is every man's duty to stay alive. To fail in that is a crime. Hence arises necessarily the right to obtain those things which are needed to sustain life; and it is only the wage for his labour which permits the man at the bottom of the ladder to exercise this right. Let workers and employer, therefore, make any bargains they like, and in particular agree freely about wages; nevertheless, there underlies a requirement of natural justice higher and older than any bargain voluntarily struck: the wage ought not to be in any way insufficient for the bodily needs of a temperate and well-behaved worker. If, having no alternative and fearing a worse evil, a workman is forced to accept harder conditions imposed by an employer or contractor, he is the victim of violence against which justice cries out. In these and similar cases—such, for instance, as the regulation of hours of labour in different industries or measures to safeguard health and safety at work—it is important to prevent the public authorities from thrusting themselves forward inconsiderately. Particularly because of the great variety of circumstances, times and places, it will be better to reserve such matters to the judgment of associations, of which more will be said later, or to find some other way by which the interests of wage-earners can be safeguarded. In the last resort appeal must be made to the help and protection of the state.

35. If a worker earns a wage which enables him to make ample provision for the needs of himself, his wife and his children, he will find it easy to practise thrift. If he is sensible, does what nature itself advises him to do and cuts out excessive expenditure, he can contrive to acquire some little property. We have seen that effective efforts to put an end to the troubles facing us must start from the principle that the right to own privately must be maintained absolutely. For that reason the law should support this right and do what it can to enable as many as possible of the people to choose to exercise it. Most valuable consequences must follow from such action, the foremost among them being a more equitable distribution of wealth. The forces of social change have split states between two classes separated by an enormous gulf. On one side stands the extremely powerful party, because extremely rich; which, being in possession of the whole of industry and trade, turns all means of production to the service of its own ends and is able to take no small part in the government of the state. On the other side stands the multitude of the weak, destitute of resources, filled with bitterness and ever ready to revolt. However, if the efforts of the people were aroused by the hope of acquiring something of what the soil contains, it would gradually come about that class would move closer to class and the gulf which separates the greatest wealth from the deepest poverty be removed. An additional benefit would be more abundant supplies of all the goods of the earth. When men work on what they know to be their own, they do so with more readiness and greater care. Indeed, they fall wholly in love with the land they cultivate and which yields them food and an abundance of other things for them and theirs. It is obvious how greatly this quickening of the will can add to the volume of production and the revenues of the state. And there is a third advantage to be looked for from this. Men prefer to remain in the land in which they were born and reared and they are less likely to leave it for foreign parts when it provides them with the means to obtain a better life.

However, one condition which must be satisfied if these benefits are to be obtained is that private means must not be exhausted by excessive taxation. Because the right to possess property privately is given by nature and not by human law, that law has no power to abolish it. All that the public authority may do is to regulate the use of property in keeping with the requirements of the common good. To take from private citizens under the guise of taxation more than is equitable is unjust and inhuman.

C. The Action of Associations

36. Finally, employers and workers can do much themselves in this matter by means of institutions which can bring timely aid to the needy and draw class closer to class. Examples of these are mutual benefit societies; foundations of various kinds to provide security for workers and their widows and orphans in cases of sudden emergency, illness and death; and welfare organizations which provide for the protection of children, adolescents and older people.

But the most important are working-men's associations, the aims of which include almost all of those listed above. The good work done by the old guilds of artisans is well known. They brought benefit to the members themselves and also did much to develop the crafts, as many monuments show. Working-men's associations have to be adapted now to the greater demands which are made on people in an age of wider education and new ways of life. It is gratifying that everywhere societies of this kind are being formed, either by workers alone or by both classes together, and it is greatly to be desired that they should become both more numerous and more efficient. . . .

37. Experience of his own weakness both impels and encourages a man to ally his forces with those of another. As the Bible puts it: "Better two than one by himself, since thus their work is really profitable. If one should fall, the other helps him up; but woe to the man by himself with no one to help him up when he falls down" (Eccles. 4:9–10); and in another place: "Brother helped by brother is a fortress, friends are like the bars of a keep" (Prov. 18:19). Just as a man is led by this natural propensity to associate with others in a political society, so also he finds it advantageous to join with his fellows in other kinds of societies, which though small and not independent are nevertheless true societies.

Because of their different immediate objectives there are many differences between these societies and the great society we call the state. The purpose for which the state exists concerns all the citizens as a whole because it comprises the common good—a good in which all and each have a right to participate in a proportionate degree. It is called a *public* society because in it "men join themselves together to form a state" (St Thomas Aquinas, *Contra impugnantes Dei cultum et religionem*, c. II). By contrast, societies which are formed within the state are said to be *private*, and rightly so because their immediate purpose is the particular interest peculiar to their own members: "A private society is one which is formed to attain private objects, as when two or three form an association to trade in common" (*ibid.*).

38. Although private societies exist within the state as parts of it, as it

were, the state does not possess the power to make a general order against their existence. It is by virtue of the law of nature that men may enter into private societies and it is for the defence of that law, not for its destruction, that the state comes into being. If the state forbids its citizens to associate together it obviously makes war upon itself, for both it and the private associations are born of one and the same principle, the natural sociability of men. There will be occasions when the law may rightly intervene against private associations, as when some among them pursue policies which are plainly contrary to honesty, justice and the good of the state itself. In cases such as these the public authority may with justice prevent the formation of associations and dissolve them where they exist. However, great care must be taken lest the rights of the citizens be emptied of content and unreasonable regulations made under the pretence of public benefit. For laws have to be obeyed only when they accord with right reason and the eternal law of God. . . .

40. Associations in immense variety and especially unions of workers are now more common than they have ever been. This is not the place to enquire into the origins of most of them, their aims or the methods they employ. There is plenty of evidence to confirm the opinion that many are in the hands of secret leaders and are used for purposes which are inconsistent with both Christian principles and the social good. They do all that they can to ensure that those who will not join them shall not eat. In this state of affairs Christian workers have but two alternatives: they can join these associations and greatly endanger their religion; or they can form their own and, with united strength, free themselves courageously from such injustice and intolerable oppression. That the second alternative must be chosen cannot be doubted by those who have no desire to see men's highest good put into extreme danger.

41. High praise is due to the many Catholics who have informed themselves, seen what is needed and tried to learn from experience by what honourable means they might be able to lead unpropertied workers to a better standard of living. They have taken up the workers' cause, seeking to raise the incomes of families and individuals, introduce equity into the relations between workers and employers and strengthen among both groups regard for duty and the teaching of the Gospel—teaching which inculcates moderation, forbids excess and safeguards harmony in the state between very differently situated men and organizations. We see eminent men coming together to learn from each other about these things and unite their forces to deal with them as effectively as possible. Others encourage different groups of workers to form useful associations, advise them, give them practical help and enable them to find suitable and well-paid employment. The bishops offer their goodwill and support; and under their authority and

guidance many of the clergy, both secular and regular, work assiduously for the spiritual interests of the members of these associations. Nor is there any lack of help from Catholics who are rich. Many have voluntarily associated themselves with the wage-earners and have spent large sums in founding and widely extending fraternal societies by means of which it becomes easy for a worker to acquire by his labour not only present advantages but also provision for honourable support in later life. . . .

42. An association has to be harmoniously organized and carefully administered if it is to arrive at agreed courses of action and a union of wills. Since citizens are possessed of a power freely to join together in associations, they must also have a right to choose freely how they shall manage their affairs and how legislate so as to attain most effectively the purposes they have set before themselves. We do not consider it possible to set forth detailed rules for the constitution and administration of these self-governing societies. These are to be largely determined in the light of careful consideration of national characteristics, past experience, the nature and efficacy of the work to be done, the stage of economic development, and many other features peculiar to the time and place. What can be done is to enunciate a general law which holds good at all times: the constitution and administration of self-governing unions of workers must be such as will enable the societies to serve their purposes most speedily and completely and thus bring to their members as great as possible an increase in physical and spiritual well-being and access to property. It is clear that perfection of faith and morals ought to be seen as being of the first importance and it is to this end that the conduct of union affairs ought to be principally aimed. Unions managed otherwise must degenerate and become like those other societies which have no place for religion. What does it profit a man if through his union he obtains a plentiful supply of material goods but finds his soul imperilled by a lack of spiritual food? "What, then, will a man gain if he wins the whole world and ruins his life?" (Matt. 16:26). Christ our Lord teaches us that this is the mark by which the Christian is to be distinguished from the heathen: "It is the pagans who set their hearts on all these things . . . Set your hearts on his kingdom first, and on his righteousness, and all these things will be given you as well" (Matt. 6:32–33). Therefore, with God as their starting point let the unions make ample provision for the religious instruction of their members to give them a thorough awareness of what is due to God—what they ought to believe, what to hope for and what to do for the sake of their eternal salvation. Particularly great care must be taken to arm them against false ideas and corrupt men who would seduce them from their path. The worker is to be urged to the worship of God and the whole-hearted practice of religion, and in particular to the observance of the holy days. Let him be led to reverence and

love the Church, the mother common to us all. Let him submit to her teaching and frequent the sacraments, the divine instruments for removing stains from his soul and preparing him for holiness.

43. When societies found their laws upon religion they can easily establish mutual relations among their members which secure their peace and prosperity. Offices should be allocated so as best to serve the common purpose, particular care being taken to ensure that distinctions do not breed discord and that the duties are distributed intelligently and defined clearly. Harm to individuals will follow if this is not done. Common funds must be properly administered and the aid appropriate to the needs of individuals be settled beforehand. The rights and duties of employers are to be suitably reconciled with the rights and duties of workers. Should a member of either class think himself to be in any way injured, nothing would be better than that the laws of the association should provide for the appointment of a committee of honest and prudent men, members of the association, whose judgment will determine the issue. It is of the greatest importance also to provide for jobs to be readily obtainable at all times and for funds to be available to relieve the needs of individuals in cases of industrial accident, sickness, old age and any other cause of distress. The willing adoption of these means will enable these Catholic societies to meet the needs of the poor suitably and sufficiently and to bring desirable aid to the prosperity of the state. It is not rash to make provision for the future in the light of past experience. Times change, but it is remarkable how far conditions remain the same because God's providence governs all. . . .

44. The condition of the workers is the question of the hour. It will be answered one way or another, rationally or irrationally, and which way it goes is of the greatest importance to the state. Christian workers can easily end matters by forming associations, choosing wise leaders and entering upon the same road as that which their fathers followed with singular advantage to themselves and to the whole community. Great though the power of prejudiced opinion and of greed may be, unless the sense of what is right be deliberately and wickedly stifled the good will of the citizens will come spontaneously to turn more and more towards those whom they see to be industrious and moderate, putting justice before gain and the sacredness of duty before all things else. A further advantage to be looked for from such a course of action is the hope and opportunity of a better life that will be offered to workers who now either altogether despise the Christian faith or live contrary to its requirements. These men know for the most part that they have been fooled by false hopes and lying appearances. They feel themselves to be treated with great inhumanity by their greedy employers who regard them as no more than so many instruments of gain; but if they are members of a union it will be of one which has no love and no affection

at its heart and is torn apart by the internal strife which is the perpetual accompaniment of proud and unbelieving poverty. Broken in spirit, worn out in body, how many wish to free themselves from servitude and humiliation! But though their desire is strong, human respect or the fear of hunger holds them back. The self-governing unions of Catholics can be of immense benefit to all of these men if they will invite them, hesitant though they are, to join them in their search for a solution to their difficulties and will receive them with faith and aid and comfort as they do so.

Conclusion

45. You know, venerable brethren, who are the people who must work hard to settle this very difficult question and how they must act. Everyone must gird himself for his part of the work and act with the utmost despatch to prevent delay from making utterly irremediable what is already so great an evil. . . .

As for the Church, whatever the time and circumstance her aid will never be looked for in vain. Those in whose hands lies the care of the general welfare must understand that the greater the freedom she is allowed, the more efficacious will be her action. All who are in holy orders must bring to the work their full strength of mind and body. Acting under your authority and inspired by your example, venerable brethren, they must never cease from setting before men of every class the pattern of life given to us by the Gospel. They must do all they can for the good of the people, particularly by way of strenuous efforts to nourish in themselves and to inspire in others the practice of charity, mistress and queen of all the virtues. For indeed it is from a great outpouring of charity that the desired results are principally to be looked for. It is of Christian charity that we speak, the virtue which sums up the whole Gospel law. It is this which makes a man ever and entirely ready to sacrifice himself for the good of others. It is this which is man's most effective antidote against worldly pride and immoderate love of self. It is of this that the Apostle Paul spoke in these words expressing its function and divine likeness: "Love is always patient and kind; it is never jealous; love is never boastful or conceited; it is never rude or selfish; it does not take offence, and is not resentful. Love takes no pleasure in other people's sins but delights in the truth; it is always ready to excuse, to trust, to hope, and to endure whatever comes: (1 Cor. 13:4—7). As a pledge of God's mercies and a sign of our good-will towards each and every one of you, venerable brethren, and to your clergy and people, we lovingly bestow upon you the apostolic benediction in the Lord.

Given at St Peter's, Rome, the 15th day of May 1891, in the fourteenth year of our pontificate.

LEO PP. XIII

34. Thomas Mann, *Buddenbrooks*

Generally regarded as one of the outstanding men of letters of the twentieth century, Thomas Mann was born in the old Hanseatic seaport of Lübeck on the Baltic coast of Germany in 1875. He was a descendant on his father's side of a long-established patrician family of merchants. His first novel, *Buddenbrooks,* published in 1901, immediately established its young author's reputation. *The Magic Mountain* (1924), the tetralogy *Joseph and His Brothers* (1933–41), and *Doctor Faustus* (1947) followed. When the Nazis came to power in Germany in 1933, Mann left his native country and settled first in Switzerland, then in the United States, finally returning to Switzerland, where he died in 1955.

Buddenbrooks is the story of four generations of a wealthy burgher family in northern Germany. It traces the family's gradual decline from the robust energy of the early mercantile ventures by which it first amassed its fortune to the ennui and nervous frailty that overtake the later descendants at the end of the nineteenth century.

This selection comes from the point in the novel at which Thomas Buddenbrook felt, Mann tells us, "inexpressibly weary and disgusted. What there was in life for him to reach, he had reached. He was well-aware that the high-water mark of his life . . . had long since passed." The family business was on the decline, and his wife, many years his junior, was having an affair with a young man. In this mood, Buddenbrook becomes convinced of his own impending death and finds himself picking up a copy of a "famous philosophical system." Although Mann does not name the text in question, it is readily identifiable as Arthur Schopenhauer's *The World as Will and as Idea* (1819), a dramatic statement of a position that might be called metaphysical pessimism.

Schopenhauer's philosophy enjoyed a vogue in Germany from the 1860s through the 1880s. Mann's fictional account of Thomas Buddenbrook's encounter with it offers an interpretation of the appeal of Schopenhauer to contemporaries.

From Thomas Mann, *Buddenbrooks,* translated by H. T. Lowe-Porter (New York: Knopf, 1924), chap. 5, pp. 508–16. Copyright 1924 and renewed 1952 by Alfred A. Knopf, Inc. Reprinted by permission of the publishers, Alfred A. Knopf, Inc., and Martin Secker and Warburg Limited.

For the truth was that Thomas Buddenbrook, at the age of forty-eight, began to feel that his days were numbered, and to reckon with his own approaching death.

His health had failed. Loss of appetite, sleeplessness, dizziness, and the chills to which he had always been subject forced him several times to call in Dr. Langhals. But he did not follow the doctor's orders. His will-power had grown flabby in these years of idleness or petty activity. He slept late in the morning, though every evening he made an angry resolve to rise early and take the prescribed walk before breakfast. Only two or three times did he actually carry out the resolve; and it was the same with everything else. And the constant effort to spur on his will, with the constant failure to do so, consumed his self-respect and made him a prey to despair. He never even tried to give up his cigarettes; he could not do without the pleasant narcotic effect; he had smoked them from his youth up. He told Dr. Langhals to his vapid face: "You see, Doctor, it is your duty to forbid me cigarettes—a very easy and agreeable duty. But I have to obey the order—that is my share, and you can look on at it. No, we will work together over my health; but I find the work unevenly divided—too much of yours falls to me. Don't laugh; it is no joke. One is so frightfully alone—well, I smoke. Will you have one?" He offered his case.

All his powers were on the decline. What strengthened in him was the conviction that it could not last long, that the end was close at hand. He suffered from strange apprehensive fancies. Sometimes at table it seemed to him that he was no longer sitting with his family, but hovering above them somewhere and looking down upon them from a great distance. "I am going to die," he said to himself. And he would call Hanno to him repeatedly and say: "My son, I may be taken away from you sooner than you think. And then you will be called upon to take my place. I was called upon very young myself. Can you understand that I am troubled by your indifference? Are you now resolved in your mind? Yes? Oh, 'yes' is no answer! Again you won't answer me! What I ask you is, have you resolved, bravely and joyfully, to take up your burden? Do you imagine that you won't have to work, that you will have enough money without? You will have nothing, or very, very little; you will be thrown upon your own resources. If you want to live, and live well, you will have to work hard, harder even than I did."

But this was not all. It was not only the burden of his son's future, the future of his house, that weighed him down. There was another thought that took command, that mastered him and spurred on his weary thoughts. And it was this: As soon as he began to think of his mortal end not as an indefinite remote event, almost a contingency, but as something near and tangible for which it behooved him to prepare, he began to investigate himself, to examine his relations to death and questions of another world. And his earliest researches in this kind discovered in himself an irremediable unpreparedness.

His father had united with his hard practical sense a literal faith, a fanatic Bible-Christianity which his mother, in her latter years, had adhered to as well; but to himself it had always been rather repellent. The worldly scepticism of his grandfather had been more nearly his own attitude. But the comfortable superficiality of old Johann could not satisfy his metaphysical and spiritual needs, and he ended by finding in evolution the answer to all his questions about eternity and immortality. He said to himself that he had lived in his forbears and would live on in his descendants. And this line which he had taken coincided not only with his sense of family, his patrician self-consciousness, his ancestor-worship, as it were; it had also strengthened his ambitions and through them the whole course of his existence. But now, before the near and penetrating eye of death, it fell away; it was nothing, it gave him not one single hour of calm, of readiness for the end.

Thomas Buddenbrook had played now and then throughout his life with an inclination to Catholicism. But he was at bottom, none the less, the born Protestant: full of the true Protestant's passionate, relentless sense of personal responsibility. No, in the ultimate things there was, there could be, no help from outside, no mediation, no absolution, no soothing-syrup, no panacea. Each one of us, alone, unaided, of his own powers, must unravel the riddle before it was too late, must wring for himself a pious readiness before the hour of death, or else part in despair. Thomas Buddenbrook turned away, desperate and hopeless, from his only son, in whom he had once hoped to live on, renewed and strong, and began in fear and haste to seek for the truth which must somewhere exist for him.

It was high summer of the year 1874. Silvery, high-piled clouds drifted across the deep blue sky above the garden's dainty symmetry. The birds twittered in the boughs of the walnut tree, the fountain splashed among the irises, and the scent of the lilacs floated on the breeze, mingled, alas, with the smell of hot syrup from a sugar-factory nearby. To the astonishment of the staff, the Senator now often left his work during office hours, to pace up and down in the garden with his hands behind his back, or to work about, raking the gravel paths, tying up the rose-bushes, or dredging mud out of the fountain. His face, with its light eyebrows, seemed serious and attentive as he worked; but his thoughts travelled far away in the dark on their lonely, painful path.

Sometimes he seated himself on the little terrace, in the pavilion now entirely overgrown with green, and stared across the garden at the red brick rear wall of the house. The air was warm and sweet; it seemed as though the peaceful sounds about him strove to lull him to sleep. Weary of lone-liness and silence and staring into space, he would close his eyes now and then, only to snatch them open and harshly frighten peace away. "I must think," he said, almost aloud. "I must arrange everything before it is too late."

He sat here one day, in the pavilion, in the little reed rocking-chair, and read for four hours, with growing absorption, in a book which had, partly by chance, come into his hands. After second breakfast, cigarette in mouth, he had unearthed it in the smoking-room, from behind some stately vol-umes in the corner of a bookcase, and recalled that he had bought it at a bargain one day years ago. It was a large volume, poorly printed on cheap paper and poorly sewed; the second part, only, of a famous philosophical system. He had brought it out with him into the garden, and now he turned the pages, profoundly interested.

He was filled with a great, surpassing satisfaction. It soothed him to see how a master mind could lay hold on this strong, cruel, mocking thing called life and enforce it and condemn it. His was the gratification of the sufferer who has always had a bad conscience about his sufferings and con-cealed them from the gaze of a harsh, unsympathetic world, until suddenly, from the hand of an authority, he receives, as it were, justification and li-cense for his suffering—justification before the world, this best of all pos-sible worlds which the master-mind scornfully demonstrates to be the worst of all possible ones!

He did not understand it all. Principles and premises remained unclear, and his mind, unpractised in such reading, was not able to follow certain trains of thought. But this very alternation of vagueness and clarity, of dull incomprehension with sudden bursts of light, kept him enthralled and breathless, and the hours vanished without his looking up from his book or changing his position in his chair.

He had left some pages unread in the beginning of the book, and hurried on, clutching rapidly after the main thesis, reading only this or that section which held his attention. Then he struck on a comprehensive chapter and read it from beginning to end, his lips tightly closed and his brows drawn together with a concentration which had long been strange to him, com-pletely withdrawn from the life about him. The chapter was called "On Death, and its Relation to our Personal Immortality."

Only a few lines remained when the servant came through the garden at four o'clock to call him to dinner. He nodded, read the remaining sen-tences, closed the book, and looked about him. He felt that his whole being had unaccountably expanded, and at the same time there clung about his senses a profound intoxication, a strange, sweet, vague allurement which somehow resembled the feelings of early love and longing. He put away the book in the drawer of the garden table. His hands were cold and unsteady, his head was burning, and he felt in it a strange pressure and strain, as though something were about to snap. He was not capable of consecutive thought.

What was this? He asked himself the question as he mounted the stairs and sat down to table with his family. What is it? Have I had a revelation? What has happened to me, Thomas Buddenbrook, Councillor of this government, head of the grain firm of Johann Buddenbrook? Was this message meant for me? Can I bear it? I don't know what it was: I only know it is too much for my poor brain.

He remained the rest of the day in this condition, this heavy lethargy and intoxication, overpowered by the heady draught he had drunk, incapable of thought. Evening came. His head was heavy, and since he could hold it up no longer, he went early to bed. He slept for three hours, more profoundly than ever before in his life. And, then, suddenly, abruptly, with a start, he awoke and felt as one feels on realizing, suddenly, a budding love in the heart.

He was alone in the large sleeping chamber; for Gerda slept now in Ida Jungmann's room, and the latter had moved into one of the three balcony rooms to be nearer little Johann. It was dark, for the curtains of both high windows were tightly closed. He lay on his back, feeling the oppression of the stillness and of the heavy, warm air, and looked up into the darkness.

And behold, it was as though the darkness were rent from before his eyes, as if the whole wall of the night parted wide and disclosed an immeasurable, boundless prospect of light. "I shall live!" said Thomas Buddenbrook, almost aloud, and felt his breast shaken with inward sobs. "This is the revelation: that I shall live! For *it* will live—and that this *it* is not I is only an illusion, an error which death will make plain. This is it, this is it! Why?" But at this question the night closed in again upon him. He saw, he knew, he understood, no least particle more; he let himself sink deep in the pillows, quite blinded and exhausted by the morsel of truth which had been vouchsafed.

He lay still and waited fervently, feeling himself tempted to pray that it would come again and irradiate his darkness. And it came. With folded hands, not daring to move, he lay and looked.

What *was* Death? The answer came, not in poor, large-sounding words: he felt it within him, he possessed it. Death was a joy, so great, so deep that it could be dreamed of only in moments of revelation like the present. It was the return from an unspeakably painful wandering, the correction of a grave mistake, the loosening of chains, the opening of doors—it put right again a lamentable mischance.

End, dissolution! These were pitiable words, and thrice pitiable he who used them! What would end, what would dissolve? Why, this his body, this heavy, faulty, hateful incumbrance, which *prevented him from being something other and better.*

Was not every human being a mistake and a blunder? Was he not in painful arrest from the hour of his birth? Prison, prison, bonds and limitations everywhere! The human being stares hopelessly through the barred window of his personality at the high walls of outward circumstance, till Death comes and calls him home to freedom!

Individuality?—All, all that one is, can, and has, seems poor, grey, inadequate, wearisome; what one is not, can not, has not, that is what one looks at with a longing desire that becomes love because it fears to become hate.

I bear in myself the seed, the tendency, the possibility of all capacity and all achievement. Where should I be were I not here? Who, what, how could I be, if I were not I—if this my external self, my consciousness, did not cut me off from those who are not I? Organism! Blind, thoughtless, pitiful eruption of the urging will! Better, indeed, for the will to float free in spaceless, timeless night than for it to languish in prison, illumined by the feeble, flickering light of the intellect!

Have I hoped to live on in my son? In a personality yet more feeble, flickering, and timorous than my own? Blind, childish folly! What can my son do for me—what need have I of a son? Where shall I be when I am dead? Ah, it is so brilliantly clear, so overwhelmingly simple! I shall be in all those who have ever, do ever, or ever shall say "I"—*especially, however, in all those who say it most fully, potently, and gladly!*

Somewhere in the world a child is growing up, strong, well-grown, adequate, able to develop its powers, gifted, untroubled, pure, joyous, relentless, one of those beings whose glance heightens the joy of the joyous and drives the unhappy to despair. *He* is my son. He is I, myself, soon, soon; as soon as Death frees me from the wretched delusion that I am not he as well as myself.

Have I ever hated life—pure, strong, relentless life? Folly and misconception! I have but hated myself, because I could not bear it. I love you, I love you all, you blessed, and soon, soon, I shall cease to be cut off from you all by the narrow bonds of myself; soon will that in me which loves you be free and be in and with you—in and with you all.

He wept, he pressed his face into the pillows and wept, shaken through and through, lifted up in transports by a joy without compare for its exquisite sweetness. This it was which since yesterday had filled him as if with a heady, intoxicating draught, had worked in his heart in the darkness of the night and roused him like a budding love! And in so far as he could now understand and recognize—not in words and consecutive thoughts, but in sudden rapturous illuminations of his inmost being—he was already free, already actually released and free of all natural as well as artificial limitations. The walls of his native town, in which he had wilfully and consciously shut himself up, opened out; they opened and disclosed to his view the entire world, of which he had in his youth seen this or that small portion, and of which Death now promised him the whole. The deceptive perceptions of space, time and history, the preoccupation with a glorious historical continuity of life in the person of his own descendants, the dread of some future final dissolution and decomposition—all this his spirit now put aside. He was no longer prevented from grasping eternity. Nothing began, nothing left off. There was only an endless present; and that power in him which loved life with a love so exquisitely sweet and yearning—the power of which his person was only the unsuccessful expression—that power would always know how to find access to this present.

"I shall live," he whispered into his pillow. He wept, and in the next moment knew not why. His brain stood still, the vision was quenched. Suddenly there was nothing more—he lay in dumb darkness. "It will come back," he assured himself. And before sleep inexorably wrapped him round, he swore to himself never to let go this precious treasure, but to read and study, to learn its powers, and to make inalienably his own the whole conception of the universe out of which his vision sprang.

But that could not be. Even the next day, as he woke with a faint feeling of shame at the emotional extravagances of the night, he suspected that it would be hard to put these beautiful designs into practice.

He rose late and had to go at once to take part in the debate at an assembly of burgesses. Public business, the civic life that went on in the gabled narrow streets of this middle-sized trading city, consumed his energies once more. He still planned to take up the wonderful reading again where he had left it off. But he questioned of himself whether the events of that night had been anything firm and permanent; whether, when Death approached, they would be found to hold their ground.

His middle-class instincts rose against them—and his vanity, too: the fear of being eccentric, of playing a laughable rôle. Had he really seen these things? And did they really become him—him, Thomas Buddenbrook, head of the firm of Johann Buddenbrook?

He never succeeded in looking again into the precious volume—to say nothing of buying its other parts. His days were consumed by nervous pedantry: harassed by a thousand details, all of them unimportant, he was too weak-willed to arrive at a reasonable and fruitful arrangement of his time. Nearly two weeks after that memorable afternoon he gave it up—and ordered the maid-servant to fetch the book from the drawer in the garden table and replace it in the bookcase.

And thus Thomas Buddenbrook, who had held his hands stretched imploringly upward toward the high ultimate truth, sank now weakly back to the images and conceptions of his childhood. He strove to call back that personal God, the Father of all human beings, who had sent a part of Himself upon earth to suffer and bleed for our sins, and who, on the final day, would come to judge the quick and the dead; at whose feet the justified, in the course of the eternity then beginning, would be recompensed for the sorrows they had borne in this vale of tears. Yes, he strove to subscribe to the whole confused unconvincing story, which required no intelligence, only obedient credulity; and which, when the last anguish came, would sustain one in a firm and childlike faith.—But would it, really?

Ah, even here there was no peace. This poor, well-nigh exhausted man, consumed with gnawing fears for the honour of his house, his wife, his child, his name, his family, this man who spent painful effort even to keep his body artificially erect and well-preserved—this poor man tortured himself for days with thoughts upon the moment and manner of death. How would it really be? Did the soul go to Heaven immediately after death, or did bliss first begin with the resurrection of the flesh? And, if so, where did the soul stay until that time? He did not remember ever having been taught this. Why had he not been told this important fact in school or in church? How was it justifiable for them to leave people in such uncertainty? He considered visiting Pastor Pringsheim and seeking advice and counsel; but he gave it up in the end for fear of being ridiculous.

And finally he gave it all up—he left it all to God. But having come to such an unsatisfactory ending of his attempts to set his spiritual affairs in order, he determined at least to spare no pains over his earthly ones, and to carry out a plan which he had long entertained.

One day little Johann heard his father tell his mother, as they drank their coffee in the living-room after the midday meal, that he expected Lawyer So-and-So to make his will. He really ought not to keep on putting it off. Later, in the afternoon, Hanno practised his music for an hour. When he went down the corridor after that, he met, coming up the stairs, his father and a gentleman in a long black overcoat.

"Hanno," said the Senator, curtly. And little Johann stopped, swallowed, and said quickly and softly: "Yes, papa."

"I have some important business with this gentleman," his father went on. "Will you stand before the door into the smoking-room and take care that nobody—absolutely nobody, you understand—disturbs us?"

"Yes, Papa," said little Johann, and took up his post before the door, which closed after the two gentlemen.

He stood there, clutching his sailor's knot with one hand, felt with his tongue for a doubtful tooth, and listened to the earnest subdued voices which could be heard from inside. His head, with the curling light-brown hair, he held on one side, and his face with the frowning brows and blue-shadowed, gold-brown eyes, wore that same displeased and brooding look with which he had inhaled the odour of the flowers, and that other strange, yet half-familiar odour, by his grandmother's bier.

Ida Jungmann passed and said, "Well, little Hanno, why are you hanging about here?"

And the hump-backed apprentice came out of the office with a telegram, and asked for the Senator.

But, both times, little Johann put his arm in its blue sailor sleeve with the anchor on it horizontally across the door; both times he shook his head and said softly, after a pause, "No one may go in. Papa is making his will."

35. Friedrich Nietzsche, *The Gay Science*

Friedrich Nietzsche (1844–1900) was, after Hegel and Marx, the most important German philosopher of the nineteenth century. Born in Prussian Saxony, Nietzsche studied theology and classics at Bonn and Leipzig, where he discovered the work of Schopenhauer and Richard Wagner, both of whom influenced greatly his early thought. Although he had not completed a conventional academic dissertation, Nietzsche was appointed to a professorship in classical philology at Basel in 1869, at the age of twenty-four. He resigned this position in 1879 and left Basel for a ten-year sojourn in Switzerland, France, and Italy, where he wrote his most important philosophical work. In 1889 he collapsed from physical and mental illness and spent the last years of his life as a total invalid in the care of his family.

Nietzsche's philosophy was marked by an aversion to Christianity and by penetrating psychological insights into the frailty and tortuousness of man's conscious destiny. He was no less a moralist for his persistent articulation of the elusiveness and deceptiveness of man's rational and ethical capacities. Indeed the fate of, and ultimately, the decadence of morality in Western culture was a principal concern of virtually all of his work. Like most great thinkers Nietzsche has had two lives: that of himself and that of his reputation, that of a genius who courageously articulated his own ideas and that of an (often misrepresented) subject whose ideas could inspire a number of divergent intellectual projects, some noble, others unfortunate.

From Friedrich Nietzsche, *The Gay Science,* translated by Walter Kaufmann (New York: Vintage Books, 1974), pp. 181–82, 306–8. Copyright © 1974 by Random House, Inc. Reprinted by permission of the publisher.

These selections present two of the starting points of Nietzsche's philo-sophical work as a whole. The first includes the announcement that "God is dead," a statement for which Nietzsche has become famous but which is often quoted out of context. Its real significance for Nietzsche is very different from that casually ascribed to it. In the second selection, Nietzsche assesses the general influence of Schopenhauer and obliquely indicates his criticism of him, a criticism Nietzsche made at length in other works.

Section 125

The madman.—Have you not heard of that madman who lit a lantern in the bright morning hours, ran to the market place, and cried incessantly: "I seek God! I seek God!"—As many of those who did not believe in God were standing around just then, he provoked much laughter. Has he got lost? asked one. Did he lose his way like a child? asked another. Or is he hiding? Is he afraid of us? Has he gone on a voyage? emigrated?—Thus they yelled and laughed.

The madman jumped into their midst and pierced them with his eyes. "Whither is God?" he cried; "I will tell you. *We have killed him*—you and I. All of us are his murderers. But how did we do this? How could we drink up the sea? Who gave us the sponge to wipe away the entire horizon? What were we doing when we unchained this earth from its sun? Whither is it moving now? Whither are we moving? Away from all suns? Are we not plunging continually? Backward, sideward, forward, in all directions? Is there still any up or down? Are we not straying as through an infinite nothing? Do we not feel the breath of empty space? Has it not become colder? Is not night continually closing in on us? Do we not need to light lanterns in the morning? Do we hear nothing as yet of the noise of the grave-diggers who are burying God? Do we smell nothing as yet of the divine decomposition? Gods, too, decompose. God is dead. God remains dead. And we have killed him.

"How shall we comfort ourselves, the murderers of all murderers? What was holiest and mightiest of all that the world has yet owned has bled to death under our knives: who will wipe this blood off us? What water is there for us to clean ourselves? What festivals of atonement, what sacred games shall we have to invent? Is not the greatness of this deed too great for us? Must we ourselves not become gods simply to appear worthy of it? There has never been a greater deed; and whoever is born after us—for the sake of this deed he will belong to a higher history than all history hitherto."

Here the madman fell silent and looked again at his listeners; and they, too, were silent and stared at him in astonishment. At last he threw his lantern on the ground, and it broke into pieces and went out. "I have come too early," he said then; "my time is not yet. This tremendous event is still on its way, still wandering; it has not yet reached the ears of men. Lightning and thunder require time; the light of the stars requires time; deeds, though done, still require time to be seen and heard. This deed is still more distant from them than the most distant stars—*and yet they have done it themselves.*"

It has been related further that on the same day the madman forced his way into several churches and there struck up his *requiem aeternam deo.* Led out and called to account, he is said always to have replied nothing but: "What after all are these churches now if they are not the tombs and sepulchers of God?"

Section 357

. . . It would be a fourth question whether *Schopenhauer,* too, with his pessimism—that is, the problem of the *value of existence*—had to be precisely a German. I believe not. The event after which this problem was to be expected for certain—an astronomer of the soul could have calculated the very day and hour for it—the decline of the faith in the Christian god, the triumph of scientific atheism, is a generally European event in which all races had their share and for which all deserve credit and honor. Conversely, one might charge precisely the Germans—those Germans who were Schopenhauer's contemporaries—that they *delayed* this triumph of atheism most dangerously for the longest time. Hegel in particular was its delayer par excellence, with his grandiose attempt to persuade us of the divinity of existence, appealing as a last resort to our sixth sense, "the historical sense." As a philosopher, Schopenhauer was the *first* admitted and inexorable atheist among us Germans: This was the background of his enmity against Hegel. The ungodliness of existence was for him something given, palpable, indisputable; he always lost his philosopher's composure and became indignant when he saw anyone hesitate or mince matters at this point. This is the locus of his whole integrity; unconditional and honest atheism is simply the *presupposition* of the way he poses his problem, being a triumph achieved finally and with great difficulty by the European conscience, being the most fateful act of two thousand years of discipline for truth that in the end forbids itself the *lie* in faith in God.

You see what it was that really triumphed over the Christian god: Christian morality itself, the concept of truthfulness that was understood ever

more rigorously, the father confessor's refinement of the Christian conscience, into intellectual cleanliness at any price. Looking at nature as if it
were proof of the goodness and governance of a god; interpreting history in
honor of some divine reason, as a continual testimony of a moral world
order and ultimate moral purposes; interpreting one's own experiences
as pious people have long enough interpreted theirs, as if everything were
providential, a hint, designed and ordained for the sake of the salvation of
the soul—that is *all over* now, that has man's conscience *against* it, that is
considered indecent and dishonest by every more refined conscience—
mendaciousness, feminism, weakness, and cowardice. In this severity, if
anywhere, we are *good* Europeans and heirs of Europe's longest and most
courageous self-overcoming.

As we thus reject the Christian interpretation and condemn its "meaning" like counterfeit, *Schopenhauer's* question immediately comes to us in
a terrifying way: *Has existence any meaning at all?* It will require a few
centuries before this question can even be heard completely and in its full
depth. What Schopenhauer himself said in answer to this question was—
forgive me—hasty, youthful, only a compromise, a way of remaining—
remaining stuck—in precisely those Christian-ascetic moral perspectives
in which one had *renounced faith* along with the faith in God. But he *posed*
the question—as a good European, as I have said, and *not* as a German.

4
Constitutionalism, Authoritarianism, and Nationalism in Germany

36. Otto von Bismarck, Speech on the Constitution of the North German Confederation (11 March 1867)

Otto von Bismarck

Otto von Bismarck (1815–98) was the principal political architect of the German Empire created in 1871. Born to an old Junker family in eastern Prussia, the young Bismarck entered the Prussian state service in 1836, but soon abandoned it to devote his time to managing his estate in Pomerania. During the Revolution of 1848 he emerged as a bitter opponent of King Frederick William IV's concessions to the Liberal revolutionists. In 1851 Bismarck was appointed Prussian minister to the Federal Diet of the restored German Confederation in Frankfurt, where he staunchly opposed Austrian schemes to dominate postrevolutionary Germany.

In September 1862 he became minister-president of Prussia, following the king's failure to get a parliamentary majority to support a new army bill, which, in addition to increasing costs, raised the number of recruits, extended the period of service to three years, and lessened the role of the national militia (*Landwehr*) in the structure of the Prussian army. By manipulating the budgetary procedures established by the Prussian Constitution of 1850, Bismarck defied the Liberal majority in the Prussian Parliament and provoked a constitutional conflict that endured for four years. At the same time he skillfully angled for popular support and achieved an overwhelming success when, through two short, victorious wars against Austria (1866) and France (1870), he made Prussia the core of a new German Empire, formed in 1870–71 by a federation of all

From *Stenographische Berichte über die Verhandlungen des Reichstages des Norddeutschen Bundes im Jahre 1867*, 11 March 1867, pp. 135–39. Translated for this volume by Paul Silverman.

German states (except Austria). Rather than confirming earlier Liberal assumptions about an inevitable linkage between liberalism and nationalism, Bismarck seemed to suggest that the two were alternatives rather than complementaries.

The first speech presented in part 4 is Bismarck's defense of his draft of a constitution for the North German Confederation, given before the constituent Reichstag of the Confederation on 11 March 1867. This constitution united the states of northern and central Germany (excluding the south German states of Baden, Württemberg, Bavaria, and Hesse-Darmstadt) and later served as the basis for the final 1871 settlement. Bismarck's comments should be read against both those of Gagern from 1848 (document 21) and the programmatic statements of his contemporaneous Liberal and Catholic opponents (documents 38 and 39). James Sheehan has noted of Bismarck's tactics that "he dropped broad hints about future foreign political dangers and opportunities and let it be known that, if the parliament did not fulfill its functions correctly, he was ready to issue the constitution by decree. Government initiative, the domestic manipulation of foreign policy, and the distant but still real threat of a coup—all of these familiar elements of the mature Bismarckian system could be seen during the first months of the new Germany's existence." [1] The final version of the constitution, modified by concessions to the Liberals, which enhanced the role of Parliament in controlling the budget and which established a very limited national executive, as well as providing for the use of the secret ballot in national elections, passed on 16 April 1867.

As chancellor of the new German Empire and as prime minister and foreign minister of Prussia, Bismarck continued to dominate German political affairs until 1890. Many of the Liberals who had opposed him in 1862–66 later came round to support the strategic (and economic) results, if not the political methods, of his work in unifying Germany. After a decade of uneasy cooperation between the Liberals and his conservative regime, which included a vicious attack on political Catholicism and the Catholic Center party (the *Kulturkampf*), Bismarck again broke with the Liberals in 1879, this time over the issue of tariff protection. To rally support Bismarck came to (uneasy) terms with the Catholic church—the worst of the *Kulturkampf* legislation was withdrawn by 1887. He also used an attempted assassination of the emperor in 1878 to push through a law repressing the emergent socialist movement in Germany, which had won significant electoral support in working-class circles (the Social

---

1. James J. Sheehan, *German Liberalism in the Nineteenth Century* (Chicago, 1978), p. 130.

Democrats won 9 percent of the national vote in the 1877 elections). Bismarck's strategy in the 1880s of suppressing the Socialists was no more successful, however, than his persecution of the Church in the 1870s: by 1890 the Social Democrats had almost tripled their vote compared with the 1877 elections.

The second speech presented here comes from the parliamentary debates in 1884 on Bismarck's bill for compulsory accident insurance for factory workers, legislation that followed on the heels of the June 1883 law establishing compulsory sickness insurance. The 1884 plan provided for the obligatory insurance on the basis of mutual liability, with employers forced to contribute the premiums and to organize themselves (for insurance purposes) into legal associations (*Berufsgenossenschaften*) with considerable self-governing powers. This scheme of intermediate state compulsion ran counter to Liberal views of the proper limitation of government intervention in society. But it also outraged Social Democratic politicians (who in spite of the anti-Socialist law still sat in Parliament), since they viewed the legislation as a ploy to discredit them before their own voters. On 15 March 1884 Bismarck appeared in the Reichstag to defend his proposals against both Liberal and Socialist objections.

. . . It could not have been our objective to produce a theoretically ideal federal constitution in which both the unity of Germany would be guaranteed for all time and freedom of movement for every particularistic stirring would be secured. Such a philosopher's stone, if it is to be found at all, must be left to the future to discover. The task of the present moment is not to come a few decimal places closer to such a squaring of the circle. Rather, recalling and, in my opinion, correctly estimating the forces of resistance upon which the earlier attempts at unification made in Frankfurt and Erfurt foundered, we have made it our business to defy those forces of resistance as little as was at all compatible with our goal. We have held it our task to discover the minimum of those concessions to the whole that the particular political entities existing within German territory must make if the whole is to be capable of surviving. Whether we want to attach the name of a constitution to the product that has thereby come into being is irrelevant. However we believe that if that product is accepted here, the road will have been cleared for the German people, and we further believe that we can have confidence in the genius of our people that it will be able to find its way along this road, which leads to its goals. (Bravo!)

Although the document under consideration here is sufficient for this purpose, at least in our view, I nonetheless fully understand that many wishes remain unsatisfied, that a great many things besides these were wished for, and that in like manner a great many others could have been wished for. But what I do not understand is how one could want to refuse what is being offered because these wishes have up to now remained unfulfilled, and at the same time assert that all one really wants is a constitution that could lead Germany to unity. To date objections have been raised and wishes have been expressed by individuals standing on two different sides. I would like to term them the *unitary* and the *particularistic* sides. From the unitary side one hears that they expected the creation of a constitutionally responsible ministry from this draft constitution in the same way as from the earlier one. But who should appoint this ministry? This task is not to be expected of a consortium of twenty-two governments; it would not be able to fulfill it. However, it is equally unacceptable to exclude twenty-one of twenty-two governments from a share in the establishment of the executive. The demand could only have been satisfied if a unified head with monarchical character had been created. But then, gentlemen, you would no longer have a federal relationship; then you would have the mediatization of those to whom this monarchical power was not given. This mediatization was neither consented to by our confederates nor sought by us. Some here have intimated that it could be exacted by force, while others have suggested that it will in part come about by itself, the latter position being found in political quarters located close to me. We do not expect this to such a degree, and we do not believe that German princes will be ready in large numbers to exchange their present positions for that of an English peer. We have never made this unreasonable demand of them, and we do not intend to do so. (Very good! Hear! Hear!) But still less can I consider it to be our task—along the lines, for instance, of what was said by the previous speaker—to rely on the power, on the superior strength of Prussia in this confederation in order to force concessions that cannot be brought about voluntarily. We could use such force least of all against allies who faithfully stood by us in the moment of danger, and just as little against those with whom we have just sealed a—we hope, as one is accustomed to use the word on this earth—perpetual peace sanctioned by international law. (Bravo!)

The basis of this relationship should not be force, neither with respect to the princes nor the people. (Bravo!) The basis should be trust in Prussia's faithfulness to treaties, (Bravo!) and this trust may not be shaken as long as this faithfulness if reciprocated. (Very good! Bravo!)

A previous speaker alluded to the declarations proposing a more unified central power, which were set down in the final protocols by a few of the governments of the Confederation. I can only regret that these declarations first saw the light of day in the final protocols. If they had been made in the discussions, before the final protocols were edited for publication, then one could have at least formed a judgment concerning the reception such views would have found with the majority of the governments. Since they first appeared only after the conclusion of the proceedings, I can only conceive of them as a lifeless confession of faith without inner substance.

In my view, the objections raised by those representing the particularistic point of view are more weighty and are advanced with greater earnestness than those made by the representatives of the unitary point of view. By particularism one ordinarily understands an oppositional dynasty or an oppositional caste in any state that, on account of special interests, places itself against the creation of common institutions. Today we have to deal with a new species of particularism, with parliamentary particularism. (Amused laughter)

In earlier times, from a dynastic standpoint, it went: "a Ghibelline, a Guelph!" Nowadays it goes: "a *Landtag*, a *Reichstag!*"

The right that the Prussian Landtag has to say *no* to the agreements we make here was emphasized a short time ago by a speaker on the other side, and I believe that no one will seriously dispute this right and appeal to force in the face of it. *Every Landtag* has this right, however small or large it may be, for we desire to live in a community that is based on law rather than force. However, until now the disagreements of the other Landtags have not been lodged at this rostrum in the same manner as those of the Prussian Landtag; these disagreements, moreover, have arisen from quarters that have surprised me. All of a sudden the advocate of a north German republic becomes enthusiastic about the monarchical Prussian Constitution (Amused laughter); then a Catholic priest, with the guidance of a text from the Bible, placed this same constitution on a plane equal with that of the salvation of his soul and spoke to us in words and tone that betrayed the deepest emotional shock at the thought that even a single article of this constitution could be altered—through legal channels mind you. I do not doubt for a moment the upright conviction with which those words were spoken, but it surprised me that he weakened their effect by including a facetious passing shot at me. "I would know how to take care of things even if nothing came to pass here" was the way he put it. Gentlemen, whether in that case I *would* be able to take care of things is something I would like to leave undiscussed. The point is that I *would not* take care of things. I have never failed to serve my king and country, but in such a case I would fail to do so, and I would leave it to those who brought on the chaos to find the way back out of the labyrinth. (Bravo!)

The proposition was advanced on the other side that the Prussian Constitution for the time being stands above the Constitution of the realm—advanced by deputies who I am aware hold some views in common with me, members of the Prussian House of Deputies, individuals who I believe truly want to see the matter come to pass. Likewise what was agreed upon here between all of the governments of the individual states following a painfully achieved union and what was agreed upon among the freely elected representatives of thirty million Germans has already been cited before the assizes of the Prussian *Landtag*. Gentlemen, I must tell you that with these things a humiliating feeling came over me that those who have newly joined us will quickly lose the illusion they could have had that a person grows as his goals become greater and that the broader mental horizon which ought to be part of a larger state is able to impart to all its members. (Bravo!)

The gentlemen who here so unceremoniously announce that the Prussian Landtag will approve or reject the product of our labors in this or that case already had their authority to do so called into question the day before yesterday. But I want to ask you, what would you say if today one of the confederated governments of its own accord declared: "If this or that does not stand in the constitution, then I do not accept it under any circumstances!" What would you say if a class or a caste made this same declaration, if, for instance, a member of the Mecklenburg *Ritterschaft* stepped forward and said: If our rights are not respected—and they weigh just as heavily on the scales of justice as do those of the Prussian Landtag—then we aren't going along! (Very good!)

I remind you, Gentlemen, that when the attempts at unification made in Frankfurt and Erfurt miscarried—the one made in Erfurt miscarried not so much, as had been argued here, through the opposition of the governments *involved,* even if I cannot assert that the Prussian government at the time undertook its mission with the energy that might have been desired; it ran aground in my opinion because Hannover and Saxony simply had more trust in the Austrian army that stood behind Olmütz than in the *Three Kings Alliance* (that was indeed the decisive factor, even if there may have been a great many other causes). To return to the point, I remind you that in the public press one could find no word strong enough to brand "the shameful lack of love for the fatherland" which led, "as a consequence of corporate interests, to a preference to establish a Junker state of the size of the Mark Brandenburg" and which was supposedly attributable to us who, under the name of the Prussian Junker party, had to take public responsibility at the time for the failure of things to come to pass. Such assertions were to be found in newspaper articles, now forgotten by you, that piled insults and accusations upon us because we hindered the project we were not in a position to fulfill. When on the day before yesterday the same right was claimed for the Prussian Landtag, I heard not a single cry of astonishment, aside from the one I repressed inside myself. I believe, gentlemen, that those who made this statement indeed underestimate the earnestness of the situation in which we find ourselves. Do you really believe that the magnificent movement that last year led into battle the peoples from the Belts to the seas around Sicily, from the Rhine to the Prut and the Dniester, which led to the iron game of dice in which the stakes were royal and imperial crowns; that the millions of German warriors who fought against each other and bled on the battlefields from the Rhine to the Carpathians; that the thousands upon thousands of those killed in battle and those who succumbed to disease, who with their death sealed this national decision, do you believe all this could be written off with the resolution of a Landtag? (Bravo!) Gentlemen if you believe that, then you really do not grasp the situation!

I do not desire to lay down any sort of threat, for I respect the rights of our Landtag, just as I gladly would have respected them from the beginning if, according to my conviction, that would have been compatible with the continued existence of the Prussian state. But I am of the firm conviction that no German Landtag will pass such a resolution if we come to an agreement here. (Bravo!) I would indeed like to see how the gentlemen who are considering these possibilities would answer, let us say, an invalid from the Battle of Königgrätz, when he inquired about the outcome of the stupendous deeds done there. They would perhaps say to him: "Yes, to be sure, with respect to German unity once again nothing has happened. When the occasion arises things will turn out all right on that count. Unity is easy to acquire. An agreement is possible at any time. However, we have rescued the right of the House of Deputies of the Prussian Landtag to approve the budget, the right annually to place in question the existence of the Prussian army (commotion on the left), a right that we, as good patriots, would never make use of, indeed should an assembly ever go so far astray as really to want to do so, then we would call to account as traitors to their country the ministers who were party to the execution of the orders. But it is, nevertheless, our right. It was for this that we struggled with the emperor of Austria outside the walls of Pressburg." With that the invalid ought to console himself over the loss of his limbs, with that the widow who has buried her husband ought to find solace?

Gentlemen, it is really a completely impossible situation that you are creating for yourselves here. I thus gladly turn from these fantastic impossibilities back to realm of reality, to a few objections that have been made here against the content of the constitution. It has already been said—I do not know whether the phrase was left in the king's address—that we consider the draft to be capable of improvement. I can at least testify here that we are receptive to any suggestion honestly intended to improve the constitution and to facilitate its enactment. (Bravo!)

However you must not hold the government—nor the governments of any of the twenty-two confederated states—under the suspicion of wishing to renounce the historical, constitutional development of Germany. You must not accuse them of perhaps wishing to use this Parliament to wear down parliamentarianism in a struggle of Parliaments against each other. What would we gain from that? Is then, in the long run, a government conceivable that sets for itself the task of forging a union in fire or even with cold metal, should the fire cool down—a union that is not viewed with favor everywhere in Europe—and, then, so-to-speak, sets for itself the systematic task of suppressing the rights of the population to participate in its own affairs, enters into a savage policy of reaction, wastes time in struggles with its own people? Gentlemen, you cannot believe it likely that a dynasty such as the one that rules over Prussia, that any of the dynasties that at present rule in Germany, would approach a national undertaking with such—I cannot call it anything else—hypocrisy. (Spirited bravo!)

We *desire* the development of freedom to the greatest degree compatible with the security of the whole. The issue can only be that of the limits. How much and what is *in the long run* compatible with this security? What is *at present* compatible with it? Is a transition stage necessary? How long must it last? (Very good! Bravo!)

It cannot be our intention to withdraw the military budget from your cognizance even for the, in my opinion, indispensable period of time in which it should be treated by yourselves as immutable. One has spoken here as if the military budget hereafter is to be treated with a certain secrecy. Insofar as I have made up my mind on this matter at all, I envision that we would in any case present a budget that includes the total expenditures of the Confederation, military expenditures not excluded. Only we would do that on the basis of an agreement, to be reached with the representatives of the people, that would last for a certain number of years and would ensure that one could strike nothing from the military budget for this period, at least nothing that had not been agreed upon with the commander in chief of the Confederation. It is indeed possible that the commander in chief could convince himself that he cannot do without this or that, that he could say: "I want that." But there must be a period of time in which the existence of the army of the Confederation does not depend upon the fortuitous oscillations of the majority. I gladly admit that it is highly improbable that in this Reichstag a majority would be found that would not approve what in *its* opinion was sufficient for the defense of the country. In this connection I am not especially fearful of the particularists in the manner referred to here. I fear much more the jumbling of the boundary between parliamentary and princely power with respect to Germany's ability to defend itself against foreign enemies. I do not think it desirable that one has the urge to exercise the kind of parliamentary influence that is being sought—and that we gladly grant to the Parliaments—chiefly on the army, while numerous other fields in which it could be exercised remain continually untouched. I believe, gentlemen, that it would be a more effective means to secure for yourself influence over the governments (which several speakers on the day before yesterday regretted not seeing), if, for example, you drew customs treaties under the sway of your legislation in such a way as to cut the realm off from its resources; if, for example, you did away with those officials who were included in the budget for the collection of customs duties; if, when you wanted to turn your activity toward setting aside a system of government that was unacceptable to you, you chose to cripple the railroad and telegraph systems. Gentlemen, I believe that these things would perhaps be more effective than reserving for yourselves the right to determine the composition and size of the army, for in the latter case the decision concerns the foundations of security and of the existence of the state, particularly in a federal state. There the government would be in the same position of finding it impossible to give in as the one in which the Prussian government has believed itself to be for several years now. Gentlemen, if this institution, the army of the Confederation, for the time being the most developed of the bases of a united Germany, the foundation that is the most indispensable to us, were to be placed in question through an annual vote, it would for me create the impression—forgive me. I use an analogy drawn from a profession that I at one time found myself in— of a dike association in which each year it was decided according to a head count, one that also included the propertyless, whether in case of high water the dikes should be broken or not. I would simply resign from such a dike association, for living would be too insecure for me, and I would not surrender myself to the danger that at some time those who wish to operate with open pastures would win the upper hand from those who work with tilled and water-free fields and that all would be ruined by a flood.

In any case, as I have already taken the liberty of indicating, we need in this connection an inviolable transition period that will last until we have grown together organically as flesh and blood (Bravo!); I believe that this idea will also not be contested by a large portion of the stricter constitutionalists who want to see the matter brought to a successful conclusion. (Bravo! Quite right!)

Aside from these things, I would like to make some remarks in connection with a few details that have been subjected to criticism, in order to prevent the discussion from straying more often than is necessary into the areas concerned. For example, there are our relations with south Germany. On the day before yesterday, Deputy Waldeck set high hopes merely on the creation of a constitutionally unitary ministry: "Then we would have the south Germans," as he put it. I believe that we could not more effectively frighten them off than if we followed such a course, a course that, as I indicated previously, would be greatly similar to the mediatization of the German princes.

Who are these south Germans? For the present they are the Bavarian, the Württemberg, and the Baden governments. Do you believe that his majesty the king of Bavaria or of Württemberg will feel himself particularly attracted to institutions such as those suggested by Deputy Waldeck? (Amused laughter.)

Gentlemen! I know the opposite to be the case.

Our relationship to south Germany will develop simply and securely, in my view, on the basis of the article concerning it in the draft constitution. To begin with we share with south Germany the community of the *Zollverein,* a community that at present hangs to a certain degree in the air because the peace treaties reserve to the parties the right to terminate their participation on six months' notice, until we have come to an agreement on the relationship between north and south Germany in this matter. The right of termination was necessary in order to make an agreement possible. Therefore, I think that as soon as we are finished with the north German Constitution we should immediately approach the south German governments and invite them to join with us in a discussion of the way in which we can attain a lasting organic *Zollverein,* not one that can be terminated every twelve years. We have secured this blessing for the North German Confederation through articles concerning customs legislation, but we can neither demand that the three or four south German states should accept without further ado all that we have decided here through legislation that they did not participate in, nor can we concede to them a veto over that which is legally decided upon in the north German Reichstag, a veto that each of the three or four governments could exercise and would share with their estates. Should the *Zollverein* continue to exist in its present dimensions, then it is inevitable that organic institutions will be created by virtue of which south Germany will participate in legislation concerning customs matters. I shall forgo suggesting the particulars, but I believe that how these institutions must be created is something that follows as a matter of course. (Quite right!)

It is difficult to believe that such common organs of legislation for customs issues, once they are created, could avoid gradually absorbing into their sphere of responsibility issues relating to most of the other sections of material welfare as well as much formal legislation, such as legislation concerning procedure, and so forth, and providing common regulations for all Germany in connection with these things. Moreover, I assuredly would not want to underestimate the issue and attach to the responsible body merely the deprecatory name "Customs Parliament." What struggles have we not fought in this regard! Only he who has participated in the course of events can judge properly here. In the years 1852 and 1864 wasn't it precisely customs interests that appeared to us as our most vital political interests? I do not want to undervalue the importance of the fact that an economic community can be created for all Germany.

Further, in connection with the question of power, I hold the unification of north and south Germany to be definitively secured against every attack in all matters where the security of German soil is concerned. In the south there can be no doubt that should its integrity be endangered, north Germany will unconditionally render it fraternal assistance (Energetic bravo!), and in the north there is no doubt that we are completely certain of the assistance of south Germany against every attack that would be made upon us. (Bravo!) . . .

I do not know whether during the general discussion I shall have further cause to take the floor or whether one of my colleagues will. For the moment I do not know of anything further to add to what I have said other than to renew the challenge: Gentlemen! Let us work quickly! Put Germany, as it were, in the saddle! It will certainly be able to ride. (Energetic applause.)

37. Otto von Bismarck, Speech on the Law for Workmen's Compensation (15 March 1884)

If in the general debate I speak about the matter under discussion, it cannot be my intention to enter into exhaustive discourse about the whole of the subject that concerns us, and even less to anticipate in any way the special debate over the great number of articles that the proposal contains. I do consider it necessary, however, to say a few words concerning the position of the allied governments[1] with respect to the genesis of the present proposal and to the intentions that they hold in regard to the bill. Indeed, I should best address my remarks to a discussion of those objections that were made in the previous debate against the principle of the law in general in order to maintain a coherent focus.

I turn first to the remarks of the first speaker, Deputy von Vollmar.[2] . . .

First, Representative von Vollmar avowed a certain satisfaction, which was not free from malicious pleasure, that the lofty socialist intentions that may have been the basis of the first version of this proposal had disap-

From *Stenographische Berichte über die Verhandlungen des Reichstages,* 5th Legislaturperiode, 4th session, 15 March 1884, pp. 72–78. Translated for this volume by John W. Boyer.

1. I.e., the states, including Prussia, which were united in the government of the German Empire.—ED.

2. Georg Heinrich von Vollmar (1850–1922), German Social Democratic leader.—ED.

peared. Yes, gentlemen, but this is only seemingly the case. . . . That which we refrain today from presenting has not been consigned to the fire, but only put back in reserve. We have to explore a *terra incognita*. This field of legislation was first set foot on by Germany in 1871 with the law on liability. . . . At that time we eventually convinced ourselves that the difficulties become all the greater, the wider the front on which we advance, while we attempt to march through the narrow gate of your consent. We have for the present restricted ourselves—and to be sure on my own motion, and therefore I believe it my duty to comment on this matter—to the most limited and necessary scope. My colleague von Boetticher already explained yesterday that we do not thereby intend to abandon and not take heed of the remaining occupational groups, but we wish only to be on guard against those dangers to which the proverb alludes, that the better is the enemy of the good. When one attempts too much at one time, one runs the danger of achieving nothing. I wish that we and the present Reichstag might have the honor of at least doing something, and at least making a beginning in this area and thereby taking the lead among European states. Restraint is justified by the consideration that the more comprehensive the proposal is, the more are diverse interests affected, . . . so that the acceptance of the law becomes that much more difficult. . . .

Deputy von Vollmar has expressed his astonishment that . . . we are making new and different proposals. Gentlemen, that is not our fault. Yesterday Deputy Bamberger[3] compared the business of government with that of a cobbler who measures shoes, which he thereupon examines as to whether they are suitable for him or not and accordingly accepts or rejects them. I am by no means dissatisfied with this humble comparison, by which you place the united governments in the perspective of a shoemaker taking measurements for Herr Bamberger. The profession of government in the sense of Frederick the Great is to serve the people, and may it be also as a cobbler; the opposite is to dominate the people. We want to serve the people. But I make the demand on Herr Bamberger that he act as my co-shoemaker in order to make sure that no member of the public goes barefoot, and to create a suitable shoe for the people in this crucial area.

(Bravo!)

Up to now I find that lacking.

Deputy von Vollmar then proceeded to the connection that he imputes between our proposal and the Socialist Law.[4] It is not correct, as he conceives it, that we made the proposal in order to win more support for the

---

3. Ludwig Bamberger (1823–99), banker and cofounder of the Liberal Party.—ED.

4. A law passed in 1878 that made the Social Democratic party illegal, though it did not prevent members of the party from being elected to the Reichstag.—ED.

Socialist Law. There is, indeed, a connection between the two, but it is quite different. At the time of the submission of the Socialist Law the government, and particularly His Majesty the Emperor and, if I am not in error, also the majority of the Reichstag, underwrote certain promissory notes for the future and gave assurances that as a corollary to this Socialist Law a serious effort for the betterment of the fate of the workers should go hand in hand. In my opinion that is the complement to the Socialist Law; if you have persistently decided not to improve the situation of the workers, then I understand that you reject the Socialist Law. For it is an injustice on the one hand to hinder the self-defense of a large class of our fellow citizens and on the other hand not to offer them aid for the redress of that which causes the dissatisfaction. That the Social Democratic leaders wish no advantage for this law, that I understand; dissatisfied workers are just what they need. Their mission is to lead, to rule, and the necessary prerequisite for that is numerous dissatisfied classes. They must naturally oppose any attempt of the government, however well intentioned it may be, to remedy this situation, if they do not wish to lose control over the masses they mislead.

Therefore, I place no value on the objections that come from the leaders of the Social Democrats; I would place a very high value on the objections that come from the workers in general. Our workers, thank God, are not all Social Democrats and are not to such a degree unresponsive to the efforts of the confederated governments to help them, perhaps also not to the difficulties that these efforts meet in the parliamentary arena. The parliament has indeed the right to prevent any progress on our legislation; you have the absolute veto with regard to legislation, and through the uncontrolled exercise of this veto you can certainly paralyze legislation, whether it be because you oppose the government on principle, or whether you do so only opportunely, but consistently in each individual case. . . . The parliamentary element, if it is used only as an obstacle, if proof is provided to the people that it refuses its cooperation to the benevolent intentions of the government, that it has only a simple no, that it makes no attempt to help the government—that must of course to a high degree prove self-destructive and self-diminishing. This I would consider a great misfortune, since I do not know how we could compensate for that. I in no way support an absolutist government. I believe properly exercised parliamentary cooperation to be as necessary and as useful as I consider parliamentary control damaging and impossible.

(Bravo, from the right.)

Parliament should be capable of preventing evil; it should be able to set its veto against the dangers that can be associated with a monarchist government and with every government marked by wastefulness, bureaucratic

narrowness, plans based on unrealistic ideas, and political corruption. . . .
It should be able to prevent bad laws from being passed, it should be capable of hindering the squandering of the nation's money; but rule, gentlemen, that it cannot do. I do not wish to enter into particulars over this; there
will be another opportunity to give a lecture on fundamental conceptions
with respect to this matter.

I also do not know what one would set in the place of the parliament in
order to guard against the dangers that would surround a nonparliamentary
government, which would have no openness, no freedom of the press. I
mean that in complete seriousness. . . .

[The real question] is whether the state—by state I always mean the
empire—whether the state has the right to abandon to chance the performance of a responsibility of the state, namely, to protect the worker from
accidents and need when he is injured or becomes old, so that private companies form that charge premiums from the workers and the employers at
whatever rates the market will bear. . . . As soon as the state concerns itself with these matters at all, however—and I believe that it is the state's
duty to concern itself—it must strive for the least expensive form and must
take no advantage from it, and above all not lose sight of the benefit for the
poor and the needy. Otherwise one could indeed relinquish the fulfillment
of certain state duties, such as among other things the care of the poor, in
the widest sense of the word, as well as schools and national defense . . .
to private stock companies. . . . In the same way one can continue to believe that the whole of the state's responsibility must in the end be left to
the voluntary formation of private stock companies. The whole problem is
rooted in the question: does the state have the responsibility to care for its
helpless fellow citizens, or does it not? I maintain that it does have this
duty, and to be sure, not simply the Christian state, as I once permitted
myself to allude to with the words "practical Christianity," but rather every
state by its very nature. It would be madness for a corporate body or a
collectivity to take charge of those objectives that the individual can accomplish; those goals that the community can fulfill with justice and profit
should be relinquished to the community. There are objectives that only the
state in its totality can fulfill. . . . Among the last mentioned objectives [of
the state] belong national defense [and] the general system of transportation. . . . To these belong also the help of persons in distress and the prevention of such justified complaints as in fact provide excellent material for
exploitation by the Social Democrats. That is the responsibility of the state
from which the state will not be able to withdraw in the long run.

If one argues against my position that this is socialism, then I do not
fear that at all. The question is, where do the justifiable limits of state socialism lie? Without such a boundary we could not manage our affairs.

Each law for poor relief is socialism. There are states that distance themselves so far from socialism that poor laws do not exist at all. I remind you
of France. From these conditions in France the theories of the remarkable
social politician, Léon Say,[5] whom Herr Bamberger referred to, are quite
naturally accounted for. This man expresses the French view that every
French citizen has the right to starve and that the state has no responsibility
to hinder him in the exercise of his right. (Hear, hear! On the right).

You see also that for many years, ever since the government of the July
Monarchy,[6] social conditions in France have been unsettled, and I believe
that in the long run France will not be able to avoid promoting somewhat
more state socialism than it has up to now. Was not also, for example, the
Stein-Hardenberg legislation[7] of glorious memory, the constitutional justification and appropriateness of which no one today doubts anymore, state
socialism? Is there a stronger state socialism than when the law declares: I
take away from the property owner a certain part of his real estate and
transfer it to the tenant farmer, whom he had on the property up to that
point? . . . Whoever censures state socialism completely must also repudiate the Stein-Hardenberg legislation. He must altogether refuse the state
the right, whenever law and privilege combine to form a chain and a coer-
cive force which hinders our free breathing, to cut with the knife of the
surgeon and create new and healthy conditions. . . .

I can pass on in general to the comments of Deputy Bamberger because
to a certain extent he has summed up the preceding speakers and can therefore serve as a guide. The Deputy mentioned in the introduction to his
speech that "yesterday," therefore the day before yesterday, "once again as
a prelude to the day's agenda the perniciousness and reprehensibleness of
any opposition was indicated." Gentlemen, it is however not correct to so
characterize my position toward the matter as if I had treated any opposition as reprehensible. I have only refused on my part to cooperate with the
goals of the opposition; my whole speech at that time can be summarized
in the sentence: I do not wish to allow myself to be harnessed to the triumphant wagon of the opposition. . . .

. . . In my opinion, a primary reason for the success that the leaders of
the real Social Democracy have had with their never clearly defined future
goals lies in the fact that the state does not promote enough state socialism;
it allows a vacuum to form in a place where it should be active, and this is
filled by others, by agitators who poke their nose into the state's business. . . . Deputy von Vollmar has for his own part admitted . . . that the

5. Jean-Baptiste-Léon Say (1826–96), French Liberal; finance minister in four cabinets
between 1872 and 1882.—ED.

6. Established 1830.—ED.

7. Laws abolishing serfdom and regulating property relations in Prussia, 1807–11.—ED.

ideals of Social Democracy could not actually be implemented in one individual state, but rather would only be attainable if a general, international foundation existed. I believe that also, and therefore I believe them to be impossible, since this international basis will never exist; but even if internationalism comes some day, the interim period might be long enough to find a modus vivendi that is somewhat more bearable and pleasant for the oppressed and suffering among us. We cannot comfort them with promises that perhaps are not even payable in the next century; we must provide something that has value from tomorrow or the next day. . . .

Deputy Bamberger has objected that the proposed organization is not compatible with the word *free* and with the concept of freedom; there would be too much compulsion therein and a motto for the whole law would be: "If you aren't willing, I'll use force!" Gentlemen, freedom is a vague concept; no one has a use for the freedom to starve. But here freedom is also in my opinion not at all limited and not in contradiction with itself. The proposal intends a freedom in the organization, but it makes the execution obligatory. . . .

The expression "If you aren't willing, I'll use force" is totally unjustified. There scarcely exists nowadays a word with which more abuse is committed than the word *free*. . . . According to my experience, everyone understands by *freedom* only the freedom for oneself and not for others, as well as the responsibility of others to refrain absolutely from any limitation of one's own freedom. In short, by *freedom* they actually mean *domination;* by *freedom of speech* they understand the domination of the speaker; by *freedom of the press* the predominant and preponderant influence of editorial offices and of newspapers. Indeed gentlemen, and I am not speaking here in confessional terms, in all confessions, by *freedom of the church* the domination of the priests is very frequently understood . . . I have no desire to speak of human weakness, but rather of the human custom which establishes the importance of the individual person, the dominance of individual persons and their influence over the general public, precisely on the pretext that freedom demands it. That is indeed more strikingly realized in our own history than in any other. In the centuries of the decay of the German Empire, German freedom was always sharply accentuated. What did this mean? The freedom of the princes from the emperor, and the power of the nobles over the serfs! They wanted for their part to be free; that means, *to be free* was for them and also for others identical with the concept *to dominate*. They did not feel themselves to be free unless they dominated. Therefore, whenever I read the word *free* before another adjective, I become very suspicious. . . .

Deputy Bamberger expressed subsequently his regret concerning the "socialist fad." It is, however, a harsh expression when one characterizes as a "socialist fad" the careful decision of the allied governments in Germany, weighed for three years, which they again, for the third time, propose to you in the hope finally to obtain your approval. Perhaps the whole institution of the state is a socialist fad. If everyone could live on his own, perhaps everyone would be much more free, but also much less protected and guarded. If the Deputy calls the proposal a socialist whim, I reply simply that it is untrue, and my assertion is as justified as his.

He uses further the expression that the old age and disability care "were chimerical plans." . . . There is nothing about our proposal that is chimerical. Our proposals are completely genuine; they are the result of an existing need. . . . The fulfillment of a state responsibility is never a chimera, and as such I recognize it as a legislative responsibility. It is in fact not a pleasant occupation to devote these public cobbler services to a customer like Deputy Bamberger, who treats us with scorn and ingratitude in the face of real exertions, and who characterizes as a "fad" and a "chimera" the proposal that was worked out in order to make it acceptable to you. I would like to suggest in general that we might be somewhat milder in the expressions with which we mutually characterize our efforts. . . .

When Deputy Bamberger indicates that for the sake of a socialist whim the long since established system of insurance in the empire is to be abolished, I reply: if the state occupies itself at all with accident insurance, then the present system is just too expensive. If it were strengthened, who would pay the cost? It would be at the cost of the suffering poor and at the cost of industry, whose export capability is reduced by the burdens laid upon it by [private] insurance. We, for our part, want to lighten these burdens by means of a general and, therefore, beneficent arrangement.

I believe that I have arrived at the end of the train of thought provided by the preceding speakers, and I have only to add . . . the request that you gentlemen meet the confederated governments halfway and serve as leaders, according to your experience and opinion, as pathfinders in an unknown land that we are entering. The entry into this realm we believe to be a responsibility of the state. Do not doubt that we are acting honorably to strengthen the domestic peace, and particularly the peace between worker and employer, and to arrive at the result that we will be in the position to renounce, on the part of the state, continuing this emergency law, which we refer to as the Socialist Law, without exposing the commonwealth to new dangers.

38. Eduard Lasker et al., Founding Statement of the National Liberal Party (June 1867)

Two German Party Programs—National Liberalism and German Catholicism

The organization of modern political parties in Prussia coincided with the founding of political institutions in which such parties might play a significant and enduring role in public affairs. Unlike the south German states, which had received constitutions after 1815, Prussia was accorded a permanent constitution only in the aftermath of the repression of the Revolution of 1848. Not surprisingly, electoral politics vegetated there for almost a decade. But with the emergence of the "New Era" in Prussia in the later 1850s, political movements again found purpose and legitimacy in defining a role within the institutions of state power. In addition to various political-interest-group associations, one of the most important political forces was the Prussian Progressive party, which in 1861 controlled 104 of the 352 seats in the Prussian Landtag and whose members bitterly opposed Bismarck's autocracy in the early 1860s.

We offer in this and the next document programmatic statements by leaders of two prominent parties from the 1860s: the National Liberal party, founded in 1867 (document 38), and the German *Zentrum*, whose origins date to the early 1850s, but whose formal establishment occurred in 1870 (document 39). Both were Prussian as well as German parties; both drew upon Prussian provinces, but both also had very substantial resources in non-Prussian lands. Together they represented a significant part of the enfranchised middle and lower middle classes of nineteenth-century Germany. The National Liberals drew upon an electoral basis of middle- and upper-middle-class Protestant voters; the *Zentrum* upon a somewhat broader mix of Catholic voters distributed across class lines in a nation where, after 1871, Catholics constituted over one-third of the population.

The National Liberal party was officially founded in February 1867, in the aftermath of the Prussian success in defeating Austria and in uniting most of north and central Germany. Some of its adherents were former Progressive politicians willing to compromise with Bismarck; others were non-Prussian Liberals dedicated to the cause of German unity. Always an

From *National-Zeitung* (Berlin, 13 June 1867), p. 1. Translated for this volume by Paul Silverman.

uneasy amalgam of divergent ideological positions (on its extreme right stood figures such as Heinrich von Treitschke and Wilhelm Wehrenpfennig), the party finally broke apart in 1880 with the secession of its left wing, led by Ludwig Bamberger and Eduard Lasker, to found the Liberal Association.

One of the principal coauthors of the original National Liberal party program from 1867 was Eduard Lasker (1829–84). A lawyer and political journalist in Berlin in the 1860s, Lasker was one of those Progressives who shifted to support Bismarck in 1866–67, in the belief that cooperation with rather than continued opposition against the chancellor might lead to the development of a truly liberal state. Lasker remained, however, an ardent defender of the ideal of the liberal *Rechtsstaat,* which often led him into collisions with Bismarck, especially after 1878. When Lasker died in 1884, Bismarck, in a typical display of Junker arrogance and covert anti-Semitism, insulted Lasker's memory in a speech before the Reichstag.

The Center party was officially founded in December 1870, on the eve of the establishment of the new Reich, but the name and concept were anchored in the history of the group of Catholic delegates serving in the Prussian Landtag between 1852 and 1866. As the party of a religious minority who feared and resented the hegemony of a unitary, Protestant state dominated from Berlin, the Center placed special emphasis on federalism and provincial rights, as well as on freedom of religious expression and of religious institutions in German society. It opposed Prussian centralizing tendencies, leading to its reputation (among its enemies) as a "collection point for all elements who opposed the unification of Germany under Prussian rule, not from a revolutionary, but from a reactionary point of view" (Franz Mehring). The Center's initial attitude toward the German state was far more complex than such reductionist judgments would allow, but its putative hostility against the new state served as a convenient excuse for Bismarck's wrath in the 1870s. As Margaret Anderson has noted, "the Zentrum was formed prior to the Kulturkampf, and at a time when Catholics, though uneasy, were still hopeful about the recognition of their interests in the new empire."[1]

One of the early leaders of the Catholic faction in the Prussian Landtag was Hermann von Mallinckrodt (1821–74), a Westphalian aristocrat and Prussian civil servant with deeply conservative social and political values. A close friend and patron of the great Center party politician, Ludwig Windthorst, Mallinckrodt was a leader of the Center delegation in the Reichstag after 1871. In 1862 he drafted a programmatic state-

1. Margaret L. Anderson, *Windthorst: A Political Biography* (Oxford, 1981), p. 136.

ment, printed as document 39, to describe the goals of his party in the Prussian Landtag. The program was never officially adopted because of quarrels within the group over Mallinckrodt's avoidance of the word *Catholic,* but it does represent, in the words of Karl Bachem, "the most important testimony for the spirit of the parliamentary group, [or] at least of its most eminent leaders" in the early 1860s.[2]

When the old Confederation broke apart last year and the Prussian government declared its earnest intention to maintain the national bond and to set German unity on firmer foundations, we felt there could be no doubt that the liberal forces of the nation must assist in the undertaking if the work of unification were to succeed and in the process satisfy the people's need for freedom. For the sake of this goal we were ready to render assistance. This assistance only became possible when the government desisted from its infractions of constitutional law, recognized the principles that have been so resolutely defended by the Liberal party, and requested and received the indemnity. The groupings within the party occasioned by the constitutional conflict were not adequate to assure the continuation of this assistance. Thus the requirements of the new situation called for the formation of the National Liberal party, a party whose purpose is the establishment, upon the foundations at hand, of a unified Germany endowed with both power and freedom.

We never harbored any illusions about the difficulties inherent in the task of promoting development along liberal lines while working in collaboration with a government that for years maintained the constitutional conflict and administered without a duly passed budget, and having to do this with imperfect constitutional weapons. But we undertook this task with the firm intention of overcoming the difficulties involved through continuous, earnest labor and with the confidence that the greatness of the goal would strengthen the energy of the people.

For we are inspired and united by the thought that, in the long run, national unity cannot be achieved and maintained without the full satisfaction of the liberal demands of the people and that, without the active and driving power of national unity, the people's instinct for freedom cannot be satisfied. Therefore our motto is as follows: the German state and German freedom must be achieved simultaneously and through the same means. It would be a pernicious error to believe that the people, its advocates, and its representatives need only protect the interests of freedom; or that, on the

From Karl Bachem, *Vorgeschichte, Geschichte und Politik der Deutschen Zentrumspartei,* vol. 2 (Cologne, 1927), pp. 219–20. Translated for this volume by Paul Silverman.

other hand, unity will be achieved without us by the government on the basis of politics made by its ministers.

For us the unification of all of Germany under one and the same constitution is the highest task of the present.

To bring a monarchical federal state into harmony with the requisites of constitutional law is a difficult assignment, something that has never yet been accomplished in the history of mankind. The constitution of the North German Confederation accomplished this task neither completely nor in a conclusively satisfactory manner. But we consider the new constitution to be the first indispensable step on the road to a German state whose freedom and power will be firmly secured. The accession of southern Germany, which the constitution holds open, must be promoted with urgency and with all available forces, but under no circumstances should it weaken or place in question the unitary central power.

A constitution that arises through the agency of practical necessities never comes into being without shortcomings. In the present instance these imperfections grew with the number of conflicting interests. However, it was always a sign of healthy vitality that the improving hand went to work immediately. We have not escaped the lot of human imperfection, but the difficulties have not discouraged us, and the imperfections have not blinded us to the good nucleus we now possess. Just as in its earliest stages our party was concerned to improve, so will it work without pause—indeed in the next session of the Reichstag—to strengthen and complete the constitution along the lines already laid out.

We saw in Parliament the union of the living active forces of the nation. Universal and equal suffrage, direct elections, and the secret ballot have with our assistance become the foundation of public life. We are not oblivious to the dangers that go along with these things, so long as freedom of the press and the rights of assembly and association are infringed upon by police power, as long as the primary schools stand under crippling regulations, and elections are subjected to bureaucratic interventions, dangers made all the more ominous by the fact that the refusal of daily allowances for deputies limits the ability of persons to stand for election. However, although these guaranties could not be achieved, the dangers have not deterred us. It is now up to the people to demand honest elections. Strenuous efforts will succeed in enabling the people to express its voice in accordance with the truth, and once this happens general suffrage will become the sturdiest bulwark of freedom. It will clear away the remnants of the estates system that have survived into modern times and will finally make guaranteed equality before the law a reality.

We are determined to secure the jurisdiction of the central government and to extend it to all matters that concern the whole. We have as a goal the most complete possible transferal of the parliamentary functions of the state to the Reichstag. In addition the Prussian Landtag should gradually come to content itself with a position that does not in any way detract from the prestige and effectiveness of the Reichstag. We want to pursue this goal by constitutional means. Until it is reached in this manner, the two parliamentary bodies must mutually respect each other's powers and display a peaceful rivalry in the fulfillment of their callings.

By following the example of the Prussian Constitution in the drafting of the Imperial Constitution, imperfections corresponding to those of the former have found their way into the latter. In both cases we must now strive in a simultaneous and uniform manner for essential reforms that can furnish the only secure foundation of public law. First and foremost, the right of approving the budget must be fully secured, so that full influence over the activities of the state falls to the representatives of the people. No less urgent is the need for laws, resting on the juristic principle that everyone must answer for his actions, which will establish effective responsibility of ministers and all officers of the state. Beyond this, a more complete representation of the responsible bearers of governmental power should be provided for on the federal level and their relationship to the governments of the individual states clarified.

Through the events of the previous year and the transformations that have now begun, the tasks of the Prussian state—of the government as well as of the people—have multiplied.

The annexation of the newly acquired territories makes a program of energetic reform legislation—which under the domination of the Conservative party has been delayed and which during the constitutional conflict was completely brought to a standstill—urgent and not postponable. Throughout the country, innumerable abuses such as the freezing of credit on real property, the limitation on the freedom of movement, and the pressures placed on the trades and labor by the chains of trade regulations, await prompt redress. The necessary merging of the old and new territories calls for comprehensive reform in the organic and other important laws. We also owe to the new provinces, which in the areas of the judiciary and administration enjoy many advantages over us, protection of their institutions. It would be impossible to allow them to be replaced by faulty old Prussian institutions. Rather, uniformity should be brought about by our following their lead in those areas where they are ahead of us. Prussia owes to all Germany a good example in the fields of law and administration in so far as both of these matters are reserved to the individual states, since the future of the entire fatherland depends on that example. For this reason we believe that we must all the more zealously strive for the development and revision of the Prussian Constitution. Now as before we call for the fulfillment of the laws promised in the constitution and the reform of the House of Lords as the precondition of all reforms. With regard to reforms themselves, by far the most important are the following: first, the removal of the estates principle from the communal, district, and provincial constitutions and the reform of these constitutions in accordance with the principles of equality of rights and self-administration; second, the abolition of local manorial authority and manorial police powers.

These secure and broad foundations are required for the vigorous advance of the fatherland. In addition, the increasing size of the state's territory increases the dangers of bureaucratic influences, and the sway of the system of communal administration which rests on preferential treatment and privileges is incompatible with the principles of modern law recognized in the constitution. The population, the urban as well as the rural, has, through the great and willing services it performed in the recent war, renewed its right to see its most urgent wishes finally fulfilled.

Among the other numerous objectives we support, we note the following: the protection of the legal system by means of an independent judiciary; the independence and expansion of legal procedure; the revision of laws dealing with conflicts of competence and the determination of the legality of actions in the administrative sphere; the extension of jury trial to all criminal matters of a political sort along with the dissolution of the *Staatsgerichtshof;* and the abolition of caution money and taxes on newspapers and journals.

Mindful of its heavy responsibility and loyal to the principles it enunciated previously, the party established internal peace during the days of danger and decision on the basis of law conforming with the constitution, and it also generously furnished the means and approved the armaments that would secure Prussia's unrestrained effectiveness in the pursuit of its destiny. For the honor and power of the fatherland, we shall continue to act in the same fashion. However, we are spurred on by the burdens of chronic war readiness to consolidate quickly the new conditions in Germany, in order that soon, in any event not later than the end of the *provisorium,* the necessary economy of a true peacetime level of military strength may be attained. In the meantime, the shortening of the required period of military service to the end of the thirty-second year, which has been secured in the constitution, must be quickly implemented, and every other possible easing of the burden in this policy area must be pursued.

We do not harbor the hope of fulfilling our numerous requirements all in a single stroke. However, we will forget none of them, and according to the propitiousness of the circumstances we shall place the one or the other in the foreground. But we consider at all times that the indispensable precondition for the successful cooperation between the government and the representatives of the people and for the prevention of new conflicts is an administration that acts in accordance with the laws and that is steadfastly respectful of the rights and freedom of the individual bodies politic as well as of the whole. Relapses into other practices characteristic of the past must be openly opposed without restraint, regardless of the danger. We can walk hand in hand only with a government that faithfully observes the law. With such a government we are ready to search out the proper paths.

Vivid experience has taught us that the same tools may not at all times be appropriate for the accomplishment of the same tasks. Where such significant and momentous goals are to be striven for simultaneously, as presently is the case in Germany and Prussia, it is not sufficient merely to hold firm to conventional maxims and to allow new and diverse needs to be neglected for the sake of a simple and convenient tradition. It requires arduous and cautious labor to master the various demands one encounters, to oversee the course of events, and to gain the advantage that can be wrought from an opportunity. The ultimate goals of liberalism are unchanging, but its demands and procedures are not cut off from life and are not reducible to fixed formulas. Its innermost being consists of observing the signs of the times and satisfying the demands they pose. The present speaks to us clearly with the message that in our fatherland every step toward unity on a constitutional basis is at the same time progress in the area of freedom or carries within it an impulse to that end.

We do not intend to oppose with malevolence other factions of the Liberal party, for we feel at one with them in the service of freedom. However, in the face of the great questions of the present moment and with a sense of responsibility that makes us conscious of how much depends on the proper choice of means, we shall endeavor and hope to bring the principles we have developed to bear within the party.

[There follow fifty-six signatures, among others those of von Bennigsen, von Forckenbeck, Lasker, H. B. Oppenheim, Twesten, and von Unruh.]

39. Hermann von Mallinckrodt, Programmatic Statement for the Prussian *Zentrum* (May 1862)

The undersigned concur in the following views:

1. The teachings and principles of Christianity constitute the essential basis of a just and free political order. Therefore all endeavors that threaten to undermine this foundation of the public welfare must be resisted. On the

From Karl Bachem, *Vorgeschichte, Geschichte und Politik der Deutschen Zentrumspartei*, vol. 2 (Cologne, 1927), p. 219. Translated for this volume by Paul Silverman.

other hand, the full, effective development of the parity characteristic of the Prussian state, rooted in its history and its constitution, is a desirable goal. To achieve this end the demand for the treatment of the equally entitled confessions and their members with equal benevolence and equal justice is to be supported.

2. The higher the respect to be accorded to the business and rights of the governmental authority, the less one can fail to recognize that its rights find their limit in the rights of individuals, families, and corporate bodies. Accordingly, we want a strong monarchy rooted in its own rights, and we want a representation of the people that is free and self-assured. Both of these elements of the state should stand solidly and loyally upon the foundation of the constitution. In addition, we desire the further development of constitutional government in a manner that is prudent and in accordance with the needs of the present, and we desire the development of corporate independence in the communes, districts, and provinces.

3. The principles of morality and law must be the guiding maxims in politics as elsewhere. He who disregards the rights of others is unworthy of his own rights. Therefore, all revolutionary tendencies are to be opposed whether they are encountered in the external relations of the state or within the state's own territory. We need a German policy that takes full account of the balance of power among states as well as the interests of our own Prussian state. Such a policy does not allow the latter to be subordinated to any outside, particularist interests, but it also does not seek the criterion for the needs and the national task of the German people in the petty cultivation of the Prussian state's own particularist interests. The national task of the German people calls for concord and firmer unity among all Germany's members; it requires reform of the Confederation and the establishment of a central power. But it does not permit, in order to achieve the closer connection of the individual members, the dissolution of the Confederation and the division of the nation. The prerequisites for the recovery of national power and greatness, the growth of material welfare in all areas of productive activity, the establishment of peace, and the lasting reduction of our own state expenditures lie precisely in the firmer union of all of Germany.

40. Hellmut von Gerlach, *A Junker Paradise*

Hellmut von Gerlach (1866–1935) was the son of a Silesian Junker family in nineteenth-century Prussia. After studying law, he entered the Prussian bureaucracy, intending to devote his life to government service—a

From *The Living Age* (Concord, N.H.) 326, no. 4238 (1925):667–70.

common career choice for sons of the East Elbian nobility. Gerlach joined
the Prussian Conservative party and became acquainted with Adolf
Stoecker, the leader of the Christian Social movement in Berlin. After
1894 Gerlach's views changed radically. He supported the faction around
Friedrich Naumann in the Christian Social movement, which wanted to
divorce the Christian Socials from the Conservative party and to create
an independent social reform movement of a more centrist, liberal, and
national orientation (the *Nationalsozialer Verein*) that might bridge the
gap between the proletarian masses and German bourgeois society. In
1903 Gerlach was elected to a seat in the German Reichstag from Hesse
as a left Liberal but with Catholic support.

Gerlach's political career stopped short when he failed to win reelection in 1907, but his agitatorial work as a journalist and political orga-
nizer on behalf of Liberal social causes continued unabated. From 1912
to 1918 Gerlach served as chairman of a liberal splinter group in Berlin,
the *Demokratische Vereinigung*. A determined pacifist during the First
World War, Gerlach served for a short time in late 1918 as a state secretary in the Prussian Ministry of Interior, but devoted most of his career in
the Weimar Republic to writing trenchant, prodemocratic articles and reviews for several Berlin newspapers. As an ardent supporter of Weimar
democracy, Gerlach was forced to flee Hitler in 1933 and died in exile in
Paris in 1935.

The following selection from Gerlach's *Erinnerungen eines Junkers*
(1925) provides an interesting, if somewhat jaundiced, view of the social
world of Gerlach's youth in Silesia and the political universe he left behind in search of a new Liberal utopia after 1895.

The first eighteen years of my life were spent in the district of Wohlau in
Silesia. This district together with Guhrau and Steinau formed an electoral
division that was called "the golden borough of the Conservatives" because it had never sent either to the Reichstag or to the Landtag a representative who did not belong to that Party. It was not necessary for the candidates to exert themselves either physically or mentally in running for
office. Any Herr von Kessel or Herr von Nitzschwitz or Graf Carmer might
be nominated by a committee of big landlords presided over by the Landrat. Thereupon his election was assured.

This department was so extremely reactionary that even the Free Conservatives were looked upon as dangerous revolutionaries. On one occasion a clergyman, who was also district school-inspector, ventured to run
for the Landtag as Free Conservative candidate with the help of some of
the public-school teachers. His presumption aroused a storm of resentment

among the country gentry. In its name a certain Herr von Seydlitz published a statement in the local paper accusing the clergyman of base ingratitude because, after having been in his younger days graciously received into the family of one of the large estate owners as a tutor for his children, he had ventured to set himself up against the will of the landed interest.

Inasmuch as the landlords enjoyed the right of appointing most of the clergymen and teachers, the latter were utterly dependent on their favor. My father's nearest neighbor was a certain Baron von Beust, a gentleman of Saxon origin. On one occasion he had to appoint a new incumbent for the parish on his estate of Herrnmotschelnitz. Several aspirants presented themselves for the position, each of whom delivered a probationary sermon. I personally heard all of them. Finally a very young clergyman, who had preached what was obviously the worst sermon of the series, was appointed. When I took Herr von Beust to task for this he merely grunted, "Well, you see the chap plays bully skat." That qualification was decisive.

My father was a Protestant, but he had the appointment to the living at the Catholic Church and school in Gross-Schmograu. He hated Catholics. He used to say, "They are even worse than the Jews." Consequently he did all in his power to get the most anti-Catholic priest he could find for the parish. Before long his policy was detected. After that the clerical aspirants for the position always represented themselves to my father as extreme freethinkers. After they were appointed, however, the lord of the parish had no control of them, and they always turned out in the end to be perfectly orthodox, and in several instances unusually zealous, priests and defenders of the Church. This only confirmed my father in his conviction that they were a breed of "Jesuitical hypocrites." My private idea was that his experience only proved the immorality of the whole institution of clerical patronage; although the Junkers considered it the very foundation stone of their power and defended it with tooth and nail.

Wohlau is in Central Silesia. We did not have the great latifundia of Upper Silesia. Our estates were for the most part of comparatively moderate size, ranging from two thousand to five thousand acres, and were usually "circulating properties"—that is, they repeatedly changed proprietors. Landlords whose families had been permanently rooted in the soil for many generations, as they were in parts of Pomerania and Brandenburg, were rare in our neighborhood. So when a family had owned and lived upon the same property for fifty years it was usual to confer upon its head the Order of the Red Eagle IV in honor of the event.

My father had no great respect for orders. One day he learned that he was about to be given one—I think it was on the occasion of completing his twenty-fifth year of service as a local magistrate. When the Landrat of

Wrochem called and notified him of the high honor that was awaiting him, my father made a deprecatory gesture and requested that the order be given instead to an elderly neighbor for whom it would be the great event of his declining years. That was done. The septuagenarian invalid, who still insisted on being called Lieutenant, was moved to tears when the Landrat, with a ceremonious speech, bestowed upon him the highest form of earthly bliss in the shape of the Order of the Red Eagle IV. As the old gentleman was no longer able to leave the house, he wore it constantly on his dressing-gown.

Much of the property in our vicinity was owned by officers who had been dropped from active service. They knew nothing whatever about farming, but they imagined that although they had failed in a military career they were at least abundantly competent to manage a large estate. Naturally they made one blunder after another, and their bailiffs robbed them right and left. Thereupon they would deliver long harangues on the depression in agriculture and clamor for higher duties upon grain. They were not consciously insincere. They regarded agriculture as a highly respectable calling that required no special preparation but that nevertheless ought to support a gentleman according to the standards of his class.

Those standards were very modest, at least in their own opinion: saddle horses, a couple of spans of coach horses, a dozen carriages, a well-stocked wine cellar, a hunting-preserve, good hunting-dinners, and ability to educate their sons as Corps students or cavalry officers. These things were assumed as a matter of course. Gambling, which was such a curse among the country gentry of Upper Silesia, was kept within bounds. A few frivolous-minded young bloods might play hazard after a hunting-dinner. On such occasions, however, they often had to use matches as chips in default of ready money. But most of the card-playing was confined to humdrum whist and skat.

Our landlords had their own economic code. If a man owned an immense park, he considered the cost of its maintenance a necessary operating-charge of his estate. Instead of sending his children to the public schools, he kept private tutors and governesses and regarded the expense as a perfectly proper cost-item in his farming-operations. He felt the same about his hunting-expenses, which first and last were very considerable—although he might have leased his hunting-rights for a goodly sum. The gentry hardly took the handsome castles and manor houses they occupied into account as revenue. I remember hearing one of our neighbors abuse the Landrat roundly at a neighborhood gathering because that gentleman had assessed his castle, which had twenty windows on the front façade, at a rental of nine hundred marks a year. He had declared it for only three hundred marks. When I asked him how he reduced it to that figure, since the interest on the cost of his residence would have amounted to several thousand marks, he said: "In my village the only other possible tenants would be farm laborers. They earn so little money that taking them altogether they couldn't pay more than three hundred marks rent." Yet this man was absolutely convinced that he was right. In fact, the country gentleman had economic theories that were all his own.

Our rural laborers were intensely ignorant and lived in a most primitive sort of way. Almost their only indulgence was liquor, which on all festal occasions, such as Christmas, Harvest Home, and the opening of the hunting-season, they obtained by litres from the landlord's distillery. The women of the gentry class would wax indignant at the farm hands' drunken orgies every Saturday and Sunday. At the same time, they took great satisfaction in the big profits that their distilleries paid. Their ethical code was well satirized in this little quatrain:—

Lern, lieber Sohn, das Leben kennen,
Sehr nobel ist es, Schnaps zu brennen,
Bedenklich schon, ihn zu verkaufen,
Ganz unmoralisch, ihn zu saufen.

(Learn, my son, this rule of conduct:
It is very noble to distill whiskey;
it is a questionable business to sell it;
it is utterly immoral to swill it.)

At that time farm laborers were politically merely tools for maintaining Conservative ascendancy. Their miserable wages prevented their indulging in the luxury of a newspaper of their own. Their landlord would let them subscribe at his expense for a little Conservative daily or a pious Sunday sheet. At Christmas he gave each of his tenants a calendar adorned with patriotic mottoes and stories or with Christian admonishments to humility, obedience, and contentedness. No village innkeeper dared to grant the use of his dancing-hall for any other than a Conservative meeting; otherwise the neighboring landlord, who was also the local magistrate, could make it exceedingly disagreeable for him. On Election Day laborers were marshaled in a column during the noon interval and marched off to the polls, with the bailiff in front and the forester behind. At the door of the polling-place the bailiff gave each laborer a Conservative ballot, which the landlord immediately collected from him in his capacity as judge of elections.

The machine worked perfectly. The only discordant notes in this political harmony came from the few villages where peasant freeholders lived. At such places a few ballots would be cast for Independent or Clerical candidates. Our Junker circle was for this reason particularly hostile to the peasants, though later the Landlords' Union managed very skillfully to bring most of them under its control. But when I was a young man the peasants in my neighborhood were looked upon as uncertain and unreliable fellows. A few of them were even presumptuous enough to refuse to lease hunting-rights over their land to the *gnädigen Herrn* because that gentleman's game had damaged their crops.

We had in our vicinity only one solitary really modern man among the Junkers. He was a certain Graf Pourtales, who was managing as trustee an estate at Glumbowitz. He had the crazy idea that the English system of government was a good one because it encouraged able men to go to Parliament. For this heresy he was roundly abused as a "Liberal." For the same reason, however, the freeholding peasants elected him to the Kreistag; and he took his seat in that body right among them.

This was going beyond all bounds. Such an offense was unforgivable. So Pourtales was ostracized by all his social equals. None of them would have anything to do with either him or his family. In fact, he was so utterly banned and isolated that he finally went off to America and stayed there ten years, until the grass could grow over the grave of his crime.

41. Max Weber, *The National State and Economic Policy*

Max Weber (1864–1920) was a man of vast learning whose scholarship was closely coordinated with his deep concern for political and social developments in Germany and the world. Born in Erfurt, he grew up in Berlin where his family moved in 1869. Weber's father rose to prominence in the National Liberal party, and the Weber home became an important meeting place for leading figures in German society and politics.

In 1882 Weber entered the University of Heidelberg to study law. He joined a student fraternity and took to dueling and beer drinking with alacrity, but also entered into wide-ranging studies in economics, history, philosophy, and theology. At this time he also came under the influence of his uncle, Hermann Baumgarten, a professor of history in Strassburg and a Liberal who had endorsed Bismarck in 1866 only to become disillusioned in the 1880s with the consequences of Bismarck's Caesarist rule. (Baumgarten was also one of Treitschke's most vigorous domestic critics.) Baumgarten's example helped Weber begin to question the self-satisfied National Liberalism of his father and to assume the stance of an independent critic whose primary concern was the security and power of the German state.

From Max Weber, *Der Nationalstaat und die Volkswirtschaftspolitik,* Akademische Antrittsrede (Freiburg, 1895). Translated for this volume by Paul Silverman.

In 1884 Weber enrolled at the University of Berlin, writing a dissertation on the law of medieval business organizations. Having decided on an academic career rather than the practice of law, Weber qualified as a lecturer in 1891 with a study on Roman agrarian history. He became an associate professor at Berlin in 1893, but was called to a professorship in economics at Freiburg in 1894.

Shortly after Weber assumed a chair at the University of Heidelberg in 1896, he endured a protracted period of serious mental problems—insomnia, anxiety, and exhaustion—forcing him to withdraw from teaching. In 1902 he had sufficiently recovered to resume a career as a scholar, although not as a teacher. He began to publish important writings on the nature and method of the social sciences and the sociology of religion. By 1913 he had completed most of his masterpiece—a treatise on general sociology published posthumously, *Economy and Society.*

At the outbreak of the war in 1914, Weber was carried away by the general nationalist enthusiasm, but later became a stern critic of German policies, especially the declaration of unrestricted submarine warfare in 1917. Following the end of the war he became a strong supporter of constitutional democracy and attempted to enter politics. He ran for office, without success, but played an important role in drafting the constitution of the Weimar Republic.

In 1892 Weber was selected by the Verein für Sozialpolitik, a social policy research association made up of academics, civil servants, and businessmen, to participate in an investigation of agricultural workers in Germany. The essay published here, *Die Freiburger Antrittsrede* (Inaugural academic lecture), was a ceremonial lecture given in May 1895 to mark the assumption of his professorship in Freiburg.

Preface

It is not the approval that the following remarks found among many of those who heard them but rather the controversy they aroused that has prompted me to present them for publication. Only in matters of detail will they provide fellow specialists as well as others with new substantive material, and the sole and special sense in which they can lay claim to the title "scientific" arises from the occasion of their formulation. Indeed, an inaugural lecture offers an opportunity for an open presentation and justification of the personal and thus "subjective" standpoint one takes when *passing judgement* upon economic phenomena. In my presentation, the remarks on pages 452–54 [of this edition] were omitted for reasons of time and in consideration of the audience of my speech, and other comments may have assumed a different form when delivered. As for the exposition, it should be noted at the outset that the processes in question are naturally depicted here in a substantially simplified form compared to what is found in reality. The period 1871–85 did not reveal any uniform population movements in the individual districts and communes of West Prussia but, rather, characteristic oscillating ones that are by no means as transparent as the examples chosen here. The tendency I have attempted to illustrate through these examples is in other cases intermingled with other factors. I shall very soon return to this issue elsewhere and deal with it at greater length. It goes without saying that the conclusions suggested by these figures rest on a much less secure foundation than those concerning the conditions of the nationalities in Posen and West Prussia, furnished us by the commendable publications of several of Neumann's students. In the absence of correct data, however, these figures will have to suffice for the time being, especially since the main features of the phenomena they illustrate have already been made known to us through the rural investigations of the last few years.

Freiburg, May 1895
Max Weber

The manner in which my subject has been formulated in the title I have chosen promises much more than I either can or wish to deal with today. What I intend to do is first to illustrate by means of a *single example* the role played in the economic struggle for existence by the physical and psychic racial differences that exist among nationalities. Then I would like to add a few observations concerning the position of a state resting on national foundations—such as our own—within the framework of study in the realm of economic policy. I have chosen as my example a group of events that are taking place in a region far from us but have been attracting public attention for a decade; I thus ask you to come along with me to the eastern marches of the empire, to the flat land of the Prussian province of *West Prussia*. This setting combines the quality of a national borderland with unusually sharp differences in economic and social conditions of existence, which makes it particularly suited for our purpose. Unfortunately, I must first try your patience with a collection of dry data.

In its rural districts, the province contains three types of contrasts. First, there are extraordinary variations in the *fertility of the soil:* between the sugar beet soil of the Vistula plain and the sandy Cassubian hill country one finds ten- and twentyfold differences in estimates of net tax yields. Even the average returns at the district level fluctuate between 4 3/4 and 33 2/3 marks per hectare.

Then there are contrasts in the *social stratification* of the population that cultivates this soil. As is generally the case in the east, alongside the "rural commune" the official records here refer to a second type of communal unit unknown in the south—the "estate district." Accordingly, between the peasants' villages the estates of the nobility stand out in bold relief on the rural landscape. These are the seats of the class that gives the east its social character—the Junkers. One sees manor houses surrounded by single-story cottages, which the lord of the manor allots, together with parcels of arable land and pasturage, to the day laborers, who for their part are obligated to work throughout the year on the manor. The province as a whole is divided almost equally between these two types of communal units; but in individual regions the estate districts' share varies from a few percent up to two-thirds of the area of a district proper.

Finally, within this population, with its twofold social stratification, one finds the third contrast—that of *nationality.* The national composition of the population of the individual communal units also varies regionally. It is *this* variation that interests us. First, the proportion of Poles rises, naturally, as one approaches the border. But it also *increases,* as any language map will show, with *decreases* in the fertility of the soil. This is something that one is first inclined to explain historically—and in many cases with justification—by reference to the way German settlement took place, a process that began with a pouring of Germans onto the fertile Vistula plain. However, if one goes on to ask which social strata on the countryside are the representatives of German and Polish culture, the figures of the most recently published population census,[1] that of 1885, present a remarkable picture. To be sure, this survey does not permit us directly to perceive the national composition of the communes. We can, however, perceive it indirectly if we are content with figures of less than perfect accuracy. We can do this by examining the membership of religious confessions, for in the nationally mixed region that concerns us here the religious groups coincide with nationality to within a few percentage points. If we separate the economic categories of peasant village and noble estate in the individual regions by identifying them—with the same sort of imprecision we have already accepted—with the communal entities,[2] rural commune and estate district respectively, one discovers that they relate to each other

1. "Gemeindelexikon," Berlin 1887.
2. From the standpoint of a consideration of social stratification, this administrative classification is, all the same, more attuned to the characteristics of the situation than is taking as one's basis the distribution of production units. On the plain, manorial operations of under one hundred and, in the hill country, peasant farms of over two hundred hectares are not uncommon.

with respect to their national composition in a *contrary* manner, which is dependent upon the fertility of the soil. In districts with high fertility, Catholics, that is, *Poles,* are relatively most numerous on the *estates,* and Protestants, that is, *Germans,* predominate in the *villages.* In districts with low fertility, the situation is precisely the reverse. For example, if one looks at districts where the average net tax yield is less than 5 marks per hectare, we find that Protestants make up only 35.5 percent of the population in the villages but 50.2 percent of the population on the estates. On the other hand, if we look at the districts where the average net tax yield per hectare is 10 to 15 marks, we find that Protestants make up 60.7 percent of the population in the villages but only 42.1 percent on the estates. Why is this the case? Why is it that on the plains the Polish element gravitates toward the estates but in the hill country it gravitates toward the villages? One thing is apparent immediately: *the Poles have a tendency to congregate in the stratum of the population that stands lowest on the economic and social scale.* On the fertile soil, especially that of the Vistula plain, the peasant farmer's standard of living was always higher than that of the day laborer on an estate, whereas on the poor soil, which could be rationally cultivated only on a large scale, the nobleman's estate has been the bearer of civilization and hence of German culture. Even today, the standard of living of the miserable small peasants who live in that area is still *below* that of the day laborers on the estates. If we did not already know this, the age structure of the population would lead us to suspect it. If one ascends from the *villages* on the plain to those on the ridges, one finds that, as the fertility of the soil declines, the proportion of the population made up of children under fourteen years of age rises from 35–36 percent to 40–41 percent. Looking at the *estates,* by comparison, one finds that on the plain the proportion of children is larger than that in the villages, that it increases as one moves up into the hill country but at a slower rate than in the villages, and that *on* the hilltops it remains below that of the villages. Here, as everywhere, the large proportion of children in the population is closely associated with a low standard of living, a condition that stifles consideration of how provisions for the future will be secured. Economic well-being, relative superiority of standard of living, and *German culture* are in West Prussia one and the same thing.

And yet the two nationalities have competed for centuries on the same soil and with the benefit of essentially the same opportunities. What, then, is the basis of this difference? One is immediately tempted to believe that there is a difference in the two nationalities, stemming from racial qualities of a physical and psychic nature, in the *ability to adapt* to different economic and social conditions. This is, in fact, the basis of the difference. The proof lies in the tendency that emerges in the *shifts* of population and nationalities observable in the region, a proof that at the same time suggests that this difference in the ability to adapt has fateful implications for German culture in the east.

To be sure, for comparative observation of population shifts in individual communes one has only the 1871–85 figures, which permit only a glimpse of the beginning of a development which since that time, according to all the information we have, has continued with an extraordinary increase in vigor. Moreover, the clarity of the picture presented by the numbers obviously suffers from the necessary but not entirely accurate equation of religious confession with nationality, on the one hand, and of administrative classifications with types of social organization on the other. Nevertheless, we can see the main point clearly enough. The rural population of the province in the period 1880–85, like that of large portions of the east as a whole, showed a tendency to *decrease*. In West Prussia this decrease amounted to 12,700 persons; in other words, while the population of the empire increased approximately 3 1/2 percent, the population of West Prussia decreased about 1 1/4 percent. This phenomenon, like the others we have already discussed, is distributed unevenly: in some districts there was an increase in the rural population. Moreover, the *manner in which* these decreases and increases are distributed is quite peculiar. If we first consider tracts of land of varying fertility, everyone would expect population decrease to have hit the *worst* land the hardest, the place where the margin of subsistence, under the pressure of sinking prices, must first become too narrow. But if one looks at the figures, it becomes apparent that the *reverse* is the case; it was precisely a group of the best-endowed districts—for example, Stuhm and Marienweder with an average net tax yield of around 15–17 marks—that experienced the greatest *population loss*, about 7–8 percent, while in the hill country the districts of Konitz and Tuchel, with a net tax yield of 5–6 marks, experienced the greatest *increase*, an increase that has been under way constantly since 1871. One searches for an explanation, and one begins by asking: Which social strata did the decrease come from, and which strata benefited from the increase? Looking at the districts with large numerical losses—Stuhm, Marienweder, Rosenberg—we find that they are always ones in which *large land holdings* are particularly dominant. If we then consider the *estate districts* of the province as a whole, it turns out that, whereas in 1880 in an area equal in size to that of the villages their population was about two-thirds smaller than that of the villages, they alone have experienced almost three-quarters of the decline of the rural population, over nine thousand persons. Their population has decreased by about 3 3/4 percent. Moreover, *within* the estates category this decrease is again distributed unevenly. In some cases there were increases, and if one singles out the regions with large decreases in the population of the estates, one finds that precisely the estates on the *fertile* soil experienced a particularly sharp loss of population.

On the other hand, the population *increase* that took place on the inferior soils of the hill country has primarily benefited the *villages,* with precisely the greatest benefit going to those villages on *inferior* soils, in contrast to the villages on the plain. *A decrease of day laborers* on the estates on the *best* soil and an *increase of peasants* on the *inferior* is thus the tendency revealed by the evidence. What is going on here and how it is to be explained becomes clear when one finally turns to the question of how the *nationalities* behave with respect to these shifts.

During the first half of the century, the Polish element in the east appears to have been slowly and continuously pushed back. Since the 1860s, however, as is well known, it has been just as slowly and continuously on the advance. Despite their faulty foundations, linguistic inquiries establish this latter fact for West Prussia in the clearest possible manner. Now a shift of the boundary between two nationalities can come about in two fundamentally distinct ways. One way is for national minorities in a nationally mixed region to have the language and customs of the majority gradually imposed upon them, for them to be "absorbed." This phenomenon can be found in the east. It is statistically demonstrable in the case of German Catholics. The bond of the church is stronger here than that of the nation, memories of the *Kulturkampf* also play a part, and the lack of a German-educated clergy permits them to be lost to the cultural community of the nation. More important, however, and more interesting for us, is the second form in which shifts of nationalities take place—*economic displacement.* This is what we are dealing with here. If one examines shifts in the proportion of the religious confessions in rural communal units between 1871 and 1885, one finds that, on the plain, an outflow of manorial day laborers is regularly associated with a relative decline of Protestants, and that in the hill country an increase of the village population is regularly associated with a relative increase of Catholics.[3] *It is primarily the German day laborers who are leaving the regions with higher levels of culture, and it is primarily Polish peasants who are multiplying in the regions where the state of culture is low.*

Both processes, however—emigration here, population growth there—are in the final analysis to be traced to one and the same cause: *the lower standard of living*—in part in connection with the material realm and in part in connection with the ideal—which the Slavic race *demands* by its

---

3. For example, the estate districts of the district of Stuhm experienced between 1871 and 1885 a population decline of around 6.7 percent, while the proportion of Protestants in its Christian population declined from 33.4 to 31.3 percent. The villages of the districts Konitz and Tuchel had a population increase of 8 percent, while the proportion of Catholics climbed from 84.7 to 86 percent.

very nature or which has been bred into it in the course of its past and has helped it to victory.

Why do the German day laborers leave? It is not for material reasons, for those who leave are not drawn from regions with low wage rates or from the categories of workers at the bottom end of the wage scale. There is hardly a situation materially more secure than that of a cottager on the estates in the east. Nor is it the often-mentioned yearning for the pleasures of the big city. This is a reason for the aimless wandering off of the younger generation, but not for the departure of day laborer families with long years of service. And why does the urge appear precisely among the people who live where large holdings predominate? Why are we able to demonstrate that the emigration of day laborers decreases as the degree to which the *peasant village* dominates the physiognomy of the countryside increases? The reason is *this:* on the estates of his homeland, for the day laborer there is only master and servant, and for his descendants to the most distant generation there is only the prospect of slaving away on someone else's land from one chime of the estate bell to the next. In this indistinct, half-conscious impulse to move off beyond the horizon there lies a hidden element of primitive idealism. He who cannot decipher it does not understand the magic of *freedom.* Indeed, its spirit seldom touches us today in the quiet of the study. The naïve ideals of freedom of our early youth are faded, and some of us have grown old prematurely, become all too wise, and believe that one of the most primordial drives within the human breast has been carried to the grave along with the slogans of a point of view regarding politics and economic policy that is on the decline.

One is dealing here with a process of a mass-psychological kind: German agricultural workers can no longer adapt to the *social* living conditions of their home. Reports out of West Prussia from the lords of the estates complain of the "self-assurance" of the workers. The old patriarchical relationship between lord and smallholder, which attached the day laborer directly to the interests of agricultural production as a small cultivator entitled to a portion of the crop, is disappearing. Seasonal work in the beet-growing districts requires seasonal workers and money wages. These workers face a purely proletarian existence, but without the possibility of the sort of vigorous ascent to economic independence that fills the industrial proletariat, crowded together in the cities, with self-confidence. It is those who take the place of the Germans who are better able to accommodate themselves to these living conditions—the Polish migrant workers, bands of nomads recruited by agents in Russia, who cross the border in tens of thousands in the spring and then depart in the autumn. They first appear in the wake of the sugar beet, a crop that transforms agriculture into a seasonal trade. Then they take over entirely, because by using them one can save on workers' housing, on expenditures for poor relief, on social obligations, and further because as foreigners they are in a precarious position and thus under the control of the landowner. These are accompanying circumstances of the economic death throes of the old Prussian Junkerdom. On the sugar beet estates, the old lord of the manor who ruled patriarchally is being replaced by a new class of industrial businessmen, while in the hill country the tracts of the estates crumble away under the pressure of the agricultural crisis from without. Tenants leasing small plots and colonies of small farmers appear on their outer reaches. The economic foundations of the old landed aristocracy's position of power are disappearing; the class itself is becoming something different from what it formerly was.

And why is it the *Polish* peasants who are gaining ground? Is it their superior intelligence in economic affairs or their greater supply of capital? It is rather the opposite of both of these. In a climate and on a soil that, along with extensive cattle raising, permit primarily grain and potato production, the person least threatened by adverse market conditions is the one who transports his products to the place where a collapse in prices will devalue them the least—to his own stomach. This is someone who produces in order to fulfill his *own requirements*. Moreover, someone who can set his own requirements the *lowest,* who with regard to his standard of living makes the least demands of a physical and ideal sort, is a person with an advantage. The Polish small farmer in the east is of a type far removed from the industrious farmer owning a tiny plot, whom you can see here in the well-endowed Rhine Valley attaching himself to the towns by means of commercial greenhouse cultivation and gardening. The Polish small peasant gains ground because he so to speak gobbles up the grass that is on it, not *in spite* of his inferior physical and intellectual living patterns but rather *because* of them.

So what we see happening here appears to be a *process of selection.* For a long time now, both nationalities have been caught up in the same conditions of existence. The consequence was *not* that they assumed the same physical and psychological qualities, as is envisioned in unsophisticated versions of the doctrine of materialism, but rather that one gave way to the other, that the victorious one was the one with the greater ability to adapt to the given economic and social living conditions.

It seems that this difference in ability to adapt is itself something that these nationalities carry with them as a constant. It could perhaps be further altered through a process of breeding lasting many generations, similar to the process through which it may have arisen over thousands of years, but as far as deliberations in the present are concerned, it is a factor that has to be dealt with as a given.[4]

4. I believe it hardly necessary for me to point out that the questions disputed in natural science concerning the scope of the applicability of the principle of natural selection, the

As we can see, the selection that takes place in the free play of forces does not, as the optimists among us believe, always redound to the benefit of the nationality that is more highly developed economically or that has greater talents in economic matters. The history of mankind contains examples of the victory of less developed types of humanity and the withering away of higher blossoms of intellectual and spiritual life when the human community that supported them lost its ability to adapt to its living conditions, whether because of its social organization or its racial qualities. In our case, the restructuring of the forms of agricultural enterprise and the enormous agricultural crisis are what is helping the nationality that is inferior in its economic development along to victory. The successful introduction of sugar beet cultivation and the unprofitability of producing cereals for the market are factors working in parallel with each other and moving in a common direction: the former breeds the Polish seasonal worker, the latter the Polish small peasant.

On reviewing the facts that have been discussed here, I readily admit that I am fully incapable of formulating theoretically the significance of the general points that might be drawn from them. The immensely difficult and for the time being certainly insoluble question of *locating* the limit of the variability of a population's physical and psychic qualities under the influence of its given living conditions is something I dare not even touch upon.

On the other hand, everyone is bound to ask: What can happen in this situation and what ought to happen?

Permit me, however, to refrain on this occasion from commenting upon this issue at length and to content myself with briefly indicating the two demands that, from the standpoint of the German nation and German cul-

---

whole of the *natural scientific* application of the concept of "breeding," and all discussions connected with this field—a field that is foreign to me—are irrelevant to the remarks made above. The *concept* of "selection" is today a part of commonly held general knowledge in the same way that a concept such as the heliocentric hypothesis is, and the idea of human "breeding" is already to be found in the Platonic state. Both concepts were, for example, already applied by F. A. Lange in his *Arbeiterfrage* and have so long been a part of our surroundings that no one familiar with our literature can possibly misunderstand their meaning. A more difficult question concerns the degree to which the most recent attempts by anthropologists to extend the applicability of the view of selection taken by Darwin and Weismann to the field of economic research possess lasting value. They are ingenious, but they raise considerable reservations with respect to their method and factual results, and they undoubtedly miscarry on account of many exaggerations. Be that as it may, the writings of, for example, Otto Ammon (*Die natürliche Auslese beim Menschen, Die Gesellschaftsordnung und ihre natürlichen Grundlagen*), deserve in any event, despite all of the provisos that must be made, more attention than they have received. A defect of most of the contributions aimed at shedding light on questions in our science furnished by writers in the natural-scientific camp lies in the misguided ambition above all else to "refute" socialism. In their eagerness to attain this goal, a supposedly "natural-scientific theory" of the social order is unintentionally transformed into an apology for it.

ture, I consider should be made and, in fact, with growing unanimity are being made. The first is that the eastern border be closed. This demand was fulfilled under Prince Bismarck and then reversed after his resignation in 1890; foreigners continued to be denied permanent residence, but they were permitted to enter as migrant workers. A "class-conscious" large landowner at the head of the Prussian government shut them out in the interests of maintaining our nationality, and the hated opponent of the agrarians let them back in, in the interests of the large landowners, who *alone* derive advantage from their influx. This demonstrates that in matters related to economic policy it is not always the "economic class standpoint" that decides the issue—what happened *here* was that the helm of the ship of state fell from a strong hand into a weaker one. The other demand is for a program of systematic purchases of land by the state, in other words the extension of the state domains, and systematic colonization by German peasants on suitable land, especially on suitable state domains. Large-scale enterprises that are being maintained only at the expense of the German element are, from the standpoint of the nation, worth allowing to perish. To leave them to their own devices means to allow nonviable Slavic hunger colonies incapable of surviving to arise through a process of gradual parceling up of the estates. Moreover, it is not only the interest we have in seeing the Slavic flood checked that calls for the transfer of significant portions of land in the east into the hands of the state; it is also the devastating criticism the landowners themselves have leveled against the continued existence of their private property by demanding, in the form of a grain monopoly and a subsidy of half a billion marks a year, the removal of the risks they face, the personal responsibility for their property, which is the sole justification for its existence.[5]

5. This demand for purchase of land by the state has now also been made within the same context by Professor Schmoller in his *Jahrbuch*. In fact, that portion of the class of large landowners whose preservation as agricultural managers is of value to the state is in many cases to be retained only as lessees of state domains, not as owners. At any rate, in my view the purchase of land makes sense in the long term only if it is organically connected with the colonization of suitable state domains, that is, in such a way that a portion of the land in the east passes through the hands of the state and, while it is in the state's hands, undergoes an energetic program of soil enrichment with the aid of state credits. The difficulty the Settlement Commission has to contend with—aside from that of being burdened with the "convalescence" of the implanted colonists, who along with their requests for extensions of the time allowed for repayment would eventually be better turned over to the somewhat more hard-hearted ordinary state treasury—lies in the fact that it would be better if a large proportion of the estates purchased first spent a decade in such a program of soil enrichment in the hands of lessees of state domains. Now the enrichment program must be introduced in great haste by the administration itself and with great losses, while numerous state domains would certainly be suitable for immediate colonization. The slow pace of the procedure, caused by these difficulties, obviously in no way justifies the judgment of its national-political im-

But, as I have already said, I do not wish to discuss today this practical question of Prussian agrarian policy. I would much prefer to take up the fact that this question has arisen for us at all, that we consider the German element in the east to be something that *ought* to be protected and in defense of which the economic policy of the state *ought* to enter into the lists. It is the fact that our state is constituted as a *national state* that allows us to feel we have the right to make this demand.

But how is the perspective from which observations concerning economic policy are made related to all of this? From that perspective, are such nationalistic value judgments prejudices that must be carefully gotten rid of, so that, without being influenced by emotional reflexes, a standard of value peculiar to that perspective can be applied to economic facts? *And what is* this standard of value that is "peculiar" to the realm of economic policy? This is the question I shall attempt to address in some further reflections.

It is evident that even in a situation with the appearance of "peace," the economic struggle between the nationalities follows its course. It is not in open conflict with a politically superior enemy that German peasants and day laborers are being pushed off the land: it is in the quiet, dreary struggle of everyday economic life that an inferior race gets the better of them and that they leave their home and head off toward submergence in a dark future. There is no *peace* in the economic *struggle* for existence. Only he who takes the appearance of peace for the reality can believe that peace and prosperity for our descendants will be born from the womb of the future. We know, of course, that in its popular conception economic policy consists of musing upon recipes for spreading happiness throughout the world. In this view the sole comprehensible goal for our work is the increase of the "balance of pleasure" in human existence. However, the sinister seriousness of the population problem is enough to prevent us from being eudaemonists, from imagining that peace and human happiness lie hidden in the womb of the future, and from believing that elbowroom in earthly existence will be won in any other way than through the hard struggle of men against men.

---

pact made by Hans Delbrück in his various well-known articles published in the *Preussische Jahrbücher*. Surely mechanical calculations comparing the number of peasant farms established with the number of Poles proves nothing for anyone who has observed the civilizing achievements of colonization on the spot: a few villages with a dozen German farms each will eventually *Germanize* several square miles, naturally under the precondition that the proletarian reinforcements from the east are dammed off and that one does not lay on the last straw by leaving the crumbling and decay of the large holdings to itself and to the free play of forces that are now acting with even less restraint on account of the laws permitting and regulating the renting of land in perpetuity.

There is certainly no work to be done in the realm of economic policy that can be based on anything other than an altruistic foundation. The vast majority of the fruits of all endeavors connected with economic and social policy taking place in the present benefit not the present generation but a future one. Our task, if it is to retain any meaning, is and can be nothing other than provision for the *future,* for our *descendants.* But there is also no work in the realm of economic policy that can be based on optimistic dreams of happiness. For the dream of peace and happiness, the following words stand inscribed above the portals of the unknown future of human history: *lasciate ogni speranza.*

It is not the question of how people will *feel* but rather of how they will *be* that moves our thinking beyond the grave of our own generation. In reality, this question forms the foundation of every task in the realm of economic policy. It is not a feeling of well-being that we wish to cultivate in people but, rather, those qualities with which we associate the sense that they constitute human greatness and the nobility of our nature.

In the realm of economics, the technical-economic problem of the production of goods and the problem of their distribution, the problem of "social justice," have alternately been pushed into the foreground as standards of value or naïvely identified with them. Yet again and again above both of these issues, half unconsciously and yet dominating everything, there arose the recognition that a science of *man,* and that is what economics is, is concerned above all with the *quality* bred into *men* through those economic and social conditions of existence. And here we must guard ourselves against an illusion.

As an explanatory and analytic science, economics is *international* in character, but as soon as *value judgments* are made in connection with it, it becomes bound to that particular variety of human nature that we find in our own being. This binding is often most complete at precisely the point at which we believe that we have most completely escaped the limitations our person places upon us. If—to use a somewhat fanciful image—we were able to return from the grave after several thousand years, it would be the distant traces of our own nature that we would seek in the visage of the future generation we encountered. Even our highest and ultimate earthly ideals are mutable and transitory. We cannot hope to impose them upon the future. But we can hope that in our species the future recognizes the species of *its own ancestors.* With our work and our nature we want to be the forebears of the future generation.

The economic policy of a German state, just as the standard of value of the German economic theorist, can therefore only be a German one.

Have things perhaps changed since economic development began to create an all-embracing economic community of nations transcending national boundaries? Is this "nationalistic" standard of value now to be thrown onto the scrap heap along with "national egoism" in economic policy? Indeed, has the struggle for economic self-assertion, for one's own wife and child, been surmounted now that the family has been divested of its former function as an association involved in production and has become enmeshed with the economic community of the nation? We know that this is *not* the case: the struggle has assumed *other forms,* forms of which one may question whether they represent not so much a moderation of this struggle as an intensification and sharpening of it. Similarly, the international economic community is simply a new form of the battle of the nations with each other, and one in which the struggle for the assertion of one's own culture has not been moderated but, rather, *made more difficult* because it enlists material interests within the very heart of the nation as allies *against* the nation's own future.

It is not peace and happiness that we have to bequeath to our descendants but *eternal struggle* for the maintenance and improvement of our national species. Moreover, we may not surrender ourselves to the optimistic hope that, with the greatest possible unfolding of culture in its economic form, our work is finished and that the process of selection in free and "peaceful" economic struggle will thereafter automatically help the more highly developed type to victory.

It will *not* be primarily for the type of economic organization we transmit to our descendants that they will hold us responsible before history but, rather, for the amount of elbowroom we win in the world and leave behind us. In the final analysis, processes of economic development are also *power* struggles; they are *power* interests of the nation, and, where they are placed in question, they are the ultimate and decisive interests in whose service the nation's economic policy has to place itself. The science of economic policy is a *political* science. It is a servant of politics, not of the day-to-day politics of whichever rulers and classes may be in power at the moment, but of the long-term power political interests of the nation. And the *national state* is not a vague something for us that some believe is made all the more majestic the more one shrouds its nature in mystical darkness. It is rather the temporal institution that organizes the nation's power, and in such an institution the ultimate standard of value for us in inquiries regarding economic policy is, as in everything else, *"reason of state."* This does not mean for us, as an odd misunderstanding has led some to believe, "state assistance" instead of "self-help," state regulation of economic life instead of the free play of economic forces. Rather, by means of this term we want to raise the demand that in questions of German economic policy—including, among others, whether and to what degree the state ought to intervene in economic life, and whether and when, on the contrary, the state ought to tear down the barriers standing in the way of the economic powers of the nation and let them loose to develop freely on their own—in individual cases the last and decisive vote ought to belong to the economic and political power interests of our nation and the entity responsible for them, the German national state.

Was it superfluous to recall these seemingly obvious truths, or, at least, for none other than a younger representative of economic science to recall them? I do not believe so, since it is precisely our generation that often seems most easily to lose sight of these simplest foundations of judgment. We are witnessing a growth, of a quite unexpected magnitude, in this generation's interest in the questions that occupy our science. In every area we are finding that the economic mode of analysis is on the advance. At the center of attention, social policy is taking the place of politics, economic power relations are taking the place of legal relations, cultural and economic history are taking the place of political history. In outstanding works produced by our colleagues in the field of history, we find today that, where earlier the martial deeds of our ancestors were related to us, the monstrosity of "mother-right" is now covering the pages and that the victory over the Huns on the Catalaunian plains has been pushed into an aside. The self-confidence of one of our most gifted theorists has led him to believe that he could characterize jurisprudence as the "handmaiden of economics." And one thing is indeed true: the economic form of analysis is penetrating jurisprudence. Even its most exclusive retreat, the handbooks of the Pandectists, is here and there beginning to be haunted by the economic perspective, and in the decisions of the courts it is not seldom that we find so-called economic considerations inserted at the point where juristic concepts have been stretched to their limits. In short, as a colleague who happens to be a jurist put it, half in reproach, we are "in fashion." A form of analysis that is so confidently forging ahead risks falling victim to certain illusions and overestimating the significance of its own point of view, in particular overestimating it in a quite specific direction. Just as the diffusion of the content of *philosophical* analysis—something that has become outwardly apparent by the fact that today we frequently find old, established chairs of philosophy entrusted to the hands of, for example, prominent physiologists—has frequently led to the opinion among us laymen that the old questions concerning the nature of human cognition are no longer the ultimate and central problems of philosophy, so too the notion has formed in the minds of the generation now coming to maturity that it is as if it were thanks to the work of economic science that not only has our *knowledge* concerning the nature of human communities been immensely expanded, but also the *standard* by which we ultimately *evaluate* the phenomena in question has become an entirely new one, that it is as if political economy were in a position to derive ideals peculiar to it from the material with which it is concerned. The optical illusion that there exist independent economic ideals or independent ideals of "social policy" becomes recognizable for what it is the moment one attempts to ascertain on the basis of the literature of our science what the canons of evaluation "peculiar" to it are. There we are confronted with a *chaos* of standards of value, both of a eudaemonistic and an ethical kind, often both kinds identified with each other in an unclear manner. Value judgments are made everywhere unabashedly, and refraining from *evaluating* economic phenomena in fact signifies refraining from providing precisely the service demanded of us. However, it is almost the exception rather than the rule that the person passing judgment clarifies to others *and to himself* the ultimate subjective core of his judgments, in other words, the *ideals* from which he departs when he proceeds to the evaluation of observed processes. Conscious self-control is lacking; the writer does not become aware of the inner contradictions in his judgment; and where he attempts to provide a general formulation of his specifically "economic" principle of evaluation, he falls into vague, indefinite propositions. In truth, what we get are *not* ideals peculiar to our science and developed independently by its practitioners but, rather, the *old, general kinds of human ideals* that we have carried into the substance of our science. Only he who approaches things solely in terms of the purely Platonic interest of the engineer or he who does the opposite and takes as his basis the current interests of a particular class, be it the ruling or the ruled, can hope to derive from the material itself his own standard for judgment.

Is it so totally unnecessary for us younger representatives of the German historical school to demonstrate these extremely simple truths to ourselves? On the contrary, it is quite necessary since we are precisely the ones who easily succumb to the power of a special illusion—the illusion that we can *completely refrain* from resorting to our own, conscious value judgments. The consequence is, of course, not that we remain true to a corresponding resolution, as one can easily convince oneself, but rather that we fall prey to uncontrolled instincts, sympathies, and antipathies. And what befalls us even more readily is that the point from which we proceed in the analysis and *explanation* of economic processes also becomes unconsciously decisive for our *judgment* of them. Perhaps we are precisely the ones who shall have to be on our guard lest the great qualities of both the living and the departed masters of our school to which they and the science owe their achievements are in our case transformed into faults. For practical purposes, essentially two different points of departure for an investigation are open for consideration.

First, we can look down upon economic development largely from above, from the heights of the administrative history of the large German states whose administration and policy in economic and social affairs we trace back through to their genesis, in the process involuntarily becoming their apologists. If—to return to our original example—the administration decides to close the eastern border, we shall be inclined and positioned to see this as the culmination of a historical sequence of development that, as a consequence of grand memories of the past, today presents the state with great tasks in the interest of fostering the culture of its nation. If, on the other hand, this decision is not made, we are more apt to observe that radical interventions of that type are in part unnecessary and in part no longer commensurable with contemporary views.

Or, second, we can view economic development more from below, observe the great spectacle of how the emancipatory struggles of rising classes emerge out of the chaos of conflicting economic interests and see how the constellation of economic power is displaced in their favor. And in so doing we unconsciously side with those who are on the rise because they are the stronger or are beginning to be. Precisely because they are victorious they seem to demonstrate that they represent an "economically" *superior* type of humanity. The historian all too easily falls under the control of the idea that the victory of the *more highly* developed element in a struggle is a matter of course and that defeat in the struggle for existence is a symptom of "backwardness." Every new instance of the numerous symptoms of the shift in power offers him satisfaction not only because it confirms his observations but also because half unconsciously he takes it as a personal triumph: history is honoring the bills he drew on it. The resistance encountered by that development is something he observes unwittingly, with a certain animosity; it appears to him, without his wishing it, not simply as the natural product of an obviously inevitable defense of specific interests, but, in a way, as a rebellion against the "judgment of history" as it was formulated by the historian. The critical analysis we have to apply to processes that appear to us the unreflective result of historical developmental tendencies fails us at precisely the point where we need it most. In any event, the temptation to join the following of the victor in the economic power struggle and thereby *to forget that economic power and the calling to political leadership of the nation do not always coincide* lies all too fully within our grasp.

For—and this brings us to a final series of observations of a more practical political sort—we economic nationalists also apply this *political standard of value,* which we hold to be the sole sovereign one, to the appraisal of the classes that hold the leadership of the nation in their hands, or aspire to hold it. What we are concerned with is their *political maturity,* that is, with their insight and their respective abilities to place the long-term economic and political *power* interests of the nation above all other considerations. Destiny bestows a kindness upon a nation when a class's naïve identification of its own interests with those of the whole actually correspond with the long-term power interests of the latter. On the other hand, it is one of the delusions that has its roots in the modern overestimation of the "economic" in the conventional sense of the word to believe that a nation's political feeling of community cannot hold up under a test of its strength imposed by divergent short-term economic interests, that if anything this feeling is itself *only* a reflection of the economic base underlying that mutable constellation of interests. It is only in times of fundamental social upheaval that this opinion assumes approximate validity. Only one thing is certain: in nations where the dependence of economic prosperity on the nation's political power position is not demonstrated daily in the manner in which it is in the case of the English, an instinctive understanding of these specific political interests does *not*, at least not as a rule, dwell in the broad *masses* of the nation's population, who are engaged in grappling with the difficulties of daily existence. It would be unfair to demand these instincts of them. On momentous occasions, in the case of a war, they too become conscious in their souls of the significance of national power. At that time it becomes clear that in the case of the broad, economically subordinate classes of the nation, as in that of the others, the national state rests on primeval psychological foundations, and that it is by no means simply a "superstructure," the organization of the economically dominant class. In the case of the masses, however, this political instinct sinks below the threshold of consciousness during normal times. At such times it is the specific function of the strata responsible for economic and political leadership to be bearers of the political instinct, the *sole* grounds capable of politically justifying their existence.

The *attainment of economic power* has, in all times, engendered in a class the notion that it *can expect to assume political leadership*. It is dangerous and, in the long run, incompatible with the interests of the nation when a class that is economically on the decline holds the nation's political power in its hands. But it is still more dangerous when classes that are beginning to *attract* economic power and thus the expectation of gaining political command are not yet politically mature enough to assume the leadership of the state. Both of these things are threatening Germany at the present time and in fact are the key to the present dangers in our situation. Moreover, the upheavals in the social structure of the east connected with the phenomena discussed at the outset also belong within this larger context.

In the Prussian state right up into the present, the dynasty has depended politically on the caste of the Prussian *Junkers*. Admittedly, the dynasty moved against them when creating the Prussian state, but, all the same, it was only with their assistance that its creation was possible. I am well aware that the Junkers' name has an unpleasant sound to South German ears. It may be felt that I am speaking a "Prussian" language if I say a word in their favor. I would not know. In Prussia even today the Junkers have open to them many paths to influence and power as well as many paths to the monarch's ear, which are not accessible to every citizen. They have not always used this power in such a way as to allow them to answer for themselves before history, and I see no reason why a bourgeois scholar ought to have any particular fondness for them. Nonetheless, the strength of their political instincts was one of the most powerful resources that could be applied in the service of the power interests of the state. Now their work is done, and today they lie in the throes of an economic death from which no economic policy of the state could ever retrieve them and lead them back to their old social status. Moreover, the tasks of the present are different from those that could be solved by them. For a quarter of a century the last and greatest of the Junkers stood at the head of Germany, and, although today some are still unable to see it, the tragic element that, alongside the incomparable greatness, was inherent in his career as a statesman will be discovered by the future in the fact that the work of his hands, the nation to which he gave unity, slowly and irresistibly changed its economic structure under him and became something other than what it was, a people who must demand social forms different from those he was able to provide it and to which his caesarist nature was able to adapt. In the final analysis, this is what brought about the partial failure of his life's work, for this life's work surely ought to have led not only to the outer but also to the inner unification of the nation, and every one of us knows that that has not been achieved. With the means he used it could not be achieved. And when in the winter of last year, ensnared by the graciousness of his monarch, he entered the capital of the empire, there were many—I know whereof I speak—who felt as though the Sachsenwald like a modern Mount Kyffhäuser had opened up its depths. But this feeling was not shared by everyone, for in the air of that January day it seemed as though the cold breath of historical transience could be detected. A strange, oppressive feeling came over us as if a ghost had climbed down out of a great period in the past and now went about among a new generation through a world that had become foreign to it.

The estates of the east were the bases of operation for the ruling class of Prussia, a class scattered over the countryside. They were the social point of contact possessed by the officialdom. But with their decay, with the disappearance of the social character of the old landed nobility, the center of gravity of the political intelligentsia is inexorably shifting to the towns. *This* shift is the decisive *political* feature of the agrarian development in the east.

But into whose hands is the political function of the Junkers slipping, and what is there to be said concerning their ability to assume the vocation of politics?

I am a member of the bourgeoisie, feel myself to be such, and have been brought up to share in its attitudes and ideals. But it is the calling of precisely our science to say what one would rather not hear—on high, down below, and in our own class too—and when I ask myself whether the German bourgeoisie is at present mature enough to become the nation's political governing class, I cannot *today* answer this question in the affirmative. The German state was not created through the power of the bourgeoisie, and on the morn of its creation there stood at the head of the nation a caesarist figure hewn from something other than bourgeois timber. Following unification, great power-political tasks were not immediately again placed before the nation; it was only much later that timidly and half unwillingly an overseas "power policy" began, a policy that does not deserve the name.

And after the unity of the nation had been thus attained and the "appeasement" of its political hunger was an established fact, the rising generation of the German bourgeoisie, drunk with success and thirsting for peace, was pervaded by a peculiarly "unhistorical" and unpolitical spirit. German history appeared to have come to an end. The present was the complete fulfillment of the millennia that had sunk into the past—Who wanted to ask whether the future might judge otherwise? Indeed it seemed as though modesty forbade world history to pass over these achievements of the German nation and proceed to the agenda of its everyday course. Today we have become sober, and it seems fitting to attempt to raise the veil of illusions that cloaks the place our generation has in the historical development of the fatherland. It seems to me that if we do this we shall judge matters differently. At our cradle stood the gravest curse history is capable of bestowing upon a generation as a birthday gift: the harsh fate of living as political *epigones*.

Do we not find at this very moment, wherever we look in our fatherland, the wretched visage of epigonism staring back at us? In the events of the past few months, for which bourgeois politicians first and foremost have to bear responsibility, in all too much of what in recent days has been said *in* the German parliament, and in some of what has been said *to* it, those of us who still possess the ability to hate pettiness recognize with the passion of enraged sorrow the petty chicanery of political epigones. The mighty sun that shone at Germany's zenith and caused the German name to shine forth in the farthest corners of the earth was, so it almost seems, too great for us and has burned out the bourgeoisie's slowly developing ability to make political judgments. After all, what have we seen of this ability lately?

A portion of the haute bourgeoisie makes no secret of its longing for a new Caesar to appear who will protect it against the masses rising from beneath and against the sociopolitical impulses that it suspects the German dynasties of harboring on high.

Another portion of the haute bourgeoisie has long since sunk into the political philistinism from which broad sections of the petite bourgeoisie have never awakened. Already when, following the wars of unification, the first beginnings of the nation's positive political tasks came into view—I am referring here to the idea of an overseas expansion—these members of the haute bourgeoisie were lacking even the simplest sort of *economic* understanding, which could have shown them what it signifies for Germany's trade on distant seas when German flags wave on the coasts around them.

The political immaturity of broad sections of the German bourgeoisie is not due to economic causes, nor is it due to "interest politics," something that is often mentioned but that other nations are no less familiar with than we are. The cause lies in this class's unpolitical past, in the fact that a century's worth of political education cannot be made up for in a decade, and in the fact that rule by a great man is not always the best means of political education. The important question for the political future of the German bourgeoisie is whether or not it is now too *late* to make up for this missed political education. No *economic* factor can serve as a substitute for it.

Will other classes become the champions of a politically greater future? The modern proletariat is self-confidently stepping forward as the heir to bourgeois ideals. What can be said of its prospective claim to the political leadership of the nation?

He who today would describe the German working class as politically mature or on the way to political maturity would be a flatterer aspiring for the dubious crown of popular acclaim.

Economically the highest strata of the German working class are far more mature than the egoism of the propertied classes would allow them to concede, and it is with justification that the working class is demanding the freedom to look after its own interests in forms that include an open, organized struggle for economic power. *Politically* that class is infinitely less mature than the clique of journalists who would like to monopolize its leadership would have it believe. Within the circles of these *déclassé* bourgeois, people are fond of toying with reminiscences from a period a hundred years back. Things have actually reached the point where certain anxious souls perceive these circles as the spiritual descendants of the men of the Convention. But such people are infinitely less capable of harm than they appear to be. There resides within them not a spark of the Convention's Catilinarian energy of the *deed,* and by the same token not a trace of the tremendous *national* passion that reverberated in the meeting halls of the Convention. They are wretched political small-timers who lack the grand *power* instincts of a class that is called to political leadership. Contrary to what the workers have been led to believe, it is not the representatives of the interests of capital alone who today make up the political opposition to their sharing in the power of the state. They would find few traces of a community of interests with capital if they searched through the studies of German scholars. Nevertheless, we *also* question the *workers* about their *political maturity.* Because there is nothing more devastating for a great nation than to be led by *politically* uneducated *philistines,* and because the German proletariat has not yet lost this character, we are its political opponents. And why is it that the English and the French proletariats are, to a degree, of a different kind? The reason is not solely the earlier and longer *economic* education to which the organized struggle for their interests subjected English workers. It is, on the contrary, above all a *political* factor that has been responsible: *the resonance of the position of world power* that constantly places before the state great tasks of power politics and supplies the individual with never-ending political schooling, schooling that in our case is administered only in the form of a crash course when our borders are threatened. Whether the pursuit of politics in the grand manner will make us again aware of the significance of the great political questions of power is likewise decisive for *our* development. We must understand that the unification of Germany was a youthful lark that the nation undertook at an advanced age and that, because of its costliness, would better have been left undone if it was supposed to be the conclusion rather than the point of departure of a German venture into world power politics.

What is *threatening* in our situation is the fact that the bourgeois classes appear to be wilting away as champions of the *power* interests of the nation, and there are still no signs that the workers are beginning to mature so that they can take their place.

The danger does *not* lie with the *masses,* as those who stare hypnotically into the depths of society believe. The ultimate content of the problem of *social* policy is not a question of the *economic* condition of the *ruled,* but on the contrary a question of the *political* qualifications of the *ruling* classes and those *on the rise.* The goal of our work in the field of social policy is not the spreading of happiness throughout the world but, rather, the *social unification* of the nation—a condition that modern economic development split apart—so that it will be possible to face the arduous struggles of the future. If a "labor aristocracy" were in fact created that would be the bearer of the political understanding we cannot now see in the workers' movement, then the spear that the arm of the bourgeoisie seems still not strong enough to carry might be transferred to those broader shoulders. But there appears to be a long way to go before that happens.

For the time being, however, one thing is clear: there is an enormous task of *political* education to be accomplished. We have no more serious duty than that each of us, within his own limited sphere, be conscious of exactly *this* task: to participate in the *political* education of the nation, something that must remain the ultimate goal of precisely our science. The economic development of periods of transition threatens natural political instincts with decay; it would be a misfortune if economic science were hurrying on toward the same goal by cultivating a soft-hearted eudaemonism, however intellectualized its form, behind the illusion of autonomous "sociopolitical" ideals.

Of course, for this reason we are the very ones who are permitted to recall that it is the contrary of political education when one seeks to formulate, paragraph by paragraph, a vote of no confidence in the peaceful social future of the nation, or when the *brachium saeculare* reaches toward the hand of the church for support for temporal authorities. But the contrary of political education is also to be heard in the mechanical yapping of that constantly growing chorus of—if one will forgive the expression—cracker-barrel social politicians as well as in the humanely kind and admirable, but nonetheless unspeakably philistine, softening of the soul that leads one to believe in the possibility of replacing political ideals with "ethical" ones and, in turn, innocently to identify these with optimistic hopes of happiness.

Even in the face of the enormous distress of the masses of the nation, which burdens the sharpened social conscience of the new generation, we must forthrightly confess that we are today even more heavily burdened by the consciousness of our responsibility *before history.* It will not be granted to our generation to see whether the struggle we are engaged in will bear fruit, whether future generations will acknowledge *us as their ancestors.* We shall not succeed in ridding ourselves of the curse that hangs over us, the curse of being sired by a great political epoch only to enter the world after our father has departed from it. We have no other recourse than to learn how to become something different—the forerunners of an even greater epoch. Will that be our place in history? I do not know and can only say that it is the right of youth to be true to itself and its ideals. Moreover, it is not years that make a man old. One is young as long as one is capable of feeling with the *great* passions that nature has placed in us. And so allow me to conclude with the observation that it is not the burden of millennia of glorious history that makes a great nation grow old. It remains young if it has the ability and the courage to remain true to itself and to the great instincts that have been given to it and if the classes that lead it can raise themselves up into the hard clear air in which the sober work of German politics can successfully follow its course, an atmosphere suffused with the solemn splendor of national sentiment.

42. Heinrich von Treitschke, *In Memory of the Great War*

Heinrich von Treitschke (1834–96) was one of the most influential political historians of late Imperial Germany. The son of a Saxon army officer,
Treitschke studied history and economics at several German universities
and eventually (in 1874) was appointed to a professorship in history at
the University of Berlin. Although exceptionally prolific in publications,
Treitschke never managed to absorb the critical historical methods of his
professional contemporaries, becoming rather a brilliant historical gener-
alist who served as the most polemical spokesman for post-Rankean,
Kleindeutsch approbation of the Bismarckian Reich.

Treitschke's early political and historical work was nominally Liberal,
but even in the 1850s and early 1860s his views of the constitutional
polity in Germany were closely circumscribed: parliamentary cooperation was not the equivalent of democratic representation; German civic
culture should not become the property of the masses; and the state itself
was a moral personality, only in the context of which could individuals
exercise personal freedom. Although initially an opponent of Bismarck's
autocracy, Treitschke soon revised his view of the man and his foreign
policy successes. Treitschke's editorship of the *Preussische Jahrbücher,*
beginning in 1866, saw his growing attachment to cultural and ideological conservatism within the Bismarckian state. After 1870 he supported
the repression of German Social Democracy and eventually advocated a
virulent cultural anti-Semitism as well as an aggressive foreign policy for
Germany in the form of a militaristic *Weltpolitik.* James Sheehan has
noted of Treitschke's abandonment of liberal values that "nationalism, not
liberalism; the army, not the parliament; war, not domestic politics—
these were to be the formative values, institutions, and experiences
through which social solidarity and political stability could be
maintained." [1]

Yet as Treitschke's *Weltanschauung* became more reactionary and hate-
ridden toward modern industrial society, his popular influence among
university students and military and government officials seemed to expand. The lecture printed below, which Treitschke delivered at a celebration of the twenty-fifth anniversary of the German victory in the Franco-
Prussian War, held at the University of Berlin in July 1895, illustrates the
profoundly troubled state of German academic culture by the early

From Heinrich von Treitschke, *Germany, France, Russia, and Islam* (New York: G. P.
Putnam's Sons, 1915), pp. 200–226.

1. Sheehan, *German Liberalism in the Nineteenth Century*, p. 274.

1890s, a culture that historian Konrad Jarausch has characterized as "academic illiberalism."

Dear Colleagues and Fellow-Soldiers,[2]

To-day's festival recalls to us of the older generation the golden days of our life—the days when the grace of God after battle and tribulation and mourning gloriously fulfilled beyond all our expectations all the longings of our youth. And yet, as I begin to speak, I feel keenly how profoundly the world has changed in this quarter of a century. It is not given to every period to do great deeds nor to understand them rightly. After the great crises of history there generally follows a generation which hears the iron voice of war, the great moulder of nations, still vibrating in its own heart, and rejoices with youthful enthusiasm over what has been gained. But without the constant work of self-recollection and self-testing, progress is impossible. New parties spring up imbued with new ideas; they ask doubtfully or scornfully whether the goal attained was worth the sacrifice made. The field-marshals of the study calculate arrangements which could certainly have been better made on the patient paper.

Industrious critics diligently spy out all the sordid and revolting details which adhere to every great human exploit, as the fungus to the oak-tree, and the preponderance of censure easily overwhelms joy and gratitude. A long period must generally elapse before a nation resolves to view the greatness of its past again on a great scale. The deep significance of the War of Liberation was not revealed to the majority of Germans till half a century afterwards through the works of Häusser, Droysen, Bernhardi, and Sybel. Let us to-day turn our eyes away from everything that is trivial and regard only the moral forces which operated in the most fortunate of all wars.

When Field-Marshal Moltke once visited his regiment, the Kolberg Grenadiers, he pointed to the portrait of Gneisenau—who had once formed this brilliant corps behind the ramparts of the unconquered Pomeranian fortress from the scattered remnants of the old army—and said, "Between us and him there is a great difference. We have had to record only victories. He has led the army to victory after a defeat. This severest test we have not yet undergone." Who can hear this utterance without admiring the profound modesty and at the same time the lofty ambition of the Field-Marshal. But we cannot merely echo the noble words; we rather thank the

---

2. Instructive mistranslation: The German text: "Liebe Collegen und Commilitonen!" "*Commilitones*" in Latin means "fellow-soldiers"; but this word has been used for centuries by German professors in addressing their students (and by students addressing each other); the correct translation would be: "fellow-students."—ED.

hero that he has himself confuted them by his deeds. So, exactly so, unerring as the hammer of Thor, had the German sword to hew down opposition, so, contrary to all experience, the changeable fortune of war had to become abiding, and garland after garland of victory had to adorn our banners if this most deeply-slandered and deeply-scorned of all nations was to win its due place in the community of States. We had been for centuries hampered and impeded in the simple task of national policy by the world-wide power of our Holy Roman Empire, just as the Italians were through their Papacy; in our Confederation of States we were obliged to let many foreign Powers co-operate, and saw ourselves at the same time linked on to a half-German Power, a disguised foreign one whose insincerity a great part of the nation, misled by old, fond recollections, would never recognize. The fame of invincibility which once no one had dared to deny the armies of Frederick, had not been restored by all the glorious contests of the War of Liberation; for foreigners always said sneeringly, "When the Prussians stood alone at Jena, they were beaten; only when allied with other Powers were they again victorious." And at the same time there grew and grew in the nation the consciousness of an immeasurable strength, a living indestructible union of both intellectual and political life. A nation in a position of such unexampled difficulty, so strong in its justifiable self-esteem, and so weak through its wretched federal constitution, must necessarily fall into confused and aimless party struggles, and pass through all the infant ailments of political life. Among the millions abroad there was only one, our faithful friend Thomas Carlyle, who, in spite of the confusion of our party divisions, recognized the nobility of the soul of the German nation. All others were unanimous in the belief that we would come to nothing, and that this central part of the Continent, on whose weakness the old society of States had so long rested, would never become strong. In the eyes of foreigners we were only the comic-looking, jovial members of singing and shooting clubs, and the German word "Vaterland" was, in England, simply a term of contempt. Then, when Prussia had again entered the old victorious paths of the Great Elector, and the Great King freed our Northern Marches, and shattered the foreign rule of the House of Austria by the cannon of Königgratz, Europe was still far from recognizing the new order of things in Germany. We had in early times aimed at the world-rule of the Roman Empire, and had been then, by the cruel justice of history, condemned to an unhappy cosmopolitanism, so that our territory provided the arena for the armies and the diplomatic intrigues of all nations. Was this state of things to continue?

What we needed was a complete, incontestable victory, won solely by German strength, which would compel our neighbours to acknowledge at last respectfully that we, as a nation, had attained our majority. This was clearly understood by the Emperor William, who so often re-echoed his people's words, when he said in his address from the throne, "If Germany silently endured violations of her rights and of her honour in past centuries, that was only because she did not realize in her dismembered condition how strong she was." For a long time past we were no longer the poor, ill-treated nation of 1813, which had seen its colours disgraced, its lands laid desolate, prayed in holy wrath, "Save us from the yoke of slavery!" and then, quietly prepared for the worst, waged the unequal strife. On the contrary, at the King's summons, a free, strong, proud nation arose in radiant exultation; she knew her power, and from amid the confused tumult of public meetings and the din of the streets, of the newspapers and the pamphlets, one cry overpowered all other sounds, "We must, we will conquer." Poets have compared the grey-haired ruler as he rode majestically before his knights to the kings of armies in German antiquity. King William was more; he was a hero of our time, the dominating monarchic leader of an immense democratic mass-movement, which shook the nation from top to bottom, and, sure of its goal, stormily swept on, regardless of the caution of hesitating Courts.

France had already lost the leading position in Europe since the overthrow of the first Empire, and then apparently recovered it through the diplomatic skill of the third Napoleon. As soon as Prussia's victories in Bohemia threatened to restore a just balance of power, there took possession of those noisy Parisian circles, which had always dominated the wavering provinces, a fantastic intoxication of national pride. There reappeared the old delusion that France's greatness depended on the weakness of her neighbours. The public opinion of the agitators compelled the sick Emperor to declare war against his will; it arrogantly controlled and disturbed every movement of the enemy; it compelled the fatal march to Sedan. After the first defeats, the imperial throne, whose only support was good fortune, fell, and the party-rule of the new revolutionary government could neither exercise justice, nor command the general respect. The fact that a superior commands and a subordinate obeys was almost forgotten in the widespread and unnatural mistrust which prevailed. Every misfortune was regarded as a piece of treachery, even when the war had seasoned men, and the army of the Loire had found a commander in Chanzy. Finally, after the surrender of Paris, the conquered people, under the eyes of the conqueror, tore each other to pieces in a terrible civil war.

Seldom has it been so clearly demonstrated that it is the will which is the deciding factor in national struggles for existence, and in unity of will we were the stronger. France, which had so often fomented and misused our domestic quarrels, all at once found herself opposed by the vital union of the Germans; for a righteous war releases all the natural forces of character, and, side by side with hatred, the power of affection. Inviolable confidence bound the soldiers to their officers, and all of them to those in supreme command.

Those who remained at home also became more generous, broaderminded, and affectionate; the seriousness of the crisis lifted them above the selfishness of every-day life. Party strife disappeared, isolated, unpatriotic fools were quickly reduced to silence, and the longer the struggle lasted the more firmly did the whole nation unite in the resolve that this war should restore to us the German Empire and our old lost western provinces. One hundred and thirty thousand Germans fell a sacrifice to war's insatiable demands, but the lines of the old Landwehr's men which followed them appeared endless, till more than a million of our soldiers gradually crossed the French frontier. The war demanded all. When the reports of deaths arrived from the West, the fathers and brothers of those who had fallen said, "Much mourning, much honour," and even the mothers, wives, and sisters had in their heavy sorrow the consolation that their little house owned a leaf in the growing garland of German glory.

But ideas alone kindle no enduring fire in the hearts of a nation; they need men. And certainly it was fortunate that the nation could look up unitedly to the grey-headed ruler, whose venerable figure will always appear greater to coming generations the more closely it is made the subject of historical investigation. "His Majesty sees everything!" the sergeant-majors used to thunder at their careless men, and they said the truth. When destiny raised him at an advanced age to the throne he had never sought, he soon perceived that Providence had determined him and his army to be an instrument for its dispensations. "If I did not believe that," he said calmly, "how could I otherwise have been able to bear the burden of this war?" As a youth, he had admired the nation under arms, when under the pressure of necessity it had collected to carry out Scharnhorst's plans though only half-drilled; as a man, he had constantly considered with Scharnhorst's successor, Boyen, how these unripe ideas might take a vital shape; finally as king, amid severe parliamentary struggles, he had carried through the three-years' service law which strengthened the troops of the line, and secured us an army which was at once popular and fully trained. He knew every little wheel-work of the gigantic machine; now he watched with satisfaction how it worked. Alone, without a council of war, he formed his resolves according to Moltke's reports. Earlier and more clearly than all those around him, he perceived that the battle of Sedan had indeed decided, but was far from ending the war. He knew the fervent patriotic pride of the French; he possessed in a special degree the rich experience of old age preserved by a powerful memory; he remembered how fifty-six years previously the armed throngs of the peasantry of Champagne had, as it

were, started up out of the ground under the eyes of the Prussians. Sooner
and more clearly than all others, he perceived the danger which threatened
from the Loire, and ordered the army in the South to be strengthened.
Thus, till the end he remained the Commander-in-Chief, and when he left
French territory, even after such victories, he seriously thought of the perpetual vicissitudes of mortal things, and warned the army of what was now
united Germany that it could maintain its position only by perpetual striving after improvement.

At last came the time of harvest. Paris surrendered, and the last desperate attempt of the French against Southern Alsace came to a pitiable end.
Four great armies were taken prisoners or disarmed, and all the German
races had an equal and glorious share in the enormous success. In these
last weeks of the war there stepped into the foreground of German history
the strong man of whom the troops had so often spoken by their bivouac-
fires. Ever since historical times began the masses of people have always
rated character and energy above intellect and culture; the greatest and
most boundless popularity was always only bestowed on the heroes of religion and of the sword. The one statesman who seems to be an exception
only confirms the rule. In the popular mind Bismarck was never anything
but the gigantic warrior with the bronze helmet and the yellow collar of the
cuirassiers of Mars la Tour, as the painters depicted him riding down the
avenue of poplars at Sedan. It was he who had once spoken the salutary
word, "Get rid of Austria!" It was he who by treaties with the South German States had in his far-sighted way prepared for the inevitable war. And
when twenty-five years ago he read to the Reichstag the French declaration
of war, all felt as though he were the first to raise the cry, "All Germany
on into France!" and it seemed to all as though he rode into the enemy's
land like a herald in front of the German squadrons. Now when the war
was over he summed up the net results of the great battles, and after
troublesome negotiations settled the constitution of the new kingdom. This
constitution seemed quite new, and yet it evoked the old sacred unforget-
table emotions of German loyalty to the Kaiser. It appeared complicated
even to formlessness, and yet it was fundamentally simple because it admitted of unlimited development. In her relations to foreign countries Germany was henceforth one, and in spite of much doubt all discerning people
hoped that the Empire, possessing an imperial head, would now attain to
its full growth.

This work of Bismarck's brought peace and reconciliation to nearly all
the old factions which had hitherto struggled on our territory. They had all
made mistakes, and almost all rediscovered in the constitution of the Empire some of their most deeply-cherished projects. Our princes especially had been in the wrong. In the course of an eventful history they had

often been the protectors of German religious freedom and the rich many-sidedness of our civilization, but had been often misled by dynastic envy and pride, even to the point of committing treachery. At the middle of the century their pride was at its height, for what else was the object of the war of 1866 except to break in pieces the State of the great Frederick, and to degrade it to the wretched condition of the petty German princedoms? But the dethroning of the sovereigns of Hanover, Hesse, and Nassau was a tremendous warning to the princes. They recollected themselves and re-membered the noble traditions of imperial sentiment in the old princely families; and as soon as the war began they gathered round their royal leader. Therefore they could, according to the old privileges of the German princes, themselves elect their emperor, and secure for themselves their proper share in the new imperial power. There in France was the first foun-dation laid for that invisible council of German princes, which is some-thing else than the Council of the Confederation, which is not mentioned in any article of the imperial constitution, and yet always works perceptibly for the good of the Fatherland. Never yet at a critical time has the honest help of the princes failed the Hohenzollern Kaisers.

The heaviest blow befell the partisans of Austria, the "Great Ger-mans."[3] So severe was it that even their party-name entirely disappeared. But those who were sincere among them had only fought against the Ger-man "rival-Emperor" because they feared a Prussian imperial power would be too weak to sustain the position of the nation as one of the Great Pow-ers. And how was it now? It was never doubtful whether a man was a Ger-man or not. We bore the mark of our good and evil qualities as distinctly impressed upon our brows as formerly did the Greeks, our kindred in tem-perament and destiny. But it was always a matter of dispute for centuries where Germany exactly was; its boundaries were constantly changing or disappearing in the fog of "rights of the Empire." Now for the first time there existed a German State whose frontiers were clearly defined. It had lost the frontier territories of the South-east, which for a long time past had only been loosely connected with the Empire, but as a compensation had finally recovered by conquest those on the Rhine and the Moselle, which had been torn away from the Empire. It had also, through the State of the Hohenzollerns, won wide territories in the East and North which had never or merely nominally belonged to the old Empire, *i.e.*, Silesia, Posen, Prussia, the land of the old Teutonic orders, and Schleswig. It was more powerful than the old Empire had been for six centuries. Who could now speak of it sneeringly as "Little Germany"? Out of the perpetual ebb and flow of races in Central Europe there had finally emerged two great Em-

3. That is, partisans of the union of Germany and Austria.

pires—one purely German with a mixture of religions, the other Catholic, and comprising a variety of races who yet could not dispense with the German language and culture. Such an outcome of the struggles of centuries could not fail to satisfy for a time even the imagination of the "Greater Germany" enthusiasts. The great majority of the nation joined in jubilantly when, in the Palace of Versailles, the acclamation of the princes and the army greeted the Emperor, who in his deep modesty accepted the new dignity only with hesitation.

In the natural course of things, after the victory, a truce was proclaimed between the German political parties. But our party strifes have become from year to year rougher and coarser. They concern themselves less with political ideas than with economic interests; they stir up the flame of hatred between class and class, and threaten the peace of society.

This coarsening of politics has its deepest source in a serious alteration which has taken place in our whole national life. Much that we considered characteristic of a decaying old world is the outcome of every over-cultivated city-civilizatıon, and is being repeated to-day before our eyes. A democratized society does not care, as enthusiasts suppose, for the aristocracy of talent, but for the power of gold or of the mob, or both together. In the new generation there is disappearing terribly fast, what Goethe called the final aim of all moral education—reverence: reverence for God; reverence for the barriers which nature has placed between the two sexes, and the limits which the structure of human society has imposed upon desire; reverence for the Fatherland which, as an ideal, is said to be yielding its place to the dream of a sensual and cosmopolitan plutocracy.

The wider culture spreads, the more shallow it becomes; the thoughtfulness of the ancient world is despised; only that which serves the aims of the immediate future seems still important. Where everyone gives his opinion about everything, according to the newspaper and the encyclopaedia, there original mental power becomes rare, and with it the fine courage of ignorance, which marks an independent mind. Science, which, once descending too deep, sought to fathom the inscrutable, loses itself in expansion, and only isolated pines of original thought tower above the low undergrowth of collections of memoranda. The satiated taste, which no longer understands the true, goes after realism, and prizes the wax figure more than the work of art. In the tedium of an empty existence the affected naturalness of betting and athletic sports gains an undeserved importance, and when we see how immoderately the heroes of the circus and the performers of the playground are over-prized, we are unpleasantly reminded of the enormous costly mosaic picture of the twenty-eight prize-fighters in the Baths of Caracalla.

These are all serious signs of the time. But no one stands so high that he can only accuse his people. We Germans, especially, have often sinned against ourselves through extravagant love of fault-finding. And no one can say that he really knows his own people. In the spring of 1870 even the most sanguine did not suppose that our young men would strike as they did. So we, also, will hope that to-day, deep in the hearts of our people, there are at work rejuvenating powers which we know not of. And how much that does not pass away has, in spite of all, remained to us from the great war. The Empire stands upright, stronger than we ever expected; every German discerns its mighty influence in the ordinary occurrences of every day, in the current exchange of the market-place. None of us could live without the Empire, and how strongly the thought of it glows in our hearts is shown by the grateful affection which seeks to console the first Imperial Chancellor for the bitter experiences of his old age. In my youth it was often said, "If the Germans become German, they will found the kingdom on earth which will bring peace to the world." We are not so inoffensive any longer. For a long time past we have known that the sword must maintain what the sword won, and to the end of history, the virile saying will hold good, βιᾷ βιὰ βιάζεται, "Force is overcome by force." And yet there is a deep significance in that old verse about the Germans. Not only was the war for Prussia's existence—the Seven Years' War,—the first European war, not only did our State combine both the old State-systems of the East and the West into a European community of States, but being at last strengthened as a central State, during a quarter of a century of dangerous diplomatic friction, it has offered peace to the Continent not by means of the panacea of the pacificists—disarming—but by the exact opposite—universal arming. Germany's example compelled armies to become nations, nations to become armies, and consequently war to be a dangerous experiment; and since no Frenchman has yet asserted that France can recover her old booty by force of arms, we may perhaps hope for some more years of peace. Meanwhile, our western frontier territory coalesces slowly, but unceasingly, with the old Fatherland, and the time will come when German culture, which has changed its place of abode so often, will again recover complete predominance in its old home.

5
Mass Politics at the Turn of the Century

43. Marx and Engels, Four Letters on the Materialist Interpretation of History

Friedrich Engels, Marx's close friend and collaborator, was born in 1820 of a prosperous commercial family in Barmen (in northeastern Rhineland). His intimate collaboration with Marx began in Paris in 1844. Having gained experience toward a business career in a Manchester cotton plant in which his father held a partnership, Engels drew together his impressions of early Victorian industrial society in his influential study *The Condition of the Working Class in England*, published in 1845. During the years 1845–50 Engels lived in France, Germany and Belgium, devoting himself, with Marx, to writing radical political and philosophical publications and participating actively in the Revolution of 1848. In 1850 he returned to what proved to be a successful business career in Manchester. In 1869 he sold the partnership in his firm and eventually joined Marx in London, devoting the rest of his life to aiding, explaining, and, later on, to editing Marx. Engels also became the mentor and advisor of the gradually emerging Socialist political movement in Germany and participated in the successful consolidation of the Second International after 1890. He died in 1895. (For Marx, see document 19.)

Developing and yet contradicting the ideas of a number of early socialist predecessors, Marx and Engels elaborated their approach to history in several writings prior to the *Communist Manifesto*. But it was in this pamphlet, published in February 1848 and destined to shake the very foundations of Liberal culture, that they most forcefully applied their materialism to the interpretation of a historical epoch as a guide to revolutionary practice, that is, to the attempt to make history as well as to understand and to explain it.

From *Karl Marx and Friedrich Engels: Correspondence, 1846–1895*, translated and edited by Dona Torr (New York: International Publishers, 1936), pp. 353–55, 472–73, 475–77, 516–19.

The four letters presented here were written between 1877 and 1894 and are concerned with a single aspect of the scientific socialism of Marx and Engels, albeit a basic one: their conception of history, frequently labeled historical materialism.

Marx to the Editor of *Otyecestvenniye zapisky* (end of 1877)[1]

In order that I might be qualified to estimate the economic development in Russia to-day, I learnt Russian and then for many years studied the official publications and others bearing on this subject. I have arrived at this conclusion: If Russia continues to pursue the path she has followed since 1861, she will lose the finest chance[2] ever offered by history to a nation, in order to undergo all the fatal vicissitudes of the capitalist regime.

The chapter on primitive accumulation does not pretend to do more than trace the path by which, in Western Europe, the capitalist order of economy emerged from the womb of the feudal order of economy. It therefore describes the historic movement which by divorcing the producers from their means of production converts them into wage earners (proletarians in the modern sense of the word) while it converts into capitalists those who hold the means of production in possession. In that history, "all revolutions are epoch-making which serve as levers for the advancement of the capitalist class in course of formation; above all those which, after stripping great masses of men of their traditional means of production and subsistence, suddenly fling them on to the labour market. But the basis of this whole development is the expropriation of the cultivators.

"This has not yet been radically accomplished except in England. . . . but all the countries of Western Europe are going through the same movement," etc. (*Capital*, French Edition, 1879, p. 315). At the end of the chapter the historic tendency of production is summed up thus: that it itself begets its own negation with the inexorability which governs the metamorphoses of nature; that it has itself created the elements of a new economic order, by giving the greatest impulse at once to the productive forces of

---

1. This letter was written by Marx in French to the editor of the Russian journal *Otyecestvenniye zapisky* (*Notes on the Fatherland*). Marx never mailed the letter, but shortly after Marx's death in 1884 Engels sent it to a Russian socialist. It was published in Russian and other languages and widely discussed. The letter grew out of a debate on whether Russia could bypass capitalism in her development toward a socialist society. The critic to whom Marx refers in his letter had attributed to Marx the view that Russia was inevitably fated to go through a phase of capitalist development.—ED.

2. I.e., the finest chance of escaping capitalist development.

social labour and to the integral development of every individual producer; that capitalist property, resting as it actually does already on a form of collective production, cannot do other than transform itself into social property. At this point I have not furnished any proof, for the good reason that this statement is itself nothing else than the short summary of long developments previously given in the chapters on capitalist production.

Now what application to Russia can my critic make of this historical sketch? Only this: If Russia is tending to become a capitalist nation after the example of the Western European countries, and during the last years she has been taking a lot of trouble in this direction—she will not succeed without having first transformed a good part of her peasants into proletarians; and after that, once taken to the bosom of the capitalist regime, she will experience its pitiless laws like other profane peoples. That is all. But that is not enough for my critic. He feels himself obliged to metamorphose my historical sketch of the genesis of capitalism in Western Europe into an historico-philosophic theory of the *marche générale* [general path] imposed by fate upon every people, whatever the historic circumstances in which it finds itself, in order that it may ultimately arrive at the form of economy which will ensure, together with the greatest expansion of the productive powers of social labour, the most complete development of man. But I beg his pardon. (He is both honouring and shaming me too much.) Let us take an example.

In several parts of *Capital* I allude to the fate which overtook the plebeians of ancient Rome. They were originally free peasants, each cultivating his own piece of land on his own account. In the course of Roman history they were expropriated. The same movement which divorced them from their means of production and subsistence involved the formation not only of big landed property but also of big money capital. And so one fine morning there were to be found on the one hand free men, stripped of everything except their labour power, and on the other, in order to exploit this labour, those who held all the acquired wealth in possession. What happened? The Roman proletarians became, not wage labourers but a *mob* of do-nothings more abject than the former "poor whites" in the southern country of the United States, and alongside of them there developed a mode of production which was not capitalist but dependent upon slavery. Thus events strikingly analogous but taking place in different historic surroundings led to totally different results. By studying each of these forms of evolution separately and then comparing them one can easily find the clue to this phenomenon, but one will never arrive there by the universal passport of a general historico-philosophical theory, the supreme virtue of which consists in being super-historical.

Engels to Conrad Schmidt

London, 5 August 1890

. . . The materialist conception of history also has a lot of friends nowadays to whom it serves as an excuse for *not* studying history. Just as Marx used to say about the French "Marxists" of the late 'seventies: "All I know is that I am not a Marxist." . . .

In general the word *materialistic* serves many of the younger writers in Germany as a mere phrase with which anything and everything is labelled without further study; they stick on this label and then think the question disposed of. But our conception of history is above all a guide to study, not a lever for construction after the manner of the Hegelians. All history must be studied afresh, the conditions of existence of the different formations of society must be individually examined before the attempt is made to deduce from them the political, civil-legal, aesthetic, philosophic, religious, etc., notions corresponding to them. Only a little has been done here up to now because only a few people have got down to it seriously. In this field we can utilise masses of help, it is immensely big and anyone who will work seriously can achieve a lot and distinguish himself. But instead of this only too many of the younger Germans simply make use of the phrase historical materialism (and *everything* can be turned into a phrase), in order to get their own relatively scanty historical knowledge (for economic history is still in its cradle!) fitted together into a neat system as quickly as possible, and they then think themselves something very tremendous. . . .

Engels to Joseph Bloch

London, 21 September 1890

According to the materialist conception of history the determining element in history is *ultimately* the production and reproduction in real life. More than this neither Marx nor I have ever asserted. If therefore somebody twists this into the statement that the economic element is the *only* determining one, he transforms it into a meaningless, abstract and absurd phrase. The economic situation is the basis, but the various elements of the superstructure—political forms of the class struggle and its consequences, constitutions established by the victorious class after a successful battle, etc.— forms of law—and then even the reflexes of all these actual struggles in the brains of the combatants: political, legal, philosophical theories, religious ideas and their further development into systems of dogma—also exercise their influence upon the course of the historical struggles and in many cases preponderate in determining their *form*. There is an interaction of all these elements, in which, amid all the endless *host* of accidents (*i.e.*, of things and events whose inner connection is so remote or so impossible to prove that we regard it as absent and can neglect it), the economic movement finally asserts itself as necessary. Otherwise the application of the theory to any period of history one chose would be easier than the solution of a simple equation of the first degree.

We make our own history, but in the first place under very definite presuppositions and conditions. Among these the economic ones are finally decisive. But the political, etc., ones, and indeed even the traditions which haunt human minds, also play a part, although not the decisive one. The Prussian State arose and developed from historical, ultimately from economic causes. But it could scarcely be maintained without pedantry that among the many small states of North Germany, Brandenburg was specifically determined by economic necessity to become the great power embodying the economic, linguistic and, after the Reformation, also the religious differences between north and south, and not by other elements as well (above all by its entanglement with Poland, owing to the possession of Prussia, and hence with international, political relations—which were indeed also decisive in the formation of the Austrian dynastic power). Without making oneself ridiculous it would be difficult to succeed in explaining in terms of economics the existence of every small state in Germany, past and present, or the origin of the High German consonant mutations, which the geographical wall of partition formed by the mountains from the Sudetic range to the Taunus extended to a regular division throughout Germany.

In the second place, however, history makes itself in such a way that the final result always arises from conflicts between many individual wills, of which each again has been made what it is by a host of particular conditions of life. Thus there are innumerable intersecting forces, an infinite series of parallelograms of forces which give rise to one resultant—the historical event. This again may itself be viewed as the product of a power which, taken as a whole, works *unconsciously* and without volition. For what each individual wills is obstructed by everyone else, and what emerges is something that no one willed. Thus past history proceeds in the manner of a natural process and is also essentially subject to the same laws of movement. But from the fact that individual wills—of which each desires what he is impelled to by his physical constitution and external, in the last resort economic, circumstances (either his own personal circumstances or those of society in general)—do not attain what they want, but are merged into a collective mean, a common resultant, it must not be concluded that their value = 0. On the contrary, each contributes to the resultant and is to this degree involved in it. . . .

Marx and I are ourselves partly to blame for the fact that younger writers sometimes lay more stress on the economic side than is due to it. We had to emphasise this main principle in opposition to our adversaries, who denied it, and we had not always the time, the place or the opportunity to allow the other elements involved in the interaction to come into their rights. But when it was a case of presenting a section of history, that is, of a practical application, the thing was different and there no error was possible. Unfortunately, however, it happens only too often that people think they have fully understood a theory and can apply it without more ado from the moment they have mastered its main principles, and those even not always correctly. And I cannot exempt many of the more recent "Marxists" from this reproach, for the most wonderful rubbish has been produced from this quarter too. . . .

Engels to H. Starkenburg

London, 25 January 1894

Here is the answer to your questions![3]

(1) What we understand by the economic conditions which we regard as the determining basis of the history of society are the methods by which human beings in a given society produce their means of subsistence and exchange the products among themselves (in so far as division of labour exists). Thus the *entire technique* of production and transport is here included. According to our conception this technique also determines the method of exchange and, further, the division of products, and with it, after the dissolution of tribal society, the division into classes also and hence the relations of lordship and servitude and with them the state, politics, law, etc. Under economic conditions are further included the geographical basis on which they operate and those remnants of earlier stages of economic development which have actually been transmitted and have survived—often only through tradition or the force of inertia; also of course the external milieu which surrounds this form of society.

If, as you say, technique largely depends on the state of science, science depends far more still on the *state* and the *requirements* of technique. If society has a technical need, that helps science forward more than ten universities. The whole of hydrostatics (Torricelli, etc.) was called forth by the necessity for regulating the mountain streams of Italy in the sixteenth

3. Starkenburg had put the following questions to Engels: (1) How far do economic conditions act *causally?* (Are they an adequate ground, motive, permanent condition, etc., of development?) (2) What part is played by the *racial* element and by historic *personality* in Marx and Engels's conception of history?

and seventeenth centuries. We have only known anything reasonable about electricity since its technical applicability was discovered. But unfortunately it has become the custom in Germany to write the history of the sciences as if they had fallen from the skies.

(2) We regard economic conditions as the factor which ultimately determines historical development. But race is itself an economic factor. Here, however, two points must not be overlooked:

(a) Political, juridical, philosophical, religious, literary, artistic, etc., development is based on economic development. But all these react upon one another and also upon the economic base. It is not that the economic position is the *cause and alone active,* while everything else only has a passive effect. There is, rather, interaction on the basis of the economic necessity, which ultimately always asserts itself. The state, for instance, exercises an influence by tariffs, free trade, good or bad fiscal system; and even the deadly inanition and impotence of the German petty bourgeoisie, arising from the miserable economic position of Germany from 1640 to 1830 and expressing itself at first in pietism, then in sentimentality and cringing servility to princes and nobles, was not without economic effect. It was one of the greatest hindrances to recovery and was not shaken until the revolutionary and Napoleonic wars made the chronic misery an acute one. So it is not, as people try here and there conveniently to imagine, that the economic position produces an automatic effect. Men make their history themselves, only in given surroundings which condition it and on the basis of actual relations already existing, among which the economic relations, however much they may be influenced by the other political and ideological ones, are still ultimately the decisive ones, forming the red thread which runs through them and alone leads to understanding.

(b) Men make their history themselves, but not as yet with a collective will or according to a collective plan or even in a definitely defined, given society. Their efforts clash, and for that very reason all such societies are governed by *necessity,* which is supplemented by and appears under the forms of *accident.* The necessity which here asserts itself amidst all accident is again ultimately economic necessity. This is where the so-called *great men* come in for treatment. That such and such a man and precisely that man arises at that particular time in that given country is of course pure accident. But cut him out and there will be a demand for a substitute, and this substitute will be found, good or bad, but in the long run he will be found. That Napoleon, just that particular Corsican, should have been the military dictator whom the French Republic, exhausted by its own war, had rendered necessary, was an accident; but that, if a Napoleon had been lacking, another would have filled the place, is proved by the fact that the man has always been found as soon as he became necessary: Caesar, Augustus,

Cromwell, etc. While Marx discovered the materialist conception of history, Thierry, Mignet, Guizot, and all the English historians up to 1850 are the proof that it was being striven for, and the discovery of the same conception by Morgan proves that the time was ripe for it and that indeed it *had* to be discovered.

So with all the other accidents, and apparent accidents, of history. The further the particular sphere which we are investigating is removed from the economic sphere and approaches that of pure abstract ideology, the more shall we find it exhibiting accidents in its development, the more will its curve run in a zig-zag. So also you will find that the axis of this curve will approach more and more nearly parallel to the axis of the curve of economic development the longer the period considered and the wider the field dealt with.

44. Maurice Barrès, *The Nancy Program*

The traditional Right in nineteenth-century France had defined itself during the revolutionary decade of 1789–99 as an elite movement made up largely of aristocrats and clerics, hostile to republicanism, and in favor of a return to monarchy. In the 1880s, a "new" Right began to emerge, distrustful of the democratic parliamentarianism of the Third Republic but drawing upon the support of the masses. Maurice Barrès was one of the prominent early spokesmen for this new political movement.

The focus of the new movement was nationalism, coupled with the charge that the republican Left, identified since 1792 with the nation, was now betraying it. The most dramatic instance of this alleged betrayal was the republicans' failure to pursue an active *revanchist* policy to restore to France the provinces of Alsace and Lorraine, which had been lost to Germany as a result of the Franco-Prussian War. The new movement crystallized for the first time around the person of Gen. Georges Boulanger, who curried favor with the crowds and seemed in 1889 on the verge of staging a coup d'état. But, apparently beset by a failure of nerve, Boulanger fled the country instead.

Maurice Barrès (1862–1923), born and educated in Lorraine, pursued his literary and political careers simultaneously, intertwining the goals of the two. Among his most influential works was the 1897 novel *Les déracinés* (The uprooted), which traces the fortunes of a group of young men who quit their native town of Nancy (in Lorraine) for Paris. Each comes to a bad end. Barrès intended to show that an individual's life

From *France: Empire and Republic, 1850–1940,* edited and translated by David Thomson (New York: Harper and Row, 1968), pp. 268–73. Copyright © 1968 by David Thomson. Reprinted by permission of Harper and Row, Publishers, Inc.

could have meaning only when the individual was rooted—*raciné*—in the community where his ancestors had lived and left their bones. (The slogan "la terre et les morts"—the soil and the dead—summed up this Barrèsian tenet.) The uprooted individual cut himself off from the instinctual basis of life and entered an arid and sterile world of abstractions. Paris, a city made up of *déracinés* trafficking in abstract ideas, became for Barrès the very emblem of decadence.

In 1889 Barrès entered the political arena. Running on a Boulangist platform, he was elected deputy from Nancy. In 1898 he ran again, on the platform printed here, keeping the label Nationalist Socialist, which he had first used in 1889, as the description of his political position. Barrès lost this particular election and reentered the Chamber only in 1906 as a deputy for Paris, holding his seat from that "decadent" capital until his death. Nonetheless, the Nancy Program of 1898 is a valuable document; spelling out the ramifications of Barrès's intense nationalism as applied to the specific issues of the day (including the Dreyfus case), it is a representative statement of the outlook of the new Right in France at the turn of the century.

ELECTORS,

The nationalist and social ideas which we brought to a joint triumph for the first time in 1889, had at that time alarmed certain minds because of the popularity of General Boulanger. Today, whether because they seem to be more matured, or whether circumstances now justify them more, they attract many adherents even among the antagonists of the previous campaign, disabused by a party which has done nothing since we left it with a free field.

The "Nationalist Socialist Republican Committee of Meurthe-et-Moselle" and a large number of independent electors have asked me to take up again the electoral battle.

To a policy having for its aim only animosities to satisfy, and for its driving force only lust for power, I come anew to oppose those *national* and *social* ideas which already you have acclaimed and which you will not today repudiate.

I. We Are Nationalists

In the top ranks of society, in the heart of the provinces, in the moral and in the material sphere, in commerce, industry, and agriculture, even in the shipyards where they are competing with French workers, foreigners are poisoning us like parasites.

One vital principle that should underlie the new French policy is to protect all its nationals against this invasion, and to beware of that brand of socialism that is so cosmopolitan, or rather so German, that it would weaken the country's defenses.

The Jewish problem is linked to the national problem. The Jews were assimilated to the native French by the Revolution, but have retained their peculiar characteristics and now, instead of being persecuted as they once were, are themselves the overlords. We believe in complete freedom of conscience; what is more, we should consider it highly dangerous to allow the Jews the chance of invoking (and so to appear to be defending) the principles of civil liberty promulgated by the Revolution. But they violate these principles by characteristically isolated behavior, by monopolies, speculation, and cosmopolitanism. There is, moreover, in the army, the magistracy, the ministries, in all branches of the administration, a far higher proportion of them than their numbers justify. They have been appointed prefects, judges, treasurers, officers—because they have money, which corrupts. We ought to destroy this dangerous disproportion, without even changing the law, by insisting on greater fairness on the part of those who govern, and so gain more consideration for our real nationals, the children of Gaul and not of Judea.

But the most urgent need is to make the process of naturalization more difficult. It is by this loophole that the worst Jews and many second-rate Frenchmen have slipped in.

Statistics show that 90 per cent of foreigners do not become naturalized until they have evaded active army service. We should insist that military service is a condition of nationality. What is more, a naturalized person (except those from Alsace-Lorraine) should be allowed just private rights, while only his descendants should be assimilated to French-born citizens and enjoy political rights.

The opportunist policy over the last twenty years has favored Jews, foreigners, cosmopolitans. The reason given by those who committed this criminal mistake was that these aliens would introduce a vigorous element into France. Fine elements these—Reinach, Cornelius Herz, Alfred Dreyfus, and the like—who have almost brought us to decay! This is the real position: French society does need vigorous new elements, it is true, but they can be found within that society, by encouraging the least privileged, the poorest, by raising their standard of living and improving their vocational training.

So nationalism leads inevitably to socialism. We define socialism as "the material and moral improvement of the largest and poorest classes."

It has taken some centuries for the French nation to give political security to its members. It must now protect them against that economic insecurity that prevails at all levels.

Let us define this insecurity.

II. We Demand Protection against Economic Insecurity

Insecurity of the worker—The elderly worker has not enough to eat. Even if he is able-bodied, he runs the risk of unemployment.

Wages are kept low by foreign competition.

Mechanization means that he is crowded into factories, subjected to military discipline under the arbitrary rule of the boss. In some districts he is reduced by certain economic organizations to real slavery.

He cannot get out. For one thing, you do not take your native earth with you on the soles of your boots, and for many of them exile is heartbreak. Again, materially speaking, if he goes, he and his family will probably starve to death for he will have no savings. Besides, where could he find work?

Insecurity of the small trader—The small trader has the same economic insecurity as the worker. They are interdependent. It is, in fact, the lower working class, black-coated and manual workers, who keep the small trader going, for the middle classes go to the big stores. The small trader helps the black-coated or manual worker to survive periods of unemployment by allowing credit. But the credit that the worker gets from the small trader—baker, butcher, grocer, or landlord—lays him open to ruin if unemployment is prolonged or too frequent.

Another cause of insecurity is that prime costs for small industrialists and tradespeople fluctuate arbitrarily, at the bidding of speculators.

We should note in passing that these traders and industrialists did not gain from the lowering of the bank rate. They still pay 8 per cent (6 per cent for three months with four renewals that cost 1/2 per cent, making 8 per cent in all). Without going so far as a State bank, which could be held to ransom in wartime, we should like to have seen commerce profit by the renewal of the charter of the Bank of France. But the Government and the financial feudality thought otherwise.

Insecurity of the farmer—The price of wheat no longer depends solely on the French harvest. At one time the producer used to get compensation for a poor harvest in the higher prices charged to the consumer. Nowadays these prices depend on the harvests of India and the United States.

They have begun to remedy this situation by protection, which is basically a socialist measure, intervention by the State in the natural course of events. (Just as the same circumstances are sweeping away parties, like a flood tide!)

We are in full agreement with the major aspects of protection. It aims at guaranteeing a minimum price to the producer. But the big middlemen absorb the profits with their fluctuations and speculative maneuvers, which should be opposed with terrorist severity. . . .

Insecurity of the bourgeoisie—The bourgeoisie is menaced by the international finance feudality, which turns financial securities into bits of paper.

I will not go back as far as Panama—I could find ten examples in the last twelve months. Take this one. The price of gold mines launched on the French market was raised to the point where their total value reached about 1.8 billion francs. Today they are worth no more than 615 million. This means that in less than two years national savings worth 1.2 billion was lost on securities held by small French investors.

No investigation followed.

ELECTORS

It is for the defense of the ideas that I have just explained that I propose for your approbation the following Program:

I. MEASURES TO BE TAKEN TO ENSURE THE UNION OF ALL FRENCHMEN

Against foreign produce: the work of protectionism must be maintained;

Against the foreign worker who, being dispensed from military service, draws every year a billion in wages from France and causes poverty and destitution, through unemployment, among the families of French workers. In particular public works, financed from taxes, must be carried out by national workers;

Against the international financial feudality which, through its joint-stock association, eliminates the worker from the country and replaces him by undercutting with foreign workers, paralyzes the action of protective measures taken in support of agriculture and industry, organizes monopoly and speculation in the basic essentials, falsifies prices, sending them up and down, and in the end ruins the real producers of wealth—our farmers, our traders, our workers;

Against the naturalized foreigner, who claims to play a role in politics and to whom we would allow only private rights, reserving political rights for his descendants. This is the best way to get at the Jew, whose invasion of State functions the executive power would otherwise have to restrict.

II. INSTITUTION OF A SUPERANNUATION FUND for workers organized by the State.

The duties which must be levied on foreign workers and the customs duties levied on basic essential goods must be specifically allotted to this superannuation fund in order to simplify somewhat these taxes where strictly no levy should be imposed.

The matter of superannuation funds is one of the most important to settle for the sake of social peace. It is urgent. It forces itself upon us. But it is complicated by a grave financial problem which has to be solved. I shall give this all my attention and care. I declare myself in favor of the principle. I shall accept any solution likely to produce the quickest and most lasting results.

III. REFORM OF TAXATION TO PROMOTE DEMOCRATIC JUSTICE aiming at lowering taxes on consumer goods and charges which hit the small growers. The land tax is charged on an estimated income which often does not exist, on the basis of assessments which no longer correspond to reality. The tax on consumer goods is infinitely heavier on the poor than on the rich.

IV. ORGANIZATION OF AGRICULTURAL CREDIT, WHICH COULD INCLUDE THE FUNDS OF THE SAVINGS BANKS, today drained away from the whole province in order to BE CENTRALIZED and riskily used for the purchase of stocks.

V. FREEDOM OF ASSOCIATION. THIS IMPLIES EXTENSION OF THE CIVIL PER-SONALITY OF THE TRADE UNIONS IN SUCH A WAY THAT WHETHER AGRICUL-TURAL OR INDUSTRIAL UNIONS, THEY CAN USE THE POWER OF CREDIT, BE-COME ASSOCIATIONS OF PRODUCERS and own the premises and working tools needed in industrial, commercial, or agricultural production.

VI. EXTENSION OF THE INDEPENDENT FREEDOMS AND THE CIVIL PERSON-ALITY OF THE COMMUNES, SO as to permit them to achieve in part certain kinds of social progress—always provided they do not infringe the rights of the State.

VII. DEVELOPMENT OF PUBLIC EDUCATION IN THE DIRECTION OF OCCUPA-TIONAL TRAINING in order to allow all national aptitudes, all forms of intel-ligence to be developed.

VIII. REVISION OF THE CONSTITUTION with the aim of giving universal suf-frage its full and complete sovereignty, particularly by means of the *muni-cipal referendum*.

ELECTORS,

It is useful that, in this region of Lorraine, where day by day they be-come more numerous, the workers in factories and in the fields should be able to express their wishes; it would be dangerous to suppress them into silence, as the old opportunists wished to do.

This program of the "National Socialist Republican Committee"—what generous and just mind would wish to misunderstand it?—corre-sponds to the needs of our population; IT IS IN TUNE WITH THE SPECIAL SPIRIT OF OUR LORRAINE and of our frontier.

Articles IV, V, VI, VIII, which concern decentralization, strongly indi-cate the direction of our demands in our region, where the "School of Nancy" matches public feeling.

In all our Articles, as anyone can see who examines them in the light of our preliminary arguments, the path of the future is prepared, and at the same time immediate interests are guaranteed. I undertake to defend them with every means at my disposal, at the same time as I place myself completely at the service of the special interests of my compatriots.

45. Theodor Herzl, *The Jewish State*

Theodor Herzl (1860–1904) was born in Budapest of a well-to-do German-Jewish family. Like his father, he believed in the promise of emancipation: in modern, liberal states, where religion was a private matter, Jews who adapted to the culture around them would become fully integrated members of society without converting to Christianity. During Herzl's childhood Jews achieved legal equality in Germany and Austria-Hungary, as they had earlier in western Europe. But at this time there emerged throughout Europe a modern anti-Semitism that argued that Jews were a foreign element whom neither cultural assimilation nor even religious conversion could change in essence, and that the essence of Judaism was disruptive and demoralizing to the national existence of the peoples among whom the Jews lived.

Although Herzl came into contact with the new anti-Semitism as a law student in Vienna, he did not abandon his liberal and assimilated views until the 1890s. After taking a law degree he devoted himself to a literary career in Vienna, becoming a modestly successful short-story writer, essayist, and playwright. In 1891 he went to Paris as the correspondent of Austria's most important newspaper, the *Neue Freie Presse*. In Paris Herzl witnessed the growth of an anti-Semitism that seemed even more virulent than that of Vienna. One decisive turning point in his life came with the trial for espionage of a Jewish army officer, Capt. Alfred Dreyfus, and the anti-Jewish mob scenes that Dreyfus's conviction and subsequent degradation unleashed in Paris in the winter of 1894–95. A second personal crisis came with the success of a group of political anti-Semites, led by Karl Lueger, in winning control of the municipal council of Vienna in late May 1895. Herzl began *The Jewish State* in June 1895. The book was published in 1896.

Since he felt that the problems facing the Jews in Europe were ultimately national in nature, Herzl focused attention on a political solution in the form of a Jewish state. His position at this time was more "territo-

From Theodor Herzl, *The Jewish State* (New York: American Zionist Emergency Council, 1946), pp. 85–97.

rialist" than rigidly Zionist: he called for a Jewish state in either Palestine or Argentina. Although he was not the first modern Zionist, his advocacy of a Jewish state, and his later popularity among the Jewish masses in eastern Europe, contributed to his reputation as the father of political Zionism.

II.—The Jewish Question

No one can deny the gravity of the situation of the Jews. Wherever they live in perceptible numbers, they are more or less persecuted. Their equality before the law, granted by statute, has become practically a dead letter. They are debarred from filling even moderately high positions, either in the army, or in any public or private capacity. And attempts are made to thrust them out of business also: "Don't buy from Jews!"

Attacks in Parliaments, in assemblies, in the press, in the pulpit, in the street, on journeys—for example, their exclusion from certain hotels—even in places of recreation, become daily more numerous. The forms of persecutions vary according to the countries and social circles in which they occur. In Russia, imposts are levied on Jewish villages; in Rumania, a few persons are put to death; in Germany, they get a good beating occasionally; in Austria, Anti-Semites exercise terrorism over all public life; in Algeria, there are travelling agitators; in Paris, the Jews are shut out of the so-called best social circles and excluded from clubs. Shades of anti-Jewish feeling are innumerable. But this is not to be an attempt to make out a doleful category of Jewish hardships.

I do not intend to arouse sympathetic emotions on our behalf. That would be a foolish, futile, and undignified proceeding. I shall content myself with putting the following questions to the Jews: Is it not true that, in countries where we live in perceptible numbers, the position of Jewish lawyers, doctors, technicians, teachers, and employees of all descriptions becomes daily more intolerable? Is it not true, that the Jewish middle classes are seriously threatened? Is it not true, that the passions of the mob are incited against our wealthy people? Is it not true, that our poor endure greater sufferings than any other proletariat? I think that this external pressure makes itself felt everywhere. In our economically upper classes it causes discomfort, in our middle classes continual and grave anxieties, in our lower classes absolute despair.

Everything tends, in fact, to one and the same conclusion, which is clearly enunciated in that classic Berlin phrase: *"Juden Raus!"* (Out with the Jews!)

I shall now put the Question in the briefest possible form: Are we to "get out" now and where to?

Or, may we yet remain? And, how long?

Let us first settle the point of staying where we are. Can we hope for better days, can we possess our souls in patience, can we wait in pious resignation till the princes and peoples of this earth are more mercifully disposed towards us? I say that we cannot hope for a change in the current of feeling. And why not? Even if we were as near to the hearts of princes as are their other subjects, they could not protect us. They would only feel popular hatred by showing us too much favor. By "too much," I really mean less than is claimed as a right by every ordinary citizen, or by every race. The nations in whose midst Jews live are all either covertly or openly Anti-Semitic.

The common people have not, and indeed cannot have, any historic comprehension. They do not know that the sins of the Middle Ages are now being visited on the nations of Europe. We are what the Ghetto made us. We have attained pre-eminence in finance, because mediaeval conditions drove us to it. The same process is now being repeated. We are again being forced into finance, now it is the stock exchange, by being kept out of other branches of economic activity. Being on the stock exchange, we are consequently exposed afresh to contempt. At the same time we continue to produce an abundance of mediocre intellects who find no outlet, and this endangers our social position as much as does our increasing wealth. Educated Jews without means are now rapidly becoming Socialists. Hence we are certain to suffer very severely in the struggle between classes, because we stand in the most exposed position in the camps of both Socialists and capitalists.

Previous Attempts at a Solution

The artificial means heretofore employed to overcome the troubles of Jews have been either too petty—such as attempts at colonization—or attempts to convert the Jews into peasants in their present homes.

What is achieved by transporting a few thousand Jews to another country? Either they come to grief at once, or prosper, and then their prosperity creates Anti-Semitism. We have already discussed these attempts to divert poor Jews to fresh districts. This diversion is clearly inadequate and futile, if it does not actually defeat its own ends; for it merely protracts and postpones a solution, and perhaps even aggravates difficulties.

Whoever would attempt to convert the Jew into a husbandman would be making an extraordinary mistake. For a peasant is in a historical category, as proved by his costume which in some countries he has worn for centuries; and by his tools, which are identical with those used by his earliest forefathers. His plough is unchanged; he carries the seed in his apron; mows with the historical scythe, and threshes with the time-honored flail. But we know that all this can be done by machinery. The agrarian question is only a question of machinery. America must conquer Europe, in the same way as large landed possessions absorb small ones. The peasant is consequently a type which is in course of extinction. Whenever he is artificially preserved, it is done on account of the political interests which he is intended to serve. It is absurd, and indeed impossible, to make modern peasants on the old pattern. No one is wealthy or powerful enough to make civilization take a single retrograde step. The mere preservation of obsolete institutions is a task severe enough to require the enforcement of all the despotic measures of an autocratically governed State.

Are we, therefore, to credit Jews who are intelligent with a desire to become peasants of the old type? One might just as well say to them: "Here is a cross-bow: now go to war!" What? With a cross-bow, while the others have rifles and long range guns? Under these circumstances the Jews are perfectly justified in refusing to stir when people try to make peasants of them. A cross-bow is a beautiful weapon, which inspires me with mournful feelings when I have time to devote to them. But it belongs by rights to a museum.

Now, there certainly are districts to which desperate Jews go out, or at any rate, are willing to go out and till the soil. And a little observation shows that these districts—such as the enclave of Hesse in Germany, and some provinces in Russia—these very districts are the principal seats of Anti-Semitism.

For the world's reformers, who send the Jews to the plough, forget a very important person, who has a great deal to say on the matter. This person is the agriculturist, and the agriculturist is also perfectly justified. For the tax on land, the risks attached to crops, the pressure of large proprietors who cheapen labor, and American competition in particular, combine to make his life hard enough. Besides, the duties on corn cannot go on increasing indefinitely. Nor can the manufacturer be allowed to starve; his political influence is, in fact, in the ascendant, and he must therefore be treated with additional consideration.

All these difficulties are well known, therefore I refer to them only cursorily. I merely wanted to indicate clearly how futile had been past attempts—most of them well intentioned—to solve the Jewish Question. Neither a diversion of the stream, nor an artificial depression of the intellectual level of our proletariat, will overcome the difficulty. The supposed infallible expedient of assimilation has already been dealt with.

We cannot get the better of Anti-Semitism by any of these methods. It cannot die out so long as its causes are not removed. Are they removable?

Causes of Anti-Semitism

We shall not again touch on those causes which are a result of temperament, prejudice and narrow views, but shall here restrict ourselves to political and economical causes alone. Modern Anti-Semitism is not to be confounded with the religious persecution of the Jews of former times. It does occasionally take a religious bias in some countries, but the main current of the aggressive movement has now changed. In the principal countries where Anti-Semitism prevails, it docs so as a result of the emancipation of the Jews. When civilized nations awoke to the inhumanity of discriminatory legislation and enfranchised us, our enfranchisement came too late. It was no longer possible to remove our disabilities in our old homes. For we had, curiously enough, developed while in the Ghetto into a bourgeois people, and we stepped out of it only to enter into fierce competition with the middle classes. Hence, our emancipation set us suddenly within this middle-class circle, where we have a double pressure to sustain, from within and from without. The Christian bourgeoisie would not be unwilling to cast us as a sacrifice to Socialism, though that would not greatly improve matters.

At the same time, the equal rights of Jews before the law cannot be withdrawn where they have once been conceded. Not only because their withdrawal would be opposed to the spirit of our age, but also because it would immediately drive all Jews, rich and poor alike, into the ranks of subversive parties. Nothing effectual can really be done to our injury. In olden days our jewels were seized. How is our movable property to be got hold of now? It consists of printed papers which are locked up somewhere or other in the world, perhaps in the coffers of Christians. It is, of course, possible to get at shares and debentures in railways, banks and industrial undertakings of all descriptions by taxation, and where the progressive income-tax is in force all our movable property can eventually be laid hold of. But all these efforts cannot be directed against Jews alone, and wherever they might nevertheless be made, severe economic crises would be their immediate consequences, which would be by no means confined to the Jews who would be the first affected. The very impossibility of getting at the Jews nourishes and embitters hatred of them. Anti-Semitism increases day by day and hour by hour among the nations; indeed, it is bound to increase, because the causes of its growth continue to exist and cannot be removed. Its remote cause is our loss of the power of assimilation during the Middle Ages; its immediate cause is our excessive production of mediocre intellects, who cannot find an outlet downwards or upwards—that is to say, no wholesome outlet in either direction. When we sink, we become a revolutionary proletariat, the subordinate officers of all revolutionary parties; and at the same time, when we rise, there rises also our terrible power of the purse.

Effects of Anti-Semitism

The oppression we endure does not improve us, for we are not a whit better than ordinary people. It is true that we do not love our enemies; but he alone who can conquer himself dare reproach us with that fault. Oppression naturally creates hostility against oppressors, and our hostility aggravates the pressure. It is impossible to escape from this eternal circle.

"No!" Some soft-hearted visionaries will say: "No, it is possible! Possible by means of the ultimate perfection of humanity."

Is it necessary to point to the sentimental folly of this view? He who would found his hope for improved conditions on the ultimate perfection of humanity would indeed be relying upon a Utopia!

I referred previously to our "assimilation." I do not for a moment wish to imply that I desire such an end. Our national character is too historically famous, and, in spite of every degradation, too fine to make its annihilation desirable. We might perhaps be able to merge ourselves entirely into surrounding races, if these were to leave us in peace for a period of two generations. But they will not leave us in peace. For a little period they manage to tolerate us, and then their hostility breaks out again and again. The world is provoked somehow by our prosperity, because it has for many centuries been accustomed to consider us as the most contemptible among the poverty-stricken. In its ignorance and narrowness of heart, it fails to observe that prosperity weakens our Judaism and extinguishes our peculiarities. It is only pressure that forces us back to the parent stem; it is only hatred encompassing us that makes us strangers once more.

Thus, whether we like it or not, we are now and shall henceforth remain, a historic group with unmistakable characteristics common to us all.

We are one people—our enemies have made us one without our consent, as repeatedly happens in history. Distress binds us together, and, thus united, we suddenly discover our strength. Yes, we are strong enough to form a State, and, indeed, a model State. We possess all human and material resources necessary for the purpose.

This is therefore the appropriate place to give an account of what has been somewhat roughly termed our "human material." But it would not be appreciated till the broad lines of the plan, on which everything depends, has first been marked out.

The Plan

The whole plan is in its essence perfectly simple, as it must necessarily be if it is to come within the comprehension of all.

Let the sovereignty be granted us over a portion of the globe large enough to satisfy the rightful requirements of a nation; the rest we shall manage for ourselves.

The creation of a new State is neither ridiculous nor impossible. We have in our day witnessed the process in connection with nations which were not largely members of the middle class, but poorer, less educated, and consequently weaker than ourselves. The Governments of all countries scourged by Anti-Semitism will be keenly interested in assisting us to obtain the sovereignty we want.

The plan, simple in design, but complicated in execution, will be carried out by two agencies: The Society of Jews and the Jewish Company.

The Society of Jews will do the preparatory work in the domains of science and politics, which the Jewish Company will afterwards apply practically.

The Jewish Company will be the liquidating agent of the business interests of departing Jews, and will organize commerce and trade in the new country.

We must not imagine the departure of the Jews to be a sudden one. It will be gradual, continuous, and will cover many decades. The poorest will go first to cultivate the soil. In accordance with a preconceived plan, they will construct roads, bridges, railways and telegraph installations; regulate rivers; and build their own dwellings; their labor will create trade, trade will create markets and markets will attract new settlers, for every man will go voluntarily, at his own expense and his own risk. The labor expended on the land will enhance its value, and the Jews will soon perceive that a new and permanent sphere of operation is opening here for that spirit of enterprise which has heretofore met only with hatred and obloquy.

If we wish to found a State today, we shall not do it in the way which would have been the only possible one a thousand years ago. It is foolish to revert to old stages of civilization, as many Zionists would like to do. Supposing, for example, we were obliged to clear a country of wild beasts, we should not set about the task in the fashion of Europeans of the fifth century. We should not take spear and lance and go out singly in pursuit of bears; we would organize a large and active hunting party, drive the animals together, and throw a melinite bomb into their midst.

If we wish to conduct building operations, we shall not plant a mass of stakes and piles on the shore of a lake, but we shall build as men build now. Indeed, we shall build in a bolder and more stately style than was ever adopted before, for we now possess means which men never yet possessed.

The emigrants standing lowest in the economic scale will be slowly followed by those of a higher grade. Those who at this moment are living in despair will go first. They will be led by the mediocre intellects which we produce so superabundantly and which are persecuted everywhere.

This pamphlet will open a general discussion on the Jewish Question, but that does not mean that there will be any voting on it. Such a result would ruin the cause from the outset, and dissidents must remember that allegiance or opposition is entirely voluntary. He who will not come with us should remain behind.

Let all who are willing to join us, fall in behind our banner and fight for our cause with voice and pen and deed.

Those Jews who agree with our idea of a State will attach themselves to the Society, which will thereby be authorized to confer and treat with Governments in the name of our people. The Society will thus be acknowledged in its relations with Governments as a State-creating power. This acknowledgment will practically create the State.

Should the Powers declare themselves willing to admit our sovereignty over a neutral piece of land, then the Society will enter into negotiations for the possession of this land. Here two territories come under consideration, Palestine and Argentine. In both countries important experiments in colonization have been made, though on the mistaken principle of a gradual infiltration of Jews. An infiltration is bound to end badly. It continues till the inevitable moment when the native population feels itself threatened, and forces the Government to stop a further influx of Jews. Immigration is consequently futile unless we have the sovereign right to continue such immigration.

The Society of Jews will treat with the present masters of the land, putting itself under the protectorate of the European Powers, if they prove friendly to the plan. We could offer the present possessors of the land enormous advantages, assume part of the public debt, build new roads for traffic, which our presence in the country would render necessary, and do many other things. The creation of our State would be beneficial to adjacent countries, because the cultivation of a strip of land increases the value of its surrounding districts in innumerable ways.

Palestine or Argentine?

Shall we choose Palestine or Argentine? We shall take what is given us, and what is selected by Jewish public opinion. The Society will determine both these points.

Argentine is one of the most fertile countries in the world, extends over a vast area, has a sparse population and a mild climate. The Argentine Republic would derive considerable profit from the cession of a portion of its territory to us. The present infiltration of Jews has certainly produced some discontent, and it would be necessary to enlighten the Republic on the intrinsic difference of our new movement.

Palestine is our ever-memorable historic home. The very name of Palestine would attract our people with a force of marvellous potency. If His Majesty the Sultan were to give us Palestine, we could in return undertake to regulate the whole finances of Turkey. We should there form a portion of a rampart of Europe against Asia, an outpost of civilization as opposed to barbarism. We should as a neutral State remain in contact with all Europe, which would have to guarantee our existence. The sanctuaries of Christendom would be safeguarded by assigning to them an extra-territorial status such as is well-known to the law of nations. We should form a guard of honor about these sanctuaries, answering for the fulfilment of this duty with our existence. This guard of honor would be the great symbol of the solution of the Jewish Question after eighteen centuries of Jewish suffering.

Demand, Medium, Trade

I said in the last chapter, "The Jewish Company will organize trade and commerce in the new country." I shall here insert a few remarks on that point.

A scheme such as mine is gravely imperilled if it is opposed by "practical" people. Now "practical" people are as a rule nothing more than men sunk into the groove of daily routine, unable to emerge from a narrow circle of antiquated ideas. At the same time, their adverse opinion carries great weight, and can do considerable harm to a new project, at any rate until this new thing is sufficiently strong to throw the "practical" people and their mouldy notions to the winds.

In the earliest period of European railway construction some "practical" people were of the opinion that it was foolish to build certain lines "because there were not even sufficient passengers to fill the mail-coaches." They did not realize the truth—which now seems obvious to us—that travellers do not produce railways, but, conversely, railways produce travellers, the latent demand, of course, is taken for granted.

The impossibility of comprehending how trade and commerce are to be created in a new country which has yet to be acquired and cultivated, may be classed with those doubts of "practical" persons concerning the need of railways. A "practical" person would express himself somewhat in this fashion:

> Granted that the present situation of the Jews is in many places unendurable, and aggravated day by day; granted that there exists a desire to emigrate; granted even that the Jews do emigrate to the new country; how will they earn their living there, and what will they earn? What are they to live on when there? The business of many people cannot be artificially organized in a day.

To this I should reply: We have not the slightest intention of organizing trade artificially, and we should certainly not attempt to do it in a day. But, though the organization of it may be impossible, the promotion of it is not. And how is commerce to be encouraged? Through the medium of a demand. The demand recognized, the medium created, it will establish itself.

If there is a real earnest demand among Jews for an improvement of their status; if the medium to be created—the Jewish Company—is sufficiently powerful, then commerce will extend itself freely in the new country.

46. Jean Jaurès, *Idealism in History*

Jean Jaurès (1859–1914) was the embodiment of French socialism before the Great War. Born in Castres in the south of France, he was by social background something between a bourgeois and a man of the people: his father, a failed businessman, had ended up as a small peasant proprietor. Jaurès was also very much a beneficiary of the meritocratic aspects of the French educational system. Once his intellectual gifts had been noticed by a local schoolmaster, he was sent on scholarship to a Paris lycée and then passed the entrance examination for the prestigious Ecole Normale Supérieure. In effect, ENS trained France's intellectual elite, and Jaurès's classmates included Emile Durkheim (who became the founder of sociology in France) and Henri Bergson (who became the influential anti-rationalist philosopher). As was required of *normaliens,* Jaurès taught in a lycée—his subject was philosophy—upon graduation. Later in life, he liked to refer to himself as a "cultured peasant."

Jaurès entered politics in 1885, when at the age of twenty-six he was elected deputy for his native department of the Tarn. He had run on an independent, moderate republican ticket. The 1892 strike by the glassworkers of Carmaux, a town in the Tarn, gave him his first direct experience of the relations between labor and management and is generally credited with the decisive leftward turn in his thought and politics. Having failed in his bid for reelection in 1889, he ran again, successfully, in 1893, now as a socialist.

Although Jaurès was henceforth to regard himself as a Marxist, he never felt entirely comfortable with the "orthodox" Marxism espoused in France by the Parti ouvrier français (POF) of Jules Guesde. Much like the German revisionist Eduard Bernstein (see document 47), he preferred to conceptualize socialism as the logical outgrowth and extension of the Jacobin democratic tradition. But he was also convinced that the cause of socialism in France could only be damaged by doctrinal squabbles

From *Socialist Thought: A Documentary History* (New York: Doubleday, 1964), pp. 405–15. Reprinted by permission of the editors, Albert Fried and Ronald Sanders.

among its adherents, and it is a tribute to his great political skill that he was able to unify all French socialists into a single party, the SFIO (French Section of the Workers' International), in 1905. Membership in the SFIO doubled beween the party's founding and 1914.

Jaurès was an impassioned and compelling orator. Larding his speeches with poetic imagery and literary allusions and able to tap the most generous sentiments of his audience, he was allowed to go on for two or three hours, on occasion for days, in the Chamber of Deputies. On the evening of 31 July 1914, shortly after he had returned from a meeting of the Second International in Brussels, Jaurès was assassinated by a crazed nationalist fanatic as he sat in a Paris café with some fellow socialists discussing how the apparently imminent war might be averted. His tragic death proved an apt augury of the immediate future of Europe.

This selection is an early articulation of Jaurès's conception of socialism. It is Jaurès's side of a formal debate with the Guesdist Paul Lafargue (Karl Marx's son-in-law) on 12 January 1894. The debate, on "Idealism and Materialism in the Conception of History," took place in the Latin Quarter before an overflow crowd of socialist students.

First I want to caution you against an error that might arise from the fact that the subject I shall deal with here before you is one on which I spoke a few months ago. At that time I expounded the thesis of economic materialism, the interpretation and movement of history that was set forth by Marx; and I made an effort to justify Marx's doctrine, in such a way that it might have appeared that I accepted it without any qualification whatsoever.

This time, on the other hand, I want to demonstrate that the materialist conception of history does not preclude an idealist interpretation of it. And since one might, in this second part of my demonstration, lose sight of the arguments in all their force that I gave in favor of Marx's thesis, I ask you, so that there be no mistake about the whole of my thought on the subject, to correct and complete each part of this exposition, that we have been obliged to split in two, by the other.

I demonstrated, last time, that one could interpret all the phenomena of History from the viewpoint of economic materialism, which, as I said then, is definitely not physiological materialism. Marx was as far as anyone could be from saying that all phenomena of the consciousness or of thought can be explained by simple groupings of molecular matter. This, in fact, is a hypothesis that Marx and, more recently Engels, regarded as metaphysical, and that has been repudiated as thoroughly by the scientific school as by the spiritualist one.

Nor is it what is sometimes called "moral materialism," which is the subordination of all of man's activity to the satisfaction of physical appetites and the search for individual well-being. On the contrary, if you will recall how Marx treats the British utilitarian conception in his book *Capital,* if you will recall with what disdain and contempt he speaks of theoreticians of Utilitarianism like Jeremy Bentham, who maintains that man always acts with a personal interest in mind that is constantly sought after by him, you will see that these two doctrines have nothing in common. Rather, one is entirely the opposite of the other; for, precisely because Marx held that the very modes of feeling and thought are determined in men by the essential form of the economic relationships of the society in which they live, he thereby introduced into the individual's conduct social forces, collective forces, historical forces, whose power transcends that of individual and egoistic motives. What this means is that the essential in history consists in economic relationships, in relationships of production between man and man.

It is according to the way in which men are linked together by one or another form of economic organization, that a society has this or that character, this or that conception of life, this or that kind of morality, and gives one or another sort of general direction to its enterprises. Furthermore, according to Marx, men do not act in accordance with an abstract idea of justice or right; they act because the social system that has been formed among them out of the economic relations of production is, at any given moment in history, an unstable system, obliged to transform itself in order to yield its place to other systems. It is the substitution of one economic system for another, for example of slavery for cannibalism, that naturally brings along in its wake an equivalent transformation in political, moral, aesthetic, scientific and religious conceptions: in other words, the deepest and most significant well-spring of historical energy is, according to Marx, the mode of organization of economic interests.

The term "economic materialism" can therefore be explained in this way: a man does not draw out of his own brain a completely formed idea of justice; he does no more than reflect within himself, within his cerebral substance, the economic relations of production.

The idealist conception in relation to the materialist one, exists in numerous forms. I will sum it up this way: it is the conception according to which humanity has, at its point of departure, an initial presentiment of its destiny and development.

Before having the experience of history, before establishing this or that economic system, humanity carries within itself a preliminary idea of justice and right, and it pursues this preconceived ideal from one form of civilization to another, higher form. When humanity acts, it is not by the automatic and mechanical transformation of the modes of production, but under the obscurely or clearly felt influence of this ideal.

This takes place in such a way that the idea itself becomes the principle of movement and of action, and that, far from the intellectual conceptions being derived from economic facts, it is the economic facts that, little by little, translate and incorporate the ideal of humanity into reality and history.

Such is the conception of idealism in history, apart from the innumerable formulas that various religious or philosophical systems have given to it. Now, you will note that these two conceptions, apparently opposed to one another and even mutually exclusive, are really, in the contemporary consciousness, almost, I would say, enmeshed in one another and completely reconciled. There is in fact not a single idealist who would not concede that it is impossible to achieve a higher ideal of man without a preliminary transformation of the economic organism, and, on the other hand, there are very few adherents of the theory of economic materialism who do not allow themselves to appeal to the idea of justice and right, or who confine themselves to depicting the communist society of tomorrow as the necessary and fatal consequence of economic evolution. Rather, they continue to hail this communist society of tomorrow as a higher realization of justice and right.

Is there a contradiction here? Marx was always anxious to maintain the somewhat harsh integrity of his formula, and had nothing but jibes for those who believed that they were strengthening economic evolution and the socialist movement by appealing to the pure idea of justice; he had nothing but jibes for those who, in his own words, "wanted to throw over the reality of history, over the body of facts themselves, a sort of veil woven of the most immaterial threads of the dialectic, embroidered with flowers of rhetoric and soaked in sentimental dew."

It is our task to see if this reconciliation between the materialist and the idealist conceptions of history, which has been realized in fact in our country through instinct, is really alien to the socialist conscience. It is our task to see if it is theoretically and doctrinally possible, or if there is an insoluble contradiction in it, if we are obliged to make a decisive choice between the two conceptions, or if we can logically and reasonably consider them as two different aspects of a single truth. . . .

There is of course no need to remind those versed in the Marxian doctrine that Marx was the intellectual disciple of Hegel; he said so himself, proclaiming it in his introduction to *Capital* (and for the past few years, Engels, following that inclination that leads men who have lived a long time back to their origins, has apparently been making a more intense study of Hegel). It is a striking application of Hegel's formula of contradictions when Marx notes the antagonism of classes in the world today, the state of economic war that opposes the capitalist class to the proletarian class; because this antagonism was born under the capitalist regime, a regime of divisiveness and war, and is preparing the way for a new regime of peace and harmony. According to the ancient formula of Heraclitus that Marx was fond of citing: "Peace is only a form, an aspect of war; war is only a form, an aspect of peace." There is no need to hold up one in opposition to the other; the battle of today is the beginning of the reconciliation of tomorrow.

Modern thinking on the identity of opposites is summed up today in this other admirable conception of Marxism: Until now, humanity has been guided, so to speak, by the unconscious forces of history; until now, men have not acted on their own. Rather, economic evolution guides their acts; they believe themselves to be producing events, or imagine themselves to be vegetating and remaining always in the same place, but economic transformations are taking place without their even realizing it, and they are being unconsciously affected. In a way, humanity has been like a sleeping person afloat on a river, carried along by the flow without contributing to it, or at least without taking account of its direction, but waking up from time to time and perceiving that the surrounding countryside has changed.

Well, once the socialist revolution has become a reality, once the antagonism of classes has ceased, once the human community has become master of the principal means of production in order to direct them to the service of the known and acknowledged needs of men, then humanity will have been torn from the long period of unconsciousness in which it had resided for centuries, pushed along by the blind course of events, and will have entered upon the era in which man will no longer be subject to things outside himself, but will govern their movement instead. But this forthcoming era of full consciousness and clarity is possible only because of a long period of unconsciousness and obscurity.

If, at the dim beginnings of history, men had consciously tried to regulate the course of events and development of things, they simply would have set everything awry, wasted their resources for the future, and as a result of having too soon aspired to act with full consciousness, deprived themselves of the means of ever acting in full consciousness. It is as if a child were summoned too soon to the fully conscious life of reflective reason; deprived of the period of the unconscious evolution of the organic life and of the first manifestations of the moral life, he would then, as a result of having been forced to think in the first moments of life, be incapable of thinking thereafter.

For Marx, this unconscious life was the very condition of and preparation for the conscious life of tomorrow, and history was charged in this way with the task of resolving an essential contradiction. I ask you then, if one may not, if one must not, without violating the spirit of Marxism, press still further this method of the reconciliation of opposites, the synthesis of contradictory elements, and seek out the fundamental reconciliation of economic materialism with idealism, as applied to the development of history.

Notice in what spirit—and I must ask your pardon for these long preliminaries, but one cannot resolve a particular question unless one's thought is based upon a general philosophical conception—notice in what spirit I seek this reconciliation of economic materialism with historical and moral idealism.

I am not trying to say that each has its place, that one part of history is governed by economic necessity, and another part is guided by a pure idea, by a concept—by the idea, for example, of humanity, of justice, or of right. I am not trying to place the materialist conception on one side of a partition, and the idealist conception on the other. I maintain that they must interpenetrate one another, the way that cerebral mechanism and conscious spontaneity interpenetrate one another in the organic life of man. . . .

Marx says: "The human brain does not produce an idea of right all by itself; such an idea would be vain and hollow. In all aspects of the life of humanity, even the intellectual and moral, there is only a reflection of economic phenomena in the human brain."

Well, I accept that. Yes, in all the development of the intellectual, moral, and religious life of humanity, there is only the reflection of economic phenomena in the human brain; yes, but there is at the same time the human brain, and therefore the cerebral preformation of humanity.

Humanity is the product of a long physiological evolution that preceded the historical one, and when man emerged, at the end of this physiological evolution, from animality, the state that was immediately below his own, he already had various predispositions and tendencies within this first brain of nascent humanity. . . .

I grant to Marx that all subsequent development would be nothing but the reflection of economic phenomena within the brain, but on condition that we agree that there were in this brain to begin with, through the aesthetic sense, through the faculty of imaginative sympathy, and through the need for unity, fundamental forces that intervene in the economic life.

Let us note, once again, that I am not juxtaposing the intellectual faculties with economic forces, that I am not trying to reconstitute that syndicate of historical factors that our eminent friend, Gabriel Deville, dispersed with such vigor a few months ago. No, I am not seeking such a juxtaposition, but I am saying that it is impossible that the observable eco-

nomic phenomena penetrate the human brain without at the same time setting primitive faculties in motion. This is why I do not grant to Marx that
religious, political and moral conceptions are solely the reflection of economic phenomena: there is within man such an interpenetration of the man
himself and his economic *milieu* that one cannot subordinate one to the
other, you must first abstract one from the other; now, this abstraction is
impossible. You can no more cut historical humanity in two and dissociate
its ideal life from its economic life, than you can cut a man in two and
thereby dissociate his organic life from the life of his consciousness. Such
is my thesis, which I find partially confirmed by Greek philosophy.

The Greeks did not begin by observing the economic antinomies, the
laws that established order in the city, the opposition and reconciliation of
the rich and the poor, and then go on to project their observations about the
economic order onto the universe. No, rather they united economic and
natural phenomena in a single view and a single conception. Look at Heraclitus, Empedocles, Anaximander; they observed the connections and contradictions between elements within single formulas, and noted that these
elements *heat* and *cold, light* and *dark,* belonged to nature, or that the elements *healthy* and *sick* belonged to the physiological organism, or that the
elements *perfect* and *imperfect, equal* and *unequal,* belonged to the intellectual life. They made a single table of these oppositions, borrowed either
from nature or from society, and for Heraclitus, the same word, "Cosmos,"
expresses at one and the same time the order in the world resulting from the
reconciliation of opposites, and the order in the city resulting from the reconciliation of factions. The Greek thinkers perceived the world order
through the chaos of society in a single, unifying conception.

Since time prevents me from doing anything more than skimming
lightly over the whole question, I will confine myself to addressing another
request for an explanation to the Marxist theoreticians, and ask them this:
What judgment do you make, if you make one (and I'm sure you do), about
the direction of economic movement and the direction of the movement of
humanity?

It is not sufficient to say that one form of production succeeds another
form—it is not sufficient to say that slavery succeeded cannibalism, that
serfdom succeeded slavery, and that the collectivist or communist regime
will succeed that of wage labor. No, you must say more than this. Is there
evolution or progress? And if there is progress, what is the final and decisive idea by which the various forms of human development are measured? And, what is more, if you want to repudiate this idea of progress as
being too metaphysical, then why has the movement of history gone from
one form to another in the direction it has, from economic stage to economic stage, from slavery to serfdom, from serfdom to wage-labor, from

wage-labor to the socialist regime, and not in some other direction? Why, by virtue of what source of energy—I won't say by virtue of what decree of Providence, because I remain attached to the materialist and positive conception of history—has the development of humanity proceeded in this fashion?

To me, the reason is easy to perceive, if you are willing to admit the activity of man as man, the activity of those human forces of which I have just spoken. The reason is that, precisely because the economic relations of production involve human beings, there is no single form of production that does not contain an essential contradiction within itself so long as the full freedom and solidarity of men have not been realized.

It was Spinoza who demonstrated admirably the fundamental contradiction within every tyrannical regime, every form of social and political exploitation of man by man, not by observing things from the standpoint of abstract right, but by showing that these situations presented a contradiction of fact. Either the tyranny will cause so much harm to those it oppresses that they will cease to fear the consequences of staging an insurrection, and so will rise up against the oppressor, or else, the oppressor, to prevent an uprising, will pay attention to some extent to the needs and instincts of his subjects, and will thus prepare them for freedom. And so, whatever course it takes, tyranny must disappear by virtue of the play of forces, *because these forces are men.*

This will be the same as long as the exploitation of man by man endures. It was Hegel, again, who said with marvellous precision: "The essential contradiction of all political or economic tyranny is that it is obliged to treat men as inert instruments, and men, no matter who they are, can never even conceive of descending to the condition of being mere machines." And let us note that this contradiction is at once a logical contradiction and a contradiction of fact.

It is a logical contradiction because there is an opposition between the very idea of man—that is, of a creature endowed with sensibility, spontaneity and the capacity for reflection—and the idea of a machine. It is a contradiction of fact because, when you use man as a tool that is alive in a way that you would use a tool that is not, you do violence to the very force that you are using, and thereby create a social mechanism that is discordant and precarious. Because this contradiction violates at the same time both man and the mechanical laws according to which a man's power can be utilized, the movement of history is at once an idealistic protest of the conscience against the regimes that debase man, and an automatic reaction of human forces against every unstable and violent social arrangement. What was cannibalism? It was a double contradiction: for, in obliging man to slaughter man even away from the excitation of combat, it did violence to man's primitive instinct of sympathy: moral contradiction;—and, further-more, it made of man, who has a certain aptitude to produce through regulated labor, a sort of beast of prey not useful for anything but his flesh: economic contradiction. At that point, slavery had to be born, because the domestication of man did less violence to the instinct of sympathy, and better served the interests of the master, by getting from the man, through his labor, far more than he could give in his substance.

And one could easily make the same demonstration for slavery, for serfdom, or for wage-labor. One could then see that, since the whole movement of history results from the essential contradiction between man and the use made of him, that this movement tends in every one of its moments, as in its over-all development, towards an economic order in which man will be made use of in a way that conforms to man. Humanity gradually realizes itself through a succession of economic forms that are more or less repugnant to its ideal. And there is not only a necessary evolution in human history, but an intelligible direction and a concept of the ideal as well. So, through the whole course of the centuries, man has been able to aspire toward justice only by aspiring toward a social order less contradictory to himself than the existing one and prepared by that existing order; thus the evolution of his moral ideas is clearly regulated by the evolution of economic forms. But at the same time, through the course of these successive configurations, humanity seeks out its nature and affirms itself, and whatever the diversity of *milieux,* of times, or economic demands, it is the same breath of reproach and of hope that escapes from the mouth of the slave, the serf, the proletarian. It is the immortal breath of humanity, which is the very soul of that which we call right. It is therefore not necessary to oppose the materialist and the idealist conceptions of history to one another. They interweave in a single and indissoluble line of development, because, if you cannot abstract man from economic relations, you also cannot abstract economic relations from man, and history, at the same time that it is a phenomenon unfolding in accordance with a mechanical law, is also an aspiration realizing itself according to an ideal law.

And is it not the same, after all, for the whole evolution of life as it is for historical evolution? Certainly life could not have passed from one form to another, from one species to another, except under the double action of *milieu* and the immediately preceding biological conditions. The whole development of life is susceptible to the materialist explanation, but at the same time one can say that the initial force of life concentrated in the first living particles, as well as the general conditions of our planetary existence, determined in advance the general outlines, the plan, so to speak, of our life on this planet. Thus, the innumerable beings that have evolved have, at the same time that they were subject to a law, also collaborated through a secret aspiration in the realization of a plan of life. The development of physiological life as well as of historical life has thus been both idealist and materialist at the same time. And the synthesis that I am proposing to you therefore forms part of a more general synthesis that I can only point out, since there is no time to elaborate upon it.

But, to return to the economic question, didn't Marx himself really reintroduce the notion of the ideal, of progress, of right, into his historical conception? He did not merely proclaim the communist society as the necessary outcome of the capitalist order, but he demonstrated that it would put an end to the antagonism of classes that uses up the energies of humanity. He also demonstrated that, for the first time, man will enjoy a full and free life, that those who labor will have at the same time the lively sensibility of the worker and the tranquil vigor of the peasant, and that humanity will rise up, happier and nobler, on an earth that has been renewed.

Isn't this to recognize that the word "justice" has meaning, even within the materialist conception of history, and that the reconciliation that I am proposing is therefore already implicitly accepted by you?

47. Eduard Bernstein, *Evolutionary Socialism*

The German Social Democrat Eduard Bernstein (1850–1932) was the son of a locomotive engineer in Berlin. After attending high school, Bernstein became a clerical employee in the Rothschild Bank in Berlin. In 1872 he joined the Social Democratic party, but was forced into exile in 1878 following the passage of Bismarck's Socialist Law. Between 1881 and 1888 Bernstein edited *Der Sozialdemokrat* in Zurich; following his expulsion from Switzerland he went to London, where he remained until 1901. Although he came to know Friedrich Engels well (becoming, along with August Bebel, the literary executor of Engels's estate), Bernstein was also greatly impressed by the work of the English Fabians, especially the Webbs, Keir Hardie, Graham Wallas, and Bernard Shaw. Such contacts may have influenced the new vision of the future of political and economic Socialism that Bernstein presented most fully in his controversial book, *Die Voraussetzungen des Sozialismus und die Aufgaben der Sozialdemokratie* (1899), a chapter of which is reprinted here.

With this work Bernstein became the principal theorist of Marxist "revisionism"—a modification of traditional doctrine that stressed the possibility of reform within capitalism, coalition by the Socialists with certain elements of the bourgeosie, and the progressive abandonment of

From Eduard Bernstein, *Evolutionary Socialism: A Criticism and Affirmation,* translated by Edith C. Harvey (New York: B. W. Huebsch, 1909), pp. 165–99. Some footnotes deleted.

an orientation directed toward the total transformation of society. Though Bernstein is sometimes placed on the extreme right wing of pre-1914 German Socialism, he was in fact much less conservative than many in his party whose ritualistic orthodoxy (and formal opposition to "revisionism") covered up an almost total abandonment of any strategy aimed at Socialist transformation. "My dear Ede," Party Secretary Ignaz Auer wrote to him, "one does not formally make a decision to do the things you suggest, one doesn't *say* such things, one simply *does* them." [1]

The Most Pressing Problems of Social Democracy

And what she is, that dares she to appear.

Schiller, *Maria Stuart.*

The tasks of a party are determined by a multiplicity of factors: by the position of the general, economic, political, intellectual and moral development in the sphere of its activity, by the nature of the parties that are working beside it or against it, by the character of the means standing at its command, and by a series of subjective, ideologic factors, at the head of them, the principal aim of the party and its conception of the best way to attain that aim. It is well known what great differences exist in the first respect in different lands. Even in countries of an approximately equal standard of industrial development, we find very important political differences and great differences in the conceptions and aspirations of the mass of the people. Peculiarities of geographical situation, rooted customs of national life, inherited institutions, and traditions of all kinds create a difference of mind which only slowly submits to the influence of that development. Even where socialist parties have originally taken the same hypotheses for the starting point of their work, they have found themselves obliged in the course of time to adapt their activity to the special conditions of their country. At a given moment, therefore, one can probably set up general political principles of Social Democracy with a claim that they apply to all countries, but no programme of action applicable for all countries is possible.

As shown above, democracy is a condition of socialism to a much greater degree than is usually assumed, *i.e.,* it is not only the means but also the substance. Without a certain amount of democratic institutions or traditions, the socialist doctrine of the present time would not indeed be possible. There would, indeed, be a workers' movement, but no Social Democracy. The modern socialist movement—and also its theoretic explana-

1. Quoted in Peter Nettl, *Rosa Luxemburg,* abridged edition (New York, 1969), p. 101.

tion—is in fact the product of the influence of the concepts of law and justice, which arose in the great French Revolution, and of the conceptions of
right which through it gained general acceptance in the wages and labour
movement. The movement itself would exist without them as, without
and before them, a communism of the people was linked to primitive
Christianity.

But this communism of the people was very indefinite and half mythical,
and the workers' movement would lack inner cohesion without the foundation of those organisations and conceptions of law which, at least to a great
part, necessarily accompany capitalist evolution. A working class politically without rights, grown up in superstition and with deficient education,
will certainly revolt sometimes and join in small conspiracies, but never
develop a socialist movement. It requires a certain breadth of vision and a
fairly well developed consciousness of rights to make a socialist out of a
workman who is accidentally a revolter. Political rights and education
stand indeed everywhere in a prominent position in the socialist programme of action.

So much for a general view. For it does not lie in the plan of this work to
undertake an estimation of individual points of the socialist programme of
action. As far as concerns the immediate demands of the Erfurt programme of German Social Democracy, I do not feel in any way tempted to
propose changes with respect to them. Probably, like every Social Democrat, I do not hold all points equally important or equally expedient. For
example, it is my opinion that the administration of justice and legal assistance free of charge, under present conditions, is only to be recommended
to a limited degree, that certainly arrangements should be made to make it
possible for those without means to seek to have a chance of getting their
rights; but that no pressing need exists to take over the mass of the property
law suits to-day and put the lawyers completely under the control of the
state. Meanwhile, although legislators of to-day will hear nothing of such a
step, as a socialist legislature cannot be achieved without a full reform of
the legal system, or only according to such newly created legal institutions,
as, for example, exist already in arbitration courts for trade disputes, the
said demand may keep its place in the programme as an indication of the
development striven after.

I gave a very definite expression to my doubt as to the expediency of the
demand in its present form as early as in 1891, in an essay on the draft
scheme of the programme then under discussion, and I declared that the
paragraph in question gave "too much and too little." [2] The article belongs
to a series which Kautsky and I then drew up jointly on the programme

2. *Neue Zeit* ix. 2, § 221.

question, and of which the first three essays were almost exclusively the mental work of Kautsky, whilst the fourth was composed by me. Let me here quote two sentences from it which indicate the point of view which I upheld at that time with regard to the action of Social Democracy, and which will show how much or how little my opinions have changed since then:—

> To demand simply the maintenance of all those without employ-
> ment out of the state money means to commit to the trough of the state
> not only everyone who cannot find work but everyone that will not
> find work. . . . One need really be no anarchist in order to find the
> eternal heaping of duties on the state too much of a good thing. We
> will hold fast to the principle that the modern proletarian is indeed
> poor but that he is no pauper. In this distinction lies a whole world,
> the nature of our fight, the hope of our victory.
>
> We propose the formula: "Conversion of the standing armies to
> citizen armies" because it maintains the aim and yet leaves the party a
> free hand to-day (when the disbanding of standing armies is utterly
> impossible) to demand a series of measures which narrow as much as
> possible the antagonism between army and people as, for example, the
> abolition of special military courts of justice, lessening of time of
> service, etc.[3]

But has Social Democracy, as the party of the working classes and of peace, an interest in the maintenance of the fighting power? From many points of view it is very tempting to answer the question in the negative, especially if one starts from the sentence in the *Communist Manifesto:* "The proletarian has no fatherland." This sentence might, in a degree, perhaps, apply to the worker of the 'forties without political rights, shut out of public life. Today in spite of the enormous increase in the intercourse between nations it has already forfeited a great part of its truth and will always forfeit more, the more the worker, by the influence of socialism, moves from being a proletarian to a citizen. The workman who has equal rights as a voter for state and local councils, and who thereby is a fellow owner of the common property of the nation, whose children the community educates, whose health it protects, whom it secures against injury, has a fatherland without ceasing on that account to be a citizen of the world, just as the nations draw nearer one another, without, therefore, ceasing to lead a life of their own.

The complete breaking up of nations is no beautiful dream, and in any case is not to be expected in the near future. But just as little as it is to be wished that any other of the great civilised nations should lose its independence, just as little can it be a matter of indifference to German Social De-

3. Pp. 819, 824, 825.

mocracy whether the German nation, which has indeed carried out, and is carrying out, its honourable share in the civilising work of the world, should be repressed in the council of the nations.

In the foregoing is shown in principle the point of view from which Social Democracy has to take its position under present conditions with regard to questions of foreign politics. If the worker is still no full citizen, he is not without rights in the sense that national interests can be indifferent to him. And if also Social Democracy is not yet in power, it already takes a position of influence which lays certain obligations upon it. Its words fall with great weight in the scale. With the present composition of the army and the complete uncertainty as to the changes in methods of war, etc., brought about by the use of guns of small bore, the Imperial Government will think ten times before venturing on a war which has Social Democracy as its determined opponent. Even without the celebrated general strike Social Democracy can speak a very important, if not decisive, word for peace, and will do this according to the device of the International as often and as energetically as it is necessary and possible. It will also, according to its programme, in the cases when conflicts arise with other nations and direct agreement is not possible, stand up for settling the difference by means of arbitration. But it is not called upon to speak in favour of renunciation of the preservation of German interests, present or future, if or because English, French, or Russian chauvinists take umbrage at the measures adopted. Where, on the German side, it is not a question merely of fancies or of the particular interests of separate groups which are indifferent or even detrimental to the welfare of the nation, where really important national interests are at stake, internationalism can be no reason for a weak yielding to the pretensions of foreign interested parties.

This is no new idea, but simply the putting together of the lines of thought which lie at the bottom of all the declarations of Marx, Engels, and Lassalle on the questions of foreign politics. It is also no attitude endangering peace which is here recommended. Nations to-day no longer lightly go to war, and a firm stand can under some circumstances be more serviceable to peace than continuous yielding.

The doctrine of the European balance of power seems to many to be out of date to-day, and so it is in its old form. But in a changed form the balance of power still plays a great part in the decision of vexed international questions. It still comes occasionally to the question of how strong a combination of powers supports any given measure in order that it may be carried through or hindered. I consider it a legitimate task of German Imperial politics to secure a right to have a voice in the discussion of such cases, and to oppose, on principle, proper steps to that end, I consider, falls outside the domain of the tasks of Social Democracy.

To choose a definite example. The leasing of the Kiauchow Bay at the time was criticised very unfavourably by the socialist press of Germany. As far as the criticism referred to the circumstances under which the leasing came about, the Social Democratic press had a right, nay, even a duty, to make it. Not less right was it to oppose in the most decided way the introduction of or demand for a policy of partition of China because this partition did not lie at all in the interest of Germany. But if some papers went still further and declared that the party must under all circumstances and as a matter of principle condemn the acquisition of the Bay, I cannot by any means agree with it.

It is a matter of no interest to the German people that China should be divided up and Germany be granted a piece of the Celestial Empire. But the German people has a great interest in this—that China should not be the prey of other nations; it has a great interest in this—that China's commercial policy should not be subordinated to the interest of a single foreign power or a coalition of foreign powers—in short, that in all questions concerning China, Germany should have a word to say. Its commerce with China demands such a right to protest. In so far as the acquisition of the Kiauchow Bay is a means of securing this right to protest, and it will be difficult to gainsay that it does contribute to it, there is no reason in my opinion for Social Democracy to cry out against it on principle. Apart from the manner in which it was acquired and the pious words with which it was accompanied, it was not the worst stroke of Germany's foreign policy.

It was a matter of securing free trade with and in China. For there can be no doubt that without that acquisition China would have been drawn to a greater degree into the ring of the capitalist economy, and also that without it Russia would have continued its policy of encircling, and would have occupied the Manchurian harbours. It was thus only a question as to whether Germany should look on quietly whilst, by the accomplishment of one deed after another, China fell ever more and more into dependence on Russia, or whether Germany should secure herself a position on the ground that she also, under normal conditions, can make her influence felt at any time on the situation of things in China, instead of being obliged to content herself with belated protests. So far ran and runs the leasing of the Kiauchow Bay, a pledge for the safeguarding of the future interests of Germany in China, be its official explanation what it may, and thus far could Social Democracy approve it without in the least giving away its principles.

Meanwhile, owing to the want of responsibility in the management of the foreign policy of Germany, there can be no question of positive support from Social Democracy, but only of the right foundation of its negative attitude. Without a guarantee that such undertakings should not be turned to account over the heads of the people's representative House for other aims than those announced, say as a means to achieve some temporary success which might surrender the greater interests of the future, without some such pledge Social Democracy can take upon itself no share in the measures of foreign policy.

As can be seen the rule here unfolded for the position regarding questions of foreign policy turns on the attitude observed hitherto in practice by Social Democracy. How far it agrees in its fundamental assumptions with the ruling mode of viewing things in the party, does not lie with me to explain. On the whole, tradition plays a greater part in these things than we think. It lies in the nature of all advanced parties to lay only scanty weight on changes already accomplished. The chief object they have in view is always that which does not change—quite a justifiable and useful tendency towards definite aims—the setting of goals. Penetrated by this, such parties fall easily into the habit of maintaining longer than is necessary or useful opinions handed down from the past, in assumptions of which very much has been altered. They overlook or undervalue these changes; they seek for facts which may still make those opinions seem valid, more than they examine the question whether in the face of the totality of the facts appertaining to it, the old opinion has not meanwhile become prejudice.

Such political *à priori* reasoning often appears to me to play a part in dealing with the question of colonies.

In principle it is quite a matter of indifference to-day to socialism, or the workmen's movement, whether new colonies should prove successful or not. The assumption that the extension of colonies will restrict the realisation of socialism, rests at bottom on the altogether outworn idea that the realisation of socialism depends on an increasing narrowing of the circle of the well-to-do and an increasing misery of the poor. That the first is a fable was shown in earlier chapters, and the misery theory has now been given up nearly everywhere, if not with all its logical conclusions and outright, yet at least by explaining it away as much as possible.

But even if the theory were right, the colonies about which there is now an interest in Germany are far from being in the position to re-act so quickly on social conditions at home, that they could only keep off a possible catastrophe for a year. In this respect German Social Democracy would have nothing to fear from the colonial policy of the German Empire. And because it is so, because the development of the colonies which Germany has acquired (and of those which it could perhaps win, the same holds good) will take so much time that there can be no question for many a long year of any reaction worth mentioning on the social conditions of Germany. Just from this reason German Social Democracy can treat the question of these colonies without prejudice. There can even be no question of a serious reaction of colonial possessions on the political conditions of Germany. Naval chauvinism, for example, stands undoubtedly in close connection with colonial chauvinism, and draws from it a certain nourishment. But the first would also exist without the second, just as Germany had her navy before she thought of the conquest of colonies. It must nevertheless be granted that this connection is the most rational ground for justifying a thorough resistance to a colonial policy.

Otherwise, there is some justification during the acquisition of colonies to examine carefully their value and prospects, and to control the settlement and treatment of the natives as well as the other matters of administration; but that does not amount to a reason for considering such acquisition beforehand as something reprehensible.

Its political position, owing to the present system of government, forbids Social Democracy from taking more than a critical attitude to these things, and the question whether Germany to-day needs colonies can, particularly in regard to those colonies that are still to be obtained, be answered in the negative with good authority. But the future has also its rights for us to consider. If we take into account the fact that Germany now imports yearly a considerable amount of colonial produce, we must also say to ourselves that the time may come when it will be desirable to draw at least a part of these products from our own colonies. However speedy socialists may imagine the course of development in Germany towards themselves to be, yet we cannot be blind to the fact that it will need a considerable time before a whole series of other countries are converted to socialism. But if it is not reprehensible to enjoy the produce of tropical plantations, it cannot be so to cultivate such plantations ourselves. Not the whether but the how is here the decisive point. It is neither necessary that the occupation of tropical lands by Europeans should injure the natives in their enjoyment of life, nor has it hitherto usually been the case. Moreover, only a conditional right of savages to the land occupied by them can be recognised. The higher civilisation ultimately can claim a higher right. Not the conquest, but the cultivation, of the land gives the historical legal title to its use.

According to my judgment these are the essential points of view which should decide the position of Social Democracy as regards the question of colonial policy. They also, in practice, would bring about no change worth mentioning in the vote of the party; but we are not only concerned, I repeat, with what would be voted in a given case, but also with the reasons given for the vote.

There are socialists to whom every admission of national interests appears as chauvinism or as an injury to the internationalism and class policy of the proletariat. As in his time Domela Nieuwenhuis declared Bebel's well-known assertion—that in case of an attack on the part of Russia Social Democracy would set up their men for the defence of Germany—to be chauvinism, so lately, Mr. Belfort Bax also found reprehensible jingoism in a similar assertion by Mr. Hyndman.

It must be admitted that it is not always easy to fix the boundary where the advocacy of the interests of one's nation ceases to be just and to pass into pseudo-patriotism; but the remedy for exaggeration on this side certainly does not lie in greater exaggeration on the other. It is much more to be sought in a movement for the exchange of thought between the democracies of the civilised countries and in the support of all factors and institutes working for peace.

Of greater importance to-day than the question of raising the demands already standing on the programme, is the question of supplementing the party's programme. Here practical development has placed a whole series of questions on the orders of the day which at the drawing up of the programme were partly considered to be lying away too far in the future for Social Democracy to concern itself specially with them, but which were also partly, not sufficiently considered in all their bearings. To these belong the agrarian question, the policy of local administration, co-operation and different matters of industrial law. The great growth of Social Democracy in the eight years since the drawing up of the Erfurt Programme, its reaction on the home politics of Germany as well as its experiences in other lands, have made the more intimate consideration of all these questions imperative, and many views which were formerly held about them have been materially corrected.

Concerning the agrarian question, even those who thought peasant cultivation doomed to decay have considerably changed their views as to the length of time for the completion of this decay. In the later debates on the agrarian policy to be laid down by Social Democracy, certainly many differences of opinion have been shown on this point, but in principle they revolved round this—whether, and in a given case to what limit, Social Democracy should offer assistance to the peasant as an independent farmer against capitalism.

The question is more easily asked than answered. The fact that the great mass of peasants, even if they are not wage earners, yet belong to the working classes, i.e., do not maintain existence merely on a title to possessions or on a privilege of birth, places them near the wage-earning class. On the other side they form in Germany such an important fraction of the population that at an election in very many constituencies their votes decide between the capitalist and socialist parties. But if Social Democracy would not or will not limit itself to being the party of the workers in the sense that it is only the political completion of trade unionism, it must be careful to interest at least a great part of the peasants in the victory of its candidates.

In the long run that will only happen if Social Democracy commits itself to measures which offer an improvement for the small peasants in the immediate future. But with many measures having this object the legislature cannot distinguish between the small and middle class peasants, and on the other hand they cannot help the peasant as a citizen of the state or as a worker without supporting him at least indirectly as an "entrepreneur."

This is shown with other things in the programme of socialist agrarian policy which Kautsky sketched at the end of his work on the agrarian question under the heading *The Neutralisation of the Peasantry*. Kautsky shows most convincingly that even after a victory for Social Democracy no reason will exist for the abolition of peasants' holdings. But he is at the same time a strong opponent of such measures, or the setting up of such demands, as aim at forming a "protection for peasants" in the sense that they would retain the peasant artificially as an independent producer. He proposes quite a series of reforms . . . which result in relieving the country parishes and in increasing their sources of income. But to what class would these measures be a benefit in the first instance? According to Kautsky's own representation, to the peasants. For, as he shows in another passage of his work, in the country, even under the rule of universal suffrage, there could be no question of an influence of the proletariat on the affairs of the parish worth mentioning. For that influence is, according to him, too isolated, too backward, too dependent on the few employers of labour who control it. "A communal policy other than one in the interest of the landowner is not to be thought of." Just as little can we think to-day "of a modern management of the land by the parish in a large co-operative farming enterprise controlled by the village community." [4] But, so far, and so long, as that is so, measures like "Amalgamation of the hunting divisions of the great landowners in the community," "Nationalisation of the taxes for schools, roads, and the poor," would obviously contribute to the improvement of the economic position of the peasants and therewith also to the strengthening of their possessions. Practically, then, they would just work as protection for the peasants.

Under two hypotheses the support of such protection for the peasants appears to me innocuous. First a strong protection of agricultural labourers must go hand in hand with it, and secondly democracy must rule in the commune and the district. Both are assumed by Kautsky. But Kautsky undervalues the influence of agricultural labourers in the democratised country parish. The agricultural labourers are as helpless as he describes them in the passage quoted, only in such districts as lie quite outside commercial intercourse; and their number is always becoming smaller. Usually the ag-

4. *The Agrarian Question*, pp. 337 and 338.

ricultural labourer is to-day tolerably conscious of his interests and with universal suffrage would even become more so. Besides that, there exist in most parishes all kinds of antagonisms among the peasants themselves, and the village community contains, in craftsmen and small traders, elements which in many respects have more in common with the agricultural labourers than with the peasant aristocracy. All that means that the agricultural labourers, except in a very few cases, would not have to make a stand alone against an unbroken "reactionary mass." Democracy has, in the country districts, if it is to exist, to work in the spirit of socialism. I consider democracy in conjunction with the results of the great changes in the system of communication, of transport, a more powerful lever in the emancipation of agricultural labourers than the technical changes in peasant farming.

I refrain from going through all the details of Kautsky's programme with which, as I have already remarked, I agree thoroughly in principle; but I believe that a few observations on it ought not to be suppressed. For me, as already observed, the chief task which Social Democracy now has to fulfil for the agricultural population can be classified under three heads, namely: (1) *The struggle against all the present remnants and supports of feudal landowners, and the fight for democracy in the commune and district.* This involves a fight for the removal of entail, of privileged estate parishes, hunting privileges, etc., as laid down by Kautsky. In Kautsky's formulation "the fullest self-government in the parish and the province," the word "fullest" does not seem to me well chosen, and I would substitute for it the word "democratic." Superlatives are nearly always misleading. "Fullest self-government" can apply to the circle of those entitled to have a say, what it means can be better expressed by "democratic self-government"; but it can also denote the administrative functions, and then it would mean an absolutism of the parish, which neither is necessary nor can be reconciled with the demands of a healthy democracy. The general legislature of the nation stands above the parish, apportioning its definite functions and representing the general interests against its particular interests.

(2) *Protection and relief of the working classes in agriculture.* Under this heading falls the protection of labourers in the narrower sense: Abolition of regulations for servants, limitation of hours of labour in the various categories of wage earners, sanitary police regulations, a system of education, as well as measures which free the small peasant as a taxpayer.

(3) *Measures against the absolutism of property and furthering cooperation.* Hereunder would fall demands like "Limitation of the rights of private property in the soil with a view to promoting (1) the suppression of adding field to field, (2) the cultivation of land, (3) prevention of disease" (Kautsky); "reduction of exorbitant rents by courts of justice set up for the

purpose" (Kautsky); the building of healthy and comfortable workmen's dwellings by the parish; "facilities for co-operative unions by means of legislation" (Kautsky); the right of the parish to acquire land by purchase or expropriation and to lease it at a cheap rent to workmen and workmen's associations.

This latter demand leads to the question of co-operation. After what has been said in the chapter on the economic possibilities of co-operative associations I need say little here. The question to-day is no longer whether co-operative associations ought to exist or not. They exist and will exist whether Social Democracy desires it or not. By the weight of its influence on the working classes, Social Democracy certainly can retard the spread of workmen's co-operative societies, but it will not thereby do any service for itself or the working class. The hard-and-dry Manchesterism which is often manifested by sections of the party in regard to co-operation and is grounded on the declaration that there can be no socialist co-operative society within a capitalist society is not justified. It is, on the contrary, important to take a decided position and to be clear which kind of associations Social Democracy can recommend, and can morally support.

We have seen what an extraordinary advance associations for credit, purchasing, dairy farming, working and selling, make in all modern countries. But these associations in Germany are generally associations of peasants, representatives of the "middle class movement" in the country. I consider it incontrovertible that they, in conjunction with the cheapening of the rate of interest which the increased accumulation of capital brings with it, could indeed help much towards keeping peasant enterprises capable of competing with large enterprises. Consequently, these peasant associations are in most cases the scene of the action of anti-socialist elements, of *petits bourgeois* liberals, clericals, and anti-semites. So far as Social Democracy is concerned, they can to-day be put out of reckoning nearly everywhere— even if in their ranks there are here and there small peasants who are nearer to the socialist than to other parties. The middle-class peasant takes the lead with them. If Social Democracy ever had a prospect of winning a stronger influence on the class of the country population referred to by means of co-operation, it has let the opportunity slip.

But if the Social Democratic party has not the vocation of founding co-operative stores, that does not mean it should take no interest in them. The dearly-loved declaration that co-operative stores are not socialist enterprises, rests on the same formalism which long acted against trade unions, and which now begins to make room for the opposite extreme. Whether a trade union or a workmen's co-operative store is or is not socialistic, does not depend on its form but on its character—on the spirit that permeates it. They are not socialism, but as organisations of workmen they bear in themselves enough of the element of socialism to develop into worthy and indispensable levers for the socialist emancipation. They will certainly best discharge their economic tasks if they are left completely to themselves in their organisation and government. But as the aversion and even enmity which many socialists formerly felt against the trade union movement has gradually changed into friendly neutrality and then into the feeling of belonging together, so will it happen with the stores—so has it already happened in some measure.

Those elements, which are enemies not only of the revolutionary, but of every emancipation movement of the workers, by their campaign against the workmen's co-operative stores have obliged Social Democracy to step in to support them. Experience has also shown that such fears, as that the co-operative movement would take away intellectual and other forces from the political movement of the workers, were utterly unfounded. In certain places that may be the case temporarily, but in the long run exactly the opposite takes place. Social Democracy can look on confidently at the founding of working men's co-operative stores where the economic and legal preliminary conditions are found, and it will do well to give it its full good-will and to help it as much as possible.

Only from one point of view could the workmen's co-operative store appear something doubtful in principle—namely, as the good which is in the way of the better, the better being the organisation of the purchase and the distribution of commodities through the municipality, as is designed in nearly all socialist systems. But first of all the democratic store, in order to embrace all members of the place in which it is located, needs no alteration in principle, but only a broadening of its constitution, which throughout is in unison with its natural tendencies (in some smaller places co-operative stores are already not far from counting all the inhabitants of the place as their members). Secondly, the realisation of this thought still lies such a long way off, and assumes so many political and economic changes and intermediate steps in evolution, that it would be mad to reject with regard to it all the advantages which the workers can draw to-day from the co-operative store. As far as the district council or parish is concerned we can only through it to-day provide clearly defined, general needs.

With that we come now to the borough or municipal policy of Social Democracy. This also for a long time was the step-child of the socialist movement. It is, for example, not very long ago that in a foreign socialist paper (which has since disappeared), edited by very intellectual folk, the following idea was rejected with scorn as belonging to the *petit bourgeois,* namely, the using of municipalities as the lever of the socialist work of reform without, on that account, neglecting parliamentary action, and the beginning through the municipality of the realisation of socialist demands.

The irony of fate has willed it that the chief editor of that paper was only able to get into the Parliament of his country on a wave of municipal socialism. Similarly in England, Social Democracy found in the municipalities a rich field of fruitful activity before it succeeded in sending its own representatives to Parliament. In Germany the development was different. Here Social Democracy had long obtained Parliamentary civil rights before it gained a footing to any extent worth mentioning in the representative bodies of the communes. With its growing extension its success also increased in the elections for local bodies, so that the need for working out a socialist municipal programme has been shown more and more, and such has already been drawn up in individual states or provinces. What does Social Democracy want for the municipality, and what does it expect from the municipality?

With regard to this the Erfurt programme says only "Self-government of the people in empire, state, province, and municipality; election of officials by the people," and demands for all elections the direct right to vote for all adults. It makes no declaration as to the legal relation of the enumerated governing bodies to one another. As shown farther back, I maintain that the law or the decree of the nation has to come from the highest legal authority of the community—the state. But that does not mean that the division line between the rights and powers of the state and the municipality should always be the same as to-day.

To-day, for example, the municipal right of expropriation is very limited, so that a whole series of measures of an economic-political character would find in the opposition, or exaggerated demands, of town landlords a positively insurmountable barrier. An extension of the law of expropriation should accordingly be one of the next demands of municipal socialism. It is not, however, necessary to demand an absolutely unlimited law of expropriation. The municipality would always be bound to keep to the regulations of the common law which protect the individual against the arbitrary action of accidental majorities. Rights of property which the common law allows must be inviolable in every community so long as, and in the measure in which, the common law allows them. To take away lawful property otherwise than by compensation, is confiscation, which can only be justified in cases of extreme pressure of circumstances—war, epidemics.

Social Democracy will thus be obliged to demand for the municipality, when the franchise becomes democratic, an extension of the right of expropriation (which is still very limited in various German states) if a socialist policy of local government is to be possible. Further, demands respecting the creation of municipal enterprises and of public services, and a labour policy for the municipality, are rightly put into the forefront of the programme. With respect to the first, the following demand should be set up as essential, that all enterprises having a monopolist character and being directed towards the general needs of the members of the municipality must be carried out under its own management, and that, for the rest, the municipality must strive constantly to increase the area of the service it gives to its members. As regards labour policy, we must demand from the municipalities that they, as employers of labour, whether under their own management or under contract, insert as a minimum condition the clauses for wages and hours of labour recognised by the organisations of such workmen, and that they guarantee the right of combination for these workmen. It should, however, be observed here that if it is only right to endeavour to make municipalities as employers of labour surpass private firms with regard to conditions of labour and arrangements for the welfare of the workers, it would be a shortsighted policy for municipal workmen to demand such conditions as would place them, when compared with their fellow-workers in the same trades, in the position of an unusually privileged class, and that the municipality should work at a considerably higher cost than the private employer. That would, in the end, lead to corruption and a weakening of public spirit.

Modern evolution has assigned to municipalities further duties: the establishment and superintendence of local sick funds, to which perhaps at a not very distant epoch the taking over of insurance against invalidity will be added. There has further been added the establishment of labour bureaux and industrial arbitration courts. With regard to the labour bureaux Social Democracy claims as its minimum demand that their character should be guaranteed by their being composed of an equal representation of workmen and employers; that arbitration courts should be established by compulsion and their powers extended. Social Democracy is sceptical of, even if it does not protest against, municipal insurance against unemployment, as the idea prevails that this insurance is one of the legitimate duties of trade unions and can best be cared for by them. But that can only hold good for well-organised trades which unfortunately still contain a small minority of the working population. The great mass of workers is still unorganised, and the question is whether municipal insurance against unemployment can, in conjunction with trade unions, be so organised that, so far from being an encroachment on the legitimate functions of the latter, it may even be a means of helping them. In any case it would be the duty of the Social Democratic representatives of the municipality, where such insurance is undertaken, to press with all their energy for the recognition of the unions.

From its whole nature, municipal socialism is an indispensable lever for forming or completely realising what I, in the last chapter, called "the democratic right of labour." But it is and must be patch-work where the franchise of the municipality is class franchise. That is the case in more than three-fourths of Germany. And so we stand here, as we do with reference to the diets of the federal states, on which the municipalities depend to a great extent, and to the other organs of self-government (districts, provinces, etc.), face to face with the question: how will Social Democracy succeed in removing the existing class franchise and in obtaining the democratisation of the electoral systems?

Social Democracy has to-day in Germany, besides the means of propaganda by speech and writing, the franchise for the Reichstag as the most effective means of asserting its demands. Its influence is so strong that it has extended even to those bodies which have been made inaccessible to the working class owing to a property qualification, or a system of class franchise; for parties must, even in these assemblies, pay attention to the electors for the Reichstag. If the right to vote for the Reichstag were protected from every attack, the question of treating the franchise for other bodies as a subordinate one could be justified to a certain extent, although it would be a mistake to make light of it. But the franchise for the Reichstag is not secure at all. Governments and government parties will certainly not resolve lightly on amending it, for they will say to themselves that such a step would raise amongst the masses of the German workers a hate and bitterness, which they would show in a very uncomfortable way on suitable occasions. The socialist movement is too strong, the political self-consciousness of the German workers is too much developed, to be dealt with in a cavalier fashion. One may venture, also, to assume that a great number even of the opponents of universal suffrage have a certain moral unwillingness to take such a right from the people. But if, under normal circumstances, a narrowing of the franchise would create a revolutionary tension—with all its dangers for the rulers—yet, on the contrary, one cannot speak of any serious technical difficulties in the way of altering the franchise so as to permit the success of independent socialist candidates only on an exceptional basis. It is simply political considerations which, on this question, determine the issue.

On this and other grounds it does not seem advisable to make the policy of Social Democracy solely dependent on the conditions and possibilities of the imperial franchise. We have, moreover, seen that progress is not so quickened by it as might have been inferred from the electoral successes of 1890 and 1893. Whilst the socialist vote in the triennial period from 1887 to 1890 rose 87 per cent., and from 1890 to 1893 25 per cent., in the five years from 1893 to 1898 it only rose 18 per cent.—an important increase in itself, but not an increase to justify extraordinary expectations in the near future.

Now Social Democracy depends not exclusively on the franchise and Parliamentary activity. A great and rich field exists for it outside Parliaments. The socialist working class movement would exist even if Parliaments were closed to it. Nothing shows this better than the gratifying movements among the Russian working classes. But with its exclusion from representative bodies the German working class movement would, to a great extent, lose the cohesion which to-day links its various sections; it would assume a chaotic character, and instead of the steady, uninterrupted forward march with firm steps, jerky forward motions would appear with inevitable back-slidings and exhaustions.

Such a development is neither in the interest of the working classes nor can it appear desirable to those opponents of Social Democracy who have become convinced that the present social order has not been created for all eternity but is subject to the law of change, and that a catastrophic development with all its horrors and devastation can only be avoided if in legislation consideration is paid to changes in the conditions of production and commerce and to the evolution of the classes. And the number of those who recognise this is steadily increasing. Their influence would be much greater than it is to-day if Social Democracy could find the courage to emancipate itself from a phraseology which is actually outworn and if it would make up its mind to appear what it is in reality to-day: a democratic, socialistic party of reform.

It is not a question of renouncing the so-called right of revolution, this purely speculative right which can be put in no paragraph of a constitution and which no statute book can prohibit, this right which will last as long as the law of nature forces us to die if we abandon the right to breathe. This imprescriptible and inalienable right is as little touched if we place ourselves on the path of reform as the right of self-defence is done away with when we make laws to regulate our personal and property disputes.

But is Social Democracy to-day anything beyond a party that strives after the socialist transformation of society by the means of democratic and economic reform? According to some declarations which were maintained against me at the congress in Stuttgart this might perhaps appear to be the case. But in Stuttgart my letter was taken as an accusation against the party for sailing in the direction of Blanquism, whilst it was really directed against some persons who had attacked me with arguments and figures of speech of a Blanquist nature and who wanted to obtain from the congress a pronouncement against me.

Even a positive verdict from the Stuttgart Congress against my declaration would not have diverted me from my conviction that the great mass of German Social Democracy is far removed from fits of Blanquism. After

518 Mass Politics at the Turn of the Century

the speech ot Oeynhausen I knew that no other attitude of the congress was to be expected than the one which it in fact adopted.[5]

The Oeynhausen speech has since then shared the fate of so many other speeches of extraordinary men, it has been semi-officially corrected. And in what sense has the party expressed itself since Stuttgart? Bebel, in his speeches on the attempts at assassination, has entered the most vigorous protests against the idea that Social Democracy upholds a policy of force, and all the party organs have reported these speeches with applause; no protest against them has been raised anywhere. Kautsky develops in his *Agrarian Question* the principles of the agrarian policy of Social Democracy. They form a system of thoroughly democratic reform just as the Communal Programme adopted in Brandenburg is a democratic programme of reform. In the Reichstag the party supports the extension of the powers and the compulsory establishment of courts of arbitration for trade disputes. These are organs for the furtherance of industrial peace. All the speeches of their representatives breathe reform. In the same Stuttgart where, according to Clara Zetkin, the "Bernstein-iade" received the finishing stroke, shortly after the Congress, the Social Democrats formed an alliance with the middle-class democracy for the municipal elections, and their example was followed in other Württemberg towns. In the trade union movement one union after another proceeds to establish funds for out-of-work members, which practically means a giving up of the characteristics of a purely fighting coalition, and declares for municipal labour bureaux embracing equally employers and employees; whilst in various large towns—Hamburg, Elberfeld—co-operative stores have been started by socialists and trade unionists. Everywhere there is action for reform, action for social progress, action for the victory of democracy. "People study the details of the problems of the day and seek for levers and starting points to carry on the development of society in the direction of socialism." Thus I wrote a year ago,[6] and I see no reason to induce me to delete a word of it.

5. A few days before the opening of the Social Democratic Party Congress in Stuttgart in 1898, Emperor Wilhelm II, speaking in Oeynhausen in Westphalia, announced a law threatening penal servitude for anyone who dared to prevent a man from working or who incited him to strike. The Reichstag rejected a diluted version of the bill.—ED.

6. *The Struggle of Social Democracy and the Revolution of Society.—Neue Zeit* xvi., 1, p. 451.

48. Rosa Luxemburg, *Mass Strike, Party, and Trade Unions*

Like the careers of many young east European Socialists in the 1880s,
Rosa Luxemburg's (1871–1919) was a product of emotional fervor, ideological commitment, and police persecution. The daughter of a bourgeois
merchant family in Zamość (in Russian Poland), Luxemburg graduated in
1887 from a prestigious girls' secondary school in Warsaw attended by
children of local Russian administrators (entrance to which was itself a
considerable achievement, in view of Luxemburg's Jewish background).
During her high school years she joined an extremist faction of Polish
socialism, the Proletariat party, and, facing arrest in 1889, left Poland for
political exile in Switzerland. She studied in Zürich, receiving her Ph.D.
with a dissertation titled "The Industrial Development of Poland"; there
she also met and worked with other émigré Marxists, especially her future husband, Leo Jogiches. In 1898 she moved to Berlin and joined the
German Social Democratic party, where as a journalist dedicated to furthering the impulses of revolution she soon became a leading protagonist
against Eduard Bernstein's Revisionism. As a brilliant orator and writer
dedicated to revolutionary praxis, Luxemburg soon moved beyond nega-
tivist anti-Revisionism toward a radical critique of the institutional conservatism of the mainline Social Democratic leadership, and especially
the tameness of the leaders of the powerful German Socialist trade unions.
Yet her running feud between 1909 and 1918 with Karl Kautsky, the
party's principal centrist theoretician, over the mass strike and other
issues, did not spare her posthumous condemnation by Stalinists and
German Communists in the 1920s and the 1930s. In January 1919, together with Karl Liebknecht, Luxemburg was murdered by rightist para-
military forces following the Spartacist uprising in Berlin.

In late 1905 Luxemburg left Germany to participate in the Russian
revolution in Poland and for a time was imprisoned in Warsaw. After her
release in the summer of 1906 she wrote her powerful analysis of the
consequences of that revolution for the German working classes: *Mass
Strike, Party, and Trade Unions,* selections from which are reprinted
here. Later Bolshevik theorists found her vision of a spontaneous process
of revolutionary fervor and organization emerging from the proletariat
itself and its party cadres both naïve and threatening, as did her Social
Democratic interlocutors at the 1906 party congress in Mannheim.

From Rosa Luxemburg, *The Mass Strike, the Political Party and the Trade Unions,* translated by Patrick Lavin. In *Rosa Luxemburg Speaks,* edited by Mary-Alice Waters (New York:
Pathfinder Press, 1970), pp. 181–82, 185, 197–218.

IV. The Interaction of the Political and the Economic Struggle

We have attempted in the foregoing to sketch the history of the mass strike in Russia in a few strokes. Even a fleeting glance at this history shows us a picture which in no way resembles that usually formed by the discussions in Germany on the mass strike. Instead of the rigid and hollow scheme of an arid political action carried out by the decision of the highest committees and furnished with a plan and panorama, we see a bit of pulsating life of flesh and blood, which cannot be cut out of the large frame of the revolution but is connected with all parts of the revolution by a thousand veins.

The mass strike, as the Russian Revolution shows it to us, is such a changeable phenomenon that it reflects all phases of the political and economic struggle, all stages and factors of the revolution. Its adaptability, its efficiency, the factors of its origin are constantly changing. It suddenly opens new and wide perspectives of the revolution when it appears to have already arrived in a narrow pass and where it is impossible for anyone to reckon upon it with any degree of certainty. It flows now like a broad billow over the whole kingdom, and now divides into a gigantic network of narrow streams; now it bubbles forth from under the ground like a fresh spring and now is completely lost under the earth. Political and economic strikes, mass strikes and partial strikes, demonstrative strikes and fighting strikes, general strikes of individual branches of industry and general strikes in individual towns, peaceful wage struggles and street massacres, barricade fighting—all these run through one another, run side by side, cross one another, flow in and over one another—it is a ceaselessly moving, changing sea of phenomena. And the law of motion of these phenomena is clear: it does not lie in the mass strike itself nor in its technical details, but in the political and social proportions of the forces of the revolution.

The mass strike is merely the form of the revolutionary struggle and every disarrangement of the relations of the contending powers, in party development and in class division, in the position of the counterrevolution—all this immediately influences the action of the strike in a thousand invisible and scarcely controllable ways. But strike action itself does not cease for a single moment. It merely alters its forms, its dimensions, its effect. It is the living pulsebeat of the revolution and at the same time its most powerful driving wheel. In a word, the mass strike, as shown to us in the Russian Revolution, is not a crafty method discovered by subtle reasoning for the purpose of making the proletarian struggle more effective, *but the method of motion of the proletarian mass*, the phenomenal form of the proletarian struggle in the revolution. . . .

. . . The movement on the whole does not proceed from the economic to the political struggle, nor even the reverse. Every great political mass action, after it has attained its political highest point, breaks up into a mass of economic strikes. And that applies not only to each of the great mass strikes, but also to the revolution as a whole. With the spreading, clarifying and involution of the political struggle, the economic struggle not only does not recede, but extends, organizes and becomes involved in equal measure. Between the two there is the most complete reciprocal action.

Every new onset and every fresh victory of the political struggle is transformed into a powerful impetus for the economic struggle, extending at the same time its external possibilities and intensifying the inner urge of the workers to better their position, and their desire to struggle. After every foaming wave of political action a fructifying deposit remains behind from which a thousand stalks of economic struggle shoot forth. And conversely, the workers' condition of ceaseless economic struggle with the capitalists keeps their fighting energy alive in every political interval; it forms, so to speak, the permanent fresh reservoir of the strength of the proletarian classes, from which the political fight ever renews its strength, and at the same time leads the indefatigable economic sappers of the proletariat at all times, now here and now there, to isolated sharp conflicts, out of which political conflicts on a large scale unexpectedly explode.

In a word: the economic struggle is the transmitter from one political center to another; the political struggle is the periodic fertilization of the soil for the economic struggle. Cause and effect here continually change places; and thus the economic and the political factor in the period of the mass strike, now widely removed, completely separated or even mutually exclusive, as the theoretical plan would have them, merely form the two interlacing sides of the proletarian class struggle in Russia. And *their unity* is precisely the mass strike. If the sophisticated theory proposes to make a clever logical dissection of the mass strike for the purpose of getting at the "purely political mass strike," it will by this dissection, as with any other, not perceive the phenomenon in its living essence, but will kill it altogether. . . .

VI. Cooperation of Organized and Unorganized Workers Necessary for Victory

. . . On a closer examination of German conditions and of the condition of the different sections of the working class, it is clear that the coming period of stormy political mass struggles will not bring the dreaded, threatening downfall of the German trade unions, but on the contrary, will open up hitherto unsuspected prospects of the extension of their sphere of power— an extension that will proceed rapidly by leaps and bounds. But the question has still another aspect. The plan of undertaking mass strikes as a serious political class action with organized workers only is absolutely hopeless. If the mass strike, or rather, mass strikes, and the mass struggle are to be successful they must become a real *people's movement,* that is, the widest sections of the proletariat must be drawn into the fight. Already in the parliamentary form the might of the proletarian class struggle rests not on the small organized group, but on the surrounding periphery of the revolutionary-minded proletariat. If the Social Democrats were to enter the electoral battle with their few hundred thousand organized members alone, they would condemn themselves to futility. And although it is the tendency of Social Democracy wherever possible to draw the whole great army of its voters into the party organization, its mass of voters after thirty years' experience of Social Democracy is not increased through the growth of the party organization, but on the contrary, the new sections of the proletariat, won for the time being through the electoral struggle, are the fertile soil for the subsequent seed of organization. Here the organization does not supply the troops of the struggle, but the struggle, in an ever growing degree, supplies recruits for the organization.

In a much greater degree does this obviously apply to direct political mass action than to the parliamentary struggle. If the Social Democrats, as the organized nucleus of the working class, are the most important vanguard of the entire body of the workers and if the political clarity, the strength, and the unity of the labor movement flow from this organization, then it is not permissible to visualize the class movement of the proletariat as a movement of the organized minority. Every real, great class struggle must rest upon the support and cooperation of the widest masses, and a strategy of class struggle which does not reckon with this cooperation, which is based upon the idea of the finely stage-managed march out of the small, well-trained part of the proletariat is foredoomed to be a miserable fiasco. . . .

The overestimate and the false estimate of the role of organizations in the class struggle of the proletariat is generally reinforced by the underestimate of the unorganized proletarian mass and of their political maturity. In a revolutionary period, in the storm of great unsettling class struggles, the whole educational effect of the rapid capitalist development and of Social Democratic influences first shows itself upon the widest sections of the people, of which, in peaceful times the tables of the organized, and even election statistics, give only a faint idea. . . .

In the case of the enlightened German worker the class consciousness implanted by the Social Democrats is *theoretical and latent:* in the period ruled by bourgeois parliamentarism it cannot, as a rule, actively participate in a direct mass action; it is the ideal sum of the four hundred parallel actions of the electoral sphere during the election struggle, of the many partial economic strikes and the like. In the revolution when the masses themselves appear upon the political battlefield this class consciousness becomes *practical and active*. A year of revolution has therefore given the Russian proletariat that "training" which thirty years of parliamentary and trade-union struggle cannot artificially give to the German proletariat. Of course, this living, active class feeling of the proletariat will considerably diminish in intensity, or rather change into a concealed and latent condition, after the close of the period of revolution and the erection of a bourgeois-parliamentary constitutional state.

And just as surely, on the other hand, will the living revolutionary class feeling, capable of action, affect the widest and deepest layers of the proletariat in Germany in a period of strong political engagement, and that the more rapidly and more deeply, the more energetically the educational work of Social Democracy is carried on among them. This educational work and the provocative and revolutionizing effect of the whole present policy of Germany will express itself in the circumstances that all those groups which at present in their apparent political stupidity remain insensitive to all the organizing attempts of the Social Democrats and of the trade unions will suddenly follow the flag of Social Democracy in a serious revolutionary period. Six months of a revolutionary period will complete the work of the training of these as yet unorganized masses which ten years of public demonstrations and distribution of leaflets would be unable to do. And when conditions in Germany have reached the critical stage for such a period, the sections which are today unorganized and backward will, in the struggle, prove themselves the most radical, the most impetuous element, and not one that will have to be dragged along. If it should come to mass strikes in Germany, it will almost certainly not be the best organized workers—and most certainly not the printers—who will develop the greatest capacity for action, but the worst organized or totally unorganized—the miners, the textile workers, and perhaps even the land workers.

In this way we arrive at the same conclusions in Germany in relation to the peculiar tasks of *direction,* in relation to the role of Social Democracy in mass strikes, as in our analysis of events in Russia. If we now leave the pedantic scheme of demonstrative mass strikes artificially brought about by order of parties and trade unions, and turn to the living picture of a peoples' movement arising with elementary energy, from the culmination of class antagonisms and the political situation—a movement which passes, politically as well as economically, into mass struggles and mass strikes— it becomes obvious that the task of Social Democracy does not consist in the technical preparation and direction of mass strikes, but, first and foremost, in the *political leadership* of the whole movement.

The Social Democrats are the most enlightened, most class-conscious vanguard of the proletariat. They cannot and dare not wait, in a fatalist fashion, with folded arms for the advent of the "revolutionary situation," to wait for that which in every spontaneous peoples' movement falls from the clouds. On the contrary, they must now, as always, hasten the development of things and endeavor to accelerate events. This they cannot do, however, by suddenly issuing the "slogan" for a mass strike at random at any odd moment, but first and foremost, by making clear to the widest layers of the proletariat the *inevitable advent* of this revolutionary period, the inner *social factors* making for it and the *political consequences* of it. If the widest proletarian layer should be won for a political mass action of the Social Democrats, and if, vice versa, the Social Democrats should seize and maintain the real leadership of a mass movement—should they become, in a *political* sense, the rulers of the whole movement, then they must, with the utmost clearness, consistency and resoluteness, inform the German proletariat of their tactics and aims in the period of coming struggle.

VII. The Role of the Mass Strike in the Revolution

We have seen that the mass strike in Russia does not represent an artificial product of premeditated tactics on the part of the Social Democrats, but a natural historical phenomenon on the basis of the present revolution. Now what are the factors which in Russia have brought forth this new phenomenal form of the revolution?

The Russian Revolution has for its next task the abolition of absolutism and the creation of a modern bourgeois-parliamentary constitutional state. It is exactly the same in form as that which confronted Germany at the March Revolution, and France at the Great Revolution at the end of the eighteenth century. But the condition, the historical milieu, in which these formally analogous revolutions took place, are fundamentally different from those of present-day Russia. The most decisive difference is the circumstances that between those bourgeois revolutions of the West and the present bourgeois revolution in the East, the whole cycle of capitalist development has run its course. And this development had seized not only the West European countries, but also absolutist Russia. Large-scale industry with all its consequences—modern class divisions, sharp social contrasts, modern life in large cities and the modern proletariat—has become in Russia the prevailing form, that is, in social development the decisive form of production.

The remarkable, contradictory, historical situation results from this that the bourgeois revolution, in accordance with its formal tasks will, in the first place, be carried out by a modern class-conscious proletariat, and in an international milieu whose distinguishing characteristic is the ruin of bourgeois democracy. It is not the bourgeoisie that is now the leading revolutionary element as in the earlier revolutions of the West, while the proletarian masses, disorganized amongst the petty bourgeoisie, furnish material for the army of the bourgeoisie, but on the contrary, it is the class-conscious proletariat that is the leading and driving element, while the big bourgeois sections are partly and directly counterrevolutionary, partly and weakly liberal, and only the rural petty bourgeoisie and the urban petty bourgeois intelligentsia are definitely oppositional and even revolutionary minded. . . .

In the earlier bourgeois revolutions where, on the one hand, the political training and the leadership of the revolutionary masses were undertaken by the bourgeois parties, and where, on the other hand, it was merely a question of overthrowing the old government, the brief battle at the barricades was the appropriate form of the revolutionary struggle. Today, when the working classes are being enlightened in the course of the revolutionary struggle, when they must marshall their forces and lead themselves, and when the revolution is directed as much against the old state power as against capitalist exploitation, the mass strike appears as the natural means of recruiting the widest proletarian layers for the struggle, as well as being at the same time a means of undermining and overthrowing the old state power and of stemming capitalist exploitation. The urban industrial proletariat is now the soul of the revolution in Russia. But in order to carry through a direct political struggle as a mass, the proletariat must first be assembled as a mass, and for this purpose they must come out of factory and workshop, mine and foundry, must overcome the levigation and the decay to which they are condemned under the daily yoke of capitalism.

The mass strike is the first natural, impulsive form of every great revolutionary struggle of the proletariat and the more highly developed the antagonism is between capital and labor, the more effective and decisive must mass strikes become. The chief form of previous bourgeois revolutions, the fight at the barricades, the open conflict with the armed power of the state, is in the revolution of today only the culminating point, only a moment on the process of the proletarian mass struggle. And therewith in the new form of the revolution there is reached that civilizing and mitigating of the class struggle which was prophesied by the opportunists of German Social Democracy—the Bernsteins, Davids, etc. It is true that these men saw the desired civilizing and mitigating of the class struggle in the light of petty bourgeois democratic illusions—they believed that the class struggle would shrink to an exclusively parliamentary contest and that street fighting would simply be done away with. History has found the solution in a deeper and finer fashion: in the advent of revolutionary mass strikes, which, of course, in no way replaces brutal street fights or renders them unnecessary, but which reduces them to a moment in the long period of political struggle, and which at the same time unites with the revolutionary period an enormous cultural work in the most exact sense of the words: the material and intellectual elevation of the whole working class through the "civilizing" of the barbaric forms of capitalist exploitation.

The mass strike is thus shown to be not a specifically Russian product, springing from absolutism but a universal form of the proletarian class struggle resulting from the present stage of capitalist development and class relations. From this standpoint the three bourgeois revolutions—the great French Revolution, the German Revolution of March, and the present Russian Revolution—form a continuous chain of development in which the fortunes and the end of the capitalist century are to be seen. In the great French Revolution the still wholly underdeveloped internal contradictions of bourgeois society gave scope for a long period of violent struggles, in which all the antagonisms which first germinated and ripened in the heat of the revolution raged unhindered and unrestrained in a spirit of reckless radicalism. A century later the revolution of the German bourgeoisie, which broke out midway in the development of capitalism, was already hampered on both sides by the antagonism of interests and the equilibrium of strength between capital and labor, and was smothered in a bourgeois-feudal compromise, and shortened to a brief miserable episode ending in words.

Another half century, and the present Russian Revolution stands at a point of the historical path which is already over the summit, which is on the other side of the culminating point of capitalist society, at which the bourgeois revolution cannot again be smothered by the antagonism between bourgeoisie and proletariat, but will, on the contrary, expand into a new lengthy period of violent social struggles, at which the balancing of the account with absolutism appears a trifle in comparison with the many new accounts which the revolution itself opens up. The present revolution realizes in the particular affairs of absolutist Russia the general results of international capitalist development, and appears not so much as the last successor of the old bourgeois revolutions as the forerunner of the new series of proletarian revolutions of the West. The most backward country of all, just because it has been so unpardonably late with its bourgeois revolution, shows ways and methods of further class struggle to the proletariat of Germany and the most advanced capitalist countries.

Accordingly it appears, when looked at in this way, to be entirely wrong to regard the Russian Revolution as a fine play, as something specifically "Russian," and at best to admire the heroism of the fighting men, that is, the last accessories of the struggle. It is much more important that the German workers should learn to look upon the Russian Revolution *as their own affair,* not merely as a matter of international solidarity with the Russian proletariat, but first and foremost, as a *chapter of their own social and political history.* Those trade-union leaders and parliamentarians who regard the German proletariat as "too weak" and German conditions "as not ripe enough" for revolutionary mass struggles, have obviously not the least idea that the measure of the degree of ripeness of class relations in Germany and of the power of the proletariat does not lie in the statistics of German trade unionism or in election figures, but—in the events of the Russian Revolution. Exactly as the ripeness of French class antagonisms under the July monarchy and the June battle of Paris was reflected in the German March Revolution, in its course and its fiasco, so today the ripeness of German class antagonisms is reflected in the events and in the power of the Russian Revolution. And while the bureaucrats of the German labor movement rummage in their office drawers for information as to their strength and maturity, they do not see that that for which they seek is lying before their eyes in a great historical revolution, because, historically considered, the Russian Revolution is a reflex of the power and the maturity of the international, and therefore in the first place, of the German labor movement.

It would therefore be a too pitiable and grotesquely insignificant result of the Russian Revolution if the German proletariat should merely draw from it the lesson—as is desired by Comrades Frohme, Elm, and others— of using the extreme form of the struggle, the mass strike, and so weaken themselves as to be merely a reserve force in the event of the withdrawal of the parliamentary vote, and therefore a passive means of parliamentary defensive. When the parlimentary vote is taken from us there we will resist. That is a self-evident decision. But for this it is not necessary to adopt the heroic pose of a Danton as was done, for example, by Comrade Elm in Jena; because the defense of the modest measure of parliamentary right already possessed is less a Heaven-storming innovation, for which the frightful hecatombs of the Russian Revolution were first necessary as a means of encouragement, than the simplest and first duty of every opposition party. But the mere defensive can never exhaust the policy of the proletariat, in a period of revolution. And if it is, on the one hand, difficult to predict with any degree of certainty whether the destruction of universal suffrage would cause a situation in Germany which would call forth an immediate mass strike action, so on the other hand, it is absolutely certain that when we in Germany enter upon the period of stormy mass actions, it will be impossible for the Social Democrats to base their tactics upon a mere parliamentary defensive.

To fix beforehand the cause and the moment from and in which the mass strikes in Germany will break out is not in the power of Social Democracy, because it is not in its power to bring about historical situations by resolutions at party congresses. But what it can and must do is to make clear the political tendencies, when they once appear, and to formulate them as resolute and consistent tactics. Man cannot keep historical events in check while making recipes for them, but he can see in advance their apparent calculable consequences and arrange his mode of action accordingly. . . .

But if once the ball is set rolling then Social Democracy, whether it wills it or not, can never again bring it to a standstill. The opponents of the mass strike are in the habit of denying that the lessons and examples of the Russian Revolution can be a criterion for Germany because, in the first place, in Russia the great step must first be taken from an Oriental despotism to a modern bourgeois legal order. The formal distance between the old and the new political order is said to be a sufficient explanation of the vehemence and the violence of the revolution in Russia. In Germany we have long had the most necessary forms and guarantees of a constitutional state, from which it follows that such an elementary raging of social antagonisms is impossible here.

Those who speculate thus forget that in Germany when it once comes to the outbreak of open political struggles, even the historically determined goal will be quite different from that in Russia today. Precisely because the bourgeois legal order in Germany has existed for a long time, because therefore it has had time to completely exhaust itself and to draw to an end, because bourgeois democracy and liberalism have had time to die out— because of this there can no longer be any talk of a *bourgeois* revolution in Germany. And therefore in a period of open political popular struggles in Germany, the last historical necessary goal can only be the *dictatorship of the proletariat*. The distance, however, of this task from the present conditions of Germany is still greater than that of the bourgeois legal order from Oriental despotism, and therefore, the task cannot be completed at one stroke, but must similarly be accomplished during a long period of gigantic social struggles. . . .

VIII. Need for United Action of Trade Unions and Social Democracy

The most important desideratum which is to be hoped for from the German working class in the period of great struggles which will come sooner or later is, after complete resoluteness and consistency of tactics, the utmost capacity for action, and therefore the utmost possible unity of the leading Social Democratic part of the proletarian masses. Meanwhile the first weak attempts at the preparation of great mass actions have discovered a serious drawback in this connection: the total separation and independence of the two organizations of the labor movement, Social Democracy and the trade unions.

It is clear on a closer consideration of the mass strikes in Russia as well as of the conditions in Germany itself, that any great mass action, if it is not confined to a mere one-day demonstration, but is intended to be a real fighting action, cannot possibly be thought of as a so-called political mass strike. In such an action in Germany the trade unions would be implicated as much as the Social Democrats. Not because the trade-union leaders imagine that the Social Democrats, in view of their smaller organization, would have no other resources than the cooperation of one and a quarter million trade unionists and without them would be unable to do anything, but because of a much more deep-lying motive: because every direct mass action of the period of open class struggles would be at the same time both political and economic. If in Germany, from any cause and at any time, it should come to great political struggles, to mass strikes, then at that time an era of violent trade-union struggles would begin in Germany, and events would not stop to inquire whether the trade-union leaders had given their consent to the movement or not. Whether they stand aside or endeavor to resist the movement, the result of their attitude will only be that the trade-union leaders, like the party leaders in the analogous case, will simply be swept aside by the rush of events, and the economic and the political struggles of the masses will be fought out without them.

As a matter of fact the separation of the political and the economic struggle and the independence of each is nothing but an artificial product of the parliamentarian period, even if historically determined. On the one hand in the peaceful, "normal" course of bourgeois society, the economic struggle is split into a multitude of individual struggles in every undertaking and dissolved in every branch of production. On the other hand the political struggle is not directed by the masses themselves in a direct action, but in correspondence with the form of the bourgeois state, in a representative fashion, by the presence of legislative representation. As soon as a period of revolutionary struggles commences, that is, as soon as the masses appear upon the scene of conflict, the breaking up of the economic struggle into many parts, as well as the indirect parliamentary form of the political struggle ceases; in a revolutionary mass action the political and the economic struggle are one, and the artificial boundary between trade union and Social Democracy as two separate, wholly independent forms of the labor movement, is simply swept away. But what finds concrete expression in the revolutionary mass movement finds expression also in the parliamentary period as an actual state of affairs. There are not two different class struggles of the working class, an economic and a political one, but only *one* class struggle, which aims at one and the same time at the limitation of capitalist exploitation within bourgeois society, and at the abolition of exploitation together with bourgeois society itself.

When these two sides of the class struggle are separated from one another for technical reasons in the parliamentary period, they do not form two parallel concurrent actions, but merely two phases, two stages of the struggle for emancipation of the working class. The trade-union struggle embraces the immediate interests, and the Social Democratic struggle the future interests, of the labor movement. The Communists, says the *Communist Manifesto,* represent, as against various group interests, national or local, of the proletariat, the common interests of the proletariat as a whole, and in the various stages of development of the class struggle, they represent the interests of the whole movement, that is, the ultimate goal—the liberation of the proletariat. The trade unions represent only the group interests and only one stage of development of the labor movement. Social Democracy represents the working class and the cause of its liberation as a whole. The relation of the trade unions to Social Democracy is therefore a part of the whole, and when, amongst the trade-union leaders, the theory of "equal authority" of trade unions and Social Democracy finds so much favor, it rests upon a fundamental misconception of the essence of trade unionism itself and of its role in the general struggle for freedom of the working class.

This theory of the parallel action of Social Democracy and the trade unions and of their "equal authority" is nevertheless not altogether without foundation, but has its historical roots. It rests upon the illusion of the peaceful, "normal" period of bourgeois society, in which the political struggle of Social Democracy appears to be consumed in the parliamentary struggle. The parliamentary struggle, however, the counterpart of the trade-union struggle, is equally with it, a fight conducted exclusively on the basis of the bourgeois social order. It is by its very nature political reform work, as that of the trade unions is economic reform work. It represents political work for the present, as trade unions represent economic work for the present. It is, like them, merely a phase, a stage of development in the complete process of the proletarian class struggle whose ultimate goal is as far beyond the parliamentarian struggle as it is beyond the trade-union struggle. The parliamentary struggle is, in relation to Social Democratic policy, also a part of the whole, exactly as trade-union work is. Social Democracy today comprises the parliamentary and the trade-union struggle in one class struggle aiming at the abolition of the bourgeois social order.

The theory of the "equal authority" of trade unions and Social Democracy is likewise not a mere theoretical misunderstanding, not a mere case of confusion but an expression of the well-known tendency of that opportunist wing of Social Democracy which reduces the political struggle of the working class to the parliamentary contest, and desires to change Social Democracy from a revolutionary proletarian party into a petty bourgeois reform one. . . .

In Germany, however, there is such a shifting of relations within the labor movement as is impossible in any other country. The theoretical conception, according to which the trade unions are merely a part of Social Democracy, finds its classic expression in Germany in fact, in actual practice, and that in three directions. First, the German trade unions are a direct product of Social Democracy; it was Social Democracy which created the beginnings of the present trade-union movement in Germany and which enabled it to attain such great dimensions, and it is Social Democracy which supplies it to this day with its leaders and the most active promoters of its organization.

Second, the German trade unions are a product of Social Democracy also in the sense that Social Democratic teaching is the soul of trade-union practice, as the trade unions owe their superiority over all bourgeois and denominational trade unions to the idea of the class struggle; their practical success, their power, is a result of the circumstance that their practice is illuminated by the theory of scientific socialism and they are thereby raised above the level of a narrow-minded socialism. The strength of the "practical policy" of the German trade unions lies in their insight into the deeper social and economic connections of the capitalist system; but they owe this insight entirely to the theory of scientific socialism upon which their practice is based. Viewed in this way, any attempt to emancipate the trade unions from the Social Democratic theory in favor of some other "trade-union theory" opposed to Social Democracy, is, from the standpoint of the trade unions themselves and of their future, nothing but an attempt to commit suicide. The separation of trade-union practice from the theory of scientific socialism would mean to the German trade unions the immediate loss of all their superiority over all kinds of bourgeois trade unions, and their fall from their present height to the level of unsteady groping and mere dull empiricism.

Thirdly and finally, the trade unions are, although their leaders have gradually lost sight of the fact, even as regards their numerical strength, a direct product of the Social Democratic movement and the Social Democratic agitation. It is true that in many districts trade-union agitation precedes Social Democratic agitation, and that everywhere trade-union work prepares the way for party work. From the point of view of effect, party and trade unions assist each other to the fullest extent. But when the picture of the class struggle in Germany is looked at as a whole and its more deep-seated associations, the proportions are considerably altered. Many trade-union leaders are in the habit of looking down triumphantly from the proud height of their membership of one and a quarter million on the miserably organized members of the Social Democratic Party, not yet half a million strong, and of recalling the time, ten or twelve years ago, when those in the ranks of Social Democracy were pessimistic as to the prospects of trade-union development.

They do see that between these two things—the large number of organized trade unionists and the small number of organized Social Democrats—*there exists in a certain degree a direct causal connection.* Thousands and thousands of workers do not join the party organizations precisely because they join the trade unions. According to the theory, all the workers must be doubly organized, must attend two kinds of meetings, pay double contributions, read two kinds of workers' papers, etc. But for this it is necessary to have a higher standard of intelligence and of that idealism which, from a pure feeling of duty to the labor movement, is prepared for the daily sacrifice of time and money, and finally, a higher standard of that passionate interest in the actual life of the party which can only be engendered by membership of the party organization. All this is true of the most enlightened and intelligent minority of Social Democratic workers in the large towns, where party life is full and attractive and where the workers' standard of living is high. Amongst the wider sections of the working masses in the large towns, however, as well as in the provinces, in the smaller and the smallest towns where local political life is not an independent thing but a mere reflex of the course of events in the capital, where consequently, party life is poor and monotonous, and where, finally, the economic standard of life of the workers is, for the most part, miserable, it is very difficult to secure the double form of organization.

For the Social Democratically-minded worker from the masses the question will be solved by his joining his trade union. The immediate interests of his economic struggle which are conditioned by the nature of the struggle itself cannot be advanced in any other way than by membership of a trade-union organization. The contribution which he pays, often amidst considerable sacrifice of his standard of living, brings him immediate, visible results. His Social Democratic inclinations, however, enable him to participate in various kinds of work without belonging to a special party organization; by voting at parliamentary elections, by attendance at Social Democratic public meetings, by following the reports of Social Democratic speeches in representative bodies, and by reading the party press. Compare in this connection the number of Social Democratic electors or the number of subscribers to *Vorwaerts* with the number of organized party members in Berlin!

And what is most decisive, the Social Democratically-minded average worker who, as a simple man, can have no understanding of the intricate and fine so-called "two-soul theory" feels that he is, even in the trade union, *Social Democratically* organized. Although the central committees of the unions have no official party label, the workman from the masses in every city and town sees at the head of his trade union as the most active leaders, those colleagues whom he knows also as comrades and Social Democrats in public life, now as Reichstag, Landtag or local representatives, now as trusted men of the Social Democracy, members of election committees, party editors and secretaries, or merely as speakers and agitators. Further, he hears expressed in the agitational work of his trade union much the same ideas, pleasing and intelligible to him, of capitalist exploitation, class relations, etc., as those that have come to him from the Social Democratic agitation. Indeed, the most and best loved of the speakers at trade-union meetings are those same Social Democrats.

Thus everything combines to give the average class-conscious worker the feeling that he, in being organized in his trade union, is also a member of his labor party and is Social Democratically organized, *and therein lies the peculiar recruiting strength of the German trade unions.* Not because of the appearance of neutrality, but because of the Social Democratic reality of their being, have the central unions been enabled to attain their present strength. . . .

In a word the appearance of "neutrality," which exists in the minds of many trade-union leaders, does not exist for the mass of organized trade unionists. And that is the good fortune of the trade-union movement. If the appearance of "neutrality," that alienation and separation of the trade unions from Social Democracy, really and truly becomes a reality in the eyes of the proletarian masses, then the trade unions would immediately lose all their advantages over competing bourgeois unions, and therewith their recruiting power, their living fire. This is conclusively proved by facts which are generally known. The appearance of party-political "neutrality" of the trade unions could, as a means of attraction, render inestimable service in a country in which Social Democracy itself has no credit among the masses, in which the odium attached to a workers' organization injures it in the eyes of the masses rather than advantages it—where, in a word, the trade unions must first of all recruit their troops from a wholly unenlightened, bourgeois-minded mass.

The best example of such a country was, throughout the whole of the last century, and is to a certain extent today, Great Britain. In Germany, however, party relations are altogether different. In a country in which Social Democracy is the most powerful political party, in which its recruiting power is represented by an army of over three million proletarians, it is ridiculous to speak of the deterrent effect of Social Democracy and of the necessity for a fighting organization of the workers to ensure political neutrality. The mere comparison of the figures of Social Democratic voters with the figures of the trade-union organizations in Germany is sufficient to prove to the most simple-minded that the trade unions in Germany do not, as in England, draw their troops from the unenlightened bourgeois-minded mass, but from the mass of proletarians already aroused by the Social Democracy and won by it to the idea of the class struggle. Many trade-union leaders indignantly reject the idea—a requisite of the "theory of neutrality"—and regard the trade unions as a recruiting school for Social Democracy. This apparently insulting, but in reality, highly flattering presumption is in Germany reduced to mere fancy by the circumstance that the positions are reversed; it is Social Democracy which is the recruiting school for the trade unions.

Moreover, if the organizational work of the trade unions is for the most part of a very difficult and troublesome kind, it is, with the exception of a few cases and some districts, not merely because on the whole, the soil has not been prepared by the Social Democratic plough, but also because the trade-union seed itself and the sower as well must also be "red," Social Democratic, before the harvest can prosper. But when we compare in this way the figures of trade-union strength, not with those of the Social Democratic organizations, but—which is the only correct way—with those of the mass of Social Democratic voters, we come to a conclusion which differs considerably from the current view of the matter. The fact then comes to light that the "free trade unions" actually represent today but a minority of the class-conscious workers of Germany, that even with their one and a quarter million organized members they have not yet been able to draw into their ranks one-half of those already aroused by Social Democracy.

The most important conclusion to be drawn from the facts above cited is that the *complete unity* of the trade-union and the Social Democratic movements, which is absolutely necessary for the coming mass struggles in Germany, *is actually here,* and that it is incorporated in the wide mass which forms the basis at once of Social Democracy and trade unionism, and in whose consciousness both parts of the movement are mingled in a mental unity. The alleged antagonism between Social Democracy and trade unions shrinks to an antagonism between Social Democracy and a certain part of the trade-union officials, which is, however, at the same time an antagonism within the trade unions between this part of the trade-union leaders and the proletarian mass organized in trade unions.

The rapid growth of the trade-union movement in Germany in the course of the last fifteen years, especially in the period of great economic prosperity from 1895 to 1900 has brought with it a great independence of the trade unions, a specializing of their methods of struggle, and finally the introduction of a regular trade-union officialdom. All these phenomena are quite understandable and natural historical products of the growth of the trade unions in this fifteen-year period, and of the economic prosperity and political calm of Germany. They are, although inseparable from certain drawbacks, without doubt a historically necessary evil. But the dialectics of development also brings with it the circumstance that these necessary means of promoting trade-union growth become, on the contrary, obstacles to its further development at a certain stage of organization and at a certain degree of ripeness of conditions.

The specialization of professional activity as trade-union leaders, as well as the naturally restricted horizon which is bound up with disconnected economic struggles in a peaceful period, leads only too easily, amongst trade-union officials, to bureaucratism and a certain narrowness of outlook. Both, however, express themselves in a whole series of tendencies which may be fateful in the highest degree for the future of the trade-union movement. There is first of all the overvaluation of the organization, which from a means has gradually been changed into an end in itself, a precious thing, to which the interests of the struggles should be subordinated. From this also comes that openly admitted need for peace which shrinks from great risks and presumed dangers to the stability of the trade unions, and further, the overvaluation of the trade-union method of struggle itself, its prospects and its successes.

The trade-union leaders, constantly absorbed in the economic guerrilla war whose plausible task it is to make the workers place the highest value on the smallest economic achievement, every increase in wages and shortening of the working day, gradually lose the power of seeing the larger connections and of taking a survey of the whole position. Only in this way can one explain why many trade-union leaders refer with the greatest satisfaction to the achievements of the last fifteen years, instead of, on the contrary, emphasizing the other side of the medal; the simultaneous and immense reduction of the proletarian standard of life by land usury, by the whole tax and customs policy, by landlord rapacity which has increased house rents to such an exorbitant extent, in short, by all the objective tendencies of bourgeois policy which have largely neutralized the advantages of the fifteen years of trade-union struggle. From the *whole* Social Democratic truth which, while emphasizing the importance of the present work and its absolute necessity, attaches the chief importance to the criticism and the limits to this work, the *half* trade-union truth is taken which emphasizes only the positive side of the daily struggle.

And finally, from the concealment of the objective limits drawn by the bourgeois social order to the trade-union struggle, there arises a hostility to every theoretical criticism which refers to these limits in connection with the ultimate aims of the labor movement. Fulsome flattery and boundless optimism are considered to be the duty of every "friend of the trade-union movement." But as the Social Democratic standpoint consists precisely in fighting against uncritical trade-union optimism, as in fighting against uncritical parliamentary optimism, a front is at last made against the Social Democratic theory: men grope for a "new trade-union theory," that is, a theory which would open an illimitable vista of economic progress to the trade-union struggle within the capitalist system, in opposition to the Social Democratic doctrine. . . .

In close connection with these theoretical tendencies is a revolution in the relations of leaders and rank and file. In place of the direction by colleagues through local committees, with their admitted inadequacy, there appears the businesslike direction of the trade-union officials. The initiative and the power of making decisions thereby devolve upon trade-union specialists, so to speak, and the more passive virtue of discipline upon the mass of members. This dark side of officialdom also assuredly conceals considerable dangers for the party, as from the latest innovation, the institution of local party secretariats, it can quite easily result, if the Social Democratic mass is not careful that these secretariats may remain mere organs for carrying out decisions and not be regarded in any way the appointed bearers of the initiative and of the direction of local party life. But by the nature of the case, by the character of the political struggle, there are narrow bounds drawn to bureaucratism in Social Democracy as in trade-union life. . . .

And finally, a result of this specialization and this bureaucratism amongst trade-union officials is the great independence and the "neutrality" of the trade unions in relation to Social Democracy. The extreme independence of the trade-union organization has resulted as a natural condition from its growth, as a relation which has grown out of the technical division of work between the political and the trade-union forms of struggle. The "neutrality" of the German trade unions, on its part, arose as a product of the reactionary trade-union legislation of the Prusso-German police state. With time, both aspects of their nature have altered. From the condition of political "neutrality" of the trade unions imposed by the police, a theory of their voluntary neutrality has been evolved as a necessity founded upon the alleged nature of the trade-union struggle itself. And the technical independence of the trade unions which should rest upon the division of work in the unified Social Democratic class struggle, the separation of the trade unions from Social Democracy, from its views and its leadership, has been changed into the so-called equal authority of trade unions and Social Democracy. . . .

Thus the peculiar position has arisen that this same trade-union movement which below, in the wide proletarian masses, is absolutely one with Social Democracy, parts abruptly from it above, in the superstructure of management, and sets itself up as an independent great power. The German labor movement therefore assumes the peculiar form of a double pyramid whose base and body consist of one solid mass but whose apices are wide apart.

It is clear from this presentation of the case in what way alone in a natural and successful manner that compact unity of the German labor movement can be attained which, in view of the coming political class struggles and of the peculiar interest of the further development of the trade unions, is indispensably necessary. Nothing could be more perverse or more hopeless than to desire to attain the unity desired by means of sporadic and periodical negotiations on individual questions affecting the labor movement between the Social Democratic Party leadership and the trade-union central committees. It is just the highest circles of both forms of the labor movement which as we have seen incorporate their separation and self-sufficiency, which are themselves, therefore, the promoters of the illusion of the "equal authority" and of the parallel existence of Social Democracy and trade unionism.

To desire the unity of these through the union of the party executive and the general commission [of the unions—ED.] is to desire to build a bridge at the very spot where the distance is greatest and the crossing most difficult. Not above, amongst the heads of the leading directing organizations and in their federative alliance, but below, amongst the organized proletarian masses, lies the guarantee of the real unity of the labor movement. In the consciousness of the million trade unionists, the party and the trade unions are actually *one*, they represent in different forms the *Social Democratic* struggle for the emancipation of the proletariat. And the necessity automatically arises therefrom of removing any causes of friction which have arisen between Social Democracy and a part of the trade unions, of adapting their mutual relation to the consciousness of the proletarian masses, that is, *of rejoining the trade unions to Social Democracy*. The synthesis of the real development which led from the original incorporation of the trade unions to their separation from Social Democracy will thereby be expressed, and the way will be prepared for the coming period of great proletarian mass struggles during the period of vigorous growth, of both trade unions and Social Democracy, and their reunion, in the interests of both, will become a necessity.

It is not, of course, a question of the merging of the trade-union organization in the party, but of the restoration of the unity of Social Democracy and the trade unions which corresponds to the actual relation between the labor movement as a whole and its partial trade-union expression. Such a revolution will inevitably call forth a vigorous opposition from a part of the trade-union leadership. But it is high time for the working masses of Social Democracy to learn how to express their capacity for decision and action, and therewith to demonstrate their ripeness for that time of great struggles and great tasks in which they, the masses, will be the actual chorus and the directing bodies will merely act the "speaking parts," that is, will only be the interpreters of the will of the masses.

The trade-union movement is not that which is reflected in the quite understandable *but irrational* illusion of a minority of the trade-union leaders, but that which lives in the consciousness of the mass of proletarians who have been won for the class struggle. In this consciousness the trade-union movement is a part of Social Democracy. "And what it is, that should it dare to appear."

49. Clara Zetkin, *On a Bourgeois Feminist Petition* (1895)

Clara Zetkin (née Eissner) (1857–1933) was one of the principal leaders of the German Social Democratic women's movement between 1892 and 1917. As editor of *Gleichheit* (Equality), Zetkin was instrumental in attracting tens of thousands of German working-class women to socialism. Zetkin was born in rural Saxony, the daughter of a village school teacher. Influenced by her mother on issues relating to women's rights, Zetkin also became a covert adherent of the Social Democrats in the 1870s. When her lover, Ossip Zetkin (1848–1889), fled Germany in 1881 in the wake of the political persecutions following Bismarck's anti-socialist law, Clara followed him. In 1882 they settled in Paris. Clara Eissner took her companion's name and had two children with him in common-law marriage.

During the 1880s Clara Zetkin was active in Paris in recruiting working women to socialism and she participated in the founding Congress of the Second International in 1889. In 1890 she returned to Germany where she soon assumed the editorship of *Gleichheit*. As the respected and admired, if not always loved, representative of feminism among the Socialists, Zetkin fought the indifference and passivity (if not outright hostility) of her male colleagues. Like her close friend Rosa Luxemburg, Zetkin was a staunch opponent of Eduard Bernstein's Revisionism, but unlike Luxemburg, Zetkin devoted her life to furthering the interests of the Socialist women's movement. Whereas Luxemburg preferred to work for a total political transformation of civil society (although she sympathized with the work of women like Zetkin), in the process of which

From Clara Zetkin, "On a Bourgeois Feminist Petition," translated by Hal Draper and Anne G. Lipow, in *The Socialist Register,* 1976, pp. 202–7.

women would also find liberation, Zetkin emphasized sexual equality as well as class liberation as components of women's emancipation. This did not mean, however, that Zetkin sanctioned collaboration with bourgeois women's groups on political or social issues. In fact she was a staunch opponent of such cooperation.

In January 1895 Zetkin was involved in a controversy with the editors of the party newspaper *Vorwärts*. A request from bourgeois German feminists to support a petition for women's political rights (specifically their right to organize meetings and associations) aroused the opposition of Zetkin, who argued that the petition reflected the narrow, class-based concerns of its authors and was both tendentious and harmful to Socialist-feminist interests. When *Vorwärts* dared to suggest that the Socialist women should sign the document, Zetkin sent the statement of protest reprinted here.

Last summer 22 women's rights organisations joined in an alliance which, in a petition to the Kaiser, "most humbly" implored the legal prohibition of prostitution and severe punishment of prostitutes, pimps, etc. by means of a cabinet order by the Kaiser and allied princes. The lackey-like tone favoured in the petition was worthily complemented by its socio-political ignorance, redolent of a beggar's plea, and by the presumptuousness with which the organisations "dared" to beg because their representatives would be accepted as "authorities on women's affairs."

Now we find three whole women who ask in a petition for the right of assembly and association for the female sex. Three whole women have taken the initiative, on behalf of bourgeois women's circles, to win a right whose lack is one of the most significant features of the social subordination of the female sex in Germany!

The petition addresses itself to women "of all parties and all classes." Even the signatures of proletarian women, of Social-Democratic women, are welcomed.

I will not raise the question whether it is necessary for proletarian women to sign a petition for the right of assembly and association at a point when the party, which represents their interests as well as the male proletariat's, has introduced a bill to this end in the Reichstag. As we know, the Social-Democratic Reichstag group has proposed that the laws on association and assembly now existing in the individual states be recognised on a national legal basis, and that equal rights for both sexes be included in this reorganisation as well as legal guarantee of the unrestricted exercise of freedom to organise. So it demands not only what the petition requests but much more besides.

It may well be that to some people, perhaps even many, support to this petition by organised workers and its signing by proletarian women appears "expedient"—expediency certainly smiles more sweetly for many in our party than principle does. Such a petition supported by a mass of signatures seems to them an excellent demonstration of favour of the Social-Democratic proposal, a proof that the widest circles of women as a whole feel the pressing need for the right of association and assembly.

From my point of view, even without the petition such a demonstration has just been given once and for all; the proof that the reform demanded is a just one was given long ago, permanently and emphatically, in the form of the dogged and bitter struggle carried on for years against the rights of association and assembly by the allied forces of police and judiciary.

In this struggle the police actively showed the full vigour which has earned the highest respect for the German officialdom's loyalty to duty in the eyes of the possessing classes. The judiciary, for their part, show an interpretive skill which ordinary human understanding has not always been able to appreciate. One dissolution of a proletarian women's organisation follows upon another; one prohibition of a women's meeting follows upon another; the exclusion of women from public meetings is an everyday affair; penalties against women for violating the law on association simply rain down. From 1st October, 1893 to 31st August, 1894, proletarian women had to pay 681 marks worth of fines for such offences; and this only in cases that came to my knowledge. Despite all, new associations regularly rise in place of the organisations that were smashed; over and over again women throng to rallies, over and over again they organise new ones.

The proletarian woman, living in straitened circumstances if not bitter poverty and overburdened with work, continues to make the sacrifice of time and energy required by organisational activity; bravely she exposes herself to the legal consequences and accepts the penalties that hang over her head "in the name of the law." These facts are to my mind the most indubitable proof that it is an urgent interest of life itself which makes the possession of freedom of association necessary for the proletarian woman and not a desire for political games or club socialising. If the Reichstag and the government do not understand the urgent language of these facts, they will bend their ears even less favourably to a petition.

Here it will perhaps be objected: "Well, even if the petition is of no use, still it does no harm. It is a question of broadening the rights of the disfranchised female sex, therefore we will support it and sign it." Very nice, I reply; but if this approach is taken, the petition must still somehow jibe with the bases of our proletarian viewpoint, or at least—to put it moderately—it must not stand in sharp contradiction with our viewpoint. This is not at all the case, on the contrary. The petition stems from bourgeois circles, it breathes a bourgeois spirit throughout—indeed, in many details, even a narrowly bourgeois spirit.

It baffles us, then, why Social-Democratic papers should push this petition and quasi-officially urge organised workers to support it and proletarian women to sign it. Since when is it the habit of the Social-Democratic Party to support petitions that stem from bourgeois circles and bear the marks of a bourgeois outlook on their forehead simply because such petitions ask for something valid, something the Social-Democracy also demands and has long demanded? Let us suppose that bourgeois democrats had put forward a petition whose purpose was the same as or similar to that of the women's petition under discussion, of the same character. The Social-Democratic press would criticise the petition but would in no way encourage comrades or class-conscious workers to trail along after bourgeois elements. Why should our principled standpoint with respect to the politics of the bourgeois world change because by chance an example of these politics comes from women and demands not a reform on behalf of the so-called social aggregate but rather one on behalf of the female sex? If we are willing to give up our principled attitude for this reason, we likewise give up our view that the women's question can only be understood, and demands raised, in connection with the social question as a whole.

In No. 7 of January 9, *Vorwärts* took a thoroughly correct attitude to the petition. It took notice of it, criticised it, and pointed out that it took up an old socialist demand. Unfortunately, and to my great amazement, *Vorwärts* changed its line overnight. Why? Because it was given to understand that the motivating preamble of the petition did not deserve the criticism made of it. That this assurance and an allusion to remarks in a "communication" decided *Vorwärts* to make a change of front—this I must emphatically deplore. And in spite of the "communication," the charge made against the petition—that its motivating preamble is most defective—remains in full force. The "communication" in fact has not the slightest thing to do with the petition and its preamble. It is nothing but an accompanying note, a circular letter to people whose signatures are solicited in support of the petition. It says: "Among the 'special interests' of women which are not detailed in the petition for the sake of brevity, the job situation of women especially requires a legislative bill in line with the petition."

Should this passage be taken as a statement of advice on the value of freedom of association and assembly for proletarian women? We say thanks for this information but we don't need it. The proletariat recognised, much earlier than the authors of this petition, the value of freedom of organisation for all its members without distinction of sex. And in conformity with this recognition the proletariat fights for the conquest of this right. Should the passage be taken as an assurance that the maternal parents of this petition are themselves conscious of the significance of this right and its basis? We hopefully note this token of a socio-political comprehension that is commonly lacking among German women's rightsers. But this passage has no significance as far as the petition itself is concerned. As far as the petition and its possible consideration are concerned, it is not a matter of what its sponsors and signers had in mind for its preamble but rather what grounds they put forward in its favour. In the preamble of the petition there is not a word about the fact that for the interests of independently employed women the possession of the right of association and assembly is an imperative necessity. The petition lacks precisely the ground on the basis of which the proletariat espouses the demand. It lacks the ground which is so essential for this legislative reform that—according to uncontradicted newspaper accounts—in Bavaria Centre Party people will introduce a bill in the next session of the state Diet which will demand the right of association and assembly for the female sex out of consideration for women's economic situation.

There is an air of embarrassment in the statement of the accompanying note that the pertinent ground was not introduced into the preamble of the petition for reasons of space. Indeed—then why didn't the saving consideration of brevity prevent the preamble from making the special point that one of the effects of women on legislation due to freedom of association is urgently presented as being on the "morality question." What the bourgeois women want from the lawmakers under the head of the "morality question" is made sufficiently clear by the abovementioned petition to the Kaiser [on prostitution].

In my opinion, proletarian women, politically conscious comrades least of all, cannot sign a petition which on the pretext of "brevity" passes over in silence the most important ground for the reform demanded from the proletarian standpoint, while regardless of "brevity" it stresses a ground which would be laughed at from a halfway clarified socio-political viewpoint, as the product of a very naive ignorance of social relations. Proletarian circles have not the least occasion to pin a certificate of poverty on their own socio-political judgment by solidarising themselves with a petition of this content.

Still another reason makes it impossible for the socialist movement to come out in favour of this petition. The petition does not call on the Reichstag or a Reichstag group for a bill along the lines of the reform in question; it simply requests the Reichstag to send the plea for such a bill to the federated German governments. The petition therefore ignores the competence of the Reichstag to introduce bills on this subject itself and assigns it the modest role of a porter who opens the door for the petitioners to the higher government authority. The Social-Democracy cannot support such a procedure and cannot join in it. The Social-Democracy has at all times fought the duality of the legislative power as it exists in Germany thanks to the fact that our bourgeoisie has not broken the power of absolutism but made a cowardly deal with it. The Social-Democracy has to put up with the fact that this duality exists; indeed, that the legislative authorities—the government and the people's representatives—do not confront one another as factors of equal power but that the latter is subordinate to the former; whereas the Social-Democracy had always fought with every legal means at its disposal for the people's representatives to be what they should be. Among the few rights and powers that parliament possesses in the noble German Reich is the right to introduce proposals that make demands in the name of the people instead of addressing pleas to the government. The petition, however, avoids the only straight route to the Reichstag. Proletarian women can have nothing to do with this and don't want to. Anyway, at the very least, not at this moment when the governments are launching the sharpest battle against the organisational activity of proletarian women and when the federated governments have introduced the Anti-Subversive bill. Proletarian women who expect a reform of the laws on association and assembly in accordance with their own interests to come from our governments would try to pick figs from thorns and grapes from thistles.

If the bourgeois women wanted temporary collaboration with proletarian women for a common goal on behalf of the petition, then it is evident that the petition would be formulated in such a way that working-women could sign it without compromising themselves and their aims. Such a formulation would have been premised on a prior understanding with the representatives of the class-conscious proletarian women. As the sponsors of the petition well know, there is a [socialist] Commission on Women's Work in Berlin. Why didn't the petition's sponsors come to this commission with the following two questions: (1) Are you perhaps prepared to support the planned petition? and (2) How does this petition have to be put so that it can be supported and signed by proletarian women without abandoning their own viewpoint?

Such a mode of procedure should have been self-evident and would have been dictated by good sense and courtesy if one wanted the signatures of proletarian women. The formulation of the petition and its sponsors' mode of procedure are characteristic of the outlook of bourgeois women and their relationship to the world of proletarian women. One is humanitarian enough to do something for one's "poorer sisters" under certain circumstances, and one is smart enough under all circumstances to accept their menial services, but to work together with them as if with a coequal power—well, that's an altogether different matter, you yokel.

The sponsors of the petition will refer to their "good intentions" and insist they were very far from having any conscious antagonism to the outlook of the proletarian women. But that cannot induce us to take a different view of their mode of procedure. In the name of good intentions people have long committed not only the greatest crimes but also the grossest stupidities. And the fact that the thought processes of the petitions' sponsors instinctively and unconsciously ran in a direction diametrically opposed to the proletarian outlook is indeed a sign of the gulf that separates us from them.

I believe that I speak not only in my own name but in the name of the majority of class-conscious proletarian women when I say:

Not one proletarian signature for this petition!

50. Rudyard Kipling, *The White Man's Burden* (1899)

Rudyard Kipling (1865–1936) was a British poet and short-story writer. Born in India, he returned there in 1882 after an abysmal education in England to work as a journalist. His stories and poems, which won him the Nobel Prize in literature in 1907, expressed his admiration for the British Empire and for an ethic of imperial domination over native and (implicitly) lesser races; all of this work merited him enormous popularity before 1914. Later in his life Kipling found himself increasingly estranged from official thought and policy in Britain toward the empire.

Take up the White Man's burden—
    Send forth the best ye breed—
Go bind your sons to exile
    To serve your captives' need;
To wait in heavy harness,
    On fluttered folk and wild—
Your new-caught, sullen peoples,
    Half-devil and half-child.

Take up the White Man's burden—
    In patience to abide,
To veil the threat of terror
    And check the show of pride;

From *Rudyard Kipling's Verse, Inclusive Edition, 1885–1918* (Garden City, N.Y.: Doubleday, 1925), pp. 371–72. Reprinted by permission of The National Trust for Places of Historic Interest or Natural Beauty, Macmillan London Ltd. and Doubleday and Company, Inc.

By open speech and simple,
    An hundred times made plain,
To seek another's profit,
    And work another's gain.

Take up the White Man's burden—
    The savage wars of peace—
Fill full the mouth of Famine
    And bid the sickness cease;
And when your goal is nearest
    The end for others sought,
Watch Sloth and heathen Folly
    Bring all your hope to nought.

Take up the White Man's burden—
    No tawdry rule of kings,
But toil of serf and sweeper—
    The tale of common things.
The ports ye shall not enter,
    The roads ye shall not tread,
Go make them with your living,
    And mark them with your dead.

Take up the White Man's burden—
    And reap his old reward:
The blame of those ye better,
    The hate of those ye guard—
The cry of hosts ye humour
    (Ah, slowly!) toward the light:—
"Why brought ye us from bondage,
    "Our loved Egyptian night?"

Take up the White Man's burden—
    Ye dare not stoop to less—
Nor call too loud on Freedom
    To cloak your weariness;
By all ye cry or whisper,
    By all ye leave or do,
The silent, sullen peoples
    Shall weigh your Gods and you.

Take up the White Man's burden—
    Have done with childish days—

The lightly proffered laurel,
  The easy, ungrudged praise.
Comes now, to search your manhood
  Through all the thankless years,
Cold, edged with dear-bought wisdom,
  The judgment of your peers!

51. The Earl of Cromer, *Modern Egypt*

Evelyn Baring (1841–1917; Baron Cromer since 1892, Earl of Cromer since 1901) was a member of a famous London family of bankers and financiers. From 1877 to 1879 he served as the British commissioner to the Egyptian public debt office. Working between 1880 and 1883 as a financial member of the viceroy's council in India, he returned to Egypt to serve as British agent and consul general at Cairo from 1883 to 1907, the principal British representative in Egypt. In Cromer's lifetime British imperialism reluctantly extended its grasp to include northeastern Africa (which lay under the nominal sovereignty of the Ottoman Empire). In 1881–82 dissidents in the Egyptian army and other nationalists tried to free the country from the control exercised by its foreign creditors. To put down the rebellion, which culminated in the battle at Tal al-Kabīr, and to protect the Suez Canal, British forces occupied Egypt in 1882. From 1914 to 1922 the country was a British protectorate.

Cromer's *Modern Egypt* is both a historical and political survey, and an influential personal memoir, expressing Cromer's views of the altruistic fate of the British to govern inferior peoples for the latters' own good. In 1883 Gladstone had originally intended that Cromer upgrade and reform Egyptian finances and then return to England. Instead Cromer stayed for twenty-four years to exercise vast personal power over the local Khedive. Like that of his contemporary, Lord Curzon in India, Cromer's paternalism produced short-term gains, but failed to lay reliable foundations for Egyptian self-government in the future.

Conclusion

Summary of This Work—Changes since the Time of Ismail—The British Reformers—Their Egyptian Allies—Stability of the Reforms

A short account has thus been given of the reforms which, during the last few years, have been carried out in all the more important branches of the

From Earl of Cromer, *Modern Egypt*, vol. 2 (New York: Macmillan, 1908), pp. 555–59, 563–71. Footnotes deleted.

Egyptian and Soudanese State administrations. The description given of those reforms is, indeed, defective. Several important subjects have not been even mentioned. No allusion has been made to the services of many officials who have done excellent work in their special spheres of action. All that has been attempted is to give a general sketch of the progress of Egyptian reform. Even this imperfect sketch may, however, suffice to indicate the main features of the work which has been accomplished. It has been shown how the extravagance and maladministration of Ismail Pasha led to his own downfall, and to the imposition of a qualified European tutelage on the Egyptian Government; how, at the moment when that tutelage was beginning to produce some beneficial results, the country was thrown back into disorder by a military mutiny, the offspring of Ismail's reckless conduct, and by the growth of national aspirations in a form which rendered them incapable of realisation; and how England finally intervened and bade disorder and administrative chaos cease. The readers of this book have been conducted, subject by subject, through the complicated mazes of the Egyptian administrative system. The degree of progress which has been made in the direction of introducing Western civilisation into the country has been described in some detail.

No one can fully realise the extent of the change which has come over Egypt since the British occupation took place unless he is in some degree familiar with the system under which the country was governed in the days of Ismail Pasha. The contrast between now and then is, indeed, remarkable. A new spirit has been instilled into the population of Egypt. Even the peasant has learnt to scan his rights. Even the Pasha has learnt that others besides himself have rights which must be respected. The courbash may hang on the walls of the Moudirieh, but the Moudir no longer dares to employ it on the backs of the fellaheen. For all practical purposes, it may be said that the hateful corvée system has disappeared. Slavery has virtually ceased to exist. The halcyon days of the adventurer and the usurer are past. Fiscal burthens have been greatly relieved. Everywhere law reigns supreme. Justice is no longer bought and sold. Nature, instead of being spurned and neglected, has been wooed to bestow her gifts on mankind. She has responded to the appeal. The waters of the Nile are now utilised in an intelligent manner. Means of locomotion have been improved and extended. The soldier has acquired some pride in the uniform which he wears. He has fought as he never fought before. The sick man can be nursed in a well-managed hospital. The lunatic is no longer treated like a wild beast. The punishment awarded to the worst criminal is no longer barbarous. Lastly, the schoolmaster is abroad, with results which are as yet uncertain, but which cannot fail to be important.

All these things have been accomplished by the small body of Englishmen who, in various capacities, and with but little direct support or assistance from their Government or its representative, have of late years devoted their energies to the work of Egyptian regeneration. They have had many obstacles to encounter. Internationalism and Pashadom have stood in the path at every turn. But these forces, though they could retard, have failed to arrest the progress of the British reformer. The opposition which he has had to encounter, albeit very embarrassing, merely acted on his system as a healthy tonic. An eminent French literary critic has said that the end of a book should recall its commencement to the mind of the reader. Acting on this principle, I may remind those who have perused these pages that I began this work by stating that, although possibly counterparts to all the abuses which existed, and which to some extent still exist in Egypt, may be found in other countries, the conditions under which the work of Egyptian reform has been undertaken were very peculiar. The special difficulties which have resulted from those conditions have but served to bring out in strong relief one of the main characteristics of the Anglo-Saxon race. Other nations might have equally well conceived the reforms which were necessary. It required the singular political adaptability of Englishmen to execute them. A country and a nation have been partially regenerated, in spite of a perverse system of government which might well have seemed to render regeneration almost impossible.

Yet, when it is said that all these things were accomplished by the Englishmen who have served the Egyptian Government, one qualifying remark should in justice be made. It should never be forgotten that many Egyptians have themselves borne a very honourable and useful part in the work of Egyptian regeneration.

Is the skilled labour, the energy, the perseverance, and the patient toil of the English reformers and their Egyptian allies to be thrown away? Is Egypt again to relapse into a semi-barbarous condition? Will posterity declare that this noble effort to elevate a whole nation ended in ultimate failure?

I cannot say what will be the future of Egypt, but I hope and believe that these questions may be answered in the negative.

According to the Eastern adage, the grass never grows again where once the hoof of the Sultan's horse has trod. In the sorely tried country of which this history treats, the hoof of the Turkish horse whether the rider were Sultan or Khedive, has, indeed, left a deep imprint. Nevertheless, I would fain hope it is not indelible. We are justified in substituting a sanguine in the place of a despondent metaphor. Where once the seeds of true Western civilisation have taken root so deeply as is now the case in Egypt, no retrograde forces, however malignant they may be, will in the end be able to check germination and ultimate growth. The seeds which Ismail Pasha and his predecessors planted produced little but rank weeds. The seeds which have now been planted are those of true civilisation. They will assuredly bring forth fruit in due season. Interested antagonism, ignorance, religious prejudice, and all the forces which cluster round an archaic and corrupt social system, may do their worst. They will not succeed. We have dealt a blow to the forces of reaction in Egypt from which they can never recover, and from which, if England does her duty towards herself, towards the Egyptian people, and towards the civilised world, they will never have a chance of recovering.

The Future of Egypt

Quo Vadis?—The Question of the Occupation—Its Duration—Egyptian Autonomy—The Capitulations—Desirability of Training the Egyptians—Importance of Finance—Display of Sympathy—Conclusion

It is probable that few Englishmen ever ask themselves seriously the question of *Quo Vadis* in connection with either Indian or Egyptian affairs. Even fewer are tempted to hazard any confident answer to this crucial question.

The practical instincts of our race lead us to deal with whatever affairs we have in hand for the moment, and to discard any attempt to peer too curiously into the remote future. That instinct seems to me to be eminently wise. Whether, however, it be wise or unwise, it certainly exercises so powerful an influence over my mind as to preclude me from endeavouring to forecast what will be the ultimate solution of the Egyptian Question. That solution, moreover, depends, in no small degree, on a factor which is at present both unknown and uncertain, viz., the conduct of the Egyptians themselves. We cannot as yet predict with any degree of assurance the moral, intellectual, and political results likely to be obtained by the transformation which is at present taking place in the Egyptian national character.

Although, however, I will not venture to predict the goal which will eventually be reached, I have no hesitation in expressing an opinion as to that which we should seek to attain So far as can at present be judged, only two alternative courses are possible. Egypt must eventually either become autonomous, or it must be incorporated into the British Empire. Personally, I am decidedly in favour of moving in the direction of the former of these alternatives.

As a mere academic question, I never have been, neither am I now in favour of the British occupation of Egypt. Looking at the matter from a purely British point of view, I believe that the opinion enunciated by Lord Palmerston in 1857 still holds good. More than this, however much I should regret to see the noble work of Egyptian reform checked, I am quite prepared to admit that, if it be in the interests of England to evacuate Egypt, we need not be deterred from doing so by the consideration that it is in the moral and material interests of the Egyptians, however little some few of them may recognise the fact, that we should continue our occupation of the country. It does not appear to me that we need stay in Egypt merely to carry out certain administrative reforms, however desirable they may be, unless those reforms are so essential that their non-execution would contribute to produce serious political or financial complications after the British garrison is withdrawn. All that we have to do is to leave behind us a fairly good, strong, and—above all things—stable Government, which will obviate anarchy and bankruptcy, and will thus prevent the Egyptian Question from again becoming a serious cause of trouble to Europe. We need not inquire too minutely into the acts of such a Government. In order to ensure its stability, it should possess a certain liberty of action, even although it may use that liberty in a manner which would not always be in accordance with our views. But it is essential that, subsequent to the evacuation, the Government should, broadly speaking, act on principles which will be in conformity with the commonplace requirements of Western civilisation. The idea, which at one time found favour with a section of the British public, that Egypt may be left to "stew in its own juice," and that, however great may be the confusion and internal disorder which is created, no necessity for European interference will arise, may at once be set aside as wholly impracticable. It is absurd to suppose that Europe will look on as a passive spectator whilst a retrograde government, based on purely Mohammedan principles and obsolete Oriental ideas, is established in Egypt. The material interests at stake are too important, and the degree of civilisation to which Egypt has attained is too advanced, to admit of such a line of conduct being adopted. Public opinion would force the most sluggish Government into action. If England did not interfere, some other Power would do so. Of the many delusions which at one time existed about Egypt, the greatest of all is the idea that England can shake herself free of the Egyptian Question merely by withdrawing the British garrison, and then declaring to the world that the Egyptians must get on as well as they can by themselves. Lord Granville pursued a policy of this sort in dealing with the affairs of the Soudan, and we know with what result.

It has sometimes been argued that, even if misgovernment were again allowed to reign supreme in Egypt, British interests would be sufficiently secured if all danger of occupation by any other foreign Power were averted. I have already alluded to this aspect of the question, but the point is one of so much importance that I need make no apology for reverting to it.

It cannot be too clearly understood that neutralisation, under whatsoever conditions, wholly fails to solve the Egyptian Question. The solution of that question would be little, if at all, advanced by merely obtaining guarantees against foreign interference in Egypt. The main difficulty would remain untouched. That difficulty is to decide who is to interfere, on the assumption that some foreign interference is indispensable. If it were thought desirable to prevent competition and rivalry amongst the different offices of the Metropolitan Fire Brigade, the object might readily be obtained by forbidding any one of them to aid in extinguishing a fire. The practical result would hardly be considered satisfactory. This, however, is the political system which would be involved in the neutralisaton of Egypt. Each member of the European Fire Brigade would be under an obligation not to turn his hose on to an Egyptian conflagration, in order to avoid wounding the susceptibilities of his neighbours. In the meanwhile, the whole edifice of Egyptian civilisation might, and probably would be destroyed, to the infinite detriment not only of the indigenous inhabitants of Egypt, but also of the large number of Europeans who would be ruined if the country were allowed to relapse into anarchy and barbarism. The failure of international action to deal effectively with misgovernment in other parts of the Ottoman dominions serves as a warning in dealing with Egypt.

Is it, however, possible to ensure the existence of a fairly good and stable government in Egypt if the British garrison were withdrawn? That is the main question which has to be answered.

I make no pretension to the gift of political prophecy. I can only state my deliberate opinion, formed after many years of Egyptian experience and in the face of a decided predisposition to favour the policy of evacuation, that at present, and for a long time to come, the results of executing such a policy would be disastrous. Looking to the special intricacies of the Egyptian system of government, to the licence of the local press, to the ignorance and credulity of the mass of the Egyptian population, to the absence of Egyptian statesmen capable of controlling Egyptian society and of guiding the very complicated machine of government, to the diminution of the influence exercised by the British officials and by the diplomatic Representative of England in Egypt which would inevitably result from the evacuation, and to the proved impotence of international action in administrative matters—it appears to me impossible to blind oneself to the fact that, if the British garrison were now withdrawn, a complete upset would most probably ensue. It has to be borne in mind that the Egypt of to-day is very different from the Egypt of the pre-occupation days. A return to personal rule of the Oriental type—and it is in this direction that events would probably trend—would create a revolution. A transfer of power to the present race of Europeanised Egyptians would, to say the least, be an extremely hazardous experiment, so hazardous, indeed, that I am very decidedly of opinion that it would be wholly unjustifiable to attempt it.

It may be that at some future period the Egyptians may be rendered capable of governing themselves without the presence of a foreign army in their midst, and without foreign guidance in civil and military affairs; but that period is far distant. One or more generations must, in my opinion, pass away before the question can be even usefully discussed.

The fact, however, that the occupation must last for a period which cannot now be defined, need not stand in the way of a gradual movement in the direction of autonomy in the sense in which I understand that term as applied to the special case of Egypt. The mere withdrawal of the British garrison would not render Egypt autonomous; on the contrary, it would diminish the prospect of eventual autonomy. It is a contradiction in terms to describe a country as self-governing when all its most important laws are passed, not by any of its inhabitants or by any institutions existing within its own confines, but by the Governments and legislative institutions of sixteen foreign Powers. Such, however, will be the condition of Egypt until the existing régime of the Capitulations is altered. There are, so far as I know, only two methods for effecting a radical alteration of that régime. One is that Egypt should cease to form part of the Ottoman dominions and should be annexed by some foreign Power—a solution which I discard. The other is that means should be devised for establishing a local legislature competent to deal with all local matters. The only real Egyptian autonomy, therefore, which I am able to conceive as either practicable or capable of realisation without serious injury to all the various interests involved, is one which will enable all the dwellers in cosmopolitan Egypt, be they Moslem or Christian, European, Asiatic, or African, to be fused into one self-governing body. That it may take years—possibly generations— to achieve this object is more than probable, but unless it can be achieved, any idea of autonomy, in the true sense of the term, will, in my opinion, have to be abandoned. I stated in the last Report I wrote from Egypt that it is well for every individual and every nation to have an ideal. The ideal of the Moslem patriot is, in my opinion, incapable of realisation. The ideal which I substitute in its place is extremely difficult of attainment, but if the Egyptians of the rising generation will have the wisdom and foresight to work cordially and patiently, in co-operation with European sympathisers, to attain it, it may possibly in time be found capable of realisation.

In the meanwhile, no effort should be spared to render the native Egyptians capable of eventually taking their share in the government of a really autonomous community. Much has already been done in this direction, and it may be confidently anticipated, now that the finances of the country are established on a sound footing and the most pressing demands necessary to ensure material prosperity have been met, that intellectual, and perhaps moral progress will proceed more rapidly during the next quarter of a century than during that which has now terminated. Only, it should never be forgotten that the rapidity of the progress must be made contingent on the means available for ensuring it. "Sound finance," as has been most truly said, "is the foundation of the independence of States." Nothing can compensate the Egyptians for a financial relapse.

Lastly, it should never be forgotten that, in default of community of race, religion, language, and habits of thought, which ordinarily constitute the main bonds of union between the rulers and the ruled, we must endeavour to forge such artificial bonds between the Englishman and the Egyptian as the circumstances of the case render available.

One of the most important of these bonds must always be the exhibition of reasonable and disciplined sympathy for the Egyptians, not merely by the British Government, but by every individual Englishman engaged in the work of Egyptian administration. This sympathy is a quality, the possession or absence of which is displayed by Englishmen in very various degrees when they are brought in contact with Asiatic or African races. Some go to the extreme of almost brutal antipathy, whilst others display their ill-regulated sympathy in forms which are exaggerated and even mischievous. The Egyptians rightly resent the conduct of the one class, and ridicule that of the other. A middle course, based on accurate information and on a careful study of Egyptian facts and of the Egyptian character, will be found more productive of result than either extreme.

Another bond may, to some extent, be forged by appealing to the person or the pocket. A proper system of justice and of police can protect the former. Material interests can be served by various means, the most effective of which is to keep taxation low. Do not let us, however, imagine that, under any circumstances, we can ever create a feeling of loyalty in the breasts of the Egyptians akin to that felt by a self-governing people for indigenous rulers if, besides being indigenous, they are also beneficent. Neither by the display of sympathy, nor by good government, can we forge bonds which will be other than brittle. Sir Herbert Edwards, writing to Lord Lawrence a few years after the annexation of the Punjab, said: "We are not *liked* anywhere. . . . The people hailed us as deliverers from Sikh maladministration, and we were popular so long as we were plaistering wounds. But the patient is well now, and he finds the doctor a bore. There is no getting over the fact that we are not Mohammedans, that we neither eat, drink, nor intermarry with them."

The present situation in Egypt is very similar to that which existed in the Punjab when Sir Herbert Edwards wrote these lines. The want of gratitude displayed by a nation to its alien benefactors is almost as old as history itself. In whatever degree ingratitude may exist, it would be unjust to blame the Egyptians for following the dictates of human nature. In any case, whatever be the moral harvest we may reap, we must continue to do our duty, and our duty has been indicated to us by the Apostle St. Paul. We must not be "weary in well-doing."

I take leave of a country with which I have been so long associated with the expression of an earnest hope that, in the future, as in the recent past, Egypt will continue to be governed in the interests of the Egyptians, and I commend to my own countrymen the advice which was given to Rome by one of the later Latin poets:

Quod regnas minus est quam quod regnare mereris.

52. Joseph Chamberlain, *Preference, the True Imperial Policy* (1 February 1905)

Joseph Chamberlain (1836–1914) was one of the most provocative and charismatic politicians of the late Victorian age. He began his career in 1873 as a dynamic, innovative mayor of Birmingham, where he instituted programs of municipal socialism that earned him the admiration of urban reformers around the world. His electoral work in the National Liberal Federation helped provide the Liberals with a modern, mass-based constituency organization. In the late 1870s and early 1880s he entered the highest echelons of Liberal politics, serving as president of the Board of Trade and then as president of the Local Government Board between 1880 and 1886 in Gladstone's second and third cabinets, where he merited a reputation for ardent nationalism and social progressivism. Chamberlain put his mark on such legislation as the Bankruptcy Law of 1883 and the Merchant Shipping Bill of 1884. A fundamental caesura in his career came in June 1886 when he broke with Gladstone over Irish home rule and joined the Liberal Unionist movement in defense of imperial parliamentary control in Ireland. In 1895 he completed his conversion by joining the coalition cabinet of Lord Salisbury as secretary of state for the colonies, a position Chamberlain retained until 1903. His jingoist patriotism during the Boer War must be balanced against his consistent progressivism in domestic social reform (the Workmen's Compensation Bill of 1897 was largely his work); indeed many historians have seen Chamberlain's campaign of 1903–6 to end free trade and to institute a mutual preferential trading system between England and its present and former colonies as a brilliant (if unsuccessful) strategy to posit an intellectual *and* mass political link between imperialism and domestic social reform.

The speech reprinted here on imperial tariff reform, a concise statement of Chamberlain's social imperialist views of empire and civil society, was delivered on 1 February 1905 at Gainsborough.

From *Mr. Chamberlain's Speeches*, vol. 2, edited by Charles W. Boyd (London: Constable and Co., 1914), pp. 294–314.

I am glad that I am not here on any party campaign, and I do not think that even my worst enemy—if I have such a person—would accuse me of seeking any party or personal gain in the great controversy in which I have engaged. Believe me, if I wish anything now, it is that I might find the words to impress upon this great meeting of men of all parties my intense conviction of the importance of the subject we are met to discuss.

I look back to my own political career, extending over thirty years, and I can see that from first to last two objects have presented themselves to my mind as the most important that can or could be dealt with by any statesman of any party. The first of these objects is the consideration of what is called the condition of the people; I mean to say the consideration of all the legislation, or suggestions, or changes, that may be made in order to improve the condition of the people, to elevate their lives, to give them, and especially the poorest of them, a better chance in the competition which is always going on. And, in the second place, what has most interested me has been a consideration of the future of the country, of the future of the Empire of which the country forms a part.

We all have our lives given to us no doubt for a good purpose; but the life of the individual, what is that to the life of the nation? Every one of us is bound by the highest of responsibilities to think, not only of himself, but also of his descendants, of his country, the life of which may be prolonged for generations after he has ceased to be in existence. Now this question about which I am going to speak to you is closely connected with both these objects. We are agreed—by we, I mean my opponents and myself—that this subject, whether my views about it are right or are wrong, touches every man, woman, and child in the kingdom; that it affects your families; that it will seriously influence your power to provide for them; that it affects the general course of life of the whole of the population of this country. It affects the Empire. It affects the life of the Empire, and the existence of the Empire; for that depends upon our ability in the next few years—in what is a mere nothing in the life of a nation—to devise a means by which this Empire, in which all of us feel the greatest pride, may be kept together in one united whole.

Now what is this Empire of ours? We are brought face to face with the greatest problem that has ever been presented to a nation. It is a new problem. We have no particular experience to go by, but there has been thrown upon us, as I believe, in the providence of God, a responsibility such as has never been placed upon any nation or any race before. We have to discover how to bring together in a great union of peace and affection territories vaster than have ever owned any common interest before. We have to unite varying races, varying interests, and different aspirations, and we have to make of them an organised whole.

We all talk of the British Empire. I think my countrymen are only just beginning—they have not got very far—to appreciate what it is. It is not an empire. We use that word; but it is not an empire in the sense in which other empires have existed on this globe. It is not an empire in the sense in which the German Empire now dominates a great portion of Europe. It is not a union in the sense in which there is union in the United States of America. It is not even a kingdom in the sense in which, let us say, Italy, with all her varying races and interests, has been united for common purposes. It is a great potentiality, the greatest that was ever given to man. But for the moment it is a loose bundle of sticks, bound together, indeed, by a thin tie of sentiment and sympathy, but a tie, after all, so slender that a rough blow might shatter it and dissolve it into its constituent elements.

Let us go back for a moment into our past history. Let us consider how this Empire has been built up. How do we—we in these two small islands—come to have this gigantic heritage, and with it, remember, these gigantic responsibilities, which are unknown in the case of other nations? The British Empire—bear this always in mind—was acquired by sacrifice from first to last. It was won by sacrifice. It can only be maintained by sacrifice. Partly it is the result of conquest and of war, and of all the sufferings that war brings; partly the result of discovery, the work of pioneers, men of courage and resolution, the men of whom we are most proud in the course of our history who obtained in the name of England a position which was not disputed, but which involved them, at any rate, in the greatest of hardships.

This Empire so acquired has been growing until it has become greater than anything that was ever known before. We talk of great empires, we talk of Rome and Constantinople in the past; we talk of modern empires, of Russia, of the great confederation of the United States. They are nothing by comparison with the inheritance which has devolved upon us, and with which we have now to deal. I am not prepared to say that we have any right to be proud of all the steps that have been taken in the acquisition of this Empire. I would go further, and say that, in the first instance, although its acquisition was accompanied by deeds of heroism and self-sacrifice to which you will hardly find elsewhere any parallel, yet the main object was the selfish object of acquiring a territory in the sense of a possession, in the sense of an estate which was to be ours, and the revenues of which were to be more or less at our disposal. That was the early history of our Colonial Empire; and that disappeared at a stroke. It disappeared absolutely and for ever when the Declaration of Independence was promulgated in America, and when what was then the greatest of our colonies repudiated altogether its political connection with the mother country.

But mark what followed. The original conception of a Colonial Empire was a possession, something which gave us privileges but involved no corresponding duties. When that was destroyed, then we fell into the opposite extreme. We could see no gain and direct advantage from these distant lands, and our statesmen, or many of the most distinguished of them, came to believe that it would be better to get rid of the responsibility. I think you may safely say that for fifty years—a period including, let me remind you, what is called the Free Trade period—the object of the statesmen of this country was to relieve themselves of the burden, instead of endeavouring to meet a new situation with new methods and with higher aspirations.

I said in a parenthesis that this period included what may be called the Free Trade period. I am not going to dwell upon it now, but it is a fact which you should always bear in mind, that the party which worked for Free Trade was, on the whole, a cosmopolitan party, that is to say, a party whose patriotism is as wide as the world—not confined to their own country, or even to their own Empire. For instance, you find Mr. Cobden—for whom I have always expressed the greatest respect; I think him to have been in part mistaken, but I have never doubted his honesty, his sincerity, or his ability—you find Mr. Cobden, in the height of the agitation, explaining frankly, as he always did, that to him a Colonial Empire was not at all an object of ambition; that he rejoiced in the federation of Canada, because he hoped that it would lead to the speedy independence of Canada; that he detested our rule in India; that he thought it almost a crime that we should make ourselves answerable for that great dependency.

Now, I am not going to argue that question, because it has been settled long ago. As regards the position of the Empire, posterity has given judgment against Mr. Cobden. And I do not think you can find any one of responsibility—be he Radical, be he Conservative, or be he Liberal Unionist—who would pretend to tell you that it would be a good thing if the Empire fell away from us, if we were once more, as in old times, an isolated kingdom of comparatively small extent.

If I refer to this at all, it is because I believe that you will find that in the present controversy the question of what is called Little Englandism—which is not a term of reproach: it only means a particular view of policy—is also closely connected with the doctrine of free imports. What one is in the financial sphere the other is in the political sphere. If you want an Empire, if you want influence in the world, I think you will find that free imports are inconsistent with them. But if you are one of those who hate the very name of Imperialism, as I think Sir H. Campbell-Bannerman said he did the other day, then I agree that you are consistent; you are honest in saying that under those circumstances you see no reason for a change in our fiscal policy. The two go together, and it is part of my object to-night to show you in what way they are connected.

Meanwhile, I only say that the policy of the middle of the last century, the policy of neglecting the colonies, of being apathetic with regard to them, of governing your arrangements with a view to getting rid of them— amicably, of course—is, in my opinion, a selfish policy, a short-sighted policy, and not the policy of the people of this country today. I believe that it has given place in these recent years to a higher conception of Imperial duty. I think the people of this country recognise now that they have something to be proud of in the undoubted influence which is wielded by Great Britain in the affairs of the world, and which, though not universally, is generally used for the advantage of peace and civilisation. I think we recognise that that influence exists, that it is on the whole an instrument for good, and that that instrument would vanish in our hands, if we were no longer part of an empire, but only an isolated kingdom.

But that is not all. It is not only these high arguments which I want to present to you, although it is to them, believe me, that I attach the greatest importance,—it is through them that I hope to touch your hearts; but I would also appeal to you on the ground of your material interests. Suppose that, owing to your apathy or inability to understand the colonies, your children abroad and your kinsmen across the seas, the gulf which at present is only a physical gulf of sea and distance, gradually became a moral gulf, and they fell away from you; your ideals no longer their ideals, and they being no longer proud of our common history, but looking forward only to a history to be made by themselves. Suppose all these things took place— and they are not impossible—then I ask you, What would be the first result? How would you feel it? These no doubt are sentimental considerations. You might harden your hearts and say, What matters it to us, provided we still have sufficient employment and sufficient wages?

But you would not have sufficient employment and sufficient wages. You would feel it directly. You would lose your best customers, you would lose what is called in business your best trade connections. Now, if by any chance you weaken the ties which hold your colonies and yourselves together, you have a very heavy loss to fear. You will lose your most promising market. You will lose a market which is quite different from a foreign market, because it is the market of your own people. You have the same wants, the same ideas, the same currency, the same measures. In every way it is easier to trade with your own kinsfolk than it is to trade with foreigners; and therefore that is the most hopeful part of your trade. That is the trade which would be immediately and seriously interfered with if anything occurred to produce a coolness between our colonies and ourselves.

What is the state of trade now? At the present moment we are told that times are prosperous, and that the exports are records. That may be so; but, meanwhile, the employment of the people in industrial and agricultural pursuits is not keeping pace with the population. If you go back twenty or thirty years you find a larger proportion of the people in continuous and remunerative employment in our principal industries than there are to-day. Although it may be true that the country is getting richer, the number of the unemployed is getting greater. I shall return to that directly; but that is not the only result.

I have spoken to you about Empire. If I had as many hours to speak to you as I have half-hours, I would say something more about the effect of the Empire upon the whole character of the people. Believe me, we should not be the people we are, we should not have had the qualities which, after all, make the name of Britain respected throughout the world, if we had remained a mere kingdom, and we had not taken these great responsibilities. But the burden is great; and it may be that the time is coming when we shall no longer be able to bear it alone. Have you thought of that? Who is going to help you when the burden becomes too great? Do you think it will be these foreign countries whom you welcome to your markets with open arms? Do you think that it is they who will help you in your time of stress?

I think it was twenty years ago that one of the most distinguished of our Liberal statesmen ventured—which is always a mistake—upon a prophecy. He said that if in the future this country of ours were ever engaged in a great war in which the colonies were not directly and immediately concerned, they would not send one man to help us, and would not pay one penny towards the cost. Yes; most prophets are false, and my friend, Mr. Morley, was no exception. What happened? There came a time not long afterwards when we were in great stress, when we undertook a task, which, remember, was forced upon us, but upon the performance of which depended the existence of the Empire, the confidence of our fellow-subjects throughout the world. When we undertook that task, and when every one turned aside from us, when the foreigners carped at our ignorance and weakness, when they did not even hide their desire that we should be defeated, then the colonies, the relations, came to the front. Then we found that blood was thicker than water. Then these men, so maligned, opened their purse to us. That was a small thing. But they gave us of their best to fight shoulder to shoulder with our own representatives. At a time when we stood the scorn of the civilised world, they came forward, and they came with no selfish and personal interest. They gave us their moral support because we were engaged in what they knew to be a just war.

Now that war has been called a stupid war. Well, I do not understand the adjective. I do not understand how any patriotic Englishman can come down after it has been fought, after it has been fought victoriously, when men have given their lives for it and endured all the hardships it involved, and tell an audience like this that it was a stupid war; that these lives were given in vain; that these sacrifices were of no account. But to me the war was a just war. To me it showed that the old British spirit was not dead amongst us, that we could still look forward to maintain that headship of the British race which we have maintained so long, and which some people have said was weakening in our hands. Be that as it may, one thing it did. It gave us experience. It showed us a new vista. It made possible an organised union of all the different parts of the British Empire for common objects.

Now, if you have followed me, you will see that the time is a critical and a creative time. I say that the position you have held hitherto cannot be permanently held unless you take your children into your counsels, and make the Empire theirs as well as yours. If that be done, then although it may be that the separate work of this kingdom may have ceased to be the guiding principle of the world, or of the civilisation in which we have taken part, yet our destiny may be continued and fulfilled in the British Empire, which will be sustained by the willing hands of all those who have contributed to make it.

You see what it is I am urging upon you. It falls upon you, the living generation, to maintain the Empire. Let us go a step further. The minds, not only of British statesmen, but of colonial statesmen, were directed by the late war to consider the circumstances of our mutual relations. They considered these circumstances, and they did not find them satisfactory. You have to take that into your serious consideration. All these statesmen, speaking from different parts of the globe, under different conditions, governing great communities, very varied in their character, they all turned their minds in the same direction. They said, in effect, "We see as we never saw before the potentialities and the obligations of the British Empire. How can we maintain that Empire?" They all came to the same conclusion. They said, "It cannot be maintained on its present footing." Sir Wilfrid Laurier, the Prime Minister of Canada, said in a memorable speech, "Either you must draw closer together, or you will inevitably drift apart." The late Prime Minister of Australia, Mr. Deakin, said, "There is no intelligent man who can view the present relations between the mother country and her colonies without anxiety and alarm." The same thing was said in South Africa by the present Prime Minister of the Cape, and, above all, by the late Mr. Rhodes, to whom no one will deny the character of a broad-minded Englishman. Mr. Rhodes, writing not for popular information, but merely to his fellow Prime Ministers, at a time when he was Premier of the Cape—the Prime Ministers of Canada and of the Australian colonies—suggested, "The object is to find some tie that will bind the Empire closer together. It must be a practical one." That is the next point.

I have given you these names. I have not time to go further. Almost without exception every leading statesman in South Africa, in Australia, in

New Zealand, in Canada, has said practically the same thing. But they have said more. They have all, thinking this matter out separately, come to the same conclusion—that a practical tie is only to be found in preferential arrangements between the mother country and her children. Now, they have not stopped there. Having come to the conclusion, without any pressure from us, separately, each in his own community, they proceed to give effect to it. They make us an offer. I dare say many of you have been told that they have made no offer. I can deal with facts, but I cannot deal with the ineradicable stupidity of some people. When Sir Wilfrid Laurier says to you, as he has said, that "we offer to meet you, and to make a treaty with you by which you shall treat us and we will treat you a little better than we both treat the foreigner," I do not know any name in the English language that I can give to that statement except to call it an offer. And the offer which Sir Wilfrid Laurier made has been repeated again and again in different words, in different forms, always to the same effect, not only by the statesmen of Canada, whichever side of politics they are on, but also by the statesmen of the other self-governing colonies.

Now, gentlemen—and especially I want to appeal to those who on ordinary occasions would, I suppose, be my opponents—what do you think of the position? You are asked to make a treaty with our own people, and to discuss the terms of that treaty. At present you do not know what the details will be. They must be a matter of bargain in the first instance. The colonies may ask too much, or we may ask too much; or the colonies may give too little, or we may give too little. You are not asked to commit yourselves. You are not asked to shut your eyes and open your mouths, and take whatever the colonies propose to give you. But you are asked to meet your own friends and relations in a friendly meeting, and to say whether, both having the same object, namely, to unite the Empire more closely together, you can find some means of doing so on the basis of this preferential policy.

It would not be possible, but for this party system of ours (which is very good at times: I do not know myself how we are to do without it, but in times of crisis like this it is utterly out of place)—it would be impossible but for that system, that men on both sides should not say, as sensible men, as men of business, as patriots—"Certainly, we will meet you, and if we cannot agree, we will part friends." Yet we find a great party in the State using all its organisation and all its machinery to misrepresent the offer and the views of those who support it in this country, refusing to treat it as a non-party matter, and refusing discussion with your best friends. Why? Because, forsooth, it is possible—and I think it is probable—that when you come to discuss the matter together you may all be convinced that the time has come to change, at all events in some slight degree, the antiquated system which has been rejected by all the rest of the world, but which you have pursued for sixty years without the slightest alteration, although everything has changed around you. There was a time when a great argument was met by the shouts of the mob, who said, "Great is Diana of the Ephesians." It seems to me that our politics are to be governed by similar considerations. All sorts of old formulae are to be brought out, as though they were a divinely inspired gospel.

What is the next step? The colonies offer to treat with you for further advantages. What have they done already? Are you aware that they have already given you a preference without asking anything from you in return, because they believe in this principle, and believe that your common sense will induce you to carry it further when you have once had experience of it? South Africa has offered you 25 per cent. preference on the duties it levies, and New Zealand 10 per cent. Canada has been gradually increasing the amount, until it now offers you 33 per cent. preference on its duties. I appeal to you working men, have you followed the result of that? How has it affected you and your families? Addressing myself now purely to your selfish instincts, I ask, Has it helped you? [A Voice: No.] I wonder whether that gentleman knows how much it has helped the country. I should be very sorry if he were not himself the better for it, and I think he is, without knowing it. But if I had to choose between him and the country, I should choose the country.

That preference has increased your trade with Canada, chiefly in manufactures, by something between £5,000,000 and £6,000,000 a year. Do you know what that means? Six millions a year of manufactures involves at least—I believe it is a great deal more, but I wish to take a moderate view—at least £2,500,000 of wages. In other words, 32,000 working men have gained wages equivalent, on an average, to 30s. per week continuously throughout the year in consequence of the preference given by Canada. Thirty-two thousand men with their families means 160,000 individuals. The improvement in their position affects members of other trades. The shopkeeper benefits if the workingman has more to spend. The man who supplies him with clothes, or with food, or anything else—all are benefited when the workingman gets employment; and unless my friend in the corner is a foreign millionaire living in this country on his income, I really do not see how he could escape being benefited by such a change as that.

That is what has been done for you. That is an example of one single act of preference on the part of one single colony. Is it not reasonable to consider whether more might not be done in the same way? When the Canadians come to us, as they do, and say, "We have given you this for nothing, now give us something, and we will give you more," how are they met? How are you asked to meet them? You are asked to meet them with a flat and an insulting refusal. We have heard a good deal about the loyalty of the colonies. There has never been any question about the loyalty of the colonies; but there is some question, it seems to me, about the loyalty of the motherland. When these children of ours come to us and say, "Discuss the terms of a treaty for our mutual advantage," and when we reply to them, "No, what we would do for any other nation if it came to us we will not do for you; we will meet you by all means, but we will under no circumstances discuss with you the only thing you care to discuss"—when we treat them in that way, then I venture to say that these are high-spirited nations, and the time may come when, if we treat them in such a spirit, they may seek elsewhere for the sympathy they ask.

What do you think is likely to be the effect of this kind of argument upon our loyal fellow-subjects? What would it be here? Put yourselves in their places. The other day there came to me a copy of a newspaper—an important Ottawa paper—which put the thing, as it seemed to me, in a nutshell. I will read what that paper said: "Canada, unless her hand be clasped anew in that of Great Britain, will proceed more and more to play a lone hand herself, and while the kindliest sentiments and affection will remain, the country, nevertheless, in her rapid growth, will become inevitably more self-centred. In a business and political way she would continue framing business and political arrangements to suit herself, each of which would render less probable and less possible any exceptional alliance with Great Britain, and would render much more uncertain than even at present what Great Britain can look to from Canada whenever any time of Imperial stress may come." The extract goes on to say: "Sneers in England about buying colonial loyalty arc utter rot. One might as well talk about a father trying to buy his sons' loyalty because he proposes to them to enter his business house, with a share in the profits. There is no buying or selling in this matter."

That is the right way to look at the matter. We want, and they want, to bring the Empire into a partnership, and, if you can secure a partnership in trade, believe me that will develop into a partnership in other things. We are asked to negotiate with such an object. But you are asked, why go into a negotiation when it is impossible to come to an arrangement? Why is it impossible? I was sorry to see that Sir Edward Grey, who is a sober and moderate politician, took the same line as Mr. Asquith. They say, you cannot make a bargain with the colonies, because they will not give you Free Trade. Well, you can make a bargain with France; you would be only too glad to do it. Mr. Cobden was glad enough to do it, and yet France did not give you Free Trade. Because you cannot get all that you would desire, why should you not take what you can get?

I quite agree that at the present moment you cannot get Free Trade from the colonies. Rightly or wrongly, they believe in a certain amount of Protection. They are not going to hand over their growing industries entirely to competition, even from the mother country. Very well, you cannot get that. But are you like a child that has set his heart on the moon? Will you not be satisfied with, say, a bun instead? You can get the bun. What will they give you if they will not give you Free Trade? They will give you, in the first place, a share in their home industry. There are many things which they do not make, and are not likely to make, or fitted to make. They will gladly buy these things from our manufacturers at home. They will keep a part of their own trade, but there will be a large margin under any circumstances which we can have if we like; but you can have much more. These colonies are doing a large trade with foreigners. It is a large and growing trade. A certain portion of it will never be taken from the foreigner, because the foreigner is the only producer. We cannot produce French claret, or coffee, or tea; and, accordingly, there is a large number of articles which they will always buy from the foreigner. But when all that is accounted for, there remains at the present moment a trade which they are now doing with the foreigners, of £30,000,000 a year, and which they might do with us, because they are all articles which we make as well as the foreigners.

Please consider what is happening now under the present system. Under our present system the foreign trade with the colonies is rapidly increasing. It is increasing much more rapidly than our trade is. I had an Australian paper sent to me the other day. In ten years, it says, the foreign exports to the colonies increased five times as much as the British. Germany and the United States increased four and a quarter millions in the last three years in their sales to Australia alone. You have increased somewhat, but the increase of the foreigner is greater than your increase. He is gaining upon you. Can you not see what will happen if that goes on? You will lose your market. You will lose your opportunity. You will never have it again. Now you have an opportunity, not only of retaining the trade you have, but of securing a reversion of a great portion of this trade which is now slipping into foreign hands, to English manufacturers and to English working men.

All that is subject of discussion at the conference which we want to see established; and our opponents, treating this as a party question, say, "No, we won't have a conference; or, at all events, we won't discuss this subject." I do not believe that in the history of any country there ever was a piece of greater pedantry and greater folly.

I come to another point. What our opponents say is not only that the colonies will not give you enough, but that they will ask too much. Those statesmen who apparently are ready to congratulate you upon the increase of the wealth of the country, which they attribute to Free Trade, pass over without the slightest observation the fact that thirteen millions of the population are on the verge of hunger and are under-fed: these people, while they tell you that the exports are increasing, yet have nothing to say about the fact that a largely decreased proportion of the population is being employed in industrial pursuits, compared with what were employed some twenty years ago. They have nothing to say about the enormous emigration which goes away from this country, and which would not go if people were satisfied at home. They have nothing to say about the increase of pauperism and the increase in crime.

But there is one thing they do say. They say it loudly on every occasion. They say it with every kind of exaggeration, and they produce a great effect. They say, "Your food will cost you more." If only they would confine themselves to saying that in public meetings like this, we could meet their inaccuracies—that is a long word. If we could meet their inaccuracies we should not be afraid of them; but they go into the house of the artisan and into the cottage of the labourer, and they talk to them, and, above all, they talk to their wives, and make assertions they ought to be ashamed to make. As I have said, they are producing a great effect, but it will not last. No party in the long run benefits by these colossal misrepresentations.

But it may be worth while once more to deal a little in detail with these questions. I assert that it is absolutely untrue, under any policy which I, at least, have proposed, that your food will cost you more.

I want to bring you all the trade the colonies can bring you. I want to bring about a closer intercourse between the colonies and ourselves, in order that our great Empire may be maintained. What do the colonies ask from you in return for this? They ask that a certain advantage should be given to them upon some of their principal products. They don't ask it upon all, but they do ask that that advantage should be given them upon corn, meat, dairy produce, and upon fruit.

That is what they ask. And, in order to give it to them, we should have to put a small tax upon these articles. They do not want a big tax. All they ask is for the turn of the scale. In trade, as no one knows better than the great industrial and manufacturing concerns, the majority of which are entirely in favour of this policy, "the turn of the scale" is a consideration. In our modern trade, transactions are so large that a farthing will make the difference where in the time of our ancestors they would have required larger consideration. The colonists believe, and I believe, that if they could get a trifling advantage they would divert the whole of our demand for these foodstuffs into their market, and out of the foreign market; and they believe that that would not involve any increase of prices at home. It would involve an increase of cost to the foreigner, but not an increase of prices paid to the colonial.

Now, remember that the colonial does a great deal for you; the foreigner does nothing. The deliberate purpose of the foreigner is to shut you out of his markets. If he does not do it, it is because trade is so complicated that he is not able to do it, but there is no want of goodwill and attention on his part. He puts on a duty to shut out your machinery. He fails, either because your machinery is so much cheaper to begin with, or because your manufacturers can afford to reduce their profits, or your working men are prepared to reduce their wages. And still you send your machinery abroad. How long will that last? When the foreigner finds that he has not succeeded, he raises the duty, and he goes on raising it until he has accomplished his desire. And that has been the history of every trade in this country in which the continental commerce has been of importance. One after another the profitable branches of your trade have been attacked; one after another they have been forcibly excluded from foreign markets. And that will go on. You have on one side the foreigner who, quite within his right, for a very obvious purpose tries to destroy your trade. On the other hand, you have the colonial, who tries to increase your trade. Which will you favour?

Let me try and make this clear. Suppose there are an ironmonger in Gainsborough and two bakers; and one of the bakers buys everything in the way of ironmongery that he wants at home and in his business from the ironmonger; and the other baker thinks he can do a little better in the stores in London, and he buys all his ironmongery from the stores in London. What do you suppose the ironmonger will do? It seems to me he will be certain to buy the greater part of his bread, if not the whole, from the baker who buys from him, even if he has to pay a little more. Well, that is your position. I say, "Buy from your colonies, who will buy from you, even if it costs you a little more."

Then I go back, and I say it will not cost you any more. There is nothing more certain than this in that most uncertain of sciences which is called political economy, that a tax imposed upon an article which is not a monopoly, in which there is competition, does not fall wholly upon the consumers. It falls in part, at any rate, upon the foreigner, or upon the producer.

I will give you one illustration of that. The matter is too large to be discussed in detail. There is the United States of America. It is one of the most Protectionist countries in the world—much too Protectionist in my opinion. Its tariff is not a scientific tariff. It goes to an extreme that I should never propose to follow. But in those circumstances, if our opponents were right, everything in America would be much higher in price than it is here. They put a duty of 25 per cent. upon this, a duty of 50 per cent. upon that, and of 60, 70, and even 100 per cent. Now, are things dearer on the whole in America than here? Some things are. Luxuries are much dearer. If you want to buy a lot of silver plate you will have to pay more for it in New York than you will in London. If you want the best clothes probably it is the same thing. But Mr. Carnegie, whom I take, not as a supporter of my own, but as a man with a great experience, said last year in an article which he wrote, that the ordinary necessaries of life of the working man were cheaper in America than they were here, that for a pound sterling you could buy more clothes and more food in America than you could buy in England.

I only quote that for the purpose of showing that, in spite of the taxes in America, you have actually cheaper necessaries than you have in this country. It is clear, therefore, that it is not merely a question of a tax, and that the tax does not necessarily increase the price of food. I do not believe it increases it at all. I could, if I had time, take Germany, France, Italy, Sweden, which are Protectionist countries, and I could show you that in no single case has the price of food gone up in proportion to any tax placed upon food. I conclude from that that if I put a small tax on food, or any kind of food, the consumer will, perhaps, pay none of it, will certainly not pay the whole of it, and at the worst will only pay part of it.

When, however, my opponents charge me with taxing food, they either misunderstand me or they misrepresent me. I am not going to tax food: that is to say, I am not going to tax food in the whole. I tax one kind of food in order that I may be able to untax another kind of food. Let me put a homely illustration to you. Suppose you go into a coffee-house and ask for tea and bread and butter, and when you have finished you are told that the cost of the tea is a penny and that the bread and butter is given in for nothing. Very well. Then the next day, let us suppose, you go to another tea shop, and again you ask for bread and butter and tea, and when you come to pay your bill you find tea charged a halfpenny and bread and butter a halfpenny. Does it make any difference to you? You pay a penny in either case. That is precisely what you will do under my system—unless you do better.

I have still something more to say. I began by saying I am not going to put you in a worse condition. I now say I am going to put you in a better position. How can I do that? By taxing things where the tax is partly paid by the foreigner, instead of taxing things where the whole tax is paid by you. If all the taxes that I have spoken of were put on to-morrow, the difference to a working man in paying these taxes would be something like fourpence or fivepence per week; that is to say, if I stopped there. If I only put on taxes the taxes would be fourpence or fivepence per week in the ordinary life of a working man or an agricultural labourer, supposing he paid the whole of them. But he won't pay the whole of them. I have already said that in every other country in the world where these taxes are put on the consumers only pay half, or less than half, of them. Therefore he will pay, it may be, twopence or twopence-halfpenny. But then I am going to take off taxes to the extent of at least as much, and probably more.

A man wants his bread; yes, but he wants his tea, too, and from one thing or another—I do not pledge myself to details now, although I have proposed a plan—from one thing or another which is necessary to the working man I am going to take off more than I put on. And while under our present system he has to pay every farthing of the tax upon tea, or coffee, or sugar, I am going to put the tax on the things in which there is competition, and in which the principal part of the tax will come out of the pocket of the foreigner. He will be made to contribute towards our expenditure. He will be made to pay a reasonable toll in order to gain entry to the biggest market on the face of the globe.

The result of my policy will be this—that the poor will pay less than they do now upon the absolute necessaries of life; that the rich, or those who approach even the class of rich people, will have to pay a little more for their luxuries; and that the foreigner will have to pay a good deal more for what I have called the privilege of entering this market. I hope I have said enough to show you that under this alteration there is no fear whatever for any man's home that he will have to suffer the starvation with which he is threatened, or that his big loaf will not be as big as ever. The whole object of my policy is not to lessen your loaf; it is to give you more money to buy it with.

The whole question of the social condition of the poor is contained in this one word—employment. In the past this country was in an exceptional position. It was the workshop of the world. We were fortunate in agriculture, we were supreme in manufactures. That is no longer the case. We are richer than ever, but in totally different circumstances. Our competitors are gaining upon us in that which makes national greatness. We may be richer, and yet weaker. We may have more millionaires and fewer working men, and that is the direction in which we are tending. Now, while our competitors are excluding us from their markets, they are gaining greatly upon ours. We see the beginning, because it is only the beginning. Are you so foolish that you are going to wait until it is too late to find a remedy? Those are the wise nations that look a little ahead and see a difficulty before it overwhelms them, prepare against fire before it breaks out, and amongst those nations may we not hope our own will be counted?

If you do not attend to these indications, if you are led astray, if you allow your party feelings to cause you to close your ears against the warnings which are given you in no party sense, then I say you will awake some day to find the source of your strength undermined, because you have mistaken a musty dogma of old-fashioned schools for the principle of your progress and of your national life. You have it in your power to avoid these evils. You have it still in your power, by your decision, to maintain the position of your country in the world. You may secure it if you will meet your children everywhere with open arms; if, at the same time, you will sharpen your weapons against those who are inclined to treat you badly; if you will hold your own against those who turn their back to you; if you will welcome those who are only anxious to co-operate with you in a greater future than any past that we have known. And then indeed you may hope to transmit to your descendants untarnished in lustre, undiminished in power, the sceptre of our Imperial dominion.

Index